JENNIE LEE

A LIFE

Patricia Hollis

OXFORD UNIVERSITY PRESS · OXFORD

1997

Oxford University Press, Great Clarendon Street, Oxford OX2 6DP
Oxford New York
Athens Auckland Bangkok Bogota Bombay
Buenos Aires Calcutta Cape Town Dar es Salaam
Delhi Florence Hong Kong Istanbul Karachi
Kuala Lumpur Madras Madrid Melbourne
Mexico City Nairobi Paris Singapore
Taipei Tokyo Toronto Warsaw
and associated companies in
Berlin Ibadan

Oxford is a trade mark of Oxford University Press

Published in the United States
by Oxford University Press Inc., New York

British Library Cataloguing in Publication Data
Data available

Library of Congress Cataloging-in-Publication Data
Hollis, Patricia.
Jennie Lee: a life / by Patricia Hollis.
p. cm.
Includes bibliographical references and index.
1. Lee, Jennie, 1904–1988. 2. Bevan, Aneurin, 1897–1960—Marriage. 3. Great Britain—Politics and government—1936– . 4. Great Britain—Politics and government—1910–1936. 5. Women legislators—Great Britain—Biography. 6. Statesmen's spouses—Great Britain—Biography. I. Title.
DA585.L44H65 1997
941.085'092—dc21 97–16087
[B] CIP

ISBN 0–19–821580–0

1 3 5 7 9 10 8 6 4 2

Typeset by J&L Composition Ltd, Filey, North Yorkshire
Printed in Great Britain
on acid-free paper by
Bookcraft Ltd., Midsomer Norton
Nr. Bath, Somerset

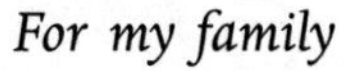

For my family

PREFACE

Most prefaces offer apologia and acknowledgment. This one, I fear, is no different.

To start with the apologia. The book is long, for it has ended up seeking to tell three stories. The first story is the political *Life* of a Scottish miner's daughter, Jennie Lee, who became a socialist MP for North Lanark in 1929 at 24, before she was even old enough to vote. Her vivid good looks and compelling style made her one of the finest platform orators in the land. She could storm a meeting to anger, move it to tears, warm it into solidarity or lift it into confidence—just as she chose. She was trained in the far-left Independent Labour Party, which made her in today's language 'oppositionist', uncompromising and sectarian. In that 1929–31 parliament, she fought Ramsay MacDonald and Snowden with all the invective at her command. She was a dissenter. Nye's 'Salvation Army lassie'. When the ILP left the Labour Party in 1932 because it would not accept Labour Party discipline, Jennie went with them out of parliament and into the wilderness. Spain, and then the Second World War, severed her from the pacifism of the ILP. She rejoined the Labour Party and won Cannock, another mining seat, in 1945. Thereafter she inevitably positioned herself on the Left, helping (well, not always) Michael Foot to run *Tribune* and Nye Bevan to run for office.

For by this time she had married Aneurin Bevan, on the rebound from the death of the great love of her life, Frank Wise. Jennie's marriage to Nye in 1934 is the book's second storyline. Jennie was reluctant to marry, but Nye pressed her. He was in love with Jennie; after Frank, she was willing to settle for something less—a marriage that was companionable, unsentimental, not too demanding. When they met, she was by far the better known. By leaving the Labour Party with the ILP, however, her career was sidelined just as his star was rising. Says Michael Foot in *Loyalists and Loners* (1986),

> Each of them had an endless capacity for enjoyment, a fierce ego, a full dose of ambition, pride and arrogance . . . The ruling passion with both of them was the way they could serve not the Party they had joined but the movement in which

they were both born, their own flesh and blood. Here, for sure, they knew how to fortify one another.

Nye had during the war remained outside the coalition government, facing abuse as he tried to hold Churchill to parliamentary account. Jennie came to see in Nye the leader of Labour's Left. The war made Nye; it also made their marriage. When Jennie re-entered the Commons in 1945, she failed to carve out a political career of her own. She had lost the shining confidence of her youth. Instead, she devoted her energies to Nye as he fought to establish the NHS in the late 1940s and to disestablish Hugh Gaitskell in the 1950s. Jennie became the dark angel at Nye's shoulder, always pulling him away from compromise, always tugging him into opposition, as he bid to become leader of the Labour Party. Jennie chose to submerge her political life in Nye's, at very considerable cost to her own well-being. She offered Nye her support with affection and generosity and he received it with tenderness and grace. Theirs was a remarkable political marriage, loving and trusting, but the costs were all Jennie's, the comforts all Nye's.

Jennie's suppression of her own career was the more remarkable precisely because as a woman in politics she had always laid claim to a 'male' life, public, itinerant, and unencumbered by family responsibilities. It was a feminism of a sort—she always walked out of dinner parties that expected the ladies to withdraw as the port circulated—but unlike other women MPs she was never a sister, never identified with women's issues, for they were irrelevant to her battle with capitalism.

Nye's premature death in 1960 broke Jennie. She was rescued by Harold Wilson who in 1964 gave her a ministerial job, the final storyline in the biography. By civil service standards she was a poor Minister; yet, with the aid of her close friend Arnold Goodman, Jennie became the first and finest Minister for the Arts. When Jennie went to a play, the audience would applaud her as she took her seat. At Wilson's request she also delivered the Open University, one of the outstanding achievements of his administration. She drove it through against almost universal hostility by steely political will. In her spare time, Jennie acquired a son, a lover, and firm friends, but in 1970 lost Cannock. So Wilson sent her to the Lords where she enjoyed some golden final years. The arts job in a sense had depoliticized her; the dissenter had come inside. She died in November 1988, gallant, feisty, and impossible to the end.

In 1989, a few months after Jennie's death, I was invited by Arnold Goodman and Michael Foot to write her biography. It was 'authorized' in the sense that I was given access—indeed temporary custody—of all her papers, some eighty boxes, mostly unsorted, which interleaved notes from Hugh Gaitskell with taxi bills from Harrods; and authorized also in that I was given every co-operation from Jennie's family and friends. They have responded to importunate requests for interviews and photographs with unfailing good humour. However, the biography has not been 'authorized' in the sense that it has been 'approved': Jennie's literary executors at no point ever asked to see the draft text. Arnold Goodman sadly died before the book was completed; Michael Foot, at my request, kindly agreed to read the draft — for the first time — when the publishers sent it out to their readers for comments and when I sent it out to friends and colleagues for theirs.

Michael Foot suggested, as did other readers, that I broke up one chapter (on the Cannock constituency) which I did; drew my attention to a recent book on Churchill's foreign policy, which I read; and corrected an error of fact on Max Beaverbrook which I had made. Apart from that, he was resolutely libertarian on all matters of interpretation, especially where he disagreed with what I had written; those who know Michael would expect nothing less.

I am perhaps labouring the point. However, my previous writing had been on Victorian radicalism. I greatly admired Tony Crosland and had been much influenced by his *Future of Socialism*, which along with Tawney and T. H. Marshall had been a formative book in my student days. I therefore expected to write about the 1950s battles between Bevan and Gaitskell over prescription charges as a retro-Gaitskellite. Political discipline, prudent budgets and all that. I could not do so. The evidence would not allow it. The more research I did, the less justifiable Gaitskell's position on charges appeared. My journey, although that is too pretentious a word for it, had everything to do with recalcitrant information, and nothing to do with any outside influence.

So my profound thanks go to all those who have read the text in whole or in part, David McKie, Meghnad Desai, Michael Foot, Jill Craigie, Betty Lockwood, Ben Pimlott, Naomi McIntosh, Ralph Toomey, Keith Jeffery, Patrick Cormack, Asa Briggs, Suse Saemann, David Grugeon, Andrew Roth, and Robert Skidelsky, as well as the anonymous but erudite readers for OUP. I am greatly indebted. Their comments have strengthened the book; its weaknesses remain my own.

The last part of the apologia is that I have found a biography very difficult to do. Perhaps that should not have surprised me as much as it did. Historical monographs now seem by comparison far more straightforward to write. For several reasons. The biographer must balance 'life' and 'times': too much background drags and the drama of the individual gets lost; but too little of it and Jennie's actions and statements become dislocated and a-historical. Others will judge whether I have got the balance roughly right. Harder still was knowing where to place one's authorial voice. Jennie, in my view, sometimes behaved very badly indeed. Writing about those occasions, one ends up sounding very censorious, and uncomfortably aware that this reveals as much about you the author as it does about your subject. One other point. In the course of research I acquired information which might have brought sex-appeal to the book, but which would none the less greatly hurt people still alive. I hesitated, as I would have preferred candour, but reluctantly I thought it right in one or two places not to name names.

To build this portrait of Jennie I am greatly indebted to the many friends, colleagues, and opponents of hers who allowed me to interview them, sometimes briefly, sometimes repeatedly. On her Labour party life, I am indebted to Richard Acland, Ian Aitken, John Beavan, Tony Benn, Donald Bruce, James Callaghan, Dennis Carter, Barbara Castle, Richard Clements, Patrick Cormack, Jill Craigie, Andrew Davidson, Mary Docherty, David Ennals, Michael Foot, Geoffrey Goodman, Denis Healey, Dennis Howell, Cledwyn Hughes, Lena Jeger, Hugh Jenkins, Roy Jenkins, Mervyn Jones, Neil Kinnock, Joan Lestor, Pat Llewelyn Davies, Betty Lockwood, Frank Longford, A. W. MacIntosh, John Mackie, Rita Mallalieu, Gordon Parry, Chris Price, Desmond Plummer, Andrew Roth, Ted Short, Renée Short, Mervyn Stockwood, David Strabolgi, G. R. Strauss, Tom Taylor, Elizabeth Thomas, Reg Underhill, Betty Vernon, Marcia Williams, Shirley Williams, Eirene White, and Woodrow Wyatt. Neil Carmichael educated me in the history of the ILP. Their tolerance as I waylaid them in the corridors of Westminster was unstinting. For her Cannock work, my thanks for interviews go especially to Derek and Muriel Davis, and to Jack Holsten, Coleen Horton, Joan Loverock, John O'Leary, Eric Roberts, Millie Rowley, and Jack Sunley. I was briefed on Jennie's arts and ministerial life by Robert Armstrong, Arnold Goodman, Michael Jameson, Keith Jeffery, Clive Saville, Neil Stuart, Nick Summers, Ralph Toomey, Arnold Wesker, Hugh Willatt (and by some very full and helpful letters from John Pope-Hennessy, Norman Reid, Roy Strong, and John Toulmin, among others). I learnt about the Open University from interviews with Asa Briggs, Jock Campbell, Chris Christodoulou, Jane Drew, Ted Graham, David Grugeon, Richard Hoggart, Bill Hughes, Naomi MacIntosh, and Walter Perry. And Jennie's personal friends and family allowed me to discuss her private life: Ushe Adams, Doreen Andrews, Constance Cummings, Mary Murray (née Wise), Suse Saemann, Bettina and Bill Stafford, Vincent Stafford, Vera Timberlake, Dorothy Vernon, and Gisella Milne-Watson. The help given me by Suse Saemann and Bettina Stafford in particular will be obvious from the text. I am also grateful to Delia Lennie for sight of the letters between Jennie and herself. Dozens and dozens of other people, from former prime ministers to general practitioners, were kind enough to supply anecdotes or to respond to letters asking for information. I hope I have faithfully acknowledged this in the endnotes. I am indebted to them all.

Particular thanks go to Stephen Bird at the National Museum of Labour History for his help with Labour Party papers, to Tony Benn for allowing me sight of papers in his private possession, to the archivists at Newcastle Public Library who located Trevelyan letters which touched on Jennie, and to the staff of the House of Lords library, who always managed to find yet another (relatively) obscure memoir. I am grateful to Dr Simon Burgess for drawing my attention to a letter of Jennie's in the Cripps papers, and to Nuffield College, Oxford, for permission to use it. Melanie Phillips has kindly allowed me to quote from her book, *The Divided House*. Jose Harris directed me to the Beatrice Webb diary references to Frank Wise. Professor Ian Taylor of Salford University generously shared with me his preliminary work on Jennie's journalism of the 1930s, Sally Creelman spent many hours sorting and annotating Jennie's papers, especially her financial papers; her help was invaluable. Jim Campbell of the Central and West Fife Local History Preservation kindly scoured local Fife newspapers for Jennie's early years. For help with photographs, my thanks to Sarah Cocke and Fred Jarvis. For help with the word-processor, without which etc., my profound thanks to Matthew. (The defining moment came when the WP's wordspell refused to recognize Enoch [Powell], on whom Jennie blamed her 1970 defeat, as a proper word, but threw up 'enoch' and then 'eunuch' instead. The machine was thereafter on side.)

To all of them I am most grateful. They will know how much I owe them. I hope they recognize the Jennie of this book.

PATRICIA HOLLIS

May Day 1997
Norwich

CONTENTS

LIST OF PLATES

(Plates 1–35 appear between pp 142–143, and plates 37–74 between pp. 302–303)

I

COWDENBEATH CHILD

WAR had been declared in August 1914. Cowdenbeath celebrated. Jennie, a dark-haired and lively child not quite 10 years old, marshalled her school friends and her younger brother Tommy to collect their broken dolls. They would play at hospitals and wave flags and march behind the town bands. Over the next few months Jennie realized her father was not cheering along with the rest. Her parents were pacifists. She was mortified, and a little frightened. Her father chaired the West Fife branch of the Scottish Independent Labour Party, and the ILP was resolutely opposed to a 'capitalist and imperialist' war. Because the Party was banned by the Defence of the Realm Act from assembling in the town centre, members took to the hills for their Sunday evening meetings. Jennie went with her parents, listening intently, struggling to understand. Then, she says, one glorious Sunday evening in late September, 'it all became clear'. That week at school, their history lesson had dwelt on the heroism of the old seventeenth-century Covenanters, who had been persecuted for their faith and had fled to the hills to hold their meetings—just like her father and the ILP.

As she wryly admitted, the analogy was not entirely complete. The ILP met not as fugitives on the lonely hillside, but as propagandists by the busy roadside, not hiding from people but urging all those passing by to join them; and even in the most vivid retelling, the treatment of conscientious objectors did not extend to thumbscrew and rack. Nevertheless, it was near enough for a romantic 10-year old. 'We were the modern Covenanters, we were fighting for conscience' sake', she told herself. 'There were only a few of us, but it was we, not the multitude, who were right.'[1]

It was a defining moment for Jennie. She was happy and proud; she was ready to fight. She was now a dissenter, and would remain so all her life. As Nye Bevan told Beaverbrook when he tried in vain to hold Jennie in the mainstream Labour Party many years later, Jennie sprang from 'Covenanter stock'.[2]

It also confirmed that black and white cast of mind, battling, sectarian, and evangelical, that led Nye famously to describe Jennie as his Salvation Army lassie. She was a dissenter not because she was a liberal, but because she wasn't. The other side was wrong. Among her undated jottings were some lines from Rebecca West written in 1911: 'A strong hatred is the best lamp to bear in our hands as we go over the dark places of life, cutting away the dead things men tell us to revere.' Her close friend Suse recalled Jennie laughingly saying within her first few weeks at university, 'Well, I'll either have to join the Salvation Army or get into the House of Commons.'[3]

Nye kept his faith (most of the time) in the mass Labour movement; he was at ease in it. Jennie never quite was. While at university she summarized Johnson's *Vanity of Human Wishes*: 'No good relying on the common people', she wrote in her notebooks. Battling with the Communist Party (CP) in Lochgelly in the late 1920s left her with something close to contempt for the spinelessness of 'the mob'. She distrusted the labour movement's instinct for unity, its willingness to fudge and to compromise in the name of solidarity. She rather doubted that truth lay with majorities. G. R. Strauss, who knew her well, said: 'she rather liked, I think, being a minority socialist. Always she was a very good minority person, indignant about anything and everything.'[4] Jennie, John Freeman told Hugh Dalton many years later, was never comfortable except in opposition. That was where truth was cherished. She would describe, admiringly, how Nye would say to a critic: 'This is my truth. Now tell me yours.' But that was Nye's style. For herself, Jennie always suspected that tolerance was the most insipid of virtues.

As the war continued, itinerant ILP lecturers discussed politics with Jennie's father at their fireside late into the evening. Jennie perched on the fender stool, her back to the grate, hoping that if she stayed silent, her father would not notice her bedtime. The long-haired and elegantly cadaverous James Maxton was a frequent guest, much given to teasing Jennie. Clifford Allen, pale and frail from his imprisonment as a conscientious objector, stayed the night, as did the former suffragette Mrs Helen Crawfurd. Jennie longed to have broken windows and to have suffered in prison with them. She wondered wistfully if there would be anything left for her to do by the time she finished school. Her much-loved grandfather, Michael Lee, who had himself led most of the labour movements in West

Fife, knew how to cheer her up. 'Lass,' he would tell her, 'there will be plenty left for you to do. It takes longer than you think.'[5]

*

Michael Lee spoke of what he knew. Born in the 1850s, his Irish Catholic parents had moved to Lochgelly for work. Father and son went down the pits. Within weeks of starting work, the pit flooded and four of Michael Lee's workmates were drowned. Determined to improve working conditions, Jennie's grandfather founded the Miners' Union in Lochgelly, becoming a member of its National Executive. Taught to read by his sons, he went on to the local school board, the first Labour man to do so, and won for Cowdenbeath's children free books and free schools. A friend of Keir Hardie, he founded the Fifeshire Federation of the ILP. He believed, wrote his granddaughter, in the brotherhood of man and the fatherhood of God. In 1898 he fought the Lochgelly Town Council elections on behalf of the ILP. The Tory candidate whom he defeated was his landlord, who took his revenge by evicting Michael Lee and his young family from their home and dumping them on the streets.[6] Grandmother Lee forgave neither landlord nor husband for putting their politics ahead of her family.

During Jennie's childhood, Michael Lee was disputes secretary of the Union, and for many years lived next door to his son James, Jennie's father—the second of his eleven children. James inherited his father's Irish looks and disputatious tastes, but, to Michael Lee's bafflement and deep distress, dispensed with his father's Irish faith (living next door to each other, father and son could only communicate on the subject by writing notes). Like his father, James Lee went down the pits at the age ot 12, where some years later he was chosen by his fellow miners to be a deputy, the men's fire and safety officer. This was a key post. Lochgelly pits were especially vulnerable to sudden combustion fires and constant flooding and the job of safety officer was dangerous and demanding. James Lee was much respected. He helped to train young men for their mining certificates, but he himself refused to become a manager. As Jennie wrote: 'In those years of crude class war between collier and coal-owner you had to be on one side or the other . . . My father had no doubts about where he stood.'[7]

The children saw another side of him. Jennie's mother, waging continual war on coal dust, did not want pets at home as well. But one day her husband brought back a still dazed, bedraggled and sooty canary, setting it down by the kitchen sink and saying: 'Poor Devil, it deserves to live.' Six times it had been sent into bad air pockets of the pits; each time it had fallen off its perch, overcome by gas fumes. The seventh time, when Jennie's father was pumping it with oxygen to revive it, he decided the colliery canary had earned its retirement, and brought it home. That evening, they went out to buy the finest cage in Cowdenbeath.

On her father's side, therefore, Jennie came from a line of outstanding local Labour leaders, Irish Catholic miners, who were educated by and cultivated in their socialist faith. They founded and sustained Fife's Independent Labour Party. They were, both of them, strong, proud, argumentative yet gentle men—Jennie's father never ever smacked her—who were adored by their family as much as they were liked and followed by their fellows.

On her mother's side, the Pollock and Greig families were shopkeepers and tradesmen, and Protestant (though nowhere in Jennie's papers is there any suggestion of religious strife between the families or within the community). The Pollock women took naturally to business. Jennie's Pollock great-grandmother ran a second-hand furniture and bric-à-brac shop, stuffed with heavy-framed pictures, ornate mirrors, chairs, chests, and chamber-pots. The Pollocks were one of the town's leading families, and Jennie's uncles and great-uncles were barbers, painters, and builders; they took the Cowdenbeath Rangers football team to the top of the League in the 1890s. Jennie's Pollock grandmother married a Greig, a kindly ineffectual man who played his fiddle and who in his later years wandered around the countryside on the tramp, resisting all efforts by his family to tidy him up into respectability.

Cowdenbeath, their home, was in 1890 a very rough and straggling mining village of around three thousand people, with dirt-roads, paraffin-lamps, and water from street wells. The miners lived in two-roomed but-and-ben cottages which they had thrown up in a week. The cottages were badly over-crowded; water ran down the walls, one 'dry' lavatory serviced several families. The coal was kept under the kitchen bed, where it soiled the sheets, and the rubbish piled up in front of the cottages, where it soiled the streets. Cowdenbeath came to be regarded as the Chicago of Fife. By 1911, coal had turned the village into a compact town of some fourteen thousand inhabitants. The town council, on which Michael Lee served, had begun to pave, light, and sewer the town. Smart new buildings were erected: shops, banks, a theatre, a lending library, as well as Beath Secondary School, which Jennie was to attend.

As Cowdenbeath grew, Grandmother Greig had seen her opportunity and opened an hotel and commercial dining room, where she offered steak-and-kidney pies, Scotch broth, and tripe and onions to commercial travellers and to the young country miners who crowded into the town to spend their wages at weekends. Jennie's mother Euphemia was a pretty and serene young woman, brown-haired, round-faced and with rosy colouring, who uncomplainingly did the cooking not only for the hotel guests, but for her family of twelve brothers and sisters as well.

One young miner who paid her particular attention, who teased her, and courted her, was James Lee, darkly handsome in his double-breasted navy suits, something of a dandy, and known as something of a ladies' man. 'An absolute devil of a man . . . talk about flashing eyes', recalled Jennie's friend, Suse.[8] They married in 1900 and moved into their own two-roomed cottage. Over the next six years, they were to have four children, two of whom died from meningitis in infancy, before Jennie was born on 3 November 1904. Her brother Tommy was born some two years later, a gentle blue-eyed fair-haired child who trotted around at the heels of his bossy and protective elder sister. Jennie remembered hearing her mother tell a friend how much she had wanted a daughter; she was, and knew she was, a greatly loved child.

Grandmother Greig saw no reason why she should lose her obliging daughter to marriage, so Ma continued to cook at her mother's hotel. In 1902, it was rebuilt as part of a smart but decidedly shoddy shopping arcade in the town centre. The hotel bedrooms stretched over the shops, and a theatre-cum-meeting-hall built at the foot of the arcade was used for music-halls, temperance lectures, bird shows, trade-union meetings, wedding breakfasts, and funeral suppers. When Grandmother Greig died, Jennie's parents reluctantly agreed to continue to run the hotel and theatre, renting it from one of Grandmother Greig's brothers. For the next few years it became Jennie's home.

Her parents worked themselves into exhaustion, Ma especially. The new hotel was ramshackle and gloomy, a fire-trap, yet so damp that Ma was for ever repapering the bedrooms. The noise was relentless. Pit engines shunted outside the bedroom windows, miners clanged as they tramped past to the pit-head cages that would take them deep underground. Jennie feared the pits. In the vivid stories she told Tommy as they lay awake at night, 'the pit became a fiery dragon or a cruel giant that swallowed up and enslaved poor mortals'.[9] Rats scurried down the corridors of the hotel. Jennie's father hated it all, and longed for a home of his own. He insisted that at the very least it be a temperance hotel. Between pressing *Clarion* newspapers on his guests on the one hand, and denying them drink on the other, he not unnaturally lost the more profitable trade. Her parents struggled to make even a modest living.

To Jennie, however, the arcade, with its toy and sweet shop, great-grandmother Pollock's treasure-trove of a furniture shop, and its theatre, was a magical place. Jennie's father attracted children into matinées by tossing out sticky, brightly coloured paper butterflies; if they stuck to your coat, you got in free.[10] The theatre folk stayed in the hotel, where Ma fed and mothered them. Jennie's playmates were drawn from these itinerant music-hall performers: magicians, plump singers in talcum powder and sequinned gowns, a ventriloquist with a doll as large as Jennie, the unimaginably tall half of a variety turn called 'The Long and the Short of It', who carried Jennie around on his shoulders with her head skimming the ceiling, and a Chinaman with a pigtail (a real one, Jennie knew; she had tugged it). In her memory they formed a frieze of brightly coloured cut-outs, a carnival of kindly grotesques. Elementary school was a drab, bleak, and grey place; but for five years Jennie came home each evening to her very own pantomime. Long afterwards she would say: 'Life is theatre, you've got to make magic, that's what you've got to do, create magic.'[11]

Finally, Jennie's father had had enough. He returned to the pits, and in 1912 the family moved out of hotel life to rent a respectable four-roomed cottage with its own indoor lavatory in Foulford Street, a quiet side street off the main Cowdenbeath to Dunfermline Road. Built on a steep slope, the terraced cottages were single-storeyed and double-fronted, with two rooms overlooking the street at the front which were used as bedrooms, and two rooms at the back overlooking their large garden. One of these was the kitchen-living-room, the other the parlour, in which reposed a piano on which Jennie bashed out 'airs' from *Rigoletto*, as well as a spare bed for visiting lecturers. Under these two living-rooms and built into the slope at the back were a wash-house, where the children played when it rained, and a coal-cellar; but as there was no back door nor internal access to washhouse or garden, the family had to trail down a draughty side passage to get to the back of the house, to collect their coal, have their baths, and deposit their refuse and their ashes. As Jennie said, the design was 'idiotic'. Ma bemoaned the inconvenience. Some years later, they moved a couple of houses down the terrace to a slightly smaller house, losing a room, but gaining an internal ladder connecting the living rooms at the back with the washhouse underneath. Jennie, now nearly 8 years old, was enchanted with the garden in Foulford Street, the first they had had, full of summer flowers and white strawberry blossom. And Ma, wherever she lived, could make a warm and loving home. Jennie would return from school to a blazing fire, a spotless white cloth on the kitchen table, and the smell of freshly baked scones and pancakes for tea.

They were golden years. The family was, by mining standards, comfortably off. Ma had brought linen, china, rugs, and furniture from the hotel, so their home was well furnished. There were flowers on the table, plants at the window. Not only did Jennie's father earn steady money, as the coal industry expanded in the years before and during the war, but, unlike most neighbouring families who had five or six children, the Lees had only two to feed. So the wages stretched to Sunday best clothes (Jennie's finery included a cream silk parasol), to bicycles, tennis racquet, dolls, and wristwatches, comics, sweets, piano and violin lessons, and modest holidays by the sea—and books, endless books. Whatever Jennie wanted, Ma somehow contrived to get for her.

Unlike most girls, Jennie entirely escaped the drudgery of cleaning and child-minding that fell on older daughters in larger families. Absorbed in a book, she would forget to do her share of the housework and Ma could never bear to remind her. Jennie suffered pangs of remorse—she meant to help—but then lost herself in another book. She never ever learnt to cook, to clean, to launder, to mend, or to housekeep. A boiled egg, and the judicious use of a safety-pin to keep up a hem, was as much as she ever managed. Someone else would always do it for her. And throughout her life someone always did—Ma, Millie Rowley of Cannock, and, after Ma died, her cousin Bettina, even Nye himself, who, despite his Welsh boyo upbringing, rather fancied himself as a cook. Jennie's lack of domestic skills was notorious. Friends coming for lunch found themselves cooking it. When one friend searched for ingredients to make a sauce for leeks, she found the cupboards bare. Asked many years later to contribute to a charity cook-book, Jennie proposed to send in a recipe for what she described as a very nourishing dish, a poached egg surrounded by mashed potato. When her secretary told her that this might not quite do, Jennie thought and then had another inspiration. On the way home from work, the busy wife should call in at a high-quality delicatessen, and buy ham and salads. She was not encouraged to send in that 'recipe' either.[12]

Jennie had a remarkable Edwardian childhood. She was brought up in a loving Scottish upper-working-class family, free of the fear of that poverty which shadowed the lives of so many neighbours' children, free (give or take a temporary fascination with hell-fire) of the private guilt and public animosities of formal religion, free of the conventional restrictions of gender, free of any parental demands to conform, and, seemingly, free of the disapproval of censorious relatives. In every way that mattered, Jennie was the son of the family, bright, brave, wilful, demanding, achieving, and self-reliant. Tommy, her younger brother, was more fragile (as a small boy he had had a few months in a sanatorium with TB), easily led, and very much in Jennie's shadow. Her mother deferred to her, but understood her not at all; her father understood her very well. Jennie adored them both. Her father was 'the God of my childhood. His songs and stories and all that he believed in were gospel to me and remained so all my life.'* Between them, she was given all the space she sought and all the attention she required. Their discipline was unobtrusive.

It could have made for a difficult adolescence. Neighbours thought she was spoiled. She was not at all tomboyish, but she was brought up unconfined by conventional notions of what it was to be a young woman. Her ILP background gave her an unusual independence of mind; her upbringing gave her a secure sense of self. She acquired a striking, even arrogant, confidence that was seldom dented. People were required to take her as she was. She was heedless of the pressure to conform. She never felt the usual feminine need to please, she was never willing to adapt to others' expectations. She was, by the usual female standards, inconsiderate and often selfish. A year or two into university she noted in her diary: 'It is high time that the idealisation of unselfishness ceased. There is no need for it.'[13] She would make demands, she would drop in and out of other people's lives without any compunction. 'Impossible' is the word her friends used. She either liked you, or she didn't, and she let you know. Jennie was not, according to girls who were at school with her, much liked by other children, because they considered she held too high an opinion of herself, and that she looked down on them.[14] They were wrong. Jennie was tactless and insensitive, but she was a compassionate child, who hated bullying at school, who worried about the acute poverty of some of her classmates, and who was indignant at injustice. She would fight their good fight. She came from the Labour aristocracy of the ILP and she had, quintessentially, a socialist childhood.

The Labour Party in Fife *was* the ILP, founded locally by Jennie's grandfather, now chaired by her father. Scotland had been Liberal. Gladstone's party had included working men, their chapels, their friendly societies and their unions. As the late nineteenth-century great depression deepened, class lines hardened and the Liberal Party could not embrace both masters and men. Wealthy Liberal employers were reluctant to select and finance working men such as Keir Hardie to be parliamentary candi-

* JL papers, undated jottings, 1970s. (In a different pen, Jennie later added—why, exactly?—'This is a very normal relationship between an attractive loving father and his small daughter.')

dates. In 1887 Hardie had run, unsuccessfully, as an independent Labour candidate in Mid Lanark. In 1893, he had federated the burgeoning network of local socialist societies into the ILP. By 1910 the Party had around 30,000 members, of whom some 5,000 were in Scotland.[15]

The ILP was a propagandist body, its sinews were its itinerant lecturers. It sought to educate Lib–Lab trade unions into socialism, and to enlist their support for an independent Labour Party in Parliament. Unlike the later Communist Party, the ILP was always committed to the parliamentary road; unlike the Fabian Society, it insisted that socialism would be built not by seducing the powerful, but by empowering working men and women. When in the 1890s the employers tried to break the trade unions by lock-outs and court cases, followed a decade later by the notorious Taff Vale and Osborne court judgements, even the more cautious Lib–Lab unions, such as coal, came in behind the fledgling parliamentary Labour Party. After the 1910 general election, forty MPs took the Labour whip. Their leader was the ILP Scot, J. Ramsay MacDonald.

The ILP was woven into every fragment of the Lees' family life: the books in the parlour glass cabinet, Paine, Marx, *The Ragged Trousered Philanthropist*; the conversations Jennie overheard between her father and grandfather as the country moved towards war; the earnest discussions with young miners refusing conscription who had received their call-up papers (James Lee had thrown his papers on the fire). Visiting ILP lecturers slept at their home on Saturday nights, some of them like David Kirkwood coming from Glasgow, others from London, and sometimes a young man on the run from the police for his anti-war activities.[16] Tommy, her younger brother, was bored by politics, and slipped off for the evening if he could cadge some extra pocket money from Ma, but Jenny, accorded a son's rights, would join her father and their guest at the tea-table, listening, questioning, and as she grew older, offering views of her own. Ma bustled around, serving them all.

After school, Jennie would haunt the bookshop in Cowdenbeath High Street of her friend the blind Mr Garvie, where together they read several volumes of *The Story of the Working Class Throughout the Ages*. It was in Garvie's back room that the ILP held their meetings. A couple of evenings a week Jennie went from house to house collecting ILP membership dues; on Sunday mornings she attended the Socialist Sunday School, which Mr Garvie led. It would open with a hymn from the Socialist Sunday School Song Book: fifty Cowdenbeath children singing cheerfully and (in Jennie's case) tunelessly:

We are children, but some day,
We'll be big and strong and say,
None shall slave and none shall slay,
Comrades all together.

Then, ever the Labour Party, the minutes of the previous Sunday School were read, followed by recitation of the ten socialist precepts (or commandments), and some fine uplifting stories. They closed with the Red Flag.[17] Jennie loved it all. On Sunday evenings she went to the great public meetings chaired by her father, which grew increasingly rowdy as the war progressed. In Benn Levy's phrase, she was 'swept into socialism long before the age of consent'. She lived and breathed the fellowship of socialism; she was wrapped in its warmth; she was, she said, 'thoroughly indoctrinated with a wealth of idealism that inspired some of us for the rest of our lives'.[18]

When a few years later Suse, her closest friend at university, came to stay with Jennie, she was overwhelmed:

> [I had] never experienced anything like Jennie's home; the loving cheerful atmosphere, people continually dropping in for a cup of tea or a chat. In the evenings sitting round the large coal fire enthusiastically discussing politics, articles to be written, where meetings were to be held. Very often we would all attend one of these unbelievably crowded meetings with a brilliant speaker like Jimmy Maxton; we would all end up by loudly singing The Red Flag and believing we were going to change the world.[19]

Meanwhile Jennie went to the local elementary school. As her father taught her sums and lessons a year ahead of the class, she sailed effortlessly through, keen to learn, irritated when she was held up by the slowness of the 'smelly children' who sat in the front rows of the classroom under the teacher's eye. She sympathized, somewhat self-righteously, with the teacher when her patience broke and the children were strapped for their stupidity. Only later did Jennie realize that, malnourished and in poor health, many of these children might neither see nor hear properly. Slowly, she became aware of the poverty of some of her schoolmates—after Christmas, for example, when children boasted of their Christmas presents. While Jennie had toys and books and clothes and confectionery, other children had in their stocking just an orange, a handkerchief, and a penny. Mary Docherty, a few classes below Jennie, for two Christmases had nothing in her stocking at all; her father was out of work. Jennie's school clothes were new; theirs were cast-offs. In winter she wore sturdy leather boots; they had plimsolls that soaked up the water and gave them chilblains. Something was wrong somewhere, Jennie decided. She consulted her father, who knew everything.

He tried to explain to her the nature of capitalism, and the need for a revolution—she could still recall the phrases he used twenty-five years later—but she remained not much the wiser. A year or two later, however, she knew something extraordinary had happened when she saw her father meeting his ILP treasurer under the railway bridge across Cowdenbeath High Street, their eyes shining, shaking hands as if they would never stop. The first news of the Russian Revolution had reached them.

Jennie moved on to Cowdenbeath's new Higher Grade School. It was a large, well-equipped secondary school, free, co-educational, and open to all children who passed their elementary school-leaving exams at the age of 12. Jennie's school uniform included a royal blue blazer, full gym kit, tennis racquets, and a straw boater in the summer. 'We were the swells', she wrote.[20]

The usual school leaving age was 14. The boys went down the pits or into a trade. Some of the girls worked at home helping with younger children. Others became pit lassies, their shawls tied around their head, pulling hutches, picking out stones, or carrying props. It was rough work. Many travelled on the special train to the Dunfermline linen factories. The more 'respectable' worked in a shop or went into domestic service; the brightest trained for office work. A very few became teachers. Jennie's parents expected her to leave school at the age of 14 along with the rest, believing against all the evidence that a course in business studies leading to office work might suit Jennie. This was not the future Jennie saw for herself. She negotiated an extra year at school by agreeing to take night classes in shorthand, typing, and bookkeeping. When at the end of that year she came top of the class, her parents relented. She could stay on, and go to university to become a teacher. Ma was determined that nothing should stand in Jennie's way.

Jennie had a classic Scottish education, broad, thorough, and didactic. In England, many women teachers of her generation were apprentice pupil teachers without the benefit of a college education; indeed, until the 1960s most teachers in England still spent only two years at training college. In Scotland, fifty years before, every male teacher and every woman Higher Grade teacher had a four-year university degree. Jennie was well taught. Her school reports noted, with entire accuracy, that she was very able, 'possessing also considerable originality of thought and independence of judgement'.[21] In her final year Jennie determined to become dux of the school. She worked very hard, pushed herself through the exams, and took the dux medal, but a week or two later collapsed with exhaustion. Never again, she vowed, would she cram so hard. She chose the University of Edinburgh rather than St Andrews. Assuming that she would become a teacher, the Carnegie Trust,[22] Fife County Council, and Fife Education Authority agreed to pay her fees and a modest maintenance grant, worth about 30*s.* (£1.50) a week in term-time. She was poised for university.

From her last year at school survive a few pages of her diary, her school essays ('Summer Twilight'), and some poems and fiction. Her diary was written in passable French, presumably to protect her privacy. She was ruthlessly honest. She fretted about her appearance—a little overweight, she ate too much, slept too much, took too little exercise, and was physically indolent. Her face and hands were 'too red', her teeth 'bad' (she must save up to go to the dentist, she told herself), but her expressive brown eyes and glossy brown hair were 'good'. She allowed that sometimes she was 'almost pretty', that the older men to whom she was attracted 'liked to look at her', and responded to her vitality (she confided that one of them had told her that she 'looked like a gypsy queen'). However, she was lonely. She found most people unbearably 'stupid'. She longed for a 'like-minded boyfriend'. 'I don't attract many friends but then I haven't the least sympathy for the other students and I don't meet many people.' She had laid down no firm friendships at school. She was often depressed, too often irritable, she told herself. Unsurprisingly, she longed for a wider world than Cowdenbeath. She was 'sick at heart with the never-ending monotony and ugliness of row-upon-row of stuffy badly built dwelling houses' that made up a mining town, the talk only 'of the weather, the wages and neighbours' doings'.

Her yearnings, at the age of 17, were less conventional than her discontents. Her fiction was barely disguised autobiography, in which a young beautiful miner's daughter gives up all for love. Jennie was for a while enamoured of her violin teacher. He took her off to a concert in Dunfermline and on walks in the local hills. Perhaps he would leave his wife and daughter for her sake. As an emancipated young woman she considered herself bound by 'no convention that she did not consider necessary and good'. Marriage, she held, was neither necessary nor good. They would live in Paris. Yet she also told her diary that she wanted to be 'a great woman', she would 'love to be an orator', to 'be able to move crowds with my eloquence'. 'I long for fame.' 'But more than anything else what I want is to be loved and admired.'[23]

*

Her parents fitted her out for university in their own inimitable ways. Her mother had swallowed her pride and the habits of a lifetime to ask for credit from Cowdenbeath's best drapery store and had put together a suitcase of new clothes for her daughter: two costumes, two blouses, a jersey, an overcoat, stockings, handkerchiefs, and even a bright blue velveteen best dress. To these Ma rather shyly added underwear drawn from her own trousseau, a voluminous embroidered nightgown, bloomers and camisoles, worn only once and then put aside in tissue paper. The underclothes were all wildly inappropriate. Jennie did not know whether to laugh or cry. She did know that she would never wear them. Her father, in his turn, wordlessly placed on her bookshelves a copy of Marie Stopes.[24]

In the autumn of 1922, she left for Edinburgh. The university had been founded in the mid-sixteenth century, built on granite stone and Calvinist principles. When Jennie arrived, its five thousand students studied in six faculties: medicine, arts, science, law, divinity, and music. The largest by far (with two thousand students) was the Faculty of Arts, where all student teachers such as Jennie were enrolled. Most arts students were therefore prospective teachers, and, unlike the other major faculties, where men outnumbered women by about ten to one, men and women were enrolled in equal numbers.[25] Education students took an 'ordinary' MA (a three-year degree), followed by a fourth year at Moray House where they obtained their teaching diploma. The honours MA, taken by an élite group of students, required a fourth, more demanding, year, and offered classified degrees.

In retrospect, Jennie was dismissive of most of her university courses ('dreary and circumspect'), and most of her fellow students. Students took five subjects. Jennie studied British history and English literature, alongside the education and psychology required for teaching. Her fifth option was law. Her lecture and tutorial notes are short, precise, impersonal, page-referenced, and functional: no nonsense. It was 'dead, disconnected parroting', she wrote, 'that earned us our University degrees'.[26]

This was not surprising. Formal Scottish education was at every level heavily didactic. Ordinary MA students were very young (they went to university at the age of 17, a year younger than in England), and academically not always very strong. Anyone who passed their final school exams could enrol; the hurdle to university entrance was money not ability. Teaching was by lectures, backed up by over-large tutorial groups of some forty undergraduates. The students themselves were seeking not a liberal education, but a degree for a job. They liked it all tidily packaged. Staff and students colluded in rote teaching and rote learning. When a new professor in education suggested that he reduce the spoon-feeding and they the note-taking, the students sat in sullen mutiny. Jennie was willing, but the majority of her fellow students had a strictly utilitarian attitude towards their degree: it was their passport to a teaching job, and they could not afford to take risks.[27] The course reverted to formal lecturing.

Jennie wondered whether to convert from an ordinary to an honours degree, but thought that the breadth of the ordinary MA would serve her better—though not for teaching: she knew she would not 'find much satisfaction' in that. 'Promises of self-realization lie in the Labour Movement', she noted in her diary.[28] She read very widely outside the curriculum, especially in contemporary literature (Wells, Huxley, Shaw, Arnold Bennett, Rose Macaulay, Rebecca West, E. M. Forster, and Eugene O'Neill were especial favourites), poetry, American literature (Emerson, Upton Sinclair), as well as Havelock Ellis, J. A. Hobson, and the socialist classics of Edward Carpenter and H. N. Brailsford. Her close friend Suse remembers her stretched out on their sitting-room sofa, reading, endlessly reading: 'She read everything. No one had read what she read . . . we were absolutely steeped in literature.'[29] She was inspired by Olive Schreiner, disapproved of D. H. Lawrence. She was much intrigued by Freud, who was endlessly debated in her circle (one of her university friends spent a weekend with John Strachey and they discussed nothing but *Totem and Taboo*). Freud's challenge to reason and rationality was deeply disturbing to scientific socialists. On balance, Jennie thought the jury was still out.

In May 1925, perhaps encouraged by J. P. M. Millar of the Scottish Labour College who had given a talk to the university Labour Club, perhaps by Herbert Grierson, she read Mansbridge's *An Adventure in Working Class Education* (1920) in which he traced the origins of the university extension movement and gloried in the liberating power of adult education.[30] It was a seminal book and he was a seminal figure. Its influence on Jennie? It would be satisfying to suggest that the book had an indelible effect, signposting her path to the Open University many years later—satisfying, but unlikely. She never refers to Mansbridge; and as she had a jaundiced view of her own education, she would not have shared his more romantic reading of what it might do. Some of her university friends taught adult evening classes, but not Jennie. Having read Tawney's *Education*, she persuaded the Labour Club to run him for rector in 1926. J. P. M. Millar coaxed her to come to one of his weekend schools for the National Council of Labour Colleges, where she met Ellen Wilkinson for the first time. None the less, she never carried a torch for adult education. When, some forty years later, Harold Wilson asked her to build a university of the air, she came to it 'cold'. She never referred to Mansbridge, Millar, or even, much, to Tawney, in her speeches. Yet Mansbridge's *An Adventure* remains an unusual book for an Edinburgh undergraduate to have read. Perhaps it left its mark.

Jennie was for many years highly critical of her university education. Over time, her views mellowed, especially when she came to compare the Scottish with the English degree. She had had a broader education than most English students, who were confined to a narrow single-subject degree course. She had had considerable freedom about what she studied. She also came to value its modularity—most courses were free-standing and examined as they went along: there was none of the make-or-break gamble of English Finals. And because most schoolteachers had to be graduates, Scottish universities were necessarily less academically selective and far more socially open than their English counterparts. Anybody with tenacity could obtain a degree, Jennie believed, with some truth; they were not difficult to get. It was the structure of Scottish higher education, therefore, rather than any obvious intellectual commitment to adult education that forty years later Jennie brought with her from Edinburgh University to the Open University

Jennie, more than most, 'read' for her degree. She also wrote well, with already half an eye to publication. In 1922 her suffragette friend Helen Crawfurd sent some of her final year school essays—such as 'The View from a Mountain Top'—to a comrade who had edited *The Young Communist*. He replied: 'Her writing gives me the impression of one with a fervently religious temperament . . . her style smacks of "The World, the devil, and the flesh" variety.'[31] Indeed so, in her writing as in her politics. The dissenting evangelical tradition of the ILP had shaped them both. Her university literature essays were often lyrical. Her history essays, in contrast to her formal notes, were sturdily partisan. Her second-year essay on seventeenth-century trade, for example, freely denounced 'the great god Profit'; she made only a half-hearted effort to argue both sides of the question, pulling the essay towards the topic on which she would clearly have preferred to write: the deplorable effect of the industrial revolution on the poor. It was polemical stuff. (The marker's comment at the end, that the essay should have been both more critical and more balanced, seems exactly right, as does its grade of 'B+?'.) Jennie wrote as though she were taking part in a student debate. She weighed in; she denounced; she supported; she appealed. No one seems to have told her that the protagonists of the past did not need her help.

Apart from history and literature, Jennie also took classes in law. Most law students were not prospective lawyers (they usually obtained their qualifications through their professional bodies), but were male clerks or women seeking government posts in the Inland Revenue or the estate duty departments. Towards the end of her third year, she won a law bursary worth £50 a year on condition she completed an LLB. So instead of staying at Edinburgh for four years, she stayed for five, graduating simultaneously with an MA, a teacher's diploma, and a law degree.

Jennie was never stretched. She did what she had to do and not much more. Little of it stayed with her. Once the termly exams were over, she forgot even that. Many of her classes bored her, most of them she found routine, though she enjoyed psychology. She was comfortably placed in the middle of the first division for most of her courses. She was no intellectual. She freely admitted: 'I have no love of study for its own sake.'[32] She was argumentative rather than speculative, racy rather than scrupulous, and made up in speed and alertness what she lacked in analytical and reflective power. She had a good but not a glittering academic career. Jennie was not particularly proud of it. She knew it had come fairly easily and, her private reading apart, that she had not invested much of herself in it. Nye, she always insisted, was much better educated than she, and he had done it by himself. She personally did not think any of her pieces of paper were worth much. On the platform, she would announce nonchalantly: 'I collected degrees as others collect postage stamps.'[33] However, Jennie sensibly had no hesitation in capitalizing on her degrees. She respected the Scottish reverence for learning, even if in her case she thought it somewhat misplaced. She always cited her degrees in her campaigning leaflets and publicity material. Even when she was speaking on a street corner, her advertisements, chalked on the pavement, would list her degrees in full. If they were left off, she would remind workers to add them. (They sometimes rebelled. One ILP man, meeting her off a train, told her if she wanted that, she must add them herself.[34])

Just one professor caught Jennie's intellectual imagination, and that was Herbert Grierson. English literature was beginning to enter the universities as a subject fit for academic study as well as private reading. However, it only engaged with poetry and prose (Chesterton, Dryden, Swift, Richardson). There was little or no fiction in the canon: as fiction carried no critical apparatus, theorizing about it was impossible (Jane Austen seems to have crept in as a neo-classicist). Grierson, who was trained at Aberdeen and Oxford in the classics and self-taught in English literature, perhaps more than any other man, says David Daiches, made 'English literature a central "liberal arts" subject at university level'.[35] Best known for his work on metaphysical poetry, Grierson was by now nearly 60 years old. Regius Professor of Rhetoric and English Literature, a shy and seemingly stern man, he still retained a freshness and warm infectious intensity that few students could resist, as he put aside his notes, tugged his right ear, let the steel-rimmed spectacles slip down his nose, and declaimed from the literature he loved. His taste was catholic: not only John Donne, but Byron and Burns. The students hung on his every word. When he dropped his voice, they strained to hear him. Leaving his lectures, Jennie would walk home with Suse, delightedly reciting Keats and Shelley. Grierson, she said, taught her to write (prose writing, of course, not 'creative' writing) and to read. Even if he did believe that 'women students are a distracting element in the University', she recalled him with pleasure and gratitude. For the rest, the university was 'the least important part of student life for me'.[36]

She loved living in Edinburgh. She was moved by the city's austere beauty, liked exploring its old streets during the day, climbing Arthur's Seat of a summer evening, and tramping over the Pentland Hills at weekends. Most female students lived in one of the women's university hostels. Jennie chose the cheaper and less restrictive alternative of Miss McLaren's lodgings, which had a bedroom (with a double bed) and a sitting-room (with a mahogany table) up a flight of stone stairs, on the far side of the Meadows. These she shared with another arts student, Suse, the daughter of a prosperous Conservative Perthshire farmer. They met in the university library and became lifelong friends. Jennie was on a tight budget. Most Saturdays, when her father did not have to work, he cycled the twenty miles over to Edinburgh, bringing a hamper of food from home, with scones, cakes, and home-made potted meat, as well as her freshly laundered clothes, and taking back with him anything Jennie needed washed or mended. Her finances eased at the end of her third year when she collected bursaries and grants. In her last terms, by student standards she was relatively affluent.

Jennie regularly exasperated and infuriated Suse—she had too little tact, too much ego, made too many demands, took too much from her—but Suse found her utterly magnetic and knew that she was destined for great things (as also did Jennie): 'Sometimes I said, "Jennie, it's just finished you know. I can't take this any more" and she would write me a long letter, saying, "Suse you're the only one I can really open my heart to". She was quite impossible . . . Yet I couldn't conceive of what life would be like if she wasn't there.'[37] They were inseparable. Together they went off to lectures in the Old Building, borrowed books from the great Carnegie

Library and read them aloud to each other in their rooms, paraded down Princes Street, ate spiced currant buns for tea at Crawford's smart tea-shop on a Saturday, and practised open-air public speaking on the Mound or in the Meadows on a Sunday (more accurately, Jennie did; Suse sometimes came along to offer moral support). Occasionally they could afford a visit to the cinema, where they paid *3d.* or *6d.* (1–$2\frac{1}{2}$p) to watch a silent movie; or sat in the gods at the theatre. After an evening Labour Club meeting, they consumed eggs or sausages and chips with the comrades at a café in Nicholson Square, where they lingered and argued until the very last tram.

Within weeks, Jennie had found her way to the university Labour Club. Here she became friends with A. W. McIntosh (Mac) who was reading history. (In the 1930s he was a member of the Communist Party before becoming Managing Director of Mars, the confectionery company.) They ran the Labour Club together. Edinburgh was a university of clubs, a hundred or more, of which a handful were what Mac describes as 'show-off clubs', debating societies such as The Dialectic, and The Diagnostic. Jennie regarded these as frivolous. She held aloof from most student activities. She took part in the Women's Debating Society and represented the Labour Club on the Students Representative Council, discussing tram fares and the War Memorial.[38] No one could accuse her of having a light touch. She was, says Mac, 'a conscious and dedicated proletarian', while 'the rest of us were already rotted and corrupted with intellectualism' and liked doing other things as well as forwarding the revolution.[39] Among the other things he would have liked to have done was have an affair with Jennie—she was 'a dazzler'—but she regarded that as frivolous too. On the walks he took her around Salisbury Crags; whatever he may have planned, she was planning the next week's Labour Club agenda.

The Labour Club had been founded the year before Jennie arrived. Edinburgh students were regarded as apolitical and conservative, much more so than at Oxford, Cambridge, or Glasgow, where there were strong Fabian and socialist societies. The new club pulled in twenty or more students to its meetings. Suse and Jennie were the only young women regularly to attend. They occasionally managed to attract a guest speaker, usually they debated among themselves: 'Labour in Office—What We Can Do and What We Cannot', 'Confiscation or Compensation', 'Civil Servants and Politicians'. (As Jennie was still arguing the same questions after the next war, they could not have come to any satisfactory conclusions.) She was soon treasurer, Mac its secretary. They agreed at their January meeting in 1925 that they should all style themselves comrade—no more Miss or Mr—except that Mac kept forgetting his socialist etiquette and had to be reproved by his treasurer and amend his manners and his minutes. There was an edge of rivalry between them. They fought for the chairmanship. Mac, with the aid of the Communists, won, but Jennie bore him no grudge.[40]

The highlight of their activities was the rectorial elections. The rector was elected by the student body every three years. It was a great university event, a cross between the hustings and rag week, a chance to politicize a lethargic student body. Could they afford to run a candidate? The minutes noted laconically: 'Much discussion took place, more or less relevant.'[41] They decided that they could, and invited Ramsay MacDonald who declined, and Bertrand Russell who accepted. Jennie edited their campaign newspaper, the *Rebel Student*, a four-page broadsheet, from her large mahogany table. It was surprisingly professional, unsurprisingly earnest. Their opening number asked its readers to agree that by choosing for Lord Rector 'a distinguished thinker rather than a careerist, profiteer, or titled parasite', the Labour Club was showing 'unusual good taste'.[42] Apart from that light note (Mac's hand, surely), the rest of its three issues carried heavyweight pieces on the nature of socialism and the writings of Russell. Even the comrades were moved to complain that it was all a bit dour.

None of the candidates appeared in person. The Tories were running Stanley Baldwin, the Liberals Lord Buckmaster. After a week of raids, ransacking, egg-pelting, and hostage-taking, from which the Labour Club with dignity abstained, Baldwin was declared the winner by a comfortable majority.[43] Three years later, the Labour Club ran R. H. Tawney but he too was roundly defeated.

Suse was ill for much of their fourth year, which she attributes partly to the intense strain of living so closely with Jennie. Jennie wrote Suse splendid, sprawling, gossipy letters, chatting about books, clothes, mutual friends, speeches she was making, news from home. The good news was that the Lees had finally moved to an attractive new pebble-dashed council house in Lochgelly—12 Paul Street, a couple of miles from Cowdenbeath, convenient to the pit where Jennie's father now worked. It was a pleasant curving street, in garden suburb style. Their house was double-fronted and semi-detached, built on a gentle slope with long gardens in front, a small garden at the back, with two bedrooms and a proper bathroom upstairs. No more tin baths in the washhouse. 'Perfect joy', wrote Jennie to Suse one Christmas. In the kitchen, Ma and Dad were bantering; 'only the ticking of the clock breaks the perfect silence, and everything from a blazing fire to the snowdrops on the polished table is just as I would have my home to be.'[44] There were only two bedrooms, and this was her sad news, because Tommy, Jennie's younger brother, had left home for Australia. On finishing school, he had become an office-boy in a Dunfermline linen works. He had a carefree boyhood, littered with temporary passions, a camera, a gramophone, a girlfriend, a violin; but he was bored and restless and wanted more. At the age of 18 he was eligible for an assisted passage to Australia, and he determined to go. Ma, amid her tears, believed it was for the best.

Jennie also kept Suse briefed on her love-life. Not that there had been much of it so far—just a tentative and delicate romance with an older student, a gentle man deeply scarred by his war experiences. Otherwise Jennie had been amused rather than overwhelmed by the clumsy advances of her fellow students. She was attracted by what she called 'potent' older men. Plenty of students were attracted to Jennie. One man recalled being:

> rather horrified with my first vision of Jennie. She sat on the table in the Union with head tilted back, a cigarette clenched between her (were they rouged?) lips talking volubly about Socialism. She wore a velvet dress, I remember, brown—her usual colour—her skirt was short (as was of course the fashion of the time), and her silk-stockinged legs were amply revealed to the disturbance of more than one male undergraduate mind. But even then she was a personality.[45]

Jennie took practical steps: 'it was time to wake up'. She learnt about birth control from a friendly woman medical student and about abortion from her forensic medicine class.* Thus equipped, she embarked on her first serious romance in the late spring of 1926, played out against the rising tension and heightened emotions of the General Strike and its aftermath.

*

The pits had been in ferment ever since the end of the war. In the eyes of the ILP Lloyd George had 'betrayed' the miners twice. After the war he had set up the Sankey commission, pledged to accept its recommendations. However, he could not accept Sankey's recommendation that the pits should not return to their former owners, but remain in public ownership. Two years later, the government abandoned its wartime control over the mines; the coal-owners promptly cut wages by scrapping the wartime bonus, triggering a three-month strike and lock-out. The battle

* Mrs J. P. Millar of the National Labour College gave her further details, which Jennie promptly passed on to Suse, then in Paris, recommending a rubber pessary together with douching, and reminding her that 'even if an accident occurred', she might 'safely evade the consequences' by abortion. 'Be greedy', Jennie commanded Suse, with all the authority of her own virginity. JL to Suse, 4 Aug. 1926. See also Lee, *My Life*, 49–50.

was fought most bitterly in Fife. Police and soldiers were drafted in to help the coal-owners resist the miners' demands.

Jennie, still a schoolgirl, was cycling home when she found herself caught between a crowd of young miners throwing stones and the police advancing with raised batons. Shop windows were broken; many men were badly hurt. Jennie's bicycle was damaged in the scrum, and she herself was lucky not to be injured. Her father ran the soup kitchen at Foulford, her old elementary school, until the lock-out ended in August 1921 with the union defeated and bankrupt. Thereafter, real wages fell below the level of 1914, pits stood idle, thousands of miners remained unemployed. A minority Labour government in 1924, coinciding with a temporary boom in demand for coal, helped the miners recover, but the return of a Tory government, together with a return to the gold standard, encouraged the coal-owners to slash wages again. The industry was losing markets abroad to the cheap coal of Germany and Poland and losing markets at home to oil, gas, and electricity. The miners threatened industrial action and were supported by railway and transport workers, who refused to move coal. On Red Friday, 31 July 1925, the Cabinet backed down and offered a temporary subsidy to coal-owners to maintain existing rates of pay. The subsidy would expire on 1 May 1926. During those nine months the government prepared for trouble. It laid in stocks of coal, revived the Emergency Powers Act, recruited volunteers, appointed regional commissioners, and briefed local authorities. This time, government and coal-owners were intransigent. On Saturday 1 May they locked out the miners who refused to accept reduced wages and dug in. On Monday night, 3 May, the TUC, unaware of 'what they were up against', in Jennie's words, 'blundered into a general strike' in support of the miners.[46]

The university term had not yet finished. With a few other members of the Labour Club, Jennie rushed down to the trade-union headquarters in Edinburgh to offer help. She was given the job of receiving and dispatching orders for the strike bulletins, sending nearly twelve thousand of them out every day by motorcycle to the West Lothian mining villages. She then found herself in charge of 'traffic control', licensing essential lorries to move on the main routes—Edinburgh to Glasgow and the ports. Her basement office was small and crowded but Jennie quickly had them organized, 'giving orders to men who had been longer in the movement than she had been in the world . . . And they meekly obeyed her.'[47] Mac, supposedly revising for Finals, was desperate to help and unable to concentrate. He abandoned cramming and turned up in Jennie's office.

Most Edinburgh students were on the side of the authorities and over two thousand of them volunteered, becoming temporary bus drivers, stokers at power stations, railway guards and porters, dock labourers, and special constables—anything to break the strike. Strikers stoned trams manned by students and pulled trolleys off the rails. A blackleg train crashed into some refuse wagons at Edinburgh's Waverley station, killing or injuring a dozen people in the worst accident of the General Strike. Pickets tried to stop blackleg transport. Student special constables armed with batons tried to stop the pickets. Throughout Scotland, hundreds of people were arrested and imprisoned. Tempers ran high. Jennie was deeply shocked when 'normally good-natured young fellows' talked 'with unholy glee of the pleasure it would give them to run a tank through one of our mining villages'. Mac was thrown down the steps of the Union for his unpatriotic behaviour by an old school friend, and told not to show his face there again.[48]

Jennie, meanwhile, was blissfully happy. Then came the awful news: the General Strike had been called off unconditionally by the TUC; the government had called its bluff.

That evening, while the Central Strike Committee attended to the last funereal rites on the floor above us, we younger ones were huddled together in the corner of our improvised office, stunned and listless, demoralised by the utter, absolute fiasco of it all. We ended the day with a cursing competition. I was shocked at the language I suddenly discovered I knew.[49]

Although the General Strike was over, the Fife miners held out until December. Jennie went home to meetings, marches led by brass and pipe bands, impromptu concerts, speeches, soup kitchens, demonstrations of the unemployed—and a love affair.

Dan Gillies, she recalled, was a 'young, tawny-haired, sturdily built, high-powered organiser and brilliant platform performer brought into West Fife to take charge of Communist activities', and to keep the miners' strike alive. He was 23, two years older than she, a rivet-heater from Glasgow by trade. A few weeks after the General Strike, she heard him on a street corner denouncing the official Labour leadership as traitors, twisters, and parasites. Meeting him again in Cowdenbeath High Street, she demanded he come home with her to settle the matter. In their front room she from the ILP and he from the CP argued passionately late into the night, until Ma, her coat wrapped around her nightdress, came in and begged them to desist. 'My friend, the enemy' accused the ILP of colluding with a right-wing Labour leadership that had betrayed the Labour movement at every turn. They had thrown away the revolutionary possibilities of the post-war years, had led the movement into the disastrously ill-planned General Strike, and then abandoned it. Jennie, in turn, found barren Communism's 'cheap quackery of infallibility' and was chilled by its diet of 'hate and mechanical Marxist clichés'. They continued to meet in public and in private as the tension between them, political and sexual, grew. He 'is the salt of my existence', she noted rather aptly.[50] She wrote ruefully to Suse:

On Saturday there was a huge demonstration in the Public Park. I was the second speaker & performed fairly well, but was jolly glad to get down from the band & run off with Dan. We thought Ma & Dad would be still in the park as there were other speakers to follow, so dashed home, expecting to have the place to ourselves.

Oh, Hell, there ever more was father, who stayed & talked & talked & talked till we were both ready to throttle him. It was raining too, so we had no excuse for going out. That night Dan was speaking at Kirkcaldy, so I saw him off.

I intended to have a play-thing Suse. Instead, I am up against a man who is stronger & cleverer than myself in every way. And yet—the chief sensation of his kisses was that of duration. Dan is, alas, a modern, & I am afraid it has got to be everything or nothing between us.

We are making arrangements to be together long enough to decide, but at the moment this love-business leaves me perfectly indifferent.[51]

So it was not to be Dan.

The miners' strike lengthened. Violence mounted, as the coal-owners introduced blackleg labour and police used their batons freely; windows were smashed, unexplained fires occurred at the pits, miners' leaders were arrested in night raids, and the women grew grey with fatigue and malnutrition.[52] Dan was everywhere, speaking, marching, organizing, blazing with anger and energy, very much the leader of the local resistance. He organized six thousand of the unemployed, men, women, and children in prams, to march the six miles to the Dunfermline poor house, each town in military formation, to demand relief. Jennie shared the platform with him. Shortly thereafter, she went to Belfast and Dublin to raise funds for the soup kitchens, and brought back a hundred pounds, mostly collected in pennies at open-air meetings, from men and women as poor as themselves.

Her infatuation cooled. At the end of June, Dan was arrested and tried for sedition—he had called on unemployed miners to fight the government and the troops. Dressed in his blue serge suit, he stood trial under the Emergency Powers Act. He defended himself ably, but was sentenced to four months imprisonment.[53]

Jennie's father had dilemmas of his own. As a safety officer, James Lee was asked by the Miners' Union not to come out. If he did, the pits would flood, gas accumulate, and the mine would become too dangerous to be worked in future. The coal-owners promptly put blacklegs to work in the pits that he was protecting. This neither he nor other safety officers could stomach. They, too, joined the strike, and were marked men.

Cowdenbeath families exhausted their savings and their health, as they struggled to hold out and survive on soup-kitchen fare, mutual help, and grudging parochial relief. For nine months they stayed out. By September the area was under informal martial law. By December the miners were finally starved into submission and returned to work on the owners' terms. The smell of surrender poisoned the air. Many families emigrated. One after another of Jennie's aunts and uncles slipped away. Her parents thought seriously of joining Tommy in Australia. Whole communities were stripped of their talent. Some men lost their jobs for ever, as coal-owners imposed new methods of work and closed less profitable pits. Families were evicted from company cottages on to the streets.[54] The comradeship that had sustained the men through 1926 was replaced by the victimizations and recriminations of 1927.

It was a bitter year. Jennie's father was blacklisted. He trudged from pit to pit, everywhere turned away. It was months before he was taken on, even for manual work. He was reinstated as safety officer only when a man lost his life due to lack of safety precautions in the Nellie pit. That summer and autumn, the Lees lived largely on Jennie's money. She fretted at her mother's 'extravagant' housekeeping. When her father saw her writing to the convenor of the ILP summer school that she could not afford to attend, he calmly added that her education expenditure was a heavy burden on the family. This, wrote Jennie to Suse in pardonable irritation, at a time when she was keeping the family, and not the family keeping her.

In September 1926 schools re-opened, and Jennie began work. Her notebooks record interminably dull hours of sums on slates, sewing lessons, a day in the life of an Eskimo interspersed with a day in the life of an owl. She had never wanted to teach, but it was her only means to a degree. She wrote despondently to Suse advising her to take a secretarial course, a cookery course, or a hairdressing course, anything other than teaching. 'I am teaching this week & feeling like Hell—only a cold grey hell with all the hot stuff burned out. What a life.'[55] It was drudgery. However, during her teaching practice, head teachers had found her 'bright and alert, keenly interested in the work', her discipline 'very satisfactory, sympathy the keynote',[56] which makes the events at Glencraig the more surprising.

Fife's Director of Education had been careful with her. She was the well-known daughter of a well-known family. On graduation, he offered Jennie a choice of local school, and she chose Glencraig, requesting a difficult class, confident that she could win them round. The school was some two miles from Lochgelly, its eight classrooms painted a depressing pea-green, the view from its windows blocked by a slag-heap that towered over the school. In it huddled some forty to fifty children, known to be something of a problem class:

> restless, nervous and not inclined to settle down quietly. It was my job to keep them interested and orderly. Every morning at nine o' clock we valiantly began the day. The first hour went quite well. But, before the end of the afternoon, I was hanging on for dear life in a losing struggle to maintain some semblance of order.
>
> I had no bent for this kind of teaching. I was too impatient; too much at war with my whole environment. I did not believe in what I was doing. I did not believe that there was any good reason why either the children or myself should come to terms with life as we found it in that bleak mining village.[57]

She exhausted herself. Her hair fell out. Discipline was usually maintained by the threat of corporal punishment, but Jennie had renounced the strap. The children tested her. They fought, they spat, they tore books, and Jennie broke. By her account, she gave the leading troublemaker two strokes of the strap. He laughed and threatened to throw his slates at her. She struggled with him and then spanked him.[58]

This was regrettable but unremarkable for a young, over-tired and inexperienced teacher in the 1920s faced with a large unruly class. Except that the ILP had denounced corporal punishment. Jennie, her father, and her grandfather were prominent figures in West Fife's ILP, and the Communist Party was seeking to discredit them and it. The incident became a local *cause célèbre*.

Since its formation in 1920, the CP had been fighting the ILP for leadership of Labour's Left, and nowhere more strongly than in Fife. The Labour Party Conference of 1924 had banned Communists from its ranks. As a result the Miners' Union split. Lochgelly was ILP, Glencraig was CP. The General Strike had ushered in a temporary truce, a popular front, but this soon unravelled amid bitter mutual recrimination. Jennie was often put up by the ILP to take on the Communists in debate. A year earlier she had written cheerfully to Suse:

There's going to be a local Waterloo tonight. I have just been asked to appear on the platform at a Communist meeting of protest against the rumour of their expulsion from the Trades & Labour Council. Till they leave, the council is maimed by being unofficial so I must support reorganisation on an official basis. Then I shall definitely join the legions of the damned, called the local reactionaries. What a lark! And of course, if I don't go, although I have no official connection with the Council, I shall be equally besmutted.[59]

The CP had already attacked Michael Lee as a trade-union official and denounced James Lee, quite unfairly, for crossing the picket lines as a safety officer. They now seized on the Glencraig incident to denounce Jennie Lee for beating children.

A former schoolmate of Jennie, 19-year-old Mary Docherty, who had been on the march to Dumfermline poor house, had founded the Communist Young Pioneers. They demanded the abolition of the strap, free school dinners, no religious education, and the teaching of 'Working Class history not Boss History'. The Glencraig children reported to Mary that one of the boys had received 'six of the belt all at one time' from Jennie. Other children, they said, had received two strokes apiece. 'Kind, kind and gentle is she', was chalked in large letters on the pavements. Leaflets circulated around Fife denouncing Jennie as a snobbish and brutal teacher. At Jennie's insistence, the Director of Education investigated the matter and demanded an apology on her behalf, but the damage to her reputation was done. She was offered a transfer to another school, but she refused. That would have seemed like running away.

The following Sunday, Jennie was taking part in an ILP debate at the Lochgelly Miners' Institute. Members of the Glencraig CP came to denounce her, and a contingent of parents turned up to support her. Jennie defended herself vigorously. The meeting remained orderly but hostile. It was an unpleasant incident, extensively reported in the local press, and it marked her. She had never before been so personally and publicly vilified. Jennie was left with an unrelenting hatred of the CP. 'Their cynicism and hypocrisy make me "sick"', she told Suse. It also made her the more determined to seek a career outside schoolteaching.[60] She never doubted what that career should be.

Pressures at school eased with the appointment of a new head teacher, but more and more of Jennie's time was being spent on the Scottish ILP circuit, helping to rebuild the Labour movement after the defeats of 1926. Jean Mann, who, like Jennie, later became an MP, stayed with the Lees in Lochgelly and noticed that their mantelpiece was covered with requests asking Jennie to speak at meetings all over Scotland.[61] From her first year at university Jennie had gone out to the villages most weekends, where she mustered the crowds and the collection; the speech she carefully prepared was invariably discarded, as she trusted to the instinct of the moment. Words spilled out, often at great length. Walking home with her from one meeting, Maxton put his arm around her shoulder, saying, 'Very good! very good! But don't try to tell them *all* you know in the one speech.'[62]

She had become a compelling speaker, much in demand, able to take to the platform on a moment's notice, and speak extempore for an hour. Patrick Dollan remarked that she was the best woman speaker in the Scottish Labour Movement. Newspapers wanted her photograph, which she willingly gave them, 'as my exit from teaching lies through publicity'. When her parents were planning to emigrate to Australia at the end of 1926, Jennie determined to stay behind, to see 'what shapes I am making towards Westminster'.[63] At the age of 23, she was appointed a delegate to the ILP national conference at Leicester in 1927. Irritated by Shinwell's defence of MacDonald's 'dithering' policies, she came to the rostrum and stormed the conference. Fenner Brockway, who was no mean judge, wrote:

> A young dark girl took the rostrum, a puckish figure with a mop of thick black hair thrown impatiently aside, brown eyes flashing, body and arms moving in rapid gestures, words pouring from her mouth in Scottish accent and vigorous phrases, sometimes with a sarcasm which equalled Shinwell's. It was Jennie Lee making her first speech at an ILP conference. And what a speech it was! Shinwell was regarded as a Goliath in debate, but he met his match in this girl David.[64]

Jennie was appointed ILP fraternal delegate to the Brussels Socialist International Conference that summer with the wealthy Charles Trevelyan,[65] who became a lifelong friend. She took advantage of her first trip abroad to travel down to Cologne.

Weekends were increasingly spent in London with T'ang Liang-Li, a young Chinese journalist and author she had met at the Leicester conference. He introduced her to Bloomsbury life and her first full love-affair. He was, recalls Suse, 'awfully attractive, a typical Chinaman, not tall. She loved his voice . . . He was different, exotic, passionately interested in politics.' Jennie found herself, in her words, 'grappling with a personality infinitely cleverer, subtler and more understanding than myself'. But not for very long. He wanted total commitment, which Jennie could not and would not give. She discouraged him from giving up his other relationships, warning him with devastating honesty that, as she was just embarking on her 'experimental phase', she might some day desert him. 'This business has a lot of pain in it, Suse, as well as pleasure. Still he says the three days (and nights) we spent together were the happiest in his life.' He wanted to support her in London while she tried her hand at journalism and national politics. Six months later, T'ang's devotion had increased, hers had cooled. 'Though fond enough and friendly enough to enjoy his company and permit his caresses', she was 'not in love with him', she reported to Suse. As suddenly as she had embarked on the affair, she ended it 'without a qualm just like that, finished, out. Absolutely incredible.' She left T'ang devastated and Suse to comfort him.[66]

T'ang had hoped to take Jennie back to China with him, but that was never a possibility. In April 1928 Jennie had turned down an invitation from Dumfries to be nominated as their parliamentary candidate. A month later she addressed a huge May Day rally of miners' families in Shotts's public park. It was cold and windy, but they warmed to her. In July Jennie arrived home from school. Her mother calmly handed her a telegram. Jennie looked startled. 'It is nothing serious, is it?', asked Ma. 'No one in trouble, no one dead?' 'No, no', Jennie reassured her. 'Just ILP business.' As Ma got her tea, she read it again: 'Labour Movement in Shotts desires to nominate you for Parliamentary Candidature of North Lanark under I.L.P. auspices reply per return as to your considering same. Dewar Secy, 5 Benhar Rd, Shotts.'[67] She was still only twenty-four years old, and not yet able to vote.[68]

2

NORTH LANARK

JENNIE was not North Lanark's first choice. In 1926 the constituency had lost its candidate when he was elected to a safe neighbouring seat. She was not their second choice either. The miners had nominated a Communist, who was unacceptable to the Labour Party, and the wrangling had cost the constituency time. With a general election due soon, most candidates were already in place. North Lanark hunted around. Since the General Strike Jennie had become the ILP's outstanding woman speaker. What else could she offer them? She had already coolly taken stock. At the age of 20 she had recorded in her diary: 'A little intelligence and what apparently are liabilities in my life might be my greatest assets e.g. being a woman, belonging to a working class family and brought up in their fashion.'[1]

On the debit side, she was admittedly very young—and to her chagrin looked even younger than she was. One incident never left her. Back in 1924, as a 19-year-old, she had been booked to speak at a mining village near Edinburgh. The large collier meeting her off the train had taken one look at her and said, 'Great God.' Both he and she made their way in mutual panic to a packed and impatient hall. As ever, she acquitted herself splendidly, but afterwards could not remember a word she had said. For years that 'Great God' rang in her ears. She tried to make herself look older in public, and took to wearing a large-brimmed hat—which made her look perhaps not much older, but even more fetching.

However, often at her meetings, 'I saw the faces of elderly and middle-aged colliers looking up towards me from the body of the hall, reconciled to my youth because of the letters after my name.' When she got her LLB, her grandfather Michael Lee had come over to Lochgelly to shake her warmly by the hand; he then said, very proudly, 'Master of Arts, Bachelor of Laws.' Scottish mining communities, she knew, revered learning. Education was a lamp for their feet, armour for the fight, and however little value she placed on her university degrees, she had no inclination to disabuse them.

She had other things going for her that were no less important. She was the daughter of a miner and the granddaughter of Michael Lee, who was honoured throughout the mining communities of Scotland. North Lanark was a mining, and a miners', constituency.[2] A miner's lassie might do. Jennie had also built no mean reputation of her own. She had packed more speaking engagements and more platform experience into the last two or three years than most politicians acquire in a decade. Although she hated it when anyone else said so, her style was 'evangelical'. As she admitted, 'MacDonald himself was not much better at painting the sorrows of the poor, the beauty and dignity of the Promised Land of socialism—and of trusting to Providence somehow to jump the gap between the distressful present and that beatific future.'[3] As MacDonald was one of the most mesmerizing leaders that Labour ever had, and could hold Conference in his hand, Jennie was making no small claim. Yet she did not overstate. She could storm a meeting to anger, move it to tears, warm it into solidarity, or lift it into confidence—as she had done at the Shotts May Day rally. She was young, passionate, and quite lovely.*

Finally, Jennie came with ILP endorsement. She was an old family friend of Glasgow's ILP Clydesiders—John Wheatley, Jimmy Maxton, David Kirkwood—who now dominated Glasgow's Trades Council, would soon take its City Hall, and since 1922 had held most of Glasgow's parliamentary seats. Their socialism was warm, militant, sharply class-conscious, and intransigent. Jennie was 'Maxton's darling', Beaverbrook noted, hastily qualifying, 'his political darling'.[4] Maxton now dominated the Clydesiders, who dominated the ILP; the ILP, in turn, was the mind and soul of the Labour Party.[5] Jennie was a sort of niece by adoption of the Clydesiders. The ILP would sponsor her, work for her, and pay her election expenses. Scottish industrial constituencies belonged either to the miners or the ILP. Jennie could plausibly lay claim to both tickets. Yes, she might reasonably conclude, she had quite a lot to offer North Lanark.

They certainly thought so. Her selection conference took place at the Keir Hardie Institute in Glasgow in mid-September 1928. In a surprisingly tranquil meeting, Jennie beat off the other candidate by a large majority.[6]

* Sara Barker, later the formidable national agent, said that when she first saw Jennie, she was 'like a rose with the dew still on her'. A Scottish MP remarked dourly: 'Its a long time since there was any dew on that rose.' Interview Lady Mallalieu.

What could North Lanark offer Jennie? It was an ugly sprawling mining constituency, much poorer than Fife, and its housing conditions much worse (half its houses, Jennie was to argue, were slums).[7] North Lanark bordered the north and east edge of Glasgow, stretched between the city's overspill and more rural communities to its east.[8] An MP who went to speak at Shotts saw 'a drear, drab, wind-swept mining community in the Lanarkshire Hills, devoid of any single redeeming natural feature. The unrelieved ugliness of it made one shiver and draw one's coat closer to keep out a chill that was more than physical.'[9] Around a fifth of its electorate had Irish Catholic roots. Of the seven Lanark seats, three were already held by Labour, four were marginal. Labour had held North Lanark until 1924, when the Tories gained it with a modest majority of 2,028. Jennie could expect to regain it for Labour at the general election. As she was young, and the election close, Jennie would not do better anywhere else (her sights, after all, had been on the general election following). North Lanark did even better for her than that. The following February, its elderly Tory MP, Col. Sir Alexander Sprot, died of a heart attack in the House of Commons lobby. Jennie faced a by-election which would deliver her huge publicity just a few weeks before she fought the general election.

The Tories had difficulty in finding a candidate, a sign that they expected to lose. They chose the unknown Lord Scone, son of a Perthshire landowner, the Earl of Mansfield, much the same age as Jennie but with none of her political experience, and down with flu for part of the campaign. The Liberal candidate was the tall lady-like figure of Miss Elizabeth Mitchell, who had fought the seat in 1924, daughter of a former sheriff of Lanarkshire and a member of Lanarkshire Education Authority. 'Tell Lord Scone', she is alleged to have said, 'that I got a First in Greats at Oxford. He is an Oxford man and knows what that means. It will frighten him.'

Neither of Jennie's opponents was particularly strong on the platform. Lord Scone was 'underdone', went the local joke, but he would be 'well done' by the time Jennie had finished with him. As Scone was as young as she, and as Miss Mitchell was the same sex as she, Jennie's age and gender were never an issue in the campaign. At the forthcoming general election, women under the age of 30 would vote for the first time, so no political party was going to alienate 'the flapper's vote', especially as no party knew which way that vote would be cast. The press grumbled that 'they have revealed their knees but not their minds'. Jennie *was* vulnerable to the loss of the important Catholic working-class vote; her replies to questions about birth control (she 'did not regard this as a political matter') were understandably more cautious than candid. However, Lord Scone was prominent in the Protestant League, so Jennie kept most of their vote. It remained a problem constituency, none the less, ready to ditch a Labour candidate who was not sound on birth control or religious schools, and Jennie was not sound on either. Rather more unexpectedly, she acquired the bookies' vote. They detested the new betting tax. As Labour had opposed it in the Commons, the bookies were now intervening in by-elections, offering cars and contributions to Labour candidates.

Jennie's main task was to enthuse traditional Labour supporters. Her election address, drafted by party managers to appeal to the centre ground vote, she rejected as too tame. She wrote a more fiery version of her own. Thus equipped, with the Catholics on side, the bookies on form, and the miners on hand, Jennie worked the constituency. It was bitterly cold. She carried with her Ma's home-made mixture of brandy, honey, and cream, to protect her voice and her enthusiasm. The press loved her; she was immensely photogenic. Even the Conservative journals carried wonderful photos: Jennie, arms outstretched, addressing large crowds from the roof of her car; Jennie returning a teething-ring to a rather surprised baby; Jennie campaigning with the stately Sir Charles Trevelyan; Jennie leaning elegantly over the table as she played billiards in a working men's club; Jennie with miners; Jennie with miners' wives. It remained a decorous and good-natured campaign. The women candidates said nice things about each other, and teased Lord Scone.

There were few outside speakers, but Lord Scone did bring over Robert Boothby, MP for East Aberdeenshire. He came to warn of the dangers of socialism. He was late for his first meeting, as he got lost in the fog, and was late for his second by taking the wrong road to the wrong village. This did not add to his powers of persuasion. Tory audiences remained sparse. The Liberals found their halls reasonably full (mainly of Labour supporters) as they called for less public spending and more free trade. Jennie's meetings were usually packed to overflowing. In the *New Leader* Patrick Dollan reported that, unsurprisingly, Jennie Lee had established herself:

> as the personality of the contest. She is proving a first rate candidate and her speeches are models of political prudence and knowledge. Her experience as an ILP propagandist is a splendid asset in a by-election campaign and enables her to deal effectively with hecklers of all kinds. Between eight and nine meetings are held daily. Collections are taken at all these to pay for expenses, and at the time of writing every meeting had paid its way . . . The whole division has been galvanised. Apathy is unknown. Veterans tell me they have never seen such enthusiasm

in the division. An encouraging feature is the large number of young people who are giving active support.[10]

The more Jennie canvassed, the angrier she became. She looked around her. A quarter of all coal-miners were unemployed, as were a quarter of iron- and steel-workers, and almost a third of Glasgow's shipbuilders.[11] Labour would tackle unemployment. How? She drew on the ILP's analysis, drawn from J. A. Hobson, and outlined in its 1926 policy document *The Living Wage*. Labour, she said, crossing her fingers, would increase home demand with higher wages and pensions; open up foreign markets, resuming trade with Russia, for example; reorganize the country's basic industries through public ownership; and use state-aided schemes to build houses and roads and, in the process, create jobs. Bitingly, she added that crofters had lost their homes in the Highland clearances; now came the Lowland clearances, as all Baldwin could offer the unemployed was emigration.

Her victory was never in doubt, but the scale of it took them by surprise. On a 75 per cent poll, Jennie took 57 per cent of the vote, a majority of 6,578 over Lord Scone. The Liberal candidate lost her deposit.[12] When the result was announced, Jennie blushed happily and turned to Ma for her kiss of congratulation. She then came out of the County Hall Buildings in Glasgow, tired, to find a large crowd waiting for her. She struggled across to her car, still decorated with its campaign balloons, and thanked them, saying that her victory had been 'a declaration of war on poverty', an indication of the general election to come. Ma wanted to telegram Tommy in Australia, Jennie to telegram her father at Lochgelly and her grandfather in Dunfermline, who were all anxiously awaiting the result. Jennie then spent the afternoon touring the constituency, Ma by her side. Red flags hung from the windows and chimneys of miners' cottages. Wherever she stopped, she was mobbed, as men and women, hysterically shouting and laughing, 'shoved and scrambled to get near the flushed, almost bewildered-looking girl, who stood on the car's leather cushions, with her dark hair tumbled by the evening breeze'. Jennie ended the day with a Labour Victory Ball at Shotts. Tea was awaiting her on the platform. Speeches were demanded. Jennie, for once, was short, and to the point. She teased them: 'I am prepared to do a lot for North Lanark, but I am dashed if I am prepared to give you a free entertainment by watching me take tea.'[13]

Her father came home from the pits, still in his working clothes, still uncertain of the outcome, to find a journalist on his doorstep with the result. The next afternoon Jennie took the train home to Cowdenbeath. Her grandfather had come to meet her. As the train steamed into the station, he scrutinized each carriage window as it passed. Jennie dismounted and started to walk along the platform, carrying her large bag. Then she saw her grandfather. She laid down her bag and waited for him. Old Mr Lee came up and hugged and kissed her, his arm around her shoulders, exclaiming over and over again: 'Jennie, my clever lassie.' Even hardened press reporters were touched. Finally, she arrived back at Lochgelly, her parents (and nearly a thousand other people) waiting to welcome her home. Jennie made a speech; Grandfather Lee made a speech. And Ma made her some tea. Two days later, Jennie left her parents in Lochgelly and took the overnight sleeper from Glasgow down to Westminster. 'Suse,' she said, 'I will have London at my feet.'[14]

*

She was met at Euston by the Trevelyan family, who took her back to their lovely old house behind Westminster Abbey where Jennie stayed for a few days. They rehearsed her introduction to the Commons—Lady Trevelyan guessed that Jennie was not used to bowing, to the Speaker or anyone else. Jennie coolly rejected the sponsors proposed for her by the Party—Margaret Bondfield, the chief woman, and Tom Kennedy, the Chief Whip. She would be introduced not by official Labour but by the 73-year-old Bob Smillie, the miners' leader who was a lifelong friend of her grandfather, and James Maxton, a lifelong friend of her own.

That afternoon, she lined up with other by-election winners at the bar of the House. Her striking good looks, extreme youth, and fiery reputation fascinated an almost entirely male House. As usual, she wore brown, a stylish brown suit. Some of the MPs had smartened themselves up for the occasion with bright new ties and waistcoats. Another had collected flowers for her from a Members' dining-room, a charming gesture, except that by mistake he gave them to the wrong woman, to the daughter of a fellow MP. Maxton's long hair was elegantly brushed for the first time MPs could recall. Jennie walked up that long carpet between her sponsors, bowed three times, took the oath, signed the book, trod accidentally on the Home Secretary's toes, and shook hands with the Speaker to loud cheers. Ramsay MacDonald was seen waiting to congratulate her. Then some of her fellow women MPs, led by Lady Astor (sporting a vast posy of Parma violets for the occasion), the Tory Lady Iveagh, Ellen Wilkinson, Susan Lawrence, and the recently elected Ruth Dalton, who had all been watching the ceremony like a bevy of aunts, swooped and carried her off to tea.[15]

Jennie had to find somewhere to live. Clifford Allen had a small top-floor furnished flat at 28 Dean Street in Soho to rent, next door to a laundry. Its two rooms were divided by a curtain, but it had a tiny roof-garden, where she sunbathed and grew flowers. Karl Marx as well as Charles Laughton had occupied it before her.[16]

In late April Jennie made her maiden speech in the budget debate. Only Lady Astor's 'maiden' had created more interest. As soon as it was known that Jennie was 'up', the Smoking Room emptied. No one apparently had told Jennie that in a maiden speech she was supposed to seem nervous, appear modest, talk about her constituency, and be non-controversial. Jennie unblushingly recycled her campaign speech, letting fly at the government. She asked whether the budget would create more employment, better conditions of labour, or higher wages for working people. It would not, she said. So she accused Winston Churchill, Chancellor of the Exchequer, and his budget, of 'cant, corruption, and incompetence'. Her gestures were dramatic, imported from the soapbox and borrowed from Maxton: the drumming fingers, the arms suddenly outflung, the toss of her head as she threw back her hair, and then the theatrical discarding of her speech notes. The Conservative who followed her generously congratulated her on 'her courageous, spirited, clever and dramatic speech'. Philip Snowden wrote her a stiff but pleasant note:

Dear Miss.

Hearty congratulations on a quite unusually successful maiden speech.
You have caused [*sic*] to be happy about it and we look forward with eagerness to your further interventions

Yrs v. truly

Philip Snowden.

(It was the only note she kept. It must subsequently have given her wry amusement, and Snowden, if he recalled it, a certain chagrin.) Maxton was well pleased, others less so. Ramsay MacDonald 'sat silent and glum'.[17]

*

She was soon overwhelmed by her constituency correspondence. It seemed that all the pent-up misery of the last twenty years in North Lanark was finding its way to her: ex-soldiers from the First World War, too ill to work but refused pensions; men who had been hurt in the pits, able only to do light work, which was unavailable, and whose compensation had been stopped; women who were living in two-roomed slum cottages with one room so wet with damp that the entire family lived, slept, and huddled in the other; women in new council houses, frightened when they found that they could not afford the high rent and costly electricity; old people who were hungry because their 10*s*. (50p) a week pension did not last to the end of the week; jobless men, footsore from seeking employment, but still cut off from benefit because they were not 'genuinely seeking work'; lads stranded abroad, penniless in Australia and Canada without the money to get home; lads unemployed at home trying in vain to get out to the Dominions.

Jennie, seemingly so buoyant and carefree, was haunted by the despair of the mining communities. It fed her own tendency to depression. Whenever she went back home, she struggled to live with it, 'galvanising myself into gaiety by some wild stimulant or other', she wrote to Frank Wise, an ILP MP and her most intimate friend. Even on trips abroad she carried 'this ugly monster' with her. 'In London I am continuously playing hide and seek with it. It is a kind of running sore that saps away most of my energy. If only I had powers to express this sense of crucifixion of the mining community or could, better still, help in any way.'[18] On a good day she turned that despair into raw anger; on a bad day it disabled her. Jennie could never be seduced by the gothic opulence of the Palace of Westminster.

Nor could she be seduced by its comforts. Jennie had no room of her own in the House—few members did. She shared the Lady Members' room, which had originally been Lady Astor's office, overlooking the Terrace. It was small and stuffy and served the ten of them. They called it 'the tomb'. If one woman used the phone, no one else could work. Later in 1929, their numbers now fourteen, they acquired a new room, still small, with a dressing-room attached, elegantly furnished with a wash-stand, a tin basin, a jug of cold water, and a bucket. They had no bath-room, as the men did, in which to recover from all-night sittings. They also had no annunciator in their room, so could not tell what was happening in the Chamber—more of a hardship than it might sound, since the women were reluctant to sit around in the bars, where the men drank, smoke, and gossiped while they waited for the vote. They were not welcome. Lady Astor made it a point to be either in her room or in the Chamber; she seldom trespassed elsewhere. The irrepressible Ellen Wilkinson, who had arrived in 1924, however, roamed the House and invaded the dining-rooms, much to male discomfort. When the first women ministers were appointed, they ventured into the Smoking Room to pick up the gossip. The lady visitors' gallery in the Commons was no longer screened off, but it was still segregated. Slowly, the facilities and geography of the House adapted to the presence of women MPs.

Jennie shrewdly camped at one of the corridor tables in the division lobbies. Maxton, seeing her struggling with a huge pile of letters, told her that she had better make up her mind whether she was going to be a socialist MP or 'another bloody welfare worker'. That was bad advice (and advice that Jennie passed on many years later to the young Joan Lestor, who had the sense to ignore it).[19] It fuelled the suspicion in North Lanark that she was more interested in building a national career for herself than in looking after the constituency. Many years later the same allegation was to cost her Cannock. More useful advice came from another Labour MP who said Jennie needed a secretary. When she replied that she could not afford one on a parliamentary salary of £400 a year, he found her a competent volunteer, who got Jennie's paperwork under control.[20]

Fortunately, given the size of the women's room, the women got on remarkably well. Nancy Astor had been the first woman MP. Rich, smart, Conservative, American, there by virtue of her husband's elevation, and with no track record in either party or women's politics, she was not exactly the first female MP that the women's movement might have hoped for. Yet, arriving at Westminster, she was met off the train by former suffragettes who had been imprisoned and forcibly fed. One of them came forward to pin a badge on her, saying; 'It is the beginning of a new era. I am glad to have suffered for this.' Lady Astor was deeply moved. The tension was lightened when an unprepossessing man in the crowd bawled: '*I* never voted for you.' 'Thank heaven for that', she retorted.[21]

Nancy Astor insisted that she was not a feminist. Indeed, virtually all the women MPs insisted that they were not feminists—Tory women because feminism was progressive, Labour women because feminism was middle class. Feminism was a dirty word. Labour men had hated what they called 'the sex antagonism' of the suffrage campaign before the war. Although women's suffrage had had strong support from Keir Hardie and the ILP, the male Labour Party was ambivalent, and male trade-unionists and doctrinaire Marxists, such as H. M. Hyndman, had opposed it. Labour had fought the 1918 election on the innocent slogan: 'Labour stands for no sex in politics.' Even Ellen Wilkinson, who had been a professional organizer for the suffrage movement before the war, was (almost) as reticent as the rest. There were no votes in evoking the suffragettes.

*

Women MPs, with the exception of the Independent Eleanor Rathbone, were Members of Parliament for their party, for their constituency, and for women and children—in that order. Ellen Wilkinson never neglected her 'important industrial constituency . . . I have women's interests to look after, but I do not want to be regarded purely as a woman's MP . . . men voters predominate in Middlesbrough East, thousands are unemployed.'[22]

Nancy Astor tentatively suggested that they might form a more structured women's group in the House. Jennie was 'violently' opposed to such an idea and would have nothing to do with it. 'Anyway', she scribbled in a rather silly aside, 'no suggestion of a man's group to deal with specifically men's affairs.'[23] None the less, women MPs banded together, regardless of party, to rectify women's disabilities. They built on their suffrage networks and worked with women's pressure groups. They were mutually supportive, well aware that some male MPs would enjoy a *frisson* if they attacked each other. However, when Margaret Bondfield became the first woman to join the Cabinet as Minister for Employment, reticence could no longer prevail. Tory women criticized her for increasing the borrowing limit for the National Insurance Fund; Labour women denounced her for cutting benefits to married women.

Although they did not shout about it, there was a woman's agenda. Most of the women MPs spoke on health, housing, and education—the same issues that dominated their work in local government. Most of them kept a watching brief on issues of women's pay, women's unemployment benefit, family allowances, and women's political and civil rights. Ellen Wilkinson tried to get more women employed in the police, while Jennie asked questions about women employed as prison officers and prison visitors. Lady Astor joined other Labour women in autumn 1930 in trying to ensure that women who married foreigners did not thereby lose their British nationality. It had been Nancy Astor and Ellen Wilkinson who between them had cornered the then Home Secretary Sir William Joynson-Hicks in February 1925 into an explicit commitment to introduce the vote for all women at the age of 21 (as the Tory Cabinet had been considering raising the voting age to 25 for both men and women, subsequent Cabinet meetings were somewhat acrimonious).[24]

The most contentious women's issue (apart from family allowances)[25] was birth control. Dorothy Jewson, the brave ILP Member for Norwich, was one of the few publicly to campaign for free family-planning advice at local maternity clinics, so that working-class wives might mitigate the poverty that came with large families. The Labour Party, however, gave more weight to the Catholic vote than to women's voices. Ellen Wilkinson was sent into the 1928 Labour Women's Conference to argue that, as birth control benefited all women, and not just working-class women, it was not a class issue and therefore not a matter for the Labour Party.[26] The issue cost Dorothy Jewson her Norwich seat in 1924, as later it lost Dr Edith Summerskill the chance of winning Bury in 1935.[27] All the churches denounced birth control as unnatural, and the Catholic Church called it murder. Jennie practised contraception, of course, as did other single women MPs in her situation, without a flicker of guilt, but with a large Catholic vote in her constituency, she kept quiet. She never doubted that women had the right to control their own fertility in any way they chose, but prudently she never spoke about such issues on the public platform.

Outside the House, women played down their interest in women's issues. Jennie spoke to distinctively women's issues rather less than most women MPs (she was too young to have taken part in the suffrage campaign and she had no background at all in the women's movement, unlike, say, Mrs Wintringham, Dorothy Jewson, Ellen Wilkinson, Marion Phillips, Ethel Bentham, Edith Picton-Turberville, Eleanor Rathbone, and even Margaret Bondfield). She had been brought up in a Scottish mining community to speak the language of class; the desperate struggle of the 1926 miners' strike was all too recent. In that setting, women's rights (as opposed to the plight of miners' wives, for example) would have seemed quite foreign. Scottish Labour did not, unlike the English Labour Party, reach out to women voters. It organized very few women's sections, and did not encourage them to affiliate to local parties. Politics was for men, and honorary men like Jennie. In every way that mattered, she had always occupied a male world—as child, as student, and as a young propagandist and politician—and she was at home in it. In North Lanark and later in Cannock she addressed working-class women like a man, proud of them, often sorry for them, sometimes fighting for them, but never one of them. She was relatively uninterested in education (more accurately, perhaps, she was heartily sick of schools); none the less, she denounced over-size classes and loyally supported her mentor, Sir Charles Trevelyan, Minister for Education, when he tried to raise the school-leaving age. She spoke passionately about the housing crisis in North Lanark and, after the war, in Cannock. And she fought to protect the rights of women, and especially of married women, to unemployment benefit.

Most women MPs, like most male MPs, had specialist issues of their own. On the Labour side, the tiny 'Red' Ellen (it denoted her hair as well as her politics) was, like Jennie, absorbed in economic and unemployment matters; Mary Agnes Hamilton, the clever and stylish MP for Blackburn, spoke to industry and finance; Edith Picton-Turberville (The Wrekin), specialized in ecclesiastical matters and argued for women priests, looking rather like a medieval abbess herself; Lucy Noel-Buxton brought with her from Norfolk an interest in horticulture; Marion Phillips (Sunderland), the Labour Party's woman officer, pressed home infant mortality figures. Two of the most able, the unhappy Margaret Bondfield (Wallsend) and the splendid Susan Lawrence (East Ham), were absorbed in their departments, and Lady Cynthia Mosley (Stoke) in her husband.

For the Tories, Lady Astor had a go at most things, which was a mistake, giving her a reputation for shallowness which she did her best to earn; but the brave and formidable Duchess of Atholl (Perth and Kinross), who had opposed women's suffrage, found herself radicalized by her time in the House. With the help of Eleanor Rathbone, she drew on the assurance of her upper-class background to discomfort male MPs in 1929, by describing to them the horrors of female circumcision in British Kenya. Eleanor Rathbone conformed most closely to the stereotype of what suffrage women had hoped for and anti-suffrage men had feared in a woman MP. An Edwardian progressive, daughter of a Liverpool merchant prince, trained in local government, she was the president of the National Union of Societies for Equal Citizenship, which grew out of Mrs Fawcett's suffragist society. She dedicated herself to women's issues, and in particular to family allowances, and to the plight of Indian women. As one (male) MP patronizingly told her in 1942, she had 'for years . . . wasted her life advocating family allowances. I suppose that is a good enough substitute for the absence of a family.' Precisely because she was an Independent, representing the Combined Universities, she was free of party priorities and able to pursue her own. She was in many ways the finest woman MP of them all.[28]

Clearly, many male MPs deeply resented their presence, and *Hansard* is littered with their offhand misogynist remarks—'My dear, if you ever become a mother, please can I have one of the kittens?'[29]—but these tended to be the older backbench Tories, for whom Parliament was a club rather than a career. Others were uneasy about engaging with women in the cut-and-thrust of debate, and to the women's exasperation, took refuge in elaborately praising their contributions, while ostentatiously ignoring their arguments. Yet at least as many other MPs were proud of and helpful towards their women colleagues, the front bench noticeably so. In the 1929 Parliament, Margaret Bondfield was in the Cabinet, Susan Lawrence in the Government, proportionately more women to their numerical strength than at any time since.

The culture of the Commons was of course exaggeratedly masculine—rowdy, boozy, assertive, and quarrelsome. For ILP women like Jennie, who had been handling rowdy, boozy, assertive, and quarrelsome men at public meetings since her student days, who had seen off hardened Communist activists, and who gave and took no quarter with more skill than most ILP men, the House presented not the faintest threat. Many of the speeches, she thought, were not up to much. She was young, fearless, fluent, impassioned, in awe of nothing, and certainly not of her fellow MPs.

Collectively, the women were as able as their male colleagues. Because they were called more often by the Speaker, they spoke more, and they worked harder. They were equally popular with the voters. Older women had often stumbled into Westminster politics at the urging of male relatives or colleagues. Of that first generation, most Tory and Liberal women took over their husband's constituency when he went to the Lords or to an early grave. As these men had held safe seats, their wives enjoyed a long political career. Labour women had a more difficult time. They had to search for seats. They were usually single and professional about their politics. Jennie was unusual only in deciding on a political career so young. Unlike male Labour MPs, few had trade-union sponsorship, which paid election costs of five or seven hundred pounds (Ellen Wilkinson, Margaret Bondfield, and Leah Manning were exceptions). Their seats were more marginal, which was often why they were vacant in the first place, so their parliamentary careers were depressingly interrupted. The 1945 election was a reunion for Labour women like Jennie who had fought and lost seats in 1931 and 1935.[30]

The women were highly visible and the subject of much speculation in the House and in the press. In this as in so much else, Nancy Astor tried to develop an appropriate style. She might arrive at the House in her furs and jewels, but then changed into her uniform, sober black with white collar, and tricorne hat. The Duchess of Atholl, in despair, brought her maid along to help her negotiate the infinite number of tiny buttons as she changed her dress. Ellen Wilkinson favoured bright green. Jennie kept to brown—brown dress, brown suit, brown jumper and skirt. When she broke this dress code, she did so magnificently. On one occasion she was seen entering the House in a scarlet cape. On another, she visibly stunned the Chamber and the Speaker as she entered in a clinging emerald velvet evening dress, which shimmered under the lights as she swept up the floor of the House, to sit by Maxton 'with all the assurance of a Bond-street mannequin, and seemed quite unconcerned by the fascinated stares of her astounded colleagues'. Charlie Chaplin turned up in the Distinguished

Strangers' Gallery, heard Jennie make a speech, and claimed he had promptly fallen in love with her. He took her out to tea.[31]

Jennie was the youngest of the women MPs, and until Frank Owen arrived, the youngest MP in the House. She fascinated the men, and on that account irritated many of the women, who did not much care for her. Mary Agnes Hamilton described her as 'almost too pretty, certainly too young'; as did Leah Manning, who said sharply that Jennie needed a few misfortunes to help her mature. Ellen Wilkinson wrote of Jennie's 'colossal self-assurance', beside which Lady Astor 'appears like a fluttering girl'.

The women MPs loathed the frank sexual appraisal to which they were exposed. Leslie Hore-Belisha, later Conservative Home Secretary, confessed to the *Daily Express* that he was 'disappointed' in most of the political women who had entered the House. Susan Lawrence, he went on, had a fine analytical brain, which showed her manly qualities; Margaret Bondfield weathered the storm of criticism like an oak, 'but the oak is a masculine tree'; the Duchess of Atholl had the knowledge and fluency of a don (and everyone knew that dons were men); only Jennie remained a member of the female sex, with her 'dark soft charm'.[32] Male MPs enjoyed being assaulted by Jennie; she was not senior enough to be intimidating, not old enough to be tiresome. They found her high spirits and high colouring equally fetching. A few weeks after Jennie arrived, she demanded that the House should not adjourn for the summer recess, but should continue sitting to deal with unemployment. Her generation, she said, would not 'perpetuate a medieval institution' like Parliament unless it responded to the crisis. The press noted that 'Ministers raised tired faces to gaze in envy on the spirit of twenty-four'.[33]

Ellen Wilkinson, although twelve years older than Jennie, became her closest female parliamentary friend. After a degree at Manchester, Ellen had joined the ILP, the suffrage movement, the Fabians, the Guild Socialists, the Plebs League, and for a few years the Communist Party, in roughly that order.[34] She had become woman's officer for the Shopworkers' Union, which sponsored her at Middlesbrough from 1924 until 1931, and then from 1935 at Jarrow. Like Jennie she was on the far left of the Party; like Jennie she was brave, combative, vivid in speech and style, and generated a flurry of noise and energy. She and Jennie acquired adjacent flats in Guilford Street, Bloomsbury, where their friends and visitors soon included Michael Foot and Nye Bevan.

*

Jennie's North Lanark by-election was followed a few weeks later by a general election. Lloyd George ensured that it was fought on the issue of unemployment. The brilliant Liberal policy document, *We Can Conquer Unemployment*, inspired by John Maynard Keynes, and signed by Lloyd George, promised a massive programme of public works, especially of road building, to be financed by public borrowing. Liberals noted that the last government to show any interest in road building in Britain had been the Romans. Better that men should be helped back to work than be paid to be idle. The Conservatives said they would do more to encourage unemployed men to move from distressed areas to more prosperous parts: a strategy recycled, so to speak, half a century later. Labour criticized the Liberal programme as extravagant and ineffectual, the Conservative programme as mean and ineffectual, and offered a perfectly sensible shopping list of economic development (more housing, more roads, more forestry, more electricity, more training), as well as 'rationalization' of depressed heavy industries so that they might regain their share of world trade. As a programme, it was a not unreasonable response to the problems of structural unemployment in the depressed areas, though it was constrained by its resolute refusal to finance works by borrowing. It was to prove hopelessly inadequate when six months later the government faced the 'economic blizzard' (MacDonald's phrase) of the slump.

In this election Jennie had a straight fight with Lord Scone. In her words, it was between the 'wealthy Party and the workers' Party'; in his, between 'Constitutionalism and Anarchy'.[35] She made housing, the coal industry, and unemployment the issues of her campaign, and they were to remain the issues of her life as an MP. Why, she asked, and not rhetorically, were pleasant modern houses standing empty at one end of town, while at the other leaned over-crowded slums, 'single-ends and but-and-bens with windows hardly a foot broad, with earth floors, without water lavatories, without wash-houses', without the most basic sanitation? In Lanark over 70 per cent of houses had only one or two rooms, so most of them were badly overcrowded, many of them officially condemned as unfit. Yet in them lived families with three or four children. Did Tories think women lived in such homes by choice? Of course not, but they could not afford the rent of anything better. North Lanark's housing problem, she insisted, was at heart a problem of poverty. She promised that a future Labour government would finance local authorities to clear the slums and to build new homes at affordable rents; which indeed it did. Housing was one of the few success stories of the 1929 government.[36]

The new register, which included all adult women for the first time, added seven million to the electorate. Jennie's vote rose, but in the absence of a Liberal candidate her majority fell, to 4,204.[37] The Labour Party was returned as the largest single party in the Commons with 287 MPs to the Tories' 261 and the Liberals' 59 Liberals. Nearly 200 Labour MPs were notionally members of the ILP: 142 of them formed the ILP parliamentary group, and 37 of them were sponsored by the ILP.[38] Of these, 17 were from Scotland. (The miners took a further 10 seats. The rest of the Labour Party in Scotland managed to secure only 7 seats.) Labour Scotland, as always, was dominated by the ILP.

Jennie had joined the House, however, just as the position of the ILP was being painfully questioned.[39] Before 1918, the only way for an individual to join the Labour Party was through an affiliated organization, such as a trade union, a co-operative society, the Fabian Society, or the ILP—the Labour Party was a federation of its societies. ILP branches therefore usually served as *de facto* local parties for individual members, simultaneously the leading constituency organization, the moral energy, and the main source of policy for the Labour Party. Labour's 1918 constitution not only gave the Party Clause 4 and some other socialist policies, but also created local constituency (or divisional) parties, which individual members could directly join. What future then had the ILP? Should it retreat back to being merely a socialist society? Did it continue to have a parliamentary role within and alongside the Labour Party, including the right to choose MPs, now that local constituency parties existed? If it did, ILP-financed MPs would be expected to abide by ILP policies, but if those policies were ahead of or at odds with the official Labour Party, whose writ should then prevail: that of the ILP who sponsored them, or the PLP of which they were members?

Such policy clashes lay in wait. Two periods of minority government were to teach the PLP that office inevitably brought with it compromises and difficulties, and that they had to trust their leaders to extract the best deal they could. The PLP became, if anything, too responsible, too cautious, and too uncritical for its own good. The ILP's cast of mind made it distrustful of leaders, suspicious of compromise, and impatient with delay. It retained its doctrinal purity, seeing itself as the guardian of the socialist flame. So far, so sectarian. But the cultures of the two parties were growing apart: while the Labour Party might organize the battalions, the ILP covenanters cherished the faith.

Out of power, such issues could be fudged. In power, party discipline was essential and standing orders tight; and such issues could not be avoided. Arthur Henderson, the Labour Party secretary, suggested the ILP should confine itself to its founding role, that of being a propagandist society, the spearhead for Labour. MacDonald had put the problem best, writing in *Forward*, the Scottish ILP paper, some ten years before: 'If the ILP were simply to become individual members of the Labour Party they would at once lose their driving force and inspiration, and their keenness would be blunted because their political faith would be obscured in the mass of indefinite opinion which, despite its declarations, is the state of mind of the huge bulk of the Labour Party.'[40]—the ILP's views precisely. The Scottish ILP, in particular, would not willingly abandon its hegemonic role within Labour.

The Labour Party took office in 1929 as a minority government, and these fissures were quickly exposed. Useful legislation was promised in that first year, reported Jennie to her local party—more money for local authority housing, for public relief works, and for pensions, reform of the trade-union laws, a commitment to raise the school-leaving age to 15 in 1931.[41] But, she went on: 'What a pity it is that these changes do not include the provision of work or maintenance for every unemployed worker.' That would require increased taxation which the Opposition in the Commons would resist. 'Timid palliatives' could not cure unemployment or abolish poverty; only socialism could do that. The government's proposals were not enough, yet it would be allowed to do nothing more. So, better that Labour suffer an early defeat, she argued, and appeal to the country, than keep watering down its distinctive policies.[42] The tensions—political, analytical, and constitutional—that were marking the ILP off from its 'host' Labour Party, were all too apparent. As unemployment grew, so did the alienation of the ILP.

No one doubted that the crucial social issue facing the country was unemployment, running at over a million, and that the critical financial issue facing the government was paying for its cost. Snowden, the Labour Party's austere Chancellor, accepted Treasury orthodoxy—classical Gladstonian economics—that economic prosperity would come from Britain regaining a greater share of world trade; and that economic depression had to be weathered by strict economy, a balanced budget financed by cuts in public expenditure if necessary, and a firm adherence both to the gold standard and to free trade.[43] Jennie and the ILP drew on the underconsumptionist writings of J. A. Hobson and came to exactly the opposite conclusion.

John Hobson moved in a pre-war Hampstead circle of progressive liberals, Fabians, and socialists, the Hammonds, Graham Wallas, Leonard Hobhouse, and H. N. Brailsford. The war had brought him into the Labour Party. His writings challenged the central tenet of Gladstonian and Treasury economics, that thrift and saving were virtuous. Such a policy might be desirable for an individual, but the collective consequences, Hobson wrote, were baleful rather than benign; saving depressed effective demand.[44] The crisis of capitalism came from the lack of effective demand in the economy, and that was due to a maldistribution of income. The wealthy saved, when instead the working class should spend. The state should therefore use taxation to check saving and encourage spending. In an analysis of unemployment that stretched back to Owenite and Chartist thought, the ILP drew on Hobson to call for a living wage, buttressed by family allowances and higher unemployment benefits, to be financed by redistributive taxation. This would inject greater purchasing power into the economy as well as into working-class homes. It was an ethical as well as an economic argument. A living income would mitigate poverty, inequality, and unemployment, all at the same time.[45]

Jennie had read Hobson as well as Marx at university.[46] She had come from the coalfields of West Fife, where destitute miners had fought but been broken by the greed of coal-owners, where class hatred was all too real and well founded. She had come from an ILP home, where she had learnt that, inevitably, class was arrayed against class, that you must choose your side, and that hers was already chosen for her. As she wrote to Suse in 1925: 'You are concerned with the problems of humanity. I am concerned with the needs and greeds of my class. You wish to judge without prejudice. I am a partisan, biased in favour of the working class.'[47] Jennie's university reading offered a theoretical framework for what she already knew. From Marx's theory of surplus value, she learnt that workers were exploited as producers; from Hobson's critique of underconsumption, that workers were impoverished as consumers, and that, in consequence, *laissez faire* capitalism must destroy itself. It was internally and inherently contradictory. There *had* to be a crisis of capitalism. Capitalist production concentrated wealth in the hands of the few, while at the same time the market economy required purchasing power to be diffused among the many. It was not only perverse, but wrong that wealth which was socially produced should be privately appropriated. From her visits to Soviet Russia, she believed that state planning could mimic the market, could match production and consumption, so that from each according to their abilities, to each according to their needs.

Her most intimate ILP colleague was the economist Frank Wise, MP for Leicester, who popularized Hobson's writings within the ILP and was an economic adviser to the Soviet Union. Jennie sat with the Clydesiders in the House; and she joined them and Frank Wise in tabling an amendment to the King's Speech in July 1929 that sought to commit the Labour

Government to a socialist attack on unemployment, demanding for every man 'an income, including Children's Allowances, sufficient to meet the human needs of himself and his family, and measures aiming at the re-organisation of the industrial system, so that it shall provide for the needs of the community, by nationalising the key sources of industrial power'. Their amendment challenged, simultaneously, party discipline and Snowden's orthodoxy.

The ILP was not alone in challenging Snowden. Apart from Hobson, there were many other voices—Keynes above all, Lloyd George, Sir Oswald Mosley, and the Political and Economic Planning Group established in 1931. They thought it futile to rely on Britain regaining a greater share of world trade as the path to prosperity; instead, they sought to stimulate the domestic market by reflation and a mix of public-work schemes funded by budgetary deficits, devaluation of the pound, cheap money policies, and tariff protection—all ways of reducing unemployment by increasing the demand for British-made goods.

Both Hobson and Keynes insisted that over-saving depressed effective demand; but there they parted. Hobson argued that over-saving meant under-spending, Keynes that over-saving meant under-investment.[48] Hobson would promote spending by raising working-class incomes; Keynes would increase investment by public-works programmes, thereby increasing working-class jobs. Hobson would finance private spending by redistributive taxation; Keynes would finance public works by borrowing and by expanding credit.[49] Hobson was not a Marxist, but became a (qualified) socialist. Keynes was an interventionist Liberal who did not favour public ownership and who rejected the class war. He wanted reformed capitalism. As Jennie ruefully told the House, he was 'among those who wish the present system to go on'.[50] As the ILP naturally preferred to tax the rich now by raising surtax, rather than tax future generations by raising loans to cover deficit finance, and as redistribution of income immediately fed its way into the economy, while public-works programmes could take years to implement, it was Hobson's policies rather than those of Keynes which were readily appropriated by Jennie and the ILP.

Given the common ground, could there have been a Lib–Lab alliance of the radical Left within Parliament strong enough to drive through reflationary policies on unemployment? Was there realistically a political alternative to the economic policies followed by government? And would it have made a difference? Jennie was a minor player and no economic theorist, but was she right and could her views have prevailed?

Not even the former 'Lib–Labs' among the PLP, nor MacDonald, and certainly not Jennie, thought a Labour government could be kept in power by a formal alliance with the Liberal Party on measures to combat unemployment. The Labour Party deeply distrusted Lloyd George—he had failed to honour the Sankey proposals after the war. As Jennie told the House: 'the miners in my constituency sit dumb and hostile whenever his name is mentioned . . . Hopes were held out to them and they have always been dashed.'[51] Trade unions were especially incensed when the Liberals wrecked the Trades Dispute Bill in the spring of 1931.[52] Furthermore, the Liberals would certainly demand electoral reform.[53] MacDonald noted in his diary: '"The bargain" proposed by Lloyd George, really amounts to this: we get two years of office from the Liberals & give them in return a permanent corner on our political stage.'[54] In any case, Labour was not persuaded that capitalism could be corrected, as Liberals believed. Labour wanted socialism, however vague it was in defining it. Yet both the PLP and the ILP accepted that this was not possible for a minority Labour government. Caught between a socialism that was impossible and a capitalism that was doomed,[55] the PLP thought their government should soldier on and put up the battered shield of decent maintenance for the unemployed; the ILP wanted the government to put more radical proposals to the test, to live dangerously, and to leave office if they were rejected. Labour's time would come again.

Even if a Lib–Lab alliance were possible in 1929, which it was not, Snowden utterly recoiled from the fecklessness of the progressives who demanded not balanced but unbalanced budgets, and that he should tax and spend his way out of the Depression. Both MacDonald and Snowden agreed that socialism could only be built on the success of capitalism and not on its failure. Socialism for Snowden was a luxury, an item of public expenditure like roads, and, in Robert Skidelsky's neat phrase; 'If the revenue was not available there could be no socialism.' Snowden told Parliament in his 1930 budget speech: 'I abate not one jot or tittle of my lifelong advocacy of great schemes of social reform and national reconstruction, but our immediate concern is to make these things ultimately possible out of a revived and prosperous industry.'[56] Snowden's 'socialism' was for good times. The ILP insisted it was the only solution for hard times.

Could and should Snowden have adopted more reflationary policies, short of full-blooded socialism, such as deficit-financed public works? And would it have made much difference had he done so? The academic literature suggests it would have had a useful impact. Keynesian public works could have alleviated the structural unemployment of depressed areas (as deficit-financed rearmament was to do from 1937), while Keynesian cheap money could have mitigated the trade cycle and stimulated domestic demand. However, the problem was as much political as economic. Free trade and the gold standard meant that Britain could not opt out of the world economy. Hence, anything which subverted 'sound money' (such as inflation, a Hobsonian living wage, balance of payments problems, deficit finance) would still further reduce financial confidence in the markets and worsen unemployment. Keynes's response was: 'Look after unemployment, and the budget will look after itself.'[57] That was beyond Snowden. He could offer only to look after unemployment benefit, and even that not for long.

Snowden was appalled by the feckless economics of the progressive Left. MacDonald likewise was unpersuaded by the political arguments of the socialist Left, that palliatives, making capitalism work, were best left to Liberals and Tories, and that Labour should go to the electorate with clean hands. Jennie had bravely argued in the Debate on the Address in October 1930:

> Rather than continue on a compromise policy which is doing nothing, which all the while is accompanied by outside events drifting more and more to disaster . . . we want a challenging line of action. We want at least an attempt made to protect and improve the position of the working masses in this country. We want it for their sakes. We want it because we believe it would be the biggest single contribution to the solution of the unemployment problem. It would be far better for us to be defeated in this House of Commons, even if that defeat meant that for a temporary period we were out of office, provided that we clearly carried on our distinctive Socialist education, and built up, for the time that is coming, that knowledge and support which will be necessary to put through the radical Socialist reorganisation which is the only means which ultimately must be resorted to, in order to bring prosperity to our country and rid our people of poverty and unemployment.[58]

When the ILP pushed such views to the vote, they attracted only eleven into the aye lobby. Not just MacDonald, but the PLP was determined to show that Labour was fit to govern and that even as a minority government it could make a modest but worthwhile difference. Against anything more, and MacDonald could pray in aid his lack of a parliamentary majority. A revolutionary party, as Jennie described the ILP, despised MacDonald's temporizing, his policy of drift. They thought he was obsessed with office and its vanities. He, in turn, saw their 'disloyalty' as undermining Labour's credibility. Every amendment the ILP moved to Labour legislation gave comfort to the enemy. He demanded their loyalty;

they insisted that their loyalty was to socialist principles and not to Labour leaders.

When the crisis between the ILP and Labour Party came to a head in 1932, it was over party discipline, as codified in standing orders; but this was an issue precisely because the ILP and the leadership of the PLP had for so long and so desperately been at odds over the response to unemployment and the 'crisis of capitalism'.

*

Until the autumn of 1929, unemployment was experienced mainly in the depressed areas of export-led heavy industry: coal, cotton, and shipbuilding. Britain was doubly disadvantaged. Not only was world demand shrinking, but compared to Germany or Poland, British industries were inefficient. The government's official policy was 'rationalization', to make such industries more competitive and thereby regain their world trade. In coal-mining, that meant modernizing profitable and closing unprofitable mines, job losses, and higher productivity, at just the time miners wanted their jobs protected and their hours reduced. The government was boxed in. So its Coal Bill in December 1929 offered an unhappy compromise between conflicting interests—a shorter day for the miners, and subsidies for the owners.

The Miners' Federation accepted the bill; Jennie did not. She pointed out at Committee that coal-owners had already received generous subsidies, which they had pocketed rather than invested in the pits. In consequence, British productivity was much lower than in Europe. She demanded that reduced hours should not be paid for by reduced wages, and that coal-owners should use their subsidies to modernize their pits. So angry did she become that she narrowly missed being the first woman MP to be named by the Speaker.[59] A year later she asked how 1,600 small private coal companies who refused to plan, refused to invest, and refused to amalgamate, could possibly compete abroad. The industry had to be put on 'a proper, unified, scientific basis under national management and control'.[60] No wonder she was to take so much pleasure as MP for coal-mining Cannock when Vesting Day finally came.

In October 1929, Wall Street crashed. World markets shrank, British exports halved over the next two years, and men were laid off. The depression widened and deepened, unemployment soared to one and a half million in January 1930, two million in July, and two and a half million in December. More people were drawing national insurance (as well as the non-contributory 'dole'), fewer people were in work to pay for it. Unemployment benefit, which had cost the Exchequer £28 million in 1928, was costing about £125 million in 1931. The National Insurance (NI) Fund was £40 million in deficit and worsening dramatically by the year.[61]

During the winter of 1929, Sir Oswald Mosley, the dazzling junior minister whom Labour had 'captured' from the Tory Party, proposed a programme to enlarge home demand and home markets: create public works, increase pensions to take the elderly out of the labour market and add to their purchasing power, and raise the school-leaving age—the package to be secured by nationalizing the banks and ringed by tariff protection. It was Keynes with Hobsonian add-ons.

Some of Labour's most talented younger MPs, including Nye Bevan, supported Mosley. But the 'Mosley Memorandum' was flatly rejected by Snowden in May 1930. Mosley appealed to the Party over Snowden's head, and was only narrowly defeated at Conference. Mosley had few allies within the ILP. They distrusted him—he had no roots in the Labour movement. They were also uneasy about the *dirigiste* powers that he would bestow upon government, enabling it to bypass the parliamentary process. As Jennie remarked perceptively to Frank Wise: 'The Mosley–Bevan group is young, vigorous, unscrupulous. They are to be reckoned with but I simply cannot conceive of myself working with them. There is something fundamentally unsound mentally and spiritually.' Mosley left the Party. Nye would not follow him on his journey into fascism.[62]

Snowden insisted that unemployment insurance was more comprehensive and generous in Britain than elsewhere; its value had risen in real terms by over a third since 1924. As the budget deficit was largely due to the NI Fund deficit, he must bring it into balance. Like all Labour members and ministers, he wanted decent maintenance for the unemployed—he never assumed unemployment was their fault, their lack of moral fibre. He did believe that there were 'abuses' in the system, including a rapidly growing number of married women, part-time and seasonal workers who were claiming benefit while not really seeking work. He did believe that the projected level of expenditure could not be afforded. But while ministers were worried about the finances of the NI Fund, Labour backbenchers were worried about the finances of the unemployed.[63] As the government possessed no coherent policies of its own with which to deal with unemployment—'unemployment is baffling us', wrote MacDonald in his diary at Christmas 1929—and as it was not about to begin borrowing Liberal ones, the debate became less about unemployment and more about unemployment benefit.[64]

The government's first move in the autumn of 1929 was to honour their election pledge by modest increases in benefit, but to offset the cost by confining it to those 'genuinely seeking work'. The onus of proof was to be on the unemployed. Facing outrage not just from the ILP but from MPs like Nye Bevan, the government backed off. The ILP, however, wanted more than that. In a series of amendments to the bill, Fenner Brockway tried to bring the increases forward, Maxton to reduce the waiting time before they could be claimed, McKinlay to raise the wife's allowance by a further 1*s*. (5p), and Jennie to raise the children's allowance from 2*s*. to 5*s*. (10p to 25p).

Family allowances, particularly for those in work, was one of the most divisive issues in the Labour movement. It arrayed men and trade unions defending a so-called 'family wage' against women, the poverty lobbies, and the ILP. During the war, Eleanor Rathbone had published a seminal article on the remuneration of women's services,[65] and H. G. Wells and H. N. Brailsford had called for the endowment of motherhood. Jennie had kept newspaper cuttings of Eleanor Rathbone's 1924 book, *The Disinherited Family.* Eleanor Rathbone had lectured to the 1924 ILP summer school and had helped to shape ILP thought. In 1926 the ILP's *The Living Wage* argued that the basic wage should meet the needs 'not of the whole family, but of a man and his wife'; family allowances and not the husband's wage would support their children.[66] In an age when large families (as well as unemployment and ill health) caused destitution, child allowances would reduce family poverty, would also give purchasing power to the mother, and strengthen the case for equal pay. The trade unions fiercely resisted family allowances as an attack on the family wage, and resisted a living wage, as it would interfere with free collective bargaining. The ILP was trespassing on 'Trade Union business', Ernest Bevin had pointedly told the Party Conference in 1927.

Now, in a highly effective speech, Jennie argued that families on relief were living below subsistence levels. Increased children's allowances would reduce ill health and malnutrition, enlarge working-class purchasing power, and aid employment. In the most perfunctory of replies, Margaret Bondfield said it would cost £4 million and could not be afforded.[67] Nye Bevan and Eleanor Rathbone were among the non-ILP MPs who joined Jennie in the lobby; trade-union MPs remained implacably hostile. Her amendment was lost by 37 votes to 210.

Loyal backbench members of the PLP had to sit in silence while Margaret Bondfield stated that they could not afford more generous National Insurance payments, and they became depressed and uneasy as they saw the ILP cheered on derisively by the Opposition. They grew increasingly irritated at 'the bitter taunts and lectures delivered to us from lofty ethical altitudes as to our failure to redeem our pledges and as to our betrayal of the working people'. The PLP chairman noted sourly that the Clydesiders had no sense of teamwork. 'Their sole method of getting "socialism in our time" was to try and embarrass the only political party that aimed to get it at any time.' They were essentially:

political individualists . . . They believed themselves to be moved by principle; whereas they were really the victims of pride. They could not play the game. What, for the sake of the Labour Party, others had to endure, they would not have. The immaculate purity of their Socialist consciences was not to be fouled by such base contacts and compromises as others had to make . . .[68]

As the PLP saw it, the ILP was courting cheap popularity within the Labour movement, demanding more than could be afforded, while they soldiered on, acting responsibly, doing what was not always popular, but was, they were told, necessary. The ILP, they said resentfully, had no monopoly of the moral high ground.[69] Jennie in return had nothing but an exasperation bordering on contempt:

[for those] solid rows of decent, well-intentioned, unpretentious Labour backbenchers. In the long term it was they who did the most deadly damage. Again and again an effort was made to rouse them from their inertia. On every occasion they reacted like a load of wet cement. They would see nothing, do nothing, listen to nothing that had not first been given the seal of MacDonald's approval.[70]

*

The issue of party loyalty and party discipline was out in the open. MacDonald angrily warned that the National Executive Committee (NEC) would go over the heads of dissidents to their constituency parties. The ILP over-responded at its Easter conference in 1930 at Birmingham. In a fateful step, it asked its MPs to accept ILP discipline, if necessary against the PLP itself.[71] Eighteen ILP MPs, including Jennie, agreed. In response, the NEC began to refuse endorsement of those ILP by-election candidates who would not accept PLP standing orders. The lines were drawn, positions were dug in.

Meanwhile, the Depression deepened. Those in work were doing perfectly well, since falling prices meant that real wages rose. The misery was borne by those out of work, especially the long-term unemployed in the depressed areas of the north, Wales, and industrial Scotland. Then, during the summer of 1931, came further assaults on the unemployed. Two official committees, one (the Gregory Commission) enquiring into the NI Fund, the other (the May Committee) into government expenditure, both recommended cuts in unemployment benefit. Snowden did not dissent from their reports.

The trade unions were outraged. They had never supported the ILP call for a living or basic wage; instead, they had fought to maintain existing wage rates, underpinned by decent unemployment benefit, together with public-work schemes for the hardest-hit areas. Margaret Bondfield, Minister for Labour, now introduced a more limited Anomalies Bill in June 1931, removing the right to benefit from seasonal and part-time workers and from many married women. This bill the trade unions could tolerate. It was left to the ILP, supported by Mosley's group, to defy standing orders, oppose their own government, and vote against the second reading. On 15 July in an all-night committee sitting, they forced thirty-two divisions. At five o'clock in the morning Jennie joined Ellen Wilkinson, Cynthia Mosley, and Eleanor Rathbone in fighting to protect the right to benefit of married women.

Led by Eleanor Rathbone, they were a formidable alliance: the tough lucid intelligence of Eleanor Rathbone glints through her closely reasoned arguments; Ellen Wilkinson provided a fine line in invective; Jennie tenaciously chased for every point. As Ellen Wilkinson said bitterly, 'If marriage is a bar against women, why not against men?' It was nothing but discrimination against women, 'which the whole women's movement' had been fighting since 1870. The minister, Margaret Bondfield, whose political life had been built in women's trade-unionism, repeated that married women abused the system; as everyone knew it, she need not provide evidence for it. That allowed her to make a very short speech, whereupon she sat down and the ILP was voted down, by 138 votes to 20.[72] No other woman went into the lobby with the minister. She was on her own, apart, that is, from the silent Labour male back-benchers. Nye and Sir Charles Trevelyan went with the women. The ILP extracted no concessions.

Worse was to come: the May Committee, made up mainly of wealthy businessmen, in its sensational report at the end of July forecast huge budget deficits for the following year. The deficits were largely notional—May had arbitrarily changed the conventions of Treasury accountancy. Keynes famously described the report as 'the most foolish document I have ever had the misfortune to read'. None the less, the Committee wanted the alleged deficits made good by cuts of 20 per cent in the level of unemployment relief, as well as substantial cuts in public sector wages.[73] There was to be little equity of sacrifice at this time of national crisis. The poor were required to save the rich from ruin. Snowden could have distanced himself from May's financial forecast, but instead praised it as thorough and exhaustive. It would force the Labour Party to read the world as he saw it.

After all the battles about unemployment insurance, the Labour Party could not believe that the government might follow May's recommendations. As Frank Wise wrote in the *New Leader*, it was 'almost unthinkable' that the government 'can identify itself with a Report which reverses the . . . principles of the Labour movement'.[74] The government hesitated, and went on holiday.

So far, London had escaped the worst of the financial crisis that was overwhelming European exchanges, and so far, Snowden, despite his flinty utterances, had not cut the basic adult male rate of unemployment insurance. Changes had been made only to marginal groups such as married women. To Snowden's surprise, the May report triggered a run on sterling. Its doomsday scenario became a self-fulfilling prophecy. Now, in the face of bitter Cabinet hostility, Snowden and MacDonald insisted that a 10 per cent cut in benefit was essential to restore financial confidence and obtain vital loans from foreign bankers. The sterling crisis was so grave that the country faced runaway inflation, the destruction of social services, and a fall in living standards of at least 20 per cent for a generation to come.[75]

The unemployment crisis had been overlaid with a financial crisis; the financial crisis in turn had become a political crisis. The Cabinet, many of whose members were barely on speaking terms with each other, by now were utterly divided. Ernest Bevin threw the TUC against the cuts, Snowden remained implacable, and MacDonald asked for his colleagues' resignation. They expected him to resign with them. So, for twenty-four hours, did MacDonald himself. (The joke around Westminster was that 'poor MacDonald has had to resign and Mosley has sent for the King'.[76]) The King shrewdly wanted to lock the Labour leadership into whatever unpalatable decisions had to be taken. MacDonald agreed to form a National Government. Snowden came with him. Most of the Labour Party went into opposition.

The run on gold escalated. On 21 September, Snowden introduced a bill to take the country off the gold standard,[77] and prepared for further deflation. Frank Wise and Nye were scathing. Jennie was withering. She told the House:

> In his concluding sentence the Chancellor of the Exchequer made what was to me a most extraordinary appeal. He asked that all Members on all sides of the House should be united in face of the present financial embarrassment. I find myself completely unable to understand how he can expect Members whose political and

economic philosophy is based on a desire to get rid of the present capitalist system to build in its place a Socialist system, to respond to his appeal that at this moment, when the capitalist system is in the greatest danger, we should lend our support to its continuance. If I understand the philosophy of the Chancellor of the Exchequer, it is that in theory he still retains his Socialist beliefs but that he does not believe the present time is suitable and opportune for pressing forward the practical application of those beliefs.

He seemed to think that capitalism must first be strengthened before it can be attacked, buttressed before it can be demolished, said Jennie, with a good effort at incredulity. She then turned on the Tories. Some, she said, still thought the answer lay in requiring working people to make yet more sacrifices, to accept wage cuts. Others, such as Churchill and Mosley, aware that this would produce widespread revolt, now called for devaluation and inflation. A 'lot' of 'tame economists' such as Keynes, were 'hurrying and scurrying hither and thither, ready to take any way out of their difficulties'. There was no shortage of options on offer, many of them contradictory. But the real division in the House, she went on, and 'the only one that counts' is between those who would 'do anything' to save the present system, and those who knew its days were numbered:

There is no way out of their difficulties . . . There is one thing with which hon. Members cannot deal, without destroying the order for which they stand, and that is the fundamental problem of the poverty of the people. You cannot have ample markets and bankrupt homes at the same time . . . Our reply to the economy proposals of the Chancellor the other day, to the Bill which he is now bringing in, and to measures of all types that are being suggested in order to save Capitalism, is that it cannot be done, and that it will not be done . . . No economist, however distinguished, could avoid the conclusion that, as Capitalism develops, the problem for the working-class was going to be worse and worse, that rationalisation and increased production were merely going to bring additional unemployment and hardship, that the class struggle was going to become more ruthless . . .

Those of us who are convinced that the present system is doomed and cannot go on, ought not to be addressing our attention at the present times to methods whereby we can prolong its life, knowing that by those methods we cannot avoid additional hardships on the people whom we are here to represent and protect.[78]

It was her last major speech in the Commons on behalf of the people she was 'here to represent'. On 28 September MacDonald was expelled from the Labour Party. On 5 October he agreed to Tory demands to call a general election. On 27 October 1931 the National Government went to the country.

*

Jennie was relieved that the election had at last been called. She had been depressed, 'suspended in a vacuum' while she waited. Now she faced 'either solid ground or a drop into the abyss'.[79] Labour had no premonition of disaster, although Jennie knew she would have a difficult time of it at North Lanark. Labour's result in 1929 as the largest single party had been fragile and rested on Liberal intervention. By the terms of the 1931 electoral pact, there would usually be just one anti-Labour candidate in each seat. The Liberals were running only a third of their 1929 candidates. In a straight fight, the Tories would pick up the Liberal votes.[80]

Had Labour gone to the country for a proper mandate within six months of taking office, it might have done rather well. As it was, the Party had exhausted its honeymoon appeal by the winter of 1929, and had thereafter been on the defensive, unwilling to do much about unemployment and unable to do much about anything else, defeated in the Commons and vetoed in the Lords. Its housing policies had been a success. Apart from that, the Labour Party was identified with failure and Jennie was tainted by it. Virtually every by-election had gone against the government. The low morale among party workers in the country was shared by MPs in the House and ministers in the Cabinet; relations with the trade-union movement had deteriorated over unemployment insurance; the PLP was splintering, with the loss of MacDonald and the Mosley Group to the Right, and men like Sir Charles Trevelyan as well as the ILP on the Left. It all suggested that the Party would fare no better at a general election than it had in its by-elections. The Tories, by contrast, were united on a programme of public economy, protection, and imperial preference, and were in good heart under Baldwin's leadership. As in the 1929 general election, Jennie faced a straight contest with the National Unionist candidate, Anstruther-Gray.[81] Lord Scone had moved on.

Over and beyond the difficulties facing any Labour candidate in 1931, Jennie had rashly acquired a few extra ones of her own—so much so that she had confided a few months before to Trevelyan that if he could help her find a better seat, 'anything really good', she would like to move.[82] North Lanark was a miners' seat. In 1929 their own Communist candidate had been refused endorsement by the Labour Party and so Jennie acquired the nomination. She had stormed the seat in her 1929 by-election, but they had begrudged it her and been reluctant to work for her. Since then, she had voted against the unhappy Coal Mines Act, which the Miners' Federation had supported as better than nothing. She could not expect much help from them this time around. She reported to Trevelyan: 'Some local officials of the miners' Union are passive, others openly hostile but nowhere are they actually helping to rally the vote as they should'; and to Frank, that the miners wanted 'to have me displaced by a miners' nominee . . . The Tory candidate is spending most of his time in the division and the Communists are also making headway. So here's to a lively winter!'[83]

Along with the Clydesiders, she had been in constant dispute with the Labour leadership over party discipline; although MacDonald had departed, the new Lansbury leadership was no more tender-minded towards what Arthur Henderson denounced as 'organized conscience'. Indeed, the fragmentation of the Party suggested that more rather than less discipline was required. Labour's annual conference at Scarborough three weeks before the election had voted by more than 2 million to fewer than 200,000 votes to strengthen disciplinary procedures against those who disregarded standing orders. Accordingly, twenty-three ILP candidates, eleven of them sitting MPs (Jennie, of course, and the Maxton group, but also Sir Charles Trevelyan) were refused endorsement by the NEC. Despite the miners, Jennie's local divisional party stood by her and re-adopted her, even though she had refused to sign the standing orders pledge. She did not have to face an official Labour candidate. The Labour Party might be moving into the gloom of official Opposition, but the ILP was moving into the outer darkness. 'A definite breach', reported Jennie's local newspapers. It was the sort of publicity that she could do without.

Her constituency party were further worried, as Jennie was also losing their substantial Catholic vote. Her friend Charles Trevelyan had, as Minister of Education, tried to raise the school-leaving age. This would cost poor families a year of their children's earnings. On top of that, a Catholic Labour back-bencher, John Scurr, argued that Trevelyan was not doing enough to aid Catholic schools. Trevelyan insisted that public money had to be accompanied by public accountability to the local authority, which Catholic schools refused. The ILP was split. Jennie was urged by Maxton to be prudent and abstain with him.[84] She must learn the facts of life, he said, grasping her by the shoulders. She could not fight both the Labour machine and Catholic prejudice in West Scotland. Jennie was livid with contempt. Along with her good friends Frank Wise and Nye Bevan, she bravely opposed Scurr's amendments as sectarian. She was not forgiven. In May that year, Pope Pius IX had denounced socialism and had encouraged Catholic priests to campaign against socialist candidates. 'Churches, chapels and press are out for blood.'[85]

Nye had become a sturdy ally and comrade since joining the House in 1929. He was unopposed at Ebbw Vale, so came up to work for Jennie, taking overspill meetings for her. 'He worked like the devil to pull me through', she told Frank.[86] Maxton did six meetings for her. Charles Trevelyan, busy defending his own Newcastle seat, sent her £200 to help with election expenses and with depressed party workers. Jennie worked desperately hard to hold the seat, driving herself in the battered baby Austin she had originally bought second-hand for her father, to every far-flung village. To add to her woes, she had six thousand new voters from a Glasgow overspill housing estate. Jean Mann, who represented them on Glasgow City Council, knew that meant trouble.[87] 'The poor little thing is very hoarse and a good deal tired', Trevelyan wrote to his wife. 'She of course is very plucky but counting all the odds against her.'[88]

On the eve of poll, she exhausted herself with twenty-seven meetings. She tried to allay Tory allegations that a Labour government would appropriate small savings held in post offices. As she wrote savagely to Suse: 'Miners & unemployed voted Tory in order to save their £10 in the Coop. & prevent the complete collapse of the £1 with which Snowden terrified them.'[89] Jennie repeatedly defended her parliamentary record. She had fought for better housing, cheaper rents, improved health services, more liberal education, higher pensions and out-of-work benefits, more public works, and a living wage: she had kept faith. 'We have lost our leaders,' Jennie would tell them, 'but the troops are still with us.'[90]

Except that they were not. The National Government entered the election with a working majority of 60 seats. They could reasonably expect a majority of 100 or more. It turned out to be not so much a landslide as a wipe-out. They took 554 seats, the entire opposition just 61.[91] The Tories lost not a single seat, Labour did not gain one. In all, 230 Labour MPs lost their seats, among them Arthur Henderson at Burnley, Herbert Morrison in Hackney, Margaret Bondfield at Wallsend, and Charles Trevelyan in Central Newcastle: the PLP was reduced to a rump of 46 members. Attlee survived at Stepney and Cripps at Bristol, with majorities of around 500; Lansbury held on to Poplar. Three ILP and three Unendorsed Labour MPs kept their seats. Jennie Lee and Frank Wise were not among them. Jennie held on to her 1929 vote and polled 19,691; the Tory candidate, however, added nearly 9,000 to his vote, to poll 24,384. Jennie was no longer MP for North Lanark.

Jennie had not expected to hold her seat. She had sent her mother back to Lochgelly the day before the poll to avoid further distress. Jennie's sheer gutsiness came out on occasions like this: 'It is all the luck of war.' She refused to slip away, but came out of Glasgow's County Hall and stood on her car roof to give a short speech, which 'bucked them a bit for they felt that anyhow we were not running away'. The day after, she made a last tour of the villages, which she found 'terrible. Both men & women were weeping & cursing, being taken completely by surprise . . . I nursed the wounded as best as I could, finishing with a funeral service in Shotts which brought a mixture of cheering & tears from crowds who blackened the streets by their numbers.'[92] Nye, who had been by her side, said as he set off for Wales, 'good-bye for five years this time', and Jennie feared he was right. She wrote to Suse: 'The political deluge has swept the Labour Movement almost out of existence & I have gone down the drain with the rest.'[93]

Jennie did expect to return to Parliament in the foreseeable future. She could do nothing else, wanted to be nothing else, except an MP. She was resilient. She would do a lecture tour in the States, learn German in Germany, train for the law, look for a job in London where 'my man is'. 'It may be that the next ten or twenty years will pass without any real challenge to capitalism but if so all the economics I believe in are utterly wrong.'[94] Had she known that she was not going to re-enter Parliament until 1945, she might have despaired.

*

With MacDonald and Snowden out of the Party, and Henderson out of the House, the Labour leadership had fallen by default to George Lansbury. Unlike Snowden, he was a man of the Left; unlike Henderson, he was not a party boss; unlike MacDonald, he could respect the dilemma that standing orders posed for the ILP. He had been through it himself: while a poor law guardian, he had refused to cut poor relief in Poplar, as instructed by government, and was imprisoned; before the war he had resigned his seat to fight it on the issue of women's suffrage (thereafter, the suffragettes poured money into his *Daily Herald*); during the war he had defended conscientious objectors; in the last two years as Commissioner for Works he had led the resistance within the Cabinet to Snowden's cuts. Of all men, he might have pulled the ILP back into the mainstream of the Labour Party, and moved the centre of the Labour Party to the Left. But power in the post-MacDonald Labour Party had shifted away from a weak PLP with weak leadership to the trade-union movement, and to powerful figures like Ernie Bevin and Walter Citrine; and their suspicions of the ILP were ineradicable. The ILP had persistently voted against the Labour government. Standing orders had been recently amended at Conference—the Party would in future withdraw the whip from persistent rebels.

The ILP had come to the parting of the ways. Never did the ILP miss its former leader, the great John Wheatley, as now. Catholic, conciliatory, and deeply respected, he had died in 1930. Had he lived, he would have pulled the ILP back from the edge. But not Maxton. He may have thought, as Gordon Brown argues, that he could use the threat of disaffiliation to extract concessions from Henderson only to find that his bluff was called.[95] Since the October 1931 general election, ILP MPs had not attended Labour Party meetings, had sat apart from the official Labour Party in the House, and were recognized as a separate party by the Speaker. At the next ILP conference, due at Easter 1932, the ILP would have to decide either to buckle under and accept PLP discipline, or to become an independent party and disaffiliate. If it disaffiliated, no member of the ILP could remain in the Labour Party. As Jennie said, it would be self-imposed exile.

The ILP's 1932 Easter conference took place at Blackpool. Delegates had before them three proposals: immediate disaffiliation, unconditional affiliation, or further negotiation. Maxton, in favour of disaffiliation, argued that the ILP sought to overthrow capitalism, the Labour Party only to modify it. They had to regain 'their Socialist soul'. He was opposed by Frank Wise, who insisted that the ILP 'could carry their policy to fruition within the Labour Party but not without it'. Jennie expected the ILP to leave the Labour Party, but wanted it to be expelled on some large issue and not to disaffiliate.[96] Delegates hesitated and chose further negotiation.[97]

This came to nothing. Perhaps Maxton never intended that it should. Henderson, on behalf of the Labour Party, would not, and probably could not, concede an inch—no 'organized conscience'. Individual conscience, yes; unorganized conscience, possibly; disorganized conscience, probably. But no party within a party. In her autobiography Margaret Bondfield quoted the Labour Party's Notes for Speakers issued under Henderson's auspices: 'The plain truth, as its history shows, is that the ILP must always be different. Its leaders have interpreted the aphorism that "minorities are always right" as meaning that the ILP, being always a minority, can never be wrong.'[98]

Henderson did not want to lose the ILP. More than any other socialist society, it had created the modern Labour Party; it had a rich tradition of educational and propaganda work; it had strong roots in the constituencies, and until recently a strong presence in the House. The ILP, Henderson argued with some justification, had brought the crisis on itself when it asked its MPs to abide by ILP discipline back in the summer of 1930, and purged those who did not. The Labour Party's standing orders, he told Maxton, had been clarified, but had not essentially changed. It was a problem for the ILP, not for the Labour Party to resolve.[99]

And it did so. At a special ILP conference in July 1932, delegates packed the splendid Jowett Hall in Bradford, where fifty years before Keir Hardie had founded the Party. After a tense debate, the ILP decided by 241 votes to 142 to disaffiliate: it went into the wilderness. Worse, militant delegates triumphantly insisted that ILP members should refrain from paying the trade-union political levy, and not take any position in the Labour movement, which would have obliged them to support Labour Party policies. They were not to attend Trades Council. They were no longer to be local councillors or members of their local Co-operative Society. All connections with the Labour Party were to be severed.

The repercussions for the ILP were disastrous.[100] Individual members had now to make their own decisions—should they stay or should they go? The ILP was split from top to bottom, branch was divided from branch, member from member. Jennie was one of six ILP rebels who toured the country urging ILP branches to disaffiliate.[101] Even the Clydesiders went their different ways, Patrick Dollan and David Kirkwood with the Labour Party, Maxton, of course, with the ILP. The issue divided friends, and it divided lovers; Frank Wise chose the Labour Party over the ILP. Jennie, to Frank's sorrow and Nye's fury, chose the ILP over the Labour Party.

Why did she do it? Those who went with the ILP, such as Fenner Brockway, afterwards regarded it as 'the worst mistake in my life'. Looking back in *My Life with Nye*, nearly fifty years later in 1980, Jennie writes that since the ILP had made the unwise and 'silliest decision' to disaffiliate, she felt bound to stay with it: 'I loathed the thought of disaffiliation but I was a prisoner of geography . . . how could I desert my friends?' It was all 'madness'.[102]

This account is at best disingenuous, and comes close to being misleading. Of course she did not *want* to leave the Labour Party. It is also entirely true that her roots and loyalties were to the ILP culture in which she had been reared. But her loyalties were not personal, not to her 'friends', but to a concept of socialism which took no prisoners, as her earlier autobiography, published in 1939, makes clear:

I did not want to leave the Labour Party. I dreaded the kind of dog fight that was bound to develop in North Lanark once rival ILP and Labour Party candidates took the field. I longed for a nice, easy, straightforward political situation in which there would be two great parties in the State and only two. The workers *versus* the rest. I had taken it for granted in all my growing years that my special job in life was to fight the coal owners and all they stand for. I loved that particular fight. It raised no divisions inside myself. It was unanswerably, triumphantly worthwhile. It was a fight for bread. It was more than that. It was a fight for status too. My grandfather and my father were proud men. So were their work-mates. The thought of them as under-dogs, mere work-beasts labouring for the greater glory and profit of a caste-ridden plutocracy was intolerable . . .

I did not want to leave the Labour Party. I wanted to take part in a political contest where the alignments were as energizingly simple as the one penny fairytale and two comic-cuts that had delighted my childhood. I wanted to slay all the dragons and set poor people free. I wanted it to be All of Us *versus* the Others.

But in 1932 the British working-class movement was in no mood to accommodate me. It had split into warring factions . . . I had to choose. It had to be either Labour Party or the ILP. It could not be both.[103]

Her own politics had by no means softened. If anything, she had moved further to the Left in the last couple of years. The only true alternative to MacDonald was not the sham opposition of the PLP (made up of 'every rat & rabbit paid by the TUC'), but 'revolutionary socialism'. She agreed that her point of view, her analysis, was 'practically identical with that of the Communists'. Not that she was ever tempted to join them: 'I detest them as a Party', its members were 'personally dirty and dishonourable', its tactics in hock to Moscow. Yet the political landscape was changing. She could not predict what might happen. 'The ILP as such may grow stronger', she wrote to her good friend Trevelyan, 'or may be strangled in the next year or two, or may split into a Communist and socialist section. I cannot tell. But for the present it allows me the right to act as I say I shall, and until the Labour Party is prepared to do that, I should feel a coward and a fraud inside it.' Trevelyan, in reproof, sent her a copy of Trotsky's *Russian Revolution*.[104]

The Shotts local party, which had first nominated her for North Lanark, loyally wrote to Jennie, inviting her to be readopted. On 5 August 1932 she replied. To be endorsed by the Labour Party, she explained, she had to give a written undertaking that she would support the policies, not of the Party itself, which she would gladly do, but of the Labour Cabinet, whether 'they act for or against socialist policy'. But, she wrote, if a Labour government ever again asked her to vote for Tory policies that would be 'used against the workers and the unemployed', she would, again, have to defy them; the right to abstain was not enough. She accepted that a united working class was essential if they were to achieve socialism, but unity required that all sections of the Party, 'high and low are pledged to carry out socialist policy'. Yet instead of the Party binding its leadership to socialism, it was instead binding prospective MPs to the leadership. She did not trust the Labour Party not to throw up another

MacDonald, or another Snowden. And if it did, she did not trust the PLP not to collude. Jennie demanded the right 'to vote and act as socialists as well as *talk* socialism'. To do that, she must work elsewhere 'for the creation of a real socialist movement'.[105]

It was an honourable letter. She would not bind herself in advance to unconditional loyalty. Frank Wise, who read her letter, told Trevelyan:

[I]t was plausible rather than convincing. But even its core pretty well collapses if the Party brings a new labour Government under effective responsibility for carrying out Party decisions. And this must be done anyhow. I don't think in the light of her local and family associations she could have refused to follow Maxton. But this is a temporary place for her and the ILPers if she keeps reasonably free of acrimonious personal discussion.[106]

Was it a silly decision, then, as she wrote in 1980, both for the ILP and for herself to disaffiliate? Not for Jennie, and not in 1932. The decision was painful, but it was not difficult, and she did not struggle with it for very long. She always expected the ILP to disaffiliate. She did not disagree with that decision, she did not think it was a mistaken decision, and she always knew that she would leave with it. She endorsed Emmanuel Shinwell's remark to the Scottish ILP conference that 'disaffiliation was the only logical, honest and possible thing'. She wrote to Suse before the special Bradford Conference in July 1932: 'After this month I shall be out of the Labour Party.'[107] Her tone was not elegiac, but matter-of-fact. She did not despairingly 'remain' with the ILP, instead she chose it; she was not a 'prisoner' of geography, but a warrior for socialism. She did not passively acquiesce in a decision made by others; she helped to shape that decision. She was not happy about it, but she did not believe she had any choice. It was a rededication to socialism. That was her covenant.

Jennie posted her letter. She felt very naked. The doorbell rang and it was Nye. She had half a mind to pretend she was not at home, for she knew what was coming. Nye berated Jennie mercilessly, the words tumbling out of him as he paced the floor of her flat:

And as for you, I tell you what the epitaph of you Scottish dissenters is going to be—pure, but impotent. Yes, you will be pure all right. But remember, at the price of impotency. You will not influence the course of British politics by as much as a hair's breadth. Why don't you get into a nunnery and be done with it? Lock yourself up in a separate cell away from the world and its wickedness. My Salvation Army lassie. Poor little Casabianca. That was a hell of an intelligent performance now, wasn't it? I tell you, it is the Labour Party or nothing. I know all its faults, all its dangers. But it is the Party that we have taught millions of working people to look to and regard as their own. We can't undo what we have done. And I am by no means convinced that something cannot yet be made of it.[108]

Nye was unshakeable in this. There was no future for fragments of the Labour movement outside the Labour Party. That was one reason why he had not joined the CP after the General Strike, why he would not follow Mosley into the New Party, and why he now tried so hard to prevent Jennie going into exile with the ILP (and why, in the 1950s, there was never a flicker of desire by Nye to establish a Bevanite party of his own).

A week or two later Jennie addressed meetings in Lochgelly and Cowdenbeath, where she was angrily heckled from both right and left. To members of the Labour Party, she insisted, of course, that it was not the ILP breaking away from the Labour Party but the Labour Party breaking away from the ILP. The Labour Party had made compromises with Liberals and Tories, thereby weakening the working-class movement and the cause of socialism. The ILP must build 'a spirit of discontent' if it was to take control of the resources of the country. It could not support a Labour government which 'only tried to get reforms inside a capitalistic society', because it could not be done, and the worker who thought it could 'had better join the Boy Scouts'. Jennie was attacked by the CP, which claimed that the ILP, with 180 MPs, had had a 'substantial majority' within the PLP—therefore the dole cuts, means test, and Anomalies Act showed that the ILP had betrayed the unemployed. Jennie grew very heated, the meeting grew very heated, and the chairman intervened to describe the Communists as 'so crooked that they could not lie straight in bed'.[109]

Nye was right. The ILP became 'a sectarian shadow of itself'. By December 1932 it had lost a third of its branches; by 1935, two-thirds, and its membership, which had stood at 17,000, now was barely 4,000. Its centre of gravity had moved from Scotland and the North to London and to its chic paper revolutionaries. Jennie had become increasingly contemptuous of Maxton's leadership, which she thought was as vacillating as MacDonald's had been. Worse still, from Jennie's point of view, Maxton and Fenner Brockway allowed the ILP to be captured by its militant Revolutionary Policy Committee, which demanded co-operation with the Communist Party in a United Front, and which insisted that socialism could not be achieved by parliamentary means: 'Parliament cannot be the main instrument for the destruction of the State of which it is the political expression.'[110] The ILP was visibly disintegrating around her.

Jennie was mockingly immortalized in the CP's songbook:

Now stand we all united, the grand old ILP
But nowadays there's two of us and soon there will be three:
We reproduce by splitting, our hearts are pure and white,
The most amoebic party, we lead the workers' fight.

From Sheffield's sooty mountains, to Brighton's pebbly strand,
We gather to deliver our class from Labour's hand,
We are not parliamentary, we are not communist,
We're used to facing both ways, we cannot now desist.

So comrades we implore you, to follow Maxton's lead,
We don't know where he's going, and nor does he indeed,
But let him lead us onwards, to where we can't quite see,
And if he doesn't get there, there's always Jennie Lee.[111]

Thus fortified, Jennie fought the 1935 parliamentary election as the ILP candidate in North Lanark.* The country was beginning to swing back to Labour.[112] In a straight fight, Jennie would have won the seat. The ILP had requested an electoral pact, and elsewhere the Labour Party had agreed not to oppose certain Liberals, such as Megan Lloyd George. Would they agree in North Lanark? Gilbert McAllister, the official Labour candidate and a Lanark man, freely admitted he could not win—the local party was deeply unhappy and divided. Party loyalists and the powerful right-wing Catholic vote insisted that McAllister ran, but at his nomination meeting the local Divisional Labour Party rebelled. They had supported Jennie through two previous elections; if the Labour vote was now split, a probable Labour gain would become a Tory victory. They asked the Scottish NEC to allow Jennie a clean run. Right up to the last moment, it looked as though she might be spared a wrecking candidate. The NEC replied that if the local party did not run McAllister, the NEC would impose its own candidate. At that point, Jennie knew she had lost the seat. McAllister collected only 6,763 votes and lost his deposit, but his intervention allowed the Tory to win by a majority of 5,034. Labour had handed the seat to the Tories.[113]

Had Jennie won, the rest of her political life would have been very different. It would have been focused. She would have fought the war from inside rather than outside the House; she would have rejoined the Labour

* Jennie's personal style was beginning to alienate some of her supporters. ILP workers stayed with a miner in his small cottage. He was still angry with Jennie, who had been there the previous weekend—she had left her shoes outside the bedroom door to be cleaned. (Information to the author.)

Party, and would probably have held a post in the 1945 government. Despite Nye's affectionate support during and after the 1935 campaign, she was deeply depressed: 'I had come to a complete dead end. I was no use as a politician.' Over the summer she had a nervous breakdown. She had been bereaved in all ways possible. She had lost her faith in the Labour movement—'reality as presented in 1929–31 was too much for me';[114] she had lost her parliamentary life; and she had lost the love of her life, Frank Wise.

3

FRANK AND NYE

FRANK Wise was twenty years older than Jennie, 45 to her 25 when their affair began. She adored him, says Barbara Castle. They may have met at ILP conferences in the late 1920s, although Jennie, absorbed with T'ang, does not say so. They came to know each other intimately in 1929 when, a few weeks after Jennie, Frank was elected to the Commons.

He came from modest background, followed by Cambridge (and a half blue in athletics), Middle Temple, the requisite stint at Toynbee Hall, and the civil service, where, says Charles Trevelyan, Frank was 'one of the young men whom Lloyd George as prime minister pitched upon for their sheer capacity' to organize supplies and army contracts during the war. Still in his early 30s, he chaired the German subcommittee of the Versailles Peace Conference and was decorated by four Allied governments for his war work, and made a CB by his own. In 1921 he joined the ILP and with J. A. Hobson started to shape the Party's economic thought. In 1923, still attached to the Board of Trade, he became economic adviser to the Russian Consumers Co-operative (Centrocoyus), and the Soviet Trading Mission, which made him essentially an employee of the Russian government. To this he added directorships in other Soviet companies trading in timber and grain. He held these posts for the next ten years, advising the inexperienced Russian government on how to develop their export trade and expand into Britain, and the British government on how to benefit from it. It was all rather unusual, even for those years, and there were some sharp exchanges in the Commons. Tory MPs denounced him for serving two masters, and demanded to know whether he was passing privileged information to the Russians. He resigned from the civil service and instead fought a Bradford seat in 1924, before winning Leicester East in 1929.[1]

When Jennie came to know him, therefore, he was already a highly influential and formidable figure, cool and self-confident, with experience of government and administration at the highest level, and with every expectation of joining the Cabinet of the next Labour government. 'It was as though someone from the City had joined the Labour Party', recalls Barbara Castle.[2] He was perhaps too 'overbearing' (Jennie's word) and 'Olympian' (Fenner Brockway's) to be entirely popular with lesser mortals, but along with Stafford Cripps he was regarded by Beatrice Webb, for example, as one of the next generation of Labour leaders*. Tall, his dark hair rapidly receding, he was not especially good looking, but undeniably he fitted Jennie's student yearnings for a 'potent' mature man, who still projected intense physicality—after his Cambridge athletics, he had captained the English amateur football team, and he was a skilled climber and rider (forty years later she told her young nephew that she had been 'overwhelmed' when she first saw him on a horse). His friends regarded him as a powerful man in every way. He was much older than Jennie, much cleverer than Jennie, with as much energy as Jennie, and as deeply in love.

Inevitably, he was married. He had four school-age children, and a wife, Dorothy, who remained fond of him and who wanted to remain married to him. She lived in the large eighteenth-century family home in the Bucks countryside, to which Frank returned for occasional weekends. His daughter Mary remembered him in her teens coming down to walk the Chilterns, take them swimming, and to entertain Russian and political friends at home.[3] Dorothy Wise was no faded *hausfrau*. She had obtained a first-class degree and a Master's at London, and then taught English at a training college. She was also a JP. In 1926 she had organized relief for Scottish miners and sent money to Fife and Cowdenbeath. She had been a loyal political partner, canvassing and speaking for Frank at elections and she chaired the local Labour party. She was an attractive, capable, mature, and serious woman, who was to learn twenty years into their marriage and two years into his affair that her husband had fallen deeply in love, and was utterly bewitched and besotted by Jennie.[4]

Their affair began within weeks of Frank joining the House. Jennie spent that first summer recess in Vienna, recovering from two elections in

* Beatrice Webb found him a 'forceful' even 'blatant' personality—she noted his burly figure, large head, heavy jaw, strident voice—'an imposing but not prepossessing man to look at and to listen to'. But she warmed to his 'bonhomie, great mental energy, high spirits—he enjoys life: he is decisive and lucid in speech, a good debater, and I think honest.' She allowed 'S. W.' the last word. 'A rough person doing rough things in a rough way.'

Diary, 27 April 1931.

(I owe this reference to Dr Jose Harris.)

quick succession. 'Vienna in the summer of 1929', she wrote evocatively, 'had luxuriant flowers in the window boxes, orchestras, large and small, playing in the open-air restaurants, a wealth of cafés providing sweet cakes and *café au lait* and lots of newspapers and magazines for leisurely customers.' The city was 'bathed in sunlight and hope'. So was Jennie. For Frank had joined her for a few days before he went to Moscow on business. In the evenings they escaped to the hills, drank wine, went dancing, and made love. Suse met them in Berlin. Never had she seen Jennie so radiant. As she strolled with Frank, every head turned. When the House resumed in the autumn, it was no longer a casual affair; they were increasingly committed to each other. On the London political scene it was discreetly understood that they were a couple. Frank took her into his world, off to Chatham House for a lecture, down to the 1917 Club for lunch,[5] over to the Mosleys for dinner, and out to Toynbee Hall.

Jennie and Frank never lived together. Jennie cherished her own space. In any case, Frank's two elder daughters attended day-school in London and lived with him in his capacious Bloomsbury flat during the week. Instead, Jennie took a new flat in Guilford Street nearby.

Nye Bevan, it was clear, also had his eye on Jennie. He was one of ten children, born in 1897, to a gentle, disputatious miner and a strong-minded mother, who brought up their family in the mining and chapel life of South Wales. At the age of 14 he went down the pits. He read his way through the Marxist literature held in Tredegar's Working Man's Library, and with the help of his closest friend, Archie Lush, made himself an education.[6] After a two-year stint at the National Labour College in London, which he found dour and regimented, he returned to South Wales, where his work on the Tredegar Council, for his union as Disputes Agent, and for the sick and unemployed, had made him, said the local newspaper, leader of the Labour movement in Ebbw Vale. He led Tredegar through the General Strike, and in 1929 he became their MP.[7]

Shortly after Nye's maiden speech, his younger sister Arianwen came to visit him. She was a trained secretary, devoted to Nye, and handled his constituency work for him back in Tredegar. Nye took her into the Strangers' Gallery. Robert Boothby was speaking, and then Jennie got to her feet. 'What do you think of her?' Nye asked his sister. 'Her features are nothing to commend her by', replied Arianwen, sensing his interest. 'I agree with you', said Nye. 'Her jaw is too heavy.' Arianwen, who was never to conceal her dislike of Jennie, was not reassured. Nye pressed her into helping Jennie with her typing, and she liked Jennie even less.[8]

Nye, like Frank, entered the House in 1929. Most miners' MPs joined the House in their 50s, decent, dependable men, taking their place on the right wing and the back benches. Nye was neither moderate nor middle-aged. He was successively angry, speculative, teasing, and taunting. He was quickly taken up and petted as an amusing bit of political rough trade by the Beaverbrook set. He prowled the West End for his affairs—his was a more raffish circle and one in which Jennie felt uncomfortable. Yet they had such similar backgrounds—he a self-taught Welsh miner, she a Scottish miner's daughter. Like her, he bitterly opposed the government's assault on unemployment insurance, and it was Nye more than any other MP who stopped Margaret Bondfield imposing a harsh test of 'genuinely seeking work' on the unemployed.

The first time Jennie saw him on the Terrace, she thought he looked awful: his mother had dressed him from the Tredegar Co-op in clothes that crossed a non-conformist Welsh minister with an aspiring stock-broker. As Jennie grew to know him better, she pressed him to join the ILP, but he refused. Nye could not take Maxton seriously, though he sometimes joined them in the lobby. One summer evening when the House was sitting late, they walked to the far end of the Terrace, talking as they leaned over the parapet, comparing notes, discussing their homes, exchanging confidences about themselves. The division bell rang and, as they hurried inside to vote, Jennie said: 'You know, Nye, we could be brother and sister.' He, with a mischievous gleam in his eye, 'Mmm—with a tendency to incest.'[9]

Nye, seven years older than Jennie, was becoming a good and strong friend. Unopposed in his own constituency in 1931, he spent the campaign fighting in hers, apart from a visit to Leicester to help Frank, only to find that there was nothing for him to do—a casualness (if that is what it was) on Frank's part for which he was roundly scolded by Jennie. Nye was 'rightly, I think, rather sore', she told Frank. He 'was also good enough to give me your instructions about tempering gratitude with discretion! My dear!'[10] Nye would drop in on her London flat. When Frank was busy elsewhere, Jennie might go for country rambles with Nye, and even visit him for the weekend in Wales.

Jennie's by-election had made her a national name. Nye was unknown, as yet just one of some fifty mining MPs, all of whom looked much the same to those outside Westminster. Despite the tease about incest, Nye was not competing with Frank for Jennie. He enjoyed 'slumming' in the West End, as he put it, and playing the field. Their friendship was light-hearted and unintense, though solid enough. Had he tried, Nye could not have rivalled the power, physical and intellectual, that Frank projected and in which Jennie delighted. Nor yet could Nye offer her the sense of warmth and security in which Frank wrapped her, and in which she basked and stretched like a young cat in the sun. She did indeed regard Nye as a surrogate brother, prone perhaps to making the occasional pass, as most men did, but cheerfully accepting her rebuffs.

Yet the speed with which Nye moved in on Jennie after Frank had gone suggests that he was waiting for her. Archie Lush told Michael Foot that Nye had girls in Pontypool, and nurses at Abergavenny—but nothing serious. Nye even told one reporter that he would never marry, as 'one cannot afford to be tied to life by one's heartstrings'. 'Until Jennie came along,' said Archie Lush, 'I never saw him really brood about a girl or ask inscrutable, revealing questions about such matters as the strength of the miners' union in Fifeshire.'[11] No one could foresee what lay ahead for Frank. However, it was not unlikely that Jennie's affair with a married man would either blow up or burn out. Frank had discussed their problems with Nye, who was in place, and not by accident. None the less, while Frank was around, Jennie had eyes for no one else.

However, since Frank was married, and often away on business, he was not always around, and then Jennie's resolve faltered. Like many men, Jennie had never put much value on sexual fidelity and none at all on sexual chastity. She warned him as, tired and fed up, she travelled north and he travelled south to their separate meetings:

> All my adult life, when feeling low, I have turned to men for companionship, forgetfulness and—other things. Now I don't really care for anyone but you, only so often when I want you most, you are simply not to be found. But other people are and I get so bad tempered and unhappy when I don't know how to fairly keep the balances. The difficulty with me is that men reach the point of wanting to sleep with me very rapidly and anything in the nature of 'platonism' is exhausted by the third evening at the latest. Don't blame me. I don't want it. I don't encourage it. I do exactly the opposite but my whole physical type, age and temperament are against me. Before I met you, since I don't care much for women's company and conversation nor yet want always to be alone, I despairingly gave in to the inevitable. Because of you I would now rather not, but you must not leave so many vacuums as I am at one with nature in abhorring them.[12]

This image of Jennie as 'despairingly' submitting to male lust requires modifying. In Vienna she stayed with Austrian friends after Frank left. She would, says Suse, 'drape herself down on the couch, and the mother would say, "For God's sake, don't seduce my son, Jennie." She just did that, she could seduce anybody. . . She was absolutely aware of it. She was quite ruthless.'

Jennie was frank, physical, and uninhibited—in ways that delighted the sophisticated and refreshed the jaded. She liked to shed her clothes and wander around her flat naked; at the theatre she would stroke the hand of a friend, man or woman. Charles Trevelyan, her wealthy mentor, she twisted around her little finger. He supplied her with cash and advice in equal proportions—not unreasonably, as he had an abundant supply of both. She aroused strongly protective instincts in him. He had to reassure his wife as he fretted over his poor little Jennie, that his feelings were strictly fatherly. (Given Trevelyan's promiscuous life, his wife had reason to worry.) On her foreign lecture tours Jennie received dozens of letters from smitten young men, many with proposals of marriage. 'Suse', she would command, 'open these' and then 'Throw them away, throw them away.' When she walked into a room, no other woman existed. Men had eyes only for her and that dark smokey beauty. They would fall in love with her, and then suddenly they found themselves rejected. 'She just goes, leaves them, drops them, finished, over, out, but no compunction, nothing.' As Jennie told Frank: 'Personal relationships must either be beautiful with me or cleanly cease to exist.'[13] There was no suggestion that she might modify her expectations, alter her behaviour, negotiate, or compromise. Men must take her as she was, and she knew they would. For she was young, beautiful and vital, entirely at ease with her sexuality. She was supremely self-confident, as she had every right to be. Countless men found her quite irresistible.

Yet there was a darker, more melancholic side to her. Jennie, so vital and radiant, was always prone to depression, not when her personal life was awry, but when her political life was going nowhere. The bleak misery of North Lanark added to her sense of oppression. She was, above all, a propagandist, urgent in her desire to bring others to the socialist faith—one of the movement's best. Politics was her calling; it gave her life meaning. Frank understood that, and soothed her, cherished her, anchored her evangelical fervour when she was up, lifted her depressions with his own buoyant optimism when she was down. All those who knew them both—George Strauss, Barbara Castle, Suse, Charles Trevelyan—recognized that they were utterly in love with each other, he even more than she. His letters to Jennie do not survive, but in November 1931 he wrote to Charles Trevelyan after staying with him and Jennie at Wallington:

J. as I daresay you well know is very clear headed and achieves an amazing combination of cool detached judgement & the warmest possible personal feelings, which at once bewilders & delights a mere Englishman . . . But she never loses sight of her main objectives. Nor generally do I. So we'll probably attain what we both want.[14]

Jennie, said Suse, sometimes drove Frank 'potty'.[15]

They tried to be discreet. Frank was a married man and Jennie feared that a scandal—let alone a pregnancy—would destroy her in Presbyterian Scotland. Frank's business trips to Russia offered Jennie some cover. In the long summer recess of 1930, Jennie joined John Strachey, George Strauss, and Nye on a visit to Moscow. 'Fascination with all things Russian' had an immense hold on her as it did on most socialists. Once there, the rest of her group understood that she would leave them to travel with Frank through to the foothills of the Caucasus. Frank introduced her to journalists and diplomats, she visited show-piece schools and theatres. Then together they travelled a thousand miles south to Tbilisi in southern Georgia, near the Armenia–Azerbaijan borders. It was a rough trip—the trains had only wooden benches and no food, and within hours of boarding they had given their own food away to famished passengers. Jennie rested and recovered in a luxury Russian sanatorium, previously the preserve of the Russian aristocracy.

Six months later, in February 1931, she embarked on a brief lecture tour of the USA, arranged for her by an agency, which also had Mary Agnes Hamilton and Ellen Wilkinson on its books. Her audiences were mainly colleges, town forums, peace groups, or business and professional women's clubs. Her lectures on Russia were the most popular. The going rate was a hundred dollars a speech, which paid for a backless corn-coloured evening frock, 'which suits me excellently', she assured Frank, as well as her hotel bills for a month. It was easy money and Jennie was generous with it. She sent regular sums home to her parents. She met up with Suse, who was having a bad time with a New York artist. They went back to Jennie's hotel, and Jennie poured money on to the bed. 'What am I going to do with all these dollars? You have them', she told Suse. 'You're looking terrible.'[16]

The American tours became increasingly important to Jennie, and were her major source of income after she lost her seat in 1931. She spent summers with Frank in Russia, climbing and tramping, rucksack on her back; and early spring in America. Her living was earned lecturing about America to the Russians, and Russia to the Americans, and selling articles on both as fast as she could write them. She travelled with Frank to parts of Russia closed to foreigners, so her pieces, said Fenner Brockway, were 'a revelation'.[17] In the States she gravitated unerringly to protest. In Kentucky in spring 1932 she visited the mining camps, rows of tumble-down wooden shacks, where for months the men had been on strike and their wives and children lived on raw cabbage and scraps. Jennie was an agitator, all agitators were Communists, and Communists were a proscribed organization, hence she found herself detained by the mayor and the police. In January 1934 she demonstrated with the hotel staff of New York's Waldorf-Astoria for better pay and union recognition. In February 1935 she and Naomi Mitchison were at Marked Tree, a small town in Arkansas, where they spoke for three hours to those 'outcasts of the south', the sharecroppers, before leading them on a march through the town, singing 'as only angels and negro-plantation workers know how', '*We shall not be Moved*'. January 1937 found her addressing automobile workers on strike in Detroit.[18]

Jennie was fascinated by the States, by its energy, its restlessness, and its contradictions. Walter Lippman and Sinclair Lewis told her that the country would defy all her predictions and confirm all her prejudices. Whatever she wanted to find and believe, she would discover there. She saw the country at the depth of the Depression; she saw Roosevelt arrive at the White House. She loved its beauty: New England under snow, the Blue Ridge Mountains, great rivers, the smell of the South, the 'faces of every race, every nation'. She noted, too, its 'problems of sharecroppers, miners, poor whites, narrow Main Streets, teachers, and preachers, not free to say what they believe in'. She confessed she could never quite make up her mind whether it was 'the finest or the damnedest [*sic*] country in the world'.[19]

Back at home Jennie had to take stock of her future. She never doubted that she would return to the House, but given the 'wipe-out' of 1931, this might be some time off. When, unlike Frank, she left the Labour Party to follow the ILP, she had marginalized herself further. She was 28 that summer of 1932. She reckoned that for a few years she could probably put together a living of lectures, propaganda work, and journalism. Trevelyan and Frank, however, pressed her to adopt a more disciplined life and think of the future. She would not return to schoolteaching, and did not consider moving into adult education. Instead, she might build on her Scottish law training, if Trevelyan would finance her. Trevelyan would. He suggested a solicitor's office, as the routine, security, and discipline would be good for her. Frank raised an eyebrow, said that Jennie should play to her strengths, and gently pushed her towards the Middle Temple where she settled in to her dinners. She soon realized just how conservative an institution she had joined. When she had to sit at women-only tables in Hall, she knew she had made a mistake, and after a year or two reverted to her peripatetic political life.

Her political life was in turmoil, and her private life was also under strain. By January 1932, her affair with Frank was common knowledge around Westminster. Jennie wrote to him from the States what a friend had reported: 'there was all kinds of gossip about you and I in Fleet Street and that if I wanted to go on in politics, I should have to be much more careful'.[20] So far Dorothy Wise had behaved with huge dignity. Their children knew nothing. But now Mrs Wise fought back. She claimed Frank in public* and threatened him with divorce if he took Jennie to Turkestan later that summer. Jennie wrote to her, pleading for her understanding.

It was messy and hurtful. Frank wanted the matter resolved. He was coming up to 50, and longed for domestic peace. Dorothy did not want a divorce, despite her threats, and neither did Jennie. She was not ready to marry anyone, let alone a divorced man. 'No hostages to fortune', she and Nye would light-heartedly remind each other, as they swopped gossip about their affairs. 'Both our lives were shaped by the same revolutionary disciplines.' Both believed that 'permanent ties' would get in the way of promoting socialism, a dedication to the cause no less real because they teased each other about it. Marriage would be an impediment; marriage following a divorce was 'impossible', she firmly told Charles Trevelyan.[21] She (and Barbara Castle and Ellen Wilkinson, who were all in romances with married men between the wars) could risk a discreet affair, even engage in a long-standing relationship, but they could not afford a divorce. It was out of the question. Marriage would limit their political freedom; divorce would destroy it. She wrote to Charles Trevelyan:

> Frank's letters are rather troubling . . . Always the trouble with me is that I know doing jobs is ever so much more important than personal relations although I crave to have these as well. I suppose that makes me seem selfish and hard in some ways but I can do no other. Even Frank I know I could and would renounce rather than pay the price of political frustration which I am sure would follow a divorce. It is all very difficult.[22]

Frank pressed her. Perhaps in 1935 after the next general election, perhaps in 1936 when she might have finished her legal training, she airily told Frank. When it was convenient. Sometime. In the future. Maybe.

* Beatrice Webb noted that Jennie was 'passionately attached to him and the scenes in the House of Commons when the rather unattractive wife appears and insists on taking possession of her husband and ignoring his friend, are a source of scandal in the Party.'
Diary, 28 June 1931

On the ship coming back from the States in March 1933, she decided to 'have it out with Frank before I arrived and was once more under strong emotional pressure'. Late at night, she wrote him a long letter 'about our personal affairs. But I don't know what to say. I seem as far as ever from any certainties.' She *was* sure that his divorce after twenty years of marriage, and then remarriage would do them both 'immense harm'. 'The hounds' would be 'at their heels':

Imagine either of us ever trying to make a speech with any reference to the welfare of children or of family happiness. Immediately the malicious or the merely critical would want to know what regard we had shown for the family life closest to us. We could easily be painted as depraved home wreckers. Now I know, dear, that as you read you are protesting, but remember I am putting the situation from the outsider's point of view . . .

Next how do I personally feel? The thought of being separated from you fills me with panic. It takes away what has been the very centre and base of my life for the past three years. And I want a definite home of my own in addition to whatever public work and activities I shall be doing. If you had been free and we had been in the same political group, I would have married you before now. Even the difference in our ages would not have stopped me, and that is quite an important item . . . I cannot, also, at twenty-eight, feel and behave as if I were forty-eight or even thirty-eight. All in good time—But for a few years more at least, I am liable to be a rather over vital animal with the temptation to love others as well as you. If I felt it was wrong to do so, I could act accordingly, but because I love you better and more completely than any other man, does not still my curiosity and even temporary infatuation for others . . .

She suspected that within marriage he might become jealous and she resentful. Already, she had seen him 'sullen, ready to leave me with a sense of your injured innocence on quite trivial matters', and it had been she and not Frank who had made the peace, 'made it because I loved you too much to see you go off to a restless unhappy night'. So, apart from public consequences, 'a free relationship is by far the better for such as us', except that public opinion would prevent them running a *ménage à deux*.

She then turned to 'the possibility of clash or co-operation in our politics'. What, she asks, 'could be more devastating between us than my cold disbelief in anything you might accomplish—if in the company that you are bound to be in if official labour gets office in the next five years'. She continued:

I admit my darling that I have no alternative group to offer you, working with whom I could believe in your success. I also am not doubting and never doubt your individual very great if dangerously lop-sided capacities. But myself presiding at your table, with the Coles, and Laskis and Cramps and Greenwoods and Cripps as typical of some of the best of your closest political colleagues, is a prospect unreal, and without belief or stimulus for me.

If I am just a twisted, perverse, incompetent person, then better you realise that now than later. Personally I do not believe I am. I am waiting, and watching and if the things and people I reject are so numerous, then I hope you will blame some of it at least on outward circumstances and not all on my jaundiced view point. Free we can agree or quarrel on those things. But bound? what would happen to us then? Of course I hope that the difference between us will prove in the end organisational rather than something more but marriage before we were quite sure that we would also be politically married, is just out of the question . . . [23]

Jennie, with her usual splendid publish-and-be-damned attitude, printed most of this letter in *My Life With Nye*, though she stopped with the reference to a *ménage à deux*. The effect of editing out the last three paragraphs is to slide over the very real political problems (and not just dinner with the Cripps and Laskis) that faced them both following the disaffiliation of the ILP. Frank had gone one way, Jennie the other. The problems of Frank's divorce aside, Jennie could never agree to a marriage which constrained in any way her own political life.

Both of them were looking out for by-elections. Frank was soon to be adopted for Nelson and Colne. With MacDonald gone, he was working to push the official Labour Party to the Left—which would, he wrote to Charles Trevelyan, bring Jennie back into the Party, and the leadership under the control of the movement. He and Brailsford brought together those ILP branches and members who would not disaffiliate from the Labour Party in the summer of 1932 to form a socialist think-tank within the Labour Party. They were joined by G. D. H. Cole's Society for Socialist Inquiry and Propaganda (SSIP), to become, in Cole's phrase, 'a home for straying intellectuals', the Socialist League.[24]

Like the ILP, the League read both domestic and foreign politics in sharp class terms. In the aftermath of 1931, Frank, 'the City man', successfully demanded at the 1932 Party Conference that they should nationalize all banks, since these were the financial arteries of capitalism. To this was added a Soviet-inspired interest in planning, to bring coherence and rationality to the chaos left by capitalism. Effective economic planning required extensive public ownership, so that the state could shape the form and content of production, the allocation of resource between consumption and investment, the supply of credit, and the direction of capital spending and purchasing power.[25] So Conference demanded that they acquire the 'vital points of power' (the 1950s 'commanding heights of the economy'—utilities, transport, steel, munitions, chemicals, textiles, and health).

The Socialist League spoke increasingly for the constituency parties, just as the old ILP had done. But could it avoid treading the same oppositionist path? He had Henderson's blessing, Frank told Trevelyan, since unlike the ILP they would not be nominating any parliamentary or municipal candidates of their own.[26] Cripps, Laski, Tawney, and Trevelyan joined the League, as did the young Barbara Betts (Castle), Barbara's lover William Mellor, and Ellen Wilkinson's lover Frank Horrobin (Jennie might have had a more congenial time hosting Frank's dinner parties than she supposed). Nye, though in sympathy with everything the League stood for, would not as yet join, perhaps, as Michael Foot suggests,[27] because the Mosley débâcle was still too fresh, perhaps also because he was unwilling to accept Frank's leadership. Ominously, neither would Ernest Bevin, a member of Cole's SSIP. Bevin's deep resentment of intellectuals was confirmed when Frank Wise, and not he, was invited to chair the new League. He did not forgive them, and prophesied that the League would go the way of the ILP.

Soon the League could claim some seventy branches and two to three thousand members: not unimpressive, but well short of the ILP. And soon, too, as Ernie Bevin had predicted, it followed the path of the ILP, questioning Labour Party policies, and becoming a faction within the Labour movement, competing for socialists.[28] Like the ILP before it and the Bevanites after it, the League thought it could operate in the space between the Labour Party's avowed tolerance of debate and the trade-union demand for discipline. Like them, it found it could not. When in the later 1930s the Socialist League increasingly operated not as a think-tank but as a political party, and sought a united front with the ILP and the CP to confront European fascism, Bevin led the move to proscribe it. In January 1937 it dissolved.

Before Jennie and Frank could work their political difficulties through, tragedy befell. Charles Trevelyan had been a sympathetic friend. Jennie and Frank sometimes stayed at his magnificent Wallington estate near Morpeth, where they read in the library, walked the bluebell woods, and enjoyed some peace and privacy. The first weekend in November 1933, Frank had travelled north to do five meetings. Before leaving London on the Friday, he had dashed round to Jennie's at breakfast to give her a birthday hug. They grumbled at being apart for the weekend, and he confessed to being tired. On the Sunday he stayed with Trevelyan. Walking in the woods, he came to a stile. Frank, apparently the most fit of men, suddenly collapsed with a brain haemorrhage. He was gone before they could bring him back to the house.

That Sunday evening Jennie received a phone call from a journalist friend—the news had just come through on the wire: Frank was dead.

Jennie was alone. She had no friends with her, no drink or sleeping tablets to help. She was 'half-unconscious' all night long, unable to understand or absorb what had happened. She neither slept nor wept. Trevelyan's first thought had been of Jennie. He went down on the overnight train from Newcastle, hoping to break the news to her in person. On the way he called in at Frank's flat to collect Jennie's letters and things. Only when he turned up at Guilford Street could Jennie break into a passion of weeping.[29] He got her up, took her out unresisting to buy a new watch to replace one she had lost, and sorted her immediate appointments. She could not even grieve in public; that was Dorothy's right. She tried, Jennie told Suse, to 'steady myself by repeating that this is my own heartbreak & loneliness that I am weeping for . . . Perhaps I was growing a bit arrogant inside the net of tenderness he wove around me. I am terrified of life yet but made myself do my *New Leader* work & on Sunday I address two anti-war meetings in Newcastle.'[30] Suse feared she was suicidal. Trevelyan steeled himself to attend Frank's funeral, taking flowers with him from Jennie. Jennie steeled herself to visit Wallington.

She wrote to Dorothy. A week later, Dorothy, who was experiencing her own share of sleepless nights, wrote back a remarkable letter to the young woman who had broken her marriage, a letter that was generous but salted with her pain:

> My dear Jennie, I do understand how intolerably hard it is for you who have no official 'right' to be considered, & who have to carry on as if it were only a great friend & not more you have lost.
>
> I feel rather a humbug getting all the official condolences—but for his sake & the children's, I've got to go on playing the game of not letting the world know—& especially the world who half knew & look to see how I take it.
>
> I think it makes it very much easier for me to feel that *you* knew I did care—that if I had loved him less, perhaps I might have made it easier for you both. If my love had been big enough, or I had been big enough, I suppose I could have carried on. But to see him just now & then, & to know I'd really lost so much, was beyond me & I was so sore. I snapped. How one blames oneself now for not always living up to the bigger selfless outlook that I got glimpses of.

Dorothy was glad that if he had to die, he had done so at Wallington and in the prime of life, the way he would have wished. And glad too that they, Dorothy and Frank, had come to a sort of peace. He had been down to see her a fortnight before, and there she had agreed to an amicable separation. The night before he left, it had been their twenty-first wedding anniversary and together they had gone to the theatre:

My last picture is of him standing on the Baker St. platform waving. Oh I'm so *thankful* we parted in that spirit—not blinking issues and covering up difficulties but agreed to face them in a spirit of friendly compromise.

I know how much you meant to him. You gave him youth & inspiration when I was middle-aged & nervy & often on edge, & too much preoccupied with the children, perhaps. I think you know I respected your love for each other. What I wanted was an end to the anomalous situation, which, quite frankly, meant that Frank wasn't facing up to issues . . .

I was facing loneliness & separation from him—& perhaps you'll understand that this separation is easier for me to bear than the other might have been. Only don't think I would have chosen this way out. He had so much to give yet to the causes we all care for—& to the children.

She is suddenly businesslike. Would Jennie come to Frank's flat next week and take away any of her books and pictures? She would like to clean out the flat and save a month's rent. And then, compassionately: 'You know, I told you I think that in my early girlhood I cared for a married man. I'm glad now though it was Hell then as well as Heaven. But it has made it easier for me to understand.'[31]

Jennie also kept another letter, a note pushed under her door by Ellen Wilkinson, still mourning the loss 'of my own Frank [Horrobin] . . . I feel sick every time I think of E.F.W. but I *am* glad to know that he was happy at the end. That *is* a big thing. There are certain miseries you are spared my dear.'*

Jennie tried to blot out any feeling by working herself into exhaustion. Three weeks of non-stop lecturing in Scotland, with two speeches a night, helped a little. Before he left London Charles Trevelyan contacted Nye, who said he would look after Jennie. He and Hubert Griffiths, the drama critic, cared for her by day and held her at night. That, too, was a way of blotting out feeling, of reaching out for human comfort. Jennie told Suse late in December:

* Ellen Wilkinson to JL, n.d. Ellen was passionately attached to Frank Horrobin; when he married, she was desolate. See Vernon, *Ellen Wilkinson*, 126. Beatrice Webb records Ellen asking her, as they walked together, whether it was 'reasonable to expect a woman in public life, who did not want to get married, to remain a celibate if she found a congenial friend who happened to have an uncongenial wife? . . . Ellen referred, I think, to her own relations with Horrobin . . . For good or for evil the political emancipation of women and their entry into public life has swept away the old requirement of chastity in the unmarried woman! The conventions (there is no code) are now the same for men and women.' *The Diary of Beatrice Webb*, vol. 4, 245 (28 July 1931), eds. N. and J. MacKenzie.

Frank's loss does not grow less. Aneurin & Griffiths are both good pals. They take me anywhere I want to go, but they are not Frank.

Did I tell you Ni wants to share the cottage with me in the summer. Frank was solid gold. Ni is quick silver. He is as unreliable as Frank was reliable. He is moody, self indulgent but in a curious way he is brother to me. Our mining background, outlooks, hopes & despairs are most similar. If I do decide to share with him it will be an emotionally & financially rocky business & perhaps now I am merely seeking another kind of pain to kill the one that is with me. But by April I count on being sane enough to make sensible decisions.[32]

Jennie's comment many years later was how little she knew Nye, and how wrong she had been about him. What is equally striking is that barely a month after Frank's death, Nye was moving in. 'Slowly I came to know that Nye loved me but would [not] knowing that Frank had died, force me in any way. We were living together in my flat in Guilford Street but Nye knew I was still restless and grieving for Frank.'[33]

In January Jennie left for her annual American lecture tour. She returned late in April, and from then to Whitsun Nye wooed her. Living together was not enough. They must marry. 'I liked him well enough and the chemistry was all right between us, but I could not believe that there would be the security that Frank had given me for a few short years, and that I had always known in my parents' home.'[34] Jennie dithered for a little longer, until one evening Nye took Jennie in her best emerald velvet dress to the Café Royal for dinner. Nye, surrounded by waiters and wine glasses, had chosen an immaculate meal. At Jennie's unspoken question, he told her, 'You can always live like a millionaire for five minutes.' She must marry him—neither could afford any further scandal.

Marry him she did. Nye went off to the USA to raise funds for German refugees, and on his return in September they announced their engagement. Nye told reporters they would marry in October. 'Miss Lee is studying for the Bar. I suppose she will study during our honeymoon, because she takes the examination in December. After marriage, we shall follow our own political paths as usual.' Jennie would change neither her name nor her Party for Nye.* Indeed, said Fenner Brockway cheerfully on behalf of the ILP, 'if anyone addresses her as Mrs Bevan on political questions the letter will not be answered'.[35]

* Women kept their 'maiden' names in the arts, but, Edith Summerskill apart, not in the world of politics and not in the 1930s. The newly married Barbara Betts attended her selection committee in Blackburn in 1944. After the meeting, the party agent said sternly: 'In Blackburn we don't like career women who use their maiden names. When you go out of here you will be Mrs Barbara Castle.' B. Castle, *Fighting all the Way* (1993), 122.

On 25 October 1934 they were quietly married at Holborn Register Office without fuss or friends. At least, that was their intention. Just Nye's friend, Archie Lush, and a woman friend (Marion Balderston) were invited to witness it. Nye's elder brother William invited himself and glowered throughout. There was no Ma or Pa Lee. But word had got round and the room was packed with pressmen and photographers; the door had to be left open for others to obtain a view. Jennie glanced at the spectators with amusement and remarked, 'I think they ought to pay for this'. She refused to wear a hat, gloves, or buy a new coat for the occasion. There was no wedding ring, not because Nye had forgotten to buy one, but because the bride did not want one. 'There is nothing in that', she told the press, 'I just don't like rings—that's all', and kept her hands stuffed in her coat pockets throughout much of the ceremony.* After lunch at The Ivy, Jennie and Nye went back to a party at the Balderstons.[36] George Lansbury and Arthur Henderson presented them with a writing desk and a filing cabinet as a wedding present from the PLP. Their honeymoon was postponed to Christmas and Spain.

Nye was undeniably in love with Jennie. Her friends (and his family) rather doubted that Jennie was ever 'in love' with Nye. She was battered and lonely; she had loved Frank profoundly and she had lost him. Now she was emotionally drained. She did not want another great romance. Something less encompassing, not exactly casual but not too demanding either. Companionable. Unsentimental. Jennie was fond of Nye—he had been a staunch friend and comrade for five years, and he made her laugh. They understood each other's background and knew where each other came from. Jennie needed Nye's gaiety and his teasing to lift her depressions; she respected his reading of the political landscape, shared his anger at the human waste of unemployment and the degradation of poverty, and confirmed his instinctive distrust of authority; she was intrigued by his philosophical musings, his range of friends inside and outside of politics, and his interest in the arts, music, painting—worlds which were unfamiliar to her. For all his Welsh mining background, she knew that Nye would never try to domesticate her and would allow her the private and the political space she demanded. He would not confine her. He would make the conventions of marriage as unoppressive as she could wish. She craved the human warmth of Frank's bed, in which she had been well loved. Nye's tender affection would do. It was, all in

* It was the wedding ring she refused; Jennie often wore dress rings—she had beautiful hands. In the 1950s a Tory MP admired a fine dress ring she was wearing. 'Oh,' she said, 'Nye gave it to me many years ago when he loved me' (information Lord Lauderdale).

all, not a bad basis for what was to become an outstanding political marriage.

Jennie later considered that Nye had been very brave to marry her. Perhaps. But Nye wanted Jennie, and he was confident that he could woo and hold her within their marriage. It was Jennie, not Nye, who was taking the risk. She had always sought the love of older mature men, who were powerful yet dependable. In 1934 it was not clear that Nye was either. He was more brother than father, their relationship, to begin with, one of equals. As for his career, Jennie was as yet the better-known public figure. By siding with the ILP, however, she sidelined herself at just the time when Nye's own star was rising. Over the years, the balance in their marriage changed. Her commitment to Nye deepened and turned into a fierce protectiveness that often irritated his friends. 'Nyedolatry', Barbara Castle was to call it.

Yet Jennie never stopped grieving for Frank. Many years after Nye had died, Jennie had lunch with her old friend, the actress Constance Cummings and Rita Mallalieu, the widow of their Bevanite friend, the delightful Bill Mallalieu. After lunch, Jennie took Mrs Mallalieu by the arm and they walked round and round Constance's garden, Jennie saying that the great love of her life, 'it wasn't Nye, you know'. And she talked about Frank.[37] Writing in 1977 to C. P. Trevelyan's daughter, she sadly recalled that 'time of immense political activity, hopes, despair, tangled private matters as Frank Wise and I were preparing to spend our lives together'.[38] As her world closed down in the 1980s, she often thought wistfully about Frank. He remained the deepest love of her life. But her future lay with Nye.

*

By Autumn 1936 Jennie was well enough to travel north with Nye to Edinburgh for the Labour Party Conference. Nye went as a delegate, Jennie was on the press table reporting for *New Leader*. That Edinburgh Conference marked the moment when the Labour Party's preoccupations moved from domestic to foreign affairs. Jennie, without a depressed mining constituency to care for, and more widely travelled than Nye, was increasingly distressed by events in Europe. She had been working with Ellen Wilkinson and alongside middle-class feminists like Vera Brittain in the Communist-led International Woman's Committee against War and Fascism. Nye, meanwhile, coming from South Wales where up to a third of the men remained unemployed, worked alongside the Communist-led National Unemployed Workers' Movement (NUWM), demanding higher unemployment benefits and the end of the hated household means test.*

The NEC disapproved. Nye joined Ellen Wilkinson and Edith Summerskill in backing the hunger marches of the unemployed.[39] The TUC and the NEC advised Labour parties and trades councils along the route of the Jarrow crusade not to help the marchers. Local branches were more generous. Said Nye in 1936: 'Why should a first class piece of work like the Hunger March have been left to the initiative of unofficial members of the Party and to the Communists and the ILP?' He told a welcoming rally in Hyde Park:

> The Hunger Marchers have achieved one thing. They have for the first time in the history of the national Labour Movement achieved a united platform. Communists, ILP-ers, Socialists, members of the Labour Party and Co-operators for the first time have joined hands together, and we are not going to unclasp them. This demonstration proves to the country that Labour needs a united leadership.[40]

None the less, in the Midlands and in the South, unemployment began slowly to fall, as the building, electrical engineering, and motor industries took off. Instead, it was the tragic events unfolding in Spain that fired the Labour movement and dominated the Edinburgh Conference.

In July 1936 civil war had broken out in Spain, when General Franco's army rebelled against the Popular Front republican government. Despite pleas from the constituency parties, the Labour leadership supported Neville Chamberlain in refusing arms to Spain's elected government, as they feared the Spanish Civil War might escalate into a European war. Jennie, who was as fond of the Catholic constituency in Scotland as she was of the Communist Party, darkly suspected that the official Labour Party was betraying Spain for a handful of Catholic votes.[41] The Vatican had thrown its support behind Franco. So had Germany, who was arming Franco and the rebels. Right-wing Tories were pro-Franco.

Ever since their honeymoon in Spain, Nye had loved the country above all others. He was distraught. At Edinburgh, he hammered away at Ernie Bevin—everybody except the platform knew that the rebels were getting arms while the republicans were denied them—but the platform swamped the constituencies with the votes of the big unions. Fraternal delegates from Spain pleaded with them, and moved Conference to tears. But the

* The means test offended every canon of working-class respectability. It forced unemployed miners to depend on the earnings of their young daughters, brothers on the earnings of their sisters. Cottages were stripped bare, down to bed, boards, cooker, table, and chairs. Grandmother's lustre jug or the mother's small garnet brooch was removed and sold for a few shillings.

policy of non-intervention was reaffirmed. Jennie and Nye were in despair:

> I crept miserably out of the hall and stumbled into Aneurin. He looked haggard and careworn. He was ill anyhow at the time[42] and in no condition to stand punishment. He looked as if he had just dragged himself out of a torture chamber. And he was not the only delegate who looked like that. Out they came, singly and in groups, the most unhappy, guilty-looking collection of people I have ever seen.[43]

Nye, Stafford Cripps, and G. R. Strauss decided they would launch *Tribune* to call for arms for Spain.

A few months later, in 1937, Jennie returned to Spain, touring the Aragon front for *New Leader.* She was joined in Barcelona by George Orwell, 'a lanky figure' with his boots slung over his shoulders. She was caught up in the war, sheltering in the kitchen of a mill-house while the fascist guns shelled them from outside. She reported the bitter hatred within the Spanish Left between Communist and POUM militia.* With her was young Bob Smillie, the brave and much-loved 19-year-old grandson of the veteran ILP MP who had introduced Jennie into the House. The young Bob had joined up. Jennie took him to the local café and fed him marzipan cake, which he adored. Within the year he was dead in a Communist jail, murdered, said Jennie, by Communists. Jennie took armfuls of red carnations to the funeral of another young soldier. 'His elderly mother', she wrote, the tears just behind her words, 'could still raise her clenched fist in revolutionary salute and bid her neighbours march on, march on.'[44]

Spain weaned the British Left away from pacifism—though not yet into rearmament. Fenner Brockway, who in 1914 had set up the No Conscription Fellowship, visited Catalonia and soon lost his pacifism. Spain, he said, was a people's war.[45] Nye was no pacifist. However, the National Government, by refusing arms to Spain in the name of 'neutrality', showed that it could not be trusted with arms of its own. British arms would not be used against European fascism; instead, said Nye at the 1937 Party Conference, 'we . . . [would] put a sword in the hands of our enemies that may be used to cut off our own heads'. The Left must unite to defeat fascism abroad and prevent the rearmament of a proto-fascist National Government at home. Rearmament was safe only in the hands of a Labour government.[46]

* The Trotskeyite Partido Obrero de Unificación Marxista (POUM), with which the ILP identified, insisted that 'the war and revolution are inseparable, and that while the war is being waged at the front, a socialist economy must be built behind the lines'. The more reactionary CP said it was a war between Fascism and the democratically elected government, and allied itself with the petit-bourgeoisie; *New Leader,* 15 Jan. 1937.

The successful launch of the Left Book Club in May 1936[47] and the growing strength of the Constituency Party Association[48] suggested a groundswell of support in the country.

Nye, a member of the Labour Party, had for years been willing to co-operate with the CP on behalf of the unemployed.[49] Jennie, a member of the more left-wing ILP, and scarred by her Cowdenbeath experiences, remained deeply distrustful of the CP, far more so than Nye. Its efforts to enter, control, recruit from, or supersede the ILP had wrecked any chance her party might have had of an honourable survival outside the Labour Party. The CP and the ILP continued a vicious fight for the membership and the leadership of the socialist Left in Britain, as in Spain.[50] (The CP, typically, denounced the ILP as 'the left hand of British fascism.)'[51] Both Nye and Jennie were equivocal about Communist bids to reaffiliate to the Labour Party. The show trials in Moscow repelled them. None the less, in January 1937 Jennie swallowed her loathing of the CP and joined Nye in launching the Unity campaign and *Tribune*, to fight fascism and arm Spain (William Mellor, Barbara Castle's lover, became *Tribune*'s first editor, aided by a young Michael Foot). Cripps provided the leadership of the one and most of the founding capital of the other. The Socialist League, the ILP, the CP, as well as the NUWM came into fragile alliance.[52]

Within days, the Unity campaign commanded huge meetings across the country that thrilled their audiences. Cripps, Bevan, Maxton, Mellor, and Pollit of the CP all on the same platform—might the Labour Party, wondered Michael Foot, be 'taken by storm?'[53] A few days later the NEC disaffiliated the Socialist League. The League dissolved. The Labour Party executive also ruled that anyone sharing a platform with the CP would be expelled.

The fears of the Left darkened when Chamberlain embarked on appeasement. In September 1938 he went to Munich; in March 1939 he recognized Franco. The Unity campaign of the Left broadened into a wider Popular Front, led by Cripps, and drawing in Liberals such as Sir Richard Acland.

This was too much for the official Labour Party, which was unwilling to contemplate electoral pacts in what was still expected to be an election year. Cripps was required either to accept PLP discipline and withdraw from the Popular Front, or be expelled. Nye claimed that the PLP was turning itself into 'an intellectual concentration camp', and joined him.[54] Denied the opportunity to defend themselves at the NEC, in March 1939 they were summarily expelled.

Nye was out of the Labour Party at the very time when it seemed possible that Jennie might rejoin it. At its Easter Conferences of 1938 and

1939, Jennie's ILP sought to negotiate reaffiliation. Jennie had been following the NEC–ILP discussions with some anxiety—her political and parliamentary future hung on them. A decent fudge now seemed possible—ILP MPs, perhaps, could speak but not vote against official Labour Party policy in Parliament. The ILP was due to call a special conference in September 1939, at which it would recommend reaffiliation, when war was declared, the conference was cancelled, and the ILP and Jennie remained in lonely isolation.[55]

Jennie retained her profound distrust of Chamberlain. When the Commons debated Munich early in October 1938 and Maxton joined in the general congratulations, Jennie wrote a bitter letter to Fenner Brockway:

> I thought we had re-affirmed a million times in the ILP that the Chamberlain breed goes to war or refrains from doing so exactly as best suits its class interests.
>
> Chamberlain was fighting the class war intelligently and with deadly effectiveness when he made terms with Hitler . . . The capitalist peace has been kept which means the victims are all on one side, on our side. But Maxton congratulates Chamberlain.[56]

As the summer lengthened, Nye and Jennie knew they were moving towards war. Their own views moved as well. Support for a Popular Front could not survive the shocking news of the Stalin–Hitler non-aggression pact in August. Britain was committed to defend Poland and Jennie and Nye could no longer resist rearmament. Those who urged peace at any price were now dismissed by Jennie as a small group:

> whose motives varied from genuine pacifism to well meaning humanitarianism to coldly calculating pro nazism. But the main flow of public opinion would have none of those. Quite quietly, almost sadly, with none of the old-fashioned jingoism, flag-waving, shouting, parading, mass hysteria of the 1914 mood, but with an utter steadiness and unbreakable conviction, this strange island had decided it must fight . . . only through and beyond war could we hope to find peace again.[57]

Since her marriage, followed by her election defeat of 1935, her growing unease with the more revolutionary tone of the ILP, and her own breakdown, Jennie had increasingly withdrawn from high politics. By default, she remained a listless and tetchy member of the ILP. In the summer of 1936 she was exchanging letters with James Carmichael, her ally and former agent in North Lanark, who was pressing her to stand again; he hoped that the 'mood for greater working class unity' would this time succeed. With no better constituency available, she agreed, and was reselected a month later.[58] She continued to brood over her own position. Could the Labour Party be brought within a united front and give her a clear run at North Lanark? It would not. Should the ILP press for reaffiliation? As yet, it did not. Should she then return to the Labour Party? She could not. She was as uneasy as ever about the authoritarian discipline and trade-union dominance of the Labour Party.

Nye, who shared her troubles, had behind him the unquestioned loyalty and political clout of the South Wales miners. He could challenge boundaries, defy, and (usually) get away with it. Jennie had no such bulwark behind her. She was on her own. If she rejoined the Labour Party she would be unable to take the risks that Nye did. When the Conference platform, buttressed by trade-union votes, insisted at Edinburgh that there should be no arms for Spain, that defined for Jennie the distance between herself and official Labour.

Yet she felt more and more alien within the ILP. On the one hand the ILP had lost its parliamentary direction under the leadership of the ineffectual Maxton. She noted in her diary that Maxton did not 'hate' enough to be a political leader, nor did he 'inspire fear'; when he spoke in the Commons, it was 'like a west end congregation listening to a gifted preacher. Feel they are not so bad that they can listen to such admonishings.' Yet on the other hand she had no confidence in an ILP led by young rank-and-file London hotheads. The ILP was compensating for its political irrelevance by increasing the extravagance and abstruseness of its political language. Ex-Liberal pacifists, anarchic democrats, paper syndicalists, revolutionary Marxists, and Moscow-disciplined Communists fought over its bones, while its numbers dwindled into insignificance. They had sacrificed influence to purity. It was falling apart.

Jennie had no difficulty in describing herself as a revolutionary socialist, but her cast of mind was essentially practical not speculative. She had a hearty dislike of abstract phrases; she preferred the concrete and the particular. She wanted to engage with the here and now, to defend her class, and fight the cause of socialism within and without Parliament. Events of 1931 had taught her two things. Unfortunately they were contradictory. The first was that there was no inevitability about gradualism. That, she had always known. Equally, 1931 had taught her that there was no inevitability about the breakdown of capitalism either. In time, she was to share with Nye a belief in a third way. But where did that leave her now? She doubted whether the Labour Party could or would change society. Yet Nye had been right in 1932 when he, and Frank also, had told her that she could do nothing outside the Labour Party. Whatever its faults, the Labour Party *was* the Labour movement. The ILP, whatever its doctrines, was irrelevant. As the international scene darkened, Jennie was isolated and impotent, unable to join the Labour Party, ineffectual outside it. 'It was like a slow paralysis.'[59]

She kept herself busy. For two years she was 'a willing prisoner' in the Tudor country cottage she and Nye had found at Lane End, fifty miles west of London. She knocked down walls, replaced the thatch, tamed the garden, and scoured the countryside for old furniture. Nye returned home at weekends. She continued to write, to take meetings, and to lecture in the States.

She started work on an autobiography, *Tomorrow is a New Day,* 'in the hope of seeing my own way more clearly through the tangle of recent years'. She wrote vividly of her childhood. She looked back at her last decade, defeated in every one of her causes: the miners after 1926, Labour in 1931, the ILP in 1932, and the British Left's Unity and Popular Front campaigns crushed along with European socialism in Italy, Germany, Austria, Spain, and Czechoslovakia. The later chapters are reflective and melancholic, infused with the sense of 'impending tragedy' in Europe. She found the final pages hard to write, wondering as she did so 'how far our defeats have been [the Labour movement's] own fault'. She went on, 'Political parties and politicians have not left me much that I feel I dare rely on.' She held fast only to her faith in the decency of ordinary working people. She hoped that would bring them a new day.[60]

She offered the book to Victor Gollancz. He read the first few chapters, and thought they were 'delightfully written and very vivid', but he missed in it any 'stress and strain, and a certain spiritual and intellectual excitement'. Jennie pressed him, but he would not commit himself, pleading 'hideous overspending on the Left Book Club'.[61] Then a new publisher, the Cresset Press, offered to publish it on the strength of a chat with Nye. Jennie circulated the manuscript for 'puffs' she could use in publicity. J. B. Priestley thought the book was 'rather messy', and as she had a gift for phrase-making, was sorry that 'you have not taken more trouble with the writing'. The book was 'alive, it is very honest, it throws a light on the political and social scene, and it will help us to think clearly about ourselves'. He added that she was welcome to use this sentence if she thought it would help. It didn't. She tried H. G. Wells. He found the book very judgemental, dividing the mob into sheep and goats; and, on the basis of a dinner they both attended at the Trevelyans, thought her views on subjects where he disagreed with her 'pert & silly & shallow'. He offered her dinner. She rallied and refused.[62] The publishers went ahead, although, with the outbreak of war, sales were inevitably limited.

What of her future? There was no question, apparently, of starting a family,[63] and no possibility, apparently, of returning to Parliament. She had come to a dead end. As Europe, in her phrase, plunged into 'the long seemingly endless night', she and Nye tried to talk of other things at the cottage—gardening, poetry, friends. She found it difficult to lift her mood. She noted: 'Ni cannot expect me to behave like a rainbow when I feel like a dumb mist.'[64] He would sometimes make her listen to music, or would read to her. One evening he pulled down a copy of A. E. Housman, quoting bitter lines from *The Shropshire Lad* that burnt into Jennie:

> Be still, be still, my soul; it is but for a season:
> Let us endure an hour and see injustice done.[65]

They thought of Spain. They thought of young Bob Smillie killed in a Communist prison in Spain.

A few months later, on the first Sunday in September 1939, Jennie and Nye tuned into the one o'clock news for official confirmation that war had been declared. Nye, who had been pacing up and down their sitting-room, rummaged through their untidy pile of gramophone records. He found what he was looking for, and what they had not dared play for a year—the marching songs of the Spanish republican army. The music rang through the cottage. They were going back to Spain, this time bearing arms.

Nye was too restless to remain at home. He sped up to London. He told Jennie that all the cars on the road that day were being driven just that little bit recklessly. Nye had no doubts, Jennie noted: 'He was all out for fighting Hitler and not particular who his allies were or what weapons he used provided he gained his end.' Jennie, true to her ILP roots, was torn:

> After the first excitement of hearing the official proclamation of war cold doubts began creeping in. Had I been carried away by the fervour of a Welsh husband? Were his truths my truths? What was the war about? Who would lead us? And for what ends? Had Spain anything to do with it? Or liberty? Or democracy? . . .
>
> Was it all a black-hearted game of power politics with ordinary men's lives and aspirations counting for nothing? What was I to do? Support the war, standing in with Chamberlain and his Cabinet, knowing all the time that whatever I might want to be fighting for, my war aims were not their war aims and it was they, not I, who were in control?[66]

4

JENNIE'S WAR

FOR the first few months of war, there was little of it. A phoney peace was followed by a phoney war and life went on as usual. The government, half-persuaded that the war might peter out, began half-heartedly to defend its people—the blackout was introduced, children were evacuated, ration books and gas masks distributed, buildings sandbagged, and men over the age of 27 conscripted. Jennie pottered around her cottage, writing occasional pieces for *Tribune*, and searched not very energetically for something useful to do.

So did the Cabinet. In the spring, they sent British forces to aid Norway and block German control of the North Sea. It was a disaster; the troops withdrew. On 10 May 1940 Chamberlain fell, Churchill became Prime Minister, and Labour entered a coalition government. Hitler invaded Holland, Belgium, and then France. At the end of May, Allied troops were evacuated from Dunkirk. Hitler prepared to invade Britain. However, he needed first to wipe out Britain's fighter command if German bombers were to subdue London and German troop ships were to cross the Channel. Beaverbrook became Churchill's Minister for Air Production, racing against the clock to produce planes, conjuring up raw materials—iron railings, aluminium saucepans—coaxing factory workers to exceed their stated hours, cutting through Whitehall red tape. And he delivered: Britain had more fighter planes by the end of the Battle of Britain than it had at its start. Beaverbrook wrought the victory that the RAF won.

Between Dunkirk in May and the Battle of Britain in August 1940, those key months on which the outcome of the War was to hinge, Jennie worked for Max Beaverbrook.

They had sparred for many years. Beaverbrook had a huge acquaintanceship, cultivated for amusement as much as for influence. He had petted and patronized Nye when he first became an MP in 1929; and he enjoyed Jennie's feistiness. On her early trips to the United States, shortly after she had lost her seat at North Lanark, Beaverbrook had furnished her with letters of introduction to his friends: 'Jenny is a great young woman. She follows Maxton; quarrels with the Labour Party; hates MacDonald; loathes Snowden; loves Russia—and may go to gaol.'[1] Over the years, Beaverbrook—brash, irresponsible, amoral, and great fun—threaded through Jennie's and Nye's lives. He was determined to extract as much mischief and pleasure out of politics as his fortunes and their dissent would afford, wickedly offering to help fund ILP by-election candidates who shared his early anti-war views, urging on Nye the use of a country cottage in which to recover his health (an offer which Nye gracefully declined), and later subsidizing *Tribune*.* Though not noticeably fastidious in such matters, even Nye and Jennie were wary of Beaverbrook's games.

In 1940 Beaverbrook phoned Jennie. To her eternal gratitude, he offered her a job. As she walked in to his office, he told her: 'You and I were against this bloody war. Now we have to win it for them.' (Not true, Jennie thought. She was not against this war, but she was not minded to contradict him.) Her job was to keep aircraft factories running during the blitz. She had to persuade them to work through the sirens and through the air raids, find out where and why there were any delays in production (men, management, materials?), and report back personally to Beaverbrook. She refused to be paid and was not part of the official civil service, so she could say what she wanted; she knew the trade-union and Labour movement backwards, she was one of them and was trusted by them, and so could move fast. She loved it. She later told Beaverbrook's biographer that working for Max taught her how to be 'a gangster's moll'; their task was 'to keep the maximum number of planes in the air, even though we sank the whole Navy and blew up the Army in the process'.[2]

She travelled the country. In her pocket she always kept a slip of paper, headed 'South Wales Miners' Federation' in bold black type, which Nye had brought back from a meeting of Welsh miners in the early days of the blitz. Its opening sentence read: 'All key men must stand by their posts

* William Mellor was sacked as editor of *Tribune* when he refused in 1938 to support the Popular Front. Michael Foot resigned in sympathy. That evening Jennie watched with interest as Nye phoned Beaverbrook to say: 'I've got a young bloody knight-errant here. They sacked his boss, so he resigned. Have a look at him.' S. Hoggart and D. Leigh, *Michael Foot: A Portrait* (1981), 68–9. Beaverbrook took Foot on to the *Evening Standard*. In the 1950s Beaverbrook's subsidy of £3,000 kept *Tribune* afloat. For Foot's relations with Beaverbrook, see M. Jones, *Michael Foot* (1994), *passim*.

throughout air raids or until relieved.' The miners had issued these instructions to themselves. What the miners decided, the transport workers agreed, and the defence workers followed. Whenever Jennie met doubt from the factory floor, she showed them her piece of paper, persuading them to keep production going as the bombs fell. 'This was their own kind calling to them.'[3] One clear night Jennie joined an aircraft spotter on the roof of a Midlands munitions factory. The men worked steadily on, ignoring the alert as enemy planes approached, depending on their spotter to sound a danger siren if they were in line for a direct hit.

She found herself knocking heads together, sorting out relations between aloof factory managers and suspicious workers, encouraging them to set up joint works production councils, resolving local grievances. 'I make them feel their work is appreciated, respected and essential, adding *my* reasons for wanting Hitler defeated.'[4] At Reading, for example, she found that the men stopped work when the sirens sounded because they were worried about their families. Jennie promised decent domestic air-raid shelters, and they promised to maintain production. 'Hell!' said Beaverbrook, when she reported this. 'Where are we going to get the cement?'—it was in desperately short supply. Beaverbrook promptly hijacked cement destined for the army. His way of doing business—improvising from one crisis to the next (his office walls carried the notice, ORGANIZATION IS THE ENEMY OF IMPROVISATION), raiding one industry after another, blasting through the systems by sheer strength of will—for the moment suited Jennie well.[5]

With the Battle of Britain won, Beaverbrook wanted to increase production of barrage balloons. Balloons stopped dive-bombing, reduced the accuracy of enemy aim, and impeded enemy planes. Jennie described it as aerial barbed wire.[6] She knew every barrage-balloon factory in the country—would she be his 'balloonatic-in-chief'? It was promotion, and it was responsibility. Yet Jennie hesitated. She was growing tired of improvising emergency responses to emergency situations, when those emergencies were by now predictable. In her travels, responsible manufacturers and sober trade-unionists had pressed on her the need to plan men, materials, and machines. They wanted a steady war effort, the long hard pull rather than the instant fix. Jennie's instinctive belief in political will clashed with her faith in more bureaucratic and Russian-style central planning. Balloons, she decided, needed planning. She asked Beaverbrook to bring together balloon manufacturers across the country to plan and coordinate their work.[7] But it was not Beaverbrook's way.

An offer from the *Daily Mirror* in late October 1940 made up her mind.

Cecil King had a couple of years back transformed the *Mirror* from being a right-wing paper for women to a noisy anti-Tory, mass-circulation, working-class newspaper. Would she accept a six-month contract as political correspondent, at £800 p. a.? The *Mirror* spoke up for the service-man and the factory worker; it was abrasive, populist, and critical of government. Jennie liked its comic strips and saucy pin-ups—she accepted the job. Beaverbrook approved, and she resigned from the Aircraft Ministry.[8] She had re-entered the House of Commons—to sit in its press gallery.

A few months later, however, the Communist *Daily Worker* was suppressed, and Churchill started to complain of the *Mirror*'s editorial line. The editor feared his paper would be the next to go. His staff were gagged, Jennie's pieces were spiked. Even 'poor little strip tease Jane' was bundled back into her clothes—'they might try to get us for pornography', the editor explained to Jennie. 'Be still my soul, be still. It is but for a day. Be still and let injustice be', Jennie wrote in her private diary, paraphrasing those biting lines of Housman that Nye had read to her during the Spanish Civil War.[9] With two months of her contract still to run, she was sacked.

Once again, Jennie was left wondering what to do. Through the autumn and winter of 1940, Britain fought on alone. However, the exile governments of Poland, Norway, Holland, and Belgium were now based in Britain, bringing with them men and ships. Meanwhile, de Gaulle was organizing the Free French. The two great 'neutrals' were the USSR and the USA, and on them the outcome would depend. How could they be brought into the war?

Stafford Cripps had been sent to Russia as Ambassador to get Stalin to enter the war. But only when Hitler invaded Russia in June 1941 did Britain have a fighting ally. Churchill and his military advisers did not expect the Soviet Union to hold out: they thought that Germany would go through Russia, in Jennie's phrase, 'like a hot knife through butter'. Russia's request for aid was seen as a burden, drawing away desperately scarce resources. Africa, in Churchill's view, remained the more vital theatre of war. Like Roosevelt, however, Beaverbrook understood the significance of Russia's war. He, Nye, and Jennie were again on the same side, mobilizing popular support for Russia, campaigning to open up a Second Front. Nye joined Victor Gollancz, Eleanor Rathbone, Sir Richard Acland, Harold Laski, J. B. Priestley, Mervyn Stockwood, H. N. Brailsford, and G. R. Strauss on the Anglo-Soviet Public Relations Committee, which organized talks, exhibitions, and pageants.

Jennie helped in the way she knew best, and dashed off a pamphlet, *Russia, Our Ally*, which drew on her memories of the Russian men and women she had met while travelling with Frank a decade before. She insisted Russia would hold out. The pamphlet sold well. 'Thank God for Russia', recorded Home Intelligence, as Russia bore the brunt of the German war effort. By early December 1941, and at a most terrible price in war dead, Stalin finally stemmed the German advance, and held Moscow.

The USA remained Britain's best hope. However, America was instinctively isolationist and Roosevelt faced an election year. The best he could offer Churchill was 'surplus' ships and supplies. So in the autumn of 1941 Brendan Bracken, Minister of Information and an acolyte of Beaverbrook's, proposed that Jennie should visit the USA to meet trade-union leaders, journalists, and party officials, and win sympathy for the British war effort. 'Don't come back', said Nye, not entirely joking, 'until you have brought America into the War.' Beaverbrook had been buying aircraft and supplies in the USA, breathing urgency into American armament manufacture, and doing everything possible to bring the country behind Britain. Jennie was a fine propagandist and knew the States. She could reach groups denied to official diplomats. She also by now had a story to tell, of her factory visits, of resilient East-Enders who made light of their sufferings, of this citizens' war. Churchill was agreeable, and in September off she went.

She travelled from East Coast to West at a frenetic pace, packing in meetings, lectures, conventions, press conferences, university gatherings, and dinners. In New York and Washington, she met politicians and journalists, La Guardia, Dean Acheson, and John Gunther. She was told that Britain would win without American intervention. She identified the growing 'America First' isolationism. She noticed rising anti-Semitism which held that 'it was the Jews who were drawing America into war'. She talked to teachers, women of the dressmakers' union, men of the maritime union. There was lots of scepticism, she recorded, that Britain was fighting 'for anything except old-fashioned imperialism'.[10] She moved on to the car belt, to Chicago, Detroit, and Michigan, where the Congress of Industrial Organizations (CIO) was in convention. Walter Reuther quietly told her that he had plans to turn automobile factories into armament factories. The shop floor, here as everywhere in the States, was deeply suspicious of British 'toffs' and saw little to choose between British capitalism and German fascism. Jennie went on to Denver, the centre of the metal-ore mining industry, and then the West Coast. While she was in San Francisco, on 6 December 1941 the Japanese bombed Pearl Harbor, two days after Stalin had halted the German invasion. Fortunately for Britain, Hitler 'gratuitously' declared war on the United States[11] and so America entered the European as well as the Far East war. The outcome would now not be in doubt.

Jennie flew home in a military plane, which, unknown to her, was tailed by a German fighter. She quietly read a book, puzzled as to why her fellow passengers, mainly military officers, were so restive. They told her it had been a close thing.

She came back to find herself in political favour. Even as Churchill was witheringly dismissing Nye in Parliament as a 'squalid nuisance', he (according to Jennie) arranged for her to appear occasionally on the BBC's *Brains Trust* to help lift public morale. This radio programme had been launched in January 1941 and soon drew audiences of ten million. No attempt was made at impartiality or political balance. The programme usefully kept Jennie in the public eye. So popular was it that listeners wrote in asking how to run their own local Brains Trust, so in 1942 the BBC filmed a panel at work. Chaired by Donald McCullough, the team included Professor Joad with his trademark pipe, buttonhole, and beard, Julian Huxley, and Jennie, in dark suit and elaborate dress rings, who was seen wincing at the chairman's rather funny and persistently 'sexist' remarks. (When asked why astrology was so popular, McCullough suggested that if the questioner was going to dabble with stars, he should make sure they were blonde.) Jennie batted strongly on the more earnest questions—the difference between left and right in politics ('human nature'), the relations between Britain and the USA after the war ('fellow-feeling'), and, from an ordnance factory girl: 'When the War is over, what will happen to us girls?'

However, Jennie soon fell from grace by choosing to break the conventions of coalition. At the end of 1942 she stood as a candidate in the Bristol Central by-election. Equally as significant, she chose to stand as an Independent, and not on behalf of the ILP. She was coming in from the cold.

Jennie had gone into the wilderness with the ILP in 1932 when it had disaffiliated, rather than accept Labour Party discipline. Frank Wise had argued with her, Nye had abused her, both men insisting that outside the Labour Party she would be impotent; but her dissenting instincts were too powerful. She distrusted Labour's 'machine politics', she disliked its trade-union bloc vote. After losing North Lanark in 1935, she knew she could not win a seat for the ILP against Labour. She contemplated rejoining the Labour Party, only to find herself in despair when it refused to support arms for Spain. Yet she also recognized that the ILP had run itself into the sands. Had there been a general election in 1939 or 1940, Jennie would no doubt have fought North Lanark on the ILP ticket. As the ILP sought to reaffiliate to the Labour Party in the autumn of 1939, Jennie might have been able to fight North Lanark as the ILP-nominated official Labour candidate, and she would have won. Because war intervened, there was no reaffiliation, and no general election. Jennie stayed out.

The war redefined Jennie's party allegiance. The ILP remained resolutely anti-war, in 1939 as in 1914. For Jennie, however, 1939 was *not* 1914. The First World War had been about the clashing imperialisms of the ruling classes. It was right then that the Labour Left should stand aside from it. The Second World War, she insisted, was very different. It was a struggle to the death of the people against fascism. She had seen it for herself in Spain. Neutrality was 'escapism'.

She had warned the ILP of her views early in 1941; in June 1942 she officially resigned. As McNair, the General Secretary of the ILP put it:

> You are not able to accept the anti-war attitude of the I.L.P. and you think we are contracting out of reality in refusing to assist in military resistance to the Fascist powers.
>
> But as Socialists we are necessarily anti-Capitalist-Imperialism and all the results therefore—whether they be Unemployment, Poverty, Fascism or War. You will surely admit that the War is a gigantic struggle on the part of two capitalist developments, one Imperialist, the other Fascist, to dominate the planet. In this struggle the workers on both sides are dying in millions and *they* are the victims. We are anti. Are you pro? You talk of 'contracting out of reality'. I don't quite know what you mean by this . . . We are not neutral. As workers' representatives we are fighting for them. We are not fighting for either of their forms of oppression Imperialist or Fascist.[12]

But Jennie had made her choice. She had made it in the months after Munich as the country moved towards war. She had not then left the ILP, she told McNair, as she hoped that her views would become those of the ILP as a whole—in vain. Since then, Jennie had worked in aircraft production in 1940, and had striven to bring the United States into the war in 1941. As she had written to McNair the day before:

> I passionately share the view of the ILP that it is to an up-rising of the workers of the world we must look for a real democratic victory and the winning of permanent peace. But that does not exempt any of us from our share of responsibility in maintaining the military front . . . It may be true that workers have never won their rights on a foreign battle field—but they can lose them there, as millions of poor people in Europe can testify today. How can they be given even the beginnings of hope until the military power of their oppressors has been broken?[13]

There could be no socialism at home or colonial independence abroad without first defeating fascism.

*

Jennie resigned from the ILP in June 1942, but did not rejoin the Labour Party. She wrote to Trevelyan in November:

> I am restive. The lack of an organised party which commands one's complete respect—or even one in which you feel there is a reasonable chance of furthering prospects you believe in, not just obstructing them—is a great deprivation for a political evangelist like myself. The Labour Party becomes progressively more disgusting. Yet for me there is no other to fill the political vacuum. Free-lancing, therefore, is all that is available for a bit yet.[14]

Free-lance she did, by fighting a seat as an Independent and breaking the electoral truce.

The three major parties had agreed an electoral truce at the outbreak of war; as seats fell vacant, they would be filled by the party that held them. However, the Labour Party refused to enter a coalition under Chamberlain. They loathed his cold sarcasm. 'He always treated us like dirt', said Attlee.[15] When he resigned in May 1940, Attlee urged the Party to recognize its responsibility in bringing him down by entering the coalition under the new Prime Minister Winston Churchill. Inevitably there would be compromises, Attlee had warned Conference, but equally there would be the opportunities offered by war to pursue socialist principles and socialist planning. Labour would be partners and not hostages in any coalition. There would be no 1931, he insisted—he would not join unless he had the support of the entire Labour movement. Conference overwhelmingly backed him.

With Labour in the coalition, the electoral truce was confirmed. By-elections would only open up party divisions which would damage the coalition. Political parties must therefore be mothballed. (Nye, who was doing his best to maintain party divisions within Westminster, called the truce a 'political blackout'.[16]) Election contests were now held to be divisive and unpatriotic, subverting the official war effort. Any government defeat would give comfort to the enemy. The government candidate at the Daventry by-election in April 1943 told his audience: 'Three countries will be pleased if I am defeated—Germany, Italy and Japan.'[17] Whether they were or not, he was.

Labour's rank and file soon grew restless with an arrangement that protected a Tory Commons majority of over two hundred, as seats came up that they believed they could win. Loyalty was strained. At the 1942

Party Conference, Nye campaigned to abandon the truce. By-election contests, he argued, did not mean abandoning the coalition government, but exposing it to the healthy test of public opinion. Tom Driberg insisted that by-elections kept alive even in wartime 'the democratic tradition of the hustings'. But, by a narrow majority of just 66,000, Conference agreed that Labour would not fight any by-election seat vacated by a Tory. In consequence, of the 141 seats that fell vacant during the war, half were filled unopposed. The rest (mainly Tory seats) were contested by the unofficial Left, a mix of variously radical Independents, ILPers, and the new Common Wealth Party, against the wishes of the official Labour Party.[18]

By now, Jennie was convinced, perhaps unfairly, that Labour had failed to fight as strongly as it should within the coalition for socialist policies.[19] She did not see much in the way of renewal and reconstruction going on. She did not believe that Labour politicians like Morrison and Attlee punched their weight within Cabinet; while Ernie Bevin, who did, had a taste for knocking out his own side. Churchill used Labour to discipline its own people, her people, and for not much more. 'The Tories in both domestic and military strategy have the whip hand', she wrote in February 1943. 'The maintenance of the electoral truce will break the spirit of organised Labour, or alternatively drive its energies into guerrilla warfare. It is better to be a guerrilla warrior than not to fight at all.'[20]

Jennie, like Nye and others on the Left, distinguished between a coalition government, which in grudging fashion she supported, and an electoral truce, which suppressed debate and dissent and which she opposed. If the Labour movement would not mobilize, she would become a guerrilla warrior. In December 1942 she agreed to fight the Bristol by-election.

Wartime by-election contestants had a difficult yet fascinating time. They were accused of damaging national unity; they were opposed by all three major parties, who withheld their workers and their funds; they also faced abnormal problems thrown up by the war. Elections were conducted on the old 1939 electoral register, which favoured the Tories, as it excluded 7 million young voters and ignored the great shifts of wartime population—the re-located key workers, evacuees, families who had moved out of damaged homes, and servicemen (during the war, there were 60 million changes of address among a population of 38 million civilians).

Much depended on the character of the constituency. Agricultural workers and miners were reserved occupations (and therefore at home to vote), textile workers were not and were dispersed to other occupations and other constituencies. There was limited petrol to get around rural constituencies, limited paper for election leaflets, few meeting halls—only one still stood in Bristol. Women were no longer at home to canvass during the day, overtime was worked late into the evening, and pitted streets, unsafe buildings, and the blackout, to say nothing of the raids, made evening meetings perilous. None the less, by-elections were great fun and much enjoyed.

From 1942 by-elections also started to flow against Tory government candidates. Undetected by most politicians, but noted by Gallup and Mass Observation, the electorate was moving left. By December 1942, Mass Observation calculated that two people in five had changed their political allegiance since the outbreak of war. The clues were there: the widespread criticism of the 'guilty men'; the demand for equality of sacrifice on the home front together with the interest in the (mildly) progressive lectures and discussions of the Army Bureau of Current Affairs on the military front; the support for Russia after it entered the war, aided by Jennie's pamphlet; the popularity of J. B. Priestley and his Postscripts; the increased circulation of the Yellow Book Club and the left-wing press; the huge enthusiasm for the Beveridge Report; and the by-election results—all suggested the growth of what Home Intelligence called 'home-made socialism'. It was not especially party-political. It was anti-toff as much as pro-Labour, against vested interests as much as for working-class interests. It was informed by a strong sense of basic fairness, and above all by a determination that the conditions of the 1930s would never happen again. The 1945 Labour victory was in the making.

Grantham was won by an Independent in March 1942, Rugby and Wallasey in April. Tom Driberg, 'William Hickey' of the *Daily Express*, won Maldon in June, a couple of days after the fall of Tobruk, with the help of Richard Acland.[21] In late July Richard Acland founded the Common Wealth Party. As its chairman R. W. G. Mackay said later: 'Common Wealth as a political movement really only exists because the Labour Party are in the Government and are not stirring the people of this country as a political opposition should so as to show them the need for a Socialist Government.'[22] Thereafter, left-of-centre by-election challengers could call on a well-funded, high-profile, and professional party machine that could parachute at short notice into any constituency.[23]

Sir Richard Acland came of a family of land, liberalism, Anglicanism, and good works.[24] Cousin of Archbishop William Temple and friend of Mervyn Stockwood, he was elected a Liberal MP for Barnstaple in 1935, read Keynes, and became an ethical socialist. The war must be a moral crusade, he argued in his paper *Forward March*; private property must be replaced by common ownership of land, class confrontation by industrial democracy, competition by fellowship, centralization by devolution, and national government by world government. By mid-1942, Acland had established a network of some two hundred local groups. They were joined by the celebrity progressives swept up by J. B. Priestley and Kingsley Martin in their 1941 Committee, and together they formed the Common Wealth Party.[25] It was more than simple Christian socialism: it was not quite Fabian, not yet green. But it drew on much the same constituency, suburban, idealistic, and professional middle class, teachers, doctors, clergy, local government staff, vaguely left, vaguely Christian, those who were uncomfortable with the trade-union class politics of Labour, and those who despised the call to greed of the Tory Party.

As the celebrity progressives progressively dropped out, Acland headhunted others to join. He particularly wanted journalists. He recruited Tom Driberg and went after Jennie who had resigned from the ILP just weeks before. She was ambivalent. Common Wealth's opposition to the electoral truce appealed to her strongly. It kept alive in the constituencies that right to dissent which Nye was defending in the Commons. As she wrote to her American publisher:

> You know the official Labour case dont you? They repeat pedantically that in May 1940 they entered into an honourable agreement with the leaders of the Liberal and Tory Party to the effect that no controversial legislation should be introduced in wartime. This standstill agreement means that since we began the war with a two thirds Tory majority we must end it with that majority still in control . . . The war is to be fought and the peace settlement arranged under the leadership of the same parliamentary gang that cheered Munich, failed either to keep us out of war or prepare efficiently for war; the gang that is bent on holding India and generally speaking restoring the pre-war status quo here and everywhere else it can make its influence felt. You see therefore why I had to fight Central Bristol and why more and more of us over here will refuse to lie down and be buried alive.

Nor did she have any problem with Common Wealth's programme—Beveridge, land reform, nationalization of major industries, comprehensive education, a redoubled housing programme, independence for India and the colonies, equal opportunities for women—policies, as she noted in a letter to Trevelyan, that were to the left of the Labour Party. She could sign up to almost all of that: 'Commonwealth [*sic*] is filling a vacuum caused by the failure of Labour to challenge. It is doing what the ILP would have been doing if I had had my way, that is supporting the military front but furiously attacking the Government's economic and social policies.'[26] However, with memories of Mosley in mind, she also rather sympathized with the graceless response of the NEC when Common Wealth later sought to affiliate to the Labour Party: Common Wealth, said the NEC in 1944, had been set up 'by a rich man who decided he would found a Party in order to become a leader'. Its middle-class image, its Christian ethic, and Acland's dominance were all uncomfortable for a class-conscious recently revolutionary socialist. Jennie much preferred that it support her rather than she support it. So she replied to Acland that she was too busy to join Common Wealth 'for the time being', but would be glad to help out on occasion 'in small ways'.[27] She never did formally join.

Common Wealth soon decided to contest all Tory by-elections. One of the earliest to occur was in Bristol Central, a seat that neighboured that of Sir Stafford Cripps (widely regarded, and not just by himself, as the next leader of the Labour Party). Its dashing Tory MP, Lord Apsley, polo player, pilot, and holder of a Military Cross (MC), had hitherto led a charmed life. His plane, and he, had been pulled out of a Polish swamp, lost in a desert, put down on a busy German autobahn, and ditched in the sea off the Isle of Wight. But in December 1942 he was killed in Malta. Common Wealth had one of its strongest branches in Bristol, and Acland wanted it to select its candidate democratically. He was not quick enough. Without setting foot in the constituency, Jennie announced that she was standing for it. Acland was not best pleased.[28]

Acland was being too hard on her. Jennie was not carpet-bagging. Although she was not local to Bristol, she was responding to local pressure. The Bristol Labour Party was anxious to contest the vacancy, but under the terms of the electoral truce could not run its official prospective candidate.[29] So it looked for an unofficial one. Jennie, with her national reputation, a former MP, friend of Cripps, supported by Acland, and married to Nye, was perfectly placed.

She was first approached by Bristol members of Common Wealth (they had obviously not told Acland); she was minded to refuse. Then several local Labour councillors, headed by the south-west regional organizer, added their support, and Jennie agreed.[30] As her candidature was illicit—she ran under the label Independent Labour—those Labour Party members who supported her were expelled. She cheerfully split two constituencies, her own of Bristol Central and the neighbouring Bristol East of Stafford Cripps, as she built up her canvassing teams.

Bristol Central was the business heart of the city and had been badly damaged by the blitz. It was not an easy seat. On paper, it looked more winnable than it was. Jennie was chasing a Tory majority over Labour in 1935 of some 1,500 votes. However, military service, industrial service, the city's own slum clearance programme, and the blitz meant that thousands of traditional Labour supporters could not be traced. Jennie told reporters that campaigning was 'like a game of hide and seek . . . Find the electors.' Yet 4–5,000 Tory voters, who lived in the suburbs but owned commercial property in the centre, had a second 'property' vote which remained unaffected by evacuation or the blitz.[31] The eventual poll was low—some 33 per cent of those on the register—though higher than at Portsmouth North two days before.

The opposition vote was further damaged because John McNair of the ILP decided to challenge Jennie, the comrade who had deserted the ILP. He and his Party could not win the seat themselves; but they were determined to stop Jennie winning it instead. The ILP ran a dirty campaign, mounting personal as well as political attacks on Jennie, while ignoring the Tory candidate altogether. As Jennie sourly noted in a letter to her American publisher: 'There is more wrath against one of the Faithful who deviates one iota on dogma than there is against the entire Infidel world.'[32] McNair had made enough money as a merchant in Paris before the First World War to devote his life to the ILP. He stood on an anti-war platform. His personal courage could not be criticized—he had been one of the first to go to Spain, where he had organized medical relief during the Civil War. A couple of servicemen, who had fought with McNair in Spain, hitched several hundred miles to help his campaign and give him publicity. Maxton joined him on the platform, to Jennie's chagrin.

The Tories had skilfully selected Lord Apsley's widow as their candidate, 'to get the sympathy vote'.[33] Lady Apsley herself had a full public life—national chairman [*sic*] of the women's section of the British Legion, active in the Auxiliary Territorial Service (ATS) and The Women's Voluntary Service (WVS), a rural councillor, and caretaker of the constituency while her husband was on active service—all the while confined to a wheelchair, the result of a hunting accident twelve years before.[34] Well known in the constituency, a war widow, disabled, and brave, she was a difficult candidate for Jennie to attack—so she didn't. Lady Apsley spent most of her election campaign calling for national unity, and waving letters of support from Churchill, Attlee, and even Harry Pollitt.

Jennie's theme was chosen for her. The Beveridge Report, which demanded that the country slay the five giants that stalked and terrified the land—the giants of Idleness, Squalor, Ignorance, Want, and Disease—had been published just a few weeks before. The Beveridge principle of contributory social insurance was by no means full-blooded socialism, but it chimed extraordinarily well with Labour's own policies for social insurance being drafted within Transport House.[35] The NEC, the TUC, and Nye himself, writing in *Tribune*, welcomed it warmly. Jennie wisely decided that this was no time for sectarian quibbles. Buoyed by the victory at Alamein, the British public were looking beyond the war to the peace. Both Beveridge and the Labour Party were demanding that planning for reform and reconstruction should start now, as part of the war effort itself. The war would be won because men and women who were inspired by a vision of a better world would struggle on and fight for victory. As Beveridge wrote, if the country 'can plan for a better peace even while waging total war, [it] will win together two victories which in truth are indivisible'.[36]

His Report generated an extraordinary response. People queued to buy their copies from HMSO, and it rapidly sold out. Coverage of the Report dominated Bristol's newspapers. Within a fortnight of its publication, 95 per cent of those polled had heard of it, and almost all of them believed that the government should implement it.[37] The government wanted to do no such thing. Beveridge put clear blue water between Jennie and Lady Apsley. Inevitably, Jennie demanded that they must not only win the war, but build on Beveridge to win the peace. In a deft reference to the circumstances of the by-election, she was, she said at her opening meeting, fighting the seat to:

> tell the man in Africa, on the seas and in the air that their widows and children and disabled were not going to be Britain's new poor. Wars were fought not only by guns, tanks and planes, but by the spirit of men and women. The Beveridge report was of supreme value . . . It provided a raft under society's weakest and most defenceless.

A vote for Lee is a vote for Beveridge, said Jennie's placards and election bills.[38]

The ILP, rather less gallantly, also suggested that a vote for Jennie was a vote for Beaverbrook.[39] Without party backing, where was Jennie's money coming from? (This was not the first and not the last time such a question was asked.) Rumours swept the constituency that Beaverbrook was funding her campaign, and when that was denied (Jennie's election agent threatened to issue a writ for slander against the ILP), then Sir Richard Acland was alleged to be bankrolling her. In fact, Common Wealth contributed little by way of cash. It was Sir Charles Trevelyan who, as always, helped her out. Jennie's Labour agent circulated the subscription list at public meetings (£100 from Trevelyan, £100 from women's organizations, £148 from individual supporters, £283 collected at meetings—and £25 from Common Wealth), as evidence that she was truly independent. The ILP tried again. Chuter Ede, later Labour's Home Secretary, noted in his diary:

> McGovern spent a scurrilous hour last Sunday on the ILP platform in personal denunciation of the Bevans' way of life—their Hyde Park mansion and its luxurious furniture etc.* He enquired why Mrs Bevan, a childless married woman aged 35 could remain outside the war effort while she drove around in a motor car urging other similarly situated women to join the services or go into factories . . . this attack had done great harm to her chances.[40]

Most wartime by-elections were low key. Jennie's was conducted in a blaze of publicity, intense canvassing, and overflowing public meetings (even if most of the audience came from outside the constituency, she noted ruefully). Despite the vindictive campaign run by the ILP, Jennie loved every minute of it. Like Tom Driberg, she confessed it was the most enjoyable campaign of her political life. Though Nye and Cripps could not come on to her platform, she had a starry list of visiting speakers, including Hannan Swaffer, Richard Acland, Clement Davies of the Liberals, the young Michael Foot, Tom Driberg, and Victor Gollancz.

The flamboyant Revd Mervyn Stockwood, later Bishop of Southwark, chaired her election committee wrapped in his great black cloak (Stockwood was brought into the Labour Party by Cripps, who was a member of his parish church. He claimed authorship of Stafford's election slogan—'Let Cripps carry your X'. He went on to become a Bristol city councillor). Stockwood thought Jennie's by-election was a 'wonderful campaign' too.[41] He was at the time local secretary of Common Wealth, which was run from rooms below his lodgings. At Jennie's meetings, as the evening wore on, 'Mervyn's speeches became shorter and shorter. A vote for Jennie Lee was a vote on the side of righteousness. A vote against her was a vote for the devil . . . Under my breath, I was thinking, "Please Mervyn, put in a few conditional clauses."'[42]

The heavy bombing of Bristol had ended by Easter 1941. Though there

* Lady Apsley, sanctified by her widowhood, joined in. 'I was warned that Lady Apsley was a one. Indeed she is,' wrote Jennie to a friend. 'Her campaign already is underground scandal. Jennie Lee is ashamed of her husband. Won't use his name. Despises the sanctity of marriage—won't wear a wedding ring (I am wearing one as a matter of fact). And lots more . . .' J. L. to Gwen, 4 Jan. 1943 (Cripps Papers 548, Nuffield College).

were half a dozen air-raid warnings while the campaign was on, no bombs fell.[43] The by-election brought carnival to the city: Jennie held daily and nightly meetings in cinemas, schools, and the sole surviving hall—she had no loudspeaker, but she had a barrel-organ that was trundled from street to street to bring people to the door; expensive advertising was bought from the press; and teams of workers drawn from the local Labour Party, some Liberals, church workers, and from Common Wealth, flooded the streets. Ten Tory MPs meanwhile spoke for Lady Apsley.

Jennie was expected to win. Against all the predictions she turned in one of the worst by-election results of the war, although she was one of the best-known and formidable figures to stand. Swings of 5–15 per cent against the government were being recorded by unknown 'private' candidates in other by-elections, and Independent Labour and Common Wealth candidates even won some seats—Eddisbury in April 1943, Skipton in January 1944, West Derbyshire in February 1944.[44] Yet in Bristol Central there was a swing *to* the Government of 4.5 per cent. In 1935 Lord Apsley had 15,774 votes to Labour's 14,258; his widow polled 5,867 to Jennie's 4,308. McNair, with 830 votes, lost his deposit. With only a third of those on the register voting, none the less Lady Apsley had a larger absolute majority than her husband in 1935.

This did not stop Jennie blaming the ILP for handing the seat back to the government, less because of the votes they took than because their dirty campaign cost her support. She explained to Trevelyan that well over a third of the electorate, disproportionately working-class people, had disappeared from the constituency. Over and beyond the loss of men and women to the services (which was common to all by-elections) Bristol had taken heavy bombing early in the war. The result surprised the press. They had expected the government to lose the seat. It was not some long-term structural change. In 1945 Bristol Central recorded as strong a swing to Labour (16.5 per cent) on its 1935 base-line as elsewhere in the country.[45]

The moral for Jennie and Nye was that Labour should abandon the electoral truce. In 1942 Conference had come close to it. In 1943 victories were won by the inch—Rommel was expelled from Africa, German troops surrendered at Stalingrad in February, the allies invaded Sicily in July, and in November Kiev was recaptured. The NEC feared that each victory strengthened Churchill's hold on the country, and that Labour had more to lose than to gain by breaking the truce. When the government was doing badly, it was unpatriotic to leave the truce; when it was doing well, it was self-defeating. Conference supported the NEC. The truce held.

Meanwhile the tide turned decisively in favour of the Allies. Official

Labour was convinced that Churchill would storm to victory at the first peacetime general election. Jennie and many on the Left feared that the Labour leadership, in order to protect the seats Labour now held, wanted to enter the election still part of the coalition, seeking the coalition 'coupon' (or ticket) to avoid being wiped out. Debates over reconstruction were showing just how far apart were Labour and Tory views on the post-war peace; the party truce was beginning to unravel; Labour was unambiguously committed to implementing the Beveridge Report. In September 1944 the NEC decided that Labour would fight the next election not as part of a coalition but on an independent ticket, and Jennie sought re-entry to the Labour Party.

Jennie and the National Agent together summarized her position:

(a) Agreed that the conditions surrounding the departure of the Independent Labour Party from the Labour Party were dead, and were no longer a guide to her political views.
(b) She indicated that her severance from the ILP arose out of the war issue. In her view the military defeat of Hitler is vital.
(c) She agreed that she had written articles in the American press, chiefly the 'New Republic', but that whilst there may have been criticism of Labour therein, there was no wickedness in it.
(d) She indicated that Labour's declaration to fight the next election as an independent Party had been the chief impulse in the steps she had taken to seek membership. She felt she understood the Party case for the General Election, and so far as she knew it she certainly approved of it. Her view was that in the Election, the rival policies of the Conservative and Labour Parties should be sharply defined and kept free from 'Splinter' issues.
(e) She was unconnected with any other Political Organization. Her loyalty to the Labour Party would be full and generous. She had no personal aims to achieve. Her activities would be devoted to supporting the broad Policy of the Party.

Having denied wickedness and renounced splinter parties and all their works, Jennie's case was brought to the NEC, and they, in the words of the National Agent, 'decided to offer no objection' to her membership.[46] She was free at last to seek a seat as an official Labour candidate. Five months later she was adopted for Cannock.

*

The terms of Jennie's recantation were less strict than Nye's. He, with Cripps, had been expelled from the Party in spring 1939 for supporting a united and then a popular front against fascism. As Nye had repeatedly told Jennie over the years, to be outside the Labour Party was to be impotent. This was not a condition that recommended itself to Nye. He was anxious to come back as soon as decency permitted. The South Wales Miners' Federation intervened on his behalf, but the NEC was underwhelmed. They insisted that he agree 'to refrain from conducting or taking part in campaigns in opposition to the declared policy of the Party'. Nye was permitted to add an addendum: 'This declaration does not interfere with my legitimate rights within the Party Constitution.' Honour was presumably satisfied on both sides, and Nye was back in the fold.[47]

Nye's war was very different from Jennie's and much harder. Neither he nor Jennie thought he should join up. His health, after two operations just before the war, was still not good. More to the point, Jennie had nothing but scorn for those MPs who combined parliamentary and military life, who would 'pop in and spend an evening with the boys in the mess' one day, and 'pop in and spend an evening with the boys at Westminster' the next. 'Armies cannot be maintained by part-time soldiers, nor Parliament by part-time MPs. To attempt to fill both positions is to make a travesty of both.' Either Parliament mattered, or it did not. And if it did not, it should be abolished—which, she suspected, was precisely what the Tories would really like. 'We have kept Parliament going in a kind of way. The men who have sustained its dignity and maintained its usefulness are those who have regarded their duties there as their highest war-time service.'[48] And that included Nye.

He got no thanks for it. Jennie, outside Parliament, was perceived to be contributing to the war effort. Nye, inside Parliament, was regarded as subverting it. Jennie wrote: 'I had an easy war. I went from one interesting job to another. It was Nye who had to stand out in the cold, abused, lied about, spied upon, as if he were an enemy agent.'[49] Nye had called for Chamberlain's resignation and had welcomed the arrival of Churchill as Prime Minister; but this was soon qualified when a few months later Churchill became leader of the Tory Party as well. Nye was highly critical—and unreasonable. In a constitution which was not presidential, there was no place for a president. Churchill had to be both leader of the country and leader of his Party. There would otherwise have been a potential power conflict between a presidential prime minister and the majority party leader. Who would give instructions to whom? Nye accepted, at least until 1942, that Churchill was irreplaceable. Yet Nye was right to be wary. With his huge majority, Churchill did not need Opposition support, as he sometimes told them. Gathering powers and ministries to himself, he might expect Parliament to rubber-stamp him, and in the name of patriotism, Parliament might acquiesce.

Churchill was the great war leader. Nye recognized this. When Churchill addressed a closed session of Parliament on the sinking of the French fleet, 'history itself seemed to come into that Chamber and address us'. But, wrote Nye:

[Churchill] saw far too much of the glory and not enough of the suffering [of war]. He saw suffering but would only describe it in poetic terms. It was the sword wound of poetry, not the sickening and degrading agony of men and women crushed in the mud by caterpillar tracks or buried alive under rubble from a bomb or slowly starving in a concentration camp. Winston was compassionate and he understood pain and suffering, but he let his mind dwell on it only if it was epic.[50]

Churchill was also the leader of the Tories, a Party which fought the war to save the world of the 1930s. Nye never allowed himself to forget that Churchill's actions were to be read through the prism of party—not just his domestic policy but his military strategy as well. Why else was Churchill so dismissive of the call to a Second Front to aid Russia if it was not about instinctive Tory hostility to the USSR? Why else did he seek to restore discredited monarchies in countries freed by the allies and the local republican movements—in Italy, Yugoslavia, and above all, in Greece? When Nye attacked Churchill he was attacking 'the Tory caucus' that draped itself 'in the national flag'.[51]

Churchill was frank. He was not only fighting for the survival of Britain, but for the survival of traditional conservative values. Nye's greatest anger was directed at those like Herbert Morrison, the Labour Home Secretary, who colluded with Churchill's Tory prejudices—on Churchill's instructions Morrison suppressed the *Daily Worker* and threatened the *Daily Mirror* where Jennie worked. Likewise, Nye found it hard to forgive Ernie Bevin for his provocative handling of the miners during the industrial strife of 1943–4, and his refusal to commit either the coalition or the Labour Party to nationalization of the mines.[52] Whenever Labour's leaders muffled proper political criticism in a spirit of misplaced patriotism, others must do their job for them. As Nye insisted, in a one-man government, the one man must be held responsible: 'Better that Ministers should be embarrassed than that Parliament should die.'[53]

Nye was loathed. He often went too far, as even Jennie confessed. Tories in the House saw him as a man of hatreds, venom, and rancour. Down in Ebbw Vale, where the Bevans were royalty, the local cinema-owner would not hire out his cinema to Nye for meetings. Nye was also suspect. He and Jennie learnt that one of their guests at Lane End Cottage was a member of MI5. Nye followed him into a cloakroom, backed him into a corner, threatened to throttle him, got him to confess, told him to make sure that his reports to his masters were more accurate than those of the tabloids, and was thereafter left alone—or trailed more discreetly. Hated and suspect though he was, as the war proceeded, he was also grudgingly respected. He entered the war dismissed as a demagogic left-wing backbencher, a cur snapping at Churchill's heels who should be kicked into docility. Stafford Cripps, with his towering integrity and austere independence, was Labour's leader in exile, not Nye. Yet Nye ended the war as one of the few men who had the measure of Churchill and the mastery of Parliament. The *Daily Mail* cartoon, which Jennie reproduced in *My Life with Nye*—showing two giant figures, Churchill and Bevan, muscling up to each other across the floor of the Commons, the rest of the benches filled by men of small stature—conveyed it all.

Nye was not quite alone in keeping the right of democratic opposition alive at Westminster, in insisting that there were other voices to be heard than Churchill's, that Churchill was not above criticism. He had the help of a handful of MPs, including Manny Shinwell, Dick Stokes, and Sydney Silverman. But it was Nye who carried it, he who led the Left. It was lonely, it was painful, and it took immense courage.

Jennie's support never wavered. She and Nye walked home one night from dinner late in 1942, when even Nye's own Welsh comrades regarded him as a failure, when he was being cold-shouldered by Labour MPs, and could count his Westminster friends (mainly Liberals) on one hand. Nye turned to Jennie in high spirits saying: 'I feel safe. Do you realise that? I feel safe—for the first time in my life. I can do absolutely what I choose to do. No one can hurt me now. That is what you have done for me.' She had married Nye in 1934, still on the rebound from Frank. 'It took him a long time to be sure of me, which is just as well', she wrote to Trevelyan. 'He has the certainties now when he most needs them. I would never dream of telling him in so many words that I feel proud of him, but he knows I entirely approve.'[54]

When she married him, she was by far the better known of the two. She came during the war to realize that Nye's contribution to the Labour movement was potentially far greater than anything she might contribute. He was more than her partner and comrade. As Cripps's reputation waned, Nye's grew. It was Nye she saw as leading the Party in the country, only Nye who had not been contaminated by the compromises of coalition, Nye who was already delineating the contours of the peace. He took everything that was thrown at him. Jennie, no coward herself, found his strength and courage awesome. Seven or eight years into their marriage, she found herself in love with her husband. The war not only made Nye the leader of the Left; it also made their marriage.

Nye was often on his own when he criticized the conduct of the war. He had more allies when, on a series of issues from pensions to family means tests, he criticized the government's failure of domestic vision. The defining issue was the Beveridge Report of December 1942.[55] Nye was not a member of the key policy-forming bodies within the wartime Labour Party which, led by Harold Laski at Transport House, were developing the economic and social agenda for the 1945 Labour government. He struck out on his own.

As Jennie fought the last days of the Bristol by-election in February 1943, demanding that the government promise to implement every letter and every line of the Beveridge Report, Nye organized a three-day debate in the House. Chuter Ede noted cynically in his diary: 'I have little doubt that Aneurin Bevan's melodramatic interruptions . . . had their inspiration from a husbandly desire to help his wife's candidature.' The coalition's Tory speakers distanced themselves from the Report; they wanted to shelve it. The PLP was outraged. Despite Bevin's threats and Morrison's blandishments, Nye was joined by ninety-seven MPs in what amounted to a vote of censure upon the domestic policies of the coalition. All the Labour ministers were in one lobby, and all but two of the Labour back-benchers either abstained or were in the Opposition lobby. Chuter Ede went on: 'Such an example of all tail and no dog was quite futile. The value of Labour Ministers to the Govt was that they represented the rank and file of the Party. It was clear that on this issue we had not done so. The Party felt that the high votes cast for Independent candidates were really Labour votes being weaned away from the Party.'[56]

Jennie concurred. She drew in *Tribune* that most unpleasant of comparisons: just as Ramsay MacDonald had been the main bulwark of the Tories through the 1931 crisis, so a socialist Herbert Morrison 'is determined to pilot a Tory dominated House of Commons safely through its present troubles'. And, she noted perceptively:

> The most tantalising feature of the whole situation is that there is a powerful Leftward current all over Great Britain, looking for effective leadership . . . Great Britain began the war with a two-thirds Tory majority in the House of Commons. If the electoral truce is to be maintained that will still be the position at the end of the war. The question we all want answered is just when does official Labour mean to take the offensive? Or are its fighting days over? Is it working its way round in a slow ambiguous curve to the position of junior partner in a British

variant of the Corporate State? . . . there is a great People's movement trying to break through. But once again it is being successfully frustrated.[57]

Nye's rebellion was well judged and, despite the embarrassment to Labour's leaders, it served the Party well. He had shown that within the coalition, Labour did indeed stand for something different, did indeed have a distinctive reading of a new moral world. Party workers were cheered. It had its effect, too, on Labour ministers. As the tide of war decisively turned, Attlee, Bevin, and Morrison began to press for reconstruction. Decisions had to be made now about the future organization of industry and the utilities, land use and agriculture, health, education, housing, employment, and the colonies. Deferring reconstruction until the end of the war, they insisted, would cause only 'chaos and confusion'. Churchill reluctantly acquiesced and in November 1943 set up the Ministry of Reconstruction under Lord Woolton, which began to plan for the peace.[58]

Nye's most damaging rebellion, both for Labour's parliamentary leadership and for his own future relations with the trade-union leadership, came a year later. During 1943 there had been a number of unofficial strikes in key industries. Ernie Bevin retaliated in spring 1944 with his notorious Regulation 1AA—which ruled that anyone who instigated or took part in an unofficial strike faced up to five years imprisonment. The Labour Party accepted it; the TUC, which disliked unofficial strikes as much as the Government, supported it; the press hailed it; Nye held out. He turned his parliamentary scorn on a fossilized trade-union leadership, 'the big bosses at the top', who had lost touch with 'the people at the bottom', and on trade-union officials who threatened their own members with gaol. Nye was right, the regulation was unenforceable, but this was unforgivable invective from a union-sponsored MP, and the General Council indeed never did forgive him. Clearly, the government could not tolerate wildcat stoppages in essential industries during the war. Equally, it had a responsibility to address the seething discontent in the coalfields, and this it refused to do. Nye took twenty-three MPs with him into the lobby; ominously, nearly ninety Labour MPs abstained.*

This time the Shadow Cabinet proposed to withdraw the whip and ask the NEC to expel Nye from the Party. The PLP, under pressure from constituency workers, did not support the leadership. Nye, it seemed, had

* After the left's clashes over Regulation 1AA, Greece, and then Morrison's release of Mosley from gaol, Driberg said to D. N. Pritt in disgust: 'That kind of thing makes one feel we've lost the War.' Pritt replied, 'Oh I don't know—it merely makes me feel we've lost Morrison, which is much less worrying.' Driberg, *Ruling Passions*, 194.

a surer sense of the views of the rank and file than had the Shadow Cabinet, the NEC, and the General Council of the TUC combined. None the less, he was required to sign an agreement to abide by standing orders. The leadership saw it as an issue of discipline, Nye as an issue of democracy. He reflected. He would not allow himself to be expelled, and silenced: he signed. That autumn he stood for election to the Shadow Cabinet and got nowhere. A few weeks later at Conference, he stood for the NEC. Laski and Shinwell, both strong critics of the government, topped the poll; Nye, in his first NEC election, came in fifth out of seven, and two years later topped the poll himself. The hold of the Left over constituency activists was confronting the hold of the Right over the trade-union bloc vote. The battles of the 1950s were being marked out.

Germany surrendered on 7 May 1945. Attlee and Bevin, fearing Labour would be swept aside, preferred to keep the coalition in place until the end of war in the Far East, for, perhaps, another year. But they were isolated—the NEC wanted and Conference demanded that the coalition should end. Churchill called the election, asking electors to 'Help Him Finish the Job'.

*

As the general election approached, local parties began to unfreeze, and Jennie needed a seat. She would not return to Scotland and she refused the offer of an 'anywhere' London seat like Slough. She wanted a 'proper' constituency, with 'some of the character of the area I grew up in'; a safe seat, free of the vitriolic infighting between ILP, CP, and the Labour Party that had scarred her in North Lanark, and in which the CP did not run the unions and the unions did not run the constituency. Above all, a full-time agent was essential: 'In North Lanark I had the experience of running a scattered county constituency with no full time agent. It was murder . . . the more you do, the more you are expected to do.'[59]

Cannock, meanwhile, needed an MP. Apart from the years 1931–5, it had been Labour since 1918. Its sitting MP, Bill Adamson of the TGWU and a Labour Whip, was a dying man. The local agent Jack Evans, and Arthur Hampton, chairman of the Cannock Party,[60] invited Jennie to visit them. They sounded each other out. Jennie pressed Jack for assurances—yes, he was building a sound organization but much needed to be done; yes, he could dispense with trade-union sponsorship if the membership worked hard and brought in the money; yes, the nomination was genuinely open—the miners had thirty-four of a possible eighty-four votes—strong, but not decisive. As for the Communist danger, that was 'not a serious one at all. They have a very small following.'[61] None the less, as an existing Labour-held seat, Cannock could expect a strong field. Jennie, with all her reputation, would still have to fight for it. However, as those so far nominated were on the right of the Party, their vote would be split, and Jennie could then come through.

Five weeks later, on a Saturday afternoon in late April, Jennie waited her turn with five others to go before the selection meeting at the Progressive Club. She had no trade-union sponsorship, and therefore no union money, bloc vote, or organization behind her; she also had the active hostility of its retiring MP. Adamson, ever the whip, was, not surprisingly, worried by her 'very erratic and at times dubious' party record: she had for years been a member of the ILP, she had fought Bristol as an Independent 'financed by a Press Lord'.[62] However, Cannock was coal, Jennie was a coal-miner's daughter and had represented a coal-mining seat, she was coming from the acceptable left, and she was the only woman. She had good looks and good connections (Nye's name was scrupulously not mentioned, but it hung in the air). Arthur Hampton took the chair.

The atmosphere, delegates recall, was 'electric'. Frank Beswick of the Co-op and the RAF put up a strong performance, but upset some of the delegates with his flying-officer style. Hector Hughes, KC, was expected to win on the back of the miners' vote, but senior members of the Party who thought he was 'a slimy little perisher', set him up. They had learned that he was 'a Man of Munich', who had written to *The Times* in 1938 supporting Chamberlain. When pressed, Hughes erupted and threatened legal action, the miners switched their vote, and on the second ballot Jennie came home.[63]

Within days Jennie held her first public meeting. To it came a young and deeply unhappy Joan Loverock. Her father had just died in a pit accident and she saw herself locked into his grim mining world, gloomy, vengeful, and without hope. She heard that 'this Jennie Lee was going to be adopted' at the Empire Cinema. As she had never seen an MP before, she cycled off to the Empire, and sat in the back. Shortly after, 'a lady came in and sat down alongside' her, with black hair, beautiful clothes, and 'a proud arrogant look', every inch, thought Joan, the film star. Arthur Hampton called Jennie on to the stage. Joan, like many in the cinema that day, was smitten: She 'gave me everything I could want in life—and the hope to change things'. Jennie was 'devastating', 'inspirational', 'enthused us while warning—here the finger would go up—that it won't be easy'. It took time to build the new Jerusalem. Joan worked for Jennie for the rest of her life. Jennie later inscribed one of her books: 'To Joan, who sometimes doubted but never faltered.'[64]

Jennie turned to her election. Across the country, it was a quiet makeshift campaign, dominated by radio broadcasts, though with a note of repressed anger to it. Many Labour candidates were still on active service and sketchy on domestic issues. Lieutenant James Callaghan, on a ship in the Indian Ocean, did not know what Labour's manifesto said, so he made his up, before hitching back to Cardiff. Few of them had ever fought an election campaign before. Major Denis Healey had been selected while fighting in Italy, Major Woodrow Wyatt while on his way from Normandy to India. Major Donald Bruce, leaving behind his post with the Army Bureau of Current Affairs and his volumes of Lenin, returned from France to fight Portsmouth North. Flying Officer Cledwyn Hughes flew himself home to Wales. There was little central guidance, limited supplies of leaflets, no petrol and no cars, no voting records; candidates fought their own contests, improvising their organization and often their views as they went along. They learnt on the job. A sort of 'political outward bound course', notes Austin Mitchell.[65] For Jennie and Nye, who had led a political life throughout the war, it was much easier. Only Labour, they insisted, would build a people's peace.

Churchill was fighting the election on international affairs. The Japanese war had still to finish; the country needed his statesmanship on the world stage. Jennie mocked Churchill's efforts at 'draping himself in the flags of all the Allies and floating, barrage balloon style, far above our vulgar workaday preoccupations with jobs and homes and a bit of all-round security'. In any case, Churchill's standing as a statesman above party was soon blown when he accused his former partner in coalition, the calm headmasterly Attlee, of being willing to usher in the Gestapo. An accusation made only weeks after the death camps were opened, it was highly offensive. Even Tory candidates were embarrassed by it; some of the more urbane tried to suggest that Churchill meant it 'as a bit of a joke'.[66]

Labour—and Jennie—looked instead to the domestic scene. Jennie reminded Cannock that having won the war 'by a mighty collective effort', they had now to decide 'what we mean to do with the peace. All of us remember the broken promises after the last war. In honour and in common sense we are bound to ensure that this time it will be different.' Her election address, like those of most Labour candidates, promised a Britain 'free from unemployment, slums and economic insecurity', with decent health services, education, and social insurance. A Britain of expanding production, up-to-date planning, and public ownership, beginning, she told Cannock, with coal. She added a personal word:

In 1940 by an act of faith combined with hard work, hard fighting and steadfastness, Great Britain astounded the world. We can do it again. But only if we are as serious about building homes as we then were about building planes. The war has helped us to understand that the wealth of a country is its men and women . . . If we are wise enough to remember that lesson, no Vested Interests, however self-seeking and powerful, can hold us back. Good politics and good ethics go hand in hand. I believe that if we make up our minds to stand by what we know to be right, we can, in helping to secure our neighbour's future, also best secure our own. That is the essence of Labour's philosophy.

Election day was 5 July. Her opponent, a Sussex accountant, fought a clean and inconspicuous campaign. Through May and June, Jennie worked a constituency which, with 110,000 voters, was one of the largest in the country. The campaign, said one worker, was 'mustard'. The morning press conference was followed by visits to shopping streets and the Women's Co-operative Guilds; midday meetings in colliery canteens; on to school gates to chat with waiting mothers; working alongside canvassers in the early evening; then to cottage meetings with women in the villages, before the evening ended in one of the two dozen working men's clubs that were the bedrock of Cannock's Labour community. The weather was lovely, canvassers remember, and open-air meetings were held at a minute's notice, often in the Cannock bandstand, or more precariously, with Jennie standing on the roof of her car. Joan Loverock led the League of Youth on her bike to schools, halls, and clubs, warming up audiences for Jennie, who often packed in three or four meetings a night, all of them lifted by Jennie's vivid warmth, style, and oratory. A Labour Party member who was working in the next-door constituency came over to find Cannock 'a mass of weekend rallies on commons and greens, almost like a country carnival. An ever-smiling Jennie walked around the small groups that gathered, and chattered with men, women and kids. It was real barnstorming.'[67]

Women members were especially protective of 'our Jennie'. When she went to a solidly Tory village, Penkridge, she was spat on while canvassing. At the next meeting in Penkridge, the Cannock women came packed in a double-decker bus, which they hid in a back street. They waited until the Tories were in the hall, blocked the exits, and made them listen to her. Children announced Jennie's arrival by ringing bells and clashing dustbin lids; they skipped to 'Vote, vote, vote for Jennie Lee: Blow the Tories away: She's sure to win the day.' To her set-piece indoor meetings Jennie brought a galaxy of talent—Nye of course; her old friend and financial support, Sir Charles Trevelyan; and J. B. Priestley, who drew crowds that spilled out of the mining college hall into adjacent rooms. Buckets were passed around for money, and overflowed. Workers remember it as the election campaign that returned a profit, as well as a Labour government.

*

Despite all the signs—Gallup polls, by-elections, newspaper sales—that the country had moved left, the Tories expected and Labour's leadership predicted that Churchill would coast to victory on a wave of patriotism and popular gratitude. Yet the Tories could win neither by fighting on their past record nor on their future promises. Their record spanned not just the last five years but the popular memory of the last fifteen. It was a memory of searing unemployment, shaming means tests, slum housing, the drift to war—all those issues on which Jennie and Nye had campaigned in and out of Parliament. People would not fatalistically acquiesce in such conditions again. The Second World War, far more than the Great War, had been a political war. Party workers at home had agreed to accept an electoral truce, but they had never agreed to a political truce. Their support for Churchill the war leader had only ever been conditional. The war had made them more confident and less afraid of change. They now believed it could be different and that their vote would make it so.

Cannock was a sour mining constituency, inward-looking, and fearful of change. Jennie switched on the lights. The young Barbara Betts (Castle) looked out from the platform at her huge eve-of-poll rally in St George's Hall, Blackburn. Three thousand people occupied every seat, lined the walls, hung over the balconies, men and women who had endured the years of depression in textiles, who were exhausted from double shifts in the munitions factories, who had suffered in the forces, suddenly believing: 'My heavens, we can win the peace for people like us.' Roy Jenkins, then a young captain in the army, found that after his meetings, people gathered round him in the twilight, outside the pub, 'a sea of tired faces looking up in hope'.[68]

The count was still three weeks away, as the service vote had to be brought home.* Cannock men serving in Burma had their voting papers dropped by parachute. The election over, the weather turned. Jennie went round in the rain thanking her supporters and voters. She stopped outside the local newsagents to sing the 'Red Flag' with some of her workers and

* Bessie Braddock knew hers ahead of the count. She borrowed the local dog track's statistician. He told workers the information to record on polling day. After the poll closed he did his sums and told Bessie she had won by 620 votes. She celebrated, the Tories dismissed it as a stunt. He was wrong, she had won by 665. J. and E. Braddock, *The Braddocks* (1963), 88–9.

got soaked. On 26 July the count began at the mining college. On a 70 per cent poll, Jennie had 48,859 votes to her opponent's 29,225, the largest Labour vote ever in Cannock.

Nationally, Labour took 393 seats with 12 million votes, the Conservatives 213 seats and nearly 10 million votes, a swing to Labour of some 12 per cent. The Party made 209 gains, 79 of them in seats never before held by Labour. To its traditional strength in southern Scotland, South Wales, and the North, the Labour Party added gains in Birmingham and the West Midlands, the London suburbs, and East Anglia. The service votes, as they tumbled out of their special boxes, were visibly Labour, as were the young new voters. Nye held Ebbw Vale, Jennie had been elected for Cannock, and a Labour government came home.

5

1945 AND MP FOR CANNOCK

JENNIE returned somewhat diffidently to the House of Commons. The landslide victory had brought in many new faces—some like John Freeman still in his major's uniform, much to Churchill's chagrin that Labour should recruit from the officer class. There were twenty-one women among Labour's intake, the highest number ever, plus one Liberal, Megan Lloyd George, one Independent, Eleanor Rathbone, and just one Tory, Viscountess Davidson.

Not all of the women were new to Parliament. Eleanor Rathbone had held the Combined English Universities seat since 1929; Jennie had campaigned with her for family allowances. Ellen Wilkinson, a good friend in the 1929 Parliament, had been re-elected in 1935; Dr Edith Summerskill won the Fulham by-election in 1938; Jenny Adamson, whom Jennie Lee knew from Fife, had captured Dartford in 1938 (her husband Bill Adamson, on retiring from Cannock, had tried to stop Jennie inheriting the seat). Leah Manning and Lucy Noel-Buxton, like Jennie, were 'recycled' members from the 1929–31 Parliament sitting for new constituencies.[1]

Those entering the House for the first time were no strangers to Jennie either. She had known Jean Mann, who had won Glasgow Gorbals, all her life. She knew Barbara Castle well. Barbara's lover, William Mellor, had joined Frank Wise's Socialist League and had edited *Tribune*. The friendship between the two couples had its tensions; Barbara and Jennie competed, and although Barbara adored Nye, Nye had not liked the fastidious William Mellor much.[2] Mellor died suddenly in 1942 and Barbara had since married Ted Castle. Alice Bacon, like Jennie the daughter of a miner and trade-union leader, sat on the NEC. The young Peggy Herbison was also the daughter of a miner, had gone to Glasgow University, and then into teaching. A burly miner had turned up at her parents' cottage in Shotts to ask her to fight Jennie's old seat of North Lanark. Unlike the young Jennie Lee, Peggy had told him to go away and 'find a man'. A week later, three burly miners turned up, and Peggy agreed to fight the seat. She was now their 'little sister' in Parliament.[3]

For women who had known, worked, and shared platforms with each other for years, 1945 was 'a great happy re-union'.[4] In the crowded Lady Members' room overlooking the Thames, they hugged, gossiped, caught up with each other's families, and skimmed the newspapers. They looked askance at the cloakroom facilities—still no place for coats and hats—and wondered cheerfully how more than twenty of them would fit into a room with only seven desks for work, two couches for rest, one small chest for storing things, and never ever enough wastepaper baskets.*

Even the solitary Liberal and the solitary Tory were made to feel welcome. Megan Lloyd George was to the left of many of the Labour women—not that that was difficult, Jennie would have muttered, and with a mischievous sense of fun. She and Barbara shocked the more staid women Members by dancing a cancan on two of the desks.[5] Joan Davidson had been selected in 1937 to take over her husband's seat when he went to the Lords—she was in the bath, 'the phone went . . . I was dripping wet and cold and so I said yes'[6]—but her Liberal father *had* devoted his life to women's suffrage. She came home one day, telling her family with glee, 'Darlings, I've finally broken through. Bessie Braddock offered me a chocolate.'[7] Only Eleanor Rathbone wrapped herself in her separateness and held aloof from the chocolates and conviviality in the women's room off the terrace.

The new MPs found their way to the Chamber and the library, looked for lockers in which to dump their papers, and wondered how to stretch their £600 a year to cover a second home and all office costs including stamps and phone calls beyond London. MPs, Jennie, Barbara, and Jean Mann argued, were underpaid. Jennie complained in *Tribune* that the more active you were in the House, the more it cost in postage and phone bills. In the past, many northern Labour MPs could only afford to attend the Commons one or two days a week.[8] Yet any irritation she felt at the archaic conditions in the House was drowned as she contemplated the work ahead. Their very first bill was to nationalize the Bank of England.

* Ellen Wilkinson, as a Cabinet Minister, moved to her own room. She died tragically in 1947. When Jean Mann was clearing out her things on retiring from the Commons in 1959, she noticed Ellen's cosmetic box in the bottom drawer of the chest where it had remained undisturbed for 14 years. She called Jennie over. 'We both stared at it for a moment, then Jennie said, "You take it, Jean."'; Mann, *Women in Parliament*, 12.

Did she think of Frank Wise, whose campaign this had been? They could expect long hours and all-night sittings. The Tories were not reconciled to defeat; they meant to fight every line of every bill. The whips were stern: MPs would not be allowed to pair. Those two couches in the Lady Members' room would come in for heavy use, and that was before the substantial figures of Bessy Braddock and Leah Manning had collapsed on to them.

Even those, like Jennie, who had known the House before the war found it confusing. Parliament had been bombed in the raid of 10 May 1941, and the Commons Chamber had been destroyed in the fire. The House of Lords only survived because its bomb did not explode. MPs moved into the red and gold gothic of the Lords, where they remained until summer 1950 under the gaze of the bronze barons of Magna Carta everlastingly on guard high above them. The Lords was temporarily democratized. The Woolsack was removed and the Speaker's chair placed at the opposite end of the Chamber to confront the throne. The Lords in turn crowded into the Robing Room off the Royal Gallery. On the day the Commons reassembled, Churchill entered to Tory cheers and a monocled colonel struck up: 'For he's a jolly good fellow.' Will Griffiths, not to be outdone, led Labour MPs in the 'Red Flag'. To the amusement of Tories opposite, many of the new MPs did not know the words, while those on the front bench who did, hesitated to sing them.[9]

The day after the King's speech, John Freeman moved the Address. The sun shone down through the stained-glass windows on to his burnished Sam Browne belt, as standing erect and confident, he told the House: 'We have before us a battle for peace, no less arduous and no less momentous than the battle we have lived through the last six years. Today, we go into action. Today may rightly be regarded as D-Day in the battle of new Britain.'[10]

Jennie was back after nearly fifteen years. She had such high hopes. For those long years she had lived a political life outside Parliament—lecturing, writing, broadcasting, campaigning, fighting elections and a by-election, all to one purpose: to return a socialist government, and herself, to the Commons. She had now finally come inside.

*

Jennie did not expect a job in Attlee's government. She wanted power for her class, but not especially for herself; she was not greatly ambitious. Time was on her side. She was barely 40—among the women MPs, only Alice Bacon, Peggy Herbison, and Barbara Castle were younger. Most of the other women were considerably older and less likely to get office.

They had, like Barbara Ayrton Gould or Lucy Middleton, long years of service in the Labour movement, in the Women's Co-operative Guild, or, like Freda Corbet, Bessie Braddock, and Jean Mann, lengthy stints in local government.

The three Labour women MPs already in Parliament in 1945 were immediately promoted. Jenny Adamson was made parliamentary secretary in the Ministry of Pensions, and then left in 1946 to become deputy chairman of the National Assistance Board; Edith Summerskill became a junior minister in Food; Ellen Wilkinson was made Cabinet Minister for Education. Of the newcomers, Barbara Castle was immediately picked out by Stafford Cripps to serve as his PPS and help with clothes rationing. Jean Mann thought Jennie would be offered a job quite quickly (she predicted either health, housing, education, possibly pensions or national insurance), and expected her progressively to move towards the Cabinet.[11] There was room. Jennie had been an MP before, she had a national reputation, a safe seat (rare for a woman MP), good health, no children, plenty of time, and plenty of domestic support. The years ahead looked good.

Admittedly, she was carrying some baggage. For fifteen years she had put her ILP loyalties ahead of the Labour Party, so her judgement was suspect in the eyes of the brothers (and sisters); she had to rebuild trust. Jean Mann, who had known her since girlhood, noted that 'many prominent members of the Labour Party were not at all pleased when Jennie Lee was adopted for Cannock'. They felt that as an 'evangelistic rebel' she should have been given 'real evangelical work like winning over the unconverted' in a difficult seat.[12] Her natural style was combative, 'oppositionist' to use today's phrase, which irritated many of her colleagues and was useful to the Party only when the enemy was in power. With a Labour government, she would have to rein back, curb herself, practise decent reticence. Naturally, the message from the whips, wrote Jean Mann, was to keep mum and let the bills go through. Not even the smallest private member's bill would be allowed.[13] Jennie was also married to Nye, and whether that would help or hinder a political career for herself had yet to unfold. She was content to regain her feel for the House, to work her way. She did not expect a job.

Nye did, but thought it would be a minor one. He and Jennie had decided that he would refuse. Better the leader of the Party in the country, than constrained in office to no very great purpose. Instead, Attlee made the bravest and most perceptive of all his appointments when he asked Nye to take on the dual ministry of housing and of health. Nye would be his youngest Cabinet Minister. He had not the flicker of any wartime ministerial experience. Would he buckle down to it?*

Housing and health were onerous and emotionally charged portfolios. The pledge to build 'millions' more houses had featured prominently in Labour's election manifesto. Ernie Bevin rashly promised five million homes 'in quick time'. Every opinion poll showed that repairing and replacing war-damaged housing, even more than jobs, came at the top of people's concerns, and on Nye's ability to deliver would be judged the success of the Attlee government's domestic programme. As for health, while in some ways it was less urgent, it was politically even more complex. Jennie was amused and impressed when Nye discarded the habits of a lifetime—going to bed well after midnight and sleeping through to mid-morning—and disciplined himself to office hours. His senior civil servants were wary of his *enfant terrible* reputation. He teased them, stroked them, inspired them, and endlessly praised them. They recalled that he was the most effective minister for whom they ever worked.

The immediate problem was housing. The war had played havoc with the housing stock. Slums that local authorities had planned to clear at the outbreak of war were still standing and had not been replaced. At least 200,000 homes had been flattened in the blitz. Over 3.5 million houses, nearly a third of the country's stock, were damaged; many had been abandoned, some could be repaired, others would have to be demolished. Even in towns unaffected by heavy bombing, there had been little new building or repair for six years. Agricultural and mining districts in particular needed decent housing if they were to attract men back to vital industries. Officials calculated that 750,000 new homes were needed just to make good the loss. Meanwhile, marriage and birth rates were rising fast, the population had grown in numbers (by a million), and in expectations. Men coming back from the war were no longer willing to live with in-laws or in a couple of damp rooms. They demanded a decent home of their own at an affordable rent.

Where did Nye start? With the Central Housing Advisory Committee (CHAC).[14] Set up in 1935, it had seldom met during the war. Its members included MPs, aldermen, architects, private builders, and the occasional parish priest, doctor, and trade-unionist. Megan Lloyd George sat on it, as

* Said Attlee: 'When he [Nye] was at his best he was a most trenchant debater. He had that extraordinary Welsh gift of just choosing the right word. Similarly, sometimes of course, he chose just the wrong word.' 'A Portrait of Nye Bevan', BBC recording, 13 July 1961.

did Lewis Silkin before he became Minister of Town, New Town and Country Planning.[15] Nye promptly appointed Jennie a member (she attributed it to her passion for doing up houses and knocking down walls). Jennie took her share of the work and learnt a lot. She attended about half the meetings of the main committee (fewer than Megan Lloyd George, or Nye come to that) and sat on several subcommittees. It was an expert and harmonious body, which by 1951 had only ever had one minority report in its life, on rural housing; and that came from Jennie.[16]

Nye chaired his first meeting of CHAC in September 1945 and from then on its minutes dance with his urgency. How could he provide homes at speed, of quality, and with economy of labour and materials? (Being Nye, he did not demand cheapness as well.) The short answer, CHAC told him, was that he could not. Reconditioned and temporary housing was quick, cheap, but of poor standard and limited life. Permanent housing was the quality solution, but it required time to gear up a programme, time which Nye did not have. It also needed a smooth flow of resources, timber, bricks, cement, craftsmen, and Nye did not have those either. The Ministry of Supply could not supply the materials, Bevin at the Ministry of Labour would not demob the skilled men. 'Where *are* all the people I need for my programme?' asked an exasperated Nye at Cabinet. 'Looking for houses, Nye', Attlee drily replied.[17] Jennie did her best to help. At CHAC, in *Tribune*, on the platform, and in the Commons she repeatedly criticized the Minister of Supply for doggedly refusing to release key building workers from the forces.[18] Nye, none the less, got the blame from every MP and every councillor in the land as the housing crisis mounted.

Squatting spread like wildfire. By the autumn of 1946 some fifty thousand people squatted in empty properties, office blocks, and abandoned army huts—as Jennie discovered in Cannock, where a former anti-aircraft camp was taken over by squatters who paid 10s. (50p) a week rent for leaking Nissen huts without partitions, dustbins, cooking facilities, or cold water tap, and with one WC for every three families. Was Nye up to it? muttered Herbert Morrison, who as a local authority man himself should have known the problems all too well. No, he was not, insisted Douglas Jay, whose instinctive centralism made him favour a national house-building corporation to bypass local government. Nye would have none of that. He respected local government and he was determined to work through it.

For Nye knew more about housing than Attlee might have surmised. From his local authority days he learned that only council housing would break the link between poverty, poor health, and bad housing. He insisted that the new building programme would be carried by local authorities who would build for rent to the most needy, and not by private builders who would sell to the affluent. When J. Laing, the builder, suggested in 1949 that local authorities permit tenants to buy their houses, he was chided by Nye's parliamentary secretary Arthur Blenkinsop: 'Houses would pass out of the control of local authorities and could then no longer be allocated to need.' Jennie was even more tough-minded. CHAC wondered if the only way to get private landlords to improve their property was to grant-aid them. Jennie, at her first CHAC meeting, immediately registered 'a major objection of principle to the private enterprise subsidy . . . in times of acute shortage dwellings ought not to be a matter of private profit. It was preferable for the local authority to acquire the property, and do the work itself.' Nye, pragmatically, would permit such grants but accompanied by strict rent control.[19]

Nye was also obsessed with quality; he knew that overcrowding as much as jerry-building created the instant slum. His houses were to be generous in space and in amenity (with two lavatories for a family house at a time when tenants were reputed still to keep coal in the bath). 'We will not build houses today which in a few years' time will be slums', he firmly told the Party Conference in 1949.[20] District councils were to use local materials and build in the local vernacular. Extra money was found for Cotswold stone, and to conserve houses of special architectural merit. When Nye was criticized for his extravagance, Jennie defended him, saying that they must build homes of beauty as well as utility, houses rooted in a sense of place and not just anywhere prefabs.[21] She served on the CHAC subcommittee which produced for him a higher definition of 'fitness', the standard to which Victorian houses should be renovated, and below which they were to be condemned.[22] CHAC issued manuals encouraging local authorities to beautify their estates; to introduce colourwashing, window boxes, creepers, forest trees, pleasing hedges and fences, and open space.

Nye was also insistent that local authorities must not throw up tracts of repetitive three-bedroomed family houses, but create the 'living tapestry' of 'balanced communities', a favourite phrase of his. No longer would council housing be designed exclusively for 'the working classes'.[23] It should serve all incomes, meet all needs. The Housing Management Subcommittee of CHAC, on which Jennie served, urged local authorities to build sheltered housing for the elderly, furnished flatlets for students and single people, and carefully designed bungalows for disabled people. Nye spent weekends touring the country, sometimes with Jennie at his side, encouraging local authorities to build homes, and opening their show council house. She brought him to Cannock, where he said all the right things.*

Much of what Nye and CHAC urged took decades to become standard local authority practice. Some of it was incorporated in his great Housing Act of 1949, which Jennie helped steer through its passage in the Commons by joining its standing committee. With the help of CHAC, Nye stretched local authority horizons and in five years propelled housing policy forward thirty years. He later observed that as Minister of Health he never spent more than five minutes a week on housing.[24] It was not true.

When, by 1947, Nye's programme had begun to roll, with 260,000 houses under construction and a further 90,000 under contract, he was forced by the government's economic crisis to cut back to 140,000 completions for 1949. He complained loudly in public, but in private he told CHAC that the housing programme needed to be brought 'into balance', its starts and its completions equalling each other. Pushing up the programme merely overstretched the men and materials; the more houses Nye started, the longer they took to complete. All too literally the country resembled a half-finished building site, in which contracts started, stopped, and started again. The foul weather of spring 1947 drove 41,000 men out of the building industry.[25] Looking back, the forced respite was no bad thing. It allowed local authorities to catch up with building programmes that were too large for them. Nye was driving them hard and not all could cope.

In the light of all this, Nye's achievements over his five years in office were impressive and are too easily underestimated.[26] Keeping a programme going, as his successors Hugh Dalton and Harold Macmillan did, is easy. Kick-starting a new progamme is harder. From acquisition and clearance of site, to design, planning, and committee approval, from obtaining regional and central government consents, letting the contract, assembling men and materials, to building, and completion, can rarely be compressed into less than eighteen months, and then only when there are no bottlenecks. To do so against the immediate post-war background of bottlenecks galore, when skilled men and materials were in desperately short supply, and for which houses, hospitals, schools, and factories were all in competition, was quite remarkable—and all this, while at the same time creating a health service. From a cold start, Nye, by late 1950, had built

* Nye's first official driver drove very fast. As they sped to yet another local authority, the driver asked Nye: 'What was on that sign-post, Sir?' 'Paint, you bugger.' JL papers, undated typescript.

almost a million new houses, mostly for rent, and had repaired into fitness a further million.[27]

Just as important, people could afford to live in them. In Jennie's youth, the poorest families living in a couple of damp rooms would refuse a good council house, as the rents were too high. Housing professionals recommended rent rebates, but Nye thought they were 'highly controversial' and kept them off the agenda.[28] He preferred to keep rents down by trebling the central government subsidy instead. Nye also encouraged CHAC to think about a quality housing service and not just quality housing. Housing staff must be trained. His houses were to be well managed and not just well built. Nye did his best. More than that, he did well. He built some of the best local authority housing of all time—garden city layout, generously proportioned, landscaped, local materials, twelve to the acre—and in a bitter-sweet tribute to Nye's (and Jennie's) efforts, they were the first houses to be sold off to sitting tenants under the right-to-buy legislation some thirty years later.

Nye moved to the Ministry of Labour early in 1951 and was replaced by Hugh Dalton. Immediately the search for economies was on.[29] CHAC's objections to smaller rooms, narrowed hallways, bedrooms opening off living-rooms, lower ceilings, and the loss of a separate WC, were brushed aside. Costs must be cut, local authorities must be encouraged to drop standards. They should install cheaper heating systems (and pass on to tenants higher heating bills). When, after the 1951 general election, Macmillan replaced Dalton, he froze council-house building, encouraged council-house sales, gave grants to build tied cottages, lowered the fitness standard, and diverted resources to the private sector. Jennie remained doggedly and noisily on the CHAC committee until autumn 1954.

*

Housing was problem enough. Health was worse. Jennie herself took little part in the health debates. It was not her field. She knew the strain Nye was under and the need he had to unburden himself when he returned home. She was, in her words, 'kept well-informed'.[30] What should he do about GPs, hospitals, and hospital consultants?

Nye had inherited from the war the experience of a national Emergency Medical Scheme, an expectation that there would be a free and general health service and a belief that it would have the support of the BMA. With the war over, the BMA withdrew its support and, in the name of clinical freedom, began an ugly war of attrition.

The structure of GP primary health care was pre-war—pre-First World War, that is. Only those workers in occupations insured under Lloyd

George's Act of 1911 were entitled to 'free' health treatment by their GPs. By 1920, some three-quarters of the workforce (a third of the adult population) were covered. Everyone else—wives, children, the elderly, the self-employed, the unemployed, the uninsured—got only what they could pay for. Even those who were insured were not covered for hospital treatment.

The Socialist Medical Association, which had drawn up Labour's health policies, wanted a universal service of salaried GPs, grouped in local authority health centres where the emphasis could be on preventative medicine. The BMA, in between denouncing Nye as a Nazi, demanded that GPs remain exactly as they were, self-employed practioners paid on a capitation basis, able to work where they wished, single-handed if they chose, with a tranche of private patients if, as GPs, they were fashionable, and buying, owning, and selling their practices. Nye judged, probably rightly, that most of these issues did not matter greatly. What mattered was that everyone, and not just the insured, should have free access to a GP. GPs did not object to that, as long as they were paid for it, and they remained self-employed. They wanted to be able to choose their patients. Nye, equally, wanted patients to be able to choose their doctor. Either approach would be difficult in a salaried service where patients and doctors were allocated to each other. Whether a GP was paid on a flat rate or on a capitation basis; whether he worked from a partnership or from a health centre—these were distinctions often more apparent than real. Nye did insist that the right to buy and sell partnerships (and patients) should end—which he did by buying them out (up?) himself. The rest was BMA bluster, Nye told Jennie, and he called their bluff when he set the appointed day.

It took steady nerves. Every time the BMA polled its members, it produced an overwhelming majority against entering the NHS. Doctors threatened to emigrate. Cabinet colleagues fretted noisily. Due to Nye's obduracy and incompetence, they said, the NHS could not possibly start on time. Should he not delay the appointed day? Nye would not. The BMA, pressured by the consultants who had got what they wanted from Nye, finally broke—barely five weeks before the official start of the NHS. Within two months 95 per cent of the population and 90 per cent of the GPs had joined it. Nye's judgement had been vindicated.

Hospitals were equally problematic. There were some three thousand of them, mostly very small (half had fewer than fifty beds) and in financial trouble. The independent voluntary hospitals (including the London teaching hospitals) were the more prestigious, and used by consultants for private patients. Alongside them and out of the workhouse infirmary wards developed the municipal hospitals, which seldom had resident medical staff, but were serviced by local GPs. Those run by the London County Council matched the best of the voluntary sector. Others still carried their pauper taint. They were warehouses of the sick and dying. They reeked of boiled cabbage and urine, an odour of poverty familiar to every medical officer of health in the land.

Unless both types of hospital were brought together to plan provision, train staff, and upgrade care, the country would be left with a grossly uneven, inaccessible, and inadequate hospital service. But which authority was to take charge? Individual voluntary hospitals could not take over the network of local authority hospitals; yet the consultants would not allow voluntary hospitals to be taken over by the local authorities, whose Labour councillors might squeeze their private practice and interfere with clinical freedom. Unlike the GPs, most of whom could not have survived on private practice, the consultants could. Unlike the GPs, they were not bluffing.

Nye cut through the deadlock with what was a brilliant piece of lateral thinking. He would not put one hospital system under the other. He would nationalize the lot. This pleased neither side. In the event, the local authorities acquiesced loyally, and the consultants acquiesced after a hefty slug of bribery—the right to retain pay beds and fractions of private practice within the NHS.

Nye's solutions carried heavy costs. By nationalizing hospitals, while leaving GPs self-employed, and all the community health services (such as school and maternity care) with the local authority, the health service was fractured, and hospital-dominated. Treatment was emphasized at the expense of prevention. The administrative structure did not prove sufficiently robust to ward off further reorganization of health services in the early 1970s and beyond. The 'democratic deficit' which had troubled Herbert Morrison remained, and remains, unaddressed.[31]

A second problem was the lack of financial discipline. NHS expenditure soon soared beyond its original estimates, raising the issue of charges. A third problem was that Nye had built private practice into the fabric of the NHS. He firmly believed that when public health care was good enough, private practice would wither away. He also believed that when the wartime residue of sickness had been treated, the cost of health care would steady and perhaps even fall.[32] He did not fully appreciate just how poor was the health of so many people—uninsured women suffering from decades of malnutrition, prolapsed wombs, and varicose veins, the elderly in need of spectacles, dentures, and hearing aids, men with bad backs and hernias from heavy work who could not afford hospital treatment—and what demands that swamp of sickness would make on the NHS. He also assumed that the demand for health care was finite, rather than infinite. He could not have foreseen that between the rock of escalating demand and the hard place of financial stringency, there would be rationing by queue, and with it the other side of rationing, its 'black-market' equivalent: the further growth of private health care.

Ideally, as Morrison argued, local authorities would provide the full seamless health service, from hospital to health centre. They were democratic. Health care would be integrated with welfare services for the elderly at one end, and with school medical services for children at the other. Yet even had that been politically acceptable, which it was not, most local authorities were then too small and their finances not sufficiently robust to cope. To overcome what Nye called the problems of borders and the shunting of patients between authorities, the structure and finance of local government would need reform, and that was a mammoth task. In any case, it was not politically acceptable to the GPs, who refused to work in local authority health centres, nor to the consultants, who refused to work in local authority hospitals. Nye might call the bluff of the GPs, but the consultants had the alternative of private medicine. Without them, there would have been a two-tier health service. As Nye well knew, services only for the poor quickly became poor services. What mattered was a free, comprehensive, and universal health service, in which health care was a service and not a commodity.[33] The rest he would negotiate, and did so. Right up to the appointed day, the BMA continued to bluster and harangue, but, having bought off the consultants, Nye could afford to ignore it. On 5 July 1948, the NHS was launched and became the most cherished of all Labour's achievements.

The strain on Nye, and on Jennie, as he was denounced by the Socialist Medical Association for selling out, by the BMA for his despotic tendencies, by the Tories for saying that those who had espoused the family means test before the war were 'lower than vermin', and by his Cabinet colleagues for incurring the wrath of them all, was immense. He came home to Asheridge for dinner in high spirits one evening saying, 'Tomorrow thirty thousand people will hear who cannot hear today.' His technicians had tested every hearing-aid on the market; one of the more expensive ones was found to be the most efficient and Nye had it mass-produced for the NHS. Yet each day he came into his office to see all the newspapers lined up for him full of false or malicious stories. The gap between what he was doing and the venom to which he was exposed, says Jill Craigie, was almost 'surreal'.

The malevolent press that Nye received licensed hooligan behaviour towards him. He was thrown down the steps of White's Club. Jill Craigie took Nye, Jennie, and Michael Foot to a film, an Ealing comedy, *The Galloping Major.* On the way in, a man roughly jostled Nye and shouted, 'You haven't a clue.' Those within earshot thought this very funny. Nye, unperturbed, laughed his way through the film. At home, bricks were thrown through their windows, and 'Vermin villa, home of a loud-mouthed rat' was painted overnight on their front door. One weekend, when Jennie was away campaigning in Cannock and Nye busy on ministerial business, she learnt that their London home had been flyposted with graffiti and her parents were much distressed. Cannock had never seen her so angry.[34]

The hate mail poured in daily through their letter box. Each morning Jennie would throw on her dressing-gown and creep quietly downstairs to sort it through, discarding the 'packets of filth' and the especially abusive and obscene. If Nye went for an evening walk, he was hounded by the press. He took to carrying a stout stick. One night, he was accosted by a prostitute, who solicited him as the cameras flashed. The next evening, Nye plucked a sleepy Jennie from the sofa and propelled her out into the street to accompany him as he took his stroll. Jennie was trailed to the shops by reporters to find out what she bought. She had been a journalist herself, but from these years dated a hatred of the press that she never lost.

*

Nye did not expect Jennie to attend dinners and dance the ministerial wife. (Formal dinners involving Nye and Jennie were always a risk. Nye refused on principle to wear a black tie, and Jennie refused on principle to withdraw with the ladies.*) Jennie had her own political life alongside his, busy if not especially distinctive.

Yet in this 1945 government Jennie seemed unable quite to find her way. Her passions were stirred by the great political dramas in foreign and domestic policy. Outside the House, she worked an audience and thrilled a

* At various times (and to note just a few) she walked out of Hugh Massingham's dinner party ('What am I supposed to do when the "ladies" withdraw? Talk about babies or something?'); from Benn Levy's, where Nye tactfully persuaded the male guests to join the women; from Mervyn Stockwood's, where his chaplain had to chase down the drive in the rain to haul her back; and had her civil servant not negotiated with the British Ambassador when she visited as minister, there would have been an 'incident' at the Washington Embassy.

rally with barely a note in front of her. Inside the House, she sat on the bench, waiting to be called, tense and uneasy, clutching a sheaf of notes in her hand. She then delivered a speech that now seems tired, without much in the way of argument. Her speeches do not read well. An anecdotal speech rambles; a well-researched one (on the cost of living, say), is stiff with information that does not quite hit the target. Her phrases do not jump off the page—unlike those of Barbara Castle, which still seem freshly minted. Jennie's articles in *Tribune* were much more effective, hard-hitting and to the point. So much depends on delivery. Jennie was never less than competent, but she set herself higher standards than that. She was no longer outstanding, no longer a Commons star; she no longer commanded the House—and she knew it. She would sit supportively in the Chamber whenever Nye had a difficult speech to make, but she now hated it if he did the same for her.

> In the 1945 parl. I had no contribution to make that Ni could not have made and with an added dimension. That is why I spoke less well than in earlier years, why I left sentences unfinished, became mildly incoherent.
>
> It was not that Ni wanted to have this effect. But he hated to be present when I was on my feet. This was his deeply protective instinct and also a masculine attitude. I was his friend & lover. He felt public occasions a violation of that private relationship. He kept out of the Chamber if he could & we both were equally resistant of all attempts to make us do 'double turns'.[35]

Precisely because she was struggling, his protectiveness made her uneasy. Like other 'recyled' MPs (Megan Lloyd George comes later to mind) Jennie was not the same. Since 1929 she had changed. She had lost her old dash and reckless self-confidence, but had not replaced it with incisiveness or authority.

Just as she had lost her old Commons voice and failed to find another, so she had also lost her old Commons role and failed to find another. In the 1929 government, she had been the shining young priestess of the ILP, guarding the flame of pure socialism. What now? She was not on the front bench. Women's issues bored her. Constituency work she regarded as drudgery, a political version of housework, which she also ignored. Although Jennie happily, and effectively on behalf of Cannock, engaged in the parliamentary bills and debates on coal, a not undemanding territory, she took no pleasure from her constituency work and cut corners when she could. She might have been a better constituency MP if Cannock had been marginal and did not turn in majorities of 19,000. However, Cannock seemed as solidly Labour as the coal on which it was built.

*

Cannock, as Jennie had found out during her election campaign, was a very large constituency, with an electorate of nearly 110,000, twice the size of most seats. At its heart was Cannock town, with some 28,000 people, around which were scattered rural and mining villages, fringed by eight urban constituencies with growing populations. Cannock was about ten miles from Stafford in the north, from Wolverhampton in the south-west, from Walsall in the south, and Lichfield in the east. The boundary commission in 1946 reduced the constituency to acceptable size by enlarging the urban seats around it and taking away the bottom half; Cannock was what was left over in the middle. It now had an electorate of 55,600, and a much tighter shape, an approximate oval rather than an elongated crescent.[36]

This new seat comprised Cannock Urban and Rural District Councils (UDC/RDC) and Brownhills UDC. Cannock Chase had been a Royal Forest, consisting of woodland, barren heath, and farmland (the name Cannock is supposed to derive from the Celtic 'cnoc', a high place) across which from the mid-nineteenth century had sprawled a coalfield. Cannock coalfield was a triangle, its base a line from Wolverhampton to Walsall, and with Rugeley, soon to be the brightest and best of its pits, forming its northern apex. The older seams in the south of Jennie's constituency, around Brownhills, were shallow, easily worked, and by now largely exhausted, leaving behind a scarred landscape and straggling street villages, built in the shadow of the pit bank, blighted with subsidence. Most of the modern pits were around Cannock itself. They produced best quality domestic coal. To the north remained what was left of the Chase.

The constituency was still largely rural, twenty-five miles of scattered mining villages and small townships, isolated, unconnected, inward-looking, clannish, conservative, distrustful of fancy notions, suspicious of change, cut off from the urban constituencies that ringed the field by poor roads and rail links which skirted rather than crossed the Chase. Its coal was hewed manually with pick and shovel, in numerous small and scattered pits, worked on the butty and gangmaster system that was virtually obsolete elsewhere. They were ageing pits worked by ageing men. Miners, some of them well over 65 years old, still crawled underground two or three miles to work. Their output was low (well below the national average), investment had been minimal, and even after nationalization Cannock pits were among the few in the Midlands to make a loss.[37]

There was other industry, though not much—small-metal workshops, brickworks, foundries, and tool shops. In 1947, 80 per cent of the insured male population of the Brownhills exchange area was employed in coal-mining. Women had to travel to Birmingham or Wolverhampton to find jobs. Cannock coal dominated the landscape, the labour, and the politics of the constituency, as well as its chapels, its football (the Hednesford town football club were known as the pitmen), and its clubs; those who worked together, also prayed together and played together. Cannock miners did not, like the pit communities of Jennie's father or husband, prize schooling, books, or the arts, as Jennie later found to her cost. Their clubs, reported one jaundiced observer, were huts clouded with smoke, reeking of beer, noisy with strumming piano to which women sang loudly, their faces flushed beetroot red, while their men shouted over them as they argued about horses and dogs. Cannock men, traditionally 'moderates', acquiesced in their fate. They did not seek to make it or escape it. Yet they had long memories. Jennie was taken to Hednesford village, where her guide pointed to a pit in the valley below saying, 'This is where Churchill brought the troops.' He was recalling 1910.[38]

The pledge to nationalize coal had been central to Jennie's campaign. Cannock pits were among the most run down in the industry. Without nationalization, she warned, they would not survive. Nye, recalling the 1920s and 1930s, said that the pits had been poisoned by their owners: 'Coal had laid the foundation of capitalist economic structures in Britain, it will now be the rock on which a socialist system of economy is built.'[39] Nationalization promised new pits, deeper shafts, new underground roads on which men could ride rather than crawl to work, fluorescent lighting, new baths, new housing, and new machinery. Vesting day was celebrated on a bitterly cold January Sunday in 1947, with hooters, crowds, and Crimmond. Jennie began her speech by delightedly addressing her 'fellow workers and fellow coal owners', as the NCB blue-and-white flag was hoisted over the pits to calls for greater partnership and productivity.[40]

With the hopes went fears. Some alarmingly frank comments from Lord Hyndley, chairman of the NCB, a few months before had suggested that Cannock fields had less than twenty-five years of reserves left, and might close. Jennie brought Manny Shinwell, Minister for Fuel and Power, to distance himself from Hyndley's remarks, and his junior minister, Hugh Gaitskell, to deny them, alleging it was all scaremongering by the press.[41] Trial boreholes sunk at Rugeley in summer 1950 found rich seams stretching towards Leicester, and Cannock's future seemed assured.

Instead, the problem became one of overproduction. Even though rationing was scrapped in 1958, Cannock again faced threats to run down its industry. At one local meeting Jennie was told that coal did not pay. She exploded. The price of coal was fixed by government,

Cannock was carrying heavy capital overheads to bring its obsolete pits up to date, and, come December, no pensioner would believe that there was a surplus of coal.[42] None the less, Jennie sensibly stressed the need to plan for alternative industry where pits were worked out. She was well aware that her constituency depended on a dwindling industry, and her votes on dwindling trade-union affiliations.

Coal extracted a high price from its community. As MP, Jennie took up numerous claims for miners' compensation and pensions with Whitehall, sometimes extracting additional money, working often with the NUM. She fought to have chronic bronchitis as well as pneumoconiosis recognized as a scheduled industrial disease with entitlement to compensation.[43] Jennie had cordial relations with the NUM, whose welfare services to its members removed much of the case-load that might otherwise have fallen on her. They both preferred it that way.

The problems of subsidence, which fractured houses, broke gas and water pipes, cracked roads, and flooded cottages with foul water, were more intractable. She visited Clayhanger in Norton Canes, where she had to walk on duckboards to reach the doors of houses, all of them flooded, some of them infested. She met one young soldier, home from Germany, who had to chase rats out of his home and bail out a foot of water. Another, with his four children, could use only the upper floor of his cottage. Next door lived two old ladies in similar conditions. The pits had taken the ground from under them, yet they were paying 10*s.* (50p) a week in rent. Jennie was appalled: 'I have seen people living in derelict houses before, but I have never seen human beings living under such conditions in all my life.' She begged them to be patient just a little longer while the NCB and the local authority cleared slums and built new homes. Some villages had no land at all free from subsidence on which it was safe to build.[44]

She reminded the Commons endlessly of the cost of coal to Cannock. Speaking on the money clauses of the Coal Industry Nationalization Bill, she explained her dilemma. If she voted the £150 million for investment, some of that would be spent on machinery used underground which undermined (literally so) the homes of the very men working it. 'It is a tragic position for a man working underground to find that he is destroying his own home.'[45] Nye's Housing Bill that same session not only increased subsidy to local authorities for council housing, but offered additional grants for works to prevent subsidence. A couple of years later Jennie extracted additional aid for local authorities to repair damaged roads, sewers, and public buildings. A year on, she happily announced a new compensation scheme for damage to houses, backdated to January 1947. Philip Noel-Baker, now Minister of Fuel and Power, speaking at the Cannock Gala in July 1951, told the crowds: 'You owe it above everybody else to Jennie Lee.'[46] The sequence of Coal Mines Subsidence Acts awarding compensation for the first time was attributed largely to Jennie's tenacity and hard work. Few MPs delivered as much for their constituency.

Other issues, including housing allocations, places in hospital, the siting of dustbins, the pounding of lorries, the planning problems of small businesses, and the pay of teachers, took her time as they did all MPs. The bitter winter of 1947, when food and fuel rationing were still in place, caught many families very badly. One couple, staunch Conservatives, he unable to work because of the arctic conditions and she six months pregnant, were living in a bitterly cold concrete block house; they ran out of coal. They turned everywhere for help, until finally they wrote to Jennie; within days she had got them extra coal and they believed saved the life of mother and baby.[47] Twenty years later, when Jennie was fighting to hold Cannock amid accusations that she neglected the constituency, they wrote to the local paper, still grateful, still in her debt.

Most of Jennie's constituency work was done by letter, in which she returned the replies she received from Whitehall without much comment, and the replies she received from the local authority with the standard line that as an MP she had not the authority to interfere in local matters. It was all perfectly courteous, careful in phrase, but somewhat perfunctory. Miners' pensions and compensation apart, Jennie rarely challenged any official reply. As with most MPs, it was post-box stuff. Her correspondence was light, and much of it handled by her agent, Jack Evans, and, when he became a welfare officer in the new NCB, by Alf Allan, ponderous, plump, slow, somewhat bumbling, but deeply loyal. He was a former railway signalman. When you shared a car with Alf, one party worker said, you felt you were physically pushing it. Another compared him and Jennie as lead to mercury, a third, no less fancifully, as elephant to gazelle. He was not much good at organizing meetings, getting out to wards, or balancing the books, but he did follow up correspondence; and he did look out for Jennie.[48]

Jennie visited the constituency every four or six weeks, mainly to open things or speak at things. She then held a surgery, but was impatient with its 'trivia'; only grudgingly did she call on people in their own home. People who came with problems found her competent, but brisk—'I'll take it up and let you know'—and would leave never quite sure whether she would help them or not. She was felt to be a bit short on tea and sympathy. Yet young couples seeking housing found her kind, and she always rose to an emergency; many a baby girl in Cannock was named after Jennie.

After a surgery she held a press conference, talking about parliamentary rather than Cannock matters, and then she changed gear. One young reporter rashly asked her about the cost of living. Jennie looked at him, and her chin went up, as she said: 'Young man, socialism isn't about the price of bread, it's about seeing that everyone has a slice.' It was accepted that she had a reputation for arrogance and a bit of a temper, but this was held to be evidence of the strength and force of her convictions.

Even by the standards of 1945, then, Jennie was not an assiduous constituency MP. Yet expectations were low. Nye, who never bothered with surgeries, told those in his constituency who wanted to see more of him: 'You must pay the price of your success.' As a Cannock woman worker said: 'We put them there, accepted them, trusted them, and let them get on with it.' What mattered to them was Jennie's integrity, which was beyond doubt. And Jennie was a star, who inspired adoration and awe in many of her workers; they would not have dreamt of criticizing her. They were 'besotted', 'mesmerized' by her looks (the men), and her beautiful clothes (the women), and all of them by the lilt of that voice which could pronounce Russia with three syllables, her audience hanging on to every one of them.

Local party members were suitably grateful when Jennie opened a Christmas fayre, or occasionally graced a General Management Committee. In January 1949, Cannock's *Labour Gazette* reported that she had attended the party AGM. Miss Jennie Lee 'was given a very cordial reception. Her charming personality always adds to any meeting, and the fact that she had travelled especially from London in order to be present, demonstrates her keen enthusiasm.'[49] The opening years were happy ones. In February 1949 there was a constituency party to welcome Alf Allan; the evening's entertainment was a contest between men and women to identify, blindfold, butter from margarine. The women won, thanks mainly to Jennie, the only one with a perfect score. It was a love affair. Only later, when party workers contrasted the way that the local Patrick Cormack, Tory MP from 1970, and then Gwilym Roberts, Labour MP from 1974, worked the constituency, did they realize that Jennie had been an MP of another era. In hindsight, they felt they had been short-changed.

Jennie was casual about the constituency and surprisingly inept at publicity; Alf, meanwhile, was hopeless. They did not make the most of what Jennie did do, and failed to invent appropriate press releases for what she did not. For someone so frequently photographed as Jennie, surprisingly few photos of her appeared in the local newspapers. Even Jennie was worried about it in 1961, and she asked Alf Allan to place more stories in the newspapers. 'As you know,' she wrote, 'in some ways I am wholly unsuited to public life. I like to get on with the job I am doing and I have a strong temperamental dislike to personal publicity. I know that it is silly but there it is.' She sent him some new photos to use.[50]

No one now can recall constituency issues other than housing (and mining) which Jennie took up and with which she was identified, and some that she missed, such as the Beeching cuts to the tenuous rail links that Cannock retained. However, there was little unemployment in the constituency; indeed, the mines were sometimes short of labour, and there was always work in the adjacent conurbation. There was, therefore, little need to attract new industries. If Jennie did not take up major local issues, that was because there were very few to address, coal-mining matters apart. The NCB and the local council worked together on housing. The local council was not short of money, in part because the outstanding Arthur Hampton bought every empty shop, built every council house, and acquired every piece of land, that would build Cannock's rateable and revenue base. Cannock was flourishing and Jennie was free to concentrate on parliamentary matters.

Usefully, Staffordshire County Council went Labour in 1946; Cannock District Council followed suit in 1947. Jennie worked in both elections, promoting their manifestos (more and better housing, planning, education, and welfare services).[51] It was housing that mattered. In September 1950, Jennie proudly brought Nye, Minister for Health and Housing, to open the one-thousandth council house to be built by Cannock after the war. It was on the Bevan–Lee estate. Normally on council matters Jennie had little desire to intervene, councillors had no desire that she should, and so a decent respect and decided reticence prevailed. Councillors claimed and obtained the credit for council work; just as the NUM claimed and obtained credit for tussles with the ministry on behalf of its members. Jennie did not need to carry a heavy constituency case-load. When, in the mid 1960s, a heavy (and well-publicized) case-load became the mark of a hard-working constituency MP, she was vulnerable, and her party workers knew it.

Jennie was well served in Cannock, not just by the loyal Alf—'every MP knows just how much it means to have a staunch man on the spot guarding your rear'[52]—but also by Millie Rowley, who mothered her.

When Jennie was selected for Cannock, she would not buy a place of her own, as she could not look after herself. She didn't care for hotels. So she stayed with Millie, who was a district nurse and Labour councillor. Millie, more shrewd than Alf, became Jennie's eyes and ears in the constituency. Millie loved Jennie. She brought her breakfast and newspapers in bed. As Jennie dressed, she dropped her clothes on the floor; Millie stalked her, picking them up, and trying to make sense of the rumple of garments spilling out of Jennie's suitcase. Jennie never managed to bring her ration book with her; nor did she go shopping. Millie's precious egg ration would sometimes go back with Jennie to London, to 'build her up', until she found Jennie stuffing the eggs into her suitcase, where on one occasion they broke all over her clothes. Jennie lived on tea, toast, and boiled eggs; otherwise she would 'pick at this and that in the pantry'; toast (over the open fire) was one of the few things Jennie could safely manage on her own.

Millie never took any money. Jennie bought her coal at Christmas; and from her royalties on *My Life with Nye* a colour TV. Millie became Jennie's Cannock Ma, scolding her, cosseting her, fixing her hair, tidying her clothes, forbidding her to smoke. Few Cannock people ever entered Jennie's London world. She did not encourage parties of schoolchildren to visit the House, nor party workers to call on her for tea—except for Millie. When Jennie retired from the Commons, Millie stayed the occasional weekend at Chester Row. She wrote thanking Jennie for her Christmas card in 1974, 'which will join all the others from you I keep, to read again and again . . .'[53] Jennie inspired great love.

Being a woman MP was an asset even among the miners. But as women MPs went, Jennie was more token than most. Perhaps because she was so undomesticated, she never showed much interest in 'women's issues', in child care, in family allowances, or in Cannock's exceptionally high infant mortality rate.[54] She gave women members the impression that she thought their concerns, housing apart, were parochial, narrow, and home-centred; real politics was about parliamentary matters and foreign policy. It was the wider canvass for her. The men were comrades; the women remained somewhat in awe of her, not patronized exactly, but belonging to a different gender from Jennie. Her tone to them was very 'male'. She thanked them effusively for fixing the sandwiches at socials, attending 'little meetings' (men attended the big ones), doing good work in the ward. 'All we want', she wrote, 'is more of the same good vintage. It is fun doing a job if you have a bunch of pals with you to share the burden, but it can be sheer drudgery if too much is left to too few.'[55] They made tea, while men, and Jennie, made policy. She never suggested that they do a different job, like stand for the council, let alone stand for Parliament. She was irritated when interviewers pressed her on what it was like being a woman MP. Her usual line was that it depended on the woman. 'Any public representative, man or woman, should not be in that position unless he or she is prepared to deal with every aspect of community life, whether it be mining or cooking . . .'[56] Cooking? Jennie?

The women never criticised her for not entering into their world. On the contrary, they were gratified when she nursed their babies or struck up a rapport with their children while they made her tea. She sometimes brought her young nephew Vincent up with her, and off they would go to a local fair, or, and this was an event that Jennie never missed, the Labour Gala, the highlight of Cannock's year. Jennie brought to the Gala a glittering array of talent: Nye and Manny Shinwell, Minister of Fuel and Power, were her first guests. Later, with fine catholicity, came Hugh Gaitskell, Harold Wilson, Michael Foot, Barbara Castle, Tom Driberg, as well as friends like Constance Cummings. The weather was always fine—the Tories said they could wash their blankets on Gala day. Amid crowds of up to 10,000, Jennie judged the races, the floats, the caged birds, and bonniest babies, the fancy dress, the blossom queen, and the May queen. She was 'the uncrowned Queen of it all'.[57]

Only a couple of political issues marred her relations with the constituency party. Nye's resignation over health charges in 1951 was one, the possibility of Nye's expulsion from the Labour Party in 1955 another. The three ministers (Nye, Harold Wilson, and John Freeman) who resigned in 1951, she told the local party, did so in protest against a defence programme so large that it required them 'to surrender hard won social gains'. She thought they had handled it gracefully: their resignation might have split the Party, but in fact it did not; might have produced an early general election, but it had not; or they could have stayed, and sold out, as in 1931, but they would not. When it came to expulsion, Cannock party members 'took her to the cleaners', one of them recalled, accusing Nye of destroying party unity, of no longer being worthy of support. Jennie was desperately upset and fought hard, but could not prevent them passing a motion that they 'did not object' to Nye's expulsion—one of the few constitutency parties in the country to hold such a view.

Relations were also a bit edgy when Jennie wanted to be sent as a party delegate to Conference in 1953 (essential if she were to take part in compositing resolutions or wanted to stand for the NEC), rather than go *ex officio*. She got only two votes while 'hectic efforts' were made to send 'anyone, absolutely anyone, rather than myself'. She darkly suspected organized plotting by Communists; she refused to believe it had anything to do with the fact that the previous year, when she had been a delegate, she had failed to turn up at the Cannock General Management Committee to 'report back'.[58] Arthur Hampton sorted it. For the most part, however, national party battles did not intrude on Cannock. Jennie, whose primary interest was international affairs, did not invite the local party's views on national or international matters, and they did not presume to offer them. Cannock was in love with her, and Jennie sailed effortlessly through a succession of general elections and boundary changes with no threat to her majority and no criticism of her in the constituency.

*

At the general election of 1950 Jennie had to defend five years of rationing, utility production, and housing shortage. Her opponent was Mrs Marjorie Hickling, described by one woman reporter as a 'jolly' housewife, a competent and centre-ground candidate who wryly recognized that Cannock was Labour territory. Bravely, she took the battle on to Jennie's territory, accusing the Labour government in general, and Nye in particular, of failing to build enough decent homes. Families had waited eleven years for a home; 200,000 of them were still in Nissen huts, or simply squatting. It was not good enough. Jennie replied indignantly that over a million homes had been built, and had Mrs Hickling not heard of the damage done by the blitz? They argued about the NHS and the cost of living. Jennie turned to the miners, who agreed that their wages had gone up; Mrs Hickling turned to their wives, who agreed that the money did not go so far. Mrs Hickling hoped that families would split their votes and that she would pick up those of the women.

Jennie was absent for much of the campaign, working in Labour marginals, and pressed most of her meetings into the last couple of days. Her good humour was seldom ruffled, until an American woman reporter asked whether Nye helped with her speeches. Jennie snapped back: 'I'm not the soft underbelly of the axis.'[59] On eve of poll, Mrs Hickling wore white heather, Jennie red tartan and a brooch that was a tiny replica of a miner's lamp. During the count, rumours swept the town. Groups gathered, dissolved, and regathered, waiting, and listening to the wireless, as they learnt of the danger to their Labour government. Finally, Jennie's result was announced: a majority of nearly 18,000, better proportionately even than in 1945. Nationwide, the Labour Party had an additional $1\frac{1}{4}$ million votes, but an overall majority of only 7 seats (with one in Manchester outstanding). The local party met almost immediately to discuss the prospect of another general election within the year.

1. Jennie's paternal grandparents, Mr and Mrs Michael Lee, in the 1870s. Michael Lee, a friend of Keir Hardie, founded the ILP and the miner's union in West Fife.

2. Jennie's first home, in Cowdenbeath (the house without dormer windows, second right). Four rooms 'idiotically arranged' said Jennie.

3. Jennie about a year old with her parents. Her father scribbled on the back, 'This does not flatter the wife. She is much prettier.'

4. Jennie aged about 12 years, with her younger brother, Tommy

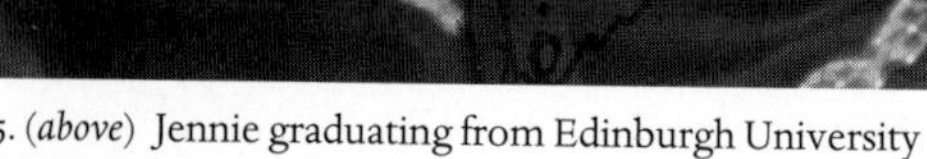

5. (*above*) Jennie graduating from Edinburgh University in 1926 as Master of Arts

6. (*top right*) 'Suse' (Mrs Saemann), Jennie's oldest and closest woman friend, *c.*1930

7. (*right*) Tommy, Jennie's brother, aged eighteen and about to emigrate to Australia

8. (*bottom*) The staff at Glencraig school (Jennie aged 22 years, back row, third from left) where she struggled as a young teacher, *c.*1927

9. (*above left*) Jennie being escorted to the House of Commons for her introduction after winning the North Lanark by-election, 1929, with James Maxton (left)

10. (*above right*) Jennie compelling her audience at Angus, 1931

11. (*left*) Campaigning for the ILP in the west of Scotland, 1930, her style 'evangelical'

12. (*main picture*) Jennie being photographed for her 1931 election material

13. (*inset*) Party workers in North Lanark displaying the resulting election poster

14. Jennie speaking at the 1931 Labour Party Conference, Scarborough

15. At an ILP summer school, Kiplin Hall, Northallerton, August 1927 with James Maxton, Jennie's ILP mentor, and T'ang Liang-Li, a Chinese journalist and Jennie's first lover

16. Jennie, a working journalist in the early 1930s

17. At the ILP summer school at Letchworth, August 1935. Back row from left: unknown, Percy Williams (Leeds), Fenner Brockway (now MP); front row from left: James Carmichael, Jennie Lee, James Maxton, John McGovern

18. Jennie on board and at work, *c.*1932

19. Jennie on board and not obviously at work, *c.*1932

20. Jennie doing her laundry while climbing in the Caucasus mountains with Frank Wise, summer 1932

21. Frank Wise, MP for Leicester (1929–1931), the love of Jennie's life, in 1924, a few years before he met Jennie. In April 1931, Beatrice Webb described him in her diary as follows. 'Unquestionably a forceful—[a] hostile critic might say—a blatant personality. Burly and formless in figure, ugly hands and feet, large head, with heavy jaw and protruding under lip dominating the face, insignificant nose and eyes, set close together, loud strident voice—he is an imposing but not prepossessing man to look at and to listen to. In-exact in his statement of fact, and slovenly in his thinking, he is not an accomplished intellectual. but he has bonhomie, great mental energy, high spirits—he enjoys life: he is decisive and lucid in speech, a good debater, and I think honest—a loyal servant and good friend.'

22. Dorothea Wise, Frank's wife

23. Jennie and Frank with friends, 1931, the only known photo of them together. Beatrice Webb's diary, June 1931, comments: 'The fascinating little Jennie Lee is the "friend" of her fellow M.P.—Wise. She is passionately attached to him and the scenes in the House of Commons when the rather unattractive wife appears and insists on taking possession of her husband and ignoring his friend, are a source of scandal in the Party.'

24. Nye aiding Jennie during the 1931 election campaign

25. Jennie with Aneurin Bevan at the 1934 Labour Party Conference in Southport, three weeks before their wedding

26. Signing the register under the eye of the registrar

FILM STARS and POLITICIANS FRATERNISE

LEFT, Benn Levy, playwright, whose film-star wife, Constance Cummings, has got in first with the ginger beer. With them are Labour M.P. Aneurin Bevan, from South Wales, and his wife, Jennie Lee, who was herself the youngest woman M.P. a few years ago.

27. Nye and Jennie picnic with good friends, the actress Constance Cummings and her husband, the playwright and Labour MP, Benn Levy, 1935

28. Jennie addressing busmen in Trafalgar Square, 1937

29. (*above*) 'Aerial barbed wire': a barrage balloon factory, *c.*1940. Jennie worked with Lord Beaverbrook, Minister for Air Production, in the early years of the war, touring barrage balloon factories for him.

30. (*right*) Jennie at work during the war

31. Jennie fought the Bristol by-election as the Independent Labour Party candidate in February 1943, demanding that the Beveridge Report be adopted by the coalition government.

(*above*) The blitzed skyline of Bristol

(*right*) Forces personnel outside Jennie's committee room

(*below*) children with Jennie's placards

32. Jennie at home in Cliveden Place after winning the Cannock seat in the 1945 general election

33. MP for Cannock: Jennie with her constituents in her campaign bus, September 1951

34. Jennie escorting the Minister for Housing around a Cannock housing site, 1950, accompanied by the local councillor, Jack Phillips

35. Jennie fighting the 1959 general election from their mobile Cannock campaign office, a 12-seater coach packed with election literature. It rained.

It came in October 1951. It was a quiet election, with half empty halls and dwindling enthusiasm. Jennie asked voters for a working majority, and promised them a fair shares society; her opponent, a teacher, called for more money for defence. The turnout was still over 80 per cent and Jennie's majority over 16,000. The Labour government, however, fell.

Thereafter, Jennie was in official opposition. She defended the seat in 1955 on new boundaries against yet another new candidate, an Orpington barrister, and won with a majority of 8,000. But by the 1959 election, even Jennie could make no dent in the 'never had it so good' mentality. Audiences even for Nye were down to thirty or forty people—they both knew that Labour was not going to take power. Barely a handful turned up for the count. Jennie had a majority of some 7,000 in Cannock; the Tories a majority of a 100 seats nationwide. Jennie's hold on Cannock was beginning to falter.

*

Constituency work within Cannock gave Jennie little satisfaction. Nor was life in the Commons as fulfilling as she had hoped. Many male back-bench MPs in Jennie's situation expected less from the Commons. They continued to work as lawyers, farmers, and businessmen. They were essentially part time. But Jennie was a full-time MP without a full time job; a politician who refused to be a constituency social worker; an orator who only felt free and uninhibited on the public platform and never in the Commons; an instinctive dissenter whose Party was in power and which therefore expected her loyalty. She was, above all, a polemicist and propagandist. The natural outlet for her talents was to seek a seat on the NEC and to work the country for the Labour movement and the Left. It was what she most wanted to do. Yet she refrained. There were only seven NEC constituency seats for which she might try (the women's section was controlled by the right-wing unions and they would never permit her on). The Bevanite Left soon held all seven. If Jennie stood and won, she would cost Nye another ally. Yes, she acknowledged, there was a price to be paid for being married to Nye.

Within the Commons, she kept fairly busy. The Tories fought their bills hard and MPs were tied to the House with late sittings night after night. Every time a controversial bill finally passed its third reading, a sigh of relief would go around the Labour benches, and 'Cwm Rhondda' would be sung in the Aye lobby. Apart from coal issues, Jennie spoke on housing (where her CHAC work gave her considerable expertise), foreign, and colonial policy. She enjoyed heckling Churchill, and the Tories enjoyed heckling her.

She made occasional forays into economic policy. She was deeply unhappy about the American loan negotiated by Keynes in the autumn of 1945. She thought its terms were impossible, and bound them to a country which might go fascist. With some twenty others, including Michael Foot, Bessie Braddock, Jim Callaghan, and Barbara Castle, she voted against the government (Barbara Castle immediately assumed, correctly, that this was 'a clear indication of how Nye voted in Cabinet').[60] Jennie's relief was palpable when she was later able to welcome the Marshall Plan. Her unease at Ernie Bevin's foreign policy deepened. Within months of the general election, she was among those on the Left denouncing it at the PLP—Greece, Palestine, Franco. Bevin made clear he would not tolerate an alternative foreign policy, nor backstabbing from so-called 'comrades'.[61] In a gesture heavy with significance, Jennie, Bessie Braddock, and Barbara Castle added their names in November 1946 to an amendment to the King's Speech, moved by Richard Crossman, demanding a foreign policy that offered a Third Way, which embodied 'socialist planning as a constructive alternative to conflict between American capitalism and Soviet communism'. It was signed by fifty-seven Labour MPs, including Nye's PPS Donald Bruce. The government put on a three-line whip. ILP MPs, sensing mischief, forced a vote. This had not been part of the signatories' intention; they wanted to change government policy, not the government. Nevertheless, 154 of Labour's 387 MPs abstained.

The protest was led by Richard Crossman, Michael Foot, Donald Bruce, and Ian Mikardo, who early in 1947 founded the Keep Left Group. The Bevanites were in the making. Ernie Bevin wanted a showdown, but given the support for the rebels reflected in the abstentions, Attlee wisely resisted. The Tories had a lovely time. The mutiny of the intellectuals, they suggested. Washing dirty ideological linen in public, they jibed. Jennie was taunted by some of them—was she speaking for Nye who was muzzled by Cabinet responsibility? Was the Minister of Health 'wobbly on this issue?' they demanded. Probably, could have been the answer. Instead, Jennie retaliated: Tories were being 'fascist' (a favourite term of abuse, this) if they believed that husband and wife could have only one mind between them and that was his; modern women had ideas of their own.[62]

As, indeed, she showed, when she spoke on the second reading of Nye's 1949 Housing Bill. She praised the minister for his 'imaginative' and 'highly civilized' proposals (which drew on CHAC reports), chided him for not giving sufficient protection to properties of special historic or architectural merit, complained that he had not done enough for people in tied cottages, and criticized him for being generous to private landlords. She teased:

> I ask the Minister to recall what he said earlier today. I took note of his words—I agree with right hon. and hon. Members opposite it is just as well not to take too much on trust. The Minister said, in a moment of eloquence, that a house was not a commodity to be bought and sold, but a social service. He added that a house was best left in the custody of a public authority.

Why then, she added ruthlessly, was he being 'less than logical' in giving grants of public money to private landlords who treated houses *exactly* like commodities? Why not give loans instead? The minister had produced a good bill, she reckoned; in Committee it must be made a better one.[63]

She kept a watching brief on colonial policy, a field which mattered to her deeply, as it did to several other women MPs, including Barbara Castle, Eirene White, and Judith Hart. She followed events in Asia and Africa, as well as other scattered bits of red, such as Cyprus and the Caribbean. Jennie's socialism was always internationalist. Precisely because the Labour movement came from an oppressed class, she expected it to have instinctive sympathy with the struggles abroad of oppressed peoples.[64] Precisely because the ILP had been a revolutionary party, she expected the Left to support revolutionary liberation movements. She became treasurer to Fenner Brockway's Movement for Colonial Freedom, a good friend of Ruth and Seretse Khama, and in due course a staunch friend of Indira Gandhi. Many years later Attlee confided to Neil Kinnock that had his 1951 government survived, he would have offered Jennie a job, though what job he did not say.[65] Had he done so, Jennie might have refused, bitterly angry as she was at the circumstances around Nye's resignation. None the less, with Jennie's fierce commitment to colonial freedom, and her evangelical style, she would have made a superb colonial office minister in an Attlee Government.

From 1947, the Labour government ran into severe difficulty. February's freezing weather and Shinwell's incompetence at the Ministry of Fuel and Power led to a crisis in coal, cuts in power, factories shut down, and two million became temporarily unemployed. Street lights were switched off, rail services closed down. Rationing was extended to bread, the staple food of working-class families. People complained more, back-benchers attacked ministers, and ministers attacked each other. The coal crisis was followed by a convertibility crisis.[66] The balance of payments situation worsened, dollar reserves haemorrhaged away. Hugh Dalton, Chancellor of the Exchequer, was worried sick, fearing a repeat of 1931, which had wrecked the Labour Party and consigned a generation of its people to the Depression.[67]

The Keep Left Group shared his fears: 'Either the Labour Government redeems the disaster of 1931 by mastering this crisis with Socialist measures and Socialist incentives, or it must sooner or later accept the necessity for deflation and for unemployment as a whip for the working class.'[68] Spending budgets, including Nye's housing programme, were slashed. There were moves to get rid of Attlee and replace him with Ernie Bevin or Stafford Cripps. Nye and Jennie were summoned to tea by the Cripps's, who were soliciting their support; but Nye made it clear they would play no part in 'palace revolutions'. Tension eased when convertibility was suspended, only for Dalton, who had gossiped about November's budget, to be replaced as Chancellor by Cripps. Cripps, on his sickbed, was forced to accept devaluation in summer 1949; then he in turn, to Jennie's and Nye's intense dismay, was replaced by Gaitskell. The Cabinet was under severe strain.

More worrying to a socialist like Jennie, the public ownership programme began to falter, as Morrison insisted that the government should now 'consolidate' its position rather than extend state intervention. Nye took it to the brink when he insisted that Labour should honour its commitment to nationalize steel. Cold weather and brinkmanship politics at home, and, equally worrying to an internationalist like Jennie, Cold War and brinkmanship threats abroad. The Marshall Plan had begun to rebuild West European economies, but at the price of isolating the USSR still further. The USSR, in turn, clamped down on Eastern Europe, quelling Czechoslovakia, and cutting off Berlin. American air bases returned to East Anglia. Ernie Bevin was helping to build NATO. Time and again Jennie had to curb herself, until the Korean War set in train a series of events that fractured the Labour Party. When Gaitskell insisted on health charges to finance an impossibly large rearmament programme, Jennie, even more than Nye, had had enough. She encouraged Nye to resign.

She had a much better time when the Tories returned to power in 1951. She piled into the attack. Her speeches on foreign and colonial policy in particular suggest some of her old fire and passion. The Cold War eased, with the stalemate in Korea and the death of Stalin in 1953. 'Butskellism' suggested that the welfare state might, after all, be safe with the Tories; unemployment remained tolerable, and Jennie's assault on the Tories subsided. By the mid-1950s Jennie was making only three or four speeches a year, one on coal, a second on health or housing, and a third, usually her best, on colonial policy in Kenya, or Cyprus. During the 1950s, defence issues as least as much as public ownership divided the Bevanite Left from the rest of the Party, and Jennie and Barbara Castle frequently defied the Party line. With many on the Left, Jennie also opposed entry into Europe in 1961.

Jennie had a wider life outside the House than many MPs, which filled out those Commons days. She attended weekly editorial *Tribune* meetings, as well as contributing pieces of her own. For the first year of the 1945 Parliament she took over George Orwell's weekly 'As I Please' column, using it to denounce demobilization arrangements, defend Nye's housing work, praise rationing, and review new plays.

In the immediate post-war years she worked with Victor Gollancz and J. B. Priestley to get food aid into central Europe. A letter smuggled back from Austrian friends, who were starving on dried peas, was quoted by her with great effect in a Commons debate on the world food shortage.* She was active in the parliamentary Anglo-German group and through them liaised with the International Rescue and Relief Committee, based in New York. More than most MPs, her internationalism was not only generous but practical as well.

Later came the Bevanite lunches at Dick Crossman's house, the *Tribune* brains trusts, galas, rallies, meetings outside London, as well as weekends at the farm to which came a flow of friends. Nye had a huge circle of friends in the arts, and Jennie acquired through them the most agreeable of educations, which she claimed later prepared her as Minister for the Arts. Every month or two there would be the visit to Cannock, every nine months or so the visit to Tredegar, as well as the foreign travel, with and without Nye, in which she delighted—to Austria, Israel, Paris, Yugoslavia, Russia, Egypt, India, and Austria.

*

It was a comfortable, varied, and not too strenuous life. There are plenty of unmarked days in Jennie's engagement diary. She was as busy as many male MPs—but less busy than most women MPs; Peggy Herbison, Eirene White, Edith Summerskill, Elaine Burton, Barbara Castle, Jean Mann, Bessie Braddock, and Alice Bacon all spoke in more debates than Jennie. They were also more conscientious about their constituency work and

* 'We now appreciate the dried peas very much, although the Russian variety gives us so much work on account on the maggots. We soak them in water over-night, and on the following day we have to cut up each single pea to get the maggots out, and that means a lot of work.' Qtd by J. Lee, *Hansard*, House of Commons 4 Apr. 1946, cols 1445–6.

more willing to cover women's issues than Jennie. Her contributions to debates on equal pay, for example, were decidedly perfunctory. Humdrum issues, such as food prices, child adoption, accidents in the home, even family allowances, were left to other women to monitor.

Was Jennie a feminist? Theorizing about patriarchy, analysing the construction of gender, challenging the separateness of public (male) and private (female) spheres, belong to the academic discourse of the 1970s. Anti-discrimination measures, access to abortion, the demand for affordable child care, employment rights for part-time (female) workers, proportionate representation on public bodies, belong to the political debate of the late 1960s and 1970s. Women MPs in the 1940s and 1950s were not going to be 'modern' feminists, members of the women's movement, before feminism's second wave. As Judith Hart was later to say, 'I am too old for Women's Lib.'[69] Those who had fought for the suffrage in the past, like Ellen Wilkinson, tended to keep quiet about it. Feminism did not win votes or friends. Only Eleanor Rathbone, who seemed to need neither, kept faith with suffragist feminism. Her torch passed to Dr Edith Summerskill, who, like Jennie, but unlike Barbara, kept her maiden name after marriage (and whose children also took her name). Edith fought and lost an ugly by-election in Bury in the 1930s on the right of women to family planning. When she was finally elected, she campaigned in the Commons to extend the right of women to matrimonial property.[70] Any male MP who talked about 'manpower' in a debate on women's war work in March 1941, felt the cutting edge of her tongue.

Though only Eleanor Rathbone and Edith Summerskill would accept the label 'feminist',* most women MPs in the 1940s and 1950s had an instinctive 'feel' for women's issues long after Edwardian feminism had become unfashionable and long before modern feminism was conceptual-

* Melanie Phillips has a very funny account of trying to interview Lady Summerskill in the late 1970s. She was invited in because Edith thought she was someone else, which she was not. 'Upon discovering this, she inquired what I had done for the feminist movement. I replied I had done nothing of any significance. She seemed much taken aback by this information. Well, what movements did I belong to, then? None at all, I replied. None at all? How old was I? And was I educated? Upon learning that I was twenty-seven and had been educated at Oxford, she drew herself up in her chair as if I had delivered some savage insult. Did I not know who she was? Did I not know that she had spent years of her life working so that girls like me could go to Oxford? . . . And what was I writing this book for anyway? Just out of interest, I replied feebly. Interest, she exclaimed! I was obviously writing it for the money. She had nothing in common with me; she would tell me nothing; and she thought I had better leave. Within ten minutes of meeting Lady Summerskill, I found myself on the other side of her front door.' Phillips, *The Divided House*, 159. Jennie refused to be interviewed.

ized. Women MPs still insisted they were members of Parliament first, with loyalties to Party and to constituency, just like men. They did not want to be ghettoized, to be confined by men to the unthreatening fields of education, social services, and consumer affairs. Herbert Morrison advised Lena Jeger to 'Stick to women's issues' when she made her maiden speech. She spoke on the Berlin conference. He chided her for not following his advice: 'Isn't peace a women's issue?' she retorted.[71] Well, not quite. Morrison was more supportive of women than most. None the less, when women spoke, men saw them as speaking for women. When men spoke, they were speaking not for men but for mankind.

Women MPs responded in their own way. Some like Barbara Castle demanded the right to range beyond the traditional housewife brief, to specialize in transport, overseas development, or in energy, just like any other MP, just like men. Yet the price of that was to accept men's definitions of what was important and what was not. Other women MPs insisted that so-called women's issues, such as health and housing, were 'human' issues and should matter equally to men and women alike. Barbara Ayrton Gould told the 1943 Conference: 'The more women they could get into parliament the sooner they could eliminate women's questions as women's questions and they would all become universal questions.' Other women MPs accepted that some issues primarily concerned women, but refused to concede that they were therefore peripheral to the 'real' matter of politics. Bessie Braddock spoke up for housewives, Jean Mann for children in care, Elaine Burton for consumers, Eirene White fought hard for widows, and Edith Summerskill for deserted wives. As women, they were motherly about other women. They waded in on their behalf. Their welfare was part of their wider constituency.[72]

Not for Jennie. She was an MP, just like any other (male) MP; she entirely shared their male views about what was politically significant and what was not. So she was neither motherly nor sisterly about women. If a policy directly attacked women's citizen rights, she would certainly take up arms. She had joined Eleanor Rathbone when the 1929 government proposed to remove unemployment benefit from married women in depressed areas. Later, she roundly attacked the Union of Post Office Workers when they voted at their 1953 conference to compel women to resign from their jobs on marriage; she pointed out that 'the shabbiest part of the whole business' was that the male unionists won the vote with the support of unmarried women delegates.[73] However, she had fought the Bristol by-election with the Beveridge Report in her hand without ever commenting on Beveridge's central assumption, that women would have their social security mediated through their husbands' national insurance, in other words that women would depend on men for their welfare benefits.

Jennie was hardly alone in this.[74] Like most women MPs of her generation, she took it for granted that women lived different lives from men. Unlike most women MPs of her generation, she did not look out for them. She occasionally mused about their situation. In the early 1950s she collected some newspaper cuttings and scribbled several pages of desultory notes for a book she thought about writing on modern women. She wrote articles about the fortitude of wives while their husbands were on strike, or the difficulty of affording a new and convenient council house on poverty wages. What mattered to Jennie about women was not their gender, but their class. Jennie, the most ardent socialist of the women MPs was also—and therefore—the least feminist of them.

It was a matter both of temperament and conviction. Temperament—in that she had little sense of sisterhood. She once said that she had never made a speech 'speaking as a woman' in her life. She did not identify with women. She had never lived a gendered life, never suffered its hardships, never had to chafe against its restrictions. While other girls of her background worked alongside their mothers to cook and clean, look after younger children, run errands for neighbours, and wait on their menfolk, Jennie had done none of that. She had been brought up as the son of the family, unencumbered by conventional notions of what it was to be womanly. She had crossed the kitchen floor and aligned herself with her father's way of life, sitting round the table to be served by Ma, collecting ILP subs, arguing with visiting lecturers late into the night. Jennie's parents took it for granted that she would be politically active.

There was nothing unusual in this. From Bessie Braddock to Barbara Castle, Shirley Williams to Margaret Thatcher and Joan Lestor, many women MPs came from political families where they learnt that politics mattered, and where they were encouraged to engage in politics for themselves.[75] Fathers (it was usually fathers) freed their daughters from any need to conform to the female stereotype. Family values gave such women the confidence to transgress domestic values, to trespass on male space (though one suspects that few of these political daughters turned out to be quite so domestically illiterate as Jennie).

Jennie had gone to university in the only way that bright working-class Scottish girls could, to train as a teacher while she built her political life. Political parties gave women the freedom to canvass and debate. Whereas the Labour Party was built on the organizational discipline of the trade-union movement, the ILP was supremely the party of campaigning, propaganda, and itinerancy. The ILP circuit gave Jennie a physical freedom unimaginable to most young women of her generation. She travelled the country, just as men did. She spoke from platforms to crowds of thousands with devastating effect, as only a few men could. Home was always provided by someone else. As a young MP, as a law student, as a journalist, as a platform speaker, and as a lecturer in America and Russia, she lived a male life, the only public life possible, and she relished it.

Her private life was at one with her public life. She was sexually independent, reluctant to settle into domesticity, ruthless in her treatment of the men who were smitten by her. She, not they, determined the terms of their affair. When after Frank's death she married Nye, both knew it would not be a conventional marriage. There were no children. Indeed, far from looking after her own children, Jennie was looked after by Ma. In that sense, there were no hard choices to be made between family and career, no shortage of money and no shortage of help. She not only lived a male life, but a comfortable male life as well.

It would have taken a huge imaginative leap for Jennie to have identified herself with the working-class women of Cannock, the endless cleaning, numerous children, and the debilitating female complaints. She could describe it, even respect it, but not identify with it. She did not really try. She talked to them in the only voice she had, which was a male voice. It was a deferential age. If, to modern ears, she patronized them, they did not mind. As Jennie was glamorous as well, they were for many years thrilled with their MP. It never occurred to Jennie that she might develop community politics. It never occured to them that their MP, a woman MP, might give *them* a voice.

To a degree, all women MPs were distanced from 'ordinary' women, since they lived lives which were not structured in the same way as ordinary women. Yet because those women MPs of 1945 were usually older, had served in local government, were bedded into their local communities, had children and even grandchildren; or because they were simply more conscientious in their constituencies than Jennie, they remained more sensitive to women's concerns than Jennie.

Like a later woman Prime Minister, there was always a touch of the queen bee about Jennie. Women MPs noticed it and did not like it. Jennie was thought to be arrogant, to have too high an opinion of herself. She seemed to prefer the company of men. Her women friends, such as Suse, held on to their friendship with her in spite of Jennie's cavalier treatment of them (though to be fair, Jennie was just as cavalier with men too).

*

Within Westminster, she had no close female friends. She had grown apart from Ellen Wilkinson, her friend and ally of the 1929 government, as Ellen had grown close to Herbert Morrison; Ellen in any case died only a couple of years into the Labour government. Barbara Castle, equally glamorous, even more gifted, and six years younger, was more competitor than friend. As members of the *Tribune* group, they were almost always on the same side, but they did not care for each other. Jennie liked Bessie Braddock, who reminded her of the sturdy matriarchs of Cowdenbeath. Bessie confessed she could find no redeeming quality in any member of the Tory Party, and told them so: 'And I don't like your faces either.'[76] These were Jennie's sentiments exactly.* Other Labour women MPs, Alice Bacon, Eirene White, Jean Mann, and Elaine Burton, collaborated in an informal women's group led by Peggy Herbison. With them, and with Edith Summerskill, Jennie was not on the same side at all. They were too right wing.

The Bevanite feuds of the 1950s played havoc with women's networking. Several women MPs (Jean Mann, Edith Summerskill, Alice Bacon, and Elaine Burton among them) sat on the National Executive. They were not, as Jennie sometimes suggested, puppets of right-wing union bosses intent on hounding Nye out of the Party. They *were* irritated at the thoughtlessness with which Nye gave hostages (such as his vermin speech) to the Tory press, angry at the dissension that Nye sowed within the Party, and furious at the bullying 'laddish' way he sometimes addressed women.

Edith Summerskill had loved inviting Nye around to her house before the war, where he enchanted her children; or going with him to the Brasserie at the Café Royal, where Nye held forth all night to political friends, artists, and the head waiter for the price of a sandwich. She could not reconcile this with the embittered Nye of the 1950s, with whom she was so often to clash on the NEC. But for Ian Mikardo's hasty return from Israel, Edith, who was chairing the NEC in 1955, would have used her casting vote to expel Nye from the Party.[77] It was a close call for Nye, as he had already alienated Jean Mann. She had heckled him at a Party meeting; he had ordered her to 'Contain your bile, woman'. Generously she refused to take revenge.[78]

Bessie Braddock regarded Nye as a good friend, but found him very difficult. Early in 1948 she was at a Labour women's conference, where Nye was being got at by the delegates complaining that in the new NHS, local authorities would no longer be able to nominate people on to

* Jennie later changed her mind about Bessie: 'Nothing left of her youth except a loud voice . . . What has life done to her to make her so vicious?' JL papers, diary (2 Sept. 1963).

hospital boards. Nye replied angrily: 'I'm not going to be dictated to by a lot of frustrated females.' There was uproar. Women demanded that Bessie sort Nye out there and then. She sat tight. She would not give the press the publicity. But next day she arranged to see him, told him what she thought of him in words unfit to print, and warned him that if he ever behaved like that again, she would take him apart in public, press or no press. The following day, Jennie went to see her. What had she said to Nye? Jennie had never seen him so upset. A grim-faced Bessie told her to ask him: 'It would serve him right if he had to tell you himself.'

A couple of years later, by which time Nye was Minister of Labour and trouble was fermenting in the docks, Bessie tackled him about the threat to arrest dockers who went on strike under the notorious Regulation 1AA. Nye blamed Hartley Shawcross, the Attorney-General; Shawcross (rightly, said Bessie) blamed Nye. She caught Nye in the Commons. 'Nye,' she told him, 'you're a bloody liar.' Nye for once had nothing to say. None the less, Bessie supported him loyally in his battle with Gaitskell over health charges. She would not, however, defy the Party whip when it came to a Commons vote. Nye, who had regarded her as a quasi-Bevanite, did not forgive her. For the next few years they snarled at each other. Bessie nearly lost her seat in Liverpool at the next election when a Bevanite caucus, led by her secretary-agent, tried to have her deselected. The NEC had to impose her on the local party. Nye finally made peace when he coaxed and charmed her into talking to him as they stood on the balcony at the Durham Miners' Gala in 1958.[79]

Nye was even more venomous towards the women MPs whom he disliked. He disliked Alice Bacon. In 1954 *Tribune* accused her of witch-hunting. She was so angry and upset that she threatened to resign from the NEC. It was not all one way. The Welsh Eirene White, MP for Flint, though no Bevanite, lost her chance of election to the women's section of the NEC in 1953 when the union bosses noted that Nye had given her a lift to the Party Conference. Eirene was fond of Nye, and nearly got engaged to his oldest friend and agent Archie Lush. She did not care for Jennie's 'adversarial style' and found it hard to establish a rapport with her.[80] Jennie was not greatly liked by other women MPs; and marriage to Nye added to the feuds within the Lady Members' room.

It was not just her temperament and upbringing that made Jennie suspicious of women's causes, oppose women's sections, and refuse to contemplate any cross-party women's politics. Above all, it was because she was a socialist. In spring 1945 she compared two womens' meetings she had recently attended:

The hall was packed, every seat occupied, and still they came trooping in. In any part of Britain they would have made a brave showing, but right there in the heart of one of London's great sprawling working-class suburbs they were superb. I watched them from the platform as they assembled and felt like getting up and giving them a cheer. They would, of course, have thought me crazy, for they did not think of themselves as anything out of the ordinary. To themselves they were just working women, mostly housewives, who belonged to a number of different Co-operative Women's Guilds in the Ealing area. All they had done that day was cope with blitzed homes, scrub, cook, see to the family, then get themselves washed, dressed, and out to an afternoon joint conference of the Guilds.

Last summer they had to live through the sustained torment of the doodlebugs. Back in 1940 there was the hell of the first great London blitz. And all between there has never been a period of real freedom from raids or expectations of raids. Yet here they were, cheerful and robust, and spoiling for another kind of fight. They were in training for the General Election.

I thought of another audience of women I had spoken to not long ago. It was a feminist group, by its constitution open to rich and poor alike, to Conservative and to Socialist. During the meeting all went well. Fine speeches were made in support of women's claim to equality of status, opportunity and reward.

Afterwards a group of us were having tea. What did we talk about? True to form, the conversation drifted to the servant problem. That can happen also when a group of Co-op. Guildswomen are having tea together. But the two conversations start from totally different premises and reach totally different conclusions. 'My dears', say the former, 'servants nowadays are awful, simply awful. There is no pleasing them, no paying them, and you are lucky, very lucky, to have anyone at all.'

'Why should our girls go into other women's houses, and do their work for them?' snort the Guildswomen. They detest the whole idea. Why? Because of the wages? Not at all. Domestic service is better paid at the present time than many factory and office jobs. It is the status that is the issue. The Guildswomen are quite right. They are not taken in by talk about the old and the ill and those with large families needing domestic help. Of course they need it, but it is those who can afford it, not necessarily those who need it, who grap the assistance. That is inevitable in a class society and the remedy is plain . . .

The problem [that] feminist movements present to Socialist women [is] ought we to belong to them? Ought we to spend time and energy working within such groups, with other women who in their general political outlook are Conservative? It is not the function of non-party feminist organizations to work for equality of status, opportunity and reward as between one woman and another. Their function is to see that the lady has the same social and economic rights as the gentleman, the near-lady as the near-gentleman, the secondary-school type as her male opposite, and the female factory-hand as the male factory-hand.

But if we are working within the Labour Movement for Socialist objectives, don't we cut through all that nonsense and go straight for the larger goal of equality of opportunity for all? . . . Conservative and Liberal feminists believe that they can achieve their aims without challenging the essential framework of capitalist society. Any Socialist knows that when they talk in those terms they are not leading women, but misleading them.[81]

An ambivalent piece of writing, surely. Jennie agrees with the public aims of the feminist women and has tea with them. 'A group of us'—the tone is one of social equals. Yet she is not having tea with the WCG women, whom she observes from the platform. They have tea, if at all, amongst themselves. As Jennie talks about the servant problem (why, exactly?) with the feminist group, she is professedly uneasy because domestic servants are employed not just by the public woman who deserves them, but by the idle lady who does not. She then turns these feminist women into those same idle ladies by attributing to them a parody ('no pleasing them, no paying them') of the drawing-room rich. No socialist would trust the idle rich. The feminist group is given the voice of the idle rich. Therefore, no socialist should work with non-party feminist organizations. If they do, they are helping the idle rich. Meanwhile, the distaste for domestic service among the WCG women comes out in talk amongst themselves rather than with Jennie; she allows herself to overhear them. She thus avoids admitting to them (and to *Tribune* readers) that she herself depended on domestic help. She can endorse the views of WCG women which, had she practised them, would have made her own life impossible.

It was a matter of class. It always was for Jennie. She did not mind that it was a man's world; most of the time she enjoyed it. She did object that it was a rich man's world. The ILP had taught her that all political issues were essentially class issues, and class was defined by (waged) work. As most women were economically dependent on men, they therefore derived their class from men, either from their fathers or from their husbands. You advanced working-class women by advancing their class. You helped them by helping their men. Women had won their political rights after the First World War thanks to the suffragettes. Women, Jennie believed, would win their economic rights after the Second World War because Labour was 'the natural ally of exploited womanhood'.

By 'economic rights' for 'exploited womanhood', it turns out, Jennie meant not equal pay for the working woman but a better deal for the married woman's family:

The wise feminist between 1945 and '50 was well content to see Labour's main energies directed to easing the lot of the married woman struggling to bring up a family on one man's income.

Improved school grants, family allowances, a free health service, income tax rebates, and priority in the queue for state subsidised homes were essential preliminaries before the principle of equal work for equal pay could be put into practice.[82]

It was a deeply conservative position, and Barbara Castle, Eirene White, and Edith Summerskill would have none of it. Barbara Castle retorted that it was not women but 'the family man' who gained from family allowances and income tax rebates, as they stretched his wage. They were no substitute for equal pay. She tackled Jennie about it privately. 'Barbara,' said Jennie, in receipt of equal pay herself, 'we cannot ask for equal pay when miners' wages are so low.' In that case, said Barbara, 'we will wait for ever'.[83]

When at Margate in 1947 Eirene White persuaded Conference by a huge four to one vote to support equal pay in the public sector 'immediately', Jennie promptly devoted a page in *Tribune* to asking, 'Are Women a Priority?' The answer, reluctantly but clearly, was no. She was, she said, 'irrationally thrilled' when the miners voted in support of equal pay: 'It was a warming gesture, symbolical of the completeness with which the Labour Movement, industrial as well as political, rejects the notion that women should be kept in positions of inferiority.' None the less, the country was facing an economic crisis. Equal pay would be inflationary. Socialists could not do all that they wanted to do. This was not the moment to press the 'sectional demands' of working women at the expense of higher unemployment benefit or better pensions. If they did, they would not only alienate the rest of the Labour movement, but set woman against woman, the professional working woman against the housewife:

Every woman of integrity must be prepared to look at the whole problem, not just at those parts of it which affect herself or her sex. It has been a long, grim fight to win through to our present status. But there will be the most deadly reaction against the woman wage and salary earner if we behave in a way that would seem to imply that ours is the only hard fight or the only worthwhile cause that has not yet won complete victory.

Trade-union leaders had to limit their members' demands: 'Women Socialists must demonstrate that they are no less responsible.'[84] On behalf of other women, Jennie would shoulder that responsibility.

When Edith Summerskill introduced her Women's Disabilities Bill in 1953, Jennie told the House that she was 'not at all in sympathy' with much of it. She 'parted company' with feminists, because they were more 'alert' to women's rights than to children's rights.[85] Perhaps—if there were any evidence that Jennie spoke up for children's rights.

Left to Jennie, women's economic rights were between a rock and a hard place. If women were married, their needs were subordinate to those of their children and subsumed within their class, as defined by the men; if they were not married, they were a sectional interest whose needs were potentially at odds with the national interest—also as defined by men.

Of course Jennie was right that most women's well-being in the 1940s and 1950s depended, as it always had done, on the well-being of their family; his wages mattered more than hers; a decent council house and the family allowance mattered more than the marriage bar; a wife's loyalty went to his struggles rather than to the struggles of other women. There was nothing new in this. But when Jennie wrote in *Tribune* that she would have been a suffragette, she was wrong. Their militancy and direct action would have attracted her, but as a socialist she would have had problems with their position. She could not have joined the Pankhursts to demand votes for 'near-ladies' on the same terms as 'near-gentlemen'; she would have insisted with Mary MacArthur and the Labour movement that women's suffrage came as part of adult suffrage. Jennie's views, in other words, remained those of the 1920s Labour movement and particularly of the 1920s Scottish Labour movement in which she had grown up. It was Mary MacArthur, after all, who persuaded women 'dilutees' to vacate their wartime jobs in 1919 to restore them to men. Caught between loyalty to their sex or to their class, women socialists were socialists first.

Yet there is a dimension missing. The shining Mary MacArthur stood alongside working-class women, shoulder to shoulder. She spent her life empowering them, helping them to slay the hobgoblins of brutal employer and brutal husband, encouraging women to have the confidence to form trade unions, to go on strike. She stood at a street corner talking to tired Lancashire women. It started to drizzle and she stopped, but they begged her to go on: ''Tis better than the seaside', they told her. She was one of them.

Jennie never was. She looked down from the platform at her WCG meeting, literally, of course, but also metaphorically. Back in Cowdenbeath days, she refused to chair a woman's section where she would be organizing 'socials etc. isolated from the main meeting where my interests lay'. She was, she explained defensively, up to her eyebrows in controversy and saw no reason to be at the same time up to her elbows in washing up.[86] Not unreasonably, she refused to be pressed into conventional women's work.* Yet it meant that she would not help women to organize for themselves or to speak for themselves. At heart, she never accepted that their interests could be at odds with those of working-class men. Nor that a socialist commonwealth might eradicate the capitalist class, while leaving the power imbalance between men and women untouched. No, Jennie was not a feminist. She was not even a 'Woman Socialist' (despite her capital letters). She was a socialist, who just happened to be a woman.

*

The 1945 Labour government was one of the great reforming administrations of all time, and Nye's establishment of the NHS its most enduring achievement. Looking back, Hugh Dalton felt there was 'a new society to be built; and we had the power to build it. There was an exhilaration among us, joy and hope, determination and confidence. We felt exalted, dedicated, walking on air, walking with destiny.'[87] Barbara Castle (with less exuberance) noted from the Left that 'our achievements had been outstanding'. No such note was sounded by Jennie when she looked back on Attlee's government. Her account in *My Life With Nye* is oddly brief, just 30 pages in a 266-page book, even though she was a minor player married to one of its most dominant figures. She describes Nye's struggles with health and housing, she says a little about her own Commons life, and rather a lot about their foreign travel, but she refuses to stand back and assess the work of that government. She damns it with faint praise. She was dissatisfied with her own contribution; depressed at the compromises forced on them; frustrated by Bevin's foreign policy and Morrison's domestic policy; and angry at the abuse and strain to which Nye was subjected. Also, and inevitably, she was writing through the prism of the 1950s, forever seeing signposts in the Attlee government to the bitter years ahead. It is a sour account. There is no joy in it and, apart from Nye's work, little sense of achievement. The Labour Left had believed in 1945 that their election victory had empowered them, that their leaders were, as the Manifesto stated, 'socialists and proud of it'. She soon shared Mikardo's 'growing disillusionment of the socialists in the Labour Party'.[88]

Yet that government had taken office facing problems of terrifying magnitude. The war had left the country with huge debts, exports down to a third, overseas investment and therefore invisible earnings

* Barbara Castle started her political life with the same views and had vehemently opposed separate women's organizations and sections, but came to believe she was wrong. Phillips, *The Divided House*, 163. Chairing a women's section and being active within the male-dominated divisional party were never, of course, alternatives, though Jennie presented them as such.

savagely depleted. Housing, health, roads, schools, as well as social security, had all to be built. When America abruptly terminated lend-lease, replacing it with a loan on punitive terms, Labour had been forced to divert resources from its domestic programmes into an export drive, 75 per cent higher than pre-war levels. Productivity had to take precedence over equality; further redistribution, it seems, would depend on the creation of further wealth.[89]

Despite this severe distortion of Labour's priorities, Nye and Jennie could have looked back in 1951 to see that Beveridge's five giants no longer strode the land with impunity. The giant of Want had been confronted with a comprehensive national insurance scheme and some dent made in child poverty by family allowances; Disease was fought by Nye's NHS; Ignorance attacked by Butler's Education Act and Ellen Wilkinson's raising of the school-leaving age; Squalor was challenged by Nye's new housing, Lewis Silkin's new towns, and by energetic local authorities using planning and housing powers to tackle bomb-sites and war blight; Idleness was slain (at least for a while) by full employment. The Party chairman could tell Conference with some pride in 1950: 'Poverty has been abolished. Hunger is unknown. The sick are tended. The old folks are cherished, our children are growing up in a land of opportunity.' When it came to the economy, transport, the Bank of England, and the utilities, 20 per cent of the economy had been taken into public ownership—not all the commanding heights, but a useful number of them. Not yet socialism, but large strides towards it. Labour had made heroic efforts against a harsh economic background. Labour's people had taken back their land from the giants.

There was another and less heroic reading. Labour's leaders had been half-hearted about socialism from the beginning, Jennie suspected. It was the Labour Left and not the Labour leadership that had wanted to end the coalition. The Left then found that most of the principles (if not the exact shape) of Labour's welfare reforms came from the wartime coalition, including the commitment to full employment, and had a fair measure of all-party agreement. The other side of that consent was compromise. Jennie was unhappy, for example, that in education, Labour had enshrined the eleven-plus and failed to tackle private schools, much as Nye had been unable to eradicate private medicine from the NHS.

The story on controlling the economy was also unimpressive. Government had inherited from the war huge planning powers, and then failed to use them. It took industries into public ownership not because they were commanding the economy, but because they were failing to do so. And then it stopped short. Was Morrison's state corporatism really a step forward to the democratic workers' control that socialists envisaged? Jennie and Nye doubted it. Taxation had increased, but the distribution of wealth remained relatively untouched. Most bitter of all to those who had fought for the Popular Front was that foreign policy in the hands of Ernie Bevin stayed pragmatic, bipartisan, pro-American, and nationalist, a far cry from the ethical foreign policy that socialism, and Jennie, called for.

In 1947, therefore, a group of Labour MPs had come together during a late sitting in the Commons believing, in Jennie's words, 'that neither the pace nor the direction of Government policy meets present needs'. Many of them had, like Jennie, signed the hostile Amendment to the Address in November 1946. Within its first year, the Labour government had thrown up a sizeable rebel group. Fearing that Keynesian economics, Bevin's foreign policy, and Cold War hostilities would blow a socialist government off course, they published *Keep Left*, and had huge sales.

Jennie reviewed the pamphlet in *Tribune*. She kept a little distance from it, and was not herself a signed-up member of the group, but there was no doubt where her sympathies lay. 'The Labour Movement', Jennie wrote, 'is getting ready to do what it has done so often in the past—to lead its leaders.'[90] The record of the Labour government had been judged by the Left and found wanting. No, it does not seem so surprising after all that Jennie, looking back in 1980, should have been so ambivalent about the Attlee government.

6

THE BEVANITE STRUGGLES

ATTLEE, everyone agreed, was tired. In the general election of February 1950, the Labour Party had been returned with a majority of only six. It had unexpectedly lost seventy-nine seats. The major boundary revision of 1948, abolishing many of Labour's inner-city constituencies, had cost it perhaps half of these, and the introduction of the postal vote was worth a further ten seats to the Tories.[1] More ominously, Labour was losing its white-collar support. That 'progressive' vote which had given Labour such a spectacular victory in 1945, had been worn away by rationing and controls; 'not liberty, equality and fraternity', complained one Labour MP, but 'utility, priority, austerity'.[2]

Attlee struggled with a tiny majority, leading a divided Party, confronting a balance of payments crisis, facing endless late-night sittings, ambush votes, limited pairing, and occasional defeats. He made a great error, says Donald Bruce, then Nye's PPS: 'He assumed that because he was tired, everyone else was.'[3] Against the advice of many of his colleagues, Attlee called a general election for late October 1951.

At the February 1950 election, the Labour Party had done much worse than it expected; in October 1951 it now did much better than it could have hoped for. Its vote rose to 14,000,000, some 200,000 more than the Tories and its highest ever. The Liberals could afford to run only 109 candidates compared to 475 the year before. Most of their votes went to the Tories, who won a small overall majority of seventeen.[4] Labour went into opposition quite cheerfully, expecting they would soon return to power.*

* Lady Astor offered to bet anyone a good cigar against one of her tiaras that the Tories would win. Jennie took up the bet, and said that if she won, she would sell the tiara for party funds. Lady Astor promptly called it off, declaring that Jennie was 'not the kind of girl I bet with'. JL papers, anon. newspaper cutting.

Nye and Jennie, however, had already gone into opposition rather less cheerfully some six months before. Jennie had been disappointed by the 1945 government, Nye's work apart. She felt increasingly betrayed by the 1950–1 Labour government. The 1950 results had been read by the Right and the Left in their own way. The Right thought Nye had frightened the voters, the Left that Morrison and company had failed to inspire them. The Right noted that Labour's middle-class vote was down by a quarter; the Left pointed out that 29 per cent of the working class voted Tory.[5] Morrison insisted that Labour could only recover the middle ground, middle-class support, and power, with a less class-conscious and more broad-based appeal. Nationalization, in particular, said the Right, had not delivered a single extra vote. The Labour government should 'consolidate'.

The Left regarded that as a euphemism for doing nothing. Labour should keep faith, keep left, and keep its nerve. Whatever Nye's disagreements with the 1945 government, he had believed they were travelling the same road to socialism; he complained only that they were rather slow at it. He and Jennie (for on this they were one) now saw the Labour front bench and party policy increasingly captured by men who in their view came from nowhere, who had not been bred in the Labour movement—rootless men like Gaitskell, who had parachuted into a party they had not built and then sought to turn it into something it was not, a social democrat party. (Nye was always baffled by the fact that the Party supported Gaitskell, the public school boy, over himself, a former miner.) The road to socialism for them was public ownership; for Hugh Gaitskell, the point of socialism was to attack inequality. They were not incompatible (and looking back, their differences seem now much narrower than they did at the time[6]) but in so far as Gaitskell's revisionism rejected Marx for Keynes and the better managment of capitalism, it appeared so.

The debate about nationalization and economic planning, in other words, was a debate about the nature of socialism; but it was also a debate about the electoral appeal and future prospects of the Labour Party, with the Right saying that the country had rejected socialism and the Left insisting that the country had not tried it. As the Cold War hardened, a third issue overlaid them both: foreign policy. When the USA, embroiled in Korea, demanded that Britain massively increase its defence expenditure, at whatever the cost to domestic programmes, the disputes over domestic and foreign policy interlocked, and the rifts between Left and Right on foreign policy, on economic planning, on welfare, on electoral appeal, and on the nature of socialism, followed the same fault line—and defined the Bevanites.

Nye and Jennie feared that the world was polarizing into two economic camps: capitalism confronted communism, the unregulated unstable market challenged the totalitarian state. British democratic socialism, they believed, could offer fairness, which capitalism could not provide, with freedom, which communism did not value. It was a 'third way', distinctive and coherent, combining political democracy with a socialist economy.

The Cold War turned the challenge of two competing economic systems into the bristling confrontation of two armed camps. With the election of Harry S. Truman in 1948, with Marshall Aid, and with Britain's economic dependence on the USA, Britain was always going to be drawn into the American camp. No Labour government could support a Stalinist Soviet regime which sealed off Eastern Europe and purged its dissidents in terror trials. No individual socialist, wrote Jennie in *Tribune*, could approve of 'a country in which you have to think as you are told, speak as you are told, change your views on history, philosophy, pedagogy, science, music, even painting, whenever your political leaders tell you to change them, [that] is my idea of hell'.[7] Friendly with America, therefore, but not a satellite of it, Nye insisted. In the age before Suez, when Britain carried more political weight than its economic or military strength justified, the Bevanites argued that in foreign policy as in domestic policy they could build a third way, allying Britain with other non-aligned nations, such as Nehru's India, Tito's Yugoslavia, even Europe itself, carving out an independent path in what they hoped would be a post-colonial world.

None the less, in the years before the 1950 election, and engrossed in his health and housing portfolio, although Nye was sometimes restive, he scrupulously respected Cabinet responsibility. He had remained loyal to Attlee and aloof from the Keep Left grouping of Crossman and Mikardo. His battles were not with the Cabinet but with the Treasury, which was understandably concerned that each year Nye not only sought considerable real growth in his budget, but needed a supplementary estimate on top. Nye's difficulties were obvious. His original estimates were stabs in the dark; they were far too low and he had then to battle to raise them. There was no base-line—no one knew what the country had spent on health before the creation of the NHS, no one could forecast the decades of pent-up demand in a demand-led service; nor could Nye refuse substantial Whitley board pay awards to the staff.

From December 1948, within six months of the launch of the NHS, Stafford Cripps was pressing Nye for cuts of £75 million.[8] But how and where? Over the next two years, every possible option—and many that weren't—was aired. As Nye refused to cut the service, staff numbers, or salaries, they had to seek income. Cripps suggested increasing National Insurance contributions, giving the NHS a more buoyant revenue to which people contributed when they were well and not when they were sick. Nye unwisely ruled that out as charging people twice over. That left charges of various sorts—'hotel' charges (never a runner), prescription charges, or charges on dentures and spectacles.

Charges had two virtues in the eyes of the Treasury: they raised income and they also depressed demand. But precisely because dentures and spectacles had been costly in the past, especially for the elderly, Nye refused to dampen demand for them. He brought home to Jennie the only present he ever kept as a minister, a blue and white cotton handkerchief on which an old lady had lovingly crocheted a blue border. With her new dentures, she wrote, 'now I can go into any company'.

Nye however did not mind dampening down demand for medicine, which he thought was being abused. 'I shudder to think of the ceaseless cascade of medicine which is pouring down British throats at the present time', he told the PLP.[9] He agreed to add a clause to the NHS Amendment Bill going through the Lords in December 1949 allowing him power by regulation to impose prescription charges. He did not object to them in principle. They could be a useful temporary deterrent to be withdrawn when demand for medicine steadied. However, as they would bring in only £6 million, Nye soon told Cripps that they were not 'worth the candle'. Attlee agreed, and the issue of charges was postponed until after the 1950 election.

The post-election shuffle brought Gaitskell to Cripps's side, where he promptly cast himself in the role of Treasury prosecutor. Nye was allowed a high budget ceiling for 1950–1, but Nye in turn accepted a Cabinet committee chaired by Attlee, on which also sat Hugh Gaitskell, to review expenditure and determine the following year's estimates. The committee sat from April 1950 to the end of the year. Jennie related that Nye would come home white with fury after his battles with Gaitskell. None the less, with a sensible baseline established, NHS finances were no longer in crisis but steady, as Nye had always predicted.

All might have been well, save that Gaitskell replaced a sick Cripps in October 1950 as Chancellor. Before 'political perceptions had time to catch up with economic reality',[10] the Korean War changed the arithmetic.

When North Korea invaded South Korea in June 1950, Nye was at one with the Cabinet in agreeing that they should resist communist advance. Memories of Chamberlain's pre-war appeasement had burnt deep in the Labour Party. Never again. This time, they would resist the aggressor. The problem was paying for it. From the start Nye expressed grave misgivings, as Gaitskell, a convinced Cold War warrior, planned to raise defence expenditure from £2,300 to £3,600 million over the three years, financed by cuts and taxes.[11] Worse was to come. General MacArthur invaded North Korea and threatened war with China; Truman was talking about using the atom bomb. Britain would be drawn in. As General Bradley famously said, it looked as though MacArthur was pushing America into the wrong war at the wrong time, in the wrong place and against the wrong enemy. America pressed Britain to increase its defence programme still higher to £4,700 million (a heavier burden per capita than in the USA itself).[12]

Gaitskell wanted to cut the NHS budget, not in order to control inflation which had been Cripps's concern, but to finance a level of rearmament that Nye (now Minister of Labour) together with Wilson at the Board of Trade, argued could neither be justified nor delivered. Britain's industrial recovery and its social wage would be deformed while America played dangerous war games. Nye was right, as Churchill himself was later teasingly to admit—the defence estimates could not be spent,[13] health charges were not needed, the budget turned out to have a surplus.

Nye was already decidedly tetchy that he had been passed over for both Chancellor of the Exchequer, where Gaitskell replaced Cripps (a job for which Nye was not a serious contender), and in March for Foreign Secretary, where Morrison took over from an ailing Bevin (a job for which Nye clearly was). He was having a miserable time at the Ministry of Labour enforcing wage restraint. Health had no one to fight for it at Cabinet; Hilary Marquand, Nye's successor,[14] would not fight charges. Gaitskell took his proposals through a series of spring Cabinet committees, building support, and was fought by Nye at every step.

Nye was not a happy man—that was perhaps understandable. He also despised and dismissed Gaitskell, and that was a profound mistake. At one of Cripps's regular dinners, Gaitskell had yet again argued for health charges ('It was a mission or an obsession with him', Wilson reported to Jennie) and Nye had shouted back. Walking home, John Strachey asked Nye why he persisted in taking on 'one of the really considerable men of the Government'. 'Considerable?' replied Nye. 'But he's nothing, nothing, nothing.' Strachey continued: 'I tried to explain to Bevan that the quiet rather slight man who sat opposite him has "a will like a dividing spear." I might have saved my breath.' Nye rather petulantly withdrew from the dinners, saying he would not sit around the table with a man 'whose aim was to destroy the Health Service'.[15] Their antipathy was almost chemical.

Nye resented Gaitskell's speedy promotion, detested his rigid Treasury rectitude, and despised his pliant Americanism.[16] Heckled at a meeting of Bermondsey dockers on 4 April 1951, Nye unwisely said publicly what he had frequently said privately, that he could not stay in a government which 'imposes charges on the patient'.[17] He had painted himself into a corner.

Nye, it seems, was spoiling for a fight, and Gaitskell obligingly arranged it for him. What had been a private row in Cabinet had gone public. Tension mounted; the tearoom and the Smoking Room filled with MPs endlessly discussing what might happen now. They bent Jennie's ear. Would Nye resign? What damage would that do the Party as they approached the election? John Freeman told Dalton that if Nye went, the government could not last more than another eight or ten weeks. George Thomas found Jennie in an almost deserted Chamber and whispered to her that she must persuade Nye not to resign, as he was too useful inside the Cabinet. Her angry reaction shook him. She was furious: 'You yellow-livered cur. You're just like all the rest! You're another MacDonald or Snowden. Go away from me!' Unable to believe what he was hearing, Thomas beat a retreat.[18]

Gaitskell knew exactly what he was doing: he had decided to make health charges a trial of strength, a contest of wills, and like a matador goaded Nye into a fight to the death. Nye, with some help from Jennie, allowed him to do it. In the absence of anything that might be regarded as leadership from Attlee or flexibility from Morrison, the more ruthless, focused, and unforgiving man won.[19]

It was never about money. As Gaitskell's most recent biographer states: '[T]he imposition of charges on false teeth and spectacles was completely irrelevant to the short-term economic well-being of the country, to the ability of the country to fulfil the rearmament programme and even to the terms of the Treasury's own forecasts . . . [it] was a symbolic political struggle.'[20] If it was only the money that mattered, Gaitskell could have obtained his savings by capping the health budget at £400 million, leaving health ministers to find the required £20 million of cuts without specifying where they were to come from. This was proposed by several Cabinet Ministers, and pressed by Attlee himself.[21] But Gaitskell, with a Cabinet decision in favour of charges behind him, refused to oblige. Why? Gaitskell noted in his diary that any proposals which produced the necessary savings without imposing charges was 'most dangerous . . . because the charges might never come into operation'.[22] Dangerous? It is a curiously intemperate word. The only danger was that Nye might not then resign.

Gaitskell deliberately raised the stakes by, in his words, 'very quietly' threatening again to resign, knowing that it would be 'rather awkward' for the Cabinet if the Chancellor resigned on the eve of the budget. Gaitskell matched Nye almost resignation threat for threat, but did so in a much more reasonable tone of voice: 'a snow peak compared to a steaming tropical swamp', noted Dalton.[23] Gaitskell was accordingly credited with the moral high ground, even though the issue for him was his political authority, while to Nye, who believed he was defending the NHS, was attributed only wounded vanity.

Of the men who might have pulled the Cabinet together, Attlee was in hospital with a duodenal ulcer, Bevin had gone, and Dalton was in decline. Even so, Dalton counselled prudence; he had been warned by Wilson that Nye was not bluffing. Nye, said Wilson, 'means business. He can't climb down after committing himself in public like that. What's more, if Nye does resign, he'll take over the leadership of the Left throughout the country.' Dalton was told privately 'by a very firm and determined' Gaitskell that they could not submit to 'blackmail' (Nye's, that is), and that if they did not 'stand up to him', Nye would destroy the Party. In any case, he believed Nye's influence in the country 'was much exaggerated'. Dalton concluded that Gaitskell was concerned to show his toughness to the electorate at the expense of the Party. Gaitskell himself claimed, not for the last time, that it was 'a fight for the soul of the Labour Party'. Nine years later he told George Brown: '[I]t was a battle between us for power—he knew it and so did I.' And so did Jennie. 'It was a power struggle.'[24] Attlee, reluctantly forced to chose between Nye and his Chancellor, backed Gaitskell.

Budget day—10 April—approached. Even then Gaitskell could have announced the imposition of charges on teeth and glasses, but deferred their implementation for six months or a year to see whether the money allocated for defence could actually be spent (and usefully taking them past the next general election). That too would have stopped Nye resigning. Gaitskell, jauntily wearing a red carnation, started his budget speech. Nye did not take his usual place on the front bench but stood with Jennie in the shadows behind the Speaker's chair to hear it. It was a very good speech. When Gaitksell came to the section announcing health charges, there was no reaction, no outcry in the Commons from the Labour benches; Nye was effectively isolated. Only Jennie's voice could be heard, just audibly, crying 'shame'.[25] Then she strode out into the passage.*

It took Nye a fortnight to decide to resign. Jennie characteristically urged him to go immediately, scribbling to him: 'Ni Darling, Hugh Delargy was saying that he hoped you would wait until after the Party meeting tomorrow but on reflection the Party meeting would certainly come down against you. I should think therefore it is better if you made your decision known before then. Jennie.'[26] But, unlike Jennie, Nye had complicated loyalties, to the NHS certainly and to the Left, but also to his Cabinet colleagues in what was certain to be an election year. The Labour Party had, after all, only a tiny majority. The outcome of the next election could swing on Nye's decision.

For their part, the Cabinet tried belatedly to keep Nye. Manny Shinwell in the unlikely role of peacemaker, suggested that the charges 'should not' be permanent. That would have kept Nye. Gaitskell would only accept that they 'need not necessarily' be permanent, which was enough to lose Nye. As Michael Foot says: '[T]he agony was drawn out through interminable days and nights at Cliveden Place where friends called one after another mostly to encourage, urge, plead with him *not* to resign.'[27] Those closest to him—Jennie, Michael Foot, his friend and agent Archie Lush of Tredegar—believed he had taken enough. He had already told Dalton that he would 'exert much more leverage outside the Cabinet than in it'.† A *Tribune* editorial which compared Gaitskell with Snowden finally signalled Nye's decision to go.[28]

Nye did not go cleanly. It was an ugly and untidy departure, which blew most of his moral authority. His House of Commons resignation speech on 23 April 1951 was heard in silence. When he argued that, although he had agreed to the possibility of charging for prescriptions two years before, he had never meant it to happen, he lost the House; when at the PLP meeting the next day he shouted and ranted, talking about 'my' Health Service, insisting 'I won't have it. I won't have it', he lost the PLP. Baited by unsympathetic colleagues—'*You* won't have it?'—Nye again

* Woodrow Wyatt adds the mocking gloss that Jennie looked 'like the tragic heroine out of Shakespeare, and no one took any notice'; W. Wyatt, *Confessions of an Optimist* (1985), 212.

† Jennie seemingly had no doubts at the time. In 1965, and by now a minister herself, she was more ambivalent: 'Could he [Nye] have been more tactful? Instead of resigning in 1951, for instance, should he have bowed his head and waited his time? There can be no absolute answer to that kind of conundrum but Ni gave the answer in part when he reported on different difficult decisions: "In public life, those who would change things must shout to be heard."' JL to M. Foot, 17 Oct. 1965.

compared Gaistkell to Snowden, whereupon Dalton and Chuter Ede (Leader of the House) promptly compared Bevan to Mosley, Jennie jumped to her feet in outrage, the meeting broke up in bitterness, and Nye, together with Harold Wilson and John Freeman, a junior minister at Supply, resigned from the Cabinet.[29]

Gaitskell, relishing the outcome—'we'd be well rid of the three of them', he had told Dalton[30]—confided to his diary that 'although I embarked on this with the knowledge that it would be a hard struggle I did not think it would be quite so tough'. Had Nye played his cards better, or had his own budget speech been less successful, 'it would have meant failure'. People were now looking to the future, he added shrewdly. 'They expect that Bevan will try and organize the Constituency parties against us, and there may be a decisive struggle at the Party Conference in October.'[31]

Two days later, the three ex-ministers, together with Jennie, went to their first meeting of the Keep Left Group. They immediately discussed whether to change their name. A week later 'it was decided for the moment the Group should remain unnamed'.[32] The caution was understandable, but no one was deceived. The Bevanites had allowed Gaitskell to push them into opposition. The effect? We can only speculate. Nye was right on all the substantive issues, as the next year was to show. Had he not been stiffened by Jennie to resign, and to do so in quite such a graceless way, it is just possible that Labour would have held on in the general election of October 1951, the Party might have been spared the civil war of the 1950s, and Nye might have inherited the leadership from Attlee.

Perhaps. There is no evidence, however, that Nye's resignation did much damage at the polls to the Labour Party—Bevanite candidates did as well as non-Bevanites. And had Nye not resigned on health charges, it seems plausible that Gaitskell might have helped him to resign over defence. A Labour Cabinet in the early 1950s could neither have excluded either man nor contained both men for long. Nye's quick temper, reinforced by Jennie's sectarian instincts, meant that he would be the one to storm out, and to be swept back in again. The rift was to dominate Labour politics for a decade.

During April 1951 Nye had come to the point of resignation several times, but had then hesitated. It was a pattern he was to repeat, usually on defence issues, several times over the next years. On each occasion, Jennie had no such doubts. 'Whenever his resolve to resign wobbled,' wrote Woodrow Wyatt, then working for *Tribune*, 'she strengthened him in it.' She was the dark angel at his shoulder.[33]

Jennie saw his path clearly. Nye was the leader of the Left and the leader of the Party in the country.[34] That role carried certain burdens. He had not borne the painful loneliness of the war only to compromise his socialist integrity in grubby deals with little men who were 'nothing, nothing'. There was no question of living to fight another day, of preferring tainted compromised power on the inside to the shining clarity of protest from the outside. Jennie was brave and strong and resolute; which meant she was also obstinate, bull-headed, sometimes wrong, and could seldom be shifted. Her first thoughts were usually her last. She was impatient with those who were indecisive, dismissive of those who could see both points of view, and contemptuous of those who were paralysed by it. She refused to understand the ambiguities that in government properly troubled Nye. It was all about political will. Enough of it, she believed, and you could blast your way through the system.

She liked to compress complex issues into a simple Right–Left alignment. In 1956, for example, Crossman recorded that the PLP was arguing about the South-East Asia Treaty Organization (SEATO). Some on the Left wanted it scrapped, Mayhew and the Right wanted it retained. Crossman proposed a working party to see if agreement could be reached. They were not to 'blur the irreconcilable difference', said one left-wing MP. 'Not blur, just see if it really exists', replied Crossman; 'Jennie Lee looked very angry', he commented.

> The psychology of Nye [and] Jennie . . . makes them instinctively feel that there is something wrong if this is the way the Party is divided. They feel happy when there is a right wing policy and a left-wing policy attacking it and they always assume that any Centre policy you produce must in fact be right-wing, in the sense that they must find a position from which to attack it as reactionary . . . they [are then] . . . forced to define their left-wing policy in very extreme terms.[35]

Jennie remained Nye's Salvation Army lassie who, even in 1951, had behind her more years in the ILP than in the Labour Party. 'Jennie', John Freeman told Dalton in April 1951, as Nye was still vacillating over whether or not to resign on health charges, 'is Opposition minded and doesn't like Nye being in the Government & has a guilt-complex about a Cabinet Minister's salary'.[36] The guilt complex about the salary may be doubted, given Jennie's relaxed attitude towards money, but Freeman was right about the rest. She scribbled herself a memo on 15 November 1952: 'I am sorry Nye is going on the front bench. Long & frequent contact with people who do not only oppose your policy but are personally hostile is more wearing, emotionally & intellectually than anything else.' He would be attending Party meetings 'in [the] spirit of engaging an enemy'.

A year later, when Nye was again returned to the Shadow Cabinet, Jennie, within a matter of weeks, was already telling their circle that 'she didn't think Nye would be able to stay on the Parliamentary Committee for the whole year'. Dalton caustically added: 'Already hunting for some pretext to resign and make trouble.' A week later, Dalton records a Shadow Cabinet meeting at which Nye spoke of the dangers of discipline, and Gaitskell spoke of the dangers of indiscipline: 'Nye fixes him across the table, with a glare of concentrated hatred, and says, "You're still too young in the Movement to know what you're talking about".' Callaghan accused Nye of seeking an excuse on which to resign, which Nye indignantly denied. 'Later he [Nye] leaves the room while we are still sitting, saying, "Whatever you agree to in your present mood, I am against it".'[37] Jennie's sentiments entirely.

Jennie reinforced both Nye's virtues and his vices. Donald Bruce says that she had 'not the slightest impact on Nye's political philosophy'.[38] Nor especially did she seek it. Nye certainly used her as his sounding-board, haranguing her late into the night as he paced up and down their sitting-room. Yet he could take her by surprise with an impulsive decision. Their friends and colleagues all concur: Nye was his own man, made his own decisions, went his own way. He was, says Mervyn Jones who worked with them on *Tribune*, 'a cat who walked by himself'. Nye Bevan was 'a reluctant Bevanite': this is a phrase that occurs time and again in the memoirs of his circle, and not just because they read each others' books. No team player him. He led, he inspired, he might debate, he sometimes discussed, he rarely confided, he seldom consulted, he was not known to listen, and he was all too careless about briefing those who supported him. Indeed, he got rather testy when reminded that he had a certain obligation to do so. His friends complained that Nye made it all too clear that he wished he could have Bevanism without the Bevanites. They added in exasperation: '[I]t was harder to be a friend of Nye's than one of his enemies.'[39]

Jennie, the most intimate of his comrades, enjoyed his confidence rather than exercised any great political influence over him. The articles she wrote, the speeches she gave, or the editorial line adopted by *Tribune*, anything striking and it was assumed that Nye was speaking through her, that she was giving voice to what he was not always able to say, bound as he was by front bench collective responsibility. She was seldom credited with virtuous views of her own. In some indefinable way, she was held to be intellectually second-rate, someone who did not need to be taken seriously, except in so far as she was an extension of Nye. The 1957 Brighton Conference, for example, overwhelmingly supported Tony Crosland's proposal that an incoming Labour government should control rather than nationalize leading industries. Jennie had denounced it, rather wittily, as 'too pink, too blue, too yellow'; but she was in a minority. It was widely assumed that her vote represented Nye's 'real' views.[40] She spoke for Nye, in other words, when his comrades approved of what she was saying; except when they didn't, and she then became a malevolent influence on him.

There is little evidence in Jennie's notes and writings that she sought to press her own opinions on Nye; she did, however, alert his instincts. And when Nye was in two minds, Jennie, who only ever had one, might shape not so much Nye's opinions, but his judgement, not so much what he thought, as what he did about it. Crossman's diaries (and to a lesser extent Dalton's) are littered with their views on the danger Jennie represented and the damage she did, isolating Nye on the farm, feeding his vanity and his paranoia, always pulling him into confrontational politics. Always pulling him away from the centre ground. As Attlee famously said, Nye needed a sedative; instead, he married a bromide. Jennie wound Nye up instead of soothing him down. In October 1954, to take one example, Crossman noted that it would be 'extremely interesting to see the development of the Left between now and Christmas . . . Everything will depend on how often he [Nye] sees us. If it is rarely, Jennie's influence on him will prevail and make him more and more the spokesman of a lunatic fringe.' And, again, this time on the issue of the H-bomb in 1957: 'Hugh Gaitskell thinks that [Nye] is not intending to bust up the Party or to get out—or rather that he wasn't yesterday afternoon before he got home to talk to Jennie.' George Wigg used to tell people: 'Nye sleeps with his politics. She's always egging him on.' When Nye told the Shadow Cabinet that he would resign after the Easter recess in 1954, Dalton noted waspishly: 'Clearly he slept with his politics last night.'[41]

Jennie also influenced Nye in a second way, in his relationships with other people. Nye, the man of the future, Labour's charismatic next leader, was greatly in demand. People always wanted to get at him, often wanted something from him, and Nye was generous. For all his worldly sophistication, he had an unworldly and joyful innocence. He needed a degree of filtering, and Jennie did that for him (much as Marcia Williams protected Harold Wilson). In the process, her judgements often became his. As Jennie's views on people were usually adverse to begin with, though they might mellow with time, she could not expect her efforts to be appreciated by Nye's male colleagues As she fought to give him some private life—Nye's biggest complaint was that he had no time to read—she had sometimes to exclude them from him.

Her fierce protectiveness was greatly resented. Among Nye's circle, Jennie aroused much male jealousy, considerable suspicion, some dislike, and not a little spite. She treated him like a paraplegic, said one; she was dubbed Lady Macbeth by others. Jennie was blamed for those aspects of Nye's behaviour that his friends found hard to take. Like many other politically committed wives of leading politicians, she was fingered for her husband's faults, in much the same way as Dora Gaitskell was blamed for some of the unattractive behaviour of Hugh Gaitskell and Marcia Williams for that of Harold Wilson. When Nye was unsure about what he should say or do (not that that was a frequent occurence), men who had argued with him in the Commons smoking-room and settled him, so they thought, could never be entirely confident that Jennie would not undo what they had done. They feared she would seduce him. They could not forgive her for possessing the last word.

*

The Keep Left Group 'was born out of a conversation among a group of Members meeting casually during a late sitting in the House of Commons', during the winter of 1946–7, worried that 'neither the pace nor the direction of Government policy meets present needs'.[42] Jennie, reviewing their manifesto in *Tribune*, was supportive but kept her distance.[43] The group started as an educational 'think-tank' for the next Labour government. Its academic resources, particularly in the field of economics, wrote Ian Mikardo, were 'better than those available to the Party leadership'.[44] As it widened into a party caucus, its members nominated each other to Commons committees and to Conference, proposed supply day ballots, co-ordinated letters to the press, defined its line on devaluation, teachers' pay, colonial policy, and, of course, the Korean War.[45] It had a dozen or so active members. Woodrow Wyatt had gone, and Michael Foot would not attend until November 1950 when he came off the NEC, but Donald Bruce, Nye's PPS until he lost his seat in February 1950, went faithfully to the early meetings (though without Nye's knowledge or approval)[46] as did Barbara Castle, Fenner Brockway, Richard Acland, and Tom Horabin. It was anchored by Crossman and Mikardo.

The arrival of the three former ministers, along with Jennie, in April 1951 gave the group a much higher profile, confirming every suspicion of the Right. Once Nye resigned, writes Michael Foot, 'all other Left-wing activities were swamped by it. And soon some steps were taken to give the Morrisonian nightmare [of a distinct Party faction] a semblance of reality.' 'It was', he added in a revealing sentence, 'necessary to engage in propaganda, to recruit, to organize.'[47]

Their first fruits of propaganda came in July, when *Tribune* published a compelling pamphlet, *One Way Only*, which reiterated the Bevan theme, that a foolish and expensive foreign policy impoverished both domestic and colonial policy. Foot and Mikardo drafted it, and the three ex-ministers, headed by Nye, signed the introduction. It sold 100,000 copies. As they were in an election year, Labour colleagues understandably were not best pleased.

They recruited. The group's numbers slowly enlarged with carefully chosen MPs, until there were attendances of around twenty most weeks, drawing on nearly fifty active members. Dalton noted sourly that 'some don't come and a lot don't count'.[48] Jennie's inclination (sensible, as it turned out) was to go for a more open membership, but this did not find favour with most of the group, who in best clubland style much preferred to draw up lists of sympathetic MPs, 'highly commended', 'commended', 'others suggested', whose names were scrutinized, crossed out, added in, and sometimes invited to join. The group was now large enough to set up separate committees to develop policy, producing and discussing more than seventy papers. Nye and Jennie were reasonably assiduous attenders.[49]

And the group also organized. The weekly Tuesday meetings were dominated by forthcoming parliamentary and party business—'The Group discussed points to be made both in the Foreign Affairs debate on Tuesday and Wednesday and in the Party meeting on Wednesday morning. It was agreed that at least one member of the Group should, if possible, speak in the debate on both days. Freeman and Bing agreed to try and get in. The importance of a division at the end of the debate was agreed on.'[50] Jennie would remind members of useful adjournment debates in which they might speak.

This was not just the support a group of friends might naturally give each other; they were handling their party business like a caucus and their parliamentary business like an alternative front bench. (As, Mikardo pointed out, the Bevanites included five ex-ministers, two future leaders of the Party, fourteen future ministers, nine current or future members of the NEC, nine who became peers on merit, six distinguished writers, and nine outstanding parliamentary orators, this was not entirely surprising.[51]) They held additional emergency meetings to agree their line on government statements, such as the sterling crisis. They co-ordinated their amendments to Tory health and pensions bills. They inherited the original Keep Left Group's formal economic advisers, Thomas Balogh and Dudley Seers, and shared speakers notes among themselves on specialized topics. They had weekends away, at Gavin Faringdon's mansion, Buscot Park, where they worked on position papers, and Nye summed up. They continued to hold meetings during the recess. For Conference they prepared resolutions, and at Conference they arranged to stay in the same hotel.

The Bevanites (as they were now known) were a group of argumentative friends. Within their resources, they were also a think-tank; and they were undeniably a caucus within the PLP. In addition, and far more than the early Keep Left Group, they were focused on Conference and constituency work. They were a campaign. They would, in Jennie's phrase, use the Labour movement 'to lead its leaders'.[52] At the Margate Conference in 1950, Keep Left had held a brains trust (modelled on the popular BBC format) as an alternative to the conventional fringe meeting; it had been a great success and they offered them around the country. When Nye, Jennie, Freeman, and Wilson joined the Keep Left Group, it was swamped with invitations. Even in high summer and even in Worthing, they could pull audiences of over nine hundred. Halls overflowed, as people came to hear four or five superb speakers, often with six views between them, and to join in themselves from the floor.* Tickets were traded outside the doors, people were turned away. Weekend after weekend, the elderly elegant green Rolls Royce of Gavin Faringdon or the noisy little red Ford of *Tribune* would set off up the A1, the A4, the A5, or A6, with Mikardo in his element as their chairman, three or four panel members, and bundles of *Tribune*, to do two or three brains trusts in two or three towns,[53] reconfirming party activists in their faith, building up commitment for Conference. Nye seldom appeared on the teams, saving himself for the big set-piece occasions, so much was he in demand, but Jennie, an experienced performer on the BBC's Brains Trust, was one of their stars, confident, stylish, and bold.

And then there was *Tribune*, which engrossed a considerable part of Jennie's political energies, and which made it all possible. Jennie wrote, in

* On the H-bomb, for example, Jennie said that what mattered was not the bomb but policy; Ted Castle, that the H-bomb must be banned; Silverman, that if you ban the bomb you must ban all weapons; John Baird, that they should not only ban all weapons but be neutral; Stephen Swingler was in favour of the bomb. 'Five contradictory positions on a Bevanite platform', noted Crossman, *Diaries* (8 March 1955).

an abandoned draft for *My Life with Nye* replete with battle images: 'After Ni's resignation in 1951, *Tribune* was our life line. In politics as in war, if you destroy communications, you destroy everything. *Tribune* was our holding point and as near as we came to having headquarters.' A few years on and the bomb issue divided Nye from *Tribune*, and the fight for possession of *Tribune* ended the Bevanites. *Tribune* made, bonded, but also broke the Bevanites.

*

Nye, Stafford Cripps, and G. R. Strauss had started *Tribune* in 1937 'to recreate Labour as a socialist Party', an objective so sufficiently remote that it never changed. It was a Popular Front newspaper, demanding arms for Spain, praising Stalin, denouncing Trotsky, calling for strong collective security pacts rather than appeasement. Within two years it was selling 30,000 copies. Nye took over as editor in 1941. The paper became ever more confident and authoritative, condemning the capitalists profiteering from the war, defending press and civil liberties, and criticizing Churchill for his oratorical successes and military defeats. Nye insisted that *Tribune* stand for decent and civilized values—what otherwise were they fighting the war for?—and strengthened its arts pages. These were to have as profound an effect on Jennie as its political columns (she herself always said, as Minister for the Arts, that she learnt about the arts in *Tribune*). She reviewed for the paper. As publishers were reluctant to waste books on the paper, she often had to borrow or buy her copies.[54] Nye gave George Orwell, then in trouble with the BBC and his *Animal Farm* rejected, a platform as its first literary editor; his obstreperous column, 'As I Please', soon brought complaints. Nye defended his freedom to write as he thought. Michael Foot believes that Jennie learnt her permissiveness towards the arts from *Tribune* as well; 'As I Please' became her column in 1945. When Nye and Strauss joined the 1945 government as ministers, the paper passed to Jennie and Michael Foot. Michael became its editor in 1948, and Jennie a featured columnist who also put considerable effort into the paper's business arrangements, planning sales strategy and securing covenants. Michael and Jennie were the mainstays of its editorial board.[55]

The paper's intellectual confidence belied its financial insecurity. *Tribune* was always in financial trouble, until it was in political trouble. Then it rallied. It needed sales of 30,000 to break even, but they seldom reached 20,000—it lived on the edge of bankruptcy. 'Somehow, always', says Peggy Duff, their business manager, Michael 'raised the money to keep it going.'[56] It was a shoe-string operation, its journalists devoted, underpaid, and overworked (Michael, the most overworked, took no pay at all). When they were hit by the Kemsley libel case, they lost their printer, faced personal bankruptcy, and could have lost the paper itself.* *Tribune* could survive only by increasing sales and, therefore, advertising; by increasing controversy and, therefore, sales; or by subsidy. *Tribune* tried all three.

It was easier to write the paper than to sell it. Small newsagents would not waste valuable shelf space on it. They treated it as political soft porn—without porn's profitability. *Tribune* staff would use their lunch hours to push the paper into yet another local newsagent. However, the paper's fortunes could always be revived by a good crisis, a noisy Conference, denunciation by the leadership, or the threat of a resignation—usually Nye's. As he managed this most years, he could be said to have done his bit for *Tribune* sales. Rob Edwards, editor in the early 1950s, wryly noted that Nye's 'sensational resignation' over health charges in April 1951 ensured that:

> [*Tribune*] as the only Bevanite organ instantly became 'must' reading for every political correspondent and commentator. Saatchi and Saatchi could not have done a better job for the paper. Messengers from all the newspapers and news agencies waited every Thursday morning for the first copies to arrive at 222, The Strand in our little red van.[57]

It does not make 'very good journalism', he added, 'to support the government'. They enjoyed similar financial success a few months later with the *Tribune* pamphlet, *One Way Only*. It was widely attacked, and therefore widely in demand. The wholesalers, W. H. Smith and Wymans, were reluctant to increase their orders. The pamphlet sold out. Peggy Duff wrote:

> [I] had heated arguments upon the telephone with W. H. Smith and even more vitriolic conversations with Jennie Lee who wanted to know why it couldn't be had. Eventually I had a brain wave and brought the two together. I suggested to Jennie that she telephone W. H. Smith and told her whom to contact. The effect was instantaneous. A very aggrieved manager rang up, asked me who she was, complained that she had accused him, quite rightly, of political prejudice, and

* Beaverbrook's *Evening Standard* had on 2 March 1950 smeared John Strachey. *Tribune* accused it of degrading press standards below those even of Kemsley. Lord Kemsley, newspaper proprietor, sued and a cynical Beaverbrook sat back 'to enjoy the fun'. *Tribune* had to defend the case right up to the House of Lords, on which sat judges who had themselves been attacked by *Tribune* in the past. Jennie and the Foots were in very real danger of bankruptcy if the case had gone against them. Jennie was desperately worried. Not just her savings, but her seat was at risk, and she had not been responsible for the article in the first place. With Beaverbrook's help, Monckton brokered a deal which left Kemsley paying costs. Lee, *My Life*, 186–7; interview Michael Foot.

proceeded to add 15,000 to their order, then another 10,000 . . . We could have sold double that if the trade had co-operated.[58]

The other path was subsidy. Early in January 1949, Michael Foot persuaded Transport House to 'rent' two pages of *Tribune*. His staff was highly scornful of its dull content, but for a while it kept the paper afloat. However, when strikes broke out among dockers and transport workers, Arthur Deakin, the TGWU boss, denounced Communist agitators, *Tribune* denounced Deakin, and the Labour Party was not best pleased. It leased Transport House from the TGWU, and only two pages from *Tribune*. Michael's previous arrangement came to an end. The death of Stafford Cripps cost the paper some of its private subsidy. Michael Foot turned to Beaverbrook, and Nye and Jennie persuaded their friends, Jack Hylton the impresario, and Howard Samuel the McGibbon and Kee publisher and property millionaire, to help out. Howard Samuel's support came at a price. He was a tall, thin, troubled man, known to *Tribune* journalists as 'the mad prince' with, in their eyes, the arrogance bestowed by money. His wife Jane painted, and the paper's art critic, all unknowingly, had slated an exhibition of hers. At the next board meeting, and without admitting to any connection, Nye denounced the review as an 'underhand and vicious attack, very wounding to the artist, unfit to appear in *Tribune*'. Howard Samuel had threatened to stop the subsidy.[59]

Jennie made it very clear that Samuel's subsidy was support for Nye, not for *Tribune*. She scribbled an oddly worded note to herself: 'Must find out how many thousands Ni contributed [*sic*] of money given him without ties of any kind to use as he thought best helped him do his job. Think £11,500 by 1956 but must check . . . The fact is without Ni, there would have been no *Tribune*.'[60] As far as Jennie was concerned, *Tribune* was Nye's paper; he founded it, helped finance it, and gave it its constituency. Where he went, it should follow. In a pre-television age, Nye also needed *Tribune* if he were to give voice and leadership to the extra-parliamentary Left. Tensions, damaging and deeply distressing, were therefore predictable when he deserted the Left over the H-bomb issue, and *Tribune*, under Michael Foot's editorship, refused to follow.[61] As Elizabeth Thomas gently noted, Jennie's personal emotions would overrule her professional responsibilities as a journalist. 'Everyone was against Nye, and everyone was wrong', Jennie announced.[62]

Bob Edwards, who edited *Tribune* between 1952 and 1955, deeply admired Nye, but 'sometimes both he and Jennie Lee shocked me a little'.

Edwards wrote a *Tribune* pamphlet on the Cresswell pit disaster called 'Dirty Coal'. He took it along to the house off Eaton Square:

> Coal fires blazed in two vast rooms. Nye sat in an armchair and Jennie on a long settee reading the galley proofs. They did not look at all enthusiastic. Eventually Jennie uttered the most inexplicable sentence I ever recall hearing. 'Only the scum are left in the mines,' she said moodily. What did Jennie mean?[63]

Edwards was stunned, but then decided that they must recently have had a row with the leaders of the NUM. A year or two later *Tribune* attacked a pro-H-bomb piece by Crossman in the *New Statesman*. Crossman dashed down to Asheridge, where Nye was in bed with flu. He ran up the stairs and, despite Jennie's attempts to stop him, burst into Nye's bedroom and violently berated him. An emergency board meeting followed, to which Edwards was summoned:

> 'What you did', spat Jennie, jabbing her fingers towards me three times, 'was damnable, damnable, damnable.' I was like a small boy caught doing something unmentionable. Everyone looked unhappy except Jennie, whose face registered black fury. Up spoke the still, small voice of Michael Foot, no doubt scratching his wrists. 'Well, he *is* the editor,' he said, putting the liberal case, as he could always be expected to do on such matters.[64]

Edwards moved on to the *Daily Express*; Jennie denounced him for selling out to Beaverbrook. Richard Clements, who took his place, had entirely cordial relations with Jennie, except when it came to pieces on Yugoslavia.

In that long summer of 1951 after Nye's resignation, Jennie and Nye had gone for a month's holiday to Yugoslavia—their first visit—where they met Tito and made formative friendships with Tito's deputy Milovan Djilas, and Vladimir Dedijer. They soon grew disenchanted with Tito, and angry and upset when in 1956 he imprisoned his socialist critics, including Djilas. Jennie covered his trial for *Tribune*.[65] She deemed it 'outrageous' when Clements visited Yugoslavia the following year. He pointed out that he was a journalist, which persuaded Jennie not at all. When *Tribune* published some friendly paragraphs on the greater liberalism being evidenced by Tito in March 1958, Jennie complained. Michael agreed the following week to add an editorial note making it clear that *Tribune* had not altered its views on the 'regime's offences against freedom. I think this will achieve the result you desire', but pointing out gently that *Tribune* welcomed small gains in freedom in other Communist states and that they should not be expected by Jennie to 'apply a different standard to Yugoslavia than to other Communist countries'. He added ruefully, knowing his Jennie: 'I do not expect I will convince you by this letter, but I hope at least I can persuade you that there may be a different point of view.'[66] Mervyn Jones himself spent a holiday there in 1959 and came back to write a sympathetic piece about Yugoslavian experiments in self-management. Jennie was 'furious'. Tito had arrested Djilas. It was 'outrageous' that Jones should write the piece he did when Djilas was in prison.[67]

There was, says Ian Aitken, 'no damn nonsense about editorial freedom' with Jennie. When during a railway strike *Tribune* supported ASLEF against the (Bevanite) NUR, Jennie was furious, and gave them all 'a vicious tongue lashing' at the next board meeting. Aitken, Geoffrey Goodman, and Michael Foot would sometimes have to ask themselves, will Jennie wear it, how will she react? They never fretted about Nye, they could always approach him; Jennie, says Goodman, had 'to see you laying bare your soul'.[68]

It was therefore not surprising that *Tribune* journalists viewed Jennie with a somewhat sardonic eye. They contrasted Nye's playfulness with her heavy-footedness. The weekly editorial lunches, with Nye, Jennie, and Howard Samuel, took place at the Cock in Fleet Street. It was not easy to park, so Nye, coming by car, decided one week to use the car park of the Inns of Court. An attendant said he could not park there, but Nye replied that 'you mustn't keep a judge waiting', and strolled away. Everyone laughed, as he repeated the story over the ham and salad, except Jennie. 'That was an untruth, Nye.' 'No, it wasn't an untruth. It was a statement of general application. You must not keep a judge waiting.' Jennie remained unamused.[69] *Tribune* staff saw Nye and Jennie as a team, loyal comrades in arms, but they did sometimes wonder amongst themselves whether Nye was irritated at Jennie's lack of subtlety, her bossiness, her literal-mindedness, her failure often to see the point.

The weekly lunches were largely social affairs. Although *Tribune* was regarded as Nye's mouthpiece and its editorials as 'signalling tactical moves', Nye seldom asked what line the paper would take, and never required its journalists to write to his instructions. He tossed off ideas that would have taken a dozen of them to follow up. The editorial board was mainly for show, its journalists now agree. *Tribune*'s editors, Michael Foot, Bob Edwards, and Dick Clements, all believed in 'omnipotent editors'.[70]

Jennie, however, did not. The departure of Bob Edwards put additional work on Michael, which Jill Craigie resented. Michael, for his part, resented the threat that Howard Samuel would, on Nye's say-so, withdraw his subsidy. The issue of Michael's editorial independence of the board was entangled with the paper's financial dependence on one of its members. There was much reference to a 'kept' paper. One Tuesday evening in 1955, tempers flared and some unforgivable things were said, leaving everyone badly scarred. Jennie's interventions, said Jill Craigie, had cost the paper several of its staff. On each occasion Michael had to pick up the pieces and train up the replacements, forever the schoolmaster. Jennie was taken aback, shocked, angry, 'and astonished by the violence of your [Jill's] attack.' As Jennie frankly admitted: 'Short of beating me up physically, nothing was left undone to drive home your attitude.' Michael, she noted to herself, could tolerate no opposition, would take no criticism. It was to Jennie's credit that she wrote to them both a day or two later, making peace. Would it help Michael, she asked, if Nye again became editor of *Tribune* and Michael returned to his book? It was, she said somewhat disingenuously, 'much better for Nye to be worried directly than indirectly'.[71] Michael soldiered on.

After the 1957 Brighton Conference, the row flared up again, irrevocably sharpened by Nye's denunciation of unilateralism, while Michael headlined *Tribune* as 'The Paper that Leads the Anti-H bomb Campaign'. Nye decided that the paper had been 'diseased' for some while, hijacked by CND. Nye, Jennie, and Howard Samuel wanted a 'proper balance' of view in *Tribune*; Michael wanted a clear editorial line, at one with the views of its readers. There followed what Michael tactfully describes as 'several awkward editorial arguments'. The board wanted Michael to be bound by its decisions, but he insisted that either he, the editor, went, or it, the board went, or that it finally accept his editorial independence. Jennie, angry and frustrated, later confessed that she wanted to stop Samuel's subsidy (threatening *Tribune* with closure), and perhaps launch another paper. 'I would have been bloody-minded', she told a *Tribune* party in 1981. 'It was Nye who restrained us despite the heartbreak he felt from *Tribune*'s attitude.'[72] Jennie and Howard Samuel backed down, and still Michael soldiered on.

A year later, in 1959, they returned to the issue. They accused Michael of using a paper subsidized by Nye's friends to attack Nye; Michael replied that Nye having rightly joined the leadership was bound by collective responsibility, but that this should not muzzle *Tribune*, which was the voice of the Left; Nye, at least on defence issues, was not. Jennie was:

> furious with Michael . . . Had he [Nye] no rights? Were only letters and comments traducing his point of view to be published? Michael is of the breed who will go to the stake for their convictions. He passionately disagreed with Nye and

refused to give equal prominence to their differing views . . . So tense was the strain on their relationship that they almost came to blows.[73]

A couple of weeks after the board fights, Nye and Jennie met Jill and Michael at a Polish embassy reception, and they went back to Jill's and Michael's for drinks. A furious row blew up between Nye and Michael, in the course of which Nye broke a Sheraton chair. Jill caught the look on Jennie's face: she was enjoying it. Jill was appalled. Deeply upset, she phoned the next morning to make peace. Nye rushed round, but things were never the same again.[74]

The subsequent exchange of letters about *Tribune* was cool, the distance too wide to bridge. Jennie's 'interference', the Samuel subsidy, and Nye's defence of the H-bomb confronted Michael's reading of editorial integrity. At Michael's suggestion, Howard and Jennie stepped down from the editorial board, and were replaced by Ian Mikardo, whose business head Michael valued. As Jennie noted, 'Michael had his way.'[75] To the distress of all, a degree of estrangment continued until Nye's last illness in January 1960, when Michael and Nye were again fully reconciled. Jennie was in no doubt that his 'friends' as well as his enemies 'hounded' Nye to his death. She told them so.

Tribune, and its brains trusts, mattered because together they bridged the parliamentary and the extra-parliamentary Left—not that, on first sight, there seemed much of either. Though the PLP included fewer manual workers than before the war, most of the PLP was instinctively loyal to its right-wing leadership, as well as anchored by its trade-union sponsorship. The Bevanites could poll thirty votes of their own, and as many again from the broad Left on certain issues, but this was seldom more than a fifth of the PLP. So the Bevanites never did well in elections to the Parliamentary Committee, as the Shadow Cabinet was then called;[76] and could not hope to capture the parliamentary leadership.

Nor did they fare much better at Conference. The constituency parties were increasingly to the left of the leadership, but Conference was dominated by six great unions which held more than half the Conference vote.[77] Ernie Bevin, the greatest trade-union leader of them all, was Labour Foreign Secretary, and his rock-like alliance with Attlee cemented the Labour movement. The Party belonged to the unions—they had founded it, they financed it—and the constitutional arrangements of the Party reflected that. Of the twenty-four seats on the NEC—the leader and deputy leader were *ex officio*—the trade unions elected not only their own twelve seats, but with their bloc vote the five women's seats as well. By upholding the sovereignty of Conference, they ensured that the leadership of the PLP was dependent on them. Never again would they allow a repeat of 1931. Only the seven constituency seats, ring-fenced in 1937, were beyond their reach. However, if the constituency activists became too uppity, that also could be changed.

As long as Conference was dominated by the unions and the unions by the Right, they continued to deliver a right-wing vote to the leadership and a right-wing NEC at Conference, locking the two together. From 1950, and for a decade, the platform was never to be defeated at party conference.

To the union leaders' innate conservatism and their insistence on unity, loyalty, and discipline in the Party as in the TUC, was added their obsessive hatred of the Communist Party, which they suspected, with some justification, of seeking to undermine full-time officials with hard-left shop stewards, and to foment wildcat strikes. They detested the Bevanites, whom they believed were anarchic and unaccountable, giving shelter to fellow-travellers. (Ernie Bevin, wrote Jennie, 'behaved towards the Soviet Union as if it were a breakaway branch of the Transport and General Workers Union.'[78]) When the Bevanites swept the constituency section at the 1952 Morecambe Conference, and when Gaitskell explained this by asserting that up to a tenth of Conference delegates were Communist-inspired, the trade unions had found their next party leader, someone not unwilling in his own words to do 'their dirty work for them and with them.'[79] Not until the very end of the decade, when a new left-wing leadership, headed by Frank Cousins, emerged within the trade unions on the one hand, and Gaitskell's efforts to revise Clause 4 brought him into conflict with trade-union leadership on the other, were the contours of Conference, constituencies, trade unions, and PLP redrawn.

Left-wing dissenters within the PLP were therefore in an especially difficult position—at odds with Conference decisions, with the majority vote both of the NEC and of the PLP, as well as with the leadership itself. In the Cold War years, it was a culture in which criticism was too easily labelled as heresy.[80] How could dissent find space, keep left, and keep faith? Every path was blocked. They were not schismatics; they would not found another party; yet they could not capture the party they were in. Standing for the Shadow Cabinet either entailed public loyalty to a right-wing leadership or a sequence of resignation crises. They must capture the constituency parties—'If Members knew [that] anti-Bevanites would not get renominated things would move.'

The Bevanites did indeed encourage local parties to select left-wing candidates, but had not the ruthlessness to unseat their right-wing parliamentary critics. Nor would the NEC have allowed it.[81] In any case, MPs were still only loosely attached to their constituencies, and constituencies did not expect to pressure their MPs into line. They elected them and let them get on with it. So although the Bevanites could, and did, take the constituency seats at Conference, that was gadfly stuff. It allowed them to criticize the leadership, but not to capture it. If the Left were to win at Conference and bind the PLP and (Shadow) Cabinet, they had to look to the unions, and try either to win the mandated vote of the rank-and-file members against their leadership, or break the unions' hold on Conference. Either strategy would intensify the hatred of the trade-union leadership and bond it more closely to Gaitskell.

So in 1954, to Jennie's dismay, Nye gave up his NEC seat to stand for the Party Treasurership against Gaitskell. He wrote to Ron Evans of the Ebbw Vale party in June:

> There seems no other way of challenging the ascendancy of the two general unions. Unless that ascendancy is challenged, there will be no hope at all for a progressive movement within the party. At the moment it is a complete stalemate. We keep on having our victories in the constituency section and defeats on the trade union side.[82]

As the *New Statesman* noted: 'The agitation in the constituencies was never closely related to the situation within the trade union movement. The militants in the local parties were organising *Tribune* meetings while the majority of trade unionists were feeling that they never had it so good.' Gaitskell took the trade-union vote and won comfortably.[83]

Although Nye and Jennie both came from mining and trade-union backgrounds, they never appeared comfortable with the trade-union movement, regarding it as a 'rotten constituency', a construct of capitalism. This was more than mere antipathy to its right-wing leadership, men like Ernie Bevin and Arthur Deakin. Solidarity they understood, but Nye and Jennie found the rigid discipline it entailed offensive, and the negative instincts and bureaucratic style it practised inimical to imaginative socialist faith.

Yet neither had they any sympathy for the Communists within the unions, who appeared to monopolize the left-wing agenda. Nye and Jennie failed to read the growth of a non-Communist Left within the trade-union movement, and neither Crossman, nor Mikardo, nor Foot had either the contacts or the inclination to do so. If there was a single reason for the failure of the Bevanites in the 1950s, it was because the parliamentary Left failed to reach out to the emerging trade-union democratic Left. The basic conflict within the Labour Party was always between Left and Right; on top of this was overlaid a struggle between the rank and file and the leadership, and a further struggle between constituency activists (often themselves active trade-unionists) and the bloc trade-union vote for possession of the leadership. The bitterness for the Left was that just as they were beginning to make inroads into the trade unions towards the end of the 1950s over the bomb, Nye deserted them. At the very point when the Left on some issues might have used the sovereignty of Conference to contain the sovereignty of the PLP and its leadership, Nye joined the leadership.

Individual conscience was always tolerated within the PLP; 'organized conscience' was not. That was schism, a party within a party, the charge levied against the Bevanites. As Mikardo wrote: 'If they [the Labour Left] get together and organise they are condemned as sectarian and as a threat to the solidarity of the Movement, and are thereby crushed, and if they remain informal and unorganised they are out-manoeuvred and picked off one at a time.'[84] Disorganized and they were ineffectual; effective and they were disloyal. The Party constitution, as amended by Morrison in 1946 to prevent the affiliation of the Communist Party, was very clear: 'Political organisations . . . having their own Programme, Principles and Policies for distinctive and separate propaganda, or possessing branches in the constituencies . . . shall be ineligible for affiliation to the Party' (the rule change also barred the re-affiliation of the ILP). Yet, as Leader of the House in the 1945 government, Morrison had that same year suspended the standing orders of the PLP, relaxing its internal discipline, tolerating active debate, preferring willing consent, and keeping only the ultimate sanction of the withdrawal of the whip.[85] The Bevanites operated in the space between the two. As free-wheeling and iconoclastic individuals, linked by friendship and hard drinking, they were in the clear; as an organized caucus, they were not.

*

Following the 1951 general election defeat, battle was joined. Nye would not stand for the Shadow Cabinet. When in spring 1952 the Tories produced their defence estimates, which differed but little from those of the previous Labour government, the Labour front bench was in a quandary. Nye, who had consistently criticized Labour's defence estimates, had no such compunction. He and fifty-six Labour MPs refused to follow the official Labour line of abstention, and voted against the government. The standing orders of the PLP were reimposed, banning voting against a three-line whip.

The atmosphere soured. Jennie and Michael in *Tribune* continued to challenge Attlee's leadership, sales increased, and demand for brains trusts grew. The constituencies were in revolt. They came to the 1952 Conference ready 'for a showdown'. It took place at Morecambe, a 'minor Blackpool', noted Crossman, 'dumped down on mud flats'. Its two main hotels were separated by a four-mile long promenade. It rained. Delegates, including Jennie, went down with streaming colds. The NEC members were mostly in the same hotel. Their wives marked out the residents' lounge much as their mates marked out the smoking-room. For the entire week, Mrs Attlee and Mrs Shinwell and their circle occupied one sofa on the left in the residents' lounge, Jennie and her circle occupied the sofa on the other side of the lounge, all of them, observed Crossman, talking in low whispers. The sofa between them was, appropriately, occupied by members of the Conference Arrangements Committee.

The Bevanites swept to victory, taking six of the seven constituency places, Dalton and Morrison lost their seats, and Gaitskell trailed in tenth. 'The Morecambe vote', writes Ben Pimlott, 'defined the Party's civil war.'[86] It was an ugly conference, cold, wet, and the worst 'for bad temper and general hatred since 1926', thought Dalton. 'We haven't had so strong hatreds since 1931—and then one section left the Party, but now everyone is staying on.'[87] There were physical fights between Bessie Braddock and John Baird, a Bevanite, and, allegedly, between Jennie and Wilfred Fienburgh, an Islington MP (and author of *No love for Johnny*). Right-wing speakers, including Deakin, boss of the TGWU, were booed; hard-left resolutions that Nye himself opposed, such as support for political strikes to bring down the government, attracted high votes (losing by 4 million to 1.7 million). A leading trade-union official rushed out of the hall yelling: 'After this there'll be no more bloody money for this bloody party.' So angry was he that he spat out his false teeth.[88]

Conspiracy theories abounded. Gaitskell explained the Morecambe results by asserting that many delegates were Communists and fellow-travellers. Trade-unionists, right-wing MPs, and finally Attlee himself called on the Bevanites to disband. 'What is quite intolerable', said Attlee, 'is the existence of a party within a party, with a separate leadership, separate meetings, supported by its own Press. It is inimical to effective action in the House. It breeds suspicion and uneasiness throughout the movement.'[89] The PLP agreed. Nye, having coffee with the young Cledwyn Hughes, one of his supporters, said in exasperation: 'This charge of trying to build up something, a party within a party, it's rubbish. I'm fed up with these people trying to make things difficult for me.' But Attlee insisted: 'You can argue a lot about groups but they're like the elephant. I may not be able to define one but I know one when I see one. Groups are all right for special purposes but what I disapprove of is an omnicompetent group like the ILP used to be.' Nye must close the group down.[90]

Nye acquiesced. They had won all they could win at Morecambe, he persuaded himself. To continue would 'perpetuate' schism, something he abhorred. An embarrassed Jennie told Crossman of Nye's decision and asked him to discuss with Michael Foot, Harold Wilson, and Ian Mikardo whether they should disband a group that officially did not exist. When they remonstrated, Nye told them robustly: 'To continue the Group now is to perpetuate schism. If you were to continue the Group in these conditions and I were the Leader I would have you expelled. The Group is intolerable.' They tried to survive by agreeing, as Jennie had once proposed, 'that members should let it be known that anyone in the PLP could come to meetings',[91] but that, Attlee decreed, would merely create a rival party meeting. They must disband. Bevanism was checked.

Was it a party within a party? It has been described by Bevan's most recent biographer as 'the awkward squad' rather than a coherent faction, and any challenge it presented was said to be merely tiresome rather than effective.[92] Crossman noted rather ruefully:

> that we are not organised, that Aneurin can never be persuaded to have any consistent or coherent strategy and that we have not even got to the beginning of a coherent, constructive policy. What we have, and it is very important, is a group of MPs who meet regularly, who know and like each other and who have come to represent 'real Socialism' to a large number of constituency members. This produces an extraordinary bitterness among those who support the Gaitskellite line.[93]

Barbara Castle similarly insists that they were not an 'organised conspiracy. We had no formal membership. Nobody paid any subscription to any central body: instead they bought *Tribune* and raised funds for it.'[94]

It is true that they were not tightly disciplined or whipped, that their Group contained many currents of left-wing thought (especially on the H-bomb), that, in Mikardo's phrases, they were more 'ideas-men than organisation men, policy formers rather than power-brokers . . . better at talking than doing, better at debating than recruiting'.[95] When Deakin called at Morecambe for them to 'get rid of their Whips, dismiss their business managers, and conform to the Party constitution', Bill Mallalieu had retorted that they had never had whips, nor managers, and could not dismiss what had never been appointed. The week after Morecambe, when the Bevanites were back in their usual corner of the Smoking Room, Tom Driberg famously remarked to Crossman that it was less a party within a party as a smoking-room within the Smoking Room.[96]

That, however, was disingenuous. The Bevanites might not have had an official membership list, but their membership was none the less by invitation only. They might not have had whips and a business manager, but they had plenty of business management. They co-ordinated their tactics, and circulated their minutes. Despite Gaitskell's wild allegations, it was not an organized conspiracy, but it was a disorganized caucus, which, as Nye admitted, held 'Group meetings'; it was a dissenting tendency.[97] If it was not a party within a party, that was not entirely for lack of trying. Those involved relished their caucusing. Mikardo took such obvious delight as he organized, Driberg gossiped, Barbara Castle rebelled, Wilson calculated, and Foot pamphleteered. Crossman could always be counted on to see the political advantage of any principle, and Foot the issue of principle in any political position. And Jennie? She had one ambition: that Nye, as leader of the Left, the guardian of the soul of the Party, should be leader of the Party—and should become so not by shabby deals within the PLP but by the will of the Labour movement.

If the Bevanites were not better at being a party within a party, that was because Nye was too wayward, too disdainful of team action, too distrustful of sectarianism, and too indolent to bother. Individual Bevanites had their own personal agenda, which, in the absence of a clear and clearly agreed line from Nye, undercut group solidarity. Friendships were strained, for example, when Nye resigned from the Shadow Cabinet over the SEATO vote in April 1954 without consulting his group, who obviously thought it a mistake, and yet he and Jennie felt betrayed when Harold Wilson, who had narrowly missed the Shadow Cabinet, took up his place. Crossman, again, wanted to move the Party left, but not necessarily to make Nye leader; and he was well aware that his own star waxed when that of Nye's waned. Harold Wilson, on the other hand, was anxious to position himself as Nye's natural heir on the Left, without compromising his links with the rest of the Party; Jennie was very downcast when, after the expulsion rows, Wilson overtook Nye in the Shadow Cabinet elections.[98]

So the Bevanites were not as coherent as they appeared to their enemies. They were a mix of the conspiratorial, the gregarious, the ambitious, and the anarchic. None the less, drawing on up to sixty votes, they had a considerable power to embarrass, and, when the Tories had only a small majority, the power to deny Labour parliamentary victories. Were they effective? The answer to that question depends on the aims attributed to them. They were not trying to displace the policy-making function of Conference. They wanted to keep Labour distinctive, not to invent new strategies for it. On domestic issues, they wanted to extend public ownership. On defence, the Bevanites did pull the Party to the left, aided by Labour's revulsion to American McCarthyism as well as by a Republican presidential victory in 1952. Gaitskell accused them of forming a party within a party, just as Attlee had done, and they agreed he had a point. They had become, wrote Shinwell, 'a second Opposition to the Shadow Cabinet'.[99] In hindsight, both Cledwyn Hughes and Donald Bruce, themselves Bevanites, thought Attlee was right to close them down. Crossman, privately, agreed.[100]

Although the leading parliamentary Bevanites, including Nye and Jennie, continued to meet informally over lunch at Crossman's house in Vincent Square on Tuesdays, and their Second Eleven[101] worked the constituencies and promoted *Tribune*, organized dissent was at an end.

However, the Bevanites still had *Tribune* and the brains trusts with which to reach out to the constituencies. The NEC and the leading unions regarded both with loathing, but despite their best efforts could find no plausible grounds to ban them. In 1954 Deakin denounced the dockers' strike against compulsory overtime as communist-inspired, and *Tribune* said that that merely showed his ignorance. Deakin demanded that the NEC bring *Tribune* into line. When the paper refused to recant, its editorial board, including Jennie, was threatened with expulsion from the Party. They stood firm and the NEC backed off.[102] But the sniping continued, endlessly. Mikardo recalled that Tom Driberg would come out of those Wednesday morning NEC meetings 'wrung out like a dish-rag and desperate for a large drink to get the taste of it out of his mouth'. Crossman detested the 'appalling dreary atmosphere of subdued bickering'. At least the meetings were very short; the Right always moved to the vote as soon as it could.[103]

Having disbanded the Bevanite group, and sought to discipline its press, the final assault of the Right was on Nye himself. Attlee would soon be standing down as leader. Gaitskell, the heir-apparent, convinced that disunity (and not merely unpopular policies) would cost the Party the next election, wanted, in Attlee's words, 'to inherit a disciplined party'. Nye was an inveterate rebel—he must go. 'It's got to be cleaned up', Gaitskell told Crossman.[104] Nye obligingly gave Gaitskell his opportunities.

On a sequence of votes on defence alliance structures—SEATO, NATO, and German rearmament—Nye refused to follow the PLP line on the floor of the House.

The debate on Churchill's defence White Paper in March 1955 brought matters to a head. It was a serious debate, as much about Churchill's foreign policy as it was about defence. Churchill, ageing, sick, and shortly to resign, warned that the USSR was fast building up its nuclear capability. Nye 'correctly' identified the logic of Churchill's position:[105] if Churchill feared that in three years time the USSR would have sufficient nuclear weapons to catch up with and annihilate the West, then Britain should be negotiating disarmament now and from a position of strength, and not let matters drift. 'We are dealing with the preservation of the human race', said Nye.

To Nye's chagrin, the official Labour amendment[106] missed the point and failed to attack Churchill's foreign policy. Instead, it accepted the need for nuclear weapons as a deterrent, and focused not on the opportunity for disarmament, but on more effective defence spending. An ageing Attlee was absent from the front bench as Nye sought clarity. Did the official Labour amendment mean that Britain would use nuclear weapons against *conventional* attack? (Attlee, in his wind-up speech, fudged: nuclear weapons would prevent war, any war.) Nye's anger grew: 'The issue is simply this. Are we to conduct a peace policy or a war policy? We could do it. We could meet the Soviet Union representatives at once. I therefore beg the Government to measure up to the magnitude of the problem . . . That is what we want from the Prime Minister.' And he went on: 'We want from my rt hon. Friends the leaders of the Opposition an assurance that the language of their Amendment, moved on our behalf, does not align the Labour movement behind that [Tory] recklessness; because if we cannot have a lead from them'—sweep of the arm—'let us give the lead ourselves.'[107]

In the vote that followed, Nye and sixty-two other Labour MPs refused to support the official Labour amendment. A furious Shadow Cabinet recognized that Nye was not only criticizing Churchill's failure to build the peace, but Attlee's failure properly to challenge him. Gaitskell (somewhat against Attlee's own inclination) led the prosecution: Nye must not only lose the whip and be expelled from the PLP, but he must be expelled from the Party itself.

Most people, even his fellow Bevanites, thought Nye had gone too far in his assault on Attlee. But Nye, the leader of the Party in the country, expelled? The Party was in uproar. The NEC was left in no doubt as to what the constituencies thought. In Pembrokeshire, one party worker,

Gordon Parry, brought dozens of members' cards to a meeting with their local MP, Desmond Donnelly, put them on the table, and stated that every one would be torn up if Nye was expelled.* Over 150 constituency parties protested to Transport House, as did regional councils and trade-union executives. Jean Mann had a sleepless night. She had known Jennie since she was a girl and had stayed with her family; but she had also been at the receiving end of Nye's chauvinist bullying. She was still undecided when the NEC meeting started, but fearing damage to the Party, abstained. Mikardo returned from attending his daughter's wedding in Israel a day early, and denied Edith Summerskill her casting vote. Attlee remained fond of Nye, and belatedly made it clear that he did not seek his expulsion. Jennie and Michael urged Nye not to 'grovel'—a cobbled-together apology was deemed to have saved face.

The row ended the Bevanites. Crossman now drew closer to Gaitskell. It also ended what chance Nye had of becoming leader. Attlee famously told Crossman that Nye 'had the leadership on the plate. I always wanted him to have it. But you know, he wants to be two things simultaneously, a rebel and an official leader, and you can't be both.'[108]

The general election followed in May 1955, a low-key affair, and the Tory majority rose from seventeen to fifty-eight.[109] Crossman noted, prophetically, that the Labour Party was 'ideologically disintegrated by the fact that Keynesian welfare capitalism is proving, for the time being, quite an adequate substitute for socialism'. And, he went on, 'We are missionaries without a mission.'[110] The Bevanites retreated back into private life, Nye and Jennie and Crossman spending more time on their farms. Gaitskell took over from Attlee in December 1955, defeating both Nye and Morrison, and settled the leadership question, apparently for a generation.

A subdued Nye rejoined the Shadow Cabinet, took over the Party Treasurership from Gaitskell in October 1956, became Shadow Foreign Secretary in November 1956, and settled his position in the Party, apparently for a generation. He began to move away from the Left over Suez, when he was far more critical of Nasser than was *Tribune*. He finally abandoned the Left at the Brighton conference of 1957 when he defended the possession of the H-bomb. A year later, the first Aldermaston marchers were carrying banners: 'No H bombs, not even Nye's.'

*

* Parry, then a young prospective candidate in South Wales, came up to Nye after a meeting: 'Any advice for me, Mr Bevan?' 'Yes. Don't worry about what sort of friends you make in politics. If you make the right sort of enemies, the right sort of friends will rally round you.'

In April 1951, Gaitskell had pushed and Jennie had pulled Nye into opposition. Now in 1957, the last phase was being played out. Jennie to her great discomfort found herself supporting Nye supporting Gaitskell.

Nye was never a pacifist and not a unilateralist; he believed in strong defence through collective security (he had favoured the use of tanks, for example, to blast into Berlin at the time of the airlift). He was not sure that nuclear bombing was morally and qualitatively different from conventional saturation bombing. He was taken by Crossman's argument that nuclear weapons were cost-effective and could cut defence spending. Above all, he believed that the world was a safer place if Britain was an independent third force, its defence not in hock to the chronically unstable USA.[111] A friendly (ex-*Tribune*) journalist reported, 'Mr Bevan has been telling his friends that Mr K[hrushchev] said to him, "Do not create a vacuum in Europe by giving up the bomb."'[112] It meant, ironically, that Gaitskell espoused the H-bomb as the basis of Britain's alliance with the USA, Nye as the basis for Britain's independence from the USA. Of course Nye wanted multilateral disarmament—all sane politicians did. But he thought it folly to throw the bomb away rather than negotiate it away for some concessions.

The NEC met the weekend before the 1957 Brighton Conference and, inevitably, decided to resist resolutions demanding the renunciation of the bomb. Nye, as Shadow Foreign Secretary, was to answer for the NEC from the platform. After two days and nights of being tormented by what lay ahead, Nye knew what he had to say. He told Jennie: 'I can just about save this Party, but I shall destroy myself in doing it.' In their hotel bedroom Jennie argued with him into the early hours of the morning; their voices could be heard next door. He was, she said, utterly alone. He did not 'even have me on his side', though she came round to his point of view. Nye was not reneging—Peggy Duff makes that clear—but the Left, in the aftermath of Suez and Hungary, had moved on beyond him. *Tribune* friends, who knew what Nye proposed to say, were in despair. Geoffrey Goodman walked up and down the promenade with Nye for nearly an hour the day before, as they 'argued and counter-argued about the political, moral and practical implications of a unilateral renunciation'. Nye was convinced that that meant impotence. Others avoided arguing with him, reluctant to add to his distress. Michael Foot still hoped that Nye might salvage the situation by the speech itself. He might still find the useful ambiguities, ask Conference to trust him to do what was right and what was best when the time came. Not so Jennie. She sought out Mervyn Jones. He wanted to talk about Algeria; she insisted on talking about Nye. 'Understand this,' she said, gripping Jones's arm, 'Nye is sixty. He can't go on resigning and walking out and isolating himself with his little band of the faithful. He can't go on like that, he can't.' The Left, she added, had become dominated by CND, 'an hysterical middle class lobby', and was out of touch.[113]

In that Brighton Ice-Rink, which served as the Conference Hall, Nye, their darling, proceeded to make a speech that was stumbling, fumbling, incoherent, a bull at bay, until the boos and the heckling fired his anger and he found his voice. He threw at them two phrases—one unforgettable, that they should not send him 'naked into the Conference Chamber',[114] and one unforgivable, that the policy of the Left was 'an emotional spasm'. Half the delegates were down with Asian flu: the rest were in tears. Loyal Bevanites searched for explanation. Gordon Parry's wife noted that Nye spoke throughout with his hand clutched to his lower stomach; she feared he had had a mild stroke. After the speech, bewildered delegates gathered in clusters and waylaid Ian Mikardo, Barbara Castle, Michael Foot, 'and asked over and over again: 'Why has he done it? Why, why, why?' . . . there was no balm to be offered.'* Jennie's emotional support was never more needed. She defended him in *Tribune*, fiercely rounded on his critics, arranged for him to visit America, took him home to the farm.

With that speech Nye had tied himself to Gaitskell. The Smoking Room circle broke up; Nye sat there alone with one or two faithful friends. He became depressed, 'encouraged only by his wife Jennie'.[115] Looking back on that time, Jennie wrote to Michael Foot in 1965:

> It was, in the last phase, a complicated kind of martyrdom. He was beset, misjudged, maligned, on every side. He was caught in an impasse from which there was no way out. Working under Gaitskell for one of Ni's intellectual arrogance and proud spirit, was plain hell. Refusal to do so was once more splitting the movement at a time when, rightly or wrongly, Ni deeply believed mankind was again and again within a hair's-breadth of nuclear war. He had sufficient confidence in his party, and in himself, as to believe it was urgently necessary to get the Tories out. As Foreign Secretary, with Gaitskell as PM he would have had a monstrous burden to carry. But he was willing to face up to this. That is, intellectually he was, rationally he was, but the emotional undercurrents were tearing his very guts to pieces.
>
> Then, although he never said this to me explicitly, in so many words, he was wounded to the very depths of his being by the refusal of so many in the party with whom and for whom he had worked, to give him their trust. No blank cheque for Ni. No room to manoeuvre. He got everything the hard way.[116]

* As one right-wing Labour MP said: 'I had to get up and go away. I couldn't stand any more. I felt as if I had been present at a murder—the murder of the enthusiasm that has built the Labour movement'; *Daily Herald*, 5 Oct. 1957, qtd in Foot, *Aneurin Bevan*, vol. 2, 576.

Two years later Nye was to rescue Gaitskell from himself. In the 1959 'You've never had it so good' general election, Macmillan had caught the public mood. Labour morale plummeted; many feared that the Party would never win another election, ever. Should it, could it, become a different sort of party?—a social democratic rather than a 'class' party? Against the advice of his own Hampstead revisionist set, and in the teeth of loyalist trade-union opposition, Gaitskell decided to scrap Clause 4.

Had Nye challenged Gaitskell to a vote at the 1959 Conference, Gaitskell would probably have been defeated. The unions were hostile; Barbara Castle in the chair had called the faithful to arms; Michael Foot had galvanized the hall. In the event, it was Nye, with superb generosity, who saved Gaitskell with one of his finest speeches, funny, far-seeing, wise, teasingly suggesting that Gaitskell and Barbara both agreed with him and therefore with each other. It was political geometry. No one was in any doubt that Gaitskell continued as leader on Nye's shoulders and with his sufferance. If they did, Jennie put them right. A beleaguered Gaitskell had had to retreat, and Nye gave him his lifeline.

In these last years Nye was impeccably loyal to Gaitskell's leadership, but it 'always concealed private reservations'. At heart, Nye believed that Gaitskell was not a socialist and that should have disqualified him from leading the Labour Party. 'Yet he saw no way of overthrowing Gaitskell's leadership, though he regarded it as a "tragedy" for the Labour Movement, because of the balance of power in and composition of the Parliamentary Labour Party.'[117] The Bevan–Gaitskell alliance was only ever coexistence rather than partnership, a truce rather than an agreement. At some point, wrote the *New Statesman*, 'they will have to resolve their contradictions'.[118] Geoffrey Goodman of the *Daily Herald*, who accompanied Nye on his national campaign during the 1959 election, says that Nye 'admitted that if Labour lost the election he would, perforce, have to challenge Gaitskell. He had no clear notion of how this was going to be done, or what the result might be; but he felt there would be a necessity to do it.'[119]

Gaitskell's leadership was no longer secure. Both Ian Mikardo and Michael Foot believed that had Nye lived, he would have broken from, confronted, and beaten Gaitskell in an outright fight for the leadership. That he would have challenged Gaitskell, as they believe, seems likely; whether, given the restlessness of the great unions at Gaitskell's tampering with Clause 4, he would have acquired their anti-revisionist vote and beaten Gaitskell, is impossible to know. Certainly he could not have overthrown Gaitskell without conciliating the unilateralists.[120] But had Nye outlived Gaitskell, few doubt that he would have become leader of the Party. He might then have become Prime Minister in 1964. Jennie, an elected politician in her own right, would have moved into 10 Downing Street at his side.

Instead, after Nye's death, Harold Wilson reluctantly took up the challenge in 1960, with Jennie's encouragment and a third of the PLP vote, and positioned himself for the future leadership. Upon Gaitskell's untimely death in January 1963, George Brown, James Callaghan, and Harold Wilson fought it out. At Wilson's victory party, he told his supporters: 'There is one toast we must drink, to the man who is not here, the man who should have done it, Nye Bevan.'[121]

*

Nye's political life placed an enormous strain on Jennie. Ever since she had lost her North Lanark seat in 1931, she had worked to return to the Commons. When she did come back in 1945, she was barely 40 and could reasonably hope for office. But it did not come, and by the late 1940s Jennie no longer expected it. She had already decided that the future of the Labour Party was only safe in Nye's hands. His career would be hers. She would, and did, run a parallel political life alongside his, but it was a political life, not a political career. 'With Jennie', wrote Jean Mann, 'we were in for a big shock. She retained her name but sank her identity, her career and her own prospects, to become Nye's background . . . She took on her husband's paper, *Tribune*, and became within Parliament and without, another Nye Bevan in all but name.'[122] Jennie's life in the 1950s was subsumed in Nye's. His life was hers.

Yet was the choice as stark as that? She had no children, a comfortable income, the flexible hours of parliamentary life, a safe and undemanding seat in Cannock, a 'homemaker' in Ma aided by other staff: if there was any woman in politics who did not, for straightforward domestic reasons, need to subordinate her career to another, that woman was Jennie. She had less responsibility, more freedom, greater affluence, and more support networks in place than most.

Jennie certainly believed she made a choice, and though it cost her dear, most of the time she did not regret the choice she had made. Yet if from the outside it seems an unnecessary one, then what was going on? This was a woman with a strong sense of herself and her mission, contemptuous of conventional femininity, who kept her own name on marriage, and refused to wear a wedding ring. Three things suggest themselves. Jennie, as the very young and very pretty MP for North Lanark, had been Labour's princess, shining, fluent, and fearless. Nye, in those days, had merely been one of an undifferentiated bunch of Welsh boyo mining MPs.

She was by far the better known. But when she returned in 1945, she had lost her nerve. She had been out of the House for too long, and she never re-mastered it. She spoke rather seldom and was not especially noticeable. House of Commons reputations are made and held in the Chamber. Though Parliament was heavily male-dominated, Jennie was not held back because she was a woman. The Labour Party was proud of its women MPs and made space for them. There were not very many of them, and they were no threat. Jennie did carry some other baggage, however: she had only recently rejoined the official Labour Party. In the eyes of the Right, therefore, she remained deeply suspect. She chose to give up a career that it was unlikely she would command; she renounced what she might well not be offered.

More profoundly, the emotional balance in their marriage changed. She had married Nye on the rebound from Frank, for comfort and comradeship. She had several affairs before she married, and rather expected to have affairs after she married. Nye was in love with Jennie; and Jennie was fond of Nye, but she had loved Frank. Yet the marriage, and the balance of power within it, changed during the war. By the time Jennie re-entered Parliament, Nye was infinitely the better-known figure, with a charismatic presence that seduced men and women alike; and Jennie became devoted to him.

The attachment, as far as anyone can judge, was as much maternal as sexual. Jennie and Ma combined to give Nye a home that was warm and welcoming, a refuge, a place of peace. As the feuds of the 1950s sharpened, so Jennie became more fiercely protective of Nye, and he became more needy. When he had an important speech to make, he would not write it but pace around the room, he talking, she taking notes, he practising his expressions in the mirror, she prodding him—that point needs stronger emphasis, don't forget to pause there. If it was a difficult speech, she would say: 'We'll rehearse it, we'll go over it', telling friends that was the way he worked best.[123]

Their circle of friends was somewhat cynical about her ministrations. They fretted when Jennie took Nye back to the farm and beyond their reach; they suspected that some of Nye's days in bed were diplomatic; they told each other that Nye needed not peace with Jennie, but peace from Jennie, from the stressful cycle of row, threat, and resignation, that she helped to provoke. Whether Jennie was 'good' or 'bad' for Nye (and almost all of the men and most of the women who knew them well believed she was 'bad' for him) was ultimately irrelevant. They (mostly) met each other's needs. A tiny incident in 1953 that Crossman reports, suggests something of the texture of their marriage:

It had been decided that we should all go to Barbara's for dinner and that I should go with Nye. When we got outside, he started driving me to his home and I said he had to go to Barbara's. 'Oh', he said, 'I'm not feeling well and I can't possibly face it. I'll go home to Jennie'. As I had hoped, Jennie sent him up with me to Barbara's dinner, where we discussed tactics.[124]

A 'we' that did not include Jennie, as far as Crossman and Barbara were concerned; Nye's feeling unwell; the wish to go home to Jennie's comfort; Jennie sending him out again; and then the evening on tactics: it is all there.

Yet Jennie was not just a somewhat frustrated MP, and not just a comrade and wife to Nye. She lived her life as a socialist, as had her father and grandfather before her, and she believed without a shred of hesitation that the finest socialist in the land, the only man fit to lead the Parliamentary Labour Party, the man who did lead the Party in the country, was Nye Bevan. She had decided during the war that: 'He was doing what I wanted done, infinitely better than I could have done it.'[125] Anything thereafter that she could do to ease his path, fight his corner, protect his privacy, advance his fortunes, was her service to the movement.* In that sense it was a truly political marriage. She maintained a semi-independent political life of her own, for their mutual sanity, but she never doubted (and nor did Nye) whose career mattered for the future of socialism. She was always there for him. She offered her support with affection and generosity, and Nye received it with tenderness and grace.

The strain told, though she did her best to conceal it from Nye. For Jennie read Nye better than Nye read her. He, in public the more subtle and complicated person, was in private simple and carefree. She, whose sectarianism and single-mindedness seemed so predictable, so black and white to outsiders, was in private the more complex, and the more torn, of the two. Nye could always handle Jennie's tempestuousness, her flouncing, her anger, and her passion. But there were aspects of her he could not fathom, that were beyond his reach. There was a darkness, a strain of deep depression in Jennie that she consciously withheld from him. Time and again when the pressures mounted she would write Nye an anguished letter, telling him how much his political life and the suppression of her own, was costing her—but she never sent him the letters; she just kept them. Nye, the Celt, romanticized this darkness into 'mystery', a need to

* 'I had in the course of years more and more accepted that to help sustain Ni's creative intelligence was much more important than aiming at the dizzy heights of maybe being a second Alice Bacon'; JL to M. Foot, 16 October 1965, JL papers.

hold on to her. He was deeply sensitive to her moods, but he was never aware of how much he drained her, how much he was taking from her, how much privately she struggled. The sacrifices were all hers. As the 1945 government drew to its close, Jennie took refuge in her diary, addressing Nye, though he never saw the note:

It is easy for me to behave in a way that would smash both our lives. I see no way in which I can save both. If only one is to be saved it must be yours for if I obey the urges of my own ego, then even I will be destroyed. You cannot adjust your leisure, your work, your periods of excessive strain, your holidays, the nature and extent of either your work or your play to suit me. You simply could not do it. Not only your own ego would be outraged. All the external pressures of the contemporary social framework would be on your side. It is the woman's part to give way, to make life smooth, to walk by your side. It is the man's part to accept the social easements on the domestic front but even in accepting to be satisfied and satiated. Dreams are reserved for the women who take not for those who give. Giving is dowdy. Taking . . .

She reflected on the deaths of Ellen Wilkinson, and an MP of the 1929 Parliament, Mavis Tate. Were there other suicides, she wondered, among public women? Was the incidence higher than normal? She assumed so. Some time later, she re-read her note, and added that it was written:

when strains at harshest. I suppose it helped me to get over a bad period but Ni did not know. I never said, still less wrote to him anything that would have added to his burdens. This resentment I felt at the time was a passing phase. Like Ni I was a disciplined warrior. What mattered then was giving him the love and support he could not live without—and he repaid in full with his love and trust.[126]

In 1950 she was writing to Charles Trevelyan, telling him that she was 'struggling to keep Ni from collapsing altogether under the strain. He is so very much alone and he cannot so long as he is in the government say very much. Still less can I.' And she continued:

Sometimes I have selfish and rebellious moods for I have too strong an ego to take easily to the role of 'backroom girl' but Ni is more than an incredibly sweet tempered husband. He is my best hope of seeing the Labour movement kept on true Socialist lines. So grumble to myself as I may, each time the storm grows intense, I can only rally, keep a small oasis of domestic tranquillity as padding to his overwrought nerves.[127]

She would have liked to have stood for the NEC constituency section in 1952, 'but I held back. If I stood at this time and had been elected, that would have meant one place less for other friends whose support Nye needed'.[128] Not until 1957 did she stand for the women's section she despised, rather than challenge a comrade in the constituency section; when Jean Mann stood down, she came on the following year.

During 1957 many of the props of her life were knocked away. Nye, having thrown in his lot with Gaitskell over defence, was preparing to distance himself formally from unilateralism and less formally from the Left. Her father was dead, her mother had cancer, her brother was a heroin addict, and she was terrified that he would bring scandal upon them. That June, Nye was staying with friends in Scotland and Jennie poured out her heart in a long anguished letter to him that she wrote, but did not send, a few paragraphs of which she published in *My Life with Nye*:

Dear Ni,
My agent telephoned to say that Cannock executive have recommended that I be a delegate to the Labour Party Conference and nominated for the women's section. Joe [*sic*] Richardson, Lena Jeger, Judith Hart of Scotland and a fifth will challenge with me, all five women asking the section to be abolished, but until that is done, that it should represent all, not just one point of view.

You know the argument. My dilemma is that this has to be done seriously, worked for or left alone. The end result we know. One year, one or other of us, most likely Lena for she has the C.P. contacts working for her more positively than the rest of us, will be elected and beyond that there is the hope that we get more radical constitutional changes. The general shift in the executive might not go your way, but there is a good chance that it would.

Anyhow, while you were in India & the Middle East, your friends thought this worth pursuing. Many people sustain you by believing in you, and no human being can go on without some encouragement. You have your doubts, your fears, but you cannot see the end anymore than any one else. Why don't you give me a little self-confidence? Or is it your real and unshakeable conviction that nothing I do matters a damn, is it just me, my personal stupidities and inadequacies, or is this your personal conviction about all socialist activity? If so, we must both think seriously about what comes next. I believe what each of us does is a contribution that alters, however infinitesimally, the general flow. I consider it conceit and ego-centricity to believe any one can do a great deal, but conversely, it is also cruel self centredness to say all you are and stand for, is without effect.

I stand back amazed when I watch you respond so ably and fruitfully to problems put to you and jobs imposed on you, against the desolation and nihilism of your spirit.* I am left naked and lame. I don't have your virtuosity. I have to have something to sustain me. Every human being can be helped to be their best

* As Jennie notes in *My Life*, 226: 'when I talk of Nye's "desolation and nihilism of spirit", I am talking of myself, not of Nye'. (The original letter has virtually no paragraphs; they have been added.)

self, or reduced by discouragement to a break down of the whole organism, physical and emotional. On the other hand, if it is not mere absentmindedness, a spilling over of your overburdened spirit that accounts for your attitude towards me, it is best I should learn the truth about myself. Others see us more clearly than we can see ourselves, and who better than you, where I am concerned, to make a judgement.

If I finish by apologising for taking up your time, you will think I am being sarcastic. But believe me Ni, you will be very wrong. I *do* apologise. I apologise to myself, for I have never felt I had a right to take liberties with you because of a personal tie. I have again and again resented how some others have done so. You must also accept that I am saying what for me is the literal truth, no double edge to it, when I say you are so much more important to your age and its people than I am—a thousand—thousand times so.

I have given more time to your problems when you are under heavy strain, which is almost always, than to my own, for I have not seen them as separate. You represent in the main—not always—certainly not always when personal relations are involved, what I believe in. But every human being must have *some* living room. The spirit has to be fed as well as the body. Food & medicine can choke and kill if that is all one is offered. We are all queer creatures. In the end the spirit dominates. I don't know what 'spirit' means precisely, neither do you, my poor sick mother could tell both of us better than any professor, but I do know that mine is not strong enough to take quite as much punishment as it has had to take in recent times.

I am tormented by the thought that in writing to you at all I am being abominably selfish. You think cowardice is an involuntary thing, selfishness something we can all do something about. I am not at all sure you are right. I am not sure about anything—except perhaps that through all the pain and frustration of these days you remain very precious to me. I don't want you hurt. I don't know quite what to do for the best. Shut up and take the consequences, sit tight on the safety valve, ease things a little by small squeals that humiliate me more than they annoy you or pretend I am being 'unselfish' by not asking for your cooperation, by deceiving you into believing that all is well, a sick woman needs only a few more vitamin pills and she will cease bothering about anything except weeds in her garden.

J.

As Jennie recognized, she was on the edge of a breakdown. Nye, who was in Scotland at the time, worried about her and made affectionate phonecalls, but he never understood just how much he took from her and how much she gave; nor how much it cost her. She not only disciplined her own pain; she loved Nye enough never to reveal it to him.

7

LIFE WITH NYE

A FEW weeks after Frank's death in 1933, Nye had moved in with Jennie, sharing her small Bloomsbury flat. They married a year later and searched for a home. Jennie liked London, but Nye wanted a home in the country. They found Lane End Cottage near Reading, fifty miles from London. It was long and low, its white-washed walls and deep thatched roof pretty enough to be used for a wartime induction film for GIs on what to expect when posted to England—Jennie and Nye in a Tudor cottage.

Although Jennie could make a home, she could not run it: she had no domestic skills. As she said herself: 'I was as helpless as an old-fashioned male.'[1] She found a 14-year-old girl for the housework, the girl's brother for the three acres of garden, and two cats for the mice. They also needed someone to cook and care for them. Jennie's lecture tours in the late 1930s would take her away for days and weeks on end, as she visited Russia, reported on Spain, lectured in the States for money and in Britain for the ILP. Jennie did not want Nye returning to a cold and empty house.

While Jennie was down south, and her brother Tommy was in Australia, Ma and Dad were still in Lochgelly. Ma's children were never out of her thoughts. Jennie's parents had met Nye fleetingly during the North Lanark 1931 election campaign, but only came to know him when Jennie took him north after the 1936 Edinburgh Party Conference to show him Scotland. Ma and Nye immediately fell for each other. Dad was more wary, until Nye began loudly to berate Jennie for buying him a box of cheap cigars in the States instead of the few decent ones he had asked for. Without a word, Dad showed Nye a box of the same unsmokeable cheap cigars that Jennie had given him. From then on, they got on famously.

Dad's health was poor: he had been in and out of hospital. If he went back down the pits, Nye told Jennie, it would kill him. That was all Jennie needed. Ma was anxious to go down south and look after them both, which Jennie wanted just as much as Ma. Dad, Jennie decided, had nothing to lose and nobody to miss by leaving Lochgelly—he would be better off living with them. How could she coax him south? She designed a two-bedroomed cottage for them in the corner of the garden. When it was well under way, they came down for a holiday, and Dad agreed to 'give it a thought'. Jennie pressed him and finally he capitulated.

All seemed to be going, in Jennie's phrase, better than well. Then, a few weeks after her parents had moved in, Nye took Jennie aside and told her coldly that she was never to talk to her father like that again. She and Dad had been engaged in their usual enjoyable over-the-top banter, Jennie telling him that he was an ignorant and silly old man. Nye, coming from a very different family with a strong mother he respected and a gentle father he shielded, was appalled. Dad was their guest, he informed Jennie, and must be treated with complete civility and respect. Jennie was stunned. Nye had never been hard and cold with her before. If he had, she would have walked out. Again, she acquiesced.

Nye misjudged. Things were never the same again between father and daughter. They stopped quarrelling. The free-and-easy camaraderie was lost and they became careful with each other. Dad withdrew, and over the years became curt and estranged from Jennie. He turned instead to Nye. He would wait up each night until Nye got home, and Nye would never fail him, however late the hour, always chatting to him about the day's events before going to bed. Relations between Dad and Jennie remained difficult—they were so alike. He once told Suse: 'I don't have a wife, Jennie has a mother.' He felt displaced: Ma was at the centre of their family, he was not. He had given up a hard life, but one which drew real meaning from the solidarity of the pits and the vitality of Fife politics. He tried to be useful, meeting them at the station in the battered old car Jennie had bought him. He retained his eye for the ladies, but his heart was not in it and his health not up to it. He was always very proud of his daughter, and they were reconciled before his death at the age of 74, in 1952, but in an arrangement that suited Jennie, Nye, and Ma very well indeed, Dad paid a price.[2]

Ma bloomed. She did not exactly share Jennie's taste for the old and the simple, the polished wood floors, white-washed walls, the lack of decorative clutter. Back in Lochgelly Ma's dresser shelves were filled with china dogs, the remains of her wedding tea-service, pink angels poised on sea-shells and simpering shepherdesses. Each week they were lovingly taken down and washed, until young Jennie sternly banished them in favour of books. Ma, anxious to please her daughter, put her knick-knacks in a large clothes basket under the bed, until Jennie returned home from school one day to find two of the pink angels timidly peering out from spaces between the books. Sensing how much the ornaments meant to Ma, Jennie was remorseful and relented. Ma, sensing how much the ornaments were detested by Jennie, insisted that the books remain.[3] For Lane End, Jennie scoured second-hand shops and markets for old pieces. Ma made cushions, curtains, and re-upholstered Jennie's finds to professional standard. Together, they made a serene and beautiful home.

Above all, Ma was a superb cook. Friends never forgot her meals; they were legendary. At weekends, Jennie would hear Nye and Ma out in the kitchen, tasting, teasing, experimenting, making new sauces, trying new dishes. Nye would preside over their refectory table, monarch of all he surveyed, a carving-knife at the ready, telling guests that he had to marry the girl in order to get the mother-in-law. Constance Cummings recalls that Ma one day had prepared a fine leg of lamb. A feast, as meat rationing was still strictly enforced. Then Nye phoned from London to say he would not be back in time, so Ma promptly returned the lamb to the fridge and found something less fine for the guests. Ma cared for Jennie, but she cooked for Nye. Surrounded in the countryside by eggs, milk, vegetables, and poultry, the war and rationing passed her by. In 1945 they moved to London, to Cliveden Place off Sloane Square, and Ma came up against rationing for the first time. For a while she was baffled. She then befriended the Italian owner of a favourite restaurant, who brought her joints of black-market meat. Jennie caught them and scolded them fiercely. If the press found out, Ma would go to prison and Jennie *absolutely* would not bail her out.[4] Some habits never left Ma: she could not bear to patronize a private shop. From Cliveden Place, Ma would take the bus halfway across London to buy groceries from the Co-op.

Jennie never took Ma for granted. She hugged her warmly each night before going to bed. Of an evening, Ma and Dad would play draughts. Ma was deeply upset if she won; it meant the world was topsy-turvy. Ma Lee, wrote a good friend, 'was everything she didn't know she was; in particular a mighty influence . . . She exuded sanity in a dotty world, she was truly the mother-figure . . . She concentrated on the trivia which are the daily stuff of living and on the loving-kindness which so rarely blesses it.'[5]

To Lane End, and then, after the war, to Cliveden Place in London, and later to Asheridge Farm in the Chilterns, came a flow of friends. For walks, garden bowls (at which Nye loved to cheat), picnics, and *Tribune* cricket matches; for Nye's quick-silver teasing and his blue-sky discourses on poetry, music, philosophy; for the warmth of Jennie's welcome, for Ma's wonderful cooking, and, inevitably, an admiring peer at the pigs. They included the utterly beautiful Constance Cummings and her husband, the playwright and Labour MP Benn Levy (Jennie had got to know them through a former lover, Hubert Griffiths, who was drama critic on the *Evening Standard*). In the early days of their friendship, Constance offered to show willing by driving Jennie to Paris so that she could report on the 1936 elections. They booked into a hotel that turned out to be a brothel, and became lifelong friends. In the 1960s Jennie was to put a poised Constance on the Arts Council; in the 1980s Constance was to put a dishevelled Jennie into her clothes and bundle her off to the theatre.

There were other friends and acquaintances from the world of the arts: Graham Sutherland, Felix Topolski, Jacob Epstein, and, later, Henry Moore, to whom they were introduced by their mutual friend Alfred Hecht, framemaker and patron of painters. Their work began to decorate Jennie's walls. Old friends—Archie Lush, Nye's oldest friend, who became chief education officer in Glamorgan and who acted as Nye's agent in Ebbw Vale (Archie who knew better than anyone how to wind Nye up, was very rude about his cows—the most miserable lot he had ever seen, he said. It was Nye's fault for relying on AI. He should get himself a decent bull[6]); Suse Robinson, close to Jennie since university days; and Jennie Duncan, an old friend from Cowdenbeath who was now a leading member of the Post Office Workers' Union. And political friends—George Russell Strauss, with whom Jennie or Nye sometimes spent the occasional night when they were stuck in London; Barbara Castle, who stayed with them for a while when in 1942 William Mellor died—Jennie was kindness itself; Mervyn Stockwood, who later coaxed Nye and Jennie to his enthronement at Southwark Cathedral. Frank and Nance Cousins, he suspicious, she over-awed;* Israel and the feminist Becky Sieff, from whom Nye and Jennie learnt their Zionism; and the fragile Jane and Howard Samuel (who helped to fund *Tribune*). Michael Foot and Jill Craigie were among their closest friends, and they spent joyful weekends at Stratford together (seeing Ashcroft, Gielgud, Richardson, and Olivier). Nye thought Michael most aristocratic because he managed to punt them down the river without mishap. Jill Craigie recalls that whenever they went out to dinner, all eyes were on their table and on Nye, as peals of laughter echoed around the

* 'For years', wrote Nance to Jennie, 'I've thought of you as socialist Gods . . . I used to dream I could have been like you and wished I was. I now know I never had the capacity but you are still my "Ideal Woman of our Movement" . . . I know Nye is good for Frank (I don't think F. has much to offer Nye except $1\frac{1}{4}$ million votes) but don't let him know I said this'. N. Cousins to JL, 1 Apr. 1959, JL papers.

restaurant. Friends who came to their home thought Nye the best company in the world.

Not only friends, but one or two refugees made their way to Lane End: Viennese Trude, pale, slender, part Jewish, and aged 18 whom Ma took under her wing; Ushe, a beautiful young Polish painter and friend of the Sieffs, whom Nye taught to cook and to whom he wrote poems; Ilse, who had been working in republican Spain, and so could not return to Hitler's Berlin—Suse, in Berlin at the time, sent her on to Jennie. Ilse made an amicable and temporary marriage of convenience to a Welsh friend of Archie's and thereby qualified for a British passport. They were all in love with Nye. Then there were the American friends: Walter Reuther, John Gunter, Walter Lippman, and friends of friends, stationed in Britain, whom Jennie had got to know on her USA trips, who often arrived bearing gifts of rare and rationed goods, and who, in return, received memorable hospitality.

A more difficult visitor was Tommy, Jennie's brother. He had been a gentle, much-loved, and easily led child. At the age of 18 he had emigrated to Australia in search of the good life, but he never found it. He could not keep a job. He married a wife who looked just like Jennie. At the outbreak of war he joined the Australian Army, and began to drink heavily. He started to mistreat his children and the police were called in. In 1946 he was hospitalized for several months. The hospital got him off drink but on to (hard) drugs. He soon returned to the drink, and stayed on the drugs. He agreed to have a lobotomy to make him, in his own words, 'sane and sober', but the evening before it was due, he fled, took a ship to England, and made his way to Ma and Jennie. For years he sailed back and forth, working his passage to England and his family, and, when things got too much, taking shelter in hospital, staying a month or two, before returning to Australia, his wife and children, and hospital. His wife could not bear it and did not want him back; she begged Jennie to keep him in England. Jennie could not bear it and did not want him home; she posted him back to his wife.

Tommy wrote endless begging letters to Jennie, who was utterly distraught. She raged at Tommy for the pain he caused Ma and the risks his addictions presented to Nye. She did not spare him. She enclosed 'eighteen pounds and with it my contempt'. He was 'a dock rat rejected by every ship that sails'. For his part, he wanted his sister's ten-pound notes 'without a spate of scornful words, which I would not read'. He asked her for 'loans' for ship uniforms, for his debts, for his 'naughty smokes'. Jennie tried to ignore him, but he would not be ignored. He wrote to Nye, he sought Suse's help, he telegrammed Jenny Duncan's son-in-law Don Revie for ten pounds, he borrowed money from Jennie's secretary, and he cadged off Ma. If Jennie would not fund him, he would pester her friends instead. Jennie's nightmare was that Tommy would turn up on the Commons Terrace or shame them in some major scandal, and feed the press piranhas who were always circling Nye. As she wrote to Arianwen: 'it is a desperate worry having him at large knowing that he is not normal, either physically or mentally.'[7] Jennie rarely kept letters written to her, but she kept Tommy's. They were an insurance policy, a record of his deterioration in case things went badly wrong.

Suse, who regularly fished Tommy out of trouble, thought Jennie was being melodramatic. Perhaps she was. Tommy only ever wanted money and affection, and Jenny and Nye had plenty of money. He never caused them any serious embarrassment, but Jennie was not to know that. During the 1950s, as her parents aged and as she and Nye came under increasing political and emotional strain, Jennie could not forgive Tommy, her adored baby brother, for making them so vulnerable. She was fiercely protective of Ma and Nye; Tommy threatened them. Part of her wanted to ban him from their home altogether, but she could not do that to Ma, who loved Tommy just as Tommy loved her. He struggled. He extracted an invalidity pension from the services and sent half of it to his wife. He cut back on the drink, but he could do little about his 'smokes'. He wrote regularly to Ma, determinedly cheerful, vacuous letters. When she complained that she was getting forgetful, he told her: 'I am sure a little forgetfulness won't do any harm. I find it helps sometimes.' When Tommy came calling, Jennie was never home.

There was another set of guests that Jennie would cheerfully have done without: Nye's Tredegar family. Nye's mother and his sister Arianwen disliked Jennie, and his brother Billy was surly. Jennie refused to take pains with them, to win them over, as Nye in her place would surely have done. The Bevans disapproved of Lane End. Mrs Bevan could not understand why they wanted thatch and daub when she herself had moved on to solid stone. She was dismayed when she inspected the cottage to find that Jennie had no plans to buy a new three-piece suite, had little in the way of furniture, and almost nothing that was new. Jennie walked up and down the lane outside telling Nye he would have to choose. Either his mother went or Jennie did. Mrs Bevan went. She came back. On her next visit Ma put herself out to win her over, after which Mrs Bevan left rebuking Nye for ill-treating his mother-in-law.[8]

The Bevans wanted Nye to have a proper wife and a conventional marriage. Jennie was an exotic, whose glamour had unfortunately turned Nye's head. Furthermore, she was promiscuous—someone had kindly sent them an anonymous letter all about Frank Wise. She would not look after Nye; indeed, she needed her own mother to look after her (Ma even took the meat out of eggs for Jennie, Arianwen said scornfully). She was 'a spoilt girl' who had been 'badly brought up', unable to cook, sew, or nurse. Ma was 'a very nice woman who had ruined her daughter'. Jennie flaunted her independence, had her own career, kept her own name. She refused to be Mrs Bevan. She did not cultivate Tredegar. She failed to have Nye's children. She was, says Arianwen, 'a terrible woman'. They always darkly suspected, and rather hoped, that the marriage would not last.

It was a poisonous relationship. Nye did not marry until the age of 36. Until then and for more than a decade, Arianwen had been his secretary, his confidante, and Tredegar comrade, always ready to do battle for him (she was no mean local politician herself, and was later the first woman to chair Tredegar's Trades and Labour Council). Jennie displaced her. Arianwen had always put Nye first, 'even over our mother'. She vied with Jennie to be useful to Nye, to do his typing, his constituency correspondence, to proof-read his writing, all the support work that Jennie refused to do. 'I'm not his secretary', said Jennie, to Arianwen's disgust (she might have added, truthfully, that she did act as Nye's editor, but she refused to justify herself to Arianwen). Instead Jennie patronized Arianwen and behaved badly, especially when she was drunk, which she tended to be when her sister-in-law was around. In one of their hilarious but pointless scraps at Asheridge Farm late in the 1950s, when Arianwen had cooked and done the washing-up, Jennie told her to put the plates away, but Arianwen resisted. Said Jennie: 'If you don't, I'll drop them.'[9]

Arianwen was endlessly censorious, Jennie was deliberately outrageous.* Arianwen, like the efficient secretary she was, kept a mental list of the wrongs Jennie did Nye, which was still raw and unforgiven fifty years later. Nye, for example, wanted a dog (a big one), but Jennie thought it would make Ma and Dad nervous; Jennie would not allow Nye his own secretary—any secretary had also to be a companion to Ma after Dad died, so

* A lifetime later and after a wearying day, Nye told Jennie tenderly: 'You are my sister.' He meant, Jennie later realized, someone who was both lover and friend. But he forgot Jennie's literalness. She was 'hopping mad. I visualised his three sisters and decided a fourth was too many. I silently planned to get my own back by encouraging a male acquaintance all too easily encouraged.' Nye sensed her indignation and roared with laughter, saying, not for the first time, 'You bloody literal Scots'. JL papers, n.d.

good secretaries would not stay; Nye, a member of the Cabinet, had to do his own packing etc. etc. It is doubtful that any of this bothered Nye. He was well aware that Jennie had claws (on marrying her, he had warned an old friend, George Russell Strauss, not to be upset by it) and their scratching probably amused him. However, some of Arianwen's criticisms did strike home. Nye had his share of ill health, and Jennie, Arianwen noted shrewdly, was 'frightened' by illness: she did not like visiting Nye in hospital, and when Nye was sick at home, she would 'escape' by going to the Commons or taking to the bottle; Jennie 'didn't want to look after my brother', she left it to others. Arianwen was not the only person to criticize Jennie for her handling of Nye's final illness. She remained very bitter about Nye's last months.

The two women also wrangled over the Tredegar house. It was a handsome double-fronted stone house in Queen's Square, which Nye helped his mother to buy in 1938. A century before it had served as the town's workhouse—the irony of domesticating it must have pleased Nye. As money was tight at the time, Jennie had tactlessly suggested to Nye's family that they might prefer a council house instead; this was not well received in a family determined to better themselves. After his mother died, the house passed to Arianwen, who lived there with her husband and son. Nye used it for his monthly constituency visits. At the end of the war, when Jennie and Nye sold Lane End and made their home in London, they hoped that the Tredegar house might serve as their country cottage for the occasional weekend and the summer break. They did not think they could afford, or justify, a second home in the country. The Tredegar house, run by Arianwen, would give Nye peace, privacy, comfort, and his beloved Wales, and would free Jennie from the need to housekeep.

It seemed a good idea at the time. The house was roomy, with four bedrooms—Nye and Jennie took over three of them. The two large front bedrooms became their bedroom and sitting-room, and they evicted Arianwen's young son Robert from his room to give themselves a private bathroom (only to find that the boiler could not cope with their bath). Robert's parents slept in a back bedroom, and Robert was banished downstairs. Grey velvet furniture, a state-of-the-art hi-fi system, and a clover-coloured carpet arrived from Heals. The carpet quickly showed wine stains. Said Jennie, on her next visit: 'I see you haven't cleaned the spots.' 'Certainly not', said Arianwen. Jennie then ostentatiously and ineffectually dusted her rooms with one of Arianwen's best pillow-cases. When Arianwen complained, Jennie apologized. She had not realized it was a pillow-case, let alone one of Arianwen's best.

Nye and Jennie were obsessive about their privacy. Given the harassment they endured from the press, they had good cause to be. They liked to go for long walks, have pub lunches, get away from people. Once, when they visited Tintern Abbey, Nye was recognized—he left immediately; his visit had been ruined. On another occasion they were about to go to Tredegar when Nye discovered that a young niece was going to be there at the same time. Nye stated that if she came, he and Jennie would stay away—she would interrupt their peace and quiet. Arianwen was outraged. It was her home and their niece. They shouted at each other, but Arianwen would not back down. Neither would Nye, and he and Jennie went to Buscot Park instead, to the home of their bachelor Labour friend Lord Faringdon.

The Bevan-Norris family blamed Jennie—they always did—even though the explosion had come from Nye. Nye was upset; he could not understand why Arianwen of all people failed to understand their need for privacy. Jennie, upset for Nye, tried to make peace. She wrote a couple of long letters to her sister-in-law; not accidentally, one suspects, she used the headed stationery of Buscot Park. Jennie was self-justifying, self-pitying even, but the undeniable strain they were under shows through as she tried to convey to Arianwen what she and Nye had to endure in London. Arianwen, she conceded, might think they had been unreasonable, but she should understand:

> in some ways we are the poorest and most vulnerable of your many friends and relatives. We are not youngsters with the world all before us, able to go off and live in hostels or even hotels. We have tried large hotels and small ones. Always we are pursued by the insensitive rubber-neckers. They simply cannot understand that the more public work people do, the more profound is their need of privacy at times. We have also friends in cottages and friends in mansions who genuinely enjoy having us to stay with them and give us a riotous welcome. But again you have to pay for that hospitality in the nervous wear and tear of endlessly going over political issues till you scream and screech inside yourself like a blunt gramophone needle playing over and over again the same old records. It would be too much to expect even the kindest of friends not to involve us in that way . . .
>
> Such is the excessive pressures of our London life that the most precious thing you have to offer is sanctuary for brief spells against the pressures of any additional egos. It is not a matter of disliking the people we must sometimes run away from. We leave behind good friends and relatives in London. It is simply that there are times when we simply *must* have room to breathe freely without too many hands clutching at us. We need a tranquil trusting and trusted atmosphere.

Jennie then turns practical. She did not expect that they would be in Tredegar for more than seven or ten weeks a year; and they would always let Arianwen know when they were coming. When they were not there, Arianwen was free to have whom she wanted to stay, providing that the dust-sheets remained undisturbed in their sitting room. When she and Nye *were* there, they must insist that there were no other guests:

> You see Arianwen, it is not true to say we have our room and the rest of the house. We do not even have our room unless there is a tranquil easy atmosphere in the whole home. If Ni and I were more selfish we would insulate ourselves and be unaffected by others under the same roof. As it is we cannot help but be aware, responsive and so invaded.
>
> . . . If you had come to us and said this is a hungry or homeless child whose need to be put up is more pressing than your need to be left in peace, you know quite well we would have been responsive. As it was, a youngster with a good home, father, mother, all the prospects and opportunities in the world before her, had to be humoured even at our psychological expense. We could not be indifferent and under the same roof, to the needs of a stranger, still less of a youngster we are attached to. So I repeat again, our need to run away from people sometimes is not a mark of dislike or indifference. It is the reverse.[10]

They also wrangled over money. The Bevan-Norris family thought Nye and Jennie were mean and did not pay their way at weekends in Tredegar. There were no gifts, no Christmas presents. Nye was very fond of Robert, his favourite nephew, who went on to read PPE at Oxford. Robert stayed with them at the farm quite often, but, to his chagrin, Jennie ignored him. Nye and Robert chatted about books together. When Robert confessed that he was bored by *Dr Zhivago*, Nye professed himself much relieved. Robert shared his mother's dislike of Jennie: she was a 'hard and selfish' woman. He remembers when his father came with him to Asheridge and they were asked what they would like to drink. His father said whisky, Robert said beer. Jennie commented immediately: 'The father's a working-class man with upper-class tastes, the son is at Oxford with working-class tastes.' Robert was mortified.[11]

Behind it all lay one very simple judgement from Tredegar: Jennie was not a proper wife to Nye. It was quickly noted that in an age when married couples invariably shared a double bed whatever the state of their marriage, Nye and Jennie had separate beds in their Lane End cottage. At Cliveden Place Nye had his own small bedroom. At Asheridge farm they had separate bedrooms, each with a double bed. Friends speculated. John Beaven, a journalist friend on the *Daily Herald*, asked Nye outright whether his marriage was in trouble. No, no, said Nye, it was just that they had 'incompatible temperatures'. He was 'fiery', Jennie was 'icy'.[12] She felt the cold. Jennie's version was that they had incompatible clocks. She was a lark, Nye an owl. This way, he could come late to bed without disturbing her. In any case, she thought a double bed was 'a recipe for staleness or worse'.

Nye had been sexually mesmerized by Jennie. He loved her vivid gypsy looks. He would stop on the street or in the underground to gaze at her and say: 'You must be painted.'[13] Despite his fast living before his marriage, he had remained somewhat puritan. Jennie, however, was sexually shameless and Nye loved it. Passionate, vibrant, and uninhibited, Jennie must have been 'fantastic in bed', commented one of her woman friends. She always gave herself generously to men, said another. When Nye was courting her, Jennie was experienced enough to note that 'the chemistry' between them was 'all right'.[14] Among her papers is an undated carbon of a letter, written to Michael Foot after Nye's death:

> Going round with Ni was like surf riding on the Niagara Falls at times. You had to be agile or you would be drowned in the sparkling, tireless movement and ebullience. I could do it and survive in the days before I became greatly emotionally involved. It amused me, it was a stimulating challenge. We both enjoyed it and kept our exchange of raffish confidences to ourselves. After all we were both suffering from an excess of virtue on the public sector. There had to be a let up somewhere.
>
> What you must understand was that neither of us quite understood what was happening to us—Ni no more than me—there was the strong undercurrent of mutual attraction, mutual understanding, but for quite a bit we were both absorbed, amused, flattered, by our separate worlds. It could be that it was my very separateness and fear of conventional bonds that kept both of us happy and carefree together until, without deliberately willing it, we had reached the point of no return. What would have happened if F. had lived, I do not know. I have always told myself that I loved him too much to leave him although I had no scruples about passing adventures but how can I be sure. How can I know that whatever the mess and heartbreaks, Ni and I would in any case have found too much in common to drift apart. I simply do not know. That was a different world, different values, different emotions, and we each became different in the more than a quarter of a century together.

Jennie and Nye both knew it would not be a conventional marriage (looking back, Jennie wrote, 'To Nye I was friend and mistress—never wife. The very word offended me as ugly. Nye would not have wanted or been content to accept a "wife" in the conventional sense').[15] Neither of them was faintly sentimental nor had romantic expectations of married life. For many years, Nye was more committed to Jennie than Jennie to Nye. He was in love with Jennie, whereas she saw in him a friend and a comrade. She was deeply fond of him, but not in love with him—having loved Frank profoundly, she knew the difference. Of the two, she was the more likely to have passing affairs. Since leaving T'ang, she had slept around. In theory, neither Nye nor Jennie placed much value on sexual fidelity; in practice, Jennie was often irritated 'by his tom-cat protectiveness'. When Nye met her off the boat-train from an overseas trip, usually with a besotted male in tow, Nye would loudly berate her for her apparent inconstancy. They enjoyed such exchanges enormously. It was their way of flirting in public.

During the early years of their marriage, Jennie remained restless and uncertain, not at all sure that it would last. Some part of her still grieved for Frank. She had not wanted to marry Nye, preferring an affair, but he browbeat her into marriage because neither of them could afford the risk of scandal as Jennie tried to find another seat. She did not trust lifelong monogamy and she was not at all sure she trusted Nye. She suffered a spell of acute depression. Nye took her to Wales for a month of walking and seabathing, teased her, made her laugh, and unobtrusively brought her through it. Her work at the time was not going well. She wanted a winnable seat, but her ILP affiliation meant that the Labour Party would not give her a clear run. She needed to be free to seek other seats and nurse them. She was a journalist and an ILP lecturer by occupation and an itinerant by temperament. She was reluctant to settle and put down roots: 'I have a lot of restlessness in me', she wrote in 1939.[16] She was apprehensive that marriage to Nye would constrain her and limit her freedom.

Had they remained cooped up for much longer in their cramped Guilford Street flat, she might have left him. When she went out of an evening, Nye could never be sure whether she would come back the same night or the next week.

> Gradually, very gradually, a reversal came about in our relationship. To begin with I needed his protection, to be shielded by him from the pain caused by the death of an earlier lover, to be brought back to living and loving again. Before we were married I did not think that I could love so much again. Ni said ruefully that nothing came to him easily. That was true of all his political battles. It was also true in his earlier relations with me. I was cavalier because I believed him to be cavalier. I reckoned marriage gave me protective colouring as I badly needed to be shielded from gossip if I was to continue in public life. But how long would it last? How soon before either or both of our wayward selves would be wandering off in all directions.

The truth is we were neither cavalier. We needed roots, deep, steady roots, that became stronger with the passing of time. We needed to be able to trust, to be emotionally secure, and we needed this increasingly . . .

Maybe too, no, not maybe, quite certainly, the fact that four years after our marriage my parents came to live with us was another steadying factor. Even if, in moments of selfishness or caprice, I might have been willing to hurt a young, strong, aggressive & seemingly indestructible Ni, I was not prepared to hurt *them*. I imagine it was the same with him.[17]

Purchasing Lane End, and bringing her parents to live there, gave her a sense of place, and a new sense of responsibility that matured her. Nye's uncomplaining tolerance of her lengthy overseas lecture tours, to New York, Moscow, Vienna, and Berlin, allayed her fears that he expected her to become a traditional stay-at-home wife: 'We never quarrelled about private, domestic matters. I could do as I pleased. I could have my own way. But there were times when he had an infuriating habit of looking at me with what I called his Mona Lisa smile, and saying, "I shall win in the end." He did.'[18]

Her respect for Nye deepened as, together, they campaigned for the Austrian socialists, for Abyssinia, for the Spanish republicans, for Czechoslovakia, for anti-Fascists from every country, always side by side, always on the losing side. Soberly, the country moved towards war. The war made Nye the leader of the parliamentary Left. He was vilified and scorned as he insisted that Churchill remain accountable to the Commons, that Churchill's handling of the war was not above reproach. Nye was now the covenanter of Jennie's childhood, who held fast to his faith, and did so with courage and grace. Marriage to Nye, Jennie came to see, was not an impediment to her socialism; it was a means of achieving it. Her affection deepened into love and utter trust.

She no longer looked elsewhere. 'Affairs aren't worth it', she told Suse. Nye had a more casual attitude to such matters. Welsh comrades wondered, as they still do, if he was bi-sexual. But, other than the jokey drunken sexual encounter that Nye allegedly had with Tom Driberg on a Commons sofa, it seems unlikely.[19] Nye did not strike his friends as lecherous. In so far as they thought about it at all, they regarded Nye as uninterested in sex, even something of a prude, with only one dirty joke in his entire repertoire, and that one pretty tame.* He disliked it if Jennie wore a low cut dress, as she often did—he did not want a tart for a wife,

* 'What did the young man give his bride for a wedding present? A nightdress with fur around the hem. To keep her neck warm' (information to the author).

he would tell her. When she bought a cheap fur coat and came home to show him, Nye, who was still in bed, opened an eye and said: 'I don't mind you looking like a prostitute; I do mind you looking like an unsuccessful one.'[20]

This was the same Nye that Jennie recalled walking round the garden at Lane End, stripped to the waist, a glass of red wine in his hand singing: 'When apples are ripe & nuts are brown, petticoats up & trousers down.' Jennie, struggling not to laugh, tried to hush him—the press haunted the public lane outside their hedge. Nye suffused their life with laughter.[21]

There is no evidence that Nye engaged in any serious affairs, but plenty to suggest that he took his chances. And his chances were considerable, for he mesmerized men and women alike. At parties, women would sit at his feet, often literally so; when the flirting got too heavy, Jennie would abruptly take him home.

Nye ran considerable risks for a seemingly perfunctory outcome. He gave one of Jennie's woman friends dinner in the Commons, and then took her on to the Savoy Hotel for the night. She awoke next morning to find he had gone—lacking in manners, she thought. She didn't think much of his style in bed either. When he next made a pass, she rejected him. That didn't stop him pouncing on her at Lane End and at Asheridge, even when Jennie was around. During the war, Barbara Castle arrived at their flat one morning to talk over some political matter with Nye, to find him alone and listening, enrapt, to Beethoven's 'Eroica' symphony, a bottle of wine half drunk on the table in front of him. He made an amorous pass at her. Barbara disentangled herself with some difficulty and much embarrassment, Nye shouting at her as she fled that she was a prissy provincial miss. Others in their circle also rebuffed him: he was too crude. Jill Craigie drove home with Nye late one night, and as they approached Hyde Park Corner, he put his arm around her and started to fumble. 'Nye', said Jill, 'what do you think you're doing? What would you say if a policeman saw you?' Unabashed came the reply, 'Officer, I would say, can you blame me?'[22]

It was widely believed that one of their refugees at Lane End was 'Nye's woman'; that an actress was his mistress. Then there was the curious case in 1954 when Nye crashed his car into a coach. There were no casualties, and he sped off. He afterwards told Jennie, who was away in the States, that he had not stopped nor called the police because he was anxious to get home to Ma; he did not want her worried. The police prosecuted. It was rumoured that he had a well-known titled woman with him in the car and he was shielding her from scandal.[23]

Did Jennie know? Not consciously perhaps. Yet she may have sensed more than she knew. She chose, said one friend who had received Nye's attentions, 'to overlook his weaknesses'. After Nye's death, Jennie said to Jill Craigie: 'I do hope Nye had some nice affairs.'[24]

Their marriage struck Shirley Williams as very much alive. In no way was it a dead marriage, an empty shell. Although they were not demonstrative in public, they remained intensely aware of each other. Nye might abuse her affectionately in front of others, call her boy or child, but he was never nasty to her, never said anything to wound her or belittle her. Nye deferred to her formally, but none of their friends doubted that he was the dominant figure in their marriage, nor did they doubt that Jennie relished the role of consort. Friends remember them on a sunny day curled up together in a hammock in the garden; they recall Nye deep in an armchair at Asheridge, gesturing expansively, Jennie sitting on the floor at his feet, her head resting against his knees. Nye's nephew Robert describes Jennie coming downstairs one morning at Tredegar, pink and flushed, saying happily: 'Nye was very loving last night.' It had surprised Jennie, thought Robert; it certainly surprised him.[25] By then, Nye was being treated for high blood pressure; and though the drugs used in the 1950s would not have affected his libido, one of their side-effects can be impotence. If that was the effect of his medication, it could have made Nye a less urgent but more tender and attentive lover.

Apart from a scrawled note, there are no letters from Jennie to Nye, and only a handful from Nye to Jennie, all of them deeply loving. Nye was acutely sensitive to her moods. In 1953 on his visit to India he was writing home worried about her health: 'I know you will have no chance of complete recovery until the Spring.' And then: 'You know I love you so much, and can think of little else when I am away from you.' Writing a couple of years later from Scotland where he was campaigning, he worried that Jennie sounded depressed on the phone:

> I went to bed full of conjectures and worries about you. I realise that your vitality is low just now, particularly when you need it most.
>
> But cheer up. It will soon be over, and you must keep in mind that the outcome, whatever it may be, will be all right for us . . .
>
> Darling I love you very much and I am always upset when I think you are worried or unwell. So please buck up and remember we have a whole summer ahead of us to spend at the farm.
>
> You must hug the thought of our secret happiness and not let public duties weigh on you too heavily.
>
> Lots of love and kisses, my darling,
>
> Ni.

In India in 1957, on a formal visit as Shadow Foreign Minister, he wished she was with him. 'We always enjoy ourselves so much more when we are away together. At least I do', he added endearingly. Instead, he would visit the Taj and whisper her name by moonlight. During the 1959 general election, he wrote to her from the West Country, signing off: 'I send you all my love my Darling and I live for the time when we can be together again.'[26] They did not have much time left.

They had no children. Tredegar believed that Nye wanted a family and they found that hardest of all to forgive. However, in their early years together Jennie was not ready for children. She was almost 30 when she married yet still unsettled. She worried about the threat of fascism darkening Europe, and did not want to bring children into such a world. More to the point, she could not look after herself, let alone small infants. As she said, with their lifestyle, their children would have had two fathers and no mother—it would have fallen to Ma to bring them up. Jennie had no urge to have children. She was not at all maternal and never went soft over small babies (nor kittens, puppies, nor lovers, come to that). She was fond of individual children: the Mackie youngsters and Pat Llewellyn-Davies's children remember her with affection. And they adored Nye. He had a fund of rhymes and stories that endlessly enchanted them. John Mackie remembers him putting the worms on the rod of his 7-year-old son and exulting with him when he caught a six-inch trout. Nye would bowl for hours to his neighbour's two sons on an improvised cricket pitch.[27] However, he would say cheerfully, a litter or none. It's a woman's choice.

And Jennie chose to have none. She was sitting on the back lawn at Tredegar in 1935, a year after her marriage, and Arianwen asked her if she and Nye expected to have children. 'Oh no,' said Jennie, 'I will not have children. I've made that very clear.' 'But what if you did', pressed Arianwen. 'These things happen.' 'If I had an accident I would have an abortion.' 'That's illegal', said Arianwen, shocked. 'I've got some money by me, a hundred pounds,' replied Jennie, 'and I would go to Holland. I know exactly what to do.'[28]

It is hard to see how children would have fitted into their lives, and not just for practical reasons. There was no emotional space within their marriage, too much else was happening. Early on Jennie did have a miscarriage (there is no suggestion that she went to Holland). Ma thereafter believed that Jennie could not have children, or so she told Arianwen. However, Jennie never told her closest women friends that she was unable to have children, only that she and Nye chose not to. Nye had 'asked me with his unfailing love if I was sure I did not want a child. If so not to leave it too late.' When, at 40, Jennie was not unwilling to become pregnant, Dan Davies, Nye's doctor, 'advised me not to have a child at that late age'.[29] A few years later she went rushing in to Suse's flat thinking she might be pregnant. She went off to Harley Street in some excitement for a check, but she was not pregnant; her age had misled her. Jennie never regretted the fact that she had no children. Among the hundreds of photos of Jennie and Nye, only a handful show them with a child. Always it was Nye who held the child, whose face was turned towards it. Jennie looks on, indulgently.

*

During the war, they lived at Lane End. There was local bombing, but nothing within a mile of the cottage. In London, they rented a small flat at Endsleigh Street, south of Euston Station, sometimes staying overnight with London friends if they could not get back home. Spare clothes were scattered in suitcases across London in case they were bombed out. As the war came to an end, they took a hard decision. Jennie now had a winnable seat at Cannock, and they both faced long hours in the Commons after the next election. Reluctantly, they realized they must make their main home in London.

Jennie decided that they should live close, but not too close, to the Commons. She scoured the streets around Sloane Square. She had a wide choice: many good houses had been abandoned during the war. Finally they bought a twelve-year remainder lease on 23 Cliveden Place, a five-storey stuccoed Regency house, tall and narrow, with enough rooms for all of them. French windows at the back opened on to a paved garden. They sold Lane End for three thousand pounds to their good friend Israel Sieff. Two days before they were due to move in, Nye phoned Jennie with the news: the street had stopped a V2 rocket: part of the front of the house was now in the back, the roof was damaged, the basement flooded, and all the windows were out.[30] Ma and Dad retreated, and Jennie and Nye camped in a couple of rooms, abandoning the rest of the house. Once the war was over, Ma and Jennie put each floor into shape.

It did not take long. By August 1945, the Bevans were at home to the *Daily Mirror*. There was a large photo of Jennie and Nye at a beautifully laid dining-table having lunch (it looks like baked potatoes with salad), and a smaller picture of them on the sofa, Nye stretched out, Jennie curled up against him. The *Mirror* approved of Jennie's taste: Cliveden Place was 'very pretty and every square inch a home'. Jennie and Ma had painted the walls and ceilings in dusky cream, the fabrics were a reseda green, there were polished wood floors, good oriental rugs, a wall lined with books, and well-used furniture brought from Lane End. In an affectionate (but surely gently teasing) article, the *Mirror* reported:

Jennie Lee might have walked out of any fashion photo. She fits perfectly into the polished little gem of a house . . . Curled up beside her husband on a settee in her bandbox Regency home in London S.W., she explains the situation quite simply. 'I'm a revolutionary Socialist', she said. 'But in my home life I'm a real Scottish Conservative. I believe that, however big a public figure one may be, your private life should be your own secret. That is the main reason why my husband and I never speak on the same platforms if we can help it—it looks too much like a circus.

'I must say that the idea has its drawbacks, though,' she added. 'The first speech I made at my old constituency was interrupted by an old Scottish farmer who wanted to know who had brought this woman into the constituency. "She's on the stage," he moaned. "She takes her clothes off in public." Me, mistaken for Gipsy Rose Lee!

'So I told Nye he would have to say something to undo the impression when he spoke, and all he could think of was to say that the way to live happily with your wife was never to see her.'

. . . Things move as fast as a news-reel in the Bevan home. Smoky, the nerve-shot Siamese cat, streaking about the place. Aneurin Bevan singing at the top of his lungs in a garden which pleases him beyond measure—it is flagged and he does not need to do any gardening. The two of them owning a type-writer each and grabbing for the one in good working order; row upon row of gramophone records. Slippery polished floors with mats to trip the unwary, treasure maps of the Empire pinned up on the study walls and 'Nye' answering questions about his share of the housework by saying, 'Only the aristocrats work—the working man dodges work all he can' . . .

As for her interests outside politics, Jennie Lee says quite unselfconsciously, 'My husband is my hobby'.[31]

Cliveden Place served them very well during those frantically busy years of a Labour government. Its lease was due to expire in the mid 1950s, and they would then have to find another home. Nye left the Cabinet in April 1950, the Labour Party left office in October 1951. There was less need to be in London, and a desperate need to be away from party feuds and press attention. Nye longed to live in the country again; Jennie, who had always preferred to live in London, now longed for some privacy. One of the drawbacks of Cliveden Place was that it had no back door. The press camped on the pavement outside and reported every movement. When in 1952 Dad was dying and a flow of friends were coming in to see him, the *Daily Express* put cameras in the house opposite to report on what they assumed were the secret cabals of the Labour Left.[32] Jennie and Nye felt under siege. One evening they returned home from the Commons to find that someone had pushed fireworks through the letter-box, setting their hall carpet on fire. They had had enough.

Jennie thought that they might buy another large cottage like Lane End. Nye had grander ideas. During the 1951 election, they had become good friends with the Mackies. John Mackie was a delightful and immensely tall man, a Scottish farmer and staunch socialist, who had advised the Labour Party on the nationalization of land. They started to share holidays in Scotland, fishing, roaming the moors, Nye of course insisting that the Scottish hills were in every way inferior to his beloved Black Mountains. Eyeing John Mackie's two thousand acres in Scotland and one thousand acres in Lincolnshire, Nye decided that farming was just the thing. Impressed by the pigs of Mackie's son, he decided that pigs were just the thing too.

Nye started to look around. To his immense delight, he came across an advertisement for Asheridge, a handsome brick and tiled period farmhouse, part of which dated back to the mid-seventeenth century. It was set high in the Chilterns, three miles from the railway station at Chesham, and only thirty miles from London. In surveyor-speak, it was originally the 'gentleman's residence' of a much larger farm. It now came with fifty-two acres, a magnificent timbered tithe barn, a pair of 1940s cottages, a range of flint, timber, and brick outbuildings, and a bed of lavender. Nye took one look and set his heart on it. John Mackie gave it his approval, and with the help of a £6,000 mortgage, they bought it for £9,000.[33]

Jennie, Nye, and Ma moved in. Almost immediately they had to call in a doctor to attend to Ma's chest cold. He found she had a suppurating abscess; cancer had eaten away part of her breast. Ma had refused to go to the doctor, and it was now untreatable. As her own mother had died of breast cancer, both Ma and Jennie knew what suffering it entailed. When the doctor broke the news to Jennie, she collapsed, crying hysterically in Nye's arms. Nye held her and calmed her, saying: 'Life will never be the same for us again. Ma leaves too many gracious memories.'[34] When she regained control of herself, Jennie firmly told Ma it was an abscess, and Ma professed to believe her. In fact, Ma was to live another eight years, to outlive Nye himself, happy, busy, and untroubled by pain.

In that summer of 1954 Nye went off to the Far East on a parliamentary delegation, and Jennie and Ma took on the house. They knocked down walls, installed central heating, and decorated and furnished it in their own inimitable way. White walls, polished wood, and stone-flagged floors (as

Constance Cummings said, all Jennie's houses looked the same); old furniture (the modern light oak of Jennie's early furnishings had been now replaced by rosewood and mahogany), and colourfully patterned rugs, cushions, and curtains. Over the years Jennie acquired some good antique stuff: a Georgian commode, a handsome Louis XIV bed, Georgian silver candlesticks and coffee service, valuable bronzes, and enamels. She also acquired paintings and lithographs by Henry Moore, Graham Sutherland, and John Piper.

Asheridge was splendidly light and spacious. The heavy front door opened into a fine double sitting-room, with its beamed ceiling and generous windows; for most of the year logs burned in its inglenook fireplace, while in summer the fragrance of Jennie's roses and tobacco plants scented the room. Off the inner hall was a dining-room where a dozen could sit around the handsome refectory table that had been a wedding present, a kitchen, and a small sitting-room (converted from the old dairy) for Ma. A wide oak staircase led to four large bedrooms, as well as dressing-rooms and bathrooms, and above these a vast attic bedroom to which Nye would retreat. An adjacent flint and brick barn became a guest cottage, complete with bar. One friend who came to stay was Pierre Mendès-France. He brought with him Henri Cartier-Bresson, who prowled around their house taking wonderful photographs of Nye and Jennie at home—Nye appears expansive, Jennie quiet and a trace wistful, their sitting-room filled with light, colour, warmth, comfort, and friends. Asheridge became the home they loved most.

They refused to sell any of the land; it gave the house the privacy they craved. It would have been sensible to have leased the land to neighbouring farmers, and forget about farming themselves, but when they bought Asheridge it was still a small working farm with fifteen pedigree Guernseys in milk and sixty hens. Nye fancied himself as a farmer, and Jennie, although no countrywoman herself, did not have the heart to veto it. The farm came with a farm manager and a cowman, who would run it on a day-to-day basis.

They hoped they would break even or better, but the farm always ran at a loss, although its capital value steadily increased.[35] John Mackie, who kept an eye on it for them, says it was too small to be profitable, let alone to offer a living. The outgoings never ended. Gutters, fencing, glazing, wiring, machinery. They upgraded the cowsheds, added to the calf-pens, extended the pullet-houses, rebuilt sheds to house foodstuffs and implements, and constructed new piggeries. Cows, they found, made a profit; poultry and pigs did not. Within three years they built up the Guernsey herd to nearly sixty cattle, added several hundred pullets whose eggs went off to the local packing-station, and two hundred and fifty sows and piglets.

They had persistent problems with staff: they could not or would not keep them. The two existing men ('neither of them particularly good', remembered John Mackie) went. Another farmhand was kicked by a pig and injured his back. He returned to work and decided to sue. Nye, worried about publicity, sought the advice of the NFU, and then sacked him, after going through due process, because his work was unsatisfactory. Other farmhands came and went in fairly rapid succession. Jennie believed that they exploited Nye, that they worked harder for employers who were harsher. Nye and Jennie, it is clear, were uneasy employers; perhaps they were unlucky employers as well.

The farm came in useful for tax purposes. Jennie, who did the accounts, quite properly claimed their farm costs and farm improvements against farm income. She also set against tax almost all of the work done to their Asheridge house, since, as she ingeniously explained to her accountant, the sitting-room was also an office, the dining-room was also used by the staff, and the kitchen supplied hot water and hot food for the farm. Their domestic rates, domestic staff, insurance, mortgage, maintenance, heating, lighting, cleaning and phone bills, as well as a new bathroom or a new car, were all necessary expenses incurred by a working farm to be set against tax.[36]

Their finances were complicated, as, in addition to their parliamentary salaries, they had extensive free-lance earnings from journalism, growing investment income, as well as the company accounts of the farm—all governed by different tax rules. As Jennie was later to confess to Arnold Goodman when he tried to sort out her financial affairs: 'Whether items that should have been farm got into private and private got into farm, I cannot be absolutely sure. Maybe that is the root of the confusion.'[37] She was never dishonest. She meticulously documented 2*s*. 6*d*. (12½p) for bone meal, and 2*s*. (10p) for brushes. However, she never learned the ground rules about allowances and expenses governing their various incomes and accounts, why some expenses were permitted and others not. She darkly suspected she was being cheated. She relied on her accountants to protect her from the tax man, and, as she had no great faith in them, relied on Arnold Goodman to protect her from her accountants. Additional tax bills always came as a great surprise.

As well as having problems with the tax man, Jennie also all her life had problems with tradesmen (which became worse as she grew older and more *grande dame*). Even where she had no quarrel with the work done or the size of the bill, she would delay payment for several months, despite letters from small firms fearful that they were going to the wall and begging to be paid. She would then tell them they were being importunate and in future she would take her business elsewhere. On one occasion the cowsheds needed new concrete floors. The final job was rather rough, and Jennie refused to pay. The contractor politely explained that the surface was pitted because they had let the cows walk on the concrete before it was set. She could see the hoof marks for herself. Jennie did not dispute this, but she delayed payment for months. On another occasion, on a contract for the bathroom of the guest cottage, Jennie altered the specification and agreed verbally to the additional cost. According to one builder, she was 'most emphatic and told our Manager he worried too much' (which sounds just like Jennie). When the bill came in, well over the original estimate, Jennie was horrified—her trust had been abused, she had been rooked: 'I am very shocked at this behaviour.' She sent a part cheque in settlement. When, after several months of acrimonious correspondence and threats of solicitors' letters, it was clear that the contractor was not going to back down, Jennie grudgingly paid up, stating: 'I do not propose to continue this correspondence . . . We will not want your services for any future work.'[38] There are many similar letters among her papers—Jennie did not behave well towards tradesmen: she was never precise about what she required and was then deeply shocked at what she got.

The farm gave Nye, especially, huge pleasure. He immersed himself in it. Jack Buchan remembered him sitting up all night nursing a sick cow, its head in his lap.[39] They acquired a new vocabulary of fertilizers and agricultural implements. On one of their picnics, John Mackie teased Jennie when she discarded the shells of her hard-boiled eggs: 'That's litter, Jennie.' 'No, John, its lime. Its good for the soil.' He was much amused.[40] They lived the country life, and used the local pub, the Blue Ball (the landlord shared their politics); they shopped locally at Chesham and ran heavy bills at the town's two wine shops. They also joined the NFU. Nye would sooner buy a new cow than a new suit, Jennie grumbled; he was a 'kulak', claimed Barbara Castle. Shortly before he died, Nye was negotiating to buy another field to enlarge the farm. Life at Asheridge gave Nye and Jennie a private life outside London politics.

It was not, however as private a life as they wanted. The press plagued them relentlessly, hiding behind their garden hedge, eavesdropping on their walks with friends, erecting floodlights on scaffolding to get better photographs of them and their house, pestering the locals to give them gossip. None the less, the farm kept them sane. It also gave them a very comfortable and stylish home to which they could retreat, bring friends, and drink Nye's cases of good Spanish rioja.

For money was not short in the mid-1950s. Although parliamentary pay was poor and there were no allowances for office costs, earnings from journalism effectively doubled their individual salaries of £1,250[41], giving them an annual reported income of over £5,000 in 1955–6. The farm ran at a loss, but it reduced their tax bill and heavily subsidized their family life. In addition, there were large undisclosed gifts from friends. Sir Charles Trevelyan had always been a generous benefactor, funding election expenses, a small car, holidays, and health care for Jennie and her family. Howard Samuel, the moody millionaire who owned large chunks of Mayfair as well as McGibbon & Kee, had underwritten many of Nye's political expenses, including the deficit on *Tribune*. One evening in 1956 after he had been gambling, he gave Nye an unsolicited and no-strings gift of £1,000. As Samuel won or lost more than that in any evening's play, Jennie had no compunction about taking the money, but was a bit baffled as to what she should do with it. She decided to open a 'special' account—special in that 'it was intended to ease the strains for us a bit . . . or when we wish to go abroad to rest or study conditions'.[42] Special also in that she failed to declare it to the tax man for many years (until the *News of the World* started to nose around in 1967). Samuel continued to contribute cash, and advised them on how to invest it. Another wealthy friend, the band-leader Jack Hylton, quietly added £2,500 in 1959, some of which went to help political friends with their election expenses. Windfalls of many pounds and five-shilling postal orders sent by anonymous admirers, all went into the special account.

In consequence, Nye and Jennie lived a more affluent lifestyle than they could earn for themselves, with first-class fares on Cunard, flowers from Moyses Stevens, and some private health care,[43] taxis from Harrods, abundant staff (their secretary paid by Howard Samuel), and quality wines. To Nye's and Jennie's own modest savings held in National Savings Certificates was now added a substantial shares portfolio in Land Securities and in blue-chip companies such as Marks and Spencer, generating a growing investment income (by the late 1960s, Jennie's investment income surpassed her parliamentary salary). It was clear to all that Nye and Jennie did not need to stint themselves, and that jibes about their champagne socialist lifestyle were not unmerited. To a degree, they were bankrolled by their friends. No favours were asked or dealt—Nye and Jennie could not be bought (Nye, after all, steered clear of Beaverbrook's offer of financial help precisely because it might carry a price). They experienced not a scrap of puritan guilt about it all, Nye because he laid claim to 'aristocratic' tastes, Jennie because she believed Nye was entitled to all the pampering she could arrange for him.

Nor were they capable of hypocrisy. Nye was the mining MP who had been the playboy of the West End world, who had taken Jennie to the Café Royale to propose to her, insisting that anyone could live like a millionaire for five minutes; he was also the minister who refused to build 'rabbit-hutches', but demanded two WCs in every council house. In Nye's New Jerusalem everyone would display aristocratic tastes, and until then he would indulge his own. Jennie, who was unpossessive about her own money, was unapologetic about enjoying other people's. She and Nye were, in her words, 'fantastically' busy in the socialist cause. If other people wanted to aid socialism by aiding them, that was fine by Jennie.

*

The 'special account' was for luxuries and trips abroad: they managed holidays in Austria and Italy during the later 1940s, and Italy displaced Spain as the country Jennie grew to love most. She rather liked it when Nye went off on trips without her, treasuring the space. Nye, however, was increasingly woebegone if she went off and left him alone. He wanted Jennie with him. As Labour was out of office during the 1950s, they could afford to travel, be briefed on international affairs at first hand, and visit old friends, to whom they remained attractively loyal. Many of these friendships began in the late 1920s and 1930s, when young students such as Pandit Nehru and Jomo Kenyatta met young MPs such as Nye and Jennie, and at meetings, conferences, and summer schools they cemented their lifelong interest in international affairs. On most of the foreign policy crises that divided the country—and the Labour Party—in the 1950s (relations with the USA, Suez and the Middle East, Yugoslavia, German rearmament, and India), Jennie and Nye could each of them talk to what they knew.

From 1951, they had happy memories of Yugoslavia. They spent a month on holiday there, the first real break Jennie and Nye had had for many years. They dined with Tito—and swam with him and his dog—while guests of the poet and partisan warrior Milovan Djilas,[44] now Yugoslavia's deputy Prime Minister, who was to become a warm friend; they climbed the mountains of Montenegro; and Nye used the long lazy days and Jennie's help to complete his draft of *In Place of Fear,* his philosophic musings on the nature of socialism. Yugoslavia, they hoped, like India, would reject alignment with the superpowers, and would follow a Third Way. Tito, Jennie believed then, was 'the conscience Stalin lost. He is more than that. He is the conscience of all poor countries that find themselves bullied by one or other of the two major world powers.'[45]

Djilas's persistent criticism of Communist leadership and its *nomenklatura* led to his eventual imprisonment. Jennie, especially, went to immense trouble to help both him and his colleague Vladimir Dedijer. Nye interceded on their behalf with the Socialist International, while Jennie travelled to Belgrade to help their families and to intercede with Yugoslavian officials. They both wrote to Tito, and they brought their families to Britain for a holiday. Milovan Djilas told the Memorial Meeting for Jennie: 'They eased my prisons, made me more secure, and indebted me. There are no ways to pay them back. But there was no need to; there are neither debtors nor debts in the struggle for freedom.'[46]

Jennie went with Nye to another troubled country at Christmas 1953: to Egypt, en route to Israel, where they would stay with the Sieffs. Nye had already incurred Tory wrath by writing in one of his syndicated articles that 'it was useless for any imperial power to garrison troops in the middle of a hostile population. Better to withdraw while there was still time to do so on friendly terms.'[47] Jennie, who edited Nye's stuff (to ensure that his sentiments as well as his syntax were not over the top), said it was one of his 'more philosophical pieces'. It was, until General Neguib and Colonel Nasser reprinted it in their Egyptian newspaper in the middle of December 1953. Nye's 'philosophical' musings on the conflict between nationalism and imperialism were now denounced at home as an unpatriotic attack on British interests and a treasonable invitation to Egyptians to attack British troops. The next day there were questions in the House, which Jennie pressed the Speaker to rule out of order. Nye and Jennie persisted with their trip, visiting Neguib (in bed with flu) and managing some sightseeing as well as official briefings before being escorted around the Canal Zone by the British military. Arriving in Israel, Nye asserted that Britain had violated Egyptian sovereignty. Jennie sighed, and told the *Daily Express*: 'He will let himself go.'[48]

It was also in the 1950s that they began to know India. Jennie's father and grandfather had campaigned for Indian independence while she was still a girl. Jennie herself met Gandhi during the 1929 Parliament: 'One day when some of us went to lunch with Gandhi after working hard all morning, we were very hungry, but when we got there we were asked to hunger-strike for twenty-four hours. We did. It taught us a lot.'[49] The campaign for Indian independence in the 1930s had been organized from the dingy India League offices across the road from *Tribune*; Nye had been among many MPs climbing to the top of its stairs to talk about Indian freedom with Krishna Menon, the League's secretary. He and Jennie had long known Nehru.[50] In the spring of 1953, Nye made his own trip to India, and thanked parliamentarians there for their efforts to secure peace in Korea. He returned again in March 1957, this time seeking to keep India in the Commonwealth after the strains of Suez and the tensions over Kashmir. Jennie first went to India for a month in January 1956 and came to know Indira Gandhi well.

Jennie's staunch (and controversial) defence of Mrs Gandhi lay in the future. More significant for the Labour Party was the foreign trip that Jennie and Nye made in the summer of 1957, travelling through Poland to Russia, where they spent a day with Khrushchev in his Crimean summer home. Jennie was startled to find that Khrushchev was not only well briefed about Nye, but about her as well, quoting her recent speech on nuclear disarmament which had swayed the (private) PLP weekly meeting. 'Not so much as a sparrow hops from branch to branch without us knowing about it', Khrushchev said, with obvious pride. Jennie believed him. They talked about the reality of the class struggle. Khrushchev dug Jennie in the ribs and said with a chuckle: 'You could not talk to Gaitskell like this.' As Jennie noted, this was both shrewd and true.[51]

From Khrushchev that day Nye learnt that the Russians were not unhappy for Britain to keep her bomb, as it would restrain the Americans. With that, the scene was set for the heart-rending Brighton Conference of 1957, the battle over unilateralism, and, Jennie believed, Nye's own death. Jennie afterwards insisted that the 'malignity' Nye endured then from some of his closest friends on the Left—and she did not exclude Michael Foot from her indictment—broke Nye's health.

*

In the spring of 1959 Nye was due to attend a meeting in Paris with Mendès-France and Pietro Nenni, but, suffering from his frequent chest-colds, the meeting instead came to him at Asheridge. For once Jennie saw Nye as he was seen by others, as Cartier-Bresson unobtrusively prowled around taking photos. 'For the first time I wondered if there might be something seriously wrong with him.'[52] Nye seemed to know it too. After their guests left, he stepped outside, wineglass in hand, gazing sadly at a favourite cherry tree that had been brutally pruned. He lifted his glass and Jennie heard him say: 'Not many more springs.' Jennie's heart turned over, but she pretended not to have heard him, Nye pretended not to have said it, and they went back in.[53] Around then, Jennie bought Nye a vast king-sized bed for his room. Nye was always wide awake at night, 'radio active', Jennie wide awake in the early morning, and drowsy at night. They had adopted separate bedrooms from early on. Nye now said, out of character: 'Why not put that other lamp on the other side (of the bed) then we can both sleep here?' Looking back, Jennie sensed that he was 'conscious of the passing of time, that we would not always be together, in the way you feel when young'.[54]

However, Nye showed his usual resilience and was soon off on a delegation to Russia with Hugh Gaitskell, generously covering for Gaitskell when he had a severe hangover the morning after. Jennie noted ruefully that Gaitskell's lapse was courteously ignored by the press; yet when Nye had been in Venice with Morgan Phillips and Dick Crossman on Labour Party business a year or two before, and they had engaged in heavy drinking, the press coverage had led to a law suit.*

Jennie's physical health was sound, although several times during her life she suffered prolonged spells of depression (from which she took refuge in bed or in drink). Winter months filled her with gloom. Both she and Nye hungered for the sun. During the later 1950s, Jennie sometimes felt unable to keep the fabric of their life going, with two careers, and two homes, the two people she most loved, Ma and Nye, becoming more dependent on her. Ma, who had always cared for Jennie, now needed care in her turn. She had a kind live-in companion-nurse, but Jennie hated to leave her with strangers. Jennie needed more help, secretarial, housekeeping, and nursing, but could not organize it—or would not organize it, perhaps, since money was no problem. For, all her life, Jennie hated to be looked after by strangers. Fiercely protective of their private life, she demanded care from friends and family, but she had no family of her own—and she detested Nye's. All this was against a background of 'despairingly difficult' politics. Nye worried for her, shopped, cooked,

* It was a sorry story. Their heavy drinking was commented on by Italian delegates and picked up by *The Spectator*. Nye was mortified, as they were on official party business. When the paper refused to apologize, Nye (unusually for him) pressed a libel action. Goodman acted for them and they won £2,500 a head. Crossman later asserted that they had been 'pissed as newts' and that they had committed perjury. Jennie noted that Crossman loved to shock. Nye did drink heavily, but he could hold his drink; and he, at least, unlike Crossman, seems to have believed he was not drunk in Venice and therefore the question of perjury did not arise. Why otherwise bring a libel suit and risk his reputation when, maligned by the press on other occasions, he had refused to act—'Let them say, let them say.' None the less, and in the light of Crossman's remark, they were fortunate to win their case.

helped nurse Ma, and bought Jennie bottles of tonic and vitamin pills. He was, says Jennie, a saint.

Nye, on the other hand, though mentally immensely strong, was less physically robust than he seemed. High blood pressure, hard drinking over many years which played havoc with his liver, a recurring weak chest, as well as nystagmus left over from his days underground,* made him vulnerable to all sorts of chills, colds, and flu. Jennie feared pneumoconiosis, tuberculosis, and bronchitis. She had had a glimpse of Nye's mortality back in Cliveden Place when late one night she found him sitting upright and gasping for breath in front of a big fire. Jennie prayed to a God that she did not believe in, Not that, not that. His father had died in Nye's arms with pneumoconiosis; they knew its every nuance. The next day Dan Davies diagnosed pleurisy. It was when Nye said that moving out of London would add ten years to his life, that Jennie gave up the London home she loved to move to Asheridge.

When the date of the October 1959 general election was announced, Nye hurried home from Moscow and set about his usual strenuous speaking tour. Jennie caught a glimpse of him on television, and his appearance panicked her. He had planned to finish his campaign tour helping Michael Foot in Devonport, but was too unwell. When it was all over he looked flushed and unhealthy—friends wondered whether he had suffered a mild heart attack or minor stroke. Nye recovered in time for the Blackpool Conference where Gaitskell divided the Party, already demoralized by election defeat, over Clause 4. Nye, wrote Jennie, 'lavished all his wit and eloquence on binding the Party together'. In sparkling style, a vintage Nye rescued Conference from depression and Gaitskell from defeat.

They returned to Asheridge. Nye, it seemed, had a stomach ulcer; he was losing weight and eating badly. In the Commons Smoking Room, as he gossiped and argued, Nye consumed ice-cubes to anaesthetize the heat and the pain. Ma and Jennie started to plan for Christmas, trying to blot out their forebodings about Nye's forthcoming operation. He went into hospital two days after Christmas: most of his stomach had to be removed. News of his illness quickly became public. Some of the less scrupulous press tried to invade his hospital room.

Nye remained in hospital for six weeks, surrounded by flowers and

* Jennie learned of his eye condition when they quarrelled about candles on the dining-room table. Nye 'literally was blinded and could not see. Also while reading he need [*sic*] a strong reading-lamp directly on the page', JL papers, undated MS jottings (1970s).

friends. At Jennie's suggestion, Michael Foot visited him there to bring books and contrive a row—'Make him feel that everything's normal.' Michael had lost Devonport. 'Why not go to Ebbw Vale?' suggested Nye. At the time, Michael thought nothing of it. Looking back, he realized that Nye believed he was dying.[55] Not until the day before Nye was due to leave hospital did his doctor, his old Welsh friend Dan Davies, tell Jennie that Nye had stomach cancer—cancer, the 'Big C', the most feared and most concealed of all illnesses. Dan Davies had promised to tell Nye if it was serious, but now doctor and wife entered into a pact. They would not tell him or anyone else—not his sister, not even his oldest and closest friend Archie Lush. Jennie feared that if Nye knew he had cancer, he would lose the will to live. She later told Michael Foot that she did confide in Howard Samuel—'I had a motive.' Samuel was to find her enough 'super-strong sleeping pills' to give Nye if his suffering became intolerable. He first promised he would, 'then felt it would be profoundly wrong'.[56] The prognosis was not good: nine to eighteen months was the professional estimate. Jennie took Nye home to Asheridge.

Every bulletin on his health was followed by scores of letters willing him well. They came from the great and the good, but also from quarry-men, nurses, workmen on a building site, from unknown men and women, some barely able to write, and others, the very elderly, barely able to see, who were thinking of Nye, praying for him, raising a glass to his recovery.* One old man wrote: 'Please fight and win Mr Bevan. I have just been discharged from hospital where I have been overwhelmed and humbled by the charity of the Health Service you have created. To preserve this service *you* must live. I pray to God that if your affliction cannot be destroyed that I might bear it for you. God bless you Sir. Please live. Many are praying.' Another announced on his card: 'So very glad that you have decided to live, and fight us all again. [signed] A Tory of the Tories.' An elderly women told him to 'buck up'; she faced the same difficulties as he did and had lived: 'so do the same my boy and get well for Jennie's sake and to spite Mr Gaitskell'. A housewife, no friend of the Labour Party, found herself praying for his recovery 'when I have been washing up, making the beds and all sorts of times when I have been

* Archie Lush was walking down Gray's Inn Road and called at a small shop to buy tobacco. 'A woman rushed in and said to the woman behind the counter, "I just saw Miss Jennie Lee leaving the hospital and she was smiling," "Oh thank God," said the woman, "Let's hope he's better."' (A. Lush to JL, n.d.)

working around the house'. Their window-cleaner sent his best wishes from Wormwood Scrubs.

Nye began to recover from the operation itself, and in March 1960 held a cheerful press call saying he would soon return to the political fight. They managed a few days of sea air in Brighton until Nye, racked with pain, had to come home. On the journey back, they stopped in Windsor Great Park for Nye to stretch his legs. He said to his Welsh driver, sadly: 'You know, Grif, before I go I must return home to see the mountains', and then, the old Nye, to Jennie: 'You know, dear, you don't know what mountains are in Scotland. My mountains of Wales are magnificent.'[57] They had planned a longer holiday in the South of France, where they would stay with Graham Sutherland while he painted Nye—Jennie bought herself a couple of bright summer frocks and Nye new white silk pyjamas as a sign of good faith—but Nye's condition deteriorated. The doctors wanted him to return to the Royal Free Hospital, but Nye refused. He loathed hospitals. So he was nursed at home, surrounded by people who loved him. John Buchan had enough medical training to administer drugs and injections.

Van-loads of flowers and sackfuls of letters flowed through Asheridge; friends flowed through Jennie. Howard Samuel visited freely, as did Archie Lush and John Mackie. Nehru called. Understandably, Jennie did not want Nye exhausted. But there were other considerations. Now that Jennie knew Nye had cancer, she punished those who had been disloyal to him, whose foul attacks had by some black alchemy turned his ulcer into cancer, who had 'caused' his final illness, who had 'murdered' him. She excluded Michael Foot, who loved Nye deeply. He was desperately upset to be kept away—it still hurts—but afterwards he and Jill vowed that never again would they quarrel with Jennie, but would always look after her.[58] Perhaps Jennie made the same resolution.

One fine June morning Nye dressed and went out into the garden before Jennie was awake. He came back bearing roses still wet with dew, which he tossed on to her bed. Jennie immediately noticed the bugs which crawled out of the roses on to her sheets.[59] Nye seems to have sensed that time was running out. A week or two later Archie Lush wheeled him to the window to look out at the Chilterns beyond. Nye talked about the Welsh mountains he and Archie had climbed together—always he returned to those mountains. Suddenly he quoted: 'God why have you made the world so beautiful and the life of man so short?' And then: 'I wish I could live. There are one or two things I want to *do*.'[60]

His spirits remained high; he never complained, never despaired. John Mackie was with him the day before he died. 'See John what happens to future prime ministers', Nye quibbed. And then gripped his arm: 'You must look after Jennie when I've gone.'[61]

Nye had enough medical knowledge to suspect the truth, and enough courage to want to know it. He cross-questioned Jennie, the doctors, and those who nursed him, but Jennie held them all to silence; she feared he might give up the fight. She loved him, and she was frightened. She was disintegrating under the strain. She was drinking heavily, her temper was filthy, and she was hard to handle. She fell down the stairs and hurt herself—'Pity she didn't break her bloody neck while she was at it', was the comment of one exasperated doctor.[62] As Nye grew worse, Jennie's dread was that he would be aware that she had deceived him. 'For days before the end, I did not say anything. I just looked at Jack [Buchan] imploringly.' Jack, entrusted with Nye's morphine, 'knew what was in my mind'. She persuaded herself that up to the moment he died, quietly in his sleep on 6 July, he never knew.[63]

Jennie refused Nye the truth, just as she had kept it from her mother five years before. For those who did know, the strain of lying to Nye was near intolerable. Those who did not found it hard to forgive Jennie for keeping them and Nye in official ignorance. Almost without exception, they believed that Nye knew he had cancer but had to pretend that he did not, in order to spare Jennie.[64] Jennie, who did know, pretended that he had not. They could not reach out to each other in all honesty. Nye professed to trust Jennie, and Jennie professed to tell him the truth. Their fictions interlocked and silenced them. Jennie insisted it was for Nye's benefit, but friends suspected it was for her own. Her drinking, her screening of friends, her denials to Nye: few of their mutual friends thought Jennie behaved well as Nye's life closed.

Such judgements were harsh. Jennie was in deep pain, and in a bad way. She did what she thought best for Nye. She wrote defensively to Archie Lush just over a year later:

> Looking back, I am sure about one thing. It would have been sheer cruelty for Nye to have known and, if those as closely attuned to him as yourself had been told, it would have been impossible to deceive him. Remember Arch that one of the things we have to keep in mind was that the mental suffering for Nye would not have been on his own account. He would have anticipated what it would all have meant to me, to you and to those very few others who were so close to him.[65]

A few months later she wrote to Michael: 'I am still obsessed by those last six months, always wondering if I did the right thing. If I had to make those decisions over again, all I know is that I would have made no other.' She said the same thing to him in 1965, in a letter she reprinted fifteen years later in the concluding chapter of *My Life with Nye*:

He did not know he was mortally ill. He guessed it sometimes. He questioned and cross-questioned his doctors, John Buchan and me, but we managed to deceive him and I am proud of that and take what comfort I can from it. He was spared at least the final sorrow of knowing that he would never complete his job, that he was beaten by illness, that I would somehow have to go on without him.

He was optimistic, he enjoyed the praise and love that encircled him, he was ready to start all over again.[66]

Jennie's *My Life with Nye* was published in 1980, only five years after Michael Foot's second volume of his life of Nye. Auberon Waugh, in a perceptive and not unkind review, suspects that Jennie wrote the book not to nail lies about Nye as she claimed, for Michael Foot had done that, but to justify her decision not to tell Nye that he was dying.[67] As Waugh says, she returned again and again to the question: 'If I had to live through that time would I have behaved differently?' It was a question that haunted her, and her answer did not comfort her.

*

The news of Nye's death stunned the nation. Michael immediately hurried to her side, their estrangement forgotten. 'Ni is asleep next door', Jennie wrote the next day to him. 'Later today he will be taken home to Wales.' Tom Driberg wrote in distress from the Commons to Jennie:

a bigger-than-usual group round the tape, a policeman—himself most distressed—whispering the news to me as I went into the Chamber . . . Then, all the evening, knots of Labour members, Welsh, miners, right-wingers, all of them, standing disconsolately in the corridors exchanging reminiscences of the most wonderful man we have ever been privileged to know.

In 'our' corner of the smoking room, Frank Bowles & Bill Mallalieu & I sat and drank several whiskies and talked of it all . . . Hugh Delargy went home as soon as the news came through; I don't think he could bear to be with anybody (and I, also, find it just a bit difficult not to be a little rude, or bitter, to one or two of our colleagues who will be among the most eloquent payers of tributes . . .).

Forgive this foolish letter. You must be absolutely exhausted & empty after your long ordeal . . . Rest for a long time, & then start to rebuild your life as an important person in your own right, which you are.[68]

'He was like a great tree hacked down, wantonly, in full leaf', wrote Michael Foot as he paid his tribute to Nye in the final pages of his biography:

> When he died, no formal or forced note was heard. The nation expressed its sense of loss unfeignedly, spontaneously, without restraint . . . It was, maybe, a sense of national guilt; a belief that he had been cheated of his destiny, that some part of his greatness had been shamefully thrown away; an awareness that he had much to say to our perplexed, polluted world, and that we had listened only fitfully.[69]

Nye was cremated. A week later a memorial service was held for him on the hills above Tredegar, where he and Archie had practised their public speaking by shouting to each other across the valley. His ashes were to be scattered high on the Duffryn hillside under a mountain ash where the bluebells grew.

That morning, Archie Lush had collected the ashes from the crematorium and then fitted in a meeting at Newport Town Hall on his way to the hillside. Time was tight, and in a hurry Archie left the car unlocked. He came out of his meeting to find the car had gone and with it Nye's ashes. The police forces of two counties were summoned to search for it. By this time, half the Welsh Labour Party were assembled on the hillside, but there was still no Nye. Archie's car was found in Gloucester, more than forty miles away, Nye's ashes still in the boot. The police of Gloucestershire rushed to the border of Monmouthshire; as the crowd of five thousand waited, a police car came speeding up the hill. Nye, says Gordon Parry, 'was a restless bugger in life and a restless bugger in death'.[70]

The crowd, subdued, had waited patiently. Jennie, exercising steely self-control, told them: 'In all the great battles of his life, Nye came home to you. He never left you. He never will.'

Jennie was desolate. For the last ten years she had, she noted, 'lived only for and through Nye'. Without him, she wrote twelve years later, 'I am homeless & alone'. She considered suicide: 'I wanted to die too. I had no strength left, no will to go on living.'[71] She had the sleeping pills that Nye had left behind, and two bottles of whisky in the dining-room cupboard. She could slip into endless sleep. Only the thought of her mother, now very frail, stopped her.

The Labour Party arranged the official memorial service in Westminster Abbey for 26 July 1960. The Abbey was packed with politicians, diplomats, businessmen, artists, as well as friends and family, but also with unknown men and women whom Nye had touched and who had never forgotten: a young black in his shirt-sleeves, the landlord of Nye's Asheridge pub, a woman with her shopping basket, and the voices from the valleys. Mervyn Stockwood gave the address, taking his text not from the Bible but from the last few pages of *In Place of Fear*: 'The frontiers of understanding are reached when our spirit fully identifies itself with the awful loneliness and finality of personal grief.'[72]

A few days later Jennie checked into an Edinburgh clinic and collapsed.

8

A WREATH FOR NYE

JENNIE dragged herself back from the Edinburgh clinic to Asheridge. In losing Nye, she had lost any will to live. He had been not just comrade and partner, but the man who might have led a socialist Labour Party to power. Those draining battles of the last decade, those personal struggles to subdue her own longings, were they all for nothing? She had disciplined herself to live for him and through him. What was now left for her? She held on, just, because Ma needed her. Ma's memory was clouding—she would wander into Nye's bedroom or around the garden in search of Nye—and her cancer was spreading; she could not have much time left. Jennie had no strength; she was utterly exhausted, unable even to weep.

When she had lost Frank, Nye had been there for her; when she had suffered her spells of severe depression, Nye had supported her through them. Now there was no one. 'I wander in and out of other people's lives. It is a strange feeling. But what else is there to do when there is next to nothing left of what could be called a life of your own?' She was oddly detached by day, tormented at night. Six months after Nye's death, she wrote: 'Came back [from London] on Thursday too tired for tears. Bad sleeps, meaningless days. When to talk and what to say?' And in September 1962, two years after Nye had gone: 'Broken sleep, constant dreams and nightmares . . . Don't know if I can go on here. But if not, where else?'[1] She could not leave Asheridge because Ma must not be uprooted, but every room was haunted with Nye's vitality. She needed a bottle or more of gin a day to blot out what she could not bear. She was in no state to look after herself, let alone Ma. She had no immediate family—no children, no sisters—and she could not stand Nye's family. She needed care, yet she hated to be looked after by strangers or paid staff.

Ma's closest sister had a daughter, Bettina, who was in her mid-40s, some ten years younger than her cousin Jennie. Bettina had spent occasional weekends at Asheridge, sometimes bringing her kindly self-effacing husband Bill Stafford, and her younger son Vincent, an enchanting 10-year-old. On Nye's death, Bettina journeyed down from Scotland for a week to cook and care for Jennie; and, just as Ma and Dad had done before them, her family stayed on for thirty years. Bettina 'uprooted her home, husband and two sons . . . and came down and took charge'.[2] With unselfconscious generosity, they gave Jennie a family.

Family resemblance played its part. Jennie looked just like Bettina's mother, Bettina took after Ma, and Vincent was a young Tommy—the same fair hair, the same build, the same artless good humour. The Staffords arrived at Asheridge; the guest cottage was ready for them. Vincent, carrying his own small suitcase, trundled up the farmhouse stairs 'and said he was going to stay there and look after Auntie Jennie. He did in his own childish way.' From that first evening, Jennie took him into her heart. She loved him as she had loved the young Tommy, unconditionally. The rest of the family slept in the cottage, Vincent with Jennie.

Vincent was acutely sensitive to her: 'He sensed my bitter sorrow about Nye.' One night, when Jennie was deeply depressed and took the whisky and sleeping tablets to bed, a sleepy Vincent came in claiming Nye had come to his bedroom telling him that Jennie needed him; he was going to sleep on Jennie's floor. Jennie did not stop him. He collected his pillow and quilt and curled up at the side of her bed. 'He had sensed my mood—how much did he know? Anyhow the child kept me from indulging my mood of total despair and desolation.' She went to sleep with her hand resting on his head. On three or four occasions Vincent stopped Jennie's depression from taking her over the edge. They went for long walks together. Jennie sat in the garden one day, wrapped in misery; Vincent 'played around with his ball, sat at my feet, said nothing, again kicked his ball around, sat at my feet, said nothing. The third time around he said, "But Auntie Jennie you have me and Dad"—and he hesitated, unsure of himself—"I think you have".'[3]

Vincent became Jennie's child. 'He was born for her', Jennie would say. She called him her 'little bastard', because in her eyes he had no father. When Jennie died, Vincent asked Bettina why she had allowed Jennie 'to become my mother'—the one and only time he asked. Bettina, who had come from a large family, told him that her own brother had been given to a childless aunt and uncle, and it had worked well. 'That's the reason I did it. I don't regret it.'[4] From the moment he moved to Asheridge, Vincent lived not with his parents but with Jennie. Bettina never spent another penny on him. Jennie bought all his clothes—down to his socks—the pony, and the car. She refused him nothing. At the age of 14 he wanted a dog, an Afghan hound. Why not have two, said Jennie? He was brought up by Jennie to think that she, her love, and her money were always there for him; he need never worry about spending any of it. He loved her without question.

Jennie decided that the local state school was not good enough for Vincent, who needed 'more individual attention, smaller classes and [to] be able to make a beginning at languages'. Arnold Goodman and Mervyn Stockwood (by now chaplain at Eton) had been designated honorary godfathers and Jennie consulted them. Mervyn Stockwood's advice, with which Jennie entirely concurred, was that 'if he is to go to a private school, then it should be the best'. Like many senior Labour MPs at the time, she felt it entirely proper to campaign to end public (that is, private) schools, while meanwhile making use of them. She sent Vincent to Michael Foot's old school at Leighton Park, not far from Asheridge.[5]

A few months after Ma died in May 1962, Jennie took Vincent with her on holiday to Paris, and later to shows and galleries; she was delighted when people assumed Vincent was her son. 'Suse', said Jennie, 'look, he's got Nye's eyes, don't you see that?' Suse could not, because Vincent had not. When friends came to Asheridge, Vincent would play the piano and sing in a pretty treble voice: 'Too young to fall in love'. Jennie's arts friends thought him very fetching. She took him to first nights at the National Theatre, where he absorbed an education. He was puzzled by *Oedipus Rex*, and back at her flat he queried this mother–son relationship. Jennie laughed and lit a cigarette. When Vincent showed a bent for film-making, she worked her networks for job openings and pressed Alan Sapper for a union card and Carl Foreman for a job. She funded Vincent generously, as he started on what was inevitably a precarious (but what became a distinguished Emmy-decorated) career.

Friends at the time were dismayed. They thought Jennie was as poor as she said and much poorer than she actually was; they worried that Vincent would cost her an impoverished old age. Arnold Goodman remonstrated with Jennie, as over the years her holdings in land securities were sold to buy Vincent a flat, to provide large 'loans', and to fund first-class train and plane tickets, five-star hotels, a sports car, and weekend visits from the States. It never occurred to Vincent to behave otherwise; he was spendthrift, he says, because he had been brought up by Jennie to believe he was wealthy. He took Jennie and the favours done to him by her friends for granted—to their intense irritation. They feared that Jennie was being charmed and exploited by her feckless nephew. 'I know I spoil him', Jennie would say, but even those who were closest to Jennie could never know what Vincent had given her in those years after Nye's death: 'Vincent's gay young face—even his naughty ways—has been my best sedative.'[6] He gave her a reason to live, and he meant everything to her. In loving him, he helped to heal her, and she lavished on him all she had.

Was Jennie aware that she had cast her new family in the image of the old? Just as she drew from Bettina some of Ma's uncritical warmth and comfort, so she transferred on to Vincent the childhood love she had borne young Tommy, and the maternal and possessive love with which she had surrounded Nye. Bill Stafford, like Dad Lee, was never fully at ease, but generously allowed himself to be displaced.

The family settled in. Bill became a charge-hand in a local factory and helped Jennie manage Asheridge, as she slowly ran down the farm, let the cottages, leased the fields, and disposed of the stock. Bettina 'underpinned Ma's life and mine with her own'.[7] She had been an aluminium welder in her youth, her Italian father a chef at the Savoy; she was lively, outgoing, and uncensorious; she did not begrudge the gift of Vincent to Jennie; and she never criticized when half her housekeeping money went on gin for Jennie. She accepted Jennie as she was, and never judged her. She cooked, shopped, and cared for her, bought her clothes, checked her lipstick before she went out, took her to the dentist, went to NFU meetings on her behalf, and saw to her accounts. Jennie knew Bettina's worth. She wrote to Archie Lush:

> [Bettina] is my lifeline. She nursed Ma tenderly, has a great deal of Ma's vitality, cheerfulness and uncalculating kindness. Bill and she make a home for me as well as for themselves . . . She keeps everything splendidly and we all lend a hand. Vincent with his apron on, cooking in the kitchen, is quite a sight. He loves cooking . . . They have all the right healthy contempt for me on the kitchen front, but I do my share in other ways.[8]

As Ma faded, Bettina would spend hours reading to her. She and Ma were much enjoying *Lady Chatterley's Lover*: 'Hurry up Bettina', said Ma, 'get on to the next bit', when she died, peacefully, and still free of pain. First Nye, and now, two years later, Ma. Jennie could not bear to enter Ma's room. Bettina took Jennie to Scotland and together they buried Ma where she wanted to be, alongside Dad in Lochgelly cemetery.

In 1969 Jennie finally sold Asheridge and made London her home. Bill and Bettina obligingly uprooted themselves again. Bettina, wisely, would not live with Jennie. Instead, they found a home a bus-ride away, and Bill took a job in a local hospital. Every day Bettina would go to Jennie's home in Chester Row, cook and shop, and lay breakfast for the following day, before going home to Bill, taking Jennie's laundry with her. Of an evening she would sometimes accompany Jennie on her arts-ministerial functions. The two were much of a height, although Jennie was a size or two larger, and she would borrow Bettina's clothes—they took it in turns to wear Bettina's brown velvet trouser-suit. In the later 1970s and 1980s Jennie's demands on the Staffords grew. Bill would be called out in the middle of the night to see to leaking pipes. He always responded.

As Jennie got better after Nye's death and became more bossy and abrasive, even Bettina sometimes found her impossible. Jennie gave her a car, a Hillman Minx in which Bettina delighted; and then took it away, sold it, and gave a sports car to Vincent. The Staffords thought the cottage at Asheridge belonged to them, but to Bettina's great distress, Jennie later decided it was only a loan. Jennie took over their lives. In 1970, after Jennie had given up Asheridge and Cannock had given up on Jennie, Bettina and Bill fled to Australia to stay with Bettina's daughter. They decided to start a new life and get away from Jennie. But Bill was injured at work, and Bettina did not care for the heat, so they returned after a couple of years, and found a flat in Streatham from where Bettina, once again, boarded the bus to look after Jennie.

It was true that Jennie 'used' Bettina; but Bettina was happy to be used. She loved Jennie's vitality, her raucous laugh, her irreverence; she took Jennie's peremptory demands and self-centredness in her stride; and, like Vincent, she loved sharing in the glamorous life that Jennie led when she became Arts Minister: the parties she hosted, the first nights and previews she attended, the well-known people she met. Jennie would not allow anyone to patronize Bettina, and told them off if they tried. She introduced her to one minor royal saying: 'This is my cousin, but she's the boss you know.' Bettina enjoyed herself enormously.[9]

Bettina's housekeeping was supplemented by cleaning help, which Jennie hired from an agency for out-of-work actors. Dorothy Vernon, an actress in her late 20s, turned up in 1968 at Chester Row. 'Are you a cook or a cleaner?' inquired Jennie. 'People are one or the other and you shall be a cleaner.' When Vincent, then aged 17, appeared in the garden, Jennie tugged Dorothy over to the window: 'Come and look, look at him, see the Scottish and Italian in him, look at the way he walks. He's lovely.' She insisted on showing her Vincent's bedroom: 'Come and look. It's not pornographic.' Then Jennie noticed there was some half-eaten toast in the bedroom: 'Now *that's* immoral.' Her temporary cleaner became fond of Jennie. She did think it odd that Jennie, Minister for the Arts, never discussed the theatre with her, and showed 'no intelligent interest' in it. She recalls only one such conversation, when Jennie was worried about the drugs culture surrounding experimental theatre, (perhaps the vulnerability of Tommy / Vincent was in her mind). When Dorothy left after six months Jennie did not ask her what she was going to do. Dorothy suspected that Jennie feared she might seduce Vincent and was glad to see her go. Jennie said it was all quite convenient and she would find someone older next time.[10]

Instead, she found a man-servant in his mid-20s, who for a couple of months cooked them wonderful dinners and ran the house, until Vincent one evening found him prostrate on the kitchen floor shooting heroin. 'Pick him up', Jennie told Vincent. He went next day, but Jennie was generous in paying him off.

Jennie talked about Ma to Bettina, and about Vincent to everybody else. She seldom talked about Nye: 'That I cannot bear.' She allowed Nye's bedroom at Asheridge to become a store room: 'I am not morbid but simply have not got the strength to bring his room back to life.' She wanted to guard Nye's reputation, but she was too close, and too ill; she felt 'unbearable pain, resentment and wrath when I recall much that Ni had to suffer', from press and political colleagues alike.[11] She did not want Nye's death to be a wasteland; no one must believe that he had died an embittered, disappointed man. He had faced his future with optimism, he expected to live, he hoped to bring his beloved party back to socialism and to power.

Jennie turned to Michael Foot. Within days of Nye's death they had agreed that Michael would write his biography. She stipulated only that 'no part of Nye's life should be falsified to suit anybody's convenience or to grind anybody's political axe'.[12] Within two years and with Jennie's help, Michael had completed the first part of his magnificent two-volume biography, written with all the love, passion, and political commitment at his command. Jennie agreed to a new edition of *In Place of Fear*, to which she added a three-thousand word introduction. It was her testament to Nye. He had, she wrote:

> a seemingly inexhaustible capacity for living, for loving, for seeing the fun and absurdity of life as well as its tragic side . . . The brusque tongue, the astringent judgement, deceived no-one who was close to him. Private living he adored. Public chores he detested. But a fierce tenderness and an inescapable involvement in all the great issues of our time impelled him onwards into one hard fight after another.
>
> I cannot remember a time in all the years we were together when he was not

fighting against impossible odds. I can hear him bounding up the stairs, two or three steps at a time, to the top flat where we lived during the first two years of our married life. The door would be thrown open, he would come hurrying in, spilling over with news and excitement. 'Here we go again. A wooden cross or a golden crown'. That was a kind of theme song. I knew it meant the beginning of a period of intense physical, emotional, intellectual exertion, no holds barred, while he was fighting to rouse public opinion, particularly in the more lethargic sections of our own Labour movement, to the imminence of war, the crime of betraying Spain, the need for the Labour Party to adopt a less drearily conservative type of socialism.

Nye's socialism had the radiant, elegant quality of his own personality.*

Five years after Nye's death, Jennie told Michael that she still flinched, still wanted to run away at the very mention of Nye's name: 'Strangers, all kinds of people, come up to me to say kind, admiring things and I am at best abrupt with them instead of taking their remarks in the spirit they are offered.' She added:

I am just sane enough to know that where Ni is concerned I am not quite sane. I have refused every offer, however seemingly profitable and worthwhile to write or talk about him. The truth would seem like the ranting of a hysterical half-wit. It is so much easier to write about faults than virtues, cruelties, insensitivities rather than humour, kindness and the rest. Ni's faults were all on the outside.[13]

She resisted contributing to any radio or television 'portraits' of Nye—not until the 1970s did she relent—and no broadcast ever satisfied her. They were crude, distorted, and downright wrong. In the early 1980s she did help one actor to capture Nye's mannerisms, only to find that the play portrayed her as Welsh, and the script, she said in a fine turn of reviewing invective, was 'a tawdry piece of mutilated history'.[14]

The Labour movement continued to mourn Nye's death. From around the country came letters to Jennie from trade-union branches, local party wards, miners' lodges, women's sections, university Labour clubs, and pensioners' groups, asking her agreement to name Labour Party halls after Nye, erect plaques, open library rooms, and acquire playing fields in his memory—and would she please come and open them? With the condolence letters often came donations. What should be done with the

* Jennie asked Neil Kinnock to write the foreword to the next reprint. He sent her a copy and she returned it, 'marked like a sixth form essay with notes in the margin and all—and three typing errors corrected'. He huffily told her he was not going to change a word. Jennie stared at him and said: 'I think it's very good. Just what was needed. But you didn't *really* expect me to let it pass without comment, did you?' Neil Kinnock, Jennie Lee Memorial Meeting, 17 Jan. 1989.

money? Jennie pondered. She thought of a memorial library, such as had been set up for Frank Wise; the Labour Party proposed an International Centre. Eventually, with Arnold Goodman and Michael Foot, she set up the Aneurin Bevan Memorial Foundation, the first claim on whose funds were overseas students wanting to study at Ruskin College, followed later by disabled students wanting to study with the Open University. It remained a very personal fund: Jennie used it to help the son of Milovan Djilas with his studies at Birkbeck College ('I can think of no student whom Aneurin Bevan would have been more eager to assist'), Michael Foot used it to help finance the National Museum of Labour History.[15]

One milestone was reached three months after Nye's death when Jennie went to Scarborough for the Party Conference. A member of the NEC, she was on the platform as delegate after delegate spoke about Nye. The spotlights played on her as tears sprang to her eyes, and then, in response to thunderous applause, she slowly rose to her feet. She told them:

> I have been watching your faces and, like me, you feel it just can't be true. You can feel the life that Nye gave us. You can feel his astringency, his wit, his laughter. You can feel the love, you can feel the vaulting intelligence that could not live with small things.
>
> All I hope is that in this coming week we will have the courage to talk to one another, to listen to one another, and not to let anyone come between us.

Then, pulling her grey cardigan around her black dress, she demanded that the Party stop bickering and, as Nye would have wanted, unite around its most precious beliefs: 'Many of you have written to me about memorials and I have been very moved. But you know the memorial you can give to any comrade you love is to see that his work is not tarnished and mocked.'[16]

A more gruelling task came late in 1964 when Jennie returned for the first time to Tredegar, to open a memorial library in St James's Hospital (Tredegar, typically, grumbled that she had not come before because she had not really loved Nye). Jennie, clearly under great strain, was photographed standing next to a bust of Nye that dominated the library. Near to tears herself, she told the audience: 'It would be false to Aneurin to make this an occasion for tears. He didn't live to bring tears into the world. You knew the strength and compassion that animated everything he did.' She hoped that doctors and nurses would use the library, and then she added: 'I dreaded it when the mountains came into sight . . . and the rest I leave to your hearts.' She broke down suddenly and sat with her head bowed as there was a slow swell of applause. Michael Foot stood to speak, Jennie fought to regain her composure; then, tired but relaxed, she left to go on to Ebbw Vale. She had, the press reported, conquered her own 'personal Everest'.[17]

In 1972 Michael, now Ebbw Vale's MP, unveiled the permanent monument to Nye at the sombre Waun-Y-Pound, on the hill overlooking the three towns of his constituency, where Nye had addressed miners and their families on every eve of election, every demonstration, and every May Day. Six thousand voices rang out in 'Cwm Rhondda'. Jennie had been asked if she preferred a statue rather than stones. She said no to a solitary statue: 'Not for Nye. Don't ever come here and think of Nye standing alone . . . he was one of a company.' Three great standing stones (for the three towns of Tredegar, Ebbw Vale, and Rhymney), hewn from a local limestone quarry, encircle a towering central stone, representing Nye himself. On it is carved: 'On this spot Aneurin Bevan spoke to the people of the constituency and to the world.' The stones look ageless; they stand, said the *Sunday Times*, as Nye did, for 'socialism, pure and simple and grand'.[18]

*

Jennie dragged herself unwillingly back to the Commons. She loathed going there, she was not naturally clubbable, and she was paired with Margaret Thatcher.* Furthermore, she detested what Gaitskell was doing to the Party. Gaitskell had vowed to 'fight and fight and fight again' at Scarborough in 1960. Though he lost the vote, his magnificent speech saved his leadership. Jennie put in appearances at the NEC and at the PLP to accuse Gaitskell of defying Party policy on defence and on Clause 4. Sitting near the back of Committee Room 14, she tried to catch Gaitskell's eye at the PLP meeting in late October, but despite some calls around the room of 'Let Jennie speak', Gaitskell would not do so.

As Wilson had made up his mind to challenge Gaitskell for the leadership, Jennie now lashed out, denouncing Gaitskell in an open letter to her Cannock agent. 'There was no hope of rallying a united and robust Socialist movement under Mr Gaitskell's leadership.'[19] Instead of fighting the Tories, she charged, Gaitskell spent his time fighting Conference. She would support Wilson. The arrival of the Polaris missile base hardened the battle between unilateralists and multilateralists. Jennie, while not opposing the base—she was not a unilateralist—insisted that the Labour Party

* Mrs Thatcher asked Jennie one day if Jennie liked her hat; Jennie said no, so Mrs Thatcher acquired another one. She also took the name of Jennie's dressmaker though Jennie warned her that she would need to wear a jacket, as Jennie's dressmaker could not manage to put sleeves in dresses. (Interview Mervyn Stockwood.)

declare it would never make first use of nuclear weapons. When the Shadow Cabinet refused, she joined Barbara Castle and Michael Foot in abstaining in December's defence debate.[20]

The spring of the following year saw her attempting to guard Nye's NHS, as Enoch Powell introduced further charges and higher NI contributions to fund the service. The House was kind as she made rather pedestrian and rambling speeches; it was left to others such as George Brown to denounce Tory policy as a poll tax on the sick.[21] She was on better form when, during 1962, she turned to colonial matters. She fought the Tory immigration bill; and on the departure of South Africa from the Commonwealth, she begged the government not to support apartheid by privileging trade with South Africa:

> We do not know when South Africa will free itself from the present racial dictatorship. But if anything in the world can be certain, it is that events will not stand still there any more than in any other part of the world.
>
> The people who are going to change conditions in South Africa are, not exclusively but dominantly, the people who are at the moment the victims of apartheid. If, one day, these victims of apartheid, together with the more enlightened liberal elements sympathising with them, are able to form a Government and dictate the policy of that Government, they may look to this island with warmth and they may want to renew their Commonwealth ties if they feel that in this, their time of darkness and persecution, we have been trying to befriend them as best we can.[22]

Apart from defence, another major issue was coming to the fore: membership of the European Economic Community. Jennie, like many on the Left, saw the EEC not as a possible Third Way, but as 'an economic shield for NATO', a capitalist club left over from the Cold War, a conspiracy of big business, which would subvert efforts to plan the economy, and which would exclude the Commonwealth and the Third World from its markets.[24] In December 1963 Harold Wilson, by then leader of the Party, paid Nye the tribute of asking Jennie to wind up the health debate for the Opposition from the front bench—her very first appearance there—where, after a flat start, she turned in a workmanlike performance.[25]

Jennie's interventions were, on the whole, sporadic. Meanwhile, letters piled up. She needed help with all the condolences as well as her constituency matters. She went rapidly through several secretaries, not always treating them properly, not paying them properly, and not aware of the work they had to do for her, until in 1961 she employed Vera Timberlake, who saw her through the next few years.

Mrs Timberlake liked working for Jennie, but she could well see why others did not. She worried about Jennie's mental health, the bitterness Jennie felt at Nye's death, the depth and length of her mourning; she also worried about the casual way Jennie handled her correspondence and neglected her constituency. The Commons apart, Jennie had largely withdrawn from public life. She saw only a few people: Arnold Goodman, who found her a new flat in Ashley Gardens (he occupied the one underneath), Suse and Constance, the Foots, occasionally Mervyn Stockwood. Arnold Wesker managed to tempt her up to his arts venue, at Centre 42. Letters still came in by the score, grieving at the loss of Nye. They upset her greatly. She would open them, and then pass them to Vera Timberlake to answer; she could not face it herself. Her secretary wondered whether Jennie was wise to remain in politics. So did Jennie. Her political as well as her private life had died with Nye. Gallantly, she tried to keep going, as she knew Nye would have wished, but she felt 'she was finished'.[25]

The 1964 general election approached, and Labour came back into government. Vera Timberlake was with Jennie in Ashley Gardens when the phone call came through from 10 Downing Street. Harold Wilson wanted to see her. Jennie came home a different woman, 'terribly excited', transformed, renewed. The Prime Minister had offered her a job. She was to be the first Minister for the Arts. It was, observers commented, a wreath for Nye.

9

MINISTER FOR THE ARTS:
'MONEY, POLICY, SILENCE'

JENNIE often quoted from J. B. Priestley's *The Arts Under Socialism*: 'The State can only clear the ground and build a wall against the cold wind. It cannot pull out of the dark soil the flower of art; only the artist can do that.' The quotation had headed the Labour Party's 1959 manifesto for the arts *Leisure and Living* (the first election, incidentally, in which parties made political statements about the arts). It was a handsomely produced document, printed on rich cream paper, with generous margins. Jennie scribbled on her copy: 'we are committed to a more coherent, imaginative and generous attitude to the arts' in the margins of one page; and at the foot of another: 'People are free to accept and enjoy—or to reject through lack of interest—the best in all of the arts. Make more generally available.' Her marginalia found their way, often word for word, into Jennie's ground-breaking White Paper for the arts in 1965. The job of the state, and the Minister for the Arts, was to support and then to stand aside; to respond, but not to impose; and always to offer the best to the most.

Though Jennie was to be the first Minister for the Arts, state patronage of the arts preceded her—it had flowered during the Second World War. Until then, government spending (at around £1 million a year) had mainly been on the national museums and galleries. Theatre was declining, under assault from the cinema; opera companies and orchestras edged close to bankruptcy. The arts were not even much supported by the upper classes. The government's involvement in the war also led to its involvement in the arts. The Entertainments National Service Association (ENSA) was revived to entertain the troops, and the Council for the Encouragement of Music and the Arts (CEMA) was devised to raise the morale of civilians at home facing the blackout, evacuation, and heavy bombing.

In December 1941, J. M. Keynes became the CEMA chairman. He was an inspired choice. Keynes moved among the Bloomsbury circle, collected books, married a ballerina, and before the war had started the London Artists Association as well as the Cambridge Arts Centre; he also became chairman of Covent Garden. CEMA's task, he said, was 'to carry music, drama and pictures to places which otherwise would be cut off from all contact with the masterpieces of happier days and times; to air-raid shelters, to war-time hostels, to factories, to mining villages.'[1] CEMA toured paintings, orchestras, and actors, and sent out six music 'travellers'—led by Vaughan Williams—who worked magic, promoting orchestral and choral groups across the country. They played in factory canteens, in munitions hostels, in Underground stations, in internment camps, in the basements of department stores, in air-raid shelters, and in church halls. 'People felt that music, the ballet, poetry and painting were concerned with a seriousness of living and dying with which they themselves had suddenly been confronted', wrote Stephen Spender. 'A little island of civilisation surrounded by burning churches—that was how the arts seemed in England during the War.' During the blitz, performers worried that they were singing and playing while England was burning; their audience arrived 'looking grey and anxious, with newspapers tucked under their arms, and an hour later they were everyone of them looking radiant and transformed'.[2]

CEMA found that it was not just 'preserving' standards and maintaining access, but giving both to those who had never before experienced it. In some munitions hostels, they found that virtually none of their audience had ever seen a live play; the concept of acting was so unreal that they treated the stage like the cinema, and talked, walked about, drank tea. Keynes and his staff thought they were replacing what the war had taken away; they soon came to realize that they were 'providing what had never existed even in peacetime'.[3] In two years, their art exhibitions had been seen by half a million, their plays by a million and a half, their concerts by thousands (and many more than that when broadcast by the BBC).

Keynes was determined that CEMA should not end with the war. In 1944 it became the Arts Council of Great Britain, and its policies began slowly to change. Whereas CEMA had been a providing body, the Arts Council became a grant-giving body. Whereas, to raise morale, CEMA had aided amateur work, the Arts Council expected amateurs to seek aid from local authorities, and confined itself to supporting only the work of professionals—buying, displaying, or touring their work. Its Treasury grant slowly rose, from £100,000 in 1942–3, to some £235,000 in 1945–6.

Its location within Whitehall also changed. CEMA had been within the Education Department, under the benign eye of Rab Butler, where Keynes wanted it to remain. It was not only a comfortable administrative fit at centre and at locality, as the Arts Council sought to coax local education authorities into partnership for 'new' arts—music and drama—alongside their existing responsibilities for 'old' arts—public libraries, local galleries, and museums; it also suited the high-minded Reithian educative tone of the enterprise. As Keynes said in a broadcast in July 1945 launching the Arts Council: 'We look forward to the time when the theatre and the concert-hall and the gallery will be a living element in everyone's upbringing, and regular attendance at the theatre and at concerts a part of organised education.'[4] Instead, the Arts Council was placed under the Treasury, where it remained until, in Jennie's time in office, it was again attached to education.

Over the next twenty years, the reach of the Arts Council was inevitably retracted. During the war it had woven its concerts and plays into the working lives of countless thousands of men and women, and supported the amateur activities of hundreds of local groups. With the war won, art and culture was again 'professionalized' and segregated into leisure time. Music clubs, set up by the Arts Council for out of hours, folded, as they faced competition from cinema, radio, TV, and professional football. The arts returned to the educated minority, and the Arts Council confined its support to the big London flagships and the leading provincial theatres. The cultural proscenium arch stood between the professional performer and the audience. The Commons Select Committee on Estimates in 1948–9 argued that the Arts Council should 'turn their energies to making the Arts more accessible, being content at first, if necessary, with less ambitious standards, and your Committee therefore suggests that the provinces, where the Arts are not so readily available to the public, provide a more valuable field than the metropolitan area for the activities of the Council'.[5]

The Arts Council developed exactly the opposite policy.[6] It saw itself as about excellence, safeguarding standards, especially of performing arts like opera which could not survive on box-office receipts alone. Excellence had to be distilled, concentrated: to diffuse it was to lose it. Diffusing—spreading—arts and culture was the job of other media, the BBC of course, and the trusts, such as Carnegie and Gulbenkian. This was not just a question about money, or the lack of it. As the Arts Council said in 1961–2: 'The essence of Arts Council policy nowadays is to sustain the best possible standards of performance at a limited number of institutions . . .

Even if its income were larger it would still prefer to consolidate those priorities than to dissipate its resources upon an extensive provision of the second-rate.'[7] Wartime's 'the best for the most' had become peacetime's 'the best for the inevitable few'.

The Arts Council was in no sense *socially* exclusive; it was happy that its audience should be a democratic élite, an audience of whatever background, educated or able to appreciate excellence. It did not intend to service the upper-middle London-living opera-loving class. Yet holding a highly Establishment view of what excellence in what arts with what artists and in what places was all about, the effect was much the same. As Hutchison has noted, membership of the Arts Council was, over the years, drawn heavily from Eton and Oxbridge (very few women), from London, and from the trustees of the great flagships, in particular the Royal Opera House (ROH) and the Tate Gallery (nearly half of whose trustees served at one time or the other on the Arts Council).[8] Panel members argued for grants for their own organizations. As the Treasury grant slowly grew, it was mostly corralled by the national companies. Few dissented. It was all very cosy, glossy, and self-referential.

There is little evidence that the Arts Council pressed the Treasury hard for increases in its budget. Probably, they underbid. Possibly, they could have got more. Certainly, the Arts Council gained no financial advantage from being placed with the Treasury. The insistence that excellence was about talent so rare that it could be cherished in only a few temples, combined with modest resources, meant that the old Arts Council (before Jennie) always positioned itself on the side of excellence as against access. It assumed instinctively that the two were antithetical.

From this assumption, everything else followed: the Arts Council would only support professionals and not amateurs; it favoured London over the provinces (as though 'the provinces' were thinned-out suburbia, mere hinterland to the metropolis); and, within London, it favoured the national companies—Covent Garden, Sadler's Wells, the Old Vic/National Theatre, and the Royal Shakespeare Company (RSC)—over smaller companies and theatres. Only the established fine arts (music, drama, painting) could be judged 'excellent'; new activities, such as children's theatre, film and photography, jazz, folk-song, even literature—all those fields where critical judgement was harder and peer review less clear cut, where performance could be controversial—were deemed not to come within the Arts Council remit. The Arts Council fastidiously distanced itself from any art form that might approximate to crafts (that was for the Board of Trade), to amateur work (that was for local government), or to popular entertainment (that was for the commercial sector). It filtered out from public subsidy most of the creative art of the country. Says one of their critics, it offered 'a very narrow response (standards) to a complex set of obligations'.[9] Had there been more money, the old Arts Council might have been somewhat puzzled how to spend it, but would probably have plumped for more of the same. Had money permitted 'a more coherent, imaginative, and generous attitude to the arts', to quote Jennie's scribble, it is not clear that it would have comprehended her language.

Jennie refused to inherit this mind-set, refused to accept that there need be any conflict between excellence and access. She defended 'excellence', as defined by those like Peter Hall whose judgement she trusted, with ferocity. 'We were all three élitists', she wrote of herself, Arnold Goodman, and Hugh Willatt (Minister, chairman, and secretary-general of the Arts Council, respectively). But with the same sublime confidence that she brought to launching the Open University, she refused to accept that more must mean worse. She did not believe that talent was so rare that it had to be carefully bunched into a handful of theatres. Let the state shield the garden (to extend Priestley's image), and artistic creativity would flower abundantly, its glories there for all to enjoy. The state could not create artists, but it could cherish them, ensure they did not wither from neglect. She was, she said, continuously pressed to take money away from the national companies and offer it elsewhere—something that she firmly resisted. She wanted to level up not down. In any case, she had no more intention of alienating influential arts grandees than she had of alienating influential vice-chancellors within higher education. 'New money' for the new initiatives, while maintaining existing levels of funding for flagships, would protect her against any charge of diluting standards.

And she got it, trebling the Arts Council grant in six years. The arts grandees were at first apprehensive about Jennie's appointment, fearful that this wild left-winger would threaten everything they valued and represented. Those fears allayed, they (some of them) took to sneering and making barbed remarks at her lack of artistic credentials. Somehow, as her civil servants mused, a Minister for the Arts was expected to be a connoisseur of the arts, a collector, and a patron, yet no one expected a Minister for Social Security particularly to love old people. When finally she and Goodman pushed through the South Bank National Theatre, a scheme that had been hanging around for half a century, she earned the art establishment's respect and even their affection.

Most of Jennie's new money went not into London's national companies, but into Scotland, Wales, and the regions (no one talked about the 'provinces' in Jennie's presence). She encouraged local authorities to support not only libraries and museums, but art, music, and drama in their schools; to aid amateur groups; to run local arts centres even in the smallest towns. A doctrine of 'response', it meant that the Arts Council would not parachute into a city to impose some version of London high culture; rather, it would only respond to and support local initiatives, local bids, grounded in the local community. Direct (and protected) funding for the flagships alongside generous support to regional arts meant Jennie could indeed brigade access with the enhancement of excellence.

Influenced by Constance Cummings, Jennie believed that the Arts Council should support only professional work—as Lord Goodman memorably said in the Lords: 'I speak for the Arts; I do not speak for amateur theatricals'[10]—but, in practice, the work of the regional arts associations and local authorities in developing community arts and local arts centres, the encouragement of new initiatives by artists who had not yet given up their day jobs, the concept of professional 'facilitators' (akin to Keynes's music travellers during the war), festivals, the use of professionals to take the lead parts in amateur choral productions of Elgar's *Gerontius*, as well as Jennie's unflagging support for young people who were inevitably amateur (the National Youth Orchestra, the National Youth Brass Orchestra, the National Youth Theatre), all blurred the amateur–professional line.

Most impressive of all was Jennie's gallant willingness to travel the length of the land, metaphorically as well as literally, to demonstrate that the arts were inclusive and not exclusive: she visited dim arts labs in Covent Garden, heavy (alleged Goodman who disliked such things) with marijuana smoke, and which offered bread, soup, and 'choreography in a bath tub' to down-and-outs; she sat in a tent being declaimed at by young bearded avant-garde poets; she went to Brighton, where she saw a play performed on stomachs, offered, said Goodman, as a great advance in artistic creativity—their spokeswoman told them: 'You are a very old lot', to which Goodman replied: 'Miss, it's the light';[11] and she travelled to the Belgrade Theatre in Coventry, to watch a production of *Lock Up Your Daughters*, where actors bravely sought to convince a sceptical audience of the truth of illusion, and where afterwards Jennie sat on stage amid the set and addressed the stalls, including a Lord Mayor with chains and trade-unionists with attitude: 'You enjoyed that, didn't you', she asked them, and, as though responding to the fairy godmother in a pantomime, they chanted back: 'Yes, yes', as she tried to persuade them of the importance and relevance of the arts.[12]

To diffuse excellence without diluting it meant cherishing the artist.

Jennie liked to think she was as much a minister for artists as she was for the arts. She secured their confidence. As Goodman wrote of her, when she lost her seat in 1970: 'They instinctively felt the profundity of her belief that the artist was the most important member of the community.' She occasionally went over the top. David Eccles, her Tory successor, heard her say to a group of artists: ' "Religion is a sham, the churches are dead; you the artists are now priests." When I said, "But religion tries to understand reality in a way that artists do not", she just looked blank.'[13]

To those who thought that money spent on artists was subsidizing the élite (this from the Left) or the layabout (this from the Right), she insisted that artists gave back infinitely more than they ever took. As she said in a party political broadcast, artists 'are not essentially takers. They are givers. They want to give us their songs, their poems, their dreams.'[14]

She and Goodman experimented with awards and bursaries for artists, but they soon learnt that the best way to support them was to create audiences for their work. That might mean purchasing paintings; subsidizing the publication of little poetry magazines; investing in buildings in which to house and hold repertory and touring theatre; it meant, especially, encouraging a taste for the arts among young people, even inviting one or two of them to sit on the Arts Council itself. Above all, it meant generating endless come-hither publicity of the sort that Jennie had a genius for—creating an image that was simultaneously glamorous (the metropolitan ease, the silver hair, the brilliant flowing kaftans in lime and orange and turquoise) yet also warm, approachable, motherly in her protectiveness of the arts and the artists. She sent a surge of energy and confidence through the arts world—she was on their side, battling against the world and the Treasury. She loved and valued the artists, responding to their insecurities with endless praise.

There were occasional tangles, of which Wesker's Centre 42 at the Roundhouse was perhaps the most painful, her failure to support public lending rights the most criticized, and the failure (not that she was culpable) to get a new opera house built in Edinburgh the most significant. Yet, overall, she did what she set out to do: she got the money, obtained the publicity, cherished the artist, and built the audiences; and then, which might have been hardest of all, stood aside. She was the first, the longest serving, the best known and most loved of all Britain's Ministers for the Arts. No subsequent holders of the post would find themselves applauded as Jennie was when she entered a theatre. The Annan Committee, summoned to consider the future of broadcasting in April 1974, was to note three years later:

> [T]he ideals of middle class culture, so felicitously expressed by Matthew Arnold a century ago, which had created a continuum of taste and opinion, always susceptible to change and able to absorb the avant-garde within its own urban, liberal, flexible principles, found it ever more difficult to accommodate the new expressions of life in the 60s. The new vision of life reflected divisions within society, divisions between classes, the generations and the sexes, between north and south, between the provinces and London, between pragmatists and ideologues. Sometimes the divisions existed but were given new publicity: sometimes they were postulated and then were brought about.[15]

What Noel Annan saw as divisions that fragmented, Jennie welcomed as a pluralism that enriched. She presided over a decade—the 1960s—which, in its mood of personal liberation and hedonism, in politics as in arts, perhaps even more than the First or Second World War, ended the hegemony of Victorian middle-class culture.[16] Jennie was not among the mourners. In her late middle age, she had the feistiness to relish it all.

*

It was the more remarkable because Nye's illness and his death in July 1960 took her out of politics and into the deepest depression for several years. Her friends sought ways of lifting her. The playwright Arnold Wesker tried to entice her out of seclusion with his Centre 42.

The first regional theatre built since the war, Coventry's Belgrade Theatre (the two cities were twinned) had opened in 1958 with the première of the Wesker Trilogy, in which working men and women found voice. Throughout the late 1950s, Wesker had continued to tilt at the anti-intellectualism of the working class. He demanded that the trade unions commission art, publish books, run theatres, recover folk-songs. At the 1960 TUC conference, he persuaded the Association of Cinematography, Television and allied Technicians (ACTT) to move Resolution 42, which called on trade unions to participate in the cultural life of the country. It was carried, against the platform.

Wesker was at the centre of a group of like-minded left-wing writers, including Doris Lessing, Bernard Kops, Shelagh Delaney, Alun Owen, and John McGrath. Together they evolved the concept of Centre 42 (after Resolution 42), a place in which to centre a pool of artists and a network of people's festivals, where artists could control their own means of expression, and where highest standards of professional work would be maintained in an atmosphere of informality, with artists close to their audiences, enabling the public to see artistic activity as a natural part of daily life. They were not seeking, says Wesker, to bring art to the masses or to promote proletarian art; rather, 'here we are, if you want us, call us'.[17] Wellingborough Trades Council promptly did, and in 1960 had a four-day festival. Half a dozen more followed the next year. Wesker wrote plays, Chris Logue read poems, Ewan McColl sang folk.

Doris Lessing had phoned Wesker to talk about Jennie: 'There's Jennie Lee, out in the wilderness, very depressed, Nye's death, there's an emptiness, why don't you contact her and involve her in Centre 42, and it might just give her a new direction?' He did, and it did. Jennie came to hear Wesker lecture at Wellingborough to an over-packed hall:

> [T]he barrier between the working classes and the artist is a monstrous illusion . . . Do you realise what the working class is saying to itself? 'We're bloody fools'. That's what its saying. 'What we don't understand we could never understand. What is strange and new to us is *not* for us. We aren't capable of a great deal of response or enthusiasm or appreciation' . . . 'Do you consider yourself morons?' he shouted at them. ''You don't tolerate bad working and living conditions. Would you tolerate bad thinking and feeling conditions? Someone once said an ugly world is a dangerous world because people become what they see.'[18]

Jennie was bowled over: 'The last time I experienced anyone lecturing with such passion to such a large audience', she told Wesker, 'was Ni.' In 1962, suppressing her personal doubts about the viability of the whole enterprise, 'in the sad hope that Wesker's faith could make us whole', Jennie joined the Council of Centre 42,[19] resigning only when she became Minister for the Arts.

Other friends were also looking out for her. Mervyn Stockwood, by now Bishop of Southwark, who had chaired Jennie's by-election in Bristol during the war, feared for her health in the years following Nye's death. She was broken, 'utterly bereft'. Stockwood knew Harold Wilson to be a kindly man, and he wrote to him asking whether he could help Jennie in any way, find her work to do.[20] Two days after the 1964 general election, Wilson did precisely that. Jennie was astonished to receive a phone call from him the day after he had appointed his Cabinet, asking her to come to Downing Street: 'I've got a job for you to do', he said. 'Find a desk and pack your handbag.'

Wilson had already offered Jennie to Richard Crossman at the Department of Housing. He did not want her—he supposed she would be good for opening bazaars.[21] The Prime Minister now suggested that Jennie might do a job in the Department of Health. He was moved by kindness; but also by calculation. It would not hurt to bring the Bevan memory on side and Jennie might well prove effective. Wilson was later to say:

To understand Jennie, Jennie was devoted to Nye. Nye died young. But Nye once said to me in a car—I think we were going to see Barbara [Castle]—and he said, 'You know Barbara gets all the publicity, but Jennie is just as good as Barbara, but because she's married to me she doesn't get any publicity.' And I think Jennie felt the need for a life and an achievement of her own.[22]

Jennie was taken aback. Health was a bitter-sweet thought, but her instinct was to refuse: 'I had been through all of that before with Aneurin Bevan eighteen years previously.' She feared 'that the P.M. was simply seeking to buy Nye's reputation at the cheapest possible price'.[23] She would be cast as the guardian of Nye's legacy, as the ultimate professional widow. Not that Harold did not owe her, she reflected afterwards. He was only leader because Nye was 'murdered', Gaitskell had died, and George Brown drank. Even so, it would mean living in the shadows. No, not that.

They discussed further. There was a junior slot as yet unfilled in the Ministry of Public Building and Works (MPBW), to which she suggested Wilson could add a loose responsibility for the arts, which up to now had been located in the Treasury. Wilson had made it clear at a Fabian meeting the year before that 'the Exchequer should not be a spending department'.[24] So he was already looking for a new home for the arts, though not necessarily for a designated minister. The MPBW, with its more general responsibility for listed buildings, historic houses, and scheduled monuments was not inappropriate, at least for the time being, while Jennie carved out a job.

Both knew it was something of a dead-end ministry and a dead-end job. Jennie had so far shown no interest in arts policy, but she and Nye had had 'artistic' friends and, although Jennie was the first to insist she was no connoisseur, her tastes were cultivated, her walls carried good paintings which had been lent to Nye, and her home overflowed with books. She had no great ambition for high political office—indeed what political future had she? She might even enjoy such a job and she could resign if she did not. Would Wilson personally support her, she asked, against the Treasury if necessary, if she tried to make a go of it? Wilson was naturally somewhat guarded. She would first have to produce a White Paper to define a policy for the arts. If the Cabinet agreed she had made a case, he would back her, and there would in future be a minister with a designated responsibility for the arts.

Jennie accepted Wilson's conditions, and was parked in MPBW while she produced her White Paper. She was a very junior minister: a parliamentary under-secretary, the lowest of the ministerial ranks. Some friends were indignant and said she was entitled to much more. Goodman, however, advised her that she had nothing to lose (by which, she deduced, he was tactfully saying that now she was 60 she could not reasonably expect preferment), and that she could use the job to give artists and arts associations much-needed help. Over the previous thirteen years, the arts had been 'starved', the great companies were deeply in debt, and not a penny had been spent on capital works for housing the arts. The press claimed that her appointment was a gimmick. But Jennie was determined to prove them wrong. She had, she decided quite quickly, two 'trump cards'. The first was the personal and political support of the Prime Minister. The second card she had yet to play. That was Arnold Goodman.[25]

She made her way to her new home in the MPBW, a splendid office in Lambeth Bridge House with fine views over the Thames, where she was welcomed warmly by her senior minister, Charles Pannell, which surprised her—back in the early 1950s he had been among the first to denounce the Bevanites as a party within a party. The MPBW was responsible for government property at home and abroad, the upkeep of all public buildings and monuments, 'heritage', and the Palace of Westminster itself. A more ambitious minister, Jennie thought, would have wanted to develop arts policy himself. Instead, Charlie Pannell took the part of the job that he most wanted, that is, deciding which Westminster rooms went to which MPs. He was wooed as assiduously as the Chief Whip. He was a very happy man.

An early parliamentary question asked Jennie what her responsibilities towards the arts were—she said she was thinking about it. After a week or two of thinking, she realized that she was not getting far; although Charlie Pannell was helpful, his permanent secretary was not. When Jennie announced that she needed the help of a senior official to prepare her White Paper, he said it was not possible. Pannell, however, said it was. Jennie wanted to know who was available—she was lucky: Antony Part, a former deputy secretary at the DES (Ellen Wilkinson's private secretary in the late 1940s) had been moved sideways into the MBPW. He had just returned from sick leave, and his desk was clear. Jennie acquired her civil servant, and they started work—'I am the Duchess of the Labour Party', she told him. Part noted with amusement that it must have been the first—and last—time in history that when the parliamentary secretary to the MPBW rang the Prime Minister, 'he stopped what he was doing and answered the telephone'.[27]

What was the arts policy of the Labour Party? It was all very vague. The

NEC had put out for comment the 1959 *Leisure for Living* manifesto; it embraced sport and open space, the media, as well as the arts. When the question had arisen as to whether it should be updated for the forthcoming general election, Wayland Young had said: 'All that is required for the Arts is money, policy and silence . . . It is no good "encouraging the arts" in the abstract. You can encourage artists but no establishment has ever shown itself able to spot infant genius.' Others called for more money and wider access. Arnold Wesker demanded 'a teaching of the arts that acknowledges the artists' work as a battle field where ideas are fought out and values affirmed'—the arts grandees would have winced. A shrewd last comment came from David Holbrook: 'It looks a little as though you are purveying posh ways of filling one's leisure.'

The Party's research department tried to pull some very discordant views together, but it was impossible. The NEC decided that an unamended *Leisure for Living* remain Party policy, and left it at that.[28] As a result, the references to the arts in the 1964 general election manifesto, *Let's Go with Labour for the New Britain*, were very brief, clearly in Wilson's hand, and suggested exactly what Holbrook feared—that the technological revolution would generate lots of leisure which should be filled with a shopping list of approved pursuits, more sport, more parks, more youth work, and 'a much more generous support to the Arts Council, the theatre, orchestras, concert halls, museums and arts galleries'.[29] The arts were indeed envisaged as the 'posh' end of leisure and should have more help. That was the extent of Jennie's formal remit.

Undaunted, she settled down to work and receded from sight. Within three months she had completed her draft White Paper, *A Policy for the Arts, the First Steps*. Antony Part skilfully piloted it through committees that Jennie did not even know existed. Before publication she had also to take it to Cabinet for approval. 'How did you get on?' Part asked. 'No problem', she said. 'I gave those boys a good talking to.'[30] To give the White Paper additional weight, and because it referred to aspects of the arts that were beyond Jennie's official remit, it was published in February 1965 under the name of the Prime Minister. It was not deemed to be of sufficient weight to merit a Commons debate until Arthur Blenkinsop MP, who had an interest in the arts, initiated a debate on 27 April 1965.

The White Paper began by outlining the state of the arts (faltering), its funding (spasmodic), and the need to do more 'to improve the quality of contemporary life'. Government support was splintered between three ministries. The DES promoted arts education in schools, colleges, and community centres; it funded the V. & A. and the National Science

Museum; and it would soon lead on public libraries. The MPBW looked after historic buildings. The Treasury directly funded most of the national galleries and museums, such as the National Gallery, the British Museum, the Tate, and the National Portrait Gallery. It also funded the Arts Council, which channelled aid 'to the living arts', music, painting, drama, festivals; sustained the flagships of the performing arts (Covent Garden, Sadler's Wells, the Old Vic/National Theatre, the Royal Festival Hall, and the RSC), and half a dozen orchestras (including the Hallé and the City of Birmingham Symphony Orchestra (CBSO)) outside of London. All three departments, together with the Ministry for Housing and Local Government, coaxed and chivvied local authorities into spending more on the arts. Finally, Jennie's White Paper outlined the next steps: four of them. The government recognized that the first call was to offer artists financial help. The second was to 'see a great increase in local and regional activity', and in particular to 'house' the arts. Complementary to that was the need to 'sustain and strengthen all that is best in the arts, and the best must be made more widely available'. The final need was for coherent planning: and that meant taking the arts remit out of the Treasury and placing it in the DES.

It was an unremarkable White Paper—low key, fairly pragmatic, not much given to purple prose, a bit anxious, as Richard Hoggart noticed, to seem 'switched on'. For the future it promised to balance the claims of the national institutions with the needs of the regions (the word 'regional' was used almost as frequently as the word 'provincial', a sure sign of Jennie's handiwork). The role and powers of the Arts Council were to remain unchanged. It promised a modest increase in funds for every participating body the following year, for bursaries, and for buildings, for purchase grants. The key insight was its recognition that 'by far the most valuable help that can be given to the living artist is to provide him with a larger and more appreciative public'.[31]

The Arts Council and its secretary general, Nigel Abercrombie, did not want to leave the Treasury. They enjoyed the prestige of negotiating direct for their grant, and they approved of the indifference of the Treasury to most of their activity. The Chancellor of the Exchequer would simply announce annually the names of any new members, would answer oral and written questions in the House, and otherwise left them alone. The Treasury kept a tight rein on their finances, but the Arts Council could and did live with that—as, indeed, could the Treasury, which, shortly before the election, considered whether there was a case for a minister with 'specific functional responsibility for the Arts', and decided there was not.[32] It was quite happy with the status quo, enjoying the bit of add-on glamour. Wilson, however, did not want the Treasury to be a spending department; meanwhile, the combination of the Arts Council's past roots and Antony Part's professional background in the DES fitted Jennie's own views. As long as she could retain an independent budget within the DES, she much preferred to have the shelter of a powerful department than set up shop as an independent, small, and probably ineffectual small department. Look what happened to the Ministry of Technology, she would say, when taxed on this.

There was one final consideration. The DES was supposed to launch Wilson's pet project, the university of the air. But nothing much was happening, so Wilson decided to entrust it to Jennie, and to brigade it with her arts portfolio, which meant, finally, placing them both and Jennie in the DES. The newspapers were trailing this new project—education and broadcasting—before Jennie had even switched ministries, making it very clear that this was at the initiative of the Prime Minister. In March 1965 she made the move, and found herself in one of Whitehall's meanest rooms, overlooking the dustbins, motorbikes, and back entrance to the Mirabelle Restaurant, in one of the drabbest buildings in London, where hundreds of wartime long, narrow offices opened off long narrow corridors. This was the Department of Education and Science.

*

The arts grandees were uncomfortable with Jennie's appointment. Lord Drogheda of Covent Garden tried to woo her, calling her, to her annoyance, by her first name, and trying out his 'winsome charm' (they later became firm allies). Nigel Abercrombie, the secretary-general of the Arts Council, who had a civil service background, tried another way. Meeting Jennie at an embassy lunch, he told her bluntly that he would refuse to do business 'below stairs'. A few days after that she met Lord Cottesloe, the chairman, a high and dry Tory; he, too, warned her off, while patronizingly refusing to take her appointment seriously. That was unwise: his five-year appointment as chairman was due for renewal. Jennie then played her second trump card. She phoned Arnold Goodman: would he, she asked, like to join the Arts Council? Light duties and all that. Thank you, that would be nice. A fortnight later, she phoned again: would he like to be chairman? Very light duties etc. After some perfunctory demurral, thank you, that would be very nice.[33]

Goodman's appointment was duly announced. Not even in *Who's Who*, was the sniffy response of civil servants. But he was known to those in power. His solicitors' practice specialized in film, theatre, and libel work—

in 1957, at Jennie's behest, he had acted for Nye, Dick Crossman, and Morgan Phillips in the infamous 'Drink in Venice' case.[34] He continued to act as Jennie's solicitor, winding up Nye's estate for her. He also advised both Gaitskell and Wilson, as they tried to stem NEC leaks to the *Guardian*. He radiated benevolence and good humour. The loveliest ugliest man in London, a friend said at a gala dinner for him. He was clever and wise, yet curiously unthreatening, as the *Sunday Times* noticed in its profile in 1977—like the schoolboy excused from all games, and therefore nobody's rival. He was worldly, but without personal ambition; independent yet discreet; liberal but not libertarian; and transparently committed to the public good. Wilson so valued his acute judgement and disinterested urbane advice that he summoned him to Downing Street every week or two, where he failed, thought Goodman ruefully, to make much use of either. The very day Wilson was elected, he tracked Goodman down to a London restaurant, to ask what should be done about the Royal Philharmonic Orchestra (RPO), which was on the edge of closure. Goodman agreed to take on his first public job, chairing the committee on London's orchestras, where in due course he took some pleasure in reporting his report to himself, as chairman of the Arts Council.[35]

Jennie trusted him utterly. He endeared himself by sharing her impatience with arrogant and dismissive senior civil servants. He was devoted to her. Their relations, he said, were 'idyllic'. She could be censorious, irritable, unfair, totally uncooperative; 'but she would only not like you if you ought not to be liked'.[36] She had spent enough time with artists to share his view that one must never compromise on standards. There should be no question of reducing quality to increase popularity and 'other abominable doctrines'; both wanted 'fervently' to make the arts 'intelligible, acceptable and available to more and more people'. He tramped the artistic highways and byways with her, less adventurous than she was, less credulous perhaps, but always there to support her.

Goodman had found a flat for Jennie above his own in Ashley Gardens. On Sunday evenings she would come down to supper in his roomy basement flat, where they would discuss the next week's business. At first Jennie would bring home her ministerial papers in the official red boxes, but she kept losing the keys. As the papers were restricted but never highly confidential, her private office would put them into large brown envelopes instead, which would then be bundled by Jennie into her capacious shopping bag, to be spilled all over the carpet of Goodman's flat. They would sit on the floor examining them, and Goodman would suggest suitable memos that she might care to write to him, and suitable replies that she might care to receive from him. The department did not like it, but there was little they could do about it. David Eccles, who followed Jennie as Minister for the Arts, said: 'Goodman will never tell you the truth about how much he was Jennie and how little she ever comprehended the arts. But it doesn't matter. She was loved by thousands.'[37] As for Goodman's views on Eccles—he suffered the double disadvantage of not being a woman, and having his enthusiasm constrained by his public school upbringing. In other words, he was not Jennie.[38]

Jennie had managed to get rid of Cottesloe as chairman, and it was not long before Goodman was determined to get rid of Abercrombie as secretary-general. He was a cold, pedantic, decent, conservative civil servant who was resentful that Cottesloe, with whom he had got on well, was not likely to be renewed. His harping on this had offended Jennie within days. When Goodman arrived to ask where the chairman's office was, Abercrombie told him: 'The chairman has never had an office, but my secretary will always type any letters you may want to write.' 'Well', Goodman replied, 'I think this room [Abercrombie's] looks just about right to be my office and my secretary will want somewhere next door.'[39] Goodman judged that either the chairman or the secretary-general had, over the years, run the Arts Council; there was not room for both. Within a couple of years, Abercrombie was moved sideways, and his place was taken by Hugh Willatt, also a solicitor (a partner in Lewis Silkin), and a long-standing member of the Arts Council, with whom Goodman and Jennie worked happily.

Apart from her sequence of very young (assistant principal) private secretaries located in her private office, Jennie also had Keith Jeffery. Jeffery had been in the Cabinet Office, one of the perks of which was that its holder could choose his next posting. Jeffery knew from the moment that Jennie went to the MPBW that there would be a Minister for the Arts. He had a love of the theatre, art, and music; he happened also to be the right rank for the job, and he set his sights on it. He was virtually a one-man band running the embryonic Office of Arts and Libraries, the first administrative civil servant to work full time on the arts. It was a great moment when he opened brand new files labelled Royal Opera House, Museums and Galleries Commission, National Theatre. Jeffery gave Jennie what, at the time neither she nor Goodman possessed, which was briefing about the catty, chatty, incestuous world of the arts. As Jennie told him: 'I rely on Michael [Foot] to give me the political gossip and you to give me the Arts gossip.'

Jennie would send him off in jeans to inspect more radical offerings and report back to her; and then, rather more soberly dressed, to escort her and her fur coat to the endless receptions required of a Minister of the Arts. Just as Goodman endeared himself to her by sharing her irritation with the obstructiveness of some senior civil servants, so she warmed to Jeffery when he briefed her in the way she liked best: pointing out from his background in the MOD that the tailplane of one aircraft cost more than a year's subsidy to the ROH and that the army spent more on military bands alone than they were spending on the entire Arts Council. He became a loyal friend, still escorting her and her fur coat to the theatre long after her political life had closed.[40]

It was not just the arts grandees who did not know what Jennie would do. Neither did the departments. The *Daily Telegraph* had the bright thought of phoning around to ask how Jennie would act as a Minister for the Arts without infringing the independence of the Arts Council. The MPBW, which she had just left, thought she would take 'a motherly interest in everything going on'; the DES simply did not know; Abercrombie at the Arts Council 'hoped she would be spending much of her time encouraging local authorities to support the arts'—that is, out of London, out of his hair.[41]

Jennie and Goodman together began to clarify priorities. Most of the national 'performing arts' flagships were in trouble (and in debt): opera, theatre, ballet, symphonic orchestras. The ROH at Covent Garden merely needed money; the rest, Sadler's Wells Opera, the Old Vic, and the London RSC, needed new homes as well. And that depended on what was built on the empty South Bank site, earmarked since the Festival of Britain back in 1951 for a new national theatre. The Old Vic hoped to go there—would it be joined by the RSC, currently cramped in Aldwych? (Not if the RSC could help it.) If not, where, then would the RSC go? Could the Arts Council afford to add a new opera house for the Sadler's Wells company, now cramped and inaccessible in Islington? If not, where should it be housed? Could it merge with the ROH? (Not if either could help it, given their mutual hostility.)[42] All possible permutations, combinations, and mergers, and many that were not, had to be explored.

The key to it, and therefore Jennie's first priority, was to sort the South Bank site. Related to this was the perennial problem of London's four symphonic orchestras (five if you included the BBC's, which underpinned the Proms) which competed for space at the South Bank's Royal Festival Hall. Were they too numerous and of indifferent quality, as Edward Heath alleged? Would they merge? If not, would one of them relocate to the despised 'provinces'? (Again, not if they could help it.)

Then there was a second set of problems, less intransigent perhaps, associated with the national galleries and museums for which Jennie had formal responsibility and which were funded from outside the Arts Council: the expansion of the Tate; the location of the British Library; the attempt to extract special purchase grants from the Treasury; and, more generally, the effort to make the national museums less forbidding and more inviting, by opening them on Sundays and to children. In addition, Jennie had her own 'new initiatives' in mind, some of them personal and dear to her, such as saving the National Youth Orchestra. Other projects—such as a National Film School—entered her agenda from the work and drive of people she respected. None of this, however, was to be at the expense of her fourth priority, which was to strengthen arts in the regions by building up arts associations, offering bursaries, and funding festivals and arts centres. This, more than anything else, she saw as her mission.

Finally, and that which would make all the rest possible, Jennie had to secure a major increase in the arts budget. Jennie and Goodman both insisted that there could be money without culture, but not culture without money—it was all about money.[43] Then, having won the money, Jennie should maintain a scrupulous silence about how the Arts Council in its turn should allocate it. As Wayland Young's paper for the NEC back in 1963 had said, for the arts 'all that is required is money, policy and silence'.

*

Jennie turned first to the South Bank, to the most intertangled of the problems she faced. It was a matter of rivalry between two opera companies, three theatre companies, four orchestras, and five sites. That was the simple part. The complexity came from its supervision by two boards (the National Theatre Board and the South Bank Board) and its finance from two authorities, the LCC/GLC and the Treasury. Without Jennie to cut her way through, there would have been no National Theatre (NT).[44]

The idea of a 'national theatre' celebrating Shakespeare had been the dream of Bernard Shaw, Henry Irving, J. M. Barrie, and Lilian Baylis since before the First World War. Nothing happened, so Lilian Baylis founded the Old Vic at Waterloo and the Shakespeare Memorial Theatre (later the RSC) at Stratford. The project of a national theatre was reopened after the Second World War: the National Theatres Bill in 1949 earmarked £1 million for it; the Old Vic formally amalgamated with the National Theatre Company; and the Cromwell Road site was swapped for a much larger site on the South Bank, cleared for the Festival of Britain and adjacent to the

Royal Festival Hall. The Queen laid the foundation stone in 1951. And then, again, nothing happened.

A decade later, Laurence Olivier tried for the third time when in the early 1960s he proposed fusing the Old Vic/National Theatre with Peter Hall's RSC, and housing them all on the South Bank. The government hesitated about the cost, Peter Hall hesitated about Laurence Olivier, but the Labour LCC, prodded by one of its members, Hugh Jenkins (a future Minister for the Arts) offered to come in with £1.3 million, more than matching the government's contribution, and enough, it hoped, also to provide for a new opera house for Sadler's Wells. In the event, the government stayed in, Peter Hall pulled out (the RSC eventually went to the Barbican), Laurence Olivier was appointed director in 1962, and Denys Lasdun the architect in 1963. The next two years were spent debating whether the NT should have an arena stage for theatre in the round, or the more focused, but also more distanced, proscenium stage. The board of directors eventually compromised and had both, adding as well a small experimental theatre. The effect of Lasdun's designs, the two years delay, and the three theatre stages, sent costs soaring. What had been estimated at just over £2 million in 1961, had now become £7.5 million, and that for the NT alone. The (Labour) government was unsure whether it could afford to fund an opera house as well—at a further £7 million—and the now Tory GLC was unsure whether it was willing even to share the cost of the NT.

Enter Jennie (one is tempted to say centre stage left). She and Goodman agreed: Edinburgh, with its prestigious international festival, needed its first opera house, a home for Scottish opera, before London got its second. If she insisted on retaining a South Bank opera house, the entire NT scheme was at risk. As the public expenditure crisis deepened, the Chancellor of the Exchequer, Roy Jenkins, became restive at the extravagant costs of the Lasdun design, and only special pleading and several meetings with Jennie and Goodman kept the NT project afloat. Sadler's Wells was furious at losing its proposed new opera house, the ROH was delighted at the discomfiture of its rival, but feelings were somewhat soothed when Goodman helped Sadler's Wells take a lease on the Coliseum just off Trafalgar Square in 1968. The company renamed itself the English National Opera (ENO).

Without the opera house, Lasdun had both to redesign and relocate the rest of the complex, causing further doubts and delays. Costs were escalating and Jennie was not at her best with issues of budgetary control. She always preferred to fight for more money than to exercise discipline over the money she had. Fortunately, most arts problems could indeed be resolved by 'throwing money' at them. By now the GLC was reluctant to put its share up front. Jennie had urgent meetings with Desmond Plummer, the GLC's Tory leader, and agreed that it would contribute its half of the cost not at tender stage, but at completion ('fatuous' was her private comment; but given the uncertain costs and the very certain delays, the GLC was being perfectly sensible). She put Goodman on the South Bank board, where he sat 'like a hooded Buddha' contemplating proceedings.[45]

Construction finally started in 1969 and the NT was completed in 1976, by now with Peter Hall as director, after it had suffered the usual problems of monumental buildings, revolving stages that would not revolve, generators that would not generate, and a cost overrun of some £16 million. But for Jennie's intervention with the Treasury and then with the GLC, the NT would have been lost. It was Jennie at her weakest, with her poor financial grasp, and Jennie at her best, with her tenacious and steely political skills.

The residual problems facing the opera and theatre companies were much simpler: they needed substantial revenue support. Opera in particular was notoriously expensive, requiring singers, ballet dancers, and orchestra. Because of its heavy demands on sets, storage, dressing-room, and orchestra pit, 'grand' opera was hard to tour, so the 'national' flagships were increasingly confined to London, creaming off nearly half the total Arts Council grant in 1964–5 for the benefit of the metropolitan wealthy, the foreign tourist, and the corporate business communities. The two opera companies were carving out very different roles. The ENO was offering productions in English to a home market with the help of some GLC subsidy. The ROH, which received double the ENO's subsidy from the Arts Council, by contrast, was judging itself by international standards—Milan, New York. Because its opera was sung in the original language, it could use foreign singers. However, the greater its insistence on international excellence, the higher the cost of its productions, sets, and artists. Even Jennie, a stout defender of 'excellence', winced when she learnt that the dragon in 'Siegfried', on stage for all of eight minutes in four performances, cost more than the entire subsidy for a theatre company in a year.[46] The Arts Council pegged the ROH revenue subsidy at a modest increase above inflation, and Sadler's Wells (for which Goodman and Jennie had a soft spot) got a little more to cover the costs of the move to the Coliseum. Most of the 'new' money went elsewhere. Even so, the two opera companies took a quarter of the much-expanded Arts Council budget in 1970–1.

Lord Drogheda, chairman of the ROH, who had been wary of Jennie, became an ally. As he said of her: 'She did not attempt to bring politics into her job. She always held that there must be certain centres of excellence, which needed generous support because it was for them to set standards, and she recognised that if they were financially starved they could not fulfil their task. As long as she was around, Covent Garden was secure.' One could see why he approved of her.[47] When later she faced a Tory motion of censure on her salary rise, Drogheda praised her in *The Times*. He wrote to her privately in 1969: 'no one can exaggerate the importance of the part you have played since you took Ministerial charge of cultural matters. You have been a triumphant success . . . sackcloth and ashes if you were to be transferred elsewhere.'[48]

Not just the opera companies and the theatre companies, but London's symphony orchestras also had an interest in what happened on the South Bank. London had four symphony orchestras: the LSO founded in 1904, the LPO founded by Thomas Beecham in 1932, the New Philharmonia Orchestra founded in 1946, which originally worked for EMI, and the RPO, a second Beecham orchestra, founded when he lost the LPO. In addition, London enjoyed the BBC Symphony Orchestra (founded in 1930), which gave a large number of public concerts, especially at the Proms, as well as the resident orchestras supporting the two opera houses, and the smaller sinfoniettas. The RPO, which had been Sir Thomas's private orchestra, was regarded as the least prestigious. Unable to get dates at the Royal Festival Hall, it resorted forlornly to playing in half-empty halls in the suburbs, and by the 1960s it was close to bankruptcy. This suggested that London had too many orchestras compared with most capital cities, which had only one or two. If some were amalgamated, would it not make for better orchestras and less subsidy? Goodman, however, was persuaded that orchestras had their own culture, and that they could not, should not, merge.

What were the alternatives? The RPO was reluctant to become a regional touring orchestra, and nor would it agree to move out of London, for instance to the East of England. The Midlands had the CBSO, the North had the Hallé, the North-West had the Liverpool Philharmonic, Scotland had its National Orchestra, and the West of England received tours from the Bournemouth Symphony Orchestra. Yet the East had nothing. Goodman (and Jennie) ducked the issue—they were not the last to do so—and decided to keep them all, and all in London. Indeed, Jennie boasted that she had 'saved' one of London's finest orchestras. As a result, their musicians remained underemployed, their standards were compared unfavourably with foreign 'competition', and East Anglia (and to some extent the South-West) remained starved of first-class music.

Goodman did persuade the Arts Council, along with the GLC, to establish the London Concerts Orchestral Board to sort out venues, rotas, and programmes. No one wanted to hear Beethoven's Fifth played four times in a week by four different orchestras, he noted.[49] There was, however, a price to pay: £250,000 a year, in subsidy to the London Orchestras Board, which took nearly a third of the Arts Council's total grant to concert and orchestras, and which heightened the disparity between London and the regions—four orchestras in the capital to the rest of the country's five. The Peacock Report of June 1970 revisited the problem, suggesting that only two orchestras be subsidized, and the rest should go commercial, but nothing was done. Efforts either to merge or relocate London's orchestras were again made in the 1980s, and in the early 1990s, and again failed. The London Orchestras Board was finally disbanded in 1986.

Jennie and Goodman had secured the future of the NT, but the rest of the theatre scene, particularly outside London, looked dire. Between 1939 and 1960, Britain had lost two-thirds of its theatres, as they fell to cinema, bombs, blitz, television, and redevelopment. Keynes had persuaded CEMA to run a few theatres during the war to keep them alive. When the last of the three theatres in Leicester was sold for commercial development in 1957, the Arts Council warned that 'in the near future, the theatre outside London will be beyond recovery and, where it manages to survive, as poignant as a museum piece . . . Must all this mean that, outside London, we are bound to accept the dissolution of the professional theatre within the new few years?'[50]

Only two new theatres had been built since 1945, both of them 'acts of faith', said the Arts Council: the Belgrade Theatre at Coventry and Bernard Miles's Mermaid Theatre at Puddle Dock, the first new theatre in the City of London for 300 years. Yet the later 1950s had seen a flowering of playwrights in search of performance. Wesker was joined by Shelagh Delaney, John Osborne, the Paris-based Samuel Beckett, and John Arden, much of their work performed at the Royal Court where in 1956 George Devine had established the experimental English Stage Company. Joan Littlewood's blazing work at Stratford (East London) had helped to generate in England a theatre of social protest, theatre as a place where the audience was challenged as much as it was entertained. But plays needed playhouses. There had been thirteen years of Tory rule and not a penny for capital projects, Jennie noted as she took up her post.

Where commercial theatres did survive, they were shabby, depressing, unwelcoming, ill-sited, and half empty. 'Housing the Arts' became one of the projects dearest to Jennie's heart. She begged local authorities to take the remaining theatres at risk into their protective ownership. She wrung from the Treasury an additional allocation over and beyond the Arts Council grant, of £250,000 in 1965, and £500,000 in subsequent years, which could be used to coax local communities to modernize old and build new theatres, adapt halls, and develop community arts centres. Hundreds of bids flooded into the Arts Council. Jennie delightedly opened the first such scheme when in August 1965 she started up the pile-drivers for the foundations of the Cygnet Theatre in Cannon Hill Park, Birmingham, part of an arts centre for young people. Afterwards, she joined the architects (young students at Birmingham's School of Architecture) and the workers (young apprentices from local building firms) in hefty mugs of tea.

By 1970 Jennie could proudly report that Housing the Arts had helped to fund over 150 projects, of which only 11 were in London. A total of £2 million of Arts Council money succeeded in levering £8 million from the local authorities in challenge funding. Beneficiaries included the Maltings at Snape, the Leeds Playhouse, Sheffield's Empire Theatre, the New Repertory Theatre at Birmingham, the Mercury Theatre at Colchester, the Harlow Playhouse, and Swindon's Wyvern Theatre. Slowly, a new sort of theatre emerged, the civic theatre, neither commercial nor repertory, but owned and subsidized by the local authority, sometimes run by a local trust, offering a varying menu of tours by the national companies, pre-West End plays, amateur performances, Sunday concerts, and pantomime.

Jennie was overjoyed. Housing the Arts was not an obsession with bricks and mortar, never about merely building buildings, but about building audiences, without which the arts perished. The cinema had taught audiences to expect new standards of comfort and plush for their night out. Producers were well aware that the more challenging and uncomfortable the play, the more comfortable needed to be the seating, if new audiences were not to find the whole occasion purgatorial. Housing the Arts also gave Jennie and Goodman the occasion to switch money into the regions; and in the name of 'response' funding, to persuade local authorities into partnership with the Arts Council and into a new responsibility for the arts. There were difficulties, as when three bids came forward simultaneously for theatres in Halifax, Huddersfield, and Wakefield. The Treasury remained its usual unhelpful self, by insisting that the balance of funds had to be raised locally before the Arts Council's share (on average around 20 per cent) was forthcoming, thus ensuring that many schemes did not come forth. Not even Jennie could get them to budge.

Bigger projects, such as the proposed new opera house for Edinburgh, were negotiated separately. George Harewood, director of the Edinburgh Festival, brought Jennie on an official visit in 1965, where she met the city leaders, mostly Tory, though with one or two Labour members present. Jennie talked at some length about the importance of the arts to the city, says Harewood:

> and not least of the need to build a great theatre to serve Edinburgh and its Festival. The Labour leader . . . started to harangue us about the prior claims of things like hospitals and road improvement, and Jennie listened in polite silence until he had finished when she said that undoubtedly hospitals and roads were highly important to the life of a community, but so too were festivals and the buildings in which to house them. In fact she had just been listening to the greatest piece of political illiteracy she had ever heard in her entire career.[51]

Goodman, undaunted, extracted a theoretical allocation of £2 million from the Treasury (an extraordinary achievement) to meet half of the cost, if the city would find the rest; but Edinburgh, he says ruefully, decided to build a new stadium, Meadowbank, for the 1970 Commonwealth Games instead (not an enterprise with which he would have instinctive sympathy).[52] He tried again, but Edinburgh kept trying to increase the government's proportion (it was, after all, a very heavy commitment for a not very large city). Like the saga of the South Bank site, no sooner had one party committed itself, then the other had doubts; by the time those doubts were resolved, costs had again soared, and the party of the first part wanted out. A new round of undertakings both from the Treasury and Edinburgh City Council were given in the mid 1970s, but 'to that city's disgrace', said Jennie, the opera house remained unbuilt, and the magnificent site opposite the castle remained empty.

If the failure to construct a new opera house at Edinburgh was the disappointment of Jennie's ministry, the vicissitudes of Arnold Wesker's Centre 42 were perhaps the most painful, and funny. Wesker and Doris Lessing had brought Jennie on to the Council of Centre 42 in 1962. They had found a building—a Victorian engine-shed in Chalk Farm, the Round House—but they needed £650,000 to convert it into a theatre and cultural centre.

Centre 42 lost Jennie as a council member when she became Minister for the Arts, but hoped it had kept a powerful friend who would send financial help its way. But, says Wesker, he was 'not a good enough hustler'.[53] He continued to go the rounds of TUC and Labour Party conferences seeking money. At Blackpool in 1966, he was standing disconsolately in the centre lobby of the Conference hotel, when Jennie came through the front entrance—she was a bit drunk, Wesker recalls—and went over to greet him. 'Come and sit down'; whereupon he poured out his complaints: the trustees of Centre 42 were idle, the project was stalling, it needed money. Could Wilson move things along 'by pulling strings?'

It was an unfortunate choice of words, and Jennie responded with tipsy outrage: 'Arnold, you want our Prime Minister to be corrupt.' Wilson came into the hotel and Jennie called him over: 'Harold, Arnold here thinks you ought to be corrupt and I'm saying we can't have a corrupt Prime Minister.' Marcia Williams, a solid friend of Centre 42, was at Wilson's side. 'How much do you need', asked Wilson, 'to start things rolling?' Wesker tried out £200,000. Wilson turned to Marcia: 'Mary must have a tea party', he said, and out he went. Jennie, says Wesker, then became contrite and helpful. She clutched him by the arm, and, as they walked up and down the lobby, she said: 'I understand you, Arnold. You come from a working-class background and your mother and father went through it all and you inherited their knowledge of working-class struggle. Well now, Harold has done this, we'll see what we can do.'

Except that 'we' did nothing. Wesker found his tea party postponed, and then postponed again. Finally, he snapped. At a meeting of the trustees in the Commons he claimed that Centre 42 was being 'sabotaged'. Just then a division bell rang. When the MPs resumed, they brought Jennie and Wilson back with them. Wesker somewhat nervously resumed his harangue: the trustees must either find the money, sell the Round House, or let it out commercially. Jennie asked the question that had been floating in the air: 'Who do you think is sabotaging the Round House?' The silence lengthened. Wesker took a deep breath and said: 'You, Jennie. And I think you have done it because you are frightened that Centre 42 is really trying to take over your function as Minister of Culture.' It was, he said, in an attempt to pun, 'Jennicide'. Jennie, not surprisingly, was very angry, leant across the table, and said, 'You know your trouble; you're still a bloody communist', and made to hit him. The rest of the group looked on in horror, amusement, and embarrassment, before they got round to soothing them both. Shortly thereafter, Wesker got a letter from Wilson offering him a CBE, which he refused, and a hostile article in *Tribune* by Ted Willis, which he resented. He suspected that Jennie was behind both.

The Wilson tea party was finally set for late July 1967. Wilson called them in, insisting there was to be no squabbling over the sandwiches. On the way out, Wesker tried to apologize to Jennie if she thought he had been unfair. 'Nye always warned me against people who make public declarations and private apologies', she said grandly; and Wesker was left feeling 'as shitty as could be'.

The tea party passed off without fireworks. Wesker spoke—for too long, grumbled Wilson—and raised promises of £80,000. It was not enough. Wesker pulled out as director of Centre 42 in November 1970, only a few months after Jennie lost her job as Minister for the Arts, and the Round House promptly showed *Oh! Calcutta*, Kenneth Tynan's profitable and commercial tilt at censorship. Why did the project fail? Lack of money. Money could be raised for one-off events, but not for unglamorous administration. Wesker sold his film rights to *Chips with Everything* to inject cash, but it was not enough. The Arts Council, which alone could have provided a reliable annual subsidy, was never on side. Wesker's intransigent manner, his offhand way with money, and his high-handed way with Jennie, alienated Goodman. Wesker would say: 'Don't mess with my idea. Either do it or don't do it.' Goodman, for his part, thought this was vanity theatre. A comment in his memoirs—Centre 42 was 'Wesker's notion of an organisation to supervise the growth of the arts in this country'—reveals the size of the gap between them. 'His scheme had not found favour in my eyes.'[54] Jennie and Wesker each continued to feel hard done by the other. When she died in 1988, Wesker wrote to Goodman, in the absence of close family: 'I'm sorry we clashed. I'm sorry I failed to make Forty Two happen. I'm sorry time passes. I'm sorry she's dead.'[55]

*

Support for the performing arts came within the remit of the Arts Council; support for the visual arts usually did not. Local authorities funded local museums and galleries, while the national institutions, such as the Tate, the National Gallery, and the National Portrait Gallery, received five yearly grants directly negotiated with the Treasury. (The British Museum/British Library complex was also part of the DES's responsibility, but Patrick Gordon-Walker, as Secretary of State for Education, seems to have retained personal responsibility for that.) This did not stop the national museums and galleries seeking Jennie's help on some occasions, and receiving her attention on others.

The Tate, for example, was still incomplete. To finish the building meant expanding on to the site occupied by the adjacent military hospital. Jennie went in to battle for the Tate. Denis Healey, Secretary of State for Defence, saw no reason to be helpful. Military doctors liked the proximity of this cancer hospital to the Westminster teaching hospital; Jennie could not understand why such a specialist hospital had to be in central London at all. Neither did Healey, when she reminded him that she understood that he was seeking to be elected to the NEC as Treasurer of the Party (she was its chair in 1968). This was old-fashioned political brutality, noted her private office admiringly. In case Healey was in any doubt, she went to Wilson, and kicked up a fuss. As a result, the military hospital moved to Woolwich, and her 'smart art chums' grabbed the site, as one doctor put it, still bitter: 'She would not have dared to have touched it, had it been an NHS hospital.'[56]

The galleries were especially attentive to Jennie when they wanted a particular acquisition. She helped the National Gallery buy the Tiepolo ceiling; she 'saved' Drake's drum for the nation. When a Gauguin landscape was offered to the Treasury in lieu of death duties, the Director of the Tate, Norman Reid, put in a strong bid and expected to get it. Jennie, however, decided she should 'look after the provinces', and proposed to offer it to Manchester. The Director was 'very cast down'—the Gauguin was important to the Tate's holdings—but by now he knew Jennie well enough through mutual friends to make one last effort, a personal letter, which he delivered to her home that evening. Jennie telephoned the next morning and agreed, 'but', she added, 'the next one must go to Manchester'. It did: it was Stubbs's *Hunters with Cheetah*. Everyone was always trying to interest her in some pet scheme or other, Reid noted, but she always listened willingly, ending such conversations by saying: 'Do be a dear and let me have a little paper on it.' She must have built up quite a portfolio, he suspects, of 'rosy hopes'.[57]

The V. & A., unlike almost all the other national galleries, was not an independent institution and had no trustees, but was run directly by the DES. So when Jennie wanted museums to be more welcoming, it was natural that she should turn first to the V. & A. Its Director John Pope-Hennessy warmly admired Jennie, and agreed with her that the V. & A. had an almost 'parental relationship' to regional museums, and should do all it could to help them, with advice, circulating exhibitions, and the like. Jennie was also determined to make the museum child-friendly. Early in April 1968, an elderly sandwich-man patrolled around South Kensington tube station, his dull raincoat somewhat at odds with the sensuous cupids that entwined on his poster-board. He was advertising the first Sunday morning opening of the V. & A. across the road. As people exited from the tube, they stared and then crossed the road to queue. At 10 o'clock in the morning, Jennie's black limousine drew up, and in she went as the doors opened so that she could greet people as they entered. Pope-Hennessy, reluctant to disappoint her, remembers 'ringing up any friend who had a child, begging them to come along to the museum' that Sunday morning. A 10-year-old son of the museum's superintendent was placed strategically at the head of the queue, wearing a CND badge on his outsize duffle coat, which he had bought at Speakers' Corner; he chatted to Jennie about his favourite section of the museum, inevitably its armoury. Around 4,500 people visited the V. & A. that day, and Jennie pronounced it a great success. But as the museum's staff establishment budget had been frozen, it meant that existing staff had to cover the extra hours, and within a year the scheme faltered.[58]

Undaunted, Jennie tried to persuade Roy Strong that the National Portrait Gallery, of which he was then the Director, should follow suit. She came to open the new nineteenth-century galleries. He did not care for her style: 'The National Portrait Gallery was not her thing at all and I knew it, shipping in a mass of Council children to keep her happy. These she lectured on the terrible times the working classes and children had in the last century, which made one groan. The children weren't entertained but one had to play up to her—as indeed all those Ministers' foibles.' And then, more sharply, he added: 'Jennie was around when the money was around. Nothing would lead me to conclude that she knew anything at all about the visual arts . . . She was a loveable opinionated champagne Socialist who always popped up at the head of the queue anywhere.' His memories may have been influenced by the occasion when she attended a V. & A. junket with Goodman in the mid-1970s, saying: 'Oh Roy, what are you here for?' To which he replied, 'Well, oddly enough, I'm the Director.'

She reigned, says Strong, over 'an illusion'.[59] It was a harsh judgement, giving Jennie no credit at all for doubling the museums' purchase grants (from an average of £850,000 a year in the mid-1960s, to £2 million in 1970–1), when all around her ministers saw their programmes being axed. 'Money, policy, silence': Jennie, even her most grudging critics agree, fought for the money. And, as Pope-Hennessy said: 'she gave directions on policy (and very sensible directions they were), but did not interfere in their implementation'.[60] Her silence came to be valued even more in retrospect when the museums enjoyed the attentions of her successor, David Eccles. Jennie often found herself unpleasantly patronized for her lack of connoisseurship; museum directors, however, found it rather more difficult when they had to deal with a minister who did make such claims and, as something of an arts grandee himself, expected them to be taken seriously.

Jennie, while mystified at some of the artistic activity that asked for subsidy, carefully kept her opinions to herself. Her civil servants noted that she would say she knew what she liked, but never said what that was. She did not intervene in, but made it clear she would not oppose, George Russell Strauss's 1968 Theatre Bill (it was, in any case, technically a matter for Roy Jenkins, then Home Secretary), which abolished the licensing powers of the Lord Chamberlain, or as Kenneth Tynan described him, the 'Royal Smut Hound'. All plays had to be submitted before performance to the Lord Chamberlain—he had banned *Cat on a Hot Tin Roof* only a few years before. Tynan noted that in six months in 1965, of 441 plays submitted, changes were required in 45, substantial changes in 15, wholesale rewriting in 3. 'Crap' had to be replaced by 'jazz', 'post-coital' by 'late evening', and 'wind from a duck's behind' became, for some reason, 'wind from Mount Zion'. A 'pee' might be permitted in Act One if 'Christ' were dropped from Act Three. A one-liner in *Look Back in Anger* ('She's as rough as a night in a Bombay brothel') was thought to be splendid—the censor would retell it himself in the Guards Club—but it was not to be heard in the theatre, 'where people don't know one another'. When eighteen passages in *Luther* were blue-pencilled, John Osborne rebelled: 'I don't write plays to have them rewritten by someone else', and the censor crumbled. Pre-censorship was to be replaced by the risk of obscenity trials, and the theatre brought into line with literature.[61]

Wilson, characteristically, was not very keen on lifting censorship—he thought playwrights might say rude things about the royals. The bill only got through the Cabinet because Wilson was away that day.[62] Goodman, equally characteristically, wanted some scheme of voluntary self-censorship, and, though he prided himself on his urbanity, did not much care, for example, to have a naked Desdemona on stage in a Bernard Miles production of *Othello*. He offered Miles the use of his credit card to clothe the lady.[63] Jennie was more robust and thought it all rather hilarious.

When David Eccles became Minister for the Arts, he made a sharp distinction between public money and private money. He was convinced that the theatre was a cesspool of filth, and that public money should not support 'disgusting blasphemy'. Sleaze joints and the like were acceptable, as they were financed by private money. When he learnt that Elizabeth Thomas, literary editor of *Tribune*, and the mildest and sanest of women, was joining the literature panel of the Arts Council, he entered into a tirade against weak-kneed liberals, the country going to the dogs, and headmasters worried about impressionable young men. When he asked to be shown around the Institute of Contemporary Arts, Goodman went to some considerable effort to insert his not inconsiderable girth between the minister and Picasso's drawings of brothel life.[64] Eccles found it very irritating to be told that the Arts Council was independent of government and therefore independent of him; and that it did not seek to impose good taste. As Jennie wrote: 'Political control is a short cut to a boring, stagnant theatre—there must be freedom to experiment, to make mistakes, to fail, to shock, or there can be no new beginnings. It is hard for any Government to accept this.'[65]

Even Jennie's tolerance had been tested, however, by one Magritte exhibition at the Tate. She arrived for the preview, where the Director Norman Reid, and Sir William Coldstream, chairman of the Art Council's art panel, were waiting to greet her. She arrived, 'puce with anger', and snapped at Coldstream: 'Who is responsible for this disgraceful invitation card?' The disgraceful card was Magritte's nude female body on which a female face (which could also be seen as female genitalia) were superimposed. Even her young private secretary thought it was 'extremely vulgar'.

Coldstream, one of the most unflappable and charming of men, replied: 'I am very sorry, Minister, it is all my fault.' Jennie, who was no fool and knew it was nothing of the sort, said tartly: 'That won't do, Bill. I want their name. Someone must pay for this.' To his eternal credit, at least in the eyes of the increasingly apprehensive Director of the Tate, Coldstream again repeated that it was entirely his fault. Jennie marched off up the Sculpture Hall with Director, chairman, and private secretary in hot pursuit. The rest of the Tate staff melted discreetly away. When she came to the pictures, she turned to Reid: 'You have to be very careful. You won't get your knighthood that way.' She then came to the Magritte picture of men with bowler hats in the rain, and turned to her private secretary: 'and there, Mr Stuart, by the grace of God goes you'. And she put up her umbrella and stomped off into the night.[66]

A few months after she had lost office, Jennie was appealed to when Eccles generated another damaging row. He believed, says Jennie, that art was a rich man's pursuit, and that they, rather than the taxpayer, should pay for it. Eccles therefore proposed to introduce charges for national galleries and museums. The National Gallery was not unhappy, neither was Pope-Hennessy at the V. & A.; but the British Museum, the Tate, and Roy Strong's National Portrait Gallery were all strongly opposed. Many of their pictures had been donated on the understanding that they would be freely displayed. Offering a day of free entry in the week was no solution—the Museum of Modern Art in New York had thirty thousand visitors on Sunday when it was free, and about a thousand a day for the rest of the week. Museums already charged for special exhibitions and collections, and that deterred three-quarters of museum visitors from attending them. The money raised would not be large—£1 million, Eccles estimated. It would be a tax on access—Tories believed that people valued what they paid for. Jennie saw it as a frontal assault on the principle she most held dear: that there should be open access to excellence.[67]

The same principle of free access at the point of use underlay Jennie's ambivalence to public lending rights (PLR), a topic on which she attracted more criticism than any other in her ministry. Writers saw their books freely circulated by public libraries, but received not a penny from it. Musicians enjoyed performance rights; why should authors not be similarly rewarded? Alan Herbert had long campaigned for PLR, and hopes were high when Jennie became minister and talked mistily of her love of books and libraries. Her White Paper promised that PLR would be examined. When the Arts Council came out in favour, authors waited hopefully, but nothing happened. Pressed in the Commons, Jennie delayed and demurred. Most of the schemes put to her, she decided, would subvert a principle even more important than justice to writers, and that was the free public lending library. Local authorities could not afford to pay royalties out of the rates; to do so, they would have to charge their readers, and this Jennie would not tolerate. Writers reminded her that library services now were not all free: there were charges for reservations and inter-library loans, for example. Why not charge for the loan of books?

Writers confronted librarians, and Jennie supported the librarians. Oddly, there is no evidence that she sought a Treasury grant to fund PLR. Writers turned on her. Michael Holroyd penned a savage piece in *The Times*: authors had trusted her, flattered her, spoken out for her, and she had betrayed them; while she delayed, the country's writers 'are dying slowly, painfully, from [your] discouragement'.[68] Jennie still refused to do anything, even though the Arts Council believed the Treasury was persuadable. Jennie almost certainly could have delivered PLR, but chose not to do so. For once, she was at odds with Goodman. Eccles, too, did nothing, similarly caught in the crossfire of conflicting views. Only when Hugh Jenkins was Minister for the Arts, and negotiated new money from the Treasury for a national fund from which to make payments (based on a sample of issues) was the problem addressed.

Jennie did try to help writers acquire readers in other ways. In discussions with Goodman, she encouraged Arts Council initiatives which sent writers on tour, into schools and universities; poets into pubs; artists into residence; gave bursaries to young writers and grants to research libraries to buy their unpublished manuscripts; and helped small presses to publish new poetry. Jennie was the first to admit that the sums were modest, but it signalled that literature and poetry, as well as the visual and performing arts, were a proper concern of the Arts Council, and that writers, too, needed cherishing. The Arts Council was somewhat nonplussed when Richard Ingrams and John Wells of *Private Eye* accordingly turned up at the Arts Council office, arguing that if the intention was to create a 'gay, fun-loving Britain', they were doing more than most; they pressed the claims of satire as a literary form, and cited Dryden, Swift, and Pope in evidence. Their attention, however, was drawn to the damage that would be done to their bold and independent image if they accepted subsidy. They took the point.[69]

Goodman did veto one poetry prize, when AMBIT, a small literary magazine kept afloat by an Arts Council grant, offered £25 for the best poem written under the influence of drugs. Angus Wilson, chairman of the literature panel, worried that they were being illiberal. When on another occasion Goodman vetoed a grant to the Covent Garden Arts Lab for the same reason, Jennie remonstrated with him, and the novelist Brigid Brophy threatened to resign. Asked by *The Times* for his response to Brophy's resignation, Goodman hoped 'to bear it with fortitude'.[70] (Goodman was known to defer to Jennie, but never to the wishes of the other members of the Council. 'It's an impasse,' he announced at one meeting, when he had been voted down nineteen to one. He brought the item back the next month and got his way.)

When Jennie was interviewed in 1969 by the *Times Educational Supplement* and in 1970 by the *Sunday Times*,[71] they both asked what her priorities had been as Minister for the Arts. She listed them: to get the National Theatre going (by then rising on the South Bank); to start the Open University (by then recruiting staff); to establish a building fund for the arts (and by now she had 140 projects underway). And she had two further ambitions: to bring arts to young people; and to bring arts to the regions. The problem with the first of these was money: arts by young people were inevitably amateur and therefore not funded by the Arts Council; the problem with the second of these was also money: finding enough new money not to threaten the London flagships.

Almost the very first issue Jennie faced when she joined the DES was the future of the National Youth Orchestra (NYO). Ruth Railton had founded it in 1947, but had stopped her subsidy when in 1962 she married Cecil King of Mirror Newspapers. As an amateur youth orchestra, it was ineligible for help from the Arts Council. Despite Jennie's eloquence, Crosland was not persuaded that it was a DES responsibility, and would not find £7,000 a year from his budget of £1.5 billion. Jennie never forgave him. She was still complaining about it to Wilson many years later.[72] She had promised the NYO that she would ensure its survival, and she did what she always did in such circumstances: turned to Goodman, who magicked the money from private funds.

Arts by and for young people wove its way through all Jennie's policies. She was keen to launch a national youth brass band, and to sustain the brass band traditions of the North; she offered grants to Menuhin's school of music (founded in 1963); and she encouraged the Arts Council to offer grants to adult theatres which worked with children. She enthused about John Neville of the Nottingham Playhouse and Bernard Miles of the Mermaid, who sent actors out to local schools. Children in Castleford, Yorkshire, never forgot the day when a friend of Jennie's, Henry Moore, turned up supposedly to talk about his work, but instead brought them lumps of clay to work on. When Laurence Olivier of the Old Vic started work as Director of the National Theatre, he pleaded at an Arts Council seminar that a national youth theatre be started—'young talent had to be trained', and a National Theatre could not survive on a few stars alone. Jennie was so moved that she asked him to write a paper for her with which she might seek to persuade the Prime Minister and the Treasury. He did, and she did—getting agreement almost by return of post. They launched the Young Vic.[73]

Jennie then turned to museums and galleries. These needed to be more friendly and more accessible. There should be Sunday morning openings, and special children's exhibitions (the directors always dreaded the task of rounding up recalcitrant children). Sir Michael Levy, the Director of the National Gallery, remembers a visit from Jennie when she scolded a mother in one of the exhibition rooms who was hushing her child, saying, 'Don't do that or she will associate the National Gallery with restrictions.' She told the staff how she had brought her young nephew Vincent in to look at some Rubens paintings, and he, studying the *Last Judgement of Paris*, had shouted: 'they're not wearing knickers'; she agreed that they were not. Levy liked her for her forthrightness; but at the gallery, 'the tendency was to despise her—I think that's not too strong—for being ignorant about art.' This view appeared to be confirmed on her first visit when she showed more interest in the coffee shop than in the pictures—'all she cared about', senior staff reported afterwards to junior staff, 'was the quality of the rock cakes'. They missed the point, as Jennie guessed they would. The café was indeed awful; no museum now, notes Levy ruefully, would be so indifferent to the comfort of parents and children.[74]

Bringing the arts to children and young people meant, above all, coaxing local education authorities into a more generous reading of the school curriculum. It is hard, so many years later, to recall just how bare that education was. A child at a rural grammar school in the late 1950s, for example, would do some painting in her junior years, might sing 'Greensleeves' in the school choir, memorize 'Daffodils', and read a Shakespeare play in English lessons—exactly as she would have done fifty years before. She would not look at a picture, read a modern novel, ever hear a symphony (on wireless, gramophone, or 'live'), or see a play performed. There would be no school orchestra, no books other than some dog-eared text books at school or at home. Such children studied, hard; they memorized, diligently; but they neither read nor wrote; neither saw nor heard nor did. Art, music, drama, literature—such things did not touch these children's lives. It was not for them. Local secondary modern schools were even more impoverished. Yet these schools were mostly within a few miles of a major city. She could not, Jennie wrote in *Socialist Commentary*,[75] give children by act of Parliament loving parents or a home with good books, but she could give them an environment rich in theatre and libraries, and perhaps an education enriched by music, drama, and art. 'Anyone', said Jennie, 'who seeks to separate education and the arts is being cruelly biased against the ordinary youngsters. I am determined that all our children should be given the kind of education which was the monopoly of the privileged minority in the past.'[76]

Such an education was a matter not for the Arts Council, but for the DES. Jennie rarely drew on the department's resources, but she did when she commissioned the HMIs to look at music and drama provision in schools, and the educational work of museums. Specialist advisers were crucial. Music advisers could, for example, organize instrumental teaching, found youth festivals and school orchestras.[77] Slowly, their numbers grew. Jennie encouraged the Arts Council to parallel her work with theirs. In 1967, they set up a Young People's Theatre Panel, which Jennie's close friend, Constance Cummings, chaired. Grants for children's theatre rose from £10,000 in 1966 to £186,500 in 1970.

Jennie's most ambitious project for young people was the National Film School. Most European countries had film schools, where they nurtured film-making talent. Britain did not, and its film industry was in sorry times. Jennie was 'got at' by Stanley Reed, the new director of the British Film Institute (BFI). She had Wilson's support—he knew about the film industry. When he was President of the Board of Trade, and worried even then by the growing dominance of Hollywood, he had instituted the National Film Finance Corporation and the Eady levy (which taxed cinema tickets) to finance independent film producers. Jennie could also count on wider support from the Labour movement.

The British film industry had produced some fine films in the late 1950s and early 1960s: for instance, *Saturday Night, Sunday Morning* (1960), *A Taste of Honey* (1961), *The Loneliness of the Long Distance Runner*, and *A Kind of Loving* (1962), all in black and white, shot against melancholy northern locations and melancholy jazz scores, and with working-class anti-heroes played by working-class actors (Albert Finney, Tom Courtenay, Alan Bates)—films which were both mainstream yet dangerous. By 1964, the 'new wave' had spent itself and audiences fell. The British film industry was under assault from TV at home, and Hollywood abroad, as well as subverted by the glamour culture of the 'swinging sixties'—of colour supplements, dolly birds, discos, and boutiques—which preferred its films hedonistic, febrile, modish.[78]

Jennie had been criticized for not mentioning film in her 1965 White Paper; but she promised the BFI she would seek support for a film school, and she honoured it. After she had started the pile-drivers at Birmingham's Cygnet theatre in August 1965, she held a press conference, and announced she was setting up a committee of inquiry into establishing a film school. Lord Lloyd of the BFI was to chair it; on it also served Carl Foreman,* Karel Reisz, Sir William Coldstream, who when he was not attending Magritte previews, was chairman of the BFI, John Davis, chairman of Rank, and George Elvin, president of ACTT. They took evidence, and reported back two years later. 'Our national culture, the film industry and the economy' would all greatly benefit, they opined, from a national film school.[79]

The report addressed four questions. First, was a film school needed, and, a version of that, would its graduates find work? The answer, they

* Jennie went to visit Carl Foreman at his home. She arrived by car and was let in by a little girl. Jennie settled into the sitting room sofa. 'Yes, little girl, do run along. I'll be alright', and helped herself to sherry and a cigarette. The little girl failed to run along so after a time Jennie asked her what she wanted. 'I usually watch television at this time.' Finally, Jennie asked the little girl when Mrs Foreman might appear. 'Oh, she lives next door.' Interview D. Andrews.

decided, was yes. The British film industry was in the state it was because it did not train and employ the talent it should. At present, recruits joined the industry where they could, learnt as they went along, and took a series of trivial jobs as they worked their way up. A better way in was desirable. Second, given the depression in the film industry (two-thirds of film technicians were under- or unemployed in 1969), would there be enough work? One hurdle was overcome when ACTT, which ran a closed shop—no job, no card, no job—agreed that (uniquely) the school's graduates should get their card, provided the union was consulted over the numbers entering the school. As for the amount of work available, not all students would make feature films. Some would join television, others do commercial and advertising work, yet others join drama or education worlds. However, as Colin Young, the school's first director said, the best hope for a film school, is 'the studios' realisation of how they have lost touch with their audiences', producing neither films nor film-makers of quality.

The third question was who and what should the school teach? This was simpler to answer. It would train film-makers, but not technicians or actors. It would teach producing, directing, editing, camera work, and screen-writing in a three-year course, stressing film as communication, film as entertainment, and film as art. It would recruit some forty students a year in their early to mid-20s, probably not straight from school, though not necessarily from university. The final question was funding. The report looked to the Treasury for capital costs, and the Eady levy for revenue support. There was little dissent about any of this. Most of the players believed a national film school would regenerate British film. The more difficult question was where such a school would be located. Jennie's instinct chimed with that of the writers of the report. There should be a prestigious, autonomous, independent, free-standing school, located suitably near London, able to develop links with the film industry.

Such a proposal was not as obvious as it might seem. There were already fledgling film courses at several art schools (such as the Royal College of Art and the Slade) and they insisted, with some justification, that a better education and better value for money would come by locating the school in one of *their* institutions, rather than start again. They objected to money being creamed off, which should be going to build those already in the field; they objected strenuously to union cards going automatically to National Film School graduates when their own film graduates were scrambling for cards and work; and they feared that a new school, separately financed, would poach the best students and the best staff. In other words, they were opposed to it. The Lloyd Committee was not persuaded. It did not want a national film school grafted on to an existing college where, given the college's other work, the film school would be underfunded and overshadowed.

It took two years before Jennie could announce that the government accepted the proposals of the Lloyd Committee, was proposing a film bill to finance the new school through the Eady levy, and that she was appointing a planning committee to take the project forward.[80] By then there were fifteen film schools in the country, all of which had built up their student numbers, many of them with courses similar to those proposed for the new National Film School, and some with funding from their local television companies. It is hard not to sympathize with her critics. Jennie blamed the delay on the 'higher reaches' of the civil service. 'What do you want a film school for?' they had asked her. 'It is a declining industry and they are all unemployed anyway.' For once, however, she had Crosland's support, now that he was in the DTI. With Wilson's help, they not only got the money, but refinanced the National Film Finance Corporation, and greatly increased the budget of the BFI.[81] The BFI financed regional film theatres (thirty-three of them by 1970–1) in much the same way as the Arts Council was funding regional drama and theatre. Jennie had done them proud.

As her civil servants noted, Jennie was determined that film—a democratic art form, she believed—should share in the real growth of the resources she had won for the arts.[82] Wilson agreed. And though Lord Lloyd and Colin Young planned the National Film School (just as Peter Venables and Walter Perry planned the Open University) no one doubted that without Jennie's drive and support, 'there would have been no School'.[83] The timing, the debates about access and excellence and national need, the legitimate complaints from those already in the field, as well as Jennie's appeal to the Prime Minister, echo the birthing problems of that much larger institution, the Open University. In the National Film School, however, even more than the OU, Jennie had a personal interest. It opened with its first twenty students in October 1971. At the launch, Jennie asked for an invitation for her nephew Vincent. She perhaps had Vincent in mind when she pressed Colin Young to ensure that admission to the Film School should be possible for youngsters without an O-level but with creative ability.[84] The National Film School became, as Lloyd predicted and Jennie hoped, a centre of excellence. It was, says Hugh Jenkins, 'a workman-like outfit existing on a shoestring without excessive complaint, no grand buildings, just a grotty collection of huts inhabited by people who knew what they were about and loved it'.[85]

*

If Jennie had a mission, over and beyond all else, it was to strengthen regional arts. In 1945 Keynes had asked that just a little of the money going into reconstruction should be used to build theatres and galleries in every blitzed town: 'There could be no better memorial of a war to save the freedom of the spirit of the individual.' They must develop a life of their own:

How satisfactory it would be if different parts of this country would again walk their several ways as they once did and learnt to develop something different from their neighbours and characteristic of themselves. Nothing can be more damaging than the excessive prestige of metropolitan standards and fashions. Let every part of Merry England be merry in its own way.[86]

During the war CEMA had established regional offices, but the Arts Council argued that these were simply very expensive postboxes—their work could all be done from London—and in the mid-1950s it closed them down. It looked very different from the other side. The embryonic Midland Arts Association noted in its first annual report,

The Midland Regional Office of the Arts Council showed us how to overcome our difficulties and, better still, gave actual practical help . . . And then, quite suddenly, the office was closed. Our friends departed, and our connection with the Arts Council seemed tenuous—a postal link with some remote body in far distant London, where we felt that no one could possibly understand the problems of Leek, or Loughborough, or Leamington. There were some who felt angry, cheated or dismayed.[87]

Closing the regional offices was not just about saving money (it took less than £30,000 of their £800,000 budget in the mid-1950s), as a revealing passage in the Arts Council annual report for 1950–1 makes clear: 'The motto which Meleager wrote to be carved over the door of a patrician nursery might be one for the Arts Council to follow . . . "Few but roses".'[88] The call on a classical education, the concern for patrician nurseries, this was arts grandee stuff indeed. It was a deeply unpopular decision.

The regions rebelled. Both the South-West, which had few theatres or concert halls, and the Midlands demanded subsidy from the Arts Council with which to federate their small arts centres, clubs, and societies into a regional arts association (RAA). In the North-East Arthur Blenkinsop MP persuaded the major local authorities to join and to bring in opera, organize festivals, and develop a regional arts strategy. It was this model that Jennie had in mind when her White Paper expressed the hope that a network of regional associations would develop to work harmoniously with the Arts Council. The new Arts Council welcomed them enthusiastically, hoping that they would promote 'distinctive regional cultures independent of London', and that 'such bodies will prove a rod for the Arts Council's back'.[89] By the time Jennie left office, every region apart from the South-East was promoting an RAA.

RAAs allowed Jennie and Goodman to square some circles. The Arts Council was committed to a doctrine of 'response'. In Wesker's phrase, it would never go where it was not invited. As Jennie wrote:

> I did not regard it as any part of my job to go into areas where nothing happened, there to impose central Government dictatorship, or even to act as a missionary. The initiative had to come from the periphery, not from the centre . . . If a community wanted a theatre, concert hall or an arts centre, it was expected to produce support, financial and otherwise, from the local council, local industry and unions, private benefactors and trusts. It was for the Arts Council to prime the pump, but not to assume whole financial responsibility.[90]

It responded to local initiative, and it funded those who shouted loudest,[91] who called for them and needed them, but, to paraphrase John Wesley, it did not respond to those who did not call them and who therefore needed them the most. Challenge funding, which was what the Arts Council offered, presumed that there was already a regional or local constituency for the arts. Places 'that were slumbering peacefully were left to slumber', wrote Jennie.[92]

The Arts Council was often criticized for this doctrine of response, and its neglect of 'real' need. Yet when it was overwhelmed with bids for aid from localities, it would have been unreasonable to refuse one bid in order to press money upon another locality which had not bid. The Council would indeed then have been accused of imposing London's judgement. The doctrine of response was not only an honest effort not to impose a London-exported culture, but an honourable effort to encourage regional distinctiveness. It also recognized that projects and companies had to have staying power to survive. Unless some of the funding and most of the enthusiasm was already in place, a project promoted by the Arts Council would become permanently dependent on the Arts Council for its artistic energy and life.

Goodman, more perhaps than Jennie, saw perfectly well the consequences of such a position:

> We must recognise—as we have over the years—that there is a considerable element of inconsistency in the distribution of the good things in the world of

theatre, arts and music in different towns and in different counties . . . That in part it is due to our deliberate policy of deferring to local requirements as they arise and only in very rare cases seeking to stimulate some activity where at least the nucleus of existing demand is not already established. I believe this policy to be basically right. I do not believe that with the immense present demand that exists in various localities, any other policy is a possibility; but it may be, as time goes on, we will have to consider a change.[93]

RAAs, precisely because they worked so closely with local authorities, could initiate that change, could awaken need, could give voice to hidden constituencies—the town that had lost its major employer, the ethnic minority without the political clout and confidence to demand funding. To encourage RAAs, which in turn encouraged partnership with local authorities, which could in turn be encouraged to read and meet gaps in provision, must have been right. Goodman was always a more metropolitan animal than Jennie. But he wrote with Jennie's firm approval in the 1967 Annual Report: 'We have, we believe, started to evolve a firm policy', encouraging 'local plans and promotions', 'sensible regionalism', which would avoid even the appearance that national subsidy should result in 'the imprint of a single body', the 'small, non-elected appointed caucus in St James Square'. That, too, was surely right.

*

Money, policy, silence: these were the imperatives demanded of Jennie. Most of the money had so far been allocated, in Hugh Jenkins's phrase, by 'custom, convenience and pull'. If Jennie was to fund her new policies, especially to build up arts in the regions, she had first to secure new money—which she did. She was rightly lauded for presiding over an Arts Council grant that trebled in size and which could therefore sponsor dozens of new initiatives. It was not only that with 'the great advantage of a small budget'[94] she was not required to make the spending cuts that faced bigger departments as the economic crisis worsened; but that, quite remarkably, she secured increases in 1966–7 and 1967–8, of nearly 50 per cent and then of a further 25 per cent—at a time when inflation was less than 5 per cent a year.

In that pre-Thatcherite age, there was all-party agreement that spending on the arts was a good thing. Only the amount was in dispute, and dispute it Jennie did—on principle. She believed in spending on the arts; she also, says Goodman, 'measured her achievement by the size of the Treasury contributions she extracted'.[95] Civil servants would have some notion of draft allocation; simultaneously, the Arts Council would be receiving bids from organizations around the country. In the light of that, the Arts

Council would disagree with the draft allocation, and Jennie, says Goodman, would think of a number and ask for more. She would then expect Goodman to try to secure that figure from the Treasury, with Jennie standing by to argue with the Chief Secretary, with the Chief Secretary's boss the Chancellor, and with the Chancellor's boss the Prime Minister (Jennie's 'hotline' to Wilson was a 'delight', said Willatt).[96]

The Chief Secretary (Jack Diamond) tried to bring some Treasury procedure into the system by seeking to subsume Jennie's estimates within the DES budget as a whole: it would no longer be a separate budget. That, said Diamond, would mean that 'money for the arts should no longer be dealt with as a separate item outside PESC'. Jennie fought him off: 'In a vast Government department with heavy pressure for all kinds of existing commitments there would be no real living room for this part of the work.'[97] She wanted, for example, to establish a film school; but if it had to take its place within the Further Education shopping list, prospects for it were 'poor'. She followed this up with indignant letters and a chat with Wilson, the result of which was a letter from the Prime Minister's office to the Treasury, a copy of which he sent to Jennie: the Prime Minister 'does not like this at all since it seems to be going back on the original idea when expenditure on the Arts was transferred to the Ministry of Public Buildings and Works and then to the DES. His view is that expenditure on the Arts is not really education expenditure and that it is dealt within the DES, mainly because "it had to have a home" somewhere.'[98] Set and match to Jennie.

Just over a year later she was fighting off another attempt by the desperate Chief Secretary to bring her budgets under control. She had asked for a 20 per cent increase on the previous year; he wanted nil growth. She and Goodman, she wrote to him indignantly, had gone through the Arts Council estimates thoroughly, and they had managed to cut back their increase from 20 per cent to 10 per cent, providing it was 'in real terms' (i.e. nearer 15 per cent). If he could not ensure that, there would be a 'blazing row' between London opera and regional arts, and he and the Party would be fingered for it. Lest there be any doubt, she also wrote to the Chancellor (Roy Jenkins), in case her colleagues were not aware of the consequences 'of cutting below a 10% increase in real terms' (only Jennie could conceive of a significant increase in real terms as 'cutting').[99] By late spring, she had won again. Goodman wrote to her saying that at dinner the previous night, Barbara Castle and Dick Crossman had talked of her victory in generous terms. Barbara Castle told Goodman 'that they had decided that this was one field where they had an absolutely uncompromised record and should not start compromising it'. The achievement was all Jennie's, 'and a chorus of importunate beggars—led by Garrett Drogheda [of the ROH], is singing your praises to high Heaven, conducted by yours ever affectionate Arnold'.[100]

Jennie conceded that her colleagues were supportive and generous. Government spending on the arts was, of course, wider than Jennie's budget. It included money spent by her old ministry, the MPBW, on grants to historic houses and the upkeep of ancient monuments (£4 million a year in the late 1960s), grants to the Royal College of Music, to the Royal College of Art, and the BFI.* The government claimed that by 1968 it was spending a total of £24 million on the arts, thus loosely defined.[101] Jennie's budget within the DES accounted for three-quarters of this, over £18 million in 1968. Rather more than half of this was going to the great national galleries, museums, and national libraries, and most of the rest (£7.2 million) to the Arts Council.

Grants to the national galleries and museums were negotiated with the Treasury for five years at a time. Jennie had little scope to exercise discretion (or, as the directors might have called it, 'interference') over this allocation. She gave them significant increases for building works (such as a public restaurant with decent rock-cakes for the BM), the transfer of its ethnological department to Burlington House, or a micro-film unit at Colindale, its newspaper library. Purchase grants, which averaged some £800,000 across the national museums in the mid 1960s, had, thanks to Jennie, risen to £2.2 million by 1970–1. Jennie would interest herself in special initiatives, such as Sunday morning openings, or special purchases, but the rest of the budget was normally a matter for the trustees, and Jennie's involvement was limited.

The Arts Council grant, on the other hand, was negotiated annually, and every year became a contest for growth. Annual allocations generated real problems for the Arts Council. It could not give assurances to the big companies such as the ROH, which had to plan several years ahead; nor

* Though whether 'heritage' was safe in the hands of the MPBW was another matter. A Liverpool sculptor asked Jennie to stop the private sale of fourteen decaying stone kings and queens taken from the south wall of the House of Lords during its renovation. They were part of a royal freeze, 130 years old. They should be weather-proofed and then reinstalled; or, if that was not possible, go to a museum. The reply he got from the MPBW was cheery: 'It is a simple exercise of deciding which ones need to be replaced by copies made by our own craftsmen. No consideration was given to preserving them. If we did that, what would happen to our craftsmen? These chaps are turning out first class work—just as good as the originals. We didn't consider offering them to the museums free' (*Guardian*, 19 Sept. 1968).

could it easily introduce a capital programme, such as Housing the Arts, when any capital sums had to come from one year's revenue budget (unlike the position of local authorities, whose capital programmes were loan-financed). When, a year after Jennie had left office, Goodman offered a forward commitment, he was summoned to the Public Accounts Committee for infringing Treasury rules. Jennie went along to give him moral support, although the civil servants tried to stop her, on the grounds that her presence was intimidating—which was, of course, what she intended. When Goodman explained the absurd accountancy imposed on him by the Treasury, the Public Accounts Committee (chaired by his friend Harold Lever) sympathized. A fortnight later, the auditor who had brought the case resigned, and in 1971–2 the Arts Council was allowed a three-year rolling programme.[102] Set and match to Goodman.

Between 1964 and 1965 (Labour's first year in office) and Jennie's last budget of 1970–1, the Arts Council grant rose from £3.2 million to £9.4 million. To keep pace with inflation, the Arts Council should only have received an additional £1 million—Jennie extracted £5 million more than that. Did Jennie and Goodman do what Jennie wanted, strengthen arts expenditure outside London? Table 1 shows where the new money went. Everybody got something. The four national companies (the ROH, the ENO, the NT, and the RSC) saw their grant rise by about 70 per cent over the period, which amounted to real growth when inflation over the same period was at 40 per cent. This not only helped to clear past deficits, but permitted subsidized touring. However, as the table shows, their percentage share of the Arts Council budget fell. The London Orchestras Board, which subsidized London's four symphonic orchestras, increased their subsidy from £88,000 to over £200,000. Other activities cannot be tidily classified: grants went to writers who might live anywhere, to small magazines published in London but with a national readership, to companies which spent much of their time on tour. None the less, over the six years, the patterns of finance clearly changed, and those changes reflect Jennie's policies.

Table 1 Arts expenditure in £ millions[103]

	1963–4	1964–5	1967–8	1970–1
National Museums & Galleries	6.60	7.00	10.60	13.00
Arts Council	2.70	3.20	7.30	9.40
(ROH, ENO, NT, RSC		1.7 (53%)	2.58 (35%)	2.89 (31%))

In the first three years, 1964–5 to 1967–8, when the Arts Council budget rose by over £4 million, around £1 million of that went to the national companies and the London Orchestral Board in growth. The other £3 million went in some expected and in some unexpected directions. Predictable was the increase to Scotland (up from £203,00 to over £700,000) and Wales (£156,000 to £448,000). Indeed, Wales became the most generously funded region outside London itself, with Scotland not far behind, though their national operas mopped up a lot of it. Scotland continued to complain that on a per capita basis it was still short-changed. Jennie told them sharply that the Arts Council responded to local initiative and that if the Scots were too mean to initiate then that was their fault and not hers.[104]

Jennie's second priority, and one which bears her fingerprint, was to fund arts in education—opera training, the Royal Ballet School, Jennie's beloved National Youth Orchestra. The third beneficiary of the new money in these three years was London: those second-tier companies which had been neglected in the past by an Arts Council obsessed with the national flagships. The English Stage Company at the Royal Court, the Mermaid at Puddle Dock, the Ballet Rambert (which toured extensively), and the Institute of Contemporary Arts now housed in Carlton House Terrace, all saw their subsidy on average treble. The Arts Council also took over responsibility for funding and displaying exhibitions in the new Hayward Gallery built by the GLC on the South Bank.

Having enjoyed a major hike in financial support to start with, from 1967–8 grants for London plateaued. As the Arts Council noted:

> London presents a special problem: it is foolish to regard it as sufficiently served by artistic and cultural amenities to a point where it can now be neglected in favour of other areas, but simple justice compels us to call a relative halt to expansion in many London plans and institutions until at least something comparable to the London 'density' of culture is available in other parts of the country.[105]

By now, the number of London orchestras and theatres was greater than anywhere in the world; London opera and ballet as good as anywhere in the world. London was the world centre for buying and selling paintings, and for publishing books. Its radio and TV were the best in the world. What London took for granted in its day-to-day cultural life, the Arts Council claimed, would amount to a major festival in any other city.

So from 1967–8, the new money went out of London, to the regions and especially to regional theatre. It went into housing the arts (from Bristol's Old Vic, to over a hundred arts centres in towns like Basildon and

Harlow); it went to theatre companies and regional reps (Chester, Manchester, Newcastle, Leeds); into travel subsidies for rural areas (so that Yarmouth pensioners could come to Norwich's Theatre Royal). It went to festivals (from the international at Bath, to the local at Little Missenden), and to sponsor exhibitions (Augustus John at Hull); to additional tours by the national companies, and to the newly emerging RAAs: in 1970–1 ten RAAs between them received £356,000—by the following year there were thirteen RAAs, and with double the grant. Drama in England, for example, received £330,000 of new money in those three years; only £50,000 went to London, the rest went to companies in the regions. The quality of performance, the new work done, and the range of plays that were revived, improved dramatically (so to speak). Midland theatres reported a box office boom, and gave the credit partly to the Arts Council. Arts Council recognition became a seal of approval—when Sunderland subsidized its Empire Theatre just as Jennie and the Arts Council had asked them to do, it was much put out when the Council ignored them in its annual report: it was 'a bit of a slight'.[106]

Sunderland notwithstanding, Jennie put considerable effort into coaxing local authorities to spend on the arts, and gave endless press interviews on the subject. Private patronage, never very strong in Britain, had dried up, and business sponsorship had not yet taken its place. Record companies like Decca, and some tobacco firms such as Wills and Peter Stuyvesant, sponsored concerts and music scholarships; but even by 1975 when business was spending some £8 million a year on sport promotion, it was spending only around £500,000 a year on the arts. The charitable trusts, such as Carnegie, Pilgrim, and Gulbenkian, probably spent less than £1 million a year on the arts, according to Lord Redcliffe-Maud, and were constrained in their objectives.[107] The only other major player alongside the Arts Council was local government.

Local authorities already spent large sums on libraries, galleries, and museums; their educational committees funded special advisers to work in schools, and subsidized evening classes in art appreciation, for example at local FE colleges. They made special grants to one-off arts projects, such as festivals, as well as financing RAAs. An Arts Council survey in 1972–3 suggested that about £15 million was spent on the arts, museums, and galleries by local authorities; at the same time they were spending £70 million on libraries, £300 million on social services, and £2,500 million on education.[108] Local arts expenditure continued to rise, however. It was increasingly seen not just as 'posh leisure', but as sound economics; it brought tourism, local jobs, and new businesses. Local authority expenditure on the arts doubled during Jennie's years, while that of the Arts Council trebled.

Money, policy, silence: Jennie exercised a virtuous silence on how the Arts Council allocated its grants. She was neither amateur critic nor Minister of Culture. 'My function is simply a permissive one', she told The *Sunday Times*. 'I keep repeating that like a gramophone record . . . permissive, permissive, permissive. I want simply to make living room for artists to work in.'[109] She believed her own language that the arts were above politics. She told Keith Jeffery that her ministry should remain small: 'I must get people used to the idea of accepting a political Minister for the Arts without that implying political control of the arts.' She appointed Conservative co-chairmen to the RAAs, and Sir Joseph Lockwood of EMI and Sir Edward Boyle to the Arts Council itself. As she recalled sardonically, 'I had powerful allies in the Tory Party, who were only too glad to see their beloved Covent Garden, ENO and much else rescued.'[110] Her success forced the Tories to appoint a Shadow Arts Minister, Paul Channon, followed by David Eccles. By insisting that arts were above politics, she ensured that, unlike the OU, the survival of her ministry would not be in doubt. She also believed that the Arts Council should be at arms length from politicians. If she had understood Wesker's view that the arts were 'a battle field where ideas are fought out and values affirmed', she would not have shared it. She understood very well that politics was about choices, about priorities, but by winning the money she did, she did not have to choose. She could (almost) do it all.

It was easier for Jennie than for her successors. As the first Minister for the Arts, she did not have to fit the conventions or expectations shaped by any predecessor. Her close friendship and Sunday suppers with Goodman, at least as much as the formal monthly briefings between her office and Arts Council staff, ensured that minister and chairman thought and spoke as one. As Goodman said, Jennie worked with him as a 'sort of super-chairman. It was not necessary for us to define the respective functions of the Department and the Arts Council. She did not get in the way and she did not allow her minions to get in the way.'[111] Their intimacy 'depoliticized' Jennie. Her views expressed in Goodman's voice took them above politics.

It was harder for her successors. Because they could not enjoy the closeness that Jennie and Goodman shared, there was inevitably a distance and potential divergence between minister and chairman. MPs had not come into politics and this job to be denied an agenda of their own, to be told that they should do as Jennie had done. The Arts Council, insisted

Goodman, operated on two very simple and splendid principles: it received its money from government without strings, and it allocated it without strings. When Eccles took an interest in the politics of the arts (and objected to some of the grants bestowed by the Arts Council on what he dubbed smutty and subversive activities), or when Hugh Jenkins took an interest in the bureaucracy of the Arts Council and tried to make it more democratic and representative (elections, he wondered?), they were both accused of gross interference. They backed off. Goodman recognized that they were elected and he was not, but he insisted that he had access to outstanding expertise (as though it were a matter of informed opinion), and they did not:

> If the Arts Council operates as it should, it has no need of Ministerial control and no means of conforming to it . . . The Minister's function is to provide the money, to seek to procure the greatest amount possible and, in discussion and consultation with the chairman, to learn of the intended policy and if necessary to express his views . . . An enthusiastic and ambitious Minister . . . wishes to direct the arts. Between him and that direction is a large independent body of people who rate him as a useful animal for finding the money, respect him if he finds it in greater abundance than hitherto, but have no real use for his views on artistic matters, since they have a duty to base their views on the best professional and public opinions that obtain.[112]

Jennie and Goodman agreed that Jennie's job was to change the climate of opinion by raising the profile of the arts; by extracting more and more money whatever the state of the economy (the country could afford the arts in good times, and needed them in hard times); by cherishing the artist; and by building his audience. If the artist needed higher prices to live, and the audience lower prices to come, then that must be bridged by subsidy.

Yet although Goodman did not concede it, Jennie's contribution was greater than that. Goodman, as he himself cheerily admitted, came to the Arts Council with some knowledge of film (he became chairman of British Lion) and some knowledge of London orchestras. For the rest, he and Jennie had both to learn on the job. Unlike Goodman, Jennie had a political history, vast political experience, much of it outside London, and firm political ideals. At policy level—moving money out of London to the regions, moving money into education in the arts, building RAAs with participation by elected local government—this was Jennie's handiwork at least as much as it was Goodman's. Specific initiatives, such as cutting through the complexities of the South Bank, launching a National

Film School, pressing money into local arts centres as much as into grander theatres and concert halls, were Jennie's work too. Goodman was the more likely to employ a metropolitan perspective on what constituted excellence, Jennie the more likely to accept the claims of the regions for investment. Yet such was their closeness and rapport that either would have been hard-pressed to say who instigated what. Goodman got the private credit, Jennie got the public credit and therefore, from her colleagues, the money.

It was perhaps not difficult to be Minister for the Arts on a rising budget, so that new initiatives were not at the expense of existing commitments, and more was not at the expense of the best. But Jennie won that budget because she raised the profile of the arts as never before or since. She had a genius for publicity. She persuaded a doubting Labour Party and a hard-pressed Cabinet that what she was doing was *politically* worthwhile. Her colleagues recognized that this was one part of Wilson's premiership that was going right for Labour, and that Jennie, by that test, was an outstanding minister. Fortunately for Jennie, nearly all her problems were resolvable by money. She and Goodman never doubted that public spending on the arts was a good thing. As Goodman put it in his annual reports, in a welfare state public patronage must 'fill the vacuum' left when the private wealth that in the past had sustained public-spirited patronage was 'garnered in' by that same welfare state. Public spending—public subsidy—was a proper task of a civilized government.

To those who feared the possibility of censorship, Kenneth Tynan, the distinguished critic, told an audience at the Royal Society of Arts that any government had two equally effective ways of controlling their artists—by direct censorship, or by the censorship that came from withholding subsidies, and thereby binding the artist to the demands of the box office to turn out loveable, undisturbing, after-dinner entertainments. 'Subsidy', he went on, 'is the missing link . . . which can occupy and colonise the great intermediate area between minority theatre based on private whim and majority theatre based on private profit.' This, he concluded, was precisely the area that the National Theatre, and the new civic theatres, should inhabit and develop.[113] Jennie never doubted it.

Her view was actually rather simple. Arts were good for people. They were readily available to the rich, so they should be made equally available to the poor. Arts were about colour, gaiety, fun, festival, and community: life-enhancing things. Richard Hoggart commented on her White Paper of 1965:

They haven't really asked themselves sufficiently, when all the public relations have ended, what the Arts really are. When we are talking about an activity which, at its most profound, explores and recreates, as nothing else can do, the splendours and miseries of our lives, then to talk so much and so exclusively about 'come to the fair' gaiety or about 'colour' sounds like blowing a tin trumpet where a full orchestra is needed. It's true that Yeats's old men were gay, but theirs was a gaiety drawn from an unswerving look at the tragic face of things.[114]

He was being unfair. Jennie took the arts seriously, but she did not believe they had to be gloomy, forbidding, and unapproachable to all but the most refined London sensibilities. 'Of course the greatest art comes from the torment of the human spirit', she said, 'and you can't legislate for that.' Yet the piano in the front room, books on the floor, the arts club, and the touring company—these all improved the quality of people's lives. She refused to 'flirt', in Nicholas Tomalin's phrase, with 'the ironic titivations of pop, op, and anti-culture'. She pushed in precisely the opposite direction. It was 'this lack of middle-class sophisticated doubt and guilt that makes her so effective'.[115]

On the contrary, she enjoyed herself enormously. She conveyed an infectious enthusiasm which endeared her to her private office as well as to the arts world. With a government majority of only three, she was tied to London most evenings in her first years, but that still allowed her to attend endless evening functions. She was seen everywhere. She did not like opera very much (she thought Wagner was 'immoral'; Goodman confessed he would have needed handcuffs to get her to one of his operas), but she liked going to first nights at the Coliseum, where she sat in the chairman's box and could bring her own party of friends. On one occasion, she was shown round while a performance was on, and burst into the back of the gods where she was loudly shushed. Covent Garden seldom invited her; when she learnt that its Royal Box was used exclusively by the directors, she decreed that the government should have first call on it for entertaining official guests. It could hold sixteen people, but had only one WC. Another must be built (her ROH critics made sure the press knew Jennie was having a special lavatory built for private convenience). She preferred ballet, and enjoyed the visual arts. Above all, she loved the theatre. Even there she was irrepressible. The last production she saw before her death was *As You Like It*. There was, says Constance Cummings, much fussy directorial activity before the cast moved into the text. Jennie whispered, very loudly, 'Are you sure we're not seeing *Much Ado About Nothing*?'[116] Film premières, exhibitions, antique fairs, previews—she graced them all.

She made full use of the royal family. The Queen Mother in particular would always turn up to an event at Jennie's bidding. Jennie regarded her as 'a trouper'. She was less pleased when one night, comfortably ensconced in the best seats of the Old Vic's dress circle, she had to vacate them for a minor royal. Questions were asked next day about the Old Vic's grant.

Weekends allowed Jennie to leave London. She enjoyed the formality of such visits; at a Midlands pottery she found herself dining off museum quality china. She visited the Dartington School of Music to meet the students; travelled down to Penzance to open an arts centre in a disused Methodist chapel; up to Edinburgh to listen to Yehudi Menuhin play Mahler's Eighth, which she said she enjoyed. She never wrote her speeches down, always spoke extempore. Her private secretary prepared the usual press release in advance, crossed his fingers, and hoped she might say some of it. She went abroad on official visits: to Italy for the film festival; to the USSR for a National Theatre tour; to Hungary for a very successful Henry Moore exhibition, the country's first cultural event since the uprising.

In her 60s, and increasingly troubled by an arthritic hip which made walking difficult, Jennie not unreasonably liked a degree of comfort. Her private office tried to be helpful, and landed her and Wilson in some embarrassment. As a parliamentary under-secretary, Jennie had the use of a pool car, but not her own car and driver. Much of her time was spent talking to people informally over dinner or after events. The office pressed for her to have her own car, although they knew this would require promotion to Minister of State. Wilson was happy to strengthen her status, but what no one seems to have appreciated was that this brought an automatic salary increase (from £5,000 to £6,575) at a time of Wilson's prices and incomes freeze. It hit the headlines while Jennie was on an official trip to the USA. Back home, she offered to forgo the pay increase; this did not stop a Tory motion of censure. She was much touched when Drogheda rallied the arts world to her aid.

When in June 1970 she lost her seat (partly because Cannock had come to believe that she was neglecting them in favour of nights at the opera), the arts world lamented. Her defeat, wrote Elizabeth Thomas in *Tribune*, is a disaster. Richard Attenborough found 'it hard indeed adequately to express to you the debt we owe . . . so much that enriches the nation's life stands as a living monument to your foresight, your judgement and your true love of people'. Over fifty actors at the National Theatre, including Maggie Smith, Anthony Quayle, Tom Baker, Olivier himself, wrote to say that 'countless generations have need to be thankful to you'. Olivier followed this up with a letter to his dear, dear Jennie, about her defeat and his bereavement 'for that is what it is'. And she received a most generous (and revealing) letter from Sir Edward Boyle, written from the Carlton Club: many like him, who had never in their lives been socialists, felt as he did (a sentiment marred only fractionally by his inability to spell socialist). He went on:

> Quite apart from your remarkable achievements for the Arts since 1964, you represented a certain individual style in politics without which Parliament would be a poor place; I'm thinking of your combination of compassion for the poor, belief in the quality of life, sensitivity to all those who—however misguidedly—genuinely wanted to improve society—and disdain for the unthinking mob.[117]

Jennie herself said that hers was the best job in government: 'All the others deal with people's sorrows . . . the tidal wave of past neglect. But I have been called the Minister of the Future.' She was, says Goodman, a minister of rare quality.[118]

10

UNIVERSITY OF THE AIR

BECOMING Minister for the Arts was Jennie's idea. Starting a university of the air was Harold Wilson's. He was lecturing at Chicago University (as the guest of Senator Benton, proprietor of the *Encyclopaedia Britannica*) when in January 1963 Gaitskell suddenly died. Wilson returned to become Party leader. A general election was due the following year. A few weeks before the Party Conference, Wilson was speaking in Glasgow. Suspecting that a speech devoted entirely to Scottish matters would not be widely reported south of the border, he tapped into the debates provoked by the Pilkington Committee on broadcasting (June 1962), and the Robbins Committee on higher education (1963), to trail his thoughts on a university of the air, a university without walls. Wilson proposed that an educational trust, on which sat universities, the BBC, and other bodies, would commission broadcasts backed by correspondence courses; these would lead to diplomas and degrees, awarded by an established university. His university of the air would harness the new broadcasting technology to meet the educational needs of adult learners—those potential students whose only mistake was to have been born too soon.

Its students, Wilson said, could be technicians and technologists seeking university qualifications, those in clerical jobs wanting new skills such as a foreign language, and, as *The Times* reported, 'Mr Wilson suggested there were even housewives who might like to secure qualifications in English literature, geography or history.'[1] *The Economist* was captivated: 'One of the best things he [Wilson] has done.'[2] Elsewhere, Wilson had a poor press. The education journals were instinctively critical—'the project could by no imaginative stretch be properly called a university'; the money would be better spent on schools.[3] The verse sent in by J. Hampden Jackson to the *Listener* summed it up for many:

> We'll call every Tech a Varsity
> And overcome the scarcity
> Of buildings, by the Arm-chair University Degree,
> The ethereal, Wireless Varsity Degree.[4]

The Labour Party was as uninterested as the press. Wilson discussed it with one or two people, including Ted Short, but it was in no sense official Labour Party policy, 'except in the sense that I was running the Party in a slightly dictatorial way; if I said something was going to happen I intended it to happen'.[5]

Michael Young remembered Wilson once telling him that he had dreamed up the complete plan for a college or a university of the air (Wilson used both terms interchangeably) on a plane returning from the USA. Wilson himself said that he drafted the outline proposals in an hour between church and lunch the previous Easter Sunday while in the Scillies.[6] Having launched the idea in Glasgow, however, Wilson made only light reference to it at the Party Conference a few weeks later, and it was not included in Labour's election manifesto the following year.

Yet it was far from a passing whim. It had its roots both in the Labour Party's passion for adult education, and in Wilson's very different enthusiasm for meeting the demands of the 'white heat' of the new scientific and technological revolution.

The Labour movement, from Chartism, through the Clarion Clubs before the Great War, to the Workers' Educational Association (WEA), left-wing summer schools, and book clubs of the 1930s, always insisted that education was liberation. It freed the individual from 'the mind-forged manacles' of oppression: 'knowledge is power'. To this, in the late 1950s, was added a politics of culture—Richard Hoggart's *The Uses of Literacy* (1957), John Osborne's *Look Back in Anger* (1956)—and a sociology of education. A succession of official and semi-official reports from Geoffrey Crowther, Lionel Robbins, and John Newsom, revealed just how few people had access to higher education in Britain. Only 4 per cent of Britain's school-leavers went to university. In Europe it was double that, in the United States four times as many.[7] Demand was increasing, there were more 18-year-olds, and more of them who wanted to go to university—Robbins forecast a shortfall of places. Each year would add to the numbers of those who, though able enough, failed to get into university. Each year would add to the backlog of those who had missed out in the past.

Higher education was not only limited, but also narrow of entry, though here the problem lay further back in the system. Working-class children started school behind middle-class children, and at school, they then fell further behind.[8] Brian Jackson reminded *The Times* that since 1944, 70,000 children had been sent by the eleven-plus to the 'wrong' school.[9] Crowther showed that nearly half in the top 10 per cent of the ability range left school at age 15 or 16; Robbins and Newsom showed that these were essentially working-class children, voting with their feet after a decade of failure in school. As Robbins famously pointed out, the child of a Welsh solicitor was twenty times more likely to go to university than the child of a London bus driver.[10]

The Robbins Report on higher education was published as the 'new' universities were added to the academic map. The Treasury back in 1958 had agreed to alleviate pressure on London University by allowing a university college at Brighton. Keith Murray, of the University Grants Committee (UGC), benevolently accepted other bids for 'new' universities. These were sunlit places set in rolling parkland on the edge of cathedral cities and seaside towns—Norwich, York, Canterbury, Lancaster, Brighton, Warwick, Stirling, Coleraine—but they reached out to the traditional university constituency, 18-year-old school leavers from middle-class backgrounds. A greater number of young women went to university, but not working-class or mature students. More did not mean worse; it did mean more of the daughters of the sharper-elbowed middle class.

With the radiant exception of Birkbeck College, London, neither the older civics nor the newer universities developed part-time degrees to suit those local people who were tied by work, marriage, children, or disability to studying from home. Instead, universities continued to send their staff out as extra-mural and WEA lecturers to local communities and village halls, where they offered courses, this year on current affairs, last year on art appreciation, next year on local history. Extra-mural work was a strong and honourable tradition by which universities reached out to their hinterlands. Many an isolated rural village was sustained intellectually through the winter by its evening class. Yet as the three-year tutorial classes withered, the short courses of the WEA and of extra-mural departments could not meet the need of the individual adult wanting sustained study and perhaps a university degree. More vocational, but with even less claim to higher education, were LEA evening classes, where over a million adults learnt typing or kept fit, and correspondence colleges, which crammed around half a million students for exams in accountancy, public administration, or GCEs. The colleges were often unbelievably bad; they made their profits from the fees of those who dropped out.

Where else could the adult distance learner turn? Only London University offered part-time 'external' degrees, and then only to students with appropriate A levels. It was all done by private study, a book list at the beginning, and nine exams five years later. That route (and Birkbeck) aside, there was no other way for mature students to take university degrees on a part-time basis, and no way at all for them to do so at their own pace, in their own home, with proper teaching, and without formal entrance qualifications. So when Tony Crosland, soon to be Secretary of State for Education (and Jennie's senior minister) wanted the leading colleges of further education to become polytechnics (rather than new universities), and to take especial responsibility for regional needs, for vocational education, and for mature and part-time students, he was surveying the same landscape of disadvantage, immobility, and denial as Harold Wilson—although without sharing Wilson's enthusiasm for new technology. For the second trend enthusing Wilson and informing a university of the air was technological, the potential for educational broadcasting.

Back in the 1920s, the BBC had contemplated a 'wireless university' with a dedicated radio channel, but had chosen not to 'ghetto' educational programmes, but to integrate them into its general channels, hoping to reach a wider 'eavesdropping' audience. Now the same debate was to face television, as additional channels became available beyond one for the BBC and one for ITV. The Pilkington Committee (1962) on the future of broadcasting, of which Richard Hoggart was a member, discussed the contribution television should make to education. So far, neither the BBC nor ITA had done very much at all. Should one of the new channels be dedicated to educational television (ETV)? Pilkington said no. The BBC and ITA were required to offer 'a service comprehensive in character . . . The subject matter of broadcasting was all embracing; each of the two services was to treat all of it.' A specialist channel which segregated education would reduce 'the serious content of the existing television services . . . for, from being unchallengeably a proper purpose, a necessary function of all broadcasting, education would have become demonstrably the particular business of one service.' It quoted approvingly and at length a paper submitted by HMI.

Education in the wide sense is part of living and not a separate activity to be confined to some ages or some times of day. But for a great mass of people education, as they understand it, *is* separate. Their formal education as children has not sufficiently nourished their imaginations or provoked a spirit of enquiry or given them an opportunity to excel in any direction by their own efforts. When they have left school, 'education' has been finished. Broadcasting, both through sound, and very much more through television, can open the doors that are closed to such people. But the doors need to be left wide open because the ill-educated will not force them open. They do not know what their own capacities for enjoyment and learning are until they are tempted to try or find that, quite inadvertently, they have stumbled on a form of education that has meaning for them . . . A service which was labelled 'educational' would tempt very few of those for whom broadcasting should have most to offer; and the non-educational service or services might see no point at aiming at a quality of programmes higher than the bare minimum which people are prepared to accept if they have no opportunity for acquiring a taste for something better.[11]

The BBC thought there was little demand for ETV. The commercial companies, eyeing the two unallocated channels, responded very differently: they wanted one channel for themselves and thought the other might safely go to ETV (thus usefully discharging their educational responsibilities and denying the BBC any expansion at the same time). Pilkington had been harsh: ITV fell 'well short' of good public service broadcasting. Yet ITV wanted another channel; at the very least, it wanted extra hours on its existing channel (it was confined to eight hours a day). It decided to strengthen its quality by including adult education in its schedules.

Associated Television (ATV) led the way with its weekly Sunday sessions (English, French, public administration), which drew regular audiences of 750,000. Anglia was then persuaded by Peter Laslett and Michael Young to mount a 'Dawn University'—six lectures at 7 o'clock in the morning by three Fellows of the Royal Society and a former Nobel prize winner. Meanwhile, Southern TV screened programmes for doctors, Westward for teachers, Border for farmers. In 1964 Southern boldly offered a prime evening slot to David Daiches of Sussex University, to lecture on English literature. As a result, 1,100 students enrolled in some 60 classes, and a further half million viewers eavesdropped.[12] By late 1963, ITV was doing much more for adult education than the BBC. But when the Tories refused to allow it additional hours, these initiatives withered. Educational programmes were not profitable. None the less, lessons had been learned. ITV had shown that adult learners could be attracted to study in considerable numbers, but they needed more hours of transmission and more tutoring than television could provide. A college of the air would need to be rooted in correspondence study.[13]

The BBC took on the third channel as BBC2, as Pilkington had proposed, coming on air in April 1964. Who would get the fourth channel? The BBC, having acquired BBC2 and reluctant to see ITV gain a second channel, was now studying whether the fourth channel should be dedicated to education. This was favoured by Sir Edward Boyle and Lord Hailsham, the education ministers. In a paper put to the Postmaster-General in July 1963, Sir Edward Boyle had said; 'I conclude that, in the long term at any rate, a separate channel for a direct teaching service will, in fact, be required.'[14] Civil servants produced drafts for a service to feed schools and colleges, but it was blocked by the Post Office, which was eyeing the potential revenues from a fourth channel if it were to go commercial. Before Boyle's paper could be put to Cabinet, the 1964 general election brought a change of government.

Wilson himself, though not interested in traditional forms of adult education such as the WEA, was clearly fascinated by the possibilities of educational television and was more knowledgeable about it than any other leading politician. On his visits to the USSR in the early 1960s, he had been impressed by the fact that 60 per cent of Soviet engineers acquired their degrees by correspondence courses backed by radio tuition, followed by a year at university. Russia had also launched the sputnik. The USA hastened to compete. In 1956 the Ford Foundation financed Chicago's college of the air, which integrated TV lectures with written work, telephone tutorials, and face-to-face teaching.[15] *Encyclopaedia Britannica* marketed its films. Wilson himself regularly lectured at Chicago University, as the guest of Senator Benton, who had destroyed McCarthy and who owned the *Encyclopaedia Britannica*. Wilson admired him for both.

When Wilson came to draft his outline proposals that Easter Sunday in 1963, he also had in front of him the Labour Party's own report into higher education, the Taylor Report, published in December 1962, which, within a wider discussion of the needs and gaps in higher education, made brief reference to a possible university of the air, sustained by both the BBC and ITV. So when Wilson delivered his speech at Glasgow in September 1963, he was well aware of the experiments in educational broadcasting in the UK and had first-hand knowledge of similar experiments abroad. It was indeed no passing whim.

And it became his public passion. Cabinet colleagues claimed that they were never in doubt that the OU would happen, because Wilson wanted it to: 'What the Prime Minister wants, he gets', said Ted Short. All they could do, say Jim Callaghan and Roy Jenkins, was to argue about the price. As Tony Benn said: 'Wilson was the real political drive behind it'—he willed it; it was therefore 'unstoppable'.[16] Benn also believed, as Wilson himself

36. Jennie's parents, *c*.1940 in the Lane End garden, Brimpton, near Reading, the first home that Nye and Jennie owned

37. (*above*) Jennie's parents, Ma Lee and Dad, shortly before they came south to Lane End Cottage

38. (*right*) Nye and Jennie at Lane End Cottage, 1946

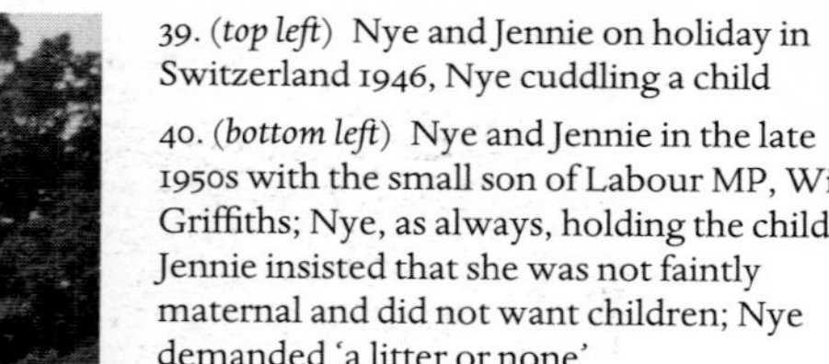

39. (*top left*) Nye and Jennie on holiday in Switzerland 1946, Nye cuddling a child

40. (*bottom left*) Nye and Jennie in the late 1950s with the small son of Labour MP, Will Griffiths; Nye, as always, holding the child. Jennie insisted that she was not faintly maternal and did not want children; Nye demanded 'a litter or none'

41. (*top right*) Asheridge Farm in the Chilterns, their favourite home, bought in 1954

42. (*bottom right*) With friends at Asheridge, 1956, and Nye (in Jennie's phrase) 'monarch of all he surveyed'

43. Pierre Mendes-France visited Asheridge in Spring 1959 bringing with him Henri Cartier-Bresson, who took these photos of Nye at home, with a sombre Jennie at his shoulder

44. Jennie's love for a frail Nye during his last illness, late Spring 1960

45. (*left*) The crowd at Nye's Welsh memorial service in the hills above Tredegar, July 1960

46. (*right*) Jennie arriving for Nye's cremation, aided by her sister-in-law Arianwen, and the funeral director

47. (*above*) Jennie, supported by Jack Buchan (who nursed Nye through his last illness) leaving Westminster Abbey after the official memorial service, 26 July 1960, to cross to the Commons. The Daily Express headline, 'Jennie Lee in the shadow of the House ALONE For the first time in 25 years . . .'

48. (*right*) Jennie, wrapped in her desolation, at the Labour party conference, Scarborough, in October 1960, three months after Nye's death

49. (*below*) The official opening of the Aneurin Bevan Memorial Library at Tredegar's St James' Hospital, 26 November, 1964. Jennie and Nye's brother, Alderman W. J. Bevan, contemplate a bust of Nye

50. (*top*) Vincent, the young 'nephew' adopted by Jennie, as a schoolboy

51. (*middle*) Jennie, with Vincent *c.*1961. His mother, Bettina Stafford, who kept house for Jennie at Asheridge, looks on

52. (*bottom*) Cup-tie final (1967?): tickets courtesy of Don Revie. Jennie, the teenage Vincent, and, on the far right, Bettina

53. (*top*) With Harold Wilson in 1968, who made her Minister for the Arts

54. (*bottom left*) Made a life-peer in 1970 by Wilson, Baroness Lee of Asheridge and Lord (Arnold) Goodman (left) introduce Lord Kissin, prominent in the Arts world, to the House of Lords in 1974

55. (*bottom right*) The Minister for the Arts meets young musicians after their concert, *c.*1968

56. (*top*) The Minister for the Arts visits Morley College Arts Centre in Lambeth, February 1969

57. (*bottom*) Jennie, with Vincent on the far right, at a smart Arts gala, early 1970, for Yehudi Menuhin (second from right)

58. Jennie receives an honorary degree at Alexandra Palace from the new Chancellor of the OU, Lord (Gerald) Gardiner, in June 1973. (*top*) On the left, seated, is 'Chris' Christadoulou, the OU's secretary and registrar, and on the right Sir Peter Venables

59. (*top*) Cannock miners from the Littlehampton pit with Jennie during the 1970 election campaign

60. (*middle*) Jennie and the victorious Tory candidate, Patrick Cormack, upon Jennie's defeat, 1970

61. (*bottom*) Visiting India in 1975, with her good friend Mrs Indira Gandhi

62. (*top*) Labour women MPs on the Commons terrace in June 1929. Back row, from left: Dr Marion Phillips, Edith Picton-Turberville, Dr Ethel Bentham, Mary Agnes Hamilton. Front row: Lady Cynthia Mosley, Susan Lawrence, the Rt Hon. Margaret Bondfield, Ellen Wilkinson, Jennie Lee.

63. (*bottom*) Women MPs on Labour's National Executive Committee, 1966. From left: Barbara Castle, Bessie Braddock, Alice Bacon, Peggy Herbison, Eirene White, Jennie Lee

64. Jennie opening the 1968 TUC exhibition of 50 years of women's suffrage. The poster shows her marching in the Durham gala, 1924. Jennie, then aged 20, walks between Dr Marion Phillips (with glasses) on the left, and Lady Cynthia Mosley, wife of Sir Oswald Mosley, on the right

65. (*above*) Jennie with Bill and Bettina (on swing)

66. (*right*) Jennie, *c*.1987, with Vincent and Michael Foot, around her dining table in the Chester Row basement

67. (*below*) One of the last photos of Jennie, walking with Vincent shortly before she died in autumn 1988

Jennie over the years:

68. (*top left*) In her early 20s (*c.*1927) wearing a trilby 'to make her look older'

69. (*top middle*) As an MP, aged 26, January 1930

70. (*top right*) In her later 30s (*c.*1940)

71. (*above right*) Jennie, aged 42, in 1946 with collar and brooch dress

72. (*above left*) Jennie in her early 60s, *c.*1966

73. (*above*) Vincent scatters Jennie's ashes in the Welsh hills, November 1988—'Fly darling fly'. From left: Vincent's wife, Laurel; Bettina Stafford; Michael Foot; Derek and (hidden behind Vincent) Muriel Davis of Cannock

74. (*right*) Jennie, aged 60, newly appointed Minister, 21 October 1964

came to believe, that it was one of the finest achievements of his premiership, 'the one for which—above almost anything else in his career—he most wished to be remembered'.[17]

One other man who could also claim authorship of the OU, and to Jennie's intense irritation often did so, was Young. In the early 1960s, Michael Young was lecturing in sociology at Cambridge, as well as chairing the Advisory Centre for Education (ACE) founded in 1959 and directing the Institute of Community Studies in Bethnal Green. Wilson had come to adult education because he was fascinated with the technology and efficiency of distance learning. Young came to it from a concern with the adult learner. One of his first thoughts was to establish a second university in Cambridge during its empty summer weeks, its teaching to be mounted by Battersea College lecturers—a Battersea university in King's Parade. This, unsurprisingly, got nowhere, though Young did run some summer schools for external London degree students in one of the Cambridge colleges.

He then outlined in *Where?* in the autumn of 1962 proposals for an 'open university' (probably the first time the term was used) built around London's external degree system, but sustained by proper teaching. A year later, and in the glow of Wilson's Glasgow speech, he, with Brian Jackson and David Grugeon, launched the National Extension College (NEC) in Cambridge from a couple of condemned workers' cottages (the young David Grugeon found himself in the scullery). The NEC was to be a comprehensive, inclusive college of the air, offering a second chance to those whose education had been interrupted by war, or by work; and it offered a dizzying range of courses, from O levels, to business technology, to tutorials for external degree students. It would offer, in other words, whatever its adult learners wanted. It would use television, but as TV costs were high and hours of output low, most teaching would be done by correspondence. Young hoped his NEC would become the core of an open university.[18]

Michael Young was certainly perceived to be the educational inspiration behind the OU. When it was clear that the NEC would not develop into a truly open university, his close friend Tony Crosland urged the Cabinet to appoint him as Vice-Chancellor (VC) of the fledgeling OU. Jennie refused. She wanted a conventional academic in the post, free of political association, who would be accepted by his fellow VCs as one of them. As Young admitted, she was probably right—though she did tell him privately that she was willing to appoint a figurehead VC, while he, as number two, 'would really run the University'. Young told her this would not work, and turned it down.[19] However, Jennie's opposition to him was more complex than that. She always paid full tribute to the crucial role played by Harold Wilson, and always denied it to Michael Young. After the conversation in 1968 about the vice-chancellorship, Jennie did not see Young again until the first graduation day in 1973; she raised a sour eyebrow when he (but not Wilson) was included in the first cohort of honorary degrees—clearly unmerited, she thought. When the *Sunday Times* ran a piece on Young's contribution to the OU in January 1977, comparing it favourably with that of Wilson,[20] Jennie sent them a lengthy letter insisting 'that he played no part in the early struggle to overcome the resistance of the educational system'; that indeed, he thought it 'too ambitious'. The *Sunday Times* declined to publish her letter. Young, in turn, believed that the OU originated with him, and that Wilson opportunistically appropriated the credit. In truth, however, knowledge of the Russian and Chicago schemes was common within Labour education circles, as were the conclusions of the Taylor Committee, Robbins, and Pilkington Reports. Wilson came to it by his own path, absorbing some of Young's thinking along the way.

In the event, the shape of the OU was determined by neither of them. Wilson's university of the air was not so much a place as a network, in which a consortium of further and higher education 'providers' rationalized and integrated their offerings and activities through the medium of an educational trust around the new technology of television and radio. It would reach out to those for whom personal physical attendance at a conventional university was impossible. Existing universities would offer them intellectual access by air. It was more comprehensive, generous, supportive, and glamorous than the existing external degree system; broadcasting technology was at its heart. It did not need to be confined to degrees, nor to mature students, though that was its natural audience.

Young came at it from the other end, from the perspective of the adult student consumer, rather than from that of the educational provider. He was, said the OU's first secretary, Anastasios Christodoulou, 'wildly enthusiastic about the idea, but he wanted not to institutionalize it, but to build on what was there'.[21] Young argued not for an open university, but for a less intimidating open college. It would be independent of existing university institutions, rather than a consortium of them; it would build, he hoped, on his own National Extension College and the external degree system, offering pre-university and FE work alongside university degrees; It would be a patchwork rather than a grand plan.

In the event, the OU drew on both visions, but was to fit neither. It was not to be Wilson's 'university of the second chance', whereby technicians and technologists could upgrade their qualifications in the national economic interest, though some students did; nor was it to be Young's 'college of the first chance' for the educationally deprived, though for a few students it was. Instead, it was an open university, accessible to all. What mattered were the degrees with which students would 'exit', rather than the reasons, routes, or background with which they entered. In contrast to Young's vision, it was to be not a college but unqualifiedly a university, offering, at least in the first instance, only degrees. There was to be no FE, no pre-university work, no access or remedial work. Indeed, it was narrower than most conventional universities, which offered in-service training for teachers, extra-mural classes, short courses, and diplomas alongside their degrees. And, unlike the proposals outlined by Wilson at Glasgow, the OU was to be an autonomous and independent university, not a trust, not run by a consortium of existing HE and FE institutions. Like the new universities, it was to have its own charter, its own degrees, its own sense of place, and in time it was to develop its research standing. It recognized that while TV was essential for its glamour and necessary for its science demonstrations, the core of its teaching would be by correspondence, backed by local study centres, tutors, and summer schools.

The OU's distinctive texture came not from Chicago (to which Wilson looked), nor from the National Extension College (on which Young wished to build) but from Scotland. It was defined by Jennie Lee. Both Wilson and Young gave her unstinting credit for it. As Young himself wrote: 'The OU was built by one person—though she had many able lieutenants and one ace card . . . the direct support of the Prime Minister . . . It was a stunning performance.' Jennie, says Asa Briggs, 'transformed everything'.[22]

*

A Labour government was returned in October 1964 with a slender majority of seven. In the Education Department, officials worked late and worked up the draft scheme for a college of the air, first prepared for Edward Boyle. It would offer, on a pilot basis, professional, vocational, and liberal courses, but not degrees. It would serve FE colleges, evening classes, and the isolated mature student in need of correspondence teaching as well. It would start with six hours of broadcasting a week, rising to eighteen hours a week by the third year.[23]

Anthony Crosland came to education as its Secretary of State in January 1965. Lord Normanbrook, chairman of the BBC, wrote to him formally offering to provide such an experimental educational service, to start that October (1965), on the understanding that the Treasury would meet the additional cost, as it did with the world overseas service. By March,

Crosland was ready to go to Cabinet. He did not do so. A few days before, Jennie had been moved by Wilson from the Ministry of Public Buildings and Works, where she held her arts portfolio, to education, with a particular brief to deliver a university of the air. Wilson, suspecting that his pet project was going nowhere, had called her in and said: 'For God's sake try to get this thing going. The DES is the most reactionary department in the Government: I can get no help from the senior officials or the ministers.' Jennie agreed to take it on, providing that she 'could count on his support especially in securing money from the Treasury'. She was officially a junior minister within a department headed by Tony Crosland, 'but *de facto* I was working on my own, dealing directly with the Treasury and with the Prime Minister. The civil service hated it: all very irregular. But it was the only way you could get a new job done.'[24]

Jennie took one look at the DES's draft proposals, and four days into her new post vetoed the lot. They would start again. The officials were aghast—had the minister thought about it? (Well no, actually, she had not.) As her senior civil servant noted: 'It was an indication of the strength of her political position that although a very junior Minister and a newcomer, she could simply throw the paper into the wastepaper basket and insist on a fresh start.'[25] On 23 March 1965, Crosland formally declined Lord Normanbrook's proposal. It was back to the drawing-board.

For better and for worse, Jennie took a grip on the project. She brought with her no known interest in adult or higher education. Indeed, by brigading the university of the air with the arts portfolio, and thereby separating it from the rest of the department's work on higher education and adult education, Wilson was clearly signalling that this was to be a free-standing project. As Brian McArthur put it:

> [Wilson] knew that by selecting Jennie Lee to steer it into being, he had chosen a politician of steely imperious will, coupled with both tenacity and charm, who was no respecter of protocol and who would refuse to be defeated or frustrated by the scepticism about the university, which persisted not only in the DES, but also in the universities, among MPs and among the community of adult educators.[26]

It meant that the university of the air was isolated from the rest of the department's concerns. (In February 1966, for example, two White Papers on higher education were published, one on polytechnics and one on the OU. Neither White Paper mentioned the existence of the other.) It also meant that no part of the civil service responsible for higher education would be reporting to Jennie. It was an independent project, neither enriched nor constrained by whatever else was going on in further and higher education, superimposed on the department's priorities, led by a junior minister with no reputation in education and with no educational support behind her, and which at best drew a studiously neutral response from her Secretary of State, who privately wished the scheme would disappear.

Jennie could, naturally, expect opposition from the Post Office, which would lose potential revenue if she acquired the fourth channel, and from the Treasury unhappy at the open-ended financial consequences of funding open access, all of which she anticipated. She might also, if she had cared to contemplate her front bench colleagues, expect resentment at money going to a project which might otherwise be available to them—as well as a lofty Oxbridge disdain for a 'telly' university, a view predictably held by (Oxbridge) newspaper editors as well. What, in her innocence, she did not expect was the hostility the project would arouse in the education world, which to a man thought that this was the wrong project for the wrong people at the wrong time. Any available monies would be far better spent on schools (the teaching journals), or on adult education (adult educationists), or on remedial and further education (the trade unions), or on expanding the existing universities (the vice-chancellors)—anything, anywhere, as long as it was not another university. Jennie was going to have a bumpy ride.

Within a few weeks, she was ready to make her position public in a Commons debate, on 2 April 1965. The department prepared her brief, as was customary, restating its view that, as broadcasting policy was being reviewed, no firm plans could at present be drawn up for the proposed university; but that, in the meanwhile, the proposals outlined in the Glasgow speech would continue to be 'vigorously explored' and an advisory committee was under consideration. It was all very cautious. Jennie was not content with that, and went far beyond her brief: 'All we are discussing', she said, 'is the timing and method of implementing the University of the Air.' She went on to describe a university that was autonomous, independent, degree-giving, with a vice-chancellor of impeccable standing and—and this is Jennie's voice—open in access, uncompromising in its standards. 'I am not interested', she told the House, 'in having the next best thing, a poor man's university of the air, which is the sort of thing which one gets if nothing else is within our reach. We should set our sights higher than that.' MPs were taken aback by the firmness of her views. The Tory Chris Chataway broke in: 'The Hon. Lady is taking this idea of a nationally organised university of the air a good deal more seriously than I expected if this is a serious proposal.' It was, said Jennie. Wilson's Glasgow speech and her appointment was evidence of that. Only the ways and means had still to be resolved.

'Ways and means', however, included a series of formidable issues in education, broadcasting, and finance. What was the educational reach of a university of the air, and how would it fit into the existing map of further and higher education? What broadcasting resource could it command? Would it, should it, annex the fourth channel for ETV? And given the high fixed overheads of broadcasting, how could Jennie secure adequate funds for a new university, not only against competing claims within education, but also against other departments, as the economic climate worsened, and as all departments were required to cut spending?

The first of these issues was educational. Could one establish a university that was open of entry, while uncompromising on standards? 'How can the ideas of open access and evaluative exit be reconciled?' asked *Education*.[27] Good staff, extended study, and proper examinations would maintain the integrity of the degree, Jennie was to reply. In any case, she had lots of degrees—they were not hard to get, people overestimated the difficulties involved. Real academic rigour would mean many would drop out, and the cost of each graduate would soar, wrote Stuart Hood, former controller of BBC TV writing in the *Spectator* and *The Times*.[28] 'The most expensive method of inefficient further education ever conceived', he concluded. Cost was not a fair test, retorted Jennie. Many who never took a degree would benefit from the programmes of a university of the air.

Based on the TV, could it be a university at all? 'A university is not a mode of mass communication, it is a community', opined the *Times Educational Supplement*.[29] Jennie recognized the force of that charge, sought to play down the significance of television in the project, and renamed it the Open University as soon as she decently could (it was as the Open University that it found its way into Labour's 1966 election manifesto).

Even if these issues could be satisfactorily addressed, was a university of the air needed? There was, said the *Times Education Supplement*, a vast network of technical colleges, evening institutes, and adult education classes; there was university extra-mural work, external degrees as well as correspondence courses: 'What real evidence is there that something more is wanted?' It was Wilson's 'pipe dream', showing socialists 'at their most endearing but impractical worst'. It was as if 'Keir Hardie were stumping determinedly into the second half of the twentieth century'.[30] It was an 'historical fossil' more appropriate to the deprived 1930s. Any spare monies would be more usefully deployed elsewhere in the education system.[31] Jennie agreed that more money was needed elsewhere in education. However, her funds were not to be at their expense; they were not available for anything else. She did not even challenge those who said that there were higher priorities within education, but said, simply: 'that was not the job I was asked to do.'[32] This was a stand-alone project entrusted to her by the Prime Minister, and that was that. Whether a university of the air was necessary, desirable, or practical was not up for debate. It was willed by the Prime Minister, and would be delivered by her.

Jennie's critics would not allow her to close down the argument in that way. The more determined she was to build a university of impeccable standards, the more enmity her scheme aroused, from those who thought she had the wrong goals to those who thought she could never obtain them. On any hard-headed assessment, Jennie's critics were right. Looking at the educational scene in the mid-1960s, it was not obvious that the greatest educational need was for yet another university, of doubtful quality, uncertain cost, dubious standing, and unknown demand, to add to the new universities recently established. Few sociologists doubted that children inherited the education of their parents. Educational deprivation began in the home and was carried into school, where inequalities widened. Money spent on nursery classes, reducing classroom size, training more teachers, or resourcing properly the raising of the school leaving age, would—to use a Victorian phrase—fence the cliff at the top rather than send an ambulance to the bottom.

There was, too, a clear and quantifiable demand for FE and sub-degree work, an open secondary school, an open college, offering remedial education for young adults and mature learners. The former principal of Ruskin College in Oxford, for example, long believed that the OU should have been an open college, geared to the needs of the 16-plus age group, instead of becoming, in his words and in the light of its initial applicants, a 'substitute training college for teachers'. Similarly, Len Murray thought it was 'unlikely to do very much to enlarge the educational opportunities of the mass of people we represent'. What was needed was a Ruskin of the Air, a Toynbee Hall of our age.[33]

Adult educationalists were even more aggrieved. 'Responsible bodies', that is the WEA and the university extra-mural departments, were the cinderella service of the DES, neglected and underfunded. The department grant of £1 million a year represented less than a tenth of 1 per cent of the total educational budget. The sums being mentioned in the context of the university of the air—£3 million for set-up costs, and £1 million plus a year for running costs—would have transformed adult education out of recognition. Neil Kinnock met Jennie for the first time in the late 1960s when he worked for the WEA. He urged its claims over the OU: 'To say the response was ferocious would be to understate the dosage of vitriol.' Neil held his ground, until Jennie finally said: 'You're utterly and totally wrong, laddie. But at least you're wrong for the right reasons.'[34]

From another quarter, Eric Robinson and Tyrell Burgess who, like Tony Crosland, were devoted allies of the polytechnic concept, were just as hostile. They wanted an independent mission for polytechnics—local, vocational, relevant to the needs of industry and technology, and pluralist in their qualifications and offerings. They were fiercely critical of the aspiration of colleges of advanced technology (CATs) to ape universities, which they saw as academic drift.[35] The OU, they thought, was a vulgar, unnecessary, expensive, and distracting hybrid that crossed the binary line.

Educational mandarins had no objection to polytechnics rounding up less able students in cheaper, separate, and inferior institutions that would stop them 'diluting' the universities. Many from the university world believed that more meant worse, and that open access certainly would. Oxbridge, the civics, and Kingsley Amis were already suspicious of the academic standards of the new universities (*film* studies—degrees by going to the cinema?). The Committee of Vice-Chancellors and Principals (CVCP) was quite clear. It did not believe a further higher education 'institution', as they carefully described the OU, was 'necessary'; it noted that there was no evidence of any demand for it; and it predicted that 'a very high proportion' of its students 'would not stay the course'. Above all, members of the CVCP did not believe it could be a proper university, and, as Peter Venables noted, 'feel that a matter of principle is involved'.[36] They felt so strongly that when Peter Venables agreed to chair the OU's Planning Committee, he felt obliged to offer his resignation as vice-chairman of the CVCP, so wide was the gap and so censorious his fellow vice-chancellors.

Those who were both more generous and better informed, who wanted university expansion and wider access, could nevertheless show that more funding for existing universities, enabling them to meet their Robbins targets, was both cost-effective and socially responsible. If broadcasting technology was to help address growing numbers, then should it not be used to create economies and expand numbers across existing universities, rather than be used to sponsor yet another independent university? As the *New Statesman* said: 'The press was lukewarm, educators were doubtful about ends, broadcasters about means, and the public was unstirred.'[37] No doubt the OU was a good idea, the *New Statesman* went on, but why single out that relatively small group, the least important among the educationally deprived, 'the men-who-missed-college group'? How many of them were there? And—a recurring theme—'How many would be house bound women? Do they want degrees? Would they make any real use of the degree style courses and, if they did, qualify?'

Jennie's critics came from all around the education world. Those on the Left were convinced that the OU could ultimately only be judged by *whom* it taught. Not by how many students it taught, not by how well it taught them, and certainly not by how cheaply it could do so; not by how innovative were its teaching methods, nor by how useful were its qualifications, nor by how impeccably austere its degrees. Its test, thought Richard Hoggart, a faithful friend of the OU and external assessor for many of its professorial appointments, was whether 'it attracted to degree work those who did not know they needed it'.[38] By that test, however, the OU looked set to fail. Precisely because it was 'open', it seemed likely to attract the wrong class—the lower-middle class; the wrong occupations—teachers and yet more teachers; the wrong gender—women (and the contempt in those pre-feminist mid 1960s for 'housewives', middle-aged, middle-class women, was unmistakable). They were baffled that Jennie, a socialist, a working-class aristocrat, as Brian Jackson dubbed her, was not only not interested in targeting educational deprivation among working-class men, but was vehemently opposed to doing so. 'I wish people would stop talking about the limited number of working class men and women who have joined', she wrote later to the university's registrar; 'I have said time and again that the most insulting thing that could happen to any working class man or woman was to have a working class university.' She made the same point repeatedly: 'It is not its function to do the work of an open secondary school as well as an open university.'[39] She refused to accept that she had any responsibility to cover the wider canvas; in any case the OU could not meet all the needs, gaps, and frustrations within education.

Her critics had a strong case. Yet, noted its first Vice-Chancellor:

> Had she given way, had she attempted to start with a scheme offering education through the media to adults at school or pre-university level, I think the concept would have disappeared. Its cost would have been no less, its status would have been much less, it would have had no glamour. It was the glamour of the university in name and in actuality that enabled her to win her way.[40]

Jennie had announced to the Commons in April 1965 proposals for an advisory committee. She wooed, deliberately, the university world. She recruited twelve members—none of them women—to a committee that was strong on senior academics (the Vice-Chancellor of Hull, the Provost of King's, the Principal of Swansea, the Professor of Economics at Strathclyde), and decidedly thin on voices from the adult education world.[41] This was not accidental. Michael Young had declined. He saw it as 'a threat', decided Jennie, to his 'less ambitious' work.[42] Peter Laslett joined instead. Norman MacKenzie came from Sussex with his expertise in educational technology, John Scupham from the BBC. Only Harold Wiltshire of Nottingham (who had worked with ATV's adult learner programmes in 1963) was a prominent member of the adult education world. Excluded were the National Labour Colleges, Ruskin College, Birkbeck College, and, remarkably, the University of London (the sole provider, after all, of external degrees). The WEA was marginalized. None of this may have been tactful; but Jennie knew that ultimately their views did not matter. It was recognition from the CVCP and its funding body, the UGC, that counted. Only they could validate the OU as a proper university in the eyes of the public, its degrees as equivalent to and comparable with their own. Only they could reassure prospective OU students that they would not be short-changed.

Civil servants prepared unenthusiastically for the first Advisory Committee meeting, convinced that nothing would come of the project, and that they were wasting their time. Jennie attended, and, to their surprise, took the chair herself. The committee was not to be independent of her or her of it. They were not advising her; she would be entirely identified with its conclusions.

She opened the meeting saying that she had just seen the Prime Minster, 'and he had confirmed that he had not changed his views about the need for a University of the Air'. She quoted his Glasgow speech and outlined her thinking so far. She was firm that the university should have open access, confer its own degrees (perhaps on the Scottish model), that its academic standards should be high and not be 'second best'. She invited members to submit their own papers as to how they might proceed. The minister might expect them to have an open mind on the project, enquired one member? No, said the minister, they might not.

The committee agreed that there should be open access, but on little else. Open access to what? To a university? Surely too limited in its appeal; a college offering intermediate qualifications would perhaps be preferable. To Scottish general degrees? Too lowly (this from the representative of the Scottish Education Department). To its own degrees? That would need supervising by the Council for National Academic Awards (CNAA). Jennie said sweetly that she had always regarded the CNAA 'as an organisation designed to enable technical colleges to gain parity with universities. Much as she sympathised with the aim, she was anxious to avoid involving the University of the Air, which she wanted to get established as a means of obtaining university degrees. There could be no compromise on standards.' And a university for whom? Should they not at least conduct a survey to identify demand? Jennie deemed that this was 'not the right time' and somewhat airily referred to casting bread upon the waters. Naturally, the view of the minister prevailed.[44]

Jennie's response may have been practical, given the time a survey would take; and it may have been sensible, given that the findings might not have said what she wanted. But it did leave her without any cards of a socialist nature—the remedying of educational disadvantage, the hunger for higher education—that might have helped her with a Cabinet fretting about cost. The committee discussed structure. Harold Wiltshire's paper helpfully proposed a chancellor (for glory), a vice-chancellor (for work and for glory), a deputy vice-chancellor (for work), honorary academic advisers (more for glory than for work), and tutorial staff (strictly for work). This was thought sensible.

Over the weeks, the committee came together. It accepted that it could not meet every need, and should not attempt to do too much. Its priority was to launch a proper university. Wiltshire said, in a line that perhaps revealed more than he intended: 'We don't want this to be a makeshift sec.mod. university.'[45] To be a proper university meant focusing on degree rather than sub-degree or intermediate work. That meant there would be less appeal to 'eavesdroppers'—a concept which did not, in any case, suggest the right note of austerity and rigour the committee were looking to convey. If eavesdropping mattered less, then so did television, the come-hither element, as Jennie put it. As television was a very expensive medium of teaching, reducing its prominence would reconcile the logistics of cost, teaching hours, and air time. Teaching would be by correspondence, backed by local tutors in local study centres. The university of the air was becoming, conceptually, an open university.

The Advisory Committee had assessed the *academic* feasibility of a university of the air. It had not consulted any interested bodies, except the BBC, and the report did not trouble itself much with costs, need, or student demand. Modern technology, it proclaimed, would allow the best in lecturing to be brought to the many who cared to look and listen, and to the minority who, unable to attend traditional universities, might wish to acquire degrees. It would provide open access by air. This seemed to brigade Labour's commitment to educational expansion, with a socialist remedying of disadvantage, with a contemporary fascination with technology and the media, and with the nation's economic need to skill its labour force. Jennie was well pleased. She had kept Wilson briefed. She wrote to Marcia Williams that she was now 'quite sure that the job the P.M. wants done can be done, but it is now for the Cabinet to consider costs and channels'.[46]

So far, the university of the air had not surfaced in Cabinet. Before it did so, and because it had major implications for broadcasting policy, the report had to be considered by the appropriate Cabinet subcommittee, the Ministerial Committee on Broadcasting, as well as by the equivalent and parallel committee of civil servants, the inter-departmental Official Committee on Broadcasting. Tony Benn, as Postmaster-General, was responsible for broadcasting policy, including licensing fees, transmission hours, allocation of channels, and finding an outlet for the university of the air. Fascinated, like Wilson, by educational technology, he was an ally.

Benn was working within the shadow of the Pilkington Report. The BBC wanted Reithian standards, arms-length independence from government, and no increase in broadcasting responsibilities without an increase in licence fee, which a Labour government was unwilling to concede. (As it was flat-rate fee, it fell heavily on pensioners.) The BBC had managed to acquire the third channel as BBC2, but it did not want to cede the fourth channel to ITV, and did not as yet want it for itself: it wanted a decision on the fourth channel deferred. It still preferred to integrate its education offerings within its general programmes; and, given the unused hours, there seemed space enough.[47] Longer hours for the BBC meant costs.

The position for ITV was the reverse: longer hours meant profits. ITV wanted more advertising revenue, for which it needed more hours, and above all the fourth channel. Tony Benn was no fan of the BBC—he thought it was too right wing.[48] He wanted more diverse voices and greater enterprise from the BBC and higher standards from commercial television. These two objectives would be met, he thought, if the BBC and ITV became 'publishing' bodies. The BBC would not only produce its own programmes, but would also commission work; ITV would no longer just receive programmes from its franchise-holders, but would itself plan and commission them. A vice-chancellor of a university of the air would commission from and show programmes on both.

In swept Jennie. Over the next few weeks she and Benn met regularly to discuss the university of the air; and to commiserate on the bloody-mindedness of their respective officials. Jennie's own views on broadcasting began to harden. She wanted prime time, not the left-over unsocial time that no one else wanted. She also wanted the fourth channel: it had glamour, and it had space. But what about the cost? She toyed with the idea of pay television. She then went for cross-subsidy: education until 8 o'clock in the evening, followed by light entertainment, whose advertising revenue would cross-subsidize ETV. This was a solution that nobody else wanted—the BBC, because it would mean extracting education from its general offerings; ITA, because it would foreclose the fourth channel; Post Office officials, because it would allow government interference with broadcasting; the Treasury, which saw lucrative revenues from the fourth channel receding; and finally, Benn himself, who thought it unnecessary. The DES was indifferent.

The Advisory Committee Report, together with Jennie's thoughts on the fourth channel, went to the Ministerial Committee on Broadcasting[49] which referred it to its Official Committee (that is, its committee of officials) to appraise its cost and viability. They calculated that it would cost £42 million to launch a fourth channel and £18 million a year to run it—impossible without advertising, but contaminated with it. In any case, advertising would remove it from the BBC and into the orbit of the ITA, and that was unacceptable. There had been no pilot scheme, so the Official Committee doubted whether there would be much demand or many completed degrees. Neither they, nor the Ministerial Committee, could summon up any enthusiasm for the project.

The situation would be no better in Cabinet, where the scheme had few friends. No one knew its cost, no one knew the potential demand. And whatever Jennie and the Prime Minister might agree, any expenditure had to be at the expense of some other project, whether within education or outside. Tony Crosland, in his first Cabinet post, believed that any money available should go first to the schools programme and the raising of the school-leaving age; he was disdainful of the whole project as well as irritated by the way that Jennie had hugged it to herself. It would be 'another Wolsey Hall',[50] he said, that is, a university correspondence college. He would neither agree with it nor engage with it.

Roy Jenkins, the Home Secretary, who was supportive of Jennie's arts work, was deeply sceptical—he confessed dryly that he had 'probably not shown great imaginative grasp of the benefits of the OU'[51]—though, as he recognized that Wilson was always going to insist on it, he would not dig himself too deeply into opposition. Jim Callaghan, Chancellor of the Exchequer and himself without a degree, was not unsympathetic. He too recognized that what Wilson wanted, he would get; his concern was to trade that for Wilson's support in other fields. When Callaghan seemed to be driving too hard a bargain, Jennie (who chaired the party in 1968) was heard to remark: 'I think, Jim, you are after being Treasurer of the Party?' after which Jim found fresh virtue in the idea of an open university.[52]

Richard Crossman, then Minister for Housing and Local Government, though an old friend of Nye and Jennie, was perhaps the most hostile. A university of the air which only taught and did not research could not be a true university. He supported Wilson's original notion of 'a kind of extension of a group of universities', but not Jennie's independent university. Its degrees, he opined, 'would not be held in high esteem'.[53] Jennie, with the help of the Chief Whip, Ted Short, tried to bring him around; Crossman agreed finally in December 1965 not to press his objections.

Only when Ted Short, with his external London degree, became Secretary of State for Education, did Jennie have unambiguous and affectionate support in the Cabinet, over and beyond the benevolent paternalism of Wilson. That was one reason, Wilson said, why he appointed him. Most of the rest, especially the former Gaitskellites, saw the OU as a 'wreath for Nye', gesture politics, a piece of misguided expensive romanticism by Harold, entrusted to an ageing woman who shamelessly manipulated Nye's memory wherever it helped her short-cut departments and Cabinet procedures. The 'tiresome widow', as she was described by the Oxbridge men, was snubbed and avoided. Infuriatingly, she appeared not to notice, and if she did, not to care. Reluctantly, they came to admire her tenacity, and retrospectively to admit she was probably right—for the wrong reasons.

The views of Cabinet critics were confirmed when the chairman of the UGC, Sir John Wolfenden, wrote to the department's permanent secretary (Sir Herbert Andrew) making it clear that the UGC had never been consulted on the project, would not support it, and in financial terms wanted nothing to do with it. Jennie then turned what might have been a devastating snub to political advantage: the university would be funded not by the UGC, which Jennie feared would treat it badly, but by the DES.

Direct funding would secure its finance; the Education Minister would be its guardian. But there were drawbacks. If the university was not financed by the UGC, its financial segregation would perpetuate its academic segregation; in a crisis, it would not be able to count on the academic support of the CVCP. It would instead be reliant on the political views of the Education Minister. Since it was a Labour Party foundation, its vice-chancellor, in order to secure its well-being, must distance himself from its Labour Party origins (quite literally so when, at the installation of the first Chancellor—Lord Crowther, in 1969—OU staff tried to keep Jennie off the platform. They should have known, and known her, better). It also meant that, to Jennie's distaste, it would have to woo Tory shadow education ministers to gain all-party support. That meant wooing Mrs Thatcher.

The general election of February 1966 loomed. A few days after the Official Committee on Broadcasting came Wilson's pre-election planning meeting of Cabinet and NEC at Chequers to determine the content of the manifesto. Wilson took them through the themes, and then, mid-afternoon, invited any other contributions. Jennie was there as a member of the NEC. She took her opportunity to speak passionately about a university of the air. She made careful and calculated references to the spin-offs that would benefit third world countries, and second chance men. She then moved into purple prose. The finest creation of the previous Labour government, said Jennie, was Nye's NHS; now they were engaged on an operation which would make just as much difference to the country. 'We were all impressed', said Wilson admiringly. 'She was a tigress.'[54]

The university of the air came formally to Cabinet two days later, on Tuesday 8 February. Jennie was there to speak to it. However, it was not quite the formality that she and Wilson had hoped for, after her Chequers *tour de force*. The Cabinet had in front of them not only Jennie's draft White Paper, but also distinctly cool appraisals from the Ministerial and Official Committees, and the Treasury. The Cabinet accepted that Wilson was determined to press on with the scheme, so debate focused, as Jennie predicted it would, on costs and channels. Its cost? Jennie hadn't a clue, she told them breezily, but then no one knew how much a tank or Concorde really cost either. And what was more she wanted the fourth channel in its entirety for her university. It was too significant a project to be confined to residual time: 'I consider that to revert to a half-baked scheme using an hour or two on BBC2 would completely undermine the whole purpose and spirit of a University of the Air', she wrote to Harold Wilson.[55]

Had Jennie persisted in demanding the fourth channel, she would have sunk the entire project. Cabinet hostility to its cost was too great. Not even Wilson could have delivered it. She capitulated. Instead the university would be launched on BBC2, with time on the fourth channel as and when it became available. Even so, the Treasury not unreasonably demanded firmer costings than Jennie would or indeed could give. Wilson stepped in. He suggested that the finances of the scheme should be independently appraised by the not-entirely independent Lord Goodman. (As Goodman chaired Jennie's Arts Council, and was the solicitor both to her and

Wilson, his independence, though not his integrity, was somewhat questionable.) It was, thought Tony Benn, 'a terrible setback for Jennie'.[56] She still did not have the necessary commitment from Cabinet, which alone would mobilize the Department of Education, the Post Office, and the Treasury behind her, and without which the project would tread water. She could, however, publish her White Paper but not mention in it costs or channels. Jennie wrote to Goodman, as Harold had proposed, though with typical panache she went well beyond her Cabinet brief (which confined the university to BBC2): 'What we need now is a realistic assessment of the relative costs of launching the University of the Air on BBC 2 and the fourth channel. The Cabinet are convinced that you are the best person to help on this and were unanimous in asking me to approach you.'[57] Goodman agreed.

The civil servants, to their immense irritation, were told nothing of the Goodman appraisal and remained for months in ignorance. They were also not told of Goodman's visit to the USA to see whether the Ford Foundation and/or *Encyclopaedia Britannica* might produce some money as they had for the Chicago scheme. Off went Goodman in early 1966 to interview Senator Benton and McGeorge Bundy, a former Kennedy aide who had recently become president of the Ford Foundation and patron of $400 million a year. Goodman learnt enough to realize that neither the *Encyclopaedia Britannica* teaching films nor the Chicago experiment easily lent themselves to export. Bundy thought Ford might offer some help but lead finance would have to come from the British government.[58]

Goodman now turned his hand to the other task set him by Wilson, which he managed with equal finesse and equal inaccuracy—that of assessing for the Cabinet the costs of the university. He treated his task as confidential, so early in 1966 he bypassed the civil servants, going straight to the BBC's Director General, Hugh Carleton Greene. BBC culture was deeply hostile to the idea of a university of the air, and Greene was uneasy, as his own Further Education Advisory Council (FEAC) was breathing down his neck. The FEAC saw itself as the educational arm of the BBC. It wanted to expand its own work, and saw the proposals for a university of the air pre-empting BBC air time as a direct competitor. A rather scratchy set of meetings and minutes followed. The FEAC wanted to supervise negotiations between the BBC and the prospective university; the university's planning bodies would have nothing to do with them—they would negotiate only with the BBC; FEAC refused to cede their existing slots to a university of the air, and would compete with it for the rest. Goodman silkily suggested to the BBC that in that case it needed 'to re-think the whole concept' of the FEAC.[59] Needless to say, Lord Goodman's view prevailed.

Greene and Goodman worked harmoniously together. Three months later, in May 1966, Goodman was able to send in his private report to Jennie and to Wilson. A university of the air could be established on BBC2 'at fairly modest cost', of £1.15 million capital and £3.7 million recurrent expenditure. Of this, £2.7 million would be needed by the BBC; the remaining £1 million would cover all other costs, from staff, to adapting TV sets. This would finance ten hours TV a week, rising to thirty hours by year three.

Goodman had reported remarkably quickly. That may have been because he and Greene were remarkably inaccurate. Greene, said Goodman, had calculated the BBC's costs down to the last penny, but between them not down to the last pound. They underestimated staff costs, ignored entirely the cost of sites, central university premises, and local centres, allowed nothing for printing and publishing equipment, or any of the infrastructure a teaching university might need. Between them, Goodman confessed, they underestimated the eventual cost of the OU some twenty-fold. But for that happy error, Goodman cheerfully explained in his memoirs, the OU would probably not have existed. When the civil servants did get to see the report several months later (in August 1966), they quickly spotted how flawed were his financial calculations, and their brief for Crosland to take to the Ministerial Committee on Broadcasting in September 1966 sounded some carefully worded financial warnings.[60]

On one point the civil servants and Goodman did agree, that the university should start on an experimental basis to allow them to assess student demand. Jennie refused. Her university was to be 'an established and firm project' from the beginning.[61] Her view was understandable, given that the costs of the BBC would be the same whether the university was experimental or established, while the political risks of closing it down increased.

Wilson wanted Jennie to publish her White Paper before the 1966 general election, even though she was under instructions from the Cabinet to fudge the issues of costs and channels. As a result, it was a less ambitious document than she wanted. In Labour's manifesto of March 1966 there was now a firm commitment to a university of the air, 'using TV and radio and comparable facilities, high grade correspondence courses and new teaching techniques. This open university will obviously extend the best teaching facilities and give everyone the possibility of study for a full degree. It will mean genuine equality of opportunity to millions of people for the first time.'

If Wilson thought the White Paper would win him friends and votes in the education world, he was much mistaken. *The Times,* the *FT,* the *Observer,* the *TES,* and *Education* were as critical as ever, now dismissing it as an election gimmick. It was impractical, costly, under-researched, grandiose. The *Teacher* could not believe that Crosland was willing to endorse 'such humbug'.[62] In Parliament, where Jennie had faced a trickle of unhelpful questions over the past year, one Tory MP said in the debate on broadcasting that there were 'no supporters for this University . . . People wish it well, but cannot see how it will work. The most truthful reason for it came to me from a Socialist, who said, "Well, Harold insists on having it."'[63] Wilson did.

With the Goodman appraisal in hand and the election secured, the Ministerial Committee on Broadcasting Policy, chaired by the Prime Minister himself and with Jennie as well as Crosland in attendance, met in October 1966 and authorized her to go ahead, and to establish a reconstituted committee (a Planning Committee) to take the scheme forward. She could acquire names for it, but not go further until the finances were sorted. Jennie, in other words, now had official Cabinet approval; but she did not yet have any identified finance, so nothing much could happen.

The Treasury remained unenthusiastic and unhelpful. Jennie tried to keep the pressure up on Callaghan, but was told that 'it was hopeless to try and arrange further meetings with the Chancellor and that it would be better to carry on discussion by correspondence'.[64] This was not surprising. Jennie's efforts to extract firm financial undertakings from the Treasury were occurring as the economic climate sharply deteriorated. Wilson and the government were, immediately after the March 1966 general election, riding high. The seamen's strike of May 1966 generated a run on sterling which by July took the Cabinet into the throes of a devaluation crisis. The price for deferring devaluation was £500 million in cuts, deflation, and austerity. New spending projects, like the OU, were not exactly welcome. Many in the DES believed the project would be axed. Meanwhile the BBC was getting impatient, as it needed a firm decision if it was to start planning. Jennie continued to stall in Parliament—in November 1966, in March, in April, and in June 1967 she was still telling the Commons that she hoped to make a full statement 'soon'. By July 1967, MPs not unreasonably wanted to know how soon was soon.

Even Jennie was getting weary. Since the general election, fifteen months before, the project had disappeared from public view, caught between Treasury, Post Office, and DES crossfire. In a moment of depression she invited to dinner John Fulton, Vice-Chancellor of Sussex University, and Norman MacKenzie, her friend of *New Statesman* days who had enthused the Advisory Committee with his own passion for educational technology. She wondered aloud whether her only hope of launching the OU was not as an independent university, but as a daughter college of Sussex University whose charter could be amended to allow it to offer external degrees. Fulton was helpful.

The crisis passed. The Treasury conducted the PESC round each July, seeking to keep the growth of public expenditure in line with the growth of the economy. Worn down, perhaps, by Jennie's persistence and an understanding that Wilson would support Callaghan (the Chancellor) in Cabinet on a tough package of cuts if Callaghan protected the OU, the Treasury conceded. In July 1967 it provided a special allocation for the OU, based on the wildly inaccurate figures of the Goodman memorandum. (DES officials, says one of them, 'realised that these estimates were far too low, but for reasons of expediency the point was not pressed home.'[66]) The Cabinet agreed. 'We're in', said Ralph Toomey, Jennie's senior civil servant, with what for him was exuberant language. This, thought civil servants, was the crucial turning point: from now on, the OU was within the Whitehall machine, and part of official policy. It would happen.

Jennie was euphoric. At a press conference a month or two later she said to Toomey: 'that little bastard that I have hugged to my bosom and cherished, that all the others have tried to kill off, will thrive.'[67] After eighteen months of stalling, they could now speed ahead. The Advisory Committee had shown that an OU was feasible. In September 1967 Jennie announced her Planning Committee, which would ensure its existence. In the preceding months she had garnered its members. She refused to interview them in 'the musty cynical atmosphere of Curzon street'. Instead, she kept a corner table for two in the Commons guest dining-room, 'and went after the people I wanted, one by one'.[68]

By any assessment, she did extraordinarily well. She acquired five vice-chancellors (including Asa Briggs of Sussex, who was also president of the WEA, Eric Ashby of Cambridge, and Brynmor Jones of Hull) as well as Lord Fulton. From the Advisory Committee came John Scupham, former education controller of the BBC, Harold Wiltshire of Nottingham, Eric Briault of the ILEA, and Norman MacKenzie from Sussex (who had, says

Ralph Toomey, been especially valuable on the Advisory Committee where his deft drafting had done much to shape its final report). They were joined by Brian Groombridge, education officer of the ITA, and by Roy Shaw, who had impressed Jennie by his work as director of Keele University's adult education department. Professor Hilde Himmelweit from the LSE, the only woman member, had written on educational television and had directed the Nuffield television enquiry in the late 1950s. Politically important was the inclusion of Sir William Alexander, who spoke for local education authorities; Ritchie Calder and Arnold Goodman were thrown in for good measure and additional weight. There were nineteen members in all, five of them coming from the Advisory Committee. It was a more impressive committee, it was noted, than the Robbins Committee itself.

Sir Peter Venables was an inspired choice of chairman. He was Vice-Chancellor of Aston University, vice-chairman of the CVCP, chaired the BBC's FEAC, and sat on the Adult Education Committee of the ITA; he had also been a member of the Crowther Committee. He came from the technological side of higher education, and combined a pragmatic Birmingham toughness with civil service lucidity. He was, says Asa Briggs, 'superb'.[69] When pressed by Jennie, Venables thought about her offer over a weekend, trying to decide whether the OU was merely a political gimmick or a serious academic enterprise. He reworked the Robbins figures: if just 10 per cent of those who had missed higher education because they were born too soon were added to the 250,000 teachers without degrees, then the OU had its market—he agreed. Jennie came to trust him completely. The Planning Committee was to meet ten times, its subgroups and working parties a further forty times.

They needed somewhere to meet, however, and this was not, Jennie decided, going to be in some dingy corner of Curzon Street. They needed stylish offices to show the world they were launching a university, not filing memos. They had to impress the visitor, 'out snob the snobs', as she put it. She looked at Richmond Terrace, but considered it was a slum inside. Her young private secretary spent lunchtime wandering around Carlton Terrace and the Mall looking for a home for the Institute of Contemporary Arts. He strayed into the filming of the ballroom scenes of *The Charge of the Light Brigade* in one grand house, and found a suitable home for the OU in another: 38 Belgrave Square.[70] Jennie and Ted Short visited it, pronounced it elegant enough, and cashed in old loyalties with Jennie's former department, the MPBW, by persuading them to send over some decent furniture to replace the dowdy stuff left behind by the

Schools Council. A huge glass-topped desk was provided for the future vice-chancellor. Puzzled OU staff found out later that it was a replica of the desk enjoyed by the British Ambassador in Stockholm. Jennie ordered that the splendid ground floor drawing-room (which was also nominally her office, complete with white carpets, pastel paint, and gilt mirrors) should serve as the staff common-room. The first time the staff sat back in her sofas and armchairs, the huge, heavy, and expensive chandelier that Jennie had also acquired came crashing down, bringing with it part of the fine ceiling on to the white carpets, though fortunately missing the equally white-faced occupants. That, for a long time, closed the only room in Belgrave Square large enough for a meeting.

The first caller at Belgrave Square was Sir William Armstrong, head of the civil service, who came to find out whether the proposed university of the air might offer courses for his staff. He was friendly, so Jennie asked for his help: 'What am I to do about those permanent secretaries?' He said, 'Oh, we'll give them a dinner.' Lord Goodman (of course) hosted it in his flat, and once it was known that Sir William had accepted the invitation, along came five permanent secretaries. The dinner party became something of a seminar, in the course of which, Jennie slyly noted, one or two people wilted. Thereafter, she thought, the Whitehall mandarins believed the scheme would happen.[71]

The Planning Committee started work. Jennie attended the buffet lunch that preceded their first meeting, but, unlike the Advisory Committee, she neither attended its regular meetings nor tried to steer its conclusions. A still sceptical DES provided the secretariat. The Planning Committee started afresh, although its recommendations did not greatly depart from those of the earlier Advisory Committee. It addressed a number of key questions. What was the function of the OU? It was to be a degree-giving body. Any thought of sub-degree work was discarded. Should it then develop, as had Exeter and Reading, as daughter colleges of London University? Or, like the Colleges of Advanced Technology, should its degrees be validated by the CNAA? Or should it be part of a consortium of universities providing degrees by distance teaching? No. It should be an autonomous independent free-standing university, like the other new universities of the decade. The difference was that students would be home-based so the teaching would come to them rather than they to the teachers, and access would be open. The first task was to appoint their executive officer, a vice-chancellor.

Jennie had been discussing possible names with Ralph Toomey for some time. Back in January 1967 his soundings had suggested Richard Hoggart, then Professor at Birmingham, Harold Wiltshire of Nottingham, Bill Hughes of Ruskin, as well as some chief education officers. Noel Annan offered further names: Norman MacKenzie of Sussex, Brian Jackson, who was running the National Extension College, and Kenneth Berrill, bursar of King's College, Cambridge, who had recently been head-hunted for the vice-chancellorship of Essex, but whose wife had not wanted to move home. Crosland favoured Michael Young.[72]

There was no obvious front runner; most (Richard Hoggart, for example) did not even know they were being considered. Venables insisted that this was a matter for the Planning Committee not the minister, and Jennie acquiesced. Unusually for the time, they advertised. Candidates were asked to set down their thoughts on the future of the OU.

They had over a hundred applications, one of which was from Walter Perry. He was 46 years old at the time, Vice-Principal and Professor of Pharmacology at Jennie's old university, Edinburgh, where he had also been an outstanding director of medical research. He was ready for a vice-chancellorship and was looking to move south with his family. His son pointed out the advertisement in the *Observer*, telling him, jocularly, that the job was made for him. On reflection, he decided it probably was, precisely because effective teaching would be at its core. Much university teaching in the 1950s and 1960s, he considered, had been unbelievably bad. Edinburgh was no exception. Staff were appointed for their scholarship—many considered students to be a nuisance, who got between them and their research; the same lectures could be delivered unchanged for twenty years, and not because they embodied eternal verities; lecturers could not always be heard, or if heard, understood. As a result, weak students floundered, while better students taught themselves. Perry knew that the OU would stand or fall by the quality of its teaching, and he saw in the OU the chance to pioneer new methods and revitalize the university teaching world. It was a challenge that he recognized and relished. So he set down his thoughts, as the advertisement required. He was short-listed, and appeared before the inner circle of the Planning Committee, who were grilling candidates at, of course, the Athenaeum Club. Neither the DES nor Jennie were consulted. Venables recommended Perry and that was enough for Jennie. He was appointed in May 1968.

Perry was a tough, practical Scot, who was something of a wine buff, a singer of Victorian ballads, and a guitar player (in the early days of the OU the last was a more prized skill than the first); he had a strong dislike of politics and a deep distrust of politicians. Like many senior academic scientists, he was both autocratic and informal, wanting top-down decision-making, and impatient of a Senate that he thought too large and too talkative, but willing to roll his sleeves up along with the rest to pack and deliver course material, especially when a seven-week postal strike occurred a couple of weeks after the OU opened. His door always stood ajar. The passing gardener might be pulled in and asked his views on a proposed new course.

The Planning Committee submitted its report to Ted Short, the Secretary of State, who, at Wilson's suggestion, made a Statement to the Commons:

> The Committee's task was to work out a comprehensive plan for an Open University, and to prepare a draft charter and statutes. This they have done with great energy and skill . . . The Government fully accept the plan of development set out in this Report. It will now be for the University authority, as an autonomous and completely independent institution, to carry the project forward, and in this way they can count on the support of the Government.[73]

A Royal Charter was granted by the Privy Council on 23 April 1969 and presented to the first Chancellor, Geoffrey Crowther, at his induction at the Royal Society on 23 July 1969. The Open University was open.

Despite sniping from the Tory back benches, the Official Opposition had been muted. Sir Edward Boyle had supported a scheme for a (sub-degree) college of the air himself in the early 1960s, and his criticism was now careful rather than forthright. Venables and Perry briefed him heavily, so he was more equivocal than his back-benchers expected. However, his comments grew more hostile. Hailsham did not hesitate; he thought the idea of an open university was decidedly 'airy-fairy'.[74] The Shadow Minister for Education, Margaret Thatcher, believed it would offer 'courses in hobbies'—flower-arranging, she seemed to have in mind. Iain Macleod, Shadow Chancellor, castigated it as 'blithering nonsense'; once elected, the Tories would scrap it.[75] Tory central office warned potential OU job applicants that they should stay away from the new venture, as its future was in doubt.

Perry was essentially a short-term man. He wanted to roll up his sleeves and get cracking with the nuts and bolts of the university. But the 1970 general election was approaching, and the university's Chancellor Geoffrey Crowther, and its new Treasurer Sir Paul Chambers (recently retired from ICI) were predicting a Tory victory. The OU was highly vulnerable, as it was funded directly by the DES. It was too closely identified with the Labour Party to survive a hostile Tory government.

The Vice-Chancellor must seek Tory support, and admit so many students that not even a determined Macleod could scrap it. If Jennie's job had been to achieve an Open University, the Vice-Chancellor's first job was to ensure its survival. He had barely two years to do it. After all those months of delay during 1966 and 1967, it had suddenly become a race against time.

II

THE OPEN UNIVERSITY

WALTER Perry had to do three things, he judged, if he were to secure the future of the OU. First, he had to distance it from the Labour Party, which meant reducing Jennie's high profile public role. Second, he had to allay the engrained hostility of the academic world, so that the OU would be judged a proper university, its degrees proper degrees, worth the having. His third task, much the most congenial, was to turn the draft of the Planning Committee into the fabric of a university. Site, staff, courses, and students had all to be acquired. He was soon working up to eighteen hours a day, seven days a week. Golf and guitar went untouched as he worked himself into exhaustion and a heart attack.

If the OU was ever to be perceived as independent, it had to be seen to be independent of the Labour Party. Devoted though Perry insisted he was to Jennie—he 'fell in love with her', he says, and she became the godmother of the daughter he never got round to christening—he had to woo Margaret Thatcher, while edging Jennie off the scene. Almost literally so. The grand Belgrave Square house that Jennie had found for the Planning Committee became the university's first home. The staff common-room with its shattered chandelier, was also Jennie's office. Not that she used it very much. But she had to be evicted. An independent university could not have a government minister sitting at its headquarters, part of its fixtures and fittings.

It was a painful lesson for Jennie to learn. For a while she continued, in Toomey's words, 'to meddle'. However she was enough of a politician to recognize that Perry was right. She tried to become more publicly self-effacing. When Peter Venables, chairman of the Planning Committee, retired in August 1969, his job done, he thanked her, delicately, for the way she 'entrusted the task fully to the Committee and myself, and yet fully supported us with advice and help as occasion required'.[1] Predictions that the Tories would win the election were all too accurate. When Jennie lost her seat, Wilson sent her to the Lords, from where she would, she said, watch Lord Eccles, Minister for the Arts, like a hawk, but leave 'Walter [Perry] severely alone, since that seems to me the friendliest thing to do'.[2] She would need to cast herself as a Goodman-like figure, fixing things behind the scenes as needed and when asked—which was not her natural style.

Perry knew Jennie's style, but that did not prepare him for Margaret Thatcher, the Shadow Minister for Education, whom he had been told to woo. The Chancellor and Treasurer of the OU together arranged a dinner at their London club. Mrs Thatcher arrived and vigorously cross-questioned Perry. He got more and more exasperated and outspoken. When she came back at him, he got heated. After she left, he turned and apologized to his hosts, for having 'blown it'. Not at all, they assured him. It was fine. She has now got her brief. Just what was necessary. All a great success. Perry was disbelieving, but dinner was followed by her visits to Walton Hall, the site at Milton Keynes. Mrs Thatcher, who had come to attack, now became an ally, albeit on her own terms. She was later to claim, with some truth: 'I did "save" the Open University.' She fought fiercely in Cabinet when Macleod threatened to scrap it; and as Secretary of State she defended it robustly in the Commons. She sent a graceful note of thanks to Toomey for the work he had put into her briefing, saying as she marched off to the Treasury: 'I do hope that somehow we shall be able to save the OU.'[3]

Mrs Thatcher approved of the OU for two reasons. She agreed with Perry that it would generate new methods of teaching and much better teaching materials, especially in maths and science, which would not only benefit the UK university world but would be of value abroad. Second, she was persuaded by Perry that the OU had a distinctive market: 'I did not think that the Open University would attract many people who lost out on education in their early years, but I did think it would help many who wished to better themselves to obtain the requisite qualifications.'[4] It would reinforce self-help, aid the occupationally mobile, rather than remedy educational deprivation. And it was likely to be cheap. Students would live at home, and require neither accommodation nor maintenance grants; they would even pay fees. They would not need the education plant (libraries, lecture halls, refectories, etc.) that made the capital costs of a university so high. Much of the cost of a conventional university to public funds would either not be incurred or be carried by the students themselves.

Jennie's OU and Thatcher's OU colluded. Thanks to Mrs Thatcher, it did indeed survive the Conservative government, though at a price—reduced grant, increased fees, and the instruction that it take a cohort of 18-year-olds to see whether it could expand higher education on the cheap.[5]

Perry's second task was to bring the established universities on side. As Peter Venables had noted before him: 'Here there was no welcome for the new institution at all.'[6] Perry had to persuade them that this was not a university selling 'telly' degrees: television would contribute only 5 per cent of its teaching time. Its original title, a University of the Air, was by now misleading. It was, instead, an Open University. Perry did the rounds, and over the next two and a half years went to twenty-two universities, propounding the mission and the academic quality of the OU. Asa Briggs and Peter Venables had to work hard to get the CVCP to accept Perry as a member. Support came slowly, and often from unexpected quarters. Older academics, including Oxbridge fellows, had taught undergraduates immediately after the war who arrived without formal qualifications for a two-year degree, yet whose motivation and maturity powered them through to upper seconds and firsts. They were tolerant of open access. More hostile were younger meritocratic dons, who had clawed their way up the system by meeting and exceeding in every test, and who were therefore deeply suspicious of the whole enterprise. They believed the OU would trivialize everything they had worked for. It would demean university degrees—and university careers. An OU regional director in his first year was at a drinks party explaining his job to a young academic: 'Oh', he said, 'that won't work, will it?' and without waiting for an answer turned on his heel.[7]

Perry sought out allies. He recruited senior faculty members from other universities to act as external assessors for his staff appointments; and employed their younger staff at summer schools. Summer school converted the sceptics. In selecting its tutors, some OU staff were upset when Perry instructed them to pass over older and more experienced adult educators; instead, they were to employ young academics, a bit brash, perhaps, usually inexperienced, but with strong paper qualifications. It would build up a cadre of the committed where it counted. When the *Telegraph* ran a story critical of the OU after that first summer, York lecturers wrote in to challenge it: 'We have never met such highly motivated students in our lives.' Others amplified their university salaries by working as local OU tutors (it became an alternative to A-level marking for the financially hard-pressed). Despite themselves, conventional universities cross-subsidized the salary bill of the OU, as they carried the overheads for its part-time staff. The tide of opinion in the academic community slowly began to turn.

Like Jennie before him, Perry took much less pains with the WEA or LEA world. Whether, had he done so, financial help to students might have been forthcoming, is hard to judge. Certainly their prejudices were as strongly held as they were ill-informed. One director of education told the OU Secretary, Christodoulou, that he was 'not going to support middle-class women in hobby education' with grants.[8] However, Sir William Alexander, who ran the National Association of LEAs, and was a member of the Planning Committee, helped coax grants for summer schools out of most LEAs, while personally remaining deeply sceptical of the entire enterprise.

Another problem constituency was the public libraries, which Jennie could have done more to bring on side. They were part of her responsibilities, but though she had been a passionate defender of them since her youth, she found the portfolio 'very boring indeed'.[9] When she was invited to address the annual library conference at Brighton, her young private secretary drafted a careful speech on library provision and brought it to her hotel. He knocked at her bedroom door. 'I'm in the bath', she said. 'Sit on the bed and declaim the speech to me.' He did, but obviously failed to do so to Jennie's satisfaction. When it came to Jennie's moment on the platform, she rose to her feet and said: 'I have a speech here written for me by my civil servants', paused, and then dramatically stuffed it back in her handbag. To her department's amusement and chagrin, she then made an unscripted speech about the Open University. The librarians were baffled, but loyally cheered.[10]

Librarians shared with adult educationalists a mutual passion for education, access, and excellence. A university of the air would bring the best lecturers within reach of all, just as libraries brought the best books to all. Branch libraries were already at the centre of much informal adult education; they reckoned they could offer the university not only lists of books, but lists of potential students, every one of them a reader.[11] OU students would make heavy demands on local libraries. Would OU students have book grants? Would the libraries? What about periodicals? Jennie had done much of her own studying in public libraries, and expected that they would not only provide books but become, along with schools, local study centres, often at unsocial hours. Who would pay for that? Not consulted about any of this, the libraries were naturally aggrieved. As the White Paper on the university of the air barely referred to books at all, they were alarmed. Libraries were invariably underfunded by local authorities (themselves experiencing tight controls on their spending in 1968), yet it was cheerily assumed that they could provide books for 50,000 serious students who had recourse to no other library. Librarians remained tetchy for years to come.

The third task facing Perry was to turn the draft of the Planning Committee into a university, and quickly. The OU was to admit its first students in January 1971, just two years after the Planning Committee reported. Perry devised his flow chart, working forwards to appointing staff and having them in place, while working backwards from the point of student admission, and therefore the need to have course material ready for them to use, and a prospectus from which to choose.

He had immediately to make a vital appointment, a secretary and registrar, who would be responsible for all the administrative and non-academic side of the university. He advertised, but though the field was abundant, it was to neither Perry's nor Venables's liking. Jennie joined in the hunt. Though her relations with Tony Crosland had been edgy, she got on well with his PPS at the Department of Education, the enthusiastic, knowledgeable, and boyish Chris Price. Jennie confessed to him that they were having 'the most ghastly time' interviewing for the OU secretary. They were 'all useless', she said dismissively; did Chris know any decent administrative staff? Chris did: Anastasios Christodoulou (always known as Chris), then deputy registrar at Leeds University and a second-row forward scrum. Within forty-eight hours Chris Price was receiving a phone call from a reluctant and somewhat fearful Christodoulou: 'Shall I apply? The Tories say it will be abolished.' Yes he should and no they wouldn't, replied the other Chris, crossing his fingers. He agreed and was appointed.[12] Chris was 'a genial clubbable swarthy Cypriot', an excellent rugby and cricket player, and a rock-solid appointment for a new university that administratively was hugely complex; it had to produce, distribute, assess, and examine course material, courses, and students in numbers beyond anyone's experience.[13]

Perry always worried that the administrative structures of the university were frail—dependent on the printing room (too small and therefore too slow), the library system (random), the postal services (on strike for seven weeks in the month the OU opened), and, above all, the computer, which 'unpersonned' its students (one wrote in complaining that he was nationality 771, mother tongue 144, occupations 05 and 12, education level L, and had last studied at 9 where he read 10). Tutors were nervous and students were vulnerable because the computer not only marked a large number of assignments, but also held the grades. It could not easily be 'got at' if mistakes were made. Their confidence was not helped when a 'not' was left out of a logic assignment; or when the computer went berserk, giving them all A grades; or when it unceremoniously expelled 600 students who could not get back into the system until the following year. Chris was a centre of calm and competence. When Perry's own health broke down from overwork and he was away for three months at the end of 1970, Chris was acting Vice-Chancellor as well.

Chris's appointment was speedily followed by senior academic staff. For the first 34 appointments, Perry had 1,200 applicants; as the only academic in post, he had to sift the lot. He was relieved at their quality. If, he noted sourly, his staff ended up politically left of centre, then Tory Central Office, which had discouraged other candidates from applying, had only themselves to blame.

When the OU was first conceived, it was expected to have a tiny central staff (perhaps 35 in all) and that most of its work would be franchised out to FE colleges. Belgrave Square would be its home. As planning proceeded, it was clear there would be at least 170 staff in post by September 1969, and they had to look for a new home. First, they were required to investigate office blocks in London, where no one wished to work; then they were instructed by Wilson to redeploy to the North, which no one wanted either (Jennie was brought in and quickly persuaded the PM to relent.) They were unable to find a site in the Thames Valley (perhaps near Reading), which almost everyone favoured. They were looking for a campus site, like the new universities, with room to expand, close to London, and close to the BBC's Alexandra Palace. They scoured heritage England, but most of the houses were either too important to permit development, or lacked the land to make it possible. They looked at Cliveden, but it went to Stanford University, and Knebworth (the Bulwer-Lytton home) near Stevenage, complete with elephant feet and discarded bits of Empire, but in poor condition. They started negotiating for Esso's training and research centre, Milton Hill, an eighteenth-century mansion near Didcot, but the BBC held that there were poor road connections to Alexandra Palace. They were, said Toomey, 'scratching around'.

Jock Campbell (made a life peer by Wilson in 1966) was president of Booker McConnell, chairman of the *New Statesman*, and also chairman of Milton Keynes Development Corporation. He was going to see Geoffrey Crowther, chairman of Trust House Forte, because he wanted a THF hotel in Milton Keynes. In the taxi he was reading *The Times* and saw that Crowther had been appointed Chancellor of this new university. He arrived, and after the usual salutations, Crowther asked: 'What can I do for you, Jock?' 'I wanted a hotel. Now I want a university'. Why, he continued, should this new pioneering university not come to the biggest and newest of the pioneering new towns? It could offer good communication links, it was close to the M1, and within an hour of London, Oxford, Cambridge, and Birmingham. Campbell could even offer a site: Walton Hall, a small yellow stuccoed Georgian mansion of considerable charm and no great distinction, which, with adjacent land, had seventy acres, a lake, some magnificent cedars of Lebanon, a church, stables, and brick outbuildings.

The managing director of Milton Keynes, who followed up Campbell's bid, assured Perry that they could negotiate 'financial terms which are entirely acceptable to you' and went on: 'We want you to come to Milton Keynes, not for income, but because we feel that your staff and activities would have a wholly desirable influence on both the short and the long term development of the new city.' A few weeks later, he was writing blandly to Perry to say that his board 'endorsed everything I have said to you about the University being very welcome'.[14]

In fact, Campbell had considerably difficulty in getting the deal through the Milton Keynes board.[15] Tory members, led by Horace Cutler of the GLC, rebelled. A general election was forthcoming, a Tory victory was expected, and then there would *be* no Open University. Why 'hypothecate this wonderful site at a peppercorn?' they asked. Campbell tried to chivvy and charm them, but they were stubborn, until he had what he thought was a brainwave. Was not Edward Boyle, the previous Tory Minister for Education and Vice-Chancellor-elect of Leeds University, a likely friend of the OU? Would his views not carry weight with the board? The board agreed they might. Campbell left the meeting and phoned Boyle, to be told in no uncertain terms: 'I'm not bloody well going to help you. I think its absolutely awful. I'm advising Conservatives not to take jobs there and not to support it.' Campbell returned to his board. What did Boyle say? Campbell told them that, regretfully, he had been unable to reach him (which in a sense was true). After further argument, the board agreed.[16]

The VC found a pretty timber and thatch cottage for himself a mile away from the site, where Jennie stayed on her visits of inspection; the Dean of Science lived in a caravan in the field; most of the new staff, who lived in adjacent university cities, preferred at first to commute. Arnold Goodman came to have a look, shook his head and feared that staff would have nothing to do 'except commune with the pigs'.[17]

They appointed as architects Fry, Drew, and partners. Maxwell Fry was one of Britain's leading modernist architects, an associate of Walter

Gropius, the founder of the Bauhaus School. His wife, Jane Drew, had designed universities, hospitals, and dams in West Africa, where she worked with Corbusier. Jennie and Jane had known each other for many years on the dinner party circuit, and their paths had crossed again when Jane launched the Institute of Contemporary Arts. Jennie had helped her raise money from the City, Sieff, and Sainsbury. Arnold Goodman had also sponsored fund-raising lunches for the ICA at the Savoy, at one of which Jennie wore a fetching low-cut dress. George Brown had to return to the Commons after one lunch, but as he left, swaying somewhat, he announced to his fellow guests: 'Now you have all had a chance of looking down Jennie's bosom you must sign up and pay up, now'. They did. Jennie was scarlet.

Goodman had, unbeknown to Jane Drew, been following her career. What sort of job, he asked her, would she most like? Something for ordinary people, she had told him. He offered her the OU. The following day she was seen by Perry and Jennie, who confirmed the offer of the job. Were they not seeing any others, Jane enquired? Yes, but they had this letter from Arnold and that was it.[18] Jane was not the first to be taken aback by the power of Lord Goodman.

Her firm was formally appointed project architects by the Planning Committee on the first Thursday in February 1969. She was told that the university needed temporary buildings for its staff by the end of the year. Jane visited the site on the Saturday; drew outline designs for the central office and the arts faculty on the Sunday; told Perry on the Monday that he could, if he wished, have permanent rather than temporary buildings by the end of the year. He took the proposals along to Jennie, who got the DES to agree a negotiated rather than a time-consuming competitive tender for the building; and work began on site on 1 April, just five weeks later.

There was the minor problem of planning permission from Newport Pagnell Council, which Jane Drew had overlooked. She went off to see the town clerk. He regretted that there was no Planning Committee meeting due, as they were in the Easter recess. Jane Drew swore. The town clerk, impressed, added helpfully that the councillor who ran the wool shop and the councillor who owned the butcher's shop might, he thought, be persuaded to summon an emergency meeting of the Planning Committee right away—like tomorrow. Jane Drew was taken aback by this turn of speed and doubted that she could have detailed plans ready in time. 'Oh they don't want plans', said the town clerk; 'they won't understand them. Do drawings instead. Lots of colour. Plenty of trees. Keep the buildings in the background. Not too visible.' To the horror of her staff, Jane did precisely that, overnight, and got her planning permission next day.[19]

The first building was a simple brick shell for the Faculty of Arts, which was completed in five months, on time, and below UGC cost, ready for the staff who were moving out of Belgrave Square in October. A fine summer, which helped the building, was followed by floods from the river which turned the site into a quagmire. Staff arrived to a building site that was a sea of mud crossed by duckboards. Perry issued them with a hundred pairs of cheap woolly black or tartan slippers to stop them carrying mud on to the new carpets. The second building, the Correspondence Services Unit, encountered more problems. It was the industrial and business heart of the OU, from where was printed, assembled, and dispatched all the course material. Steel was by now virtually unobtainable and had trebled in price. Permits to import it took time, which, with an election looming, they did not have. Jennie cleared the way for the university to get its steel from Belgium in advance of official authorization; Perry apprehensively signed the contracts.

The men were working against time. Christmas approached. Their union not unreasonably expected them to enjoy the customary extended holiday. Jane summoned Jennie, who gave them an impassioned speech: they were building a university not for the rich, but for themselves. The men, says Jane, would have kissed her feet; and worked through Christmas to meet the deadline.

A campus in the middle of nowhere much, with few buildings, no students with which to justify a library, no sports or social facilities, in an embryonic new town, was a gloomy place in mid-winter. A refectory was built, belatedly, which had to serve building workers as well as OU staff, but even that was chopped back in size by the UGC and could only serve people in shifts. Money from the American Benton Foundation might stretch to a senior common-room and a squash court. Jennie and Jane decided that the dark cobwebbed basement in Walton Hall would do splendidly. They remarked on the fine vaulted ceiling, but Perry could only notice the pipes and the junk at his feet. Jennie negotiated an additional grant from the Bevan Memorial Fund, which went on curtains, furnishings, and carriage-lamps. Jane Drew transformed the basement into a 'cellar bar', with games room and lounge. Success was ensured when Jennie ceremoniously placed Nye's flat cap on a peg to hang above his picture in the bar.

The speed was extraordinary. The glorious summer helped. Buildings were commissioned, designed, approved, constructed, furnished, and occupied in less time than it took the average spec housing development to get from first consideration to planning permission. The buildings were undeniably functional. Rayner Banham said they were two- or three-storey brick structures 'that would have served equally for a nationalised industry or a cautiously pushy electronics company—small standard offices opening via equally standard doors along both sides of featureless corridors', and with the usual new university problem of poor sound insulation.[20] He was being unfair. The grander new universities, whose architects were making 'cathedral' statements, were no more comfortable to work in and often less adaptable to future academic needs.

Academic planning decisions were being taken just as quickly. If teaching was to start in January 1971, then, working backwards, admissions had to be completed by summer 1970 so that local study centres could be acquired and local tutors put in place. That meant, still working backwards, that the course prospectus for the students had to be with potential applicants by January 1970, and therefore with the printer by October 1969. Yet the core staff would not be free from their own universities and employed by the OU until September 1969. Which meant that the prospectus had to be written before the courses had been devised by the staff who would teach them. The Planning Committee, with Perry's help, had already agreed on the broad shape: open access, sustained by a foundation year from which students went on to course credits, which built into their ordinary six-unit and honours eight-unit degree. Perry brought the staff together and they planned the foundation course in one day.

Many crucial decisions had yet to be made. Yes, the degree would be broad based, but multidisciplinary rather than interdisciplinary (the OU was not going to innovate on too many fronts all at the same time). Its academic year would run from January to December, putting the summer school at its heart (residential teaching was only possible when other universities' buildings were empty). Perry had other questions to resolve. Should degrees be classified? How should they be examined (essential to ensure that the work was unaided by spouse or partner)? And what about fees?[21] And alongside the more traditional academic decisions, Perry had also to devise arrangements with the BBC. Who would control programme content? The OU agreed to take responsibility for academic content, the BBC for production value. Perry's coronary of December 1970 was waiting to happen.

Perry, looking back, was grateful he did not have a senate or any democratic structures to hold him up; he would never have met the deadline. He and Venables did need a chancellor, however. They wanted a man of great public stature, free of party affiliations, with business experience and educational interests. They invited Geoffrey Crowther, now a cross-bench peer, to be their first Chancellor; and Sir Paul Chambers, formerly of ICI, to be their first treasurer. Venables insisted there be no consultation with the DES or with ministers; an independent university made its own decisions on such matters. Jennie was not consulted, neither was Ted Short, nor Harold Wilson. They were merely informed of the decision, and Ralph Toomey had an uncomfortable quarter of an hour with Jennie when she lashed out at him for not briefing her on a matter he knew nothing about. She was not happy about their politics and was not looking forward to the outrage on Labour back benches when 'Tory' old-boy appointments were made to 'their' university.

In fact, Crowther and Chambers were both happy choices and helped Perry in his dealings with the Official Opposition, which they predicted correctly, was the government in waiting. Jennie warmed to Crowther. When he suddenly died in 1972, he was replaced by Lord (Gerald) Gardiner, the former Labour Lord Chancellor. Six months later Gardiner enrolled for an OU degree himself, saying he could learn about the university and make good his own inadequate education (he had graduated from Oxford with a fourth) at the same time. He was fretting one evening as he waited to speak in the Lords. Jennie asked what was wrong. He feared he would be late for his 7 o'clock local study class.[22]

So, by the end of 1969, the key staff were in place; course material was being designed; the site was under mud, but showed evidence of buildings; they had a Chancellor and a royal charter. However, as the election drew closer, Tory threats to the survival of the university became more outspoken. The final stage in Perry's flow chart was the admission of students. Only if they applied in their thousands would a future government deem it politically unwise to close the OU. Would the students apply?

What demand was there? It had long been an article of faith that they should meet the educational rights of the generation born too soon. Robbins had suggested that one million adults would benefit from higher education and 100,000 might wish to; there were also known to be 250,000 non-graduate teachers in England and Wales, of whom 25,000 might want to gain degrees. Even when that need was met, Robbins calculated that around 40,000 young people a year would be leaving school able to benefit from higher education, but not reached by it. The next question was, how many students should they seek to admit? If they took too few, it would be too expensive. The OU was carrying a very high fixed cost, especially the £2 million a year subvention to the BBC and the start-up costs of publishing course textbooks. With more students, the unit costs would fall sharply. Yet if they sought to admit too many, and if they did not reach their target, this would be read as failure in the current edgy political climate.

The new universities had started with an intake of a few hundred and were slowly building towards their target of 3,000 students each in total. Perry consulted Venables, they took a deep breath, and proposed 25,000 for their first year's intake, building up to and plateauing at 75,000 students in all. Jennie and Ted Short immediately accepted their figures. DES civil servants and the Treasury thought this was far too ambitious. Roy Jenkins, Chancellor of the Exchequer, counter-proposed 10,000. Although this might have been politically prudent and could be justified as a pilot scheme, it meant that the cost per student would soar. On Perry's figures, a student would cost £140 a year; on Jenkins's, £700 a year, higher than the conventional undergraduate cost of £670. Perry and Venables took an even deeper breath and guaranteed an intake of 25,000.

The OU started advertising in January 1970. Within the first fortnight it received 10,000 enquiries. A whiteboard went up in the entrance of Walton Hall, on which were scribbled each week's number of enquiries and each week's number of firm applications. Anxious staff scrutinized the board as they came and went. By Easter there were 50,000 provisional applications. By July, a few days after the general election they had had 140,000 enquiries and 43,000 firm applications. They knew they were home. Staff now reckoned the university was unstoppable.[23]

But not quite and not yet. Jennie was actually at Walton Hall helping Lord Mountbatten lay the foundation stone when her staff heard on the car radio that Wilson was going to the country. She immediately phoned Ralph Toomey, her senior civil servant: 'For God's sake, get out the letter giving the OU its grant'—and she urged Jane Drew and Perry to make sure any contracts that were outstanding were speedily tied up. Three hundred staff wondered whether they and the OU had a future.

Jennie was wise to be worried. Unknown to her, Toomey had already been told by his department head, Herbert Andrew, to draw up draft plans to close the university. Toomey must calculate the cost of unscrambling it so that, should incoming ministers want to know, the department could tell them. It was not a job that Toomey relished, as he, more than any other senior official of the DES, had been identified with the project, helping it to frame its statutes, negotiating a grant regime from the Treasury, and smoothing the way with other government departments.[24] But he set about it. He was not worried about the buildings: they could be sold. Nor even about the number of students-in-waiting: they had not yet started any courses and their disappointment could presumably be weathered. His concern was for the staff, many of them distinguished academics who had given up safe careers for this experiment. And what exactly was the legal status of a royal charter? Could it be revoked? No one had ever closed a chartered university before; and no one knew whether it could legally be done.

The new ministers did indeed want to know the costs of closing the OU. Perry hoped that Margaret Thatcher and her junior ministers were on side, along with David Eccles who had direct access to Edward Heath; but Macleod was determined to close it. Three weeks into his appointment as Chancellor of the Exchequer, the papers were on his desk for him to sign; that evening (Edward Boyle told Richard Hoggart) he had a fatal heart attack. Whether he would have managed to close the OU is unclear, but that he had decided to do so is without doubt. The junior education minister, William van Straubenzee, later recalled that 'the very existence of the OU was in doubt', but that Thatcher's 'advocacy, sometimes almost single-handed' saved it.[25] Jennie, looking back, thought that Macleod would have come round in the end, as Thatcher had done. 'He accepted the views of Roy Jenkins and the Treasury officials—all prisoners of their early home life and early schooling', she jotted down. She recalled that Macleod had made his reputation twenty-five years before by fighting Nye's NHS, but when he became Minister of Health he had confessed to Nye that he could find nothing to change.[26]

If the OU was to survive, the Treasury was determined to tie down its costs, which were open-ended. Maurice Macmillan, Chief Secretary to the Treasury, was, on Macleod's death, acting Chancellor when Ralph Toomey escorted Margaret Thatcher to the Treasury to argue for more money. Not for the first or for the last time, she won the day, but at a price: a 7 per cent cut in budget, and an experimental cohort of 18-year-olds. OU staff hated the idea. They believed that 18-year-olds needed more support for long distance learning than staff could offer, while at the same time they would dilute the distinctive mission of the OU. Said Perry: 'she kept us open but for all the wrong reasons. She saw us as a cheap short cut to degrees.'[27]

None the less, the future of the OU was secured and on the record. Any subsequent political challenge—and there were to be many—was reflected in cuts rather than threat of closure. This did not stop right-wing Tories from denouncing it. Having discouraged Tory academics from joining the OU staff, they then complained that the university was staffed entirely by left-wingers. Jock Campbell of Milton Keynes was a trustee of

Chequers; this brought him into contact with Margaret Thatcher when she became Prime Minister. He recalls being buttonholed by her in the early 1980s, as rows about the OU's 'left-wing' courses were fomented by the Black Paper group—'How is that awful University of yours? It's a nest of Marxism. Anyone who can get an O-level in Scripture can get a degree there.' 'That's simply not true, Prime Minister', replied Campbell. 'I know', said Mrs Thatcher, her hand resting on his arm, 'I'm being feminine.'[28]

Jennie continued to keep a watchful and benevolent eye on the OU from the House of Lords. Being a peer was thought somehow to make her less party-political. Perry invited her to parties, and sought her help as he tried to build up research and post-graduate degrees at the OU, without which it was not a proper university. Jennie became trustee of the new Crowther Trust, which offered OU students bursaries and travelling fellowships and laid the foundation stone for the new library. Although she was not of much use while the Tories were in power, Perry used her as an intermediary from 1974 onwards when Labour returned. She urged Reg Prentice, at the Department of Education, to fund further development at the OU;[29] she intervened in some ill-tempered arguments between the OU and the Association of University Teachers in December of that year; and she challenged both Tory and Labour governments as fees began to rise. In 1974, 1975, and 1976 she initiated debates on the OU in the Lords.[30]

She was also in demand as a speaker at forums on the OU. Talking in January 1978 about its foundation at Walton Hall, Perry said: 'I always listen spellbound to what went on before I came, and then I listened spellbound again to what she says went on after I came.' This didn't stop her, a few days later, 'spitting blood' (in her phrase) at a further increase in fees, making the OU a retreat for the leisured rich, and accusing Perry (by now a beetroot red), that he had become respectable, part of the academic establishment, and any moment now would join her in the Lords.[31] He did, in 1979.

*

Geoffrey Crowther had been one of the first to welcome Wilson's university of the air back in 1963. As its first Chancellor, Crowther famously described the university at the Charter ceremony in July 1969 as open—open as to people, open as to places, open as to methods, open as to ideas. They could have been Jennie's words. In her House of Lords debates on the university during the mid-1970s, she fought to protect the vision that she and Crowther shared—'the very essence of the OU is that it should not be for the rich or the poor, for black or white, for men or for women, but it should be judged on its academic standards and be available to all.'[32] How far were her hopes realized?

Open access—open as to people—shaped the university's design. It entailed foundation courses of graduated learning which would prepare its students, many of whom were twenty years away from formal study, for the course units that would build their degree. It meant taking mature students, rather than 18-year-olds They doubted whether an 18-year-old could cope with the long haul of solitary study. Nor did they wish to compete with conventional universities, or pick up their 'rejects'. (When the OU was required to take experimental cohorts of 18-year-olds to see whether it provided higher education on the cheap, Jennie was scornful, but the staff found to their surprise that these students were not 'rejects' at all, but a younger version of their mature students. A young single parent. A musician wanting a degree. A footballer wanting to ensure a future. They were the immobile young, in work, in marriage, with children, with disabilities, unable to move to a conventional university.[33])

Combining open access with impeccable standards in its degrees risked a very high drop-out rate, most of which occurred in the first three months, so, shrewdly, the university offered provisional registration which was only confirmed three months into the course. Would-be students could see whether the OU was for them. Pass rates of those who finally registered and sat their exams steadied at over 90 per cent, and almost all of those students moved on to the next year's credit course. The OU calculated that for ten applicants, five typically would be accepted, four confirmed their enrolment three months on, three got credits at the end of their foundation year, and after six years of study two would graduate—about the same proportion as those registered for external degrees at London University, but much lower than those completing conventional degrees.[34]

Jennie never defended the OU on grounds of cheapness. None the less, its value for money was increasingly prayed in aid. The high drop-out rate together with the high fixed cost of BBC time make it very difficult to calculate the cost-effectiveness of the OU. It was generally reckoned by the late 1970s, that the cost of an OU student was half that of a conventional student, much more than the 10 per cent proportion originally envisaged, but still much lower than standard universities. The OU's second Vice-Chancellor, Dr John Horlock, in 1981–2 compared the cost of a conventional arts graduate with an OU arts graduate taking an ordinary degree.[35] The conventional graduate, he estimated, cost £11,500 to public funds (including plant, fees, and maintenance grants, minus parental contribution); the OU graduate cost £7,100. However, the OU graduate was carrying £750 worth of fees and the equivalent of some £3,600 in maintenance. Added together and the full cost of the OU ordinary degree was much the same as a conventional degree; the cost of an OU honours degree, taking two years longer, probably outstripped its conventional equivalent. The charge to *public* funds of the OU degree was lower only because a hefty proportion of its cost was borne by students.

Jennie was well aware of this, and became increasingly angry as OU fees were forced upwards; she was not mollified by a hardship fund. Open access had meant entry without hindrance. Now Labour and Tory governments were alike putting financial hurdles in place, which the unwaged, and women, would find impossible to leap. She had refused, she told the Lords, to found a university only for the poor; she now refused to be associated with a university only for the well-to-do: 'We have established a university which ought to be open to all. It is open to the better off, but it is not open to the poor.'[36]

OU students were carrying the high fixed cost of BBC transmission (which accounted for 20 per cent of its running costs, but contributed only 5 per cent of its teaching); on the other hand they were not carrying the cost of university plant, libraries, dining-rooms, or teaching blocks. In addition most of the OU's tutorial staff came on the cheap, as they were often full-time teachers at other HE institutions, which carried their payroll, pension, and research overheads. If the cost of the OU degree suffered by comparison with the conventional arts degree, this was not because the former was expensive but because the British conventional degree, compared to Europe, was highly cost-effective. This was partly because it was so 'élitist'—admission standards were high, and drop-out rates were low; and also because maintenance awards meant that students did not need to work their way through college, so the degree could be completed in three years rather than in four years or more.

The downside of the OU's costs—its BBC transmissions, its high drop-out rates—could be read very differently. They added to the eavesdropper audience for higher education, and they diffused at least some of the benefits of university study to those who, for whatever reason, did not complete their OU degree but were none the less enriched by what they had done. Increasingly, some OU students transferred after the first year to join their local university, their foundation course serving as their access course. More degrees could probably have been obtained for the money by expanding conventional universities at marginal cost, and certainly by expanding their part-time degrees. None the less, the OU, because it was open, served a population that conventional universities, however much they expanded, could not reach. Was it a population that the OU *should* serve?

As applications flooded in, they far exceeded the places available. Jennie pointed out in the Lords that for 1975 only 3,000 new applicants, together with 11,000 postponed applicants from the previous year, could be accepted. 'We are now finding that the [OU] is meeting a very real need, and when applicants come along we are actually saying to over 30,000 of them, "We cannot take you on." This country', she added sharply, 'has a genius for throwing away its assets.'[37]

With over-subscription, decisions had to be made on whom to accept, whom to reject. Open access required a first-come-first-served principle, in which those rejected this year headed next year's queue. The OU needed to modify its entry procedures to ensure there were enough students in the four main lines of study (arts, social science, maths, and science) and enough students in each region to sustain the network of study centres and local tutors. But should open access be 'adjusted' for other reasons? Perry expected that demand for OU places would be 'very large indeed', far surpassing its financial and teaching resources.[38] Should preference be given to the population that Wilson had originally in mind: the technicians and technologists, whose skills needed upgrading if the nation was to adapt to scientific change and experience economic growth? Or should priority go not to those for whom it was a second chance, but to those who now had a first chance—the semi- and unskilled? Should, for example, any limit be placed on the number of those over the age of 50? or on women? or on those with a middle-class background and already possessing a university degree?—in other words, those for whom a degree was deemed to be neither necessary, useful, nor liberating.

The housewife question obsessed critics of the OU, convinced as they were that it would become a 'hobbies university' for the middle-aged middle-class leisured woman, taking time off from flower-arranging and bridge parties. The contempt, from trade-unionists, adult educationalists, and LEA directors of education (all of course male) was unmistakable and unpleasant. The OU's correspondence course teaching, after all, lent itself more easily to arts rather than to science courses, which needed labs and practicals; and arts degrees attracted women.

The University need not have fretted. In the event, those over the age of 50 were under-represented, and 'housewives' formed only 10 per cent of all students. Women initially comprised 25 per cent of applicants, rising to 42 per cent by 1975, still below their proportion in the population.[39] Even so,

Jennie rejoiced. She stoutly defended the right of housebound women who were young mothers or middle-aged carers and who often 'feel intellectually starved' to join the OU. She was, she said, 'very proud' of them.[40] In fact, most women students were not 'housewives'. Around 60 per cent of them were already in work, very often as teachers; and of those who were not, over a third entered or re-entered the labour market on the back of their OU degree. Often without any money of their own, they paid their way with part-time work fitted around child care, doing market research, gardening, or grading eggs. Those who could taught something they knew—music or a language—so that they might pay to learn something else.[41] In its first ten years 9,000 women graduated from the OU, and it was soon providing a third of all places for women in higher education.

Once admitted, women did well, better than men even in maths and science, more of them graduating and with better results. In part, this was because they took their degrees more slowly; but it was also because they were in general better educated and more 'middle class' to start with (the OU estimated that two-thirds of its women and half of its men were middle class). That in turn was because many of the female students were teachers. Nearly half of all women in work who applied to the OU, and just under a quarter of all men, were certificated teachers in search of a degree.[42] This merely compounded the OU's problem. If women applicants were 'leisured' housewives, they were wasting an OU place; if they were teachers, they were already well educated and in less need of a place; if they were neither leisured nor salaried, then they might neither afford the fees nor stay the course. Few people, apart from Jennie, pointed out that women suffered as much educational deprivation as working men, and had as much claim to educational opportunity.

The OU was defensive about the proportion of its students (a third in the early years) who were teachers, even if one overlooked the fact that they were also women. Yet it was entirely predictable. Robbins had insisted that the country needed more teachers and that non-graduate teachers would want degrees. Less than a quarter of all teachers were graduates—because so many of them were women; bright girls went to training college, their brothers to university. There was, predicted Robbins, both a need for more teachers to bring down classroom sizes and to raise the school-leaving age (ROSLA); and for better educated ones.[43] Most secondary modern and virtually all primary schoolteachers went to training college and not to university. From 1963, training colleges lengthened their courses from two to three years; B.Ed. degrees were being piloted; the secondary modern schools were becoming comprehensive and their pupils might wish to take O levels and even A levels, for which non-graduate teachers were underqualified. Graduate teachers were also paid more. The James Committee was shortly to recommend that teaching become an all-graduate profession. So it was not surprising that women who wanted to become teachers, and existing teachers who wanted degrees, should flock to the OU. Birkbeck, after all, was performing a similar role—some 40 per cent of *its* students were teachers.

The OU was ambivalent. On the one hand, teachers were risk-free students, highly desirable when a new university had to establish itself quickly. They would not drop out, they would pay their fees, they would pass their exams, and their existing teaching diplomas would give them credit exemptions which meant they would graduate satisfyingly quickly (half of the first year intake had credit exemptions, mainly because they were teachers).[44] But were they the people for whom Harold Wilson had envisaged a university of the second chance? And was educating the already well educated really expanding educational opportunity, and meeting educational need? Jennie replied that it was an *open* university, available to all. As she wrote to Perry: 'I could climb the walls when I get letter after letter the gist of which is that it is failing in its purposes because there ought to be 90% dustmen instead of 90% teachers. I want to emphasise once again that the OU has to be judged by its academic standards like any other university.'[45]

It took Ted Short to point out the obvious. If the DES wanted to improve the quality of education in schools as well as reduce classroom sizes, then educating teachers to degree level in their own time and at their own expense was a highly effective way of addressing educational need further down the system. If children brought educational deprivation with them from the home, then the best chance there was of remedying it at school was to have better educated teachers. 'Today we are often asking teachers in this country to teach subjects that they themselves were never taught', Jennie said, and it was essential that they be equipped to do so. 'That was exactly how we planned it', she added, lying through her teeth.[46] In its first ten years, 100,000 teachers registered with the OU.

None the less, the more the OU attracted women with good qualifications, the less it attracted men with poor qualifications. The OU wanted more social class 'Ds' and 'Es'—Michael Young proposed that it should recruit at the factory gate—but their educational aspirations were low, fees for the unemployed seemed high, and their drop-out rate even higher. The worry was that the 'open door' would (in Naomi McIntosh's phrase) become for them a 'revolving door'.[47] Others hoped the OU might empower the working-class activist who would remain firmly rooted in his work, family, and social class, but free of 'false consciousness' and able to see society for what it was.[48] 'A very strong case' could be made out, Perry admitted, for starting an open school or college in advance of the OU, but the idea was 'not politically viable at the time. It would have filled an even bigger social need.'[49] However, his first task was to establish the university's credibility, so that students were not short-changed by their degrees, their academic currency not debased.

Students, as their letters to the OU newspaper *Sesame* make clear, shared Perry's view. They objected to any notion that the OU might be a remedial university, a 'secondary modern' amid grammar school and public school players. For them the OU remedied the lack of educational opportunity, rather than made good any educational deprivation. They wanted a degree like everyone else, but more so.

A student who was a factory worker and now on a higher degree course, pondered why the OU failed to attract blue-collar workers. Maybe it should reconsider its foundation course which repelled those who had been taught to dislike learning: 'For once let an educational establishment say, "What really matters is your desires, your interests, your concerns" instead of, "Come to us and we will teach you what we have decided that you are to learn." Let the OU demonstrate that education is something a person gets for himself, not that which someone else gives or does to him.' And, he added, 'The OU has concentrated so much on being accepted by the academic world that it has wasted the opportunity of taking a fresh look at education. If our aim is conventionality we are bound to end up as a second rate university, because we cannot possibly compete.'[50] Letters the following week in *Sesame* were baffled, cynical, or angry. If the OU was not about excellence, and getting a better job, they did not want to know, nor would they study with it for six long years. They were not part of the class struggle. Indeed, they were rather keen to leave the working class as far behind as possible.

However, when the OU researched the background of its students, it found that the matter was not straightforward. While few were current members of the educationally deprived working-class, most had working-class parents and working-class backgrounds. Had the snapshot been taken when they were all aged 18, they would have been deemed working class.[51] As mature students in their 30s, they were climbing up the occupational ladder out of their parents' social class; but they had got 'stuck'—blocked, if they were women, by marriage, or, if they were men, by their lack of formal educational qualification—and unable to do anything about it. The

OU gave mobility to those whose mobility was checked, rather than advantage to the educationally disadvantaged. It was about opportunity, not deprivation.

Perry, whose own medical career had a strong vocational element, like Margaret Thatcher, instinctively sympathized with their efforts at self-help and towards a better job. The McIntosh research showed that well over half the OU students had two A levels (enough to have taken them to university), and over half had been to a grammar school, but their education had been interrupted by war, sickness, marriage, or moves. They were committed to self-improvement. They had already taken adult evening classes, and they moved in the world of voluntary societies, clubs and churches, serious newspapers and sustained reading. They came better educated and better prepared than the OU expected. They included the teacher who wanted a degree, the home help who wanted to become a social worker, the barmaid with five children and almost as many A levels who wanted to teach, and the window-cleaner who was determined to remain a window-cleaner.[52] Wistfully, they wanted access to great thought as well as a sound degree. They were at one with Jennie when she insisted: 'It is *not* a working class university. It was never *intended* to be a working class university. It was planned as a *university*. It is the *Open* university.'[53]

Open access meant that the students chose rather than that they were chosen. It was open in the sense that entry was not competitive. It also meant that in its early years the university responded to the market, to the constituency that already existed—a pool of well-qualified applicants—rather than create a new hunger, a new demand. It was open and accessible not so much to those rejected by conventional universities because they were of the wrong age, wrong education, wrong gender, or wrong class (the OU did little better than the new universities in admitting these); rather, it was open to the immobile, those unable to climb on and upwards, those unable to move sideways. The OU was as much about distance learning as it was about open access. As Crowther said, it was open as to place.

In an obvious sense, the OU came to its students, by air, by mail (twenty to thirty tons of it a week), rather than they to it. It came to the housebound, and the hospitalized, women with young children, carers with aged parents, and the long-term sick. It came to the disabled, those who were blind, deaf, in wheelchairs, who suffered from MS, asthma, arthritis. Jennie noted that the OU did more 'for the physically disabled than all our other universities put together'.[54] Disabled students received preferential admission, tutorials by phone, worked at the speed they wanted, and were aided to summer school. One weary staff member noted that forty disabled students with forty different sets of disability created as much work in those first summer schools as the other 20,000 put together. On one occasion, a disabled woman student was given a ground-floor bedroom, and was asked to share the gents toilet. When she protested, she was told that it was 'alright' as all the men were blind.[55] Another disabled student exulted: 'It's the possum that makes it possible; it is the OU that is the fulfilment. I could not do without either. Both are essential to my sanity.'[56]

The OU went into prisons. Prison students identified with Kafka and found Socrates a revelation. They wanted teeshirts proclaiming 'Socrates is Innocent'. They experienced their own renaissance.[57] One prison student complained that he was refused permission to study experimental psychology, because his electric measuring device might manipulate the electronic security doors; but really, he said, it was because he might learn to manipulate prison staff.[58] Other OU students toured abroad as army corporals, toured at home as bit-part actors. Fathers and partners painstakingly taped and transcribed the broadcasts they missed. The OU expanded Mansbridge's College of the Sea, which for over twenty-five years had seen deckboys become captains after studying English and Maths, radio officers write novels, and ship stewards go to Ruskin College.[59] Jennie reported that the daughter of one of her Asheridge farm workers took an OU degree followed by a school headship; her husband also took an OU degree while in the Navy, and then taught navigation at Ipswich FE college. Ted Graham, the university's first MP, studied on the underground; a football commentator wrestled with logic while reporting on Celtic; one naval officer took his exams in Polaris at the bottom of the sea; and an army officer took his high up in the Himalayas, smuggling his exam papers back through the diplomatic bag. Welsh hill farmers and lighthouse-keepers taught goldfish to distinguish red from blue, left from right; learnt the binary system from a pinball machine; and constructed traffic lights as an exercise in logic. Secretaries struggling with Descartes on the train or Copernicus in the launderette were helped by those sitting next to them, who were often prompted to join the OU themselves.

Jennie herself quoted a Scottish student whose nearest library stocked not one of her books and who had to pay a pound for each one they ordered; she could not get to a study centre, so relied on phone tutorials from the only public phone box in the village, surrounded by local youngsters listening in fascination through the booth's broken panes of glass. An insurance officer, having studied a course entitled 'Understanding Society', said: 'I now detest economics, know something of politics, feel involved in sociology, am entranced by geography, and can spell psychology.'[60]

They melded at the summer school. At one of the first summer schools in Norwich, Roger Thompson, a lecturer from the University of East Anglia, found himself teaching energetic great-grandmothers, a former hospital patient 'pitting my experience against your knowledge', an Orkney islander, and city councillors, artists, doctors, salesmen, hairdressers, a dog-breeder, an antique-dealer, pregnant mothers, and men from the Pru, as well as one lady who would rather not say. He had a tense time:

> [with] a group containing an Anglican school chaplain who spoke as though he were addressing an open-air congregation of thousands in a high and contrary wind, a retired 'international civil servant' currently engaged on historical research the like of which mere mortals such as we would never appreciate. He wore his grey hair in a pony tail. Add to these a neurotically uptight spinster who refused to reveal her forename, home town or intended specialism as irrelevant, an unemployed printer who adopted the role of cheeky chappie and a primary school headmaster who opened a huge notebook and produced four immaculately sharpened pencils.

None of this, he thought ruefully, was what Saturday nights were made for. But by the end of the week, 'the chaplain boomed less, the pony tail seemed to have something to learn, the uptight, if not exactly down loose, no longer flared her nostrils when the sobered printer spoke, and the notebook had disappeared'. Tutors went away overwhelmed by students' eagerness to learn, their staying power, and their ability.[61]

Crowther said the OU was also open as to methods and ideas. In a literal sense it was a visible university; its lectures were on national radio and TV, its course books sold in bookshops. Jennie had won for the OU prime time on television. We 'made it quite clear that we were having no truck with those who wanted us to have a kind of "dawn patrol", with the idea that the time that no one else wanted on radio or television was good enough for a great university. We got rid of that idea.' Traditional universities, she went on, had some murky corners, out of sight. 'But you cannot have dark corners in an open university.'[62] The OU demystified higher education.

It was flexible in its teaching mode—television, correspondence work, radio, summer school, tutor-marked and computer-marked assessment; and multidisciplinary in its course credits. Students could go as fast or as slow as they wanted, stop or start, take unusual combinations of courses, and build their own degree.[63]

Inevitably the OU took an 'efficient' attitude to knowledge. There was little time for academic scepticism. Adult students wanted to get on with it: they were matter-of-fact, and, instrumental about their work, did what was necessary, cutting corners when they could. They respected, and feared, the hegemony of the computer. They firmly believed, in an almost Victorian sense, that there was a deposit of knowledge out there for them to appropriate and own. It was for many a humanities version of 'training'. They were not interested in a 'University without Walls'. The student debates of the 1960s about grades and exams, about deschooling and relevance, passed them by. They sensed that the OU was an academic factory of mass education. One course in social science in 1972 had 22,000 applicants, 8,000 enrolments, 85,000 essays to mark, 64,000 assignments for the computer, 24 summer schools in 5 different universities, supported by 1,000 part-time tutors in 300 study centres. As Michael Drake said: 'It is the numbers that numb.'[64] They were studying 'to get on'.

Yet there was also Jim, in the ranks of the RAF, who had been reading all his life, grasshopper-style. When he returned home he plucked up courage to enrol in the OU:

> By the time I had completed A100 it had pushed and guided me into gathering up great quantities of clutter in my mind and throwing it out for ever. It supervised and criticised, commanded and demanded, ensuring always that my wages of academic respectability were being properly earned . . . In the courses that followed, my mind was richly fed . . . Through the Reformation, via Calvin and Knox I found the meaning of my childhood socialisation, and through Kant a moral philosophy that is now an essential part of my everyday criteria. War and Society gave deeper meaning to my RAF days and to my post-war experience of the misery and destitution I had seen among the rubble and desolation of the German cities. It linked with the multitudinous beggary I had tried to ignore in India and it interrelated with my A401 research into pauperism in mid-Victorian England and what I had seen of the Depression in the early Thirties. Essentially the OU brought cause to what I had experienced only as effect, giving me not only illumination but engendering in me a deep awareness of the human condition. Of those doors that were closed to me in my boyhood the only ones which matter to me now are the doors of perception. For me, the OU opened them wide. Somewhere inside, the mermaids sing to me. This is what the OU has meant to me.[65]

On 23 June 1973, nine hundred graduands in their hoods and gowns assembled in Alexandra Palace to receive the first degrees awarded by the

Open University. Their new Chancellor, Lord Gardiner, was installed; honorary degrees were awarded to Richard Hoggart and Michael Young who had thought up the concept (though not to Harold Wilson); to Sir Peter Venables who had chaired its planning; to Hugh Greene and Lord Hill who had brought the BBC into partnership; to Lord Campbell, who had found the site; to Jane Drew who had built the buildings; and to Jennie Lee. As James Callaghan said: Jennie was 'the fortunate one who was given the responsibility of setting it up'.[66] She had made it possible, she had made it happen. In their gold and sky blue gowns, they processed out to Copland's glorious trumpet piece, *Fanfare for the Common Man*.

12

JENNIE THE MINISTER
IN PUBLIC AND IN PRIVATE

JENNIE's way of being a minister was to use the Prime Minister. She quoted him, phoned him, wrote to him, went to see him, as she deemed the occasion demanded. It never failed, and he never failed her. However hard-pressed, Wilson always gave her his time and almost always his public support. She was undoubtedly his 'wreath for Nye'; but they were also old Bevanite comrades. Wilson rightly respected her determination and her presentational skills. He was, Jennie said, her 'trump card'. Had Wilson withdrawn his active support, she would have gone.

He gave her two jobs to do—the arts and the OU—and in both she was extraordinarily effective. She had requested the arts portfolio. Wilson himself had no interest in the arts. He enjoyed reading political history, and as a former President of the Board of Trade, he knew about films, but to music, painting, and theatre, he was culturally colour-blind. He knew, however, that London's political and intellectual élite were not, that they valued what he did not perceive, and he had the political confidence and the personal modesty to be unthreatened by it.

The arts were traditionally the preserve of the public school, Oxbridge-educated male. Places like Cannock thought that the arts were nothing to do with them; northern MPs repeatedly told Jennie that there were no votes in the arts, that Labour should concentrate on bread-and-butter issues. Since the arts were, for Labour, a new political territory, it was an inspired piece of casting against the grain to entrust it to Jennie, to an outsider, a Scottish woman, robust, down to earth, who clearly enjoyed the arts without being faintly pretentious about them, and who infected others with her enthusiasm; who had enough acquaintanceship among the arts world not to look out of place or say silly things, but, equally, who was resolutely amateur in her enjoyments, who would not condescend, or be exclusive in her tastes. Precisely because it was Nye who had created the NHS, it mattered that someone like Jennie should be saying 'bread *and* roses'.

Jennie was the ideal person to rid the Labour Party of any hang-ups it had about supporting the arts, when other priorities, in health, education, and housing, loomed so large. That mixture of indolent earthy peasant and decidedly impatient dowager duchess served her very well. She would not tolerate being patronized, she did not need to be liked, she expected to get her own way, and she knew when to leave well alone. Her reticence about her own tastes was only matched by her uninhibitedness about those by whom she was surrounded. She was not easily shocked, not easily manipulated, not easily flattered, not easily impressed, and not easily deflected either. She was abrasive and supportive, censorious and generous in suitable proportions. She was disliked by most of her political colleagues, and much loved in the world of the arts.

Whereas Jennie herself chose the arts, Wilson chose her for the university of the air. Again, he judged extraordinarily well. There was at least a constituency for the arts, noisy and importunate, even if one doubted that it was a Labour constituency. There was none for the OU. It had no natural allies either from potential users—no one knew who they might be—or from traditional 'providers', the universities, FE colleges, adult educationalists. To a man, they all believed that any extra money should go to them. Jennie faced over two years of carping, criticism, disbelief, and downright obstruction. No one expected her to deliver a university; even Ralph Toomey, Arnold Goodman, and Harold Wilson, her closest allies, only expected an open college and FE work. That refusal to listen to counter-arguments, to brook criticism, which so exasperated her civil servants, meant that Jennie drove the project through on the back of her own energy. She was never mistily romantic about education, any more than she was about the arts. Almost anyone could make a go of it, get a degree, providing they had determination and staying power—just like her.

The OU and the arts jobs meshed well. Neither required Jennie to attend to detail, as an executive job in health or social security would have done. Both required the same stance from their minister—a broad policy-frame, money, come-hither publicity, and then the silence of standing aside—a language of permissiveness in the arts world, of autonomy in the university world. The conceptual languages of the two jobs also meshed. Just as her mission within the arts was to shift resources out of

London to the regions and to open it up to new audiences, new activities, and new places, so, too, the OU was about a university without walls, bringing learning to new students and by new means: television, radio, and correspondence. The same vocabulary applied to both—words like access and excellence, the best for the most, élitist in standard, while democratic in appeal.

Wilson's support was central to her relations with colleagues. She had little opposition, though little support from them, for her arts work. They were not out to thwart her. Her budget was small, it was not at their expense, and they too enjoyed going to the opera or the theatre, and sharing in the plaudits at Hampstead and Highgate dinner parties. They recognized that she was an outstanding arts minister. Roy Jenkins, for example, found himself impressed by her work despite himself. The people whose judgement he valued, valued Jennie. Their only concern was to make sure that Jennie's budget was not top-sliced from other budgets (Crossman), from their own departmental budget (Crosland), and that it could be traded for prime ministerial support for other deals (Jenkins and Callaghan). Jennie was not above some old-fashioned brutality herself, as her private office noted admiringly; she put it both to Callaghan over the OU, and Healey over the arts, that they might want her support as chairman of the Party when they stood for the Party Treasurership.

The OU was a very different matter. No one but Jennie believed the enterprise could succeed, should succeed, and would be of any value if it did. Wilson wanted a sort of FE college. Most of her colleagues did not want even that. Reading the educational pressures and priorities of the time, it is hard not to sympathize with them. However, they knew that Wilson wanted it, and, they repeated, what the Prime Minister wanted, he usually got. All they were really arguing about was the price: how much and who paid.

Jennie had, in her words, a second trump card, and that was Arnold Goodman. Quite remarkably, he enjoyed the confidence of every senior Labour politician he encountered. He was reticent about his political sympathies, but his instincts, if not his politics, at the time were Gaitskellite. Yet he was trusted by Jennie to sort Nye's affairs; Tony Benn sought his help on his Broadcasting White Paper; Hugh Jenkins, deeply suspicious of the Establishment in all its manifestations, had Goodman's protective support when he became Minister for the Arts. Above all, Goodman was simultaneously a confidant of both Wilson and Jennie. Not only did he hold the formal position of chairman of the Arts Council; he also sat on the Planning Committee of the OU, the Planning Committee of the National Film School, and the South Bank Theatre Board, all at Jennie's behest. He endlessly sorted her problems—her public (and private) finances, leases, contracts, appointments, and press stories. He behaved as her permanent secretary and personal assistant at the same time. He adored her.

Because Jennie had Wilson and Goodman on her side, she never learnt how to be a minister, how Whitehall operated, with its complex network of ministerial and official committees, its expenditure rounds, its hierarchies, procedures, and structures. She worked instead through people, collecting the voices, as she put it, on policy matters. If a distinguished committee told Jennie that something ought to be done, that was normally enough. If a director she respected told her that a production or an exhibition was of high quality, she believed him. She did want to be effective, she did want to deliver her projects, she did like to work in an atmosphere of serenity, but that would have required her to find her way around the Whitehall machine, and that she would not do. Because she had Harold Wilson's active support, for example, she never properly understood the financial constraints on his position, that he had no independent budget of his own to allocate. He could only lean on other departments, on the Chancellor, on the DES. So, despite his Glasgow speech of September 1963, it took until July 1967 before a budget was agreed for the OU.

Jennie confined herself to her projects and played a minimal role in the DES. Her private secretaries thought she was underemployed and that her job was 'not very onerous'. By the late 1960s, when Venables and Perry were running the OU, Goodman and Willatt the Arts Council, and Lloyd the proposals for a film school, her workload sharply reduced. She came into the office several days a week, not too early, and did not stay too late. There was not much paperwork to clear; she had little official correspondence, few delegations, few debates, and no bills to steer through the House. The annual reports of the national companies, galleries, and museums would be in the office, but Jennie did not read them unless she had to bone up on a problem or prepare for a visit. Her main task was publicity, at which she was superb, giving interviews, visiting towns, theatres, and festivals, attending evening functions; her visits absorbed considerable office energy, but they did not require much preparation from her. She descended, a bit like royalty. Unlike royalty, Jennie never needed to prepare a speech in advance; she picked up an audience instinctively and had them hanging on her every word.

Although her workload was relatively light, she ignored those parts of her official responsibilities which she found boring. She was not interested in library matters (she had nothing to do with the British Library site), and Keith Jeffery was left to get on with it. She had occasional meetings with the national commission on museums and galleries, but that bored her. She did not try to extend her remit either into related 'heritage' matters, architecture for example, or historic buildings and monuments (which belonged to the MPBW); nor did she use her position in the DES to interest herself in such issues as local authority discretionary awards to music and dance students, or the dual use of school premises for arts events. Her private office was quite clear that she did 'not want to take on other jobs'. She had no ambitions for herself, no wish for a ministerial career. She wanted to see her projects through and then gracefully retire. They were *her* projects. The Secretary of State must understand that, and not interfere.

Tony Crosland accepted that. He came to a small department in Whitehall terms, drab and isolated like its buildings, low in prestige and political clout. The DES had to work through the LEAs for schools, and through the UGC for universities; their autonomy limited its influence. There seemed little scope for innovation. Previous ministers had lacked dynamism. Crosland, senior civil servants reckoned, was the first of real stature.

Jennie and Crosland did not like each other. Jennie frequently called him Chief Secretary (aligning him with the Chief Secretary to the Treasury, responsible for controlling public expenditure); and persistently misspelt his name 'Crossland'—the double 's' allowing a satisfyingly drawn-out Scottish hiss in the middle. (It also allowed her, in best Labour Party fashion, to composite him with Richard Crossman, when it suited her to refer to Oxbridge 'snobs'.) Jennie was indifferent to what Crosland thought, or what he thought of her, as long as he left her alone. She was angry with him at their first departmental brush when he refused to support the National Youth Orchestra; and exasperated when he did not give the OU the support she wanted. But it was difficult for him. It was his job as Secretary of State to get the money, a job he took very seriously. Crosland knew that Jennie did not understand public expenditure; and because Jennie went direct to the Prime Minister, he did not know what she was negotiating or where she wanted to go. If she did not like the answer Crosland gave her, she ignored it and went off to Harold.[1] Jennie's private office thought he exhibited 'enormous tact' in not getting in her way, which Jennie came grudgingly to recognize when she scribbled: 'Of course it was a punishment for Crossland [*sic*] when I became one of the junior ministers in his department. It was one more mouth to feed and although *de jure* I was a junior minister, *de facto* I had a closer relationship to the prime minister than he had.'[2]

Crosland, says Chris Price who was his PPS for a year, was 'quite scared' of Jennie. It was Crosland's first Cabinet post and he had a tough agenda of his own—headed by comprehensive reorganization—to get through. He had been devoted to Hugh Gaitskell, who had died only two years before, and he continued to mourn him. Gaitskellites and Bevanites neither forgave nor forgot. Jennie was no junior minister in the usual sense, that is younger, relatively unknown, with a career to make, dependent on the Secretary of State for her workload, his patronage, her promotion, his policy steer, and his ability to find her resources. Jennie belonged to Labour Party history. She was a *grande dame*, better known in the country than he was, more senior within the Labour Party than he was, far closer to the Prime Minister than he was. He did not want Jennie in his department, he did not want the arts in his department, and he did not want the OU in his department—or, come to that, anywhere else. When Jennie was moved into the DES, he gloomily told his wife that evening that Jennie believed 'that everything in the entire Department should be subservient to the Arts', adding that he would no doubt have to forfeit his private lavatory so that Jennie could have one for her own use.*

Political dislike was allied to personal irritation. Crosland was annoyed by Jennie's style of not working the system, but, in Chris Price's phrase, of 'blasting her way through it'; of thinking that procedures and committees were for everybody else; he suspected she would eat into and erode his budget. She believed he was 'bitterly hostile' to her. Jennie was wrong. Crosland paid her the lesser compliment of finding her tiresome, but he would not sabotage her. He argued alongside her with the Treasury; helped her 'jazz up' (in his words) the language of her White Paper on the OU to make it sound more exciting. If he failed to put more departmental weight behind her and bring the senior DES officials into line, that was partly because Jennie did not ask him to do so. He gave her more support than she gave him credit. When the press wrote a critical

* Jennie, on reading Susan Crosland's biography, did not dispute the story; merely commented on how 'carefully' Susan Crosland managed her husband. 'Lavatory' stories (at least their provision) followed Jennie around; but that was mainly because government and public bodies were used only to men at the top. Not that Jennie ever used lavatories, or WCs; they were always 'the little girl's room'; S. Crosland, *Tony Crosland* (1982), 147; Interview Elizabeth Thomas.

piece on the OU, he sent her a note, both sympathetic and self-justifying, making it clear he had not talked to journalists: 'As you know, I have consistently left the entire matter to you, and have supported every paper you've put forward. Besides, I've always assumed that the source of finance for the U/air would be a broadcasting & not an educational one.' When journalists did ask him about the OU, Crosland would always tell them: 'You can go down the passage for that one.'[3]

Jennie took a minimal part in the life of the department. She seldom attended team meetings—'breezing in, breezing out, usually late', says Dennis Howell, also a junior minister in the DES—and when she came, she did not stay until the end; she was no team player. An exasperated Dennis Howell never made an education speech without praising Wilson, and highlighting their work on arts and sport; he asked Jennie to do the same for him, but she refused. Nor would she undertake departmental chores, opening schools or attending speech days.[4] As far as she was concerned, she was attached to rather than in the DES, because she and her portfolios had to be put somewhere. The rest of its work did not concern her.

Yet Crosland's educational agenda should have commended itself to Jennie, and would have gained from her support. Three issues dominated the DES: comprehensive reorganization, about which Jennie had doubts; teacher supply, on which she was silent; and higher education post-Robbins, on which she and Crosland were at odds. Crosland was determined to push through comprehensive reorganization against the wishes of the department. Jennie seldom spoke on it, although she could have drawn analogies between open rather than selective universities, and open rather than selective schools. At the 1966 Party Conference, however, as a member of the NEC (which Crosland was not), she had to make his speech for him as she wound up for the platform on education. She told Conference that they were making 'dramatic progress' on comprehensive education. Only a handful of local authorities were being uncooperative.

In private, Jennie was more scathing. Crosland thought he could get rid of the eleven-plus and integrate private schools, she wrote, without bringing 'the commanding heights' of the economy into the public sector:

> He encouraged the belief that we could have classless education in a class society. Nye, myself and many others scoffed at this delusion . . .
>
> Crossland [*sic*] hated the private fee paying schools such as he had attended. It was probably this more than anything else that brought him into the labour

movement. Others of us had a rougher baptism. The class war was a daily reality in the mining areas where we had grown up.[5]

It was an odd voice and an odd tone. Jennie, perhaps because of her Scottish upbringing, did not condemn the divisiveness of the 1944 Act, nor did she empathize with the pain of children who failed the eleven-plus. She knew that private education perpetuated privilege, and that class structures were strengthened by class-stratified education. However if one could not eradicate the class system, she seemed to argue that there was no point in mitigating its worst effects. Crosland encouraged his stepdaughters to go to the local comprehensive. Jennie sent her nephew Vincent to a private school.

On Crosland's second problem, that of teacher supply, Jennie contributed nothing to the debate, though her OU was to contribute to the solutions. DES civil servants recall that the teacher shortage dominated the later 1960s and 1970s. Every woman teacher who left to start a family, said the DES, 'meant one teacher less, one baby more'. Proposals to raise the school-leaving age (ROSLA) would add to the problem and the cost. The country needed not only more teachers but better educated ones, able to meet the challenge of comprehensive education. Less than a fifth had degrees. The OU, like Birkbeck, proved well poised to meet that need. Over a third of its early intake were teachers seeking degrees, and many more were people seeking to become teachers, a contribution that Jennie came belatedly to endorse.

Crosland's third concern was higher education in the aftermath of the Robbins Report. He believed that the last thing the country needed was another university (the OU) alongside the existing, the expanding, and the new universities. Instead, he favoured a binary system, polytechnics alongside universities, each with their own distinctive mission: 'There is an ever increasing need and demand for vocational, professional and industrially-based courses in higher education—at full-time degree level, at full-time just below degree level, at part-time added level and so on . . . In our view it requires a separate sector with a separate tradition and outlook within the higher education sector.'[6] It would be the summit of the local authority route. In 1966 Crosland proposed twenty-eight polytechnics—Wilson added to the list and scribbled in Huddersfield—that would meet the needs of students and the economy alike. Given educational provision at the time, Crosland was not wrong. But when Jennie persisted with her plans for the OU, Crosland was generous in defeat. When he left for the DTI, he acknowledged Jennie's farewell note, saying how sorry he was to leave education, 'which I loved . . . and before your announcement of the Open University, about which the press always told lies; don't let anything stop you. It was one of the last pleasures to have got money in the Public Expenditure exercise which gives the green light.'[7]

With Patrick Gordon-Walker, Jennie had even less to do. As he 'ballsed up' the British Library site (said one civil servant), delayed ROSLA, and failed to negotiate the admittedly large mantraps over comprehensive education, this was just as well. He made the foolish mistake of thinking that as he was the senior minister, she was the junior minister, and accountable to him. He tried to bring the arts under his own remit and Jennie 'had to have him reminded of her own area of responsibility in the arts, she did not have to report to him on this'.[8] She called on Wilson to stop Gordon-Walker from agreeing with the Chancellor that Jennie's budget should be subsumed in his. She quarrelled with him when he made appointments which she thought were properly hers. When she was in hospital for a few days, he appointed people to the South Bank National Theatre Board without consulting her. She was furious:

> I take the strongest possible exception to decisions being taken concerning any project for which I am fully responsible without my knowledge or consent . . . I made it quite clear to my private secretary, who visited me daily in hospital, that I was not sick, nor out of my mind, and as easily accessible as if I were over at the House of Commons . . . I have been unhappy about a number of matters affecting my job for some time now. When I return next week I hope we can get these cleared up.[9]

This was not the normal tone of junior to senior minister. She was happy to see him go, and her views may have influenced Wilson when Gordon-Walker was replaced by Ted Short, previously Wilson's Chief Whip, who, say the department, cleared up the mess, urged comprehensives forward, pressed for nursery education,[10] prepared for ROSLA, sorted the BL site, and gave Jennie unconditional support for the OU.

If Jennie's dealings with her senior colleagues were edgy, those with her senior civil servants were disastrous. She came to her job with an engrained suspicion of their obstructiveness; as Goodman said, the civil service lost no time in vindicating her views. Goodman came to share them: 'To outmanoeuvre the civil service, which is indispensable if you are to continue in a sensible way of life, is to arouse their bitterest hatred.' They were, he concluded, 'miserable creatures'.[11] The most miserable creatures, they agreed, were to be found in the Treasury. Jennie had a modest budget for the arts already; but obtaining money for the OU against a deteriorating economic situation was very difficult. Until she got it in 1967, she was not supposed to make public statements. This did not stop her from touring the country quoting Wilson's 1963 Glasgow speech on the OU with complete confidence and absolutely no authority. Every time she did so, the Treasury would ring up her permanent secretary Herbert Andrew, or Ralph Toomey, the assistant secretary responsible for universities, to tell them, as if they did not know: 'Your Minister is sounding off again.' It was, says Toomey, 'a magnificent juggling act'.[12]

Jennie expected trouble with the Treasury, she predicted difficulty with her own departments. As always, the difficulties were partly of her own making. She chaired a Cabinet committee serviced by two civil servants, one from the Cabinet Office, the other from the Treasury. She was so deeply suspicious of them that she could not bear to reach any conclusions in front of them. She simply would not understand that if she did not give them a summary to minute and circulate, nothing would happen. She would say: 'We'll discuss this further outside this room.' She was then exceedingly cross when nothing happened.[13] Her difficulties were also personal. She was unlucky with her permanent secretaries, and they were unfortunate with her.

Herbert Andrew, Jennie's permanent secretary at the DES, was a working-class Yorkshireman, deeply opposed to comprehensive organization, and much given to studying *Who's Who*. He had reluctantly come from the DTI. To his juniors he seemed cynical and jaundiced. He told Ralph Toomey that 'the only thing going right for Miss Lee at the moment is the OU. It's your job to keep her happy.' It was not, says Toomey, the most precise of briefs. Andrew regarded Jennie as a plague visited upon the department, a 'damn nuisance' to him. When a new private secretary was appointed to her office, Herbert Andrew called him in. The private secretary saw a very small man with a very large pipe, his feet on his desk, who said, through a haze of smoke: 'I am sending you to Miss Lee. Miss Lee thinks all civil servants are malign and malicious, and your job is to keep her away from me.' He did, and so nine months later was promoted and left. The young private secretary of Shirley Williams (the other Minister of State in the DES) was given exactly the same instruction: to keep Mrs Williams away.[14] They were women and Andrew was frightened of women, they were intellectually untidy, and they had policies he did not like. When, on one or two occasions, Jennie reluctantly felt she ought to communicate with Andrew, the private secretary would persuade her that he was not well, and Jennie colluded in the fiction. Andrew, his deputy, and his deputy's deputy, would all move 'heaven and earth' not to see her. Another private secretary remembers only one formal communication between Jennie and Andrew in his entire year, even though both were on the same corridor.

Andrew was even less interested in Jennie's arts work. Keith Jeffery submitted a Cabinet brief on the siting of an Army Museum; he proposed (and Jennie agreed) that it be in central London rather than in the remoter suburbs. Andrew, who saw the arts only as an adjunct to education, substituted for Jeffery's recommendation a one-line sentence—such a museum 'was unsuitable for children' and should therefore go to the suburbs. He and his colleagues, commented Jeffery, never knowingly attended an arts event.

The only smoothly run aspect of Jennie's work was the OU, handled by a middle-ranking assistant secretary, Ralph Toomey, whose brisk, dry, terse, clear style rightly inspired Jennie's confidence and the admiration of all the juniors around him. He sometimes had to take the rough edge of Jennie's tongue, but that did not stop her trusting him completely.

The OU education work had a departmental structure but no money; the arts work had money but no departmental structure. Jennie, without previous government experience, did not know what to ask for or how to do it. She was given a private secretary (she never chose her own), a succession of young men in their mid-20s, clever, obliging, often interested in the arts, picked out for their potential as high-flyers, and for whom this was often their first real departmental job. One came from the Plowden Committee on primary education—his father had been Nye's private secretary in years past; another came from the Dainton Committee on the British Library. They stayed a year or so before moving smoothly up the departmental ladder. Their job, they understood, was to keep both Jennie and Andrew happy, and to keep them apart.

Jennie got on well with all her private secretaries. They enjoyed her company, her feisty iconoclastic style, the starry evening events, the 'hairy' foreign trips. She hijacked them for escort duty, or dished out spare tickets for *Hamlet* or the Bolshoi Ballet. Often they would join her for drinks and a light supper afterwards where they acquired an unrivalled and deeply prejudiced education in politics and modern history. They were fascinated, as she talked about Tito, Stalin, and the 1930s. They saw her as a living legend, someone who had suffered, yet who remained gallant and indomitable. They were protective. Her courage, they thought, took a lot out of her. She was surprisingly formal. Because they could not call her Jennie, she would not use their first names.

On all but major issues, when they would phone her first, they would invent policy as they went along and she would then scribble any amendments on to their draft. They were constantly frustrated: she could not and would not work the system, and they were too junior to do it for her. When she was angry that the Director of the National Gallery was appointed without her knowledge, for example, she wrote a strong letter of complaint to her Secretary of State. What she should have done, they realized too late, was to require that the minister approve all short lists, but neither of them thought of it. One private secretary remembers a bad period when 'not a single mandarin would speak to us—so the office was run by an old lady and a child'—they were left to get on with it; another, that they were 'a strung-together little outfit'. Jennie was poorly served; a new minister in her first job in a newly invented post with only young assistant principals to steer her, all of them learning on the job as they went, each staying for barely a year, and none with any knowledge of the arts. Jennie was on her own; but as long as she had Goodman and Wilson with her, she preferred it that way.

The more senior civil servants were uncertain how to handle her. They had been trained to think in straight lines, whereas Jennie worked by free association—on her good days it allowed her to see around corners. She was 'difficult', impatient, and forthright (about one nomination, 'Not that sod'). She sometimes behaved badly. When she saw one under-secretary smiling at a meeting, she announced: 'I'll wipe that grin off your face'; Toomey knew exactly what was in her mind. She was censorious and did not hesitate to tear a strip off them in front of the Prime Minister, or complain loudly in public about their behaviour. She did not want to know the counter-arguments, she would brook no criticism. They found her bossy, noisy, and not very clever. Roy Shaw said to one civil servant that they must find it a great disappointment to work with Lord Eccles, after Jennie. 'Not really', he was told. 'It's nice to work with a Minister who listens.'[16]

In Parliament she had a light ride. She had little Commons work to do, which was as well, for she was not at ease there. Whenever she spoke in the Commons, she never completed a sentence; Hansard writers despaired. They would throw their transcripts at her private secretary and ask him to reconstruct the entire speech. She encountered little political opposition. The Tories did not object to money on the arts; she was 'quite their pin-up girl', she said, for aiding Covent Garden. Hugh Jenkins became her unofficial PPS for the arts, scolded by her on occasion for being too political, and the newly elected Renée Short also gave her support. The OU was more controversial, but as it was submerged from sight for most of the time, she escaped fairly lightly there too.

As a departmental minister, Jennie by conventional civil service standards was hopeless. Even though she was Arts Minister for six years (longer by far than any of her successors), she refused to learn the rules or to play by them. She wasn't effective on paper, wasn't constructive in meetings, wasn't good with the department, wasn't helpful to her colleagues, wasn't persuasive in the Commons. She wouldn't compromise, couldn't negotiate. She simply went outside the system to Wilson and Goodman. Her private secretaries say that they learnt two things from her: the need to understand the system if you are to deliver what you want, and the importance of political will if you refuse to do so.

Outside the department, and Jennie was the first, and the finest, minister the arts ever had. She persuaded her Party that arts mattered. She offered money and esteem and endless publicity. They loved it and they loved her. Every minister thereafter was judged against Jennie, and every minister failed. She gave the arts their Golden Age.

*

A year or two into her ministry and friends noted how well Jennie looked. She was happier, crisper, she laughed more, and she had lost nearly two stone in weight. Her clothes were brighter—more turquoise, lime, and tangerine—and her necklines lower. Her arthritic hip had ceased to trouble her. To one journalist she appeared the 'earthy indolent peasant' crossed with the Queen Mother.[16] She loved her job, and she was also in love.

Not, however, with Arnold Goodman. He loved her devotedly and, her family insist, would have married her fifty times over. He rang her early every morning, sent fresh flowers every week, gave her a birthday party every year. He escorted her, scolded her, cuddled her, sorted her finances, and cherished her in sickness and in health. What Jennie wanted, Arnold fixed, whether, as chairman of the Arts Council, it was money for the National Youth Orchestra, or, as her lawyer, a splendid and splendidly cheap house for herself. Friends speculated. They seemed so suited, behaved so affectionately, and Arnold was so rich. Vincent asked Jennie outright why she did not marry Arnold. 'You do not just marry the mind, you marry the body as well', she told him. 'How can I love that body?'

She continued to attract admirers. There were rumours of affairs, with a noted film producer, with a novel-writing MP. What friends did not know was that Jennie, a minister, now in her early 60s, had fallen in love with a senior civil servant, a man witty, elegant, self-assured, not entirely 'sound', by nature something of pirate (according to colleagues), and many years younger than herself. He pursued her, endlessly phoning her, sometimes several times a day. Fellow civil servants noted that he was fascinated by her and her vitality. He gave her yellow curtains for her flat in Ashley Gardens, azure curtains for Chester Row. Vincent admired them—he thought they were 'fabulous'. 'My lover gave them to me', Jennie said with a toss of her head. She introduced Vincent to him; revealingly, the young Vincent understood that this man was the selfsame Frank Wise of Jennie's youth, her 'most wonderful lover', 'her solace'. Jennie then added, carefully: 'but I love you [Vincent] in a different way'.

It was a passionate love affair, intensely physical. She adored him, and the sexual games they played. 'It was like a bonfire', she told a friend: it consumed them. They were discreet; his career was at risk. Jennie confided in one or two friends, adding: 'Don't tell Arnold, for God's sake.' She believed he wanted to marry her, but he was a married man and Jennie eventually sent him back to his family. They remained friends and managed the occasional lunch. She continued wistfully to follow his career and kept a few things among her private papers.

In 1978, the affair long over, Jennie was struggling with the final chapters of *My Life with Nye*. 'Every morning when I woke & every night before sleep came he [Nye] was in my thoughts. I knew what he would want me to do and what was the only sane thing to do—that is to accept all the love, sacred and profane, all the friendships, all the possibilities for work that life offered.'[17] That she had done. Her last was not the least love of her life.

Ashley Gardens, where they played, was her London *pied-à-terre*. It was tiny (just two main rooms); Arnold, who found it for her, lived in the flat below. Asheridge, meanwhile, remained her home. When she became a minister she decided that she could no longer maintain the farm and would make her main home in London. She left Asheridge in autumn 1968, and moved out of Ashley Gardens into a double house, 65–7 Chester Row, a smart address previously occupied by a Tory MP.[18]

The conversion (of two houses into one) had left it with some structural defects: Jennie had constant problems with bulging walls, ineffectual plumbing, and a leaking roof—and, being Jennie, with the builders and tradesmen who did the repairs. Arnold negotiated from the Grosvenor Estate a very modestly priced lease and ground rent on condition that Jennie did not enfranchise. The house had spacious rooms, large windows, and high ceilings; her basement kitchen and dining-room had French doors opening on to a lovely walled garden where she grew yellow roses. She furnished it in House and Garden style, with parquet flooring, washed Chinese rugs, white walls, antique furniture, deep sofas, richly coloured fabrics, and pictures stacked against overflowing bookcases. On the polished side-table art-gallery catalogues mingled with *Country Life*, a glossy volume on Himalayan art, and books inscribed by Henry Moore.[19] It was a wonderful setting for memorable parties, where the Dom Perignon flowed and guests perched on hired gilt chairs. She was a generous and warm hostess, and she made it a beautiful home.

Her pleasure in the house was marred by being burgled twice. The first time, says Bettina darkly, was an inside job, and some of Jennie's silver went: Jennie was notoriously casual about leaving her keys around. The second was distinctly more unpleasant. Two teenage girls broke in through the kitchen window while Jennie was in India, found her supply of drink and rampaged around the house. They broke valuable Chinese porcelain bowls, stubbed out cigarettes on her antique furniture, soiled her clothes, fouled the bed linen, and stained the carpets with vomit and spilt drink. They were caught by the police as they sashayed forth wearing Jennie's fur coats. They were given eighteen months in jail.

*

Jennie's political and private lives were going well. Her arts job was not demanding in parliamentary and office time (a couple of hours in the morning, a couple of hours in the afternoon) and her paperwork was blessedly light. Instead she turned all her great polemical and platform gifts into publicizing the arts. Typically, of a morning she would give interviews to the press or meet some delegation from the arts; a couple of times a week there would be a formal lunch with publishers or patrons; afternoons she might work with officials, attend a Party meeting, descend on the House of Commons, before going home around 4 o'clock, returning perhaps for a late vote. Two or three nights a week came the openings, first nights, previews, and receptions that she adored. When whipping allowed, she would leave London to open libraries and lay foundation stones. With Arnold, she visited Bath, Venice, and Edinburgh for their festivals. She had a rich private life, a son, a lover, a family, and admiring friends. She had a safe seat and a conscientious and experienced secretary in Doreen Andrews to look after it. In June 1966 her contribution to the arts as well as her standing in the Labour Party were recognized when she was made a Privy Councillor. And from October 1967, she was also chairman [*sic*] of the NEC and therefore of the Labour Party.

Jennie had come on to the NEC in 1958. She had long wanted to stand: it was a natural outlet for her platform talents. She had disciplined herself not to run for the constituency section, as she would have displaced another Bevanite. That left the women's section, but this was controlled by the trade unions, who returned women on the right of the Party, such as Alice Bacon, Peggy Herbison, Bessie Braddock, and the Scottish Jean Mann. Jennie disapproved of a women's section and strongly disapproved of the fact that it was controlled by the unions, but she gritted her teeth, stood for it, and in 1957 was runner-up.[20] When Jean Mann resigned in the summer of 1958, Jennie automatically took her place.[21] At Conference a few weeks later, she was elected in her own right.

Membership of the NEC gave Jennie independent standing within the Party, magnified from 1961 when Conference began to be televised; NEC members commanded prime time as they responded on behalf of the platform to debates. Apart from Barbara Castle, the other women NEC MPs lacked Jennie's charisma, her looks, her oratory, her passion, her grief. The soul of the Labour Party was always on the left. After Nye's death, Barbara Castle, six years younger than Jennie, was now its Joan of Arc; Jennie was its widowed Queen. While Nye was alive, whatever Jennie said was thought to come from Nye; it belittled her. With Nye dead, whatever Jennie said was still assumed to be in Nye's voice, but now she was the guardian of his flame. She could reach out over the leadership to the constituencies in the country in his name.

She had always been an impressive conference performer. Her speeches seldom *read* well; on paper they lack depth, originality, or argument. To hear her, however, was transforming. She trusted to the moment—she could talk for forty minutes about the price of two oranges—and could establish a bond with her audience like few others. Jennie stayed with the simple truths of the faith (unlike Nye who enlarged the faith) but she made those truths sound fresh and newly minted. She could make magic and inspire. Crossman shared a rally at Wolverhampton:

> I listened to Jennie who really is a superb orator. She was talking about the cost of living and, in the course of fifty minutes, only showed that it had gone up under the Tories. But what a speech, describing in detail everything on the table of a miner in Cannock, with that intimate working class familiarity, half way between laughing and crying.[22]

Dennis Howell believed that she was the finest platform orator in the land.

Nye would physically unfold to make a point, first bending the knee and then uncurling into his full upright strength. The young Jennie spoke with her hands—and her arms and her head and her feet—but never with notes. The mature Jennie slowed her delivery and restrained her body movements, apart from occasionally wagging a finger as she scolded her audience. Instead, she coloured and inflected that wonderful Scottish voice; its soprano top note gave her projection, its underlying mezzo pitch stopped her sounding shrill. She spoke in chords. Other platform speakers would naturally lift and drop, lighten and darken their voice within a sentence; Jennie did it within a single word. She would swoop an octave as she lengthened and caressed the long words—'our financial philosophy'—in which she delighted. She sounded the language. She might pause, fractionally, to place a word, but she never fumbled a line or had to restart a sentence. She did not shout, but her compelling emphatic delivery, the slight lift of that dark eyebrow, commanded the hall. With it, she could caress, denounce, or cajole. Tom Driberg thought she had a better feel for the mood of Conference than anyone he knew. In 1961, for example, she wound up from the platform a debate on Angola. She described men, women, and children being hunted through burning grass like wild animals; their suffering and her tears lay just behind her voice, and Conference rose to her.

After Nye's death, Jennie had neither the power nor, any more, the wish to initiate policy; but she had considerable capacity to embarrass. What—and whom—Jennie denounced was news. When in 1960 Gaitskell was struggling after the Party Conference to unify a deeply divided NEC, it was Jennie who threw him his lifeline, the phrases which, coming from her, would bind left and right behind nationalizing the commanding heights within a mixed economy. When Harold Wilson challenged Gaitskell for the Party leadership, Jennie's endorsement helped to ensure that he was positioned as Nye's heir and the next leader.

Within the Labour government she had a totemic weight—which she did not hesitate to employ—far beyond the parliamentary under-secretaryship she had in the Ministry of Works. Membership of the NEC gave her authority; becoming Minister for the Arts added glamour; being Nye's widow lent her grace. It was a heady mix. Harold Wilson was deeply apprehensive when in 1968 Jennie threatened to resign over health charges. Frank Longford, Labour leader of the Lords, also told Wilson he would resign, an event that bothered Wilson not at all; it was Jennie who mattered.[23]

Jennie scrupulously attended the NEC. She served alongside Nye on the Commonwealth and International Subcommittees of the NEC, which he chaired. Nye's death did not bridge the chasm between Gaitskell and the Bevanites. The NEC meetings of the early 1960s were fraught and the votes often narrow, as its former Bevanites, led by Barbara Castle, tried to bind Gaitskell to Conference decisions over Clause 4 and over defence. Jennie usually took her lead from Ian Mikardo. NEC members remonstrated when the PLP withdrew the whip in spring 1961 from five MPs, including Michael Foot, 'in view of the conflict between majority decisions on Defence of the Party Conference and the Parliamentary Party'.[24] When the USA followed the USSR in resuming nuclear tests, Jennie supported Barbara Castle in denouncing both the resumption of tests and Britain's insistence on remaining an independent nuclear power. They were easily beaten off by Gaitskell.[25] These were unhappy years.

When Gaitskell unexpectedly and tragically died in January 1963, Wilson became Party leader, and tensions within the NEC eased. Few issues were now pushed to the vote. In October 1967 Jennie became, by length of service on the NEC, Party chairman. On its behalf she attended congresses abroad and the circuit of conferences at home—women at Llandudno, co-operators at Brighton, local government at Derby, and various trade unions at various resorts. Highlights included opening in February 1968 the exhibition at Congress House to celebrate fifty years of women's suffrage. Jennie excelled as ambassador for the Party.

She took the chair in a difficult year for Labour.[26] Rhodesia, Nigeria/Biafra, and especially Vietnam led to widespread street and student protest; devaluation at home followed by cuts, wage restraint, and health charges brought Jennie herself, as minister and as chairman of the Party, to the brink of resignation. Her Cannock agent announced she would resign over prescription charges, and the constituency, cheered by this display of socialist principle, sent a telegram of support. The press camped on her door. She was hauled back by Arnold Goodman. Twenty-six other Labour MPs, however, did rebel; as no one wanted a fuss, they lost the whip for only a few weeks. The NEC, calmly chaired by Jennie, duly noted the fact.[27]

The government was battered by poor opinion polls, a run of by-election losses, and a bad press. Trade-union loyalty was strained by Labour's incomes policy. By early September 1968, the mood at the TUC Congress was distinctly sour. Jennie made a guest appearance, bringing greetings from the political to the industrial wing of the movement. Jennie, so close to resignation herself a few months before, tried 'to woo the Congress from their disenchantment' with the Labour government. 'It was a superb attempt', noted Geoffrey Goodman in the *Sun*: 'An artist's performance of skating round the cracks with masterly skill and at the same time injecting a revivalist message in old style to a Congress which traditionally is reluctant to respond to "political" speeches.'[28]

Jennie refused to talk about incomes policy. Instead, to a Labour movement focused on economic and social problems she talked about her job as Arts Minister and her concern with the quality of life, how to make more widely available the graces, beauty, and privileges of life. She then unashamedly moved into a rhetorical ramble. A look back to her grandfather, a reference to 'the man I married', and her peroration, 'Don't let anyone dirty our dreams.'[29] She was met with polite applause. As many of her front bench colleagues would have been howled off the platform, it was a triumph of sorts. No one could have done more.

Her year finished with the great set piece of the Blackpool Party Conference. It was not an easy body to chair. It can be tetchy, sentimental, and inconsistent, all within the space of an hour. The Labour Party in 1968 believed that their government had lost its way. There was potential for a blazing row. Wage restraint was loathed by the unions, and it was they who commanded Conference. Jim Callaghan, siding with the unions, was at war with Barbara Castle, Secretary for Employment[30] (the turmoil of *In Place of Strife* was only a few months away). Jennie had already made herself unpopular with union leaders when she used her casting vote at the pre-Conference NEC to reject a TGWU composite condemning the government's incomes policy. The Conference vote would go with the unions, but Jennie judged that for the NEC to disown the government for the first time in its history was unthinkable. Morale was low. Could Jennie turn the mood around?

Procedurally, she was not a good chairman. She got her composite motions muddled, took amendments in the wrong order, and when it came to card votes, made it up as she went along.[31] The camera sometimes caught the acting general secretary (Sara Barker) shaking her head ruefully as Jennie yet again departed from the rule book. However, Jennie did not appear nervous, she remained crisp and good-humoured, the men (for Conference back in 1968 was almost entirely male) were tolerant and thought she was 'sweet'. As Jennie welcomed delegates at the opening session, some fifty angry miners protesting against pit closures broke through the stewards' cordon and charged the proceedings. A few Biafrans were pulled along in their wake, bearing placards of their own—'to give them a chance', said the miners. Jennie, taken completely by surprise, handled them with confidence and charm; she first applauded them—'hold up your banners'—and then persuaded them to withdraw. Monday was the Prices and Incomes debate; despite strong speeches by Roy Jenkins and Barbara Castle, the TWGU motion passed overwhelmingly against the advice of the platform, and tension then subsided. During the rest of the week, the platform suffered its customary handful of defeats, including one on Rhodesia (Conference demanded no further negotiations), a defeat blamed on Jennie, who allowed a card vote which overturned the show of hands. However, flanked on one side by Sara Barker, the acting general secretary, and on the other by Betty Lockwood, the chief women's officer, they steered Jennie who, in her turn, steered Conference somewhat erratically through its debates.

A sulky Conference became an unremarkable Conference, and that was no mean achievement. As she closed the proceedings, she called on the Party to combine efficiency with compassion, never to forget its internationalism, nor its instinct for unity: 'It is we who are tuned in to the great music of humanity.' As Geoffrey Goodman remarked in the *Sun*: 'From some politicians that could sound corny, but not from Jennie.'[32] The camera panned to an applauding Tony Benn, a beaming Joan Lestor, a pained Roy Jenkins, a cynical Frank Chapple, and an inscrutable Harold Wilson wreathed in pipe smoke, as they all stood to link hands for Auld Lang Syne.

*

Jennie's ministerial work was absorbing, her party work demanding. In consequence, she neglected Cannock. She had never been an assiduous constituency MP—in that respect she was not so very different from many MPs of her generation. In the later 1950s, against a background of Macmillan's 'Never had it so good' sloganizing, constituency politics in Cannock had stagnated; publicity dried up. Jennie was occasionally reported opening fairs, neighbourhood centres, attending school speech days. Three months after the autumn 1959 general election, Nye went into hospital with cancer. By the summer of 1960 he was dead. After this, Jennie's own health broke, and the constituency saw little of her until she picked herself up to fight the autumn 1964 election. Photos taken during the campaign show how deeply she had suffered. Her glossy black hair, already beginning to silver in the late 1950s, was now snow white. The 1959 photos had shown a highly attractive mature woman of energy, good humour, and determination; these election photos reveal a wistful, frail, and melancholic figure, beautiful but barely able to summon a smile for the camera. She looked much older than she was; she had aged fifteen years in the last five.

At least this time, however, she scented victory. Like Labour candidates around the country, she fought the election on the theme of a bankrupt government and thirteen wasted years,. Her opponent played the race card: immigration was 'the biggest question' facing Wednesfield.[33] The constituency was changing. The electorate had grown to 72,000, many of the pits had closed, there was more light industry, back-to-backs were being replaced by modern semis and pleasant council houses. The rural area was still basically agricultural, but some villages were growing rapidly with 'overspill' from the conurbation whose outer suburbs were invading Cannock. Cannock was still a working-class constituency, but less dependent on coal, less held together by old loyalties. The 'incomers' owed nothing to Labour, coal, Cannock, or Jennie.

Jennie was returned in 1964 with a majority of 8,000. The result was announced in the local paper at the same time as her appointment as a junior minister with special responsibility for the arts. With Labour's tiny majority, it was clear there would soon be another election. Alf Allan, her agent, tried hard to increase Jennie's profile in the constituency. He issued press releases portraying Jennie's ministerial work as she travelled around the country; touched memories when he described her visit to Tredegar to unveil a bust of Nye; and had her walk down a bumpy road to call for its resurfacing. Eighteen months later she was calling for a proper working majority, pointing to her own work in building an Open University, pointing to Wilson's work in reversing an unfavourable balance of trade. She wanted to raise wages, reduce arms expenditure, modernize industry, invest in housing, and have fairer taxation. Her opponent, Mr Elliston, was for the first time a local man, who pointedly remarked that an MP was elected not only to determine national issues, but also 'to promote constituency interests. An election address that does not even mention Cannock by name is an insult to the electorate.' The grammar school had been closed against local wishes; the branch railway line had closed, and the buses had not improved. Elliston argued: '£1 million for a Cannock hospital would be more important than £5 million for Culture in London.'[34] Jennie's majority was 11,000 on a slightly lower poll.

But the constituency was growing restless. She had withdrawn from them in the years immediately following Nye's death, which they could understand, and about which they silently sympathized. Now, as Minister for the Arts, 'she began to slip away', says one faithful party worker. Older people felt she had forgotten them, the 'incomers' that they never saw her. She had lost her faithful Alf Allan when, after the 1964 general election, he had moved to Nuneaton to work for Frank Cousins—Nuneaton could afford to pay him. Cannock could not afford to replace him. Allan left behind a party whose organization was weak and in debt. The local party offices had to be sold. By the late 1960s, General Committee meetings were down to nine or twelve of the possible forty delegates; one or two were cancelled because they were inquorate. By Spring 1970, the party debts had grown to £900.

Jennie visited the constituency every six to eight weeks (though during 1967–8 nine months went by without a visit to Cannock).[35] In the late 1940s and 1950s, this was acceptable. Quarterly visits were not uncommon. However, expectations rose. Labour MPs newly elected in 1964 nursed their seats with care.[36] MPs were expected to live in their constituencies, to hold weekly or fortnightly surgeries, to act as lobbyists for their constituency interests. The political culture began to change; Jennie would not change with it. Unfavourable comparisons were drawn with Renée Short, another Labour woman in a nearby Wolverhampton seat, elected for the first time in 1964, who held weekly surgeries and took trouble with her constituency. Jennie's private office in London was astonished at how little she bothered with constituency matters. She was not worked very hard as junior Minister for the Arts; all her private secretaries noted that she did not 'have a lot to do', 'the job was not very onerous'. Jennie's London secretary left her partly because she was exasperated by Jennie's casual way with Cannock.[37]

It is true that Jennie was holding down not just a junior ministerial post, but in 1968 the chairmanship of the Party. This entailed committees in London and conferences elsewhere. On occasion, the load could be heavy, for which Jennie was given no credit at all in Cannock; there was barely a mention of the Party chairmanship at local meetings or in the press. Far from congratulating itself and its MP, the local party begrudged the time it took. Meanwhile, Jennie made no effort to take the party with her or into her confidence. As the Cannock party grew more surly, Jennie grew more off-hand. When her Party chairmanship came to an end, the local party pressed her to come to Cannock on Fridays in October or November 1969, when the House was not sitting. Jennie studied her diary, but regretfully reported that her autumn Fridays were taken up with speaking at a conference in the Eastern Region; attending a reception for Israel's Minister of Arts; attending another reception, this time for Walter Perry, Vice-Chancellor of the Open University. A fourth Friday was booked with a courtesy visit to the National Portrait Gallery for readings by Sir John Gielgud; a fifth was taken by a dinner for Sir John Barbirolli's 70th birthday; and another, in going to the annual dinner of the Association of University Teachers. She could offer them just one Friday in eight weeks. Cannock felt snubbed. Clearly Jennie received and replied to invitations well in advance; but it was also clear that the constituency was an afterthought, the left-over bit of her political life.

Alf, for all his faults, had watched Jennie's back for her, told her things she did not always want to hear, and was conscientious about constituency correspondence. The load was not onerous; perhaps a dozen letters a week required Jennie's attention. Most MPs had a heavier constituency correspondence—up to twenty letters a week during the 1950s, fifty letters a week or more during the later 1960s.[38] Jennie's constituency mail was light, but increasingly chaotic. Doreen Andrews, her new secretary, tried to bring order, but there was no co-ordination between Jennie's London and Cannock diaries; case notes were lost, letters went missing. Doreen Andrews found herself ringing Cannock, for example, to ask someone to call on two constituents; Jennie had seen them but had forgotten what their problems were.[39] Constituents complained that nothing happened. They stopped turning up to her rare surgeries—many of her interview slots remained unfilled. There was no one to staff the Cannock office.

With a ministerial salary and no family to support, Jennie could have bought professional help. It seems never to have crossed her mind or that of the Cannock party, that she should. She paid her London secretaries poorly and her Cannock help nothing at all. So she was left dependent on volunteers, an enthusiastic, overworked, and inexperienced young husband and wife team, Derek and Muriel Davis, who did their best to fit in Labour party work around full-time jobs and a young family. They were driven to distraction inventing semi-mythical doings: opening a mysterious event in Belgium to cover one unexplained absence. Local newspaper coverage dried up. It did not report even those events Jennie did attend, let alone those she might have done. The Davis's could not protect her from criticism within the constituency, or from the charge that she was out of touch: that she preferred the Coliseum to Cannock. At its General Committee in November 1969:

> Many views were expressed on Miss Lee's visits to the constituency. After a very long discussion it was decided that interview sessions should in future be advertised, that Miss Lee should be notified of complaints about unanswered letters, that more publicity handouts should be received in plenty of time from Miss Lee and her secretary in London and that as many visits as possible to the constituency should be arranged.[40]

When Jennie did come to Cannock, her style seemed anachronistic, to belong to another generation, long past; she had lost her sureness of touch. She still tried to inspire workers with the old rhetoric of exploitation, but they were now embarrassed by it. They turned on her. One miner told a party worker after Jennie had visited their canteen: 'Who the bloody hell does Jennie Lee think she is, talking about 1926?'—as though they were still in cloth caps, when now they drove to work in cars. In the past, Jennie had been treated as royalty. She was now met with remarks like: 'Where have you been these last four years?' And from an older man, 'Jennie we love you, we'll vote for you, but where have you been?' Party worker after party worker grumbled that Jennie had grown away from them, that she didn't want to know about Cannock any more. She visited other constituencies more frequently than she did her own.

As for her ministerial job, they accepted that it made demands on her, but they sourly noted that others who were Cabinet Ministers and more hard-pressed than Jennie worked harder in their constituencies than she did. In any case, what benefit were the arts to Cannock? Had Jennie done a different job—housing, pensions, education—they would have understood. It would have touched their concerns. The arts did not; they touched raw nerves instead. Arts, Cannock people held, were a luxury, enjoyed in London, by the cultural equivalent of the landed gentry—on all three counts, they had nothing to do with Cannock. One former local Labour Party secretary and AEU member wrote to the *Advertiser* to denounce Jennie's arts work and budget of £12 million, extracted, he said, from working men's pockets, but spent not on pensions or on cleaning up coal spoil mountains as in Aberfan, but on an Institute of Contemporary Arts exhibition for children, which included 'pornographic' films by John Lennon; she made much of her Open University work, while at the same time spending £26 million on subsidizing overseas (coloured) students at British universities.[41]

Cannock's world was narrow and limited, and Jennie made no effort to raise its sights. They were ungenerous, but Jennie did not encourage them to be anything more. She would not enter their concerns, and they could not enter hers. Much of her time as a minister was spent proselytizing for the arts, insisting on the best for the most, enthusing Labour councils with their power to enrich humdrum lives, trying to encourage even the small village to have its own community arts centre—everywhere, except in Cannock.

It was whispered that she was a part-time MP, that she did not put in the hours in the Commons either: she did not speak very much, did not show local people around very often, did not ask questions or present petitions, did not invoke Cannock's name. (The fact that, as a junior minister, she could not ask questions or speak on any other portfolio than her own, was not understood, and she did not explain it.) As one correspondent to the local paper put it: 'Miss J. Lee having represented Cannock in silence for twenty-five years in the House of Commons asks again for the support of the electorate.'[42] In Cannock's eyes, having a minister as their MP was nothing but a nuisance. David Ennals was a minister, but lost his Dover seat in 1970. In 1972 he was in the running for a seat next door to Cannock's, but he did not get it because they did not want to carry a minister like Jennie Lee.[43]

She refused after all these years to woo the constituency. They could take her or leave her, so to speak; they felt she held them in contempt. She was always immaculately dressed, but where in the 1950s this gave her film star appeal, it was now held against her, evidence that she had succumbed to London's aristocratic embrace. There were rumours of private wealth, and of a very different London lifestyle, of drinking, smoking, opera, evening dress. Her fur coat seemed to suggest it all. Jennie, who felt the cold, had always worn fur or furry coats, fake or real (for months with the lining held in place with a safety pin, until it was mended by a motherly Cannock woman). When her fur was stolen from Yehudi Menuhin's house during a dinner party, she shivered for a few months in a wool coat. The Tories put around a rumour that was widely believed: Jennie went to her constituency in her fur coat, but as the train approached Cannock she changed into cloth. Her party office tried to deny that she had two wardrobes and two lifestyles, but the story acquired mythic status (as it did for many women MPs). The fur coat impressed the constituency in the 1950s; it was resented by the late 1960s. Deference was declining.

At the beginning, Cannock would have forgiven her anything, but as she grew older and tired, as her constituency work was neglected, as she lost her electrifying glamour, Cannock became highly critical. It was 'time for a change', they felt. Rumours swept the constituency that she might voluntarily stand down (perhaps going to the Lords as Minister for the Arts there), making way for a local man who would look after the constituency properly. To their dismay, Jennie insisted on fighting one more election. She wanted, she said, to see through her work for the Open University. The changes in the political economy of the constituency, the unpopularity of Wilson's government, and the lack of enthusiasm for Jennie among party workers, all made her vulnerable. When the Tories selected as their candidate a local family man and history master, 31-year-old Patrick Cormack (who had fought Antony Crosland at Grimsby in 1966), Jennie was very vulnerable indeed.

A good campaign might have pulled it back for her, but it did not go well from the start. Nationally, the Labour Party had started the year well behind the Tories in the opinion polls, but by May Labour was showing a

7.5 per cent lead. In Cannock, however, the mood was sour, and Jennie had no full-time staff to help her in the hardest fight of her twenty-five years. The party workers had neither the energy nor the inclination to do a proper canvass. They did what tired activists always do, which was mark up the electoral register from personal knowledge of how people usually voted—but their knowledge of young voters and the more recently arrived Wednesfield voters was slight.[44] Without a doorstep canvass, they could not gauge, or engage with, the incipient racism that spilled out from Wolverhampton when Enoch Powell sparked the immigration row.

Racism alone was not enough to cost Jennie her seat (Renée Short, in a more vulnerable constituency, held hers), but it hung in the air.[45] The tolerance of Cannock miners barely extended to Poles and Italians, let alone to 'coloureds', as they were described in Cannock. That notorious Powellite slogan first used in Smethwick—'If you want a nigger for a neighbour, vote Labour'—tainted the campaign. In an understandable but unpleasant incident, Jennie (who for years had fought for colonial freedom) dismayed idealistic party workers when she rejected the graphics for her election address. Its draft front cover featured Cannock people against a stylized backdrop of mines, factory, and Cannock Chase trees. It included a West Indian in a neat blazer and a Sikh in a neat turban. Jennie took one look and said: 'If I put this out, I will get really crucified.' The address, which was already colour-printed, was shredded, the printer sworn to secrecy, and the front cover was redesigned. The Sikh was lightened, the West Indian disappeared, the working men became brawnier, the children happier, a white-coated technologist joined them, and the Cannock pines bloomed more luxuriantly. Party funds were now so depleted that the revised election address was published as a flimsy, black-and-white, folded piece of A4, amateur and unimpressive, its only photo a snapshot of her taken by her nephew Vincent. Patrick Cormack's address was a very different affair, glossy, with colour over-printing, surrounded by a handsome family. Lee for Labour as against Cormack for Cannock, said the posters: 'Time for a Change.' The contrast could not have been more marked.[46]

Jennie was also forced to defend a government's record of which she herself had at times been critical. When prescription charges were introduced for medicines in 1968, she threatened to resign her ministerial post, only to be dissuaded by Arnold Goodman who had no affection for the grand gesture. Jennie was bitterly criticized, and the Tories used it. She was attacked by the Catholic and pro-life lobby for supporting David

Steel's abortion bill. Meanwhile, Patrick Cormack hammered away at local issues: where was Cannock's hospital? where were the recreational facilities to accompany its housing programme? the swimming baths? (Jennie's reply, that she wanted a bath in each house before there was a bath in the park, was, coming from her, inept.) Mortgages, the length of the council waiting list, the state of the A5, the need to improve facilities in local school—'the sort of problems with which a local MP should concern himself'—dominated his speeches. He put in the work, and pressed all the right buttons; 'it is time we had a young active MP who could look after us like this'. He promised his supporters they would win Cannock for the first time since 1935; and they were coming to believe him.[47]

Jennie's young agent worked desperately hard for her, not getting to bed until 4 a.m., trying to get extra literature out on a duplicator in the bedroom that kept breaking down, sending copying ink splashing all over his bedroom walls. Everything went wrong. He could not find enough people even for the count, let alone to distribute literature. Local meetings attracted only a handful, and these tended to be only the loyal old-time members. Without a proper canvass to warn her, and with all the national polls still projecting a substantial Labour victory, Jennie had no inkling of the disaster that was looming. As the overnight results came in, seat after seat fell to the Tories. Jennie, though depressed, was not alarmed. She had an 11,000 majority and the same boundaries as in 1966.

As always, Cannock counted the morning after. Jennie swept into the Mining College quite late. Her agent was becoming more and more worried, as the votes stretched in long rows of equal length down the long trestle tables. 'My dear Derek, don't panic', she reassured him. He told her he had good reason to panic. He had seen the clerk to Cannock council 'smirking' and the clerk was Tory. 'Sit back', she said, 'you keep panicking about these things.' The result was a Conservative majority of 1,529. Derek Davis was stunned. Unable to believe it, he thought he should ask for a recount. No, said Jennie, give it to them. She made a dignified speech, insisting that the seat was only 'leased' to the Conservatives and that she had paid the price for a Powellite mood in the constituency. At this, there were cries of 'nonsense' from the crowd, which Cormack hushed. Patrick Cormack in turn paid graceful tribute to her twenty-five years work as an MP, promised to be in the constituency every weekend and vigorously to take up local issues.[48]

The news broke about lunch-time, and sped round the town—Jennie Lee has lost—she's gone. The agent's wife heard it at school and was desperately upset. Women, shopping, stood stunned and frozen. Joan

Loverock was numb with shock for two days, unbelieving, convinced even now that had there been another election the day after, Jennie would have been swept back in, as people wanted to make amends for the wrong they had done her. At 4.30 p.m., Jennie, Vincent, and the workers went back to the Davis's house, all except Jennie in tears. She found herself consoling everybody else. She had expected this to be her last campaign, but she had wanted to choose the timing of her abdication. She had even thought she might take a hand in choosing her successor.

Eleven government ministers and three Labour women MPs lost their seats in 1970: Gwyneth Dunwoody, Anne Kerr, and Jennie; Jennie was the only Labour woman minister to do so, and in a seat not even thought to be marginal. Along with George Brown's defeat in Belper, it was the shock result of the election. An 11,000 Labour majority had become a 1,500 Conservative lead. Jennie had an 11 per cent swing against her, the highest in the country, nearly double the regional swing in the West Midlands of 5.8 per cent, and more than double the national average of 4.8 per cent. Some of it was due to a declining mining industry and a changing constituency, even though Cannock still remained strongly working class; some of it was due to weak organization; and a little of it (perhaps 1,000 votes or more, enough to tip the seat) was due to the racist issue. Writers to the local newspaper, however, suggested 'that the vote against her was not really a political one but . . . a personal one'.[49] With Vincent, she fled to Scotland.

Among her papers is an unsigned letter from an anonymous Labour MP on Commons stationery, dated 23 June 1970:

Dear Jennie,

Of course I am very sorry that you have lost your seat but not at all surprised. In fact you yourself assisted more than anyone to achieve this. You were much more concerned in 'seeking the limelight' attending First nights etc etc and 'doing the town' than you were in fighting for Socialist principles.

Had you resigned over Prescription Charges etc, so-called Prices and Incomes policy, 'bashing the Trades Unions' etc you would have been loyal to your real beliefs, would no doubt have saved the Party from defeat but most certainly have saved your own seat.

How dear old Nye must be turning in his grave.

I send my sympathy but wished that you had not made certain that I had to do this.

Jennie returned to Cannock for one last visit, the July gala. She wore a white suit, she walked with a stick. She had lost Cannock, she said, because she was not local. In any case, she had no wish to go into opposition. Out of power, politics was nothing. 'Look', she had said to a Labour stalwart at the count, 'it's going to be another era.'[50] She went to the Lords, where, with a final snub to Cannock, she took the title of Baroness Lee 'of Asheridge', from her country home, rather than 'of Cannock', her constituency for twenty-five years.

A few months later came the Party Conference. For the last time Jennie replied for the NEC, this time on the NHS debate. With lips compressed and her anger barely controlled, she told Conference that at the last election it was a 'sin against man and God' that prescription charges had blurred the difference between them and the Tories. Charges were 'a primitive piece of self-mutilation' that ought 'never to have happened'. Nye had wanted a brave party, strong in its idealism, a party for lions not sheep.

It was an emotional moment. Jennie was met with warm applause, which developed into a rare standing ovation. She had lost her Cannock seat; she was coming off the NEC; Conference was paying Jennie its final tribute.

13

TWILIGHT YEARS

JENNIE was badly shaken by her defeat at Cannock, and the scale of it was mortifying. She took to her bed, ill with depression. Barbara Castle commiserated with her 'horrible, horrible luck. I don't suppose the Philistines of Cannock had a clue about the marvellous work you've been doing.' Barbara Wootten thought that 'of all the disasters, yours I find the most tragic, both in public and in private terms'. She recalled the thrill of Jennie's first election back in 1929. And went on:

I expect you will be offered a seat in the Lords and I do hope you will find it possible to accept it. There seems not the slightest prospect that the House will be abolished, as it ought to be, but while it survives, I really don't think it ought to be an exclusive Tory platform. One doesn't achieve much there, but if you did feel you could join us there, it would mean that your wisdom would still be at the service of the Party and it would mean a great deal to have you still in close touch (though whether you could stand sitting opposite to that self-satisfied ass David Eccles is another matter). Of course, I may be quite wrong, but I cannot believe that Harold won't suggest it, or that Heath would refuse if he did, so I shall keep on hoping.

Barbara Wootten was right. Just as Harold Wilson had helped lift Jennie off the floor of her depression in 1964 by giving her a job, so he again looked out for her in his resignation honours. A jaunty note returned to her letters. Jennie sat on the stairs at Chester Row as she waited for the official phone call to come through; she and Bettina celebrated with a drink. The condolences gave way to congratulations. Warm letters, from 'Dickie Mountbatten', 'Larry O', and a typical telegram from Arnold Goodman: 'Looking forward to introducing you to high living and high eating in the Lords stop but delighted you are joining us stop a delightful compensation for the other acolytes.'[1]

Jennie, the revolutionary socialist, the lifelong dissenter, had not hesitated for a second. Her view on the Lords was that if you can't lose it, you should use it. When Lena Jeger left the Commons at the 1979 election, Jennie wrote to her just as Barbara Wootten had written to Jennie: 'Don't refuse the Lords. You know my views about it but why not make use of it while it is still there. Good library and as Reg. Paget said to me on arrival, "All my life I have had to pay to belong to a good club, but they actually pay me for coming here!"'[2]

Over the past century, the Lords had slumbered through Tory governments, only to be prodded irritably awake with the arrival of progressive Governments. Labour had curtailed its power to delay legislation (from two years down to one) in 1949 when the Lords unwisely threatened to block iron and steel nationalization. As Jennie had sharply said, that still left the Tory governments with five full years of power, Labour only with four.[3] Its powers reduced, the Lords none the less remained hereditary, Tory, and male. Progressive reformers could not make up their minds which of these caused greatest offence. None of this concerned the Tories. However, it was also a House whose numbers, as well as whose members, were in decline, and that did concern them. Fifty years before, the Lords had been a powerful House with attendances of two or three hundred a day. By the mid-twentieth century, although the Lords remained nominally eight hundred strong, on most days fewer than eighty members attended. The House did not have enough regular and active members to function properly. Important votes went through by majorities of forty to ten.

The preferred solution for all these problems was for life peers, which, while ring-fencing the hereditaries, would enhance the red benches, reward the deserving, and add a few women and non-Tories for interest.[5] The Tories took the initiative. Hereditary peerages did not provide 'an adequate field of recruitment', said Rab Butler in February 1958, drawing revealingly on the Tory obsession both with blood lines and with field sports; they should enlarge 'the field' and inject 'new blood' by offering life peerages to men and women who were 'people of distinction in the public service'.

The official Labour Party thought it was a good idea. Jennie did not. She bridled, she said, at the 'quiet insolence' whereby Tories took it for granted that the Lords should always have a Tory majority. She did not want to 'build up in a second Chamber a barrage behind which they can defy the will of the majority of the people'. She was an abolitionist. She therefore opposed all improvements to the Lords; she opposed life peers;

and, because women hereditary peers were not allowed to take their seats, she particularly opposed women becoming life peers. She cheerfully embarrassed Herbert Morrison by moving amendments to that effect. What was wrong, she teased, with the daughters of hereditary peers? Why did their fathers hold them in contempt? More seriously, she raised the questions that concerned democrats. What popular control would exist over appointments of 'superior people'? Life peers could change their politics, party, or religion. There they would stay, 'for better for worse . . . in sickness and in health . . . till death' do them part from the House of Lords. Rebels, she noted, were unlikely to be appointed. She added: 'My right hon. Friend [Hugh Gaitskell] might even decide to invite me to become a peeress. If he does so, do I go into the second Chamber saying that I do not believe in a second Chamber?'[6] The Commons thought that was a great joke.

In 1970 Jennie did precisely that. As she acknowledged to Marcus Sieff: 'The Lords will suit me very well—better hours than the Commons so I shall have time to write.'

She was introduced in November 1970. George Brown, defeated in the neighbouring constituency to Jennie's by almost as large a swing, was introduced the same day. They occupied separate corners of the Moses room as they put on their scarlet robes. They squared up to each other, observers noted, 'like boxers in a ring'. Jennie insisted that as a 'peeress' she should go first; he insisted on the privilege of the alphabet. To the consternation of the attendants, they slanged each other off mercilessly. To even greater consternation, Jennie turned up for her introduction wearing a bright pink crimplene trouser-suit.[7] The pink clashed with the scarlet, the crimplene subverted the ermine, and a trouser-suit on a somewhat plump woman defied all lordly and most sartorial conventions (it was the crimplene that allegedly gave the greatest offence). On her head she wore the tricorne hat, modelled, say the irreverent, on Virginia McKenna's war films as a Wren. Jennie paraded, affirmed, and bowed. She was now a baroness.

She went to the Lords, she announced, to keep an eye on the arts and on the Open University. She liked to think she was Arts Minister in exile. As there were some perfectly good arts ministers, not just in the government but on the opposition benches as well, this produced tension—had Wilson appointed her to the Lords Front Bench in an official capacity? Eddie Shackleton, Labour leader in the Lords, asked Harold Wilson to clarify her exact position: 'This has caused some stirring in the House of Lords dovecotes.' Harold Wilson replied soothingly that front bench appointments in the Lords were a matter for the Lords; but he had assumed that 'for Arts debates you would bring her down to the Front Bench on a major debate, and clearly with the Phillistine [*sic*] philosophy of the Tories, we would be foolish to lose the enormous standing she has in the Arts world'. He would 'certainly not have sent her to the Lords if I thought she was going to be relegated permanently to the back benches. But there was no question of her being permanently a front-bench spokesman.' Fortunately, David Strabolgi, Labour's Shadow Arts Minister, liked Jennie, and they worked cordially together.[8] On the big set-piece arts debates she would open, and he wind up. He would then run her home to Chester Row.

Unlike Edith Summerskill and many Labour MPs who never felt comfortable in the Lords, Jennie rather enjoyed it. She never complained about the flummery, or the lack of attack and tension in debates. She liked the attentiveness of the attendants, who watched over their elderly and sometimes faltering charges with kindness and discretion. Edith Summerskill, who had kept her maiden name through marriage, tried but failed to retain her name as Dr Edith when she went to the Lords.[9] Jennie did not even try. On the contrary. People who wrote to Miss Jennie Lee were reproved; she was Baroness Lee of Asheridge. Her *grande dame* style which so irritated colleagues in the Commons was more appropriate in the Lords. She was widely liked and approved of. Her arts work endeared her to Tory hereditaries who cherished their paintings, great houses, and Covent Garden. They found her charming, pretty, lively, and, on arts and heritage issues, one of them.

For the first few years Jennie attended once or twice a week and virtuously guarded her old brief. In November 1971 she spoke movingly and effectively when she assaulted the Tory proposal to raise one million pounds from museum charges. Charges undermined the intention of the donors; they were opposed by all trustees and staff; they would not even be cost-effective. Free access, she said, was 'a gracious thing' which affirmed that men did not live by bread alone.[10] She spoke to the British Library bill, she called for a Welsh national opera house, she demanded better funding for the Open University, and she steered the bill permitting Sunday theatre opening through the House. When the railway museums at York and Clapham merged into a National Railway Museum, Jennie urged that it should go to York, 'as our Labour policy was to make the best of the arts more generally available'. There was heavy counter-lobbying from London museums, the GLC, and the press, to locate the railway museum in London, which Jennie urged Wilson to ignore.[11]

Unconstrained by office, she roamed widely. She weighed in on industrial relations, India, coal, education, disability, and foreign affairs. The

Lords were tolerant of her propensity to make long speeches—twenty-five or thirty minutes, when the going rate was nearer ten. She was busy and happy, surrounded by many old friends, such as Arnold Goodman, Pat Llewellyn-Davies (Labour's Chief Whip in the 1974 government), Eirene White, Ted Willis, and later Lena Jeger and John Mackie, her Scottish farming friend. She enjoyed the blessed freedom from constituency work. Like Edith Summerskill, she approved of the way the Lords could debate homosexuality, pornography, or abortion without fear of the constituency vote. The Lords was also far less competitive and 'laddish' than the Commons, its life peers highly distinguished and its style altogether more stately, as befitted a middle-aged and elderly House.

She continued to enjoy an active social life centred on the arts and embassies—lunches, receptions, shows. She gave interviews on the arts to the BBC. She became a founding trustee of the Milton Keynes Foundation which promoted arts in the new town, and faithfully attended its meetings; in June 1974 she opened its Jennie Lee theatre, and she persuaded Henry Moore to become its president and John Dankworth its music adviser. She joined the advisory council of the Association of Business Sponsorship for the Arts (ABSA), entirely happy to see business sponsorship of the arts.[12] 'We live in a mixed economy', she said. Public bodies supported the arts; so should private industry.

Having been semi-detached from the Commons for some years, she did not pine for it as many former MPs did. She entertained family and friends in the Lords and made heavy use of its library. Staff winced when she rang up to borrow books (mainly current political biography), as they came back ordained with coffee rings. Her interest in the Lords faded in the late 1970s. From 1985, by then in poor health, she stopped going altogether.

The 1970s were good years. Being Minister for the Arts for so long had in a certain sense de-politicized her, brought her within the walls of the Establishment. The dissenter enjoyed, literally as well as metaphorically, the aristocratic embrace. She made much of the fact:

> [F]or six years I never once, when I had responsibility for the Arts, made a Party speech; I never once made a political appointment. I was sometimes criticised by close friends in my own Party that I did not make Party capital out of it. That was not my philosophy. I believe that there is a field in public life which belongs to the world of consensus. There is a humanistic field, and surely this is something your Lordships care and know about, because you have done such a good job dealing with humanistic issues such as capital punishment, homosexuality, and all sorts of issues which the other place sometimes found too hot for them to handle. In your

Lordships' House such subjects were dealt with seriously by people from all quarters who had knowledge and who had compassion. I tried to extend this field to the Arts.[13]

So the Lords suited her very well. She enjoyed the gallantry, she rightly basked in the glow of her arts work. She received complimentary tickets for theatre first nights, for gallery previews, and exhibitions. She was cherished and fêted both inside and outside the House.

*

Only one thing marred these years for Jennie: she had lost Vincent. She had lavished love and money on Vincent, and she doted on him. Whatever he wanted she gave him, as long as he then did what she wanted him to do. If he defied her or tried to go his own way, she punished him. Friends visiting Jennie would know immediately where matters stood. She had a large framed photo of Vincent on display; if she was cross with him, the photo was turned to the wall. Vincent had canvassed with Jennie in Cannock and he had been at her side when she lost her seat. Gisella, his girlfriend, first met Jennie a few days later, at a grand May Day concert in Festival Hall, when Jennie was still shattered at the result. Later in May came Vincent's twenty-first birthday. Jennie gave him a garden party. Gisella gave him a Jack Russell terrier, which promptly did an Andrex lavatory-paper commercial in the garden, entangling itself in yards of paper. Jennie loathed the dog and the dog loathed Jennie. She kicked it whenever she could.

A few months later, in September 1970, Vincent and Gisella married—his 'only rebellious act'.[14] By now, Vincent was working on a film, *Cat Weazle*; Gisella, trained at art school, was a designer. Guessing all too correctly Jennie's reaction, they did not tell her they were getting married until a few days before; she was horrified. Why marry, Jennie wanted to know, why not live together instead? Gisella was shocked, her parents would have been mortified.

Jennie behaved towards them very badly indeed. She invaded their marriage. She darkly predicted that it would not last—as she told Gisella's parents over lunch while their daughter was still on honeymoon. 'Our young Romeo and Juliet have for the present four feet planted firmly in mid-air . . . My worry is that although Vincent is a charming youngster, whom I dearly love, he lives too much in a fantasy world . . . and I am concerned for your young daughter's happiness.'[15] Jennie unhesitatingly used her influence and her money to indulge those fantasies, and bind him to her. When Vincent needed money, as he frequently did, Jennie would arrange a large overdraft or loan for him, and subvert any efforts by Gisella to live within their income or take responsibility for their own affairs. Vincent saw no reason to give up the glamorous lifestyle he associated with Jennie. She, for her part, was not going to give up her hold on Vincent without a struggle, and she used her money as a weapon in the fight.

She would remind them of how much she had given them and how much they owed her. She would ring Vincent at any hour. Early of a Sunday morning, she would demand that he come over with a packet of Rothmans and a newspaper, or butter and a bottle of gin. When she had had too much to drink, she would spend long hours on the phone ranting and shouting. Vincent was patient, Gisella understandably resentful. If Vincent misbehaved, Gisella would blame Jennie for his upbringing, Jennie, in turn, would blame Gisella for her effect on him. At parties, Jennie would introduce Vincent and then 'thingy his wife'. Bettina liked Gisella very much; but those friends of Jennie who disapproved of Vincent snubbed his wife.

Gisella had inherited Jennie with Vincent, and although she became fond of her, she never liked her; she judged that there was not much to like. Jennie, she thought, was not a 'good' person, because she bought people, with money, with a job; she used them; and then discarded them. It was a bleak (and inevitably one-sided) judgement from Jennie's surrogate daughter-in-law, but an imperious Jennie caused the young Gisella much pain, as Jennie in turn worked out her own pain at losing Vincent.

Jennie became more reconciled to the marriage when their daughters were born. The elder one reminded Jennie of the young Vincent. (Aged three, she went with her parents to one of Mervyn Stockwood's parties. The Bishop upset wine on his robes. The child piped up: 'Oh Mervyn you've spilt your drink all down your party frock.') To the children Jennie seemed sometimes fairy godmother and sometimes (when she had been drinking) the wicked witch.

When the marriage ended in the early 1980s, Vincent moved back to Chester Row, to Jennie's transparent delight; he had come home to her. Jennie's engagement diaries chart his every movement—'V. sleeps in—V. sleeps out—V. returns—V. [crossed out]'—in obsessional detail. Within a year, however, Vincent remarried, this time to an American, and followed his work to the States. If Jennie had been horrified by Vincent's first marriage, she was devastated by his second, which all too literally—and irrevocably—took Vincent away from her. She was heartbroken, recalls Bettina. Her health was now too poor for her to contemplate visits to the

States and Vincent's film-making brought him back only occasionally to see Jennie. She continued to sell her assets to help Vincent buy a house, pay school fees, fund his career. As she said to Arnold when he remonstrated with her, Vincent would get it when she died; she was happy for him to have it while she was alive.[16]

She lived to see Vincent win his Emmy and Montreux film awards. Gisella faithfully visited Jennie every month or two bringing the children with her, and sat with Bettina through the night at Westminster Hospital when Jennie broke her hip. When Gisella remarried, Jennie was supportive and affectionate. 'Do you mind?' 'No, very good.' Now that Gisella was no longer Jennie's rival as Vincent's wife, they settled into a wary but amicable relationship.

*

Other friendships filled out these years. Jennie loved staying with Italian friends in Fiesole, where she rested, read, lay in the sun, and was allowed her privacy.[17] The Mackies took her to Scotland; Arnold Goodman and Keith Jeffery escorted her to arts events. Michael Foot relived old times as he completed his second volume of Nye's life. And she gave her friends warm support, as one by one they too were widowed.

A more equivocal, and competitive, friendship developed with Angela Fox. After Jennie had sold Asheridge, she looked for a country cottage. Angela Fox had a garden cottage at Cuckfield, which Jennie rented for two years in the mid-1970s. Vincent and Gisella spent summer weekends with Jennie. According to Angela Fox in her wickedly funny memoirs,[18] their weekends were full of sound and fury, if not from noisy friends and fast cars, then from the rows that ended their marriage. As their marriage was, at the time, happy and lasted another seven years, and as Angela Fox miscounted their children (and gave them a spare one), her account may be judged unreliable. None the less, she understood Jennie's lonely arrogance and approved of her defiance. 'We would wander together in my part of the garden telling each other how happy we were. We were lying.' Each morning, Jennie would 'totter' across the courtyard to Angela's for coffee, 'wearing an old-fashioned black bathing dress. As far as I know, she had never been near the sea or a pool. And very, very shabby, immensely high-heeled white sandals that had seen better days.' The lease ended in tears, and Jennie went back to Chester Row.

The most significant—and controversial—friendship Jennie developed during the 1970s was with Indira Gandhi. Jennie's and Nye's interest in India went back to before the war and the struggle for independence. They had warmly supported Nehru's policy of non-alignment. On Nye's death,

Nehru had set up a visiting fellowship in his memory. In 1964 Jennie sent a message on Nehru's 75th birthday: 'An India socialist, democratic and secular was his great dream. This is still India's challenge and hope.'[19] In 1973 Jennie went back to India for three weeks with Michael Foot and Jill Craigie. At the end of 1975 she returned to deliver the first Krishna Menon Memorial lecture, and stayed a month. She crossed the subcontinent nine times by plane, spending every night in a different hotel. Her notes record the 'jostling of centuries' in the morning street markets, and the splendour of India's monuments, its forts, carvings, and mausoleums. In a typical day she might visit a weaving factory, inspect a school, tour the local museum, have a working lunch with a chief minister, applaud a performance of traditional dance, and be shown around a rural community development project, before, in the evening, giving a talk about the Open University. It was a punishing schedule for someone over 70 years of age.

Indira Gandhi joined her on the tour. They admired each other deeply—two outstanding socialist women. Their friendship ripened, and they became, says Bettina, 'almost like sisters', bantering affectionately with each other. Gifts of saris were made into stunning evening dresses (held together with safety pins); a silver and amber necklace given her by Mrs Gandhi was one of the few pieces of jewellery that Jennie wore. When Mrs Gandhi visited London for the seven-month festival of Indian arts in 1982, Jennie was at her side.

Nehru's daughter had become Prime Minister in 1966. Aiding Bangladesh (East Pakistan) against (West) Pakistan brought her in June 1971 a landslide election victory. However, in June 1975 the High Court disqualified Mrs Gandhi from office because she had improperly used Government facilities in the campaign. As she clung on to power, protests mounted. The opposition leader, the revered J. P. Narayan, called on the police and the army not to repress public protest and demonstrations; on 25 June 1975 Mrs Gandhi declared a state of emergency. Jennie, an instinctive dissenter, in a letter to another hardened dissenter, Milovan Djilas, rallied immediately and fiercely to her defence:

> I am no authority, but on first principles I give my confidence to Indira Gandhi. When a situation had arisen in which the troops were incited to revolt, the workers not to work, and when a small minority in Congress were bringing Government business to a standstill, a responsible Prime Minister had to take draconian measures. Some of the pious protesters in our relatively cosy island would have been the first to demand the imprisonment of any British Opposition leader who incited the troops to revolt.[20]

*

Jennie was always loyal to her friends. She also believed that the British press was giving a very one-sided account of the emergency. Supporters of Mrs Gandhi late in 1975 founded the Indo-British Association[21] and endowed the Krishna Menon Memorial lecture. In the *Observer* in April 1976 Jennie demanded 'A Fair Deal for Mrs Gandhi'. To be pure but impotent, she wrote, quoting Nye, was the luxury of armchair commentators; she had no patience with the pink conscience.[22] Mrs Gandhi had to suspend democracy in order to save it. She alone stood between the country and its collapse into chaos. The West had done nothing to relieve India's dire poverty which sapped its democracy. 'Don't preach sermons to India', Jennie concluded.

Observer readers were outraged. Thousands of Indian protesters were being detained without trial, including Narayan, who was seriously ill with diabetes. The press was censored, trade unions broken, Parliament had acquiesced in its own curtailment, and Mrs Gandhi had put herself beyond the law—although even her critics conceded that the emergency was only mildly authoritarian by Third World standards, and had wide popular support. Freedom was indivisible.[23] Jennie now rather thought it was. She took her line from Nye, who had argued in *In Place of Fear*:

> What is the use of taunting underdeveloped countries with the absence of democratic institutions if these can survive only by a slower rate of economic progress or by help from outside? When we were at their economic level we were hanging children and driving them into mines and into the mills and organising labour camps in the countryside. Freedom is the by-product of economic surplus . . . If democratic institutions are to be helped to take root in the Orient, it can be done, not by sending professors to teach the virtues of democratic constitutions, but by sending the means to raise their material standards. Man must first live before he can live abundantly.[24]

She sent Mrs Gandhi a copy of *In Place of Fear* to cheer her up, worried about 'the appalling physical and nervous strain you are having imposed on you'. She sought further briefing from the Indian High Commissioner, who, not surprisingly, was 'most appreciative' of her efforts. Jennie was prepared even to defend Sanjay Gandhi's hated sterilization programme. She replied to one Indian correspondent: 'Of course at the base is the outrage caused by family planning, and the abrasive way it appears to have been carried out. Alas, whoever is Prime Minister of India must solve this problem, or the poor will continue to become poorer. Personally I do not see how it can be done by entirely voluntary methods.' She insisted to

Victor Reuther that 'from all I know and have seen she took the only possible step to avoid chaos when she declared the emergency'.[25]

Jennie and Michael Foot rightly predicted that Mrs Gandhi would soon lift the state of emergency. Indira Gandhi kept Jennie briefed: 'The emergency is being gradually but steadily liberalised, not always with good results.' And then: 'The talk of the town is that I am sure to be murdered since there seems to be no other way of suppressing me!'[26] In February 1977 Mrs Gandhi held free elections, which she lost, but came back to power in 1979. In 1980 Jennie wrote to her jubilantly: 'Your good friend Michael Foot may well be our next Prime Minister. Some of us had to take him by the scruff of his neck and force him into opposing Denis Healey for the leadership of the Party.' Jennie visited her again in 1983, though by then even Jennie admitted that, aged almost 80, the strain of travelling around India was getting too much. When in 1984 Mrs Gandhi was assassinated, Jennie was devastated. In a book of commemorative essays she states simply: 'I loved and admired Indira Gandhi more than any other world leader.'[27]

*

When Jennie attended the Lords, her colleagues noted that she was endlessly scribbling. She was drafting *My Life with Nye*.

In 1970 Archie Lush had stayed with her. Ten years had passed since Nye's death. Tredegar people, he reported, 'hungry for knowledge about Ni, have thought that because I have not given interviews, written articles, a book or had a book ghosted for me, there was something wrong between us'. She was wounded—Tredegar was always harsh on Jennie—but it made her reflect. When Nye was alive, they had fiercely protected their privacy. When he died, she had refused to 'sell' him. Now, she slowly decided that it was 'wrong of me to be so reserved, so unready to talk about him to friends, who had loved him', and to allow those with little knowledge of him to weave their fictions around him. Michael had written superbly about the public man; she would write about the private Nye. 'Ni is so much with me, such an indestructible part of me that I know now I cannot escape the pain—maybe in the end, the release—of setting down much about him that so few know.' It had taken her a long time to decide to write 'as candidly as I have done', she wrote in her final chapter of *My Life with Nye*. 'I hope I have made the right decision.'[28]

The reviewers thought so. Her memoir was sparkling and outspoken (*Daily Express*), intelligent, often penetrating, gossipy, tough, lively and warm (Gwyn Williams in the *Guardian*). Jill Craigie loved her 'wicked perceptions of human frailties' (*The Times*); Edna Healey wrote that Jennie was a good hater whose hate never became corrosive (*Sunday Times*). The *Tablet* put it well:

This is in a good sense an 'amateur' book, meaning that it is both loving and non-professional, written out of love and loyalty and straight from the heart, without too many corrections (one suspects) or too much neatness . . . [It has] the passionate personal commitment that on the whole makes good reading, a moving narrative. Above all it is on the side of humanity.[29]

The politicians and political historians were perhaps a shade disappointed that they did not learn more of Nye's political life; several thought that the best bit of the book was Jennie's early years, her life without Nye. Fenner Brockway rejoiced that those who had always depicted Nye as a rough, tough, uncouth, intolerant rebel, would come to know him as a man who loved poetry, philosophy, and mountains, and who found his happiness in human fellowship. The *Economist*, in an interesting but unsigned review, thought it the story of one powerful personality dominated by another even more powerful; that Jennie resented what she also loved, and that for her own sanity turned that resentment outwards on to Nye's foes. Ben Pimlott recognized the problem for Jennie of maintaining some living space; her book was 'a monument not only to her courage but also to a kind of victory. If he was a visionary, she was a life-force. Arrogant, extrovert, wilful, generous like him, she was less egocentric and more capable of humility . . . [it was] an account of unblinkered affection . . . full of gaiety, faith and a love of doing.' And, said a fellow MP Phillip Whitehead: 'This account of how a proud, stubborn, impulsive couple stayed the course, sustained by the home they made together, is no bad survival manual.'[30]

When Penguin produced a paperback version, Jennie was required to publicize it in interviews. These were not always the mutual admiration sessions her publishers hoped for. Reporters emerged from Chester Row as often cowed as charmed. The *Birmingham Post* piece opened with Jennie saying: 'What a stupid question', when asked whether the parliamentary process would survive; on reflection, her interviewer rather agreed it was. 'That's a damned stupid question', she told a young woman from the *Sunday Standard* who asked whether she was a feminist: 'I am the oldest living example of liberated womanhood.' Had she not walked out of dinner parties that asked ladies to withdraw?[31]

The book brought Jennie a sense of financial security.[32] She sent out dozens of copies to friends and their appreciative letters lifted her spirits.

Yet writing it, and writing especially about the last three years of Nye's life, says Elizabeth Thomas, 'emotionally tired her out'. Among her papers is a note to herself: 'Depressed—feeling weak & remember Nye quoting from Yeats—"The years like great black oxen tread me down & I am broken by their passing feet."' From 1980 Jennie, now aged 76, seems to enter old age. She became noticeably more frail. Within a year, Vincent's marriage began to break up, and on remarriage he went to live in the States. Jennie was bereft.

Her appearances in the Lords dropped off. When she did attend, she was still scribbling notes and jottings, for her second volume, the years after 1960. Scattered among the scrawls of many years were possible titles, which chart her moods and her reading of her life after Nye:

It takes longer than you think	In love Again
Roses in December	My life line
Love in December	No other way
Many a green Isle	Looking forward
Lest We forget	Naked to laughter
One lovely June day	Worth Fighting for.
Sunshine and Shadow	Time Remembered
One more summer	No holier than thou
It is hard to say	All over again
Head above water	I did it my way
Love in late December	First and last love
Out of the wind and rain	My worldly wealth
Passionate commitment	There was always love
Worth fighting for	Nothing to worry about
Changing life styles	In Love again (a possible title)
The best of Life	The long enchantment
Times Revenge	How lucky can you be?
In place of pity	With all our faults
In place of grandeur	Good luck or good guidance

One can see why many of them occurred to her. A reference to *In Place of Fear*, thoughts of Nye's last weeks (One lovely June day; One more summer), a phrase from her grandfather (It takes longer than you think) or Nye (All over again), a popular song (I did it my way), a political phrase (Worth fighting for; Passionate commitment; No other way). And those titles of late love—Love in December, First and last love, Roses in December, In love Again (twice), Love in late December—which were for a book on the years *after* Nye's death. Jennie never wrote this second book, but left hundreds of pages of disjointed musings and reworked stories, undated and often barely legible, a sentence, a paragraph, occasionally a few pages of diary. It became compulsive.

She began to come off committees, such as ABSA; she resigned as a trustee of the Milton Keynes Foundation in 1980, and, significantly, as trustee of the Open University early in 1982. She sidestepped one row. *Tribune* was edited from 1982 by Chris Mullin, who was critical of both Michael Foot and Neil Kinnock. Jennie placed her shareholding with John Silkin, who fought to bring the paper back into centre-left politics. *Tribune* had become 'too extremist' for her taste, she said, but she no longer had the stamina for a fight.[33]

She refused invitations to literary festivals out of London, then to art exhibitions in London, and a year later to receptions at friendly embassies. One of her last appearances in the Lords was to vote on the government's bill to abolish the Greater London Council in July 1984. She gave few interviews, and resolutely refused, as she always had done, the innumerable requests from importunate academics wanting help with their theses. Her political world was closing down. She still managed a sprinkling of treats. She went to Brecht's *Threepenny Opera* at the National Theatre, saw Constance Cummings open in a new play, visited Keith Jeffery's country home, applauded Arnold Goodman at the Gala Dinner given for him when he retired from the ENO.

As she became more frail, friends had to come to her. From the time of Nye's death she had been troubled by an arthritic hip, and in the mid-1970s by a cracked femur that came from falling off her garden wall while pruning her yellow roses. She defied it all by refusing to use a stick, but limped into the Lords on the arm of John Mackie and stomped round India on an umbrella.

With *My Life with Nye* finished, her health rapidly deteriorated. She grew old quickly. In a series of accidents, she dislocated her hip, fell off the edge of the bath and hurt her spine, injured an ankle, and fell and cracked two ribs. More serious worries threatened. She developed breast cancer like her mother and grandmother before her: 'So must get my affairs in order', she noted calmly. 'It is twenty years since I have had a life of my own. Since then have just wandered in and out of other people's lives. At seventy-six I have had a long enough innings.'[34] She had surgery, but avoided a mastectomy. She also developed stomach pains, like Nye, and suspected the worst, but unlike Nye she had an ulcer cured by medication. She became a familiar patient to her local Pimlico GPs, who thought of her fondly 'as the wife of the founder'. She would go to the surgery and wait her turn patiently, chatting away; on one occasion she lent her doctor a copy of Michael Foot's biography of Nye.[35]

Jennie was brave and offhand about it all. She never complained, never confessed to pain, there is not a shred of self-pity in her notes or letters. She is gutsy and optimistic. She determinedly noted 'the attractions of old age. I can read, write, listen to music, see more of our family and friends.'[36] She was asked by a journalist whether she was lonely. 'Lonely?' she asks incredulously. 'My dear, it's my privacy I have to fight for.'[37] Even Jennie's fortitude was tried, however, when cataracts developed on both eyes, and for four months in 1984 she could not read the biographies she enjoyed or see well enough to go out. In a brave understatement, she found this 'infinitely tiresome'. She listened to hours and hours of radio. The delight when her vision was partially restored rings through letters to friends.

By now, she no longer used the whole house. The stairs were beyond her. Bill and Bettina brought over a single bed, and she moved downstairs. Her basement was roomy, but had no central heating. Jennie called it her summer cottage, her garden room. She lived her last years in a couple of rooms full of books that she could no longer read, with a television set that she no longer looked at, but the windows were wide open on to her lovely small garden.[38] She fed the birds and they would come and perch on her head. She had good days and good times. In February 1985 she wondered whether she would see the spring and the summer; but with the coming of sunshine she felt well enough to go in May to *Pravda* at the National Theatre ('far too long') and on to the Garrick for supper ('far below standard'). She was clearly on form. Bettina managed to get her to Lochgelly for a last visit.

Each birthday Arnold would bring flowers, cake, and champagne; each year she seems slightly surprised to be still alive. She had one of her last birthdays in bed, surrounded by Arnold Goodman and friends. After a fair amount of champagne, Jennie decided she would use the bathroom. She got out of bed stark naked—she never slept in nightclothes. Her guests turned scarlet. Jennie was genuinely puzzled: 'I was born with nothing on, I will go out with nothing on.' She had vivid recurring dreams of Frank, who had died fifty-two years before. She thought of Nye and his last years. She told Michael, as she had done so many times before: 'At 80 I have no regrets. I would make the same choices over again.'[39]

Indira Gandhi's assassination killed whatever dwindling interest she still had in political events and public affairs. The world was too evil, 'it is a terrible place', and she would shut it out. Those loyal friends who came to her basement now found she wanted to talk only about Vincent and his children, an enthusiasm they did not share. Arnold Goodman, himself scarcely able to walk, would bump himself down the stairs one at a time to keep company with her. Bettina and Bill managed, with the aid of a home help. Jennie appreciated what they did but had no compunction at all about depending on them. When the Staffords moved into a small flat and Bill retired from his hospital job, 'Bettina and he [will] have more time than ever to look after me', she wrote to a friend. 'They like coming here and would be bored stiff just looking at one another in their little home.' She refused to be effusive about their care, and they did not expect her to be, yet she knew her debt: 'I have Bettina and Bill to save me from the horrors of having to engage a stranger to look after me . . . They look after me like a baby.'[40] Jennie was spared the indignity she most feared, of being nursed by strangers in a residential home.

Even so, those last few years were miserable for her, and for her friends. She was desperately lonely. The basement got gloomier, the rooms colder, the house shabbier, and Jennie in her dressing-gown more unkempt. She could barely walk, and only barely see. She was depressed and in considerable pain. She kept both at bay by drinking heavily; after eleven in the morning, friends knew not to phone. Jennie retained a mordant humour about the indignities of it all. Each Christmas, as the cards came flooding in, she would look at them morosely, and they would look back in reproach. '"Before my time. A Welshman wasn't he", was the comment of a young plumber when I gave him a copy of *My Life with Nye*' she noted ruefully.[41]

In the autumn of 1988 Bettina and Bill went away for a much-needed holiday, and the friend who looked after Jennie had to send her into St Thomas's for care. When Bettina brought her home, Jennie had pneumonia, and they both knew she was dying. Jennie told Bettina she would wait for her 'up there' though she doubted that they would both get in. She slipped in and out of consciousness. Bettina sat by her and stroked her hand. 'Do you think I am a bloody cat?' came from the bed. The doctor assured Bettina she would not give up until Vincent arrived from the States. He flew in overnight, on the plane writing a prose poem for her, 'Tomorrow is a New Day', which he read to her. Later that evening, a cheerful Jennie sat up in bed and asked Bettina for a drink. Gin, and colour it, no more, just colour it. Bettina handed Jennie her martini, and with a glass in her hand and a smile on her face, Jennie died.

*

Jennie's ashes joined Nye's, scattered at the same spot on the Welsh hillside. It was grey and overcast. Only a few friends were there. A distressed Bettina huddled against Michael Foot, who looked gaunt and sombre; Derek and Muriel Davis came over from Cannock. Jennie had asked Vincent to say: 'Peace, perfect peace, with my loved ones far away.' And as the wind whirled around and picked up her ashes, he added, 'Fly, darling, fly.'[42]

NOTES

Chapter 1

1. J. Lee, *Tomorrow is a New Day* (1939), 38. For ILP views, Christian, internationalist, pacifist, and socialist, see R. Dowse, *Left in the Centre, The Independent Labour Party 1893–1940* (1966), ch. 2.
2. Bevan to Beaverbrook, 14 May 1935.
3. Interview Mrs S. Saemann (Suse).
4. Interview G. R. Strauss.
5. Lee, *Tomorrow*, 37–9, 53–4. See also J. Lee, *My Life with Nye* (1980), 28–9.
6. J. Lee, *Labour Gazette*, May 1949.
7. Lee, *My Life*, 18.
8. Interview Mrs S. Saemann.
9. *Lochgelly Times*, 7 Jan. 1931.
10. *People's Journal*, 21 Oct. 1961.
11. Interview Mrs S. Saemann.
12. Interview Jill Craigie, Doreen Andrews.
13. JL papers, diary (14 Aug. 1924).
14. Interview Mary Docherty.
15. C. Harvie, 'Before the Breakthrough, 1886–1922', in I. Donnachie *et al.* (eds.), *Forward! Labour Politics in Scotland, 1888–1988* (1989).
16. Of the 1,191 trials for conscientious objectors, 805 were members of the ILP and most of the rest were Quakers. A. Marwick, *Clifford Allen. The Open Conspirator* (1964), 45.
17. M. Docherty, *A Miner's Lass* (1992), 27–9. Mary Docherty, four years younger than Jennie, moved on from the Cowdenbeath ILP Sunday School to the (Communist) Proletarian Sunday School, which she much preferred. It was less formal, more 'working class and down to earth'. Above all, it did not bother with minutes of the meeting.
18. Benn Levy, Introduction, *My Great Journey* (1939); J. Lee, *My Life*, 26. Benn Levy was a dramatist and Labour MP, and husband of Jennie's friend, the actress Constance Cummings.
19. Interview Mrs S. Saemann.
20. JL papers, MS autobiographical writings.
21. Ibid., School reports.
22. Andrew Carnegie had donated $10 million to the universities of Scotland in 1901, much of which was spent on financial assistance to students. About half the women in Edinburgh's Faculty of Arts received Carnegie grants, and all those from poorer families studying to become teachers. A. Logan Turner, *The History of the University of Edinburgh, 1883–1938*, *passim.*

23. JL papers, French diary (July, Dec. 1921, Jan., July 1922); fictional jottings, 'A Greater Right', 'The Soul of a Woman'.
24. Lee, *Tomorrow*, 69–70.
25. Logan Turner, *University of Edinburgh*, *passim*. The 1919 Education (Scotland) Act permitted the new local education authorities to grant aid to students: women were the main beneficiaries, able to acquire funding to teach in the higher grade schools. Three-quarters of the women students and half of the men in the Arts Faculty were prospective teachers. 'The Arts Faculty has thus tended to become a place of training for one particular vocation'; loc. cit., 168.
26. Lee, *Tomorrow*, 78.
27. Ibid., 76–80.
28. JL papers, diary (23 May 1924).
29. Interview Mrs S. Saemann.
30. Albert Mansbridge came out of the co-operative movement. In the years before the war he had founded the WEA, drawing on the Christian socialists and progressives of Edwardian Oxford as tutors and lecturers. Most of the inter-war initiatives in adult education can be traced to him. See J. F. C. Harrison, *Learning and Living, 1790–1960* (1961), 261–6. The line went through R. H. Tawney to Michael Young and the Open University (OU).
31. Anon. (the last page of the letter is missing) to Mrs Helen Crawfurd, 17 March 1922. JL papers.
32. JL papers, diary (7 Jan. 1924).
33. Interview J. Craigie.
34. Interview Lord (Neil) Carmichael.
35. D. Daiches, *Sir Herbert Grierson, 1866–1960*, Proceedings of the British Academy (1960).
36. Lee, *Tomorrow*, 75.
37. Interview Mrs S. Saemann.
38. *The Student*, 25 Oct., 13 Dec. 1922; Edinburgh University Labour Party (EULP) Minute Book (22 Nov 1922).
39. Interview A. W. McIntosh.
40. EULP Minute Book, *passim*; interview A. W. McIntosh.
41. EULP Minute Book (19 Jan. 1923).
42. *Rebel Student*, June 1923.
43. *The Student*, 7 Nov. 1923. Baldwin had 1,236, Buckmaster 488, Russell 261 votes.
44. JL to Suse, n.d., 1926, 1928.
45. Anon, *Sunday Mail*, n.d., Sept. 1934.
46. Lee, *Tomorrow*, p. 81 ff.
47. Anon, *Sunday Mail*, n.d. Sept. 1934.
48. Aberdeen, St Andrews, and Edinburgh universities (but not Glasgow) all postponed examinations to help the 'volunteers' who were breaking the strike. I. MacDougall, 'Some Aspects of the 1926 General Strike in Scotland', in I. MacDougall (ed.), *Essays in Scottish Labour History* (1979), 181–2. Interview A. W. McIntosh; *The Student*, 2 June 1926.
49. Lee, *Tomorrow*, 83.
50. JL to Suse, 21 June 1926.
51. JL to Suse, n.d. (May 1926); see also *Tomorrow*, 107–11; *My Life*, 47.

52. JL to Suse, 13 Sept., 23 Nov. 1926.
53. The *West Fife Echo*, 23 June, 7 July 1926 (I owe this and many later references to the *West Fife Echo* and the *Wishaw Press* to the kindness of Mr Jim Campbell of the Central & West Fife Local History Preservation).
54. S. Macintyre, *Little Moscows. Communism and Working-class Militancy in Inter-war Britain* (1980). Between 1924 and 1927 the number of miners employed in Fife fell from 30,089 to 22,546, and by 1931 there were only 27 pits working compared with 64 in 1924. loc. cit., 63.
55. JL to Suse, n.d. (autumn 1925).
56. J. Masterton, head teacher, Foulford School, 20 Sept. 1923 (JL papers).
57. Lee, *Tomorrow*, 96.
58. *Lochgelly Times*, 29 Feb. 1928.
59. JL to Suse, 29 Dec. 1926.
60. *Lochgelly Times*, 29 Feb., 7 March 1928; Docherty, *A Miner's Lass*, 53 ff. M. Docherty to the author, 11 Apr. 1995. See also Jennie's account of the same incident in Lee, *My Life*, 56–7, JL to Suse, 12 Jan., 25 Apr. 1928. She left the story out of her *Tomorrow*. More generally on ILP and CP rivalry, see R. Page Arnot, *A History of the Scottish Miners* (1955), ch. 8; R. Selkirk, 'Fife Miners and the Communist Party', *The Communist Review* (March 1929); J. Macdougall, 'The Scottish Coalminer', *The Nineteenth Century* (Dec. 1927).
61. J. Mann, *Woman in Parliament*, 104.
62. JL papers, undated MSS.
63. *West Fife Echo*, 12 Jan., 17 Aug. 1927; JL to Suse, 29 Dec. 1926, 29 March 1927; *Lochgelly Times*, 29 Feb. 1928.
64. F. Brockway, *Inside the Left* (1941), 185–6.
65. C. P. Trevelyan, a former Liberal, had joined the Union of Democratic Control during the war, and then the ILP. He was twice Minister of Education, resigning from the Labour Cabinet in 1930. See A. J. A. Morris, *C. P. Trevelyan 1870–1958* (1977).
66. JL to Suse, 17 June 1927; interview Mrs S. Saemann. T'ang returned to China, married a Western-educated Chinese girl in 1931, and continued writing. When revolution convulsed the country, he was imprisoned.
67. JL to Suse, 25 Apr. 1928; Lee, *Tomorrow*, 120.
68. The 1918 Reform Act confined women's suffrage to local government electors or the wives of local government electors over the age of 30. The Equal Suffrage Act of 1928 swept away these restrictions in time for the 1929 general election.

Chapter 2

1. JL papers, diary (11 Aug. 1924).
2. Labour Party constituency organization was weak in Scotland, compared to England; instead, miners fought the ILP for the right to nominate to industrial seats. See Gordon Brown, 'The Labour Party and Political Change in Scotland 1918–29', Ph.D. thesis, University of Edinburgh (1981), 394–7.
3. Lee, *Tomorrow*, pp. 112–13. The father of historian Gwyn Williams heard Jennie speak at Dowlais Recreation Ground, and 'was in a trance for a week. My

mother thought of citing the Labour Party as co-respondent', *Guardian*, 20 Nov. 1980.

4. Lee, *My Life*, 86.
5. R. K. Middlemas, *The Clydesiders* (1965). The Clydeside group also included Emmanuel Shinwell, Revd Campbell Stephen, George Buchanan, and Patrick Dollan.
6. *Motherwell Times*, 19 Sept. 1928. Her opponent was Baillie Archibald of Glasgow, the miners' candidate. See Page Arnot, *A History of the Scottish Miners*, 213 ff.
7. *Hansard*, House of Commons, 10 Apr. 1930, col. 2437.
8. It stretched from Cadder in the north, around through New Monklands, down to Shotts and Auchter Water.
9. *New Leader*, 20 June 1930.
10. *New Leader*, 8 March 1929.
11. J. Stevenson and C. Cook, *The Slump. Society and Politics During the Depression*. (1979 edn), 55. The Pilgrim Trust estimated that of the 53,000 men who had been out of work for more than a year in 1929, 38,000 were coal-miners. By mid-1932, when male unemployment had risen to over 25 per cent, in coal-mining it was over 40 per cent.
12. Lee: 15,711; Scone: 9,133; Mitchell: 2,488.
13. *Wishaw Press*, 29 March 1929; *Sunday Mail*, 24 March, 1929.
14. *Lochgelly Times*, 27 March 1929; interview Mrs S. Saemann.
15. Jennie joined a House which already had 4 Labour women MPs: Ellen Wilkinson, Margaret Bondfield, Susan Lawrence, Ruth Dalton; 4 Conservative: Lady Astor, Lady Iveagh, the Duchess of Atholl, Mrs Mabel Philipson; and 1 Liberal: Mrs Runciman.
16. *The Star*, 23 June 1931.
17. *Hansard*, House of Commons, 25 Apr. 1929, cols 1114–19; *Lochgelly Daily Record and Mail*, 4 May 1929; *Lochgelly Times*, 1 May 1929.
18. JL to Frank Wise, 12 Oct. 1930.
19. Interview Joan Lestor.
20. Lee, *Tomorrow*, 127–9. Jennie was contributing to her agent's costs in North Lanark, as well as sending money home. See also E. Picton-Turberville, *Life is Good. An Autobiography* (1939), 186, who had the same problem.
21. Quoted in P. Brookes, *Women at Westminster* (1967) pp. 19–20. Lady Astor had heard Mrs Pankhurst in the States and been much impressed, (interview Jill Craigie). Lady Astor's wit was not always intentional. An MP had asked a question of the Minister of Health about the birth rate, which he thought should rise. 'Lady Astor in a clear penetrating voice said: "Is the Minister aware that in Italy Mussolini coupled with the Pope has been unable to redress the birth rate?"' The House was convulsed. Picton-Turberville, *Life is Good*, 233.
22. *Yorkshire Evening News*, 10 Dec. 1924, qtd in B. Vernon, *Ellen Wilkinson* (1982), 79–80.
23. JL papers, undated MS jottings (1970s).
24. Brookes, *Women at Westminster*, 62–3.
25. See p. 52.

26. P. Graves, *Labour Women. Women in British Working-Class Politics 1918–39* (1994), 81 ff; H. Smith, 'Sex versus Class: British Feminists and the Labour Movement, 1919–29', *The Historian*, 47 (Nov. 1984).
27. M. Pugh, *Women and the Women's Movement in Britain, 1914–1959* (1992), 172, 188.
28. Qtd in B. H. Harrison, 'Women in a Men's House. The Women MPs 1919–45', *The Historical Journal* (1986), 628. This paragraph draws on Brookes, *Women at Westminster.*
29. Mann, *Woman in Parliament*, 18.
30. See Pugh's admirable *Women and the Women's Movement*, ch. 6. See also Harrison, 'Women in a Men's House' for a detailed analysis of women's contributions to Commons debates.
31. *Daily Record*, 10 March 1931.
32. M. A. Hamilton, *Remembering my Good Friends* (1944), 181; L. Manning, *A Life for Education* (1970), 92; E. Wilkinson, *Peeps at Politicians* (1930), 50; L. Hore-Belisha, 'Letters to a Lady', *Daily Express*, 6 Dec. 1929.
33. *Wishaw Press*, 19 July 1929.
34. Vernon, *Ellen Wilkinson*, on which this paragraph draws. The Plebs League was the propaganda voice of the Labour College Movement. See also Jennie's moving obituary of Ellen in *Tribune*, 14 Feb. 1947.
35. *Wishaw Press*, 24 May 1929.
36. Ibid.; 7 Aug. 1931; see also *Hansard*, House of Commons, 12 Feb. 1930, cols 496–500; 10 Apr. 1930, cols 2435–41; 25 June 1931, cols 735–40.
37. Lee: 19,884; Scone: 15,680.
38. ILP Annual Conference Report (1930), 5.
39. See Dowse, *Left in the Centre*, *passim.*
40. *Forward*, 12 June 1920, qtd in Dowse, *Left in the Centre*, 46.
41. The public relief works found jobs for only 60,000, the trade-union bill restoring contracting-out was savaged by the Liberals, the education bill thrown out by the Lords. Trevelyan was Minister for Education; Jennie (aged 25) was one of a handful from whom he hoped to choose his under-secretary. C. Trevelyan to Lady Trevelyan, 6 June 1929.
42. *North Lanark Labour News*, Oct. 1929, 3.
43. Peter Clarke notes that the well-thumbed Treasury copy of the Liberal *We Can Conquer Unemployment* had scribbled on its cover the Treasury's verdict: 'Extravagance, Inflation, Bankruptcy'. P. Clarke, *The Keynesian Revolution in the Making, 1924–1936* (1988), frontispiece.
44. On Hobson, see H. N. Brailsford. *The Life-work of J. A. Hobson* (1947); J. A. Hobson, *Confessions of an Economic Heretic* (1938); P. Clarke's seminal *Liberals and Social Democrats* (1978), 46–54 and *passim*. Hobson was no Marxist; he was concerned with the the relations of distribution but not the relations of production on which they might be held to rest. He thought that democracy could 'control capitalism' (when, of course, it was not being jingoistic). It was left unclear whether the Living Wage could be obtained within a reformed capitalist society or whether, as Jennie assumed, it required the supersession of capitalism. Clarke, loc. cit., 96–7.
45. See H. N. Brailsford *et al.*, *The Living Wage* (1926), 20–6.

46. Her private reading list had included two of Hobson's major works, *The Evolution of Modern Capitalism* (1894), *The Industrial System* (1909), as well as his journalism.
47. JL to Suse, n.d. (Sept 1925).
48. Clarke, *Liberals and Social Democrats*, 234.
49. With the help of a circle of younger Cambridge economists, Keynes was to feel his way later to the multiplier principle implied by a massive public-works programme. Had the concept of the multiplier been more fully developed, it might have refuted the argument that such programmes cost too much or that unemployment benefit was preferable because it was cheaper. What mattered in reducing unemployment was the effect of government spending on demand, not the intrinsic value of the projects on which government money was spent. 'A living wage' also required a concept of the multiplier; with hindsight, it seems unlikely that it could have done much to alleviate unemployment without generating a flight of capital.
50. Hobson, *Confessions*, 126; *Hansard*, House of Commons, 21 Sept. 1931, col. 1342.
51. *Hansard*, House of Commons, 6 July 1931, col. 1777.
52. The 1927 Trades Dispute Act, passed after the General Strike, banned sympathy strikes and required trade-unionists to opt in to the political levy. This had reduced the Labour Party's income from affiliation fees by a quarter.
53. The Liberals in 1929 had won over 5 million votes (23.6% of the total), but only 59 seats. They wanted PR, but the Labour Party only offered the alternative vote (AV), which was not proportional, but would give the Liberals some extra seats. PR would allow the Liberals to fight the whole country with 200 candidates. They could remain a national party despite limited finance. See A. Thorpe, *The British General Election of 1931* (1991), 59. The ILP did not believe any measure of electoral reform should be pursued 'while the social condition of the people is so bad', ILP Annual Conference Report, Scarborough (April 1931), 80.
54. Qtd in D. Marquand, *Ramsay MacDonald* (1977), 529.
55. R. Skidelsky's phrase, in his splendid *Politicians and the Slump, The Labour Government of 1929–1931* (1994 edn.), 395, to which this account is heavily indebted.
56. *Hansard*, House of Commons, 14 Apr. 1930.
57. See R. McKibbin, 'The Economic Policy of the Second Labour Government, 1929–1931', *Past and Present*, 68 (Aug. 1975); R. Middleton, *Towards the Managed Economy. Keynes, the Treasury and the Fiscal Debate of the 1930s* (1985), in defence of Snowden. More recent experience suggests that expansion of demand or devaluation could not alone have solved the fundamental problems. However, £100 million of loan-financed public works, it is argued, could have generated up to 500,000 jobs—not a trivial number—at an additional cost to the budget of £30–40 million. See W. R. Garside, *British Unemployment 1919–39* (1990), 373. See also A. Thorpe, *Britain in the 1930s* (1992) and Robert Skidelsky's introduction to the 1994 edition of *Politicians and the Slump*, where he reviews the arguments.
58. *Hansard*, House of Commons, 31 Oct. 1930, col. 422.
59. *Hansard*, House of Commons, 11 Feb. 1930, col. 273 ff. Germany produced

26 cwt a man-shift on a shorter working day, Poland 27½ cwt for the same working day, Britain could only manage 21 cwt a man-shift.

60. *Hansard*, House of Commons, 6 July 1931, col. 1775.
61. McKibbin, 'Economic Policy', 112. The deficit was £75 million in 1930, £100 million in 1931.
62. JL to Frank Wise, 12 Oct. 1930. Mosley resigned from government in May 1930, lost his case at the Party Conference in October, issued his manifesto in December, signed by seventeen MPs, including Nye Bevan and John Strachey, and in February 1931 announced the formation of his New Party. He was expelled from the Labour Party. Only four Labour MPs, including his wife and Strachey, followed him. For an account of Nye's position, see M. Foot, *Aneurin Bevan*, vol. 1 (1975 edn.), 121 ff. For Jennie's, see her *Tomorrow*, 149–50.
63. Skidelsky, *Politicians and the Slump*, 82. The NI Fund was financed by one-third each from employers, employees, and the Exchequer. The Treasury had to meet the deficit. A man received 17*s*. (85p) for himself, 9*s*. (45p) for his wife, 2*s*. (10p) a child, or 32*s*. (£1.60) a week for a family of five.
64. MacDonald went on: 'The simple fact is that our population is too great for our trade . . . I sit in my room in Downing Street alone and in silence. The cup has been put to my lip—and it is empty.' qtd in Marquand, *Ramsay MacDonald*, 537. The trade unions had no alternative agenda. 'Their acceptance of unemployment as the price to be paid for maintaining wages made them less interested in increasing employment than in increasing unemployment benefits, thus complementing the "palliative" notions of the parliamentary Socialists.' Skidelsky, *Politicians and the Slump*, 395.
65. *Economic Journal*, March 1917.
66. *The Living Wage*, 33.
67. *Hansard*, House of Commons, 3 Dec. 1929, cols 2243–9.
68. Lord Snell, *Men, Movements and Myself* (1938), 230 ff.
69. *Hansard*, House of Commons, 3 Dec. 1929, col. 2316.
70. Lee, *Tomorrow*, 144.
71. ILP Annual Conference Report, Birmingham (April 1930), 7.
72. *Hansard*, House of Commons, 15 July 1931, cols 667–82. By March 1932, over 80 per cent of married women's claims and 75 per cent of seasonal workers claims were being disallowed. See also loc. cit., 21 July 1931, when Jennie tried to secure the right to benefit for married women whose husbands were unable to work, and for widows. One difficulty, though the minister did not trouble herself to explain it, was that it was hard to apply the 'available for work' test when married women were not mobile.
73. The May Committee forecast a deficit of £120 million by 1932 on a budget in 1931 of some £800m.; to balance the budget it said would require increased taxes of £24 million and economies of £96 million, of which £66 million was to come from unemployment expenditure. The deficit was a construct of accountancy. It treated £55 million to the Sinking Fund, and £40 million of borrowing for the NI Fund, as current expenditure, contrary to Treasury practice.
74. *New Leader*, 7 Aug. 1931.
75. Thorpe, *Britain in the 1930s*, 85–6

76. Picton-Turberville, *Life is Good*, 198
77. Snowden noted laconically in his autobiography a few years later: 'The suspension of the gold standard had not the serious consequences which might have been expected' (*An Autobiography*, 977). Frank Wise had been one of the few economists to query the need to keep it. It benefited rentiers and the City. *Hansard*, House of Commons, 10 Sept. 1931, cols 332–41.
78. *Hansard*, House of Commons, 21 Sept. 1931, cols 1339–45.
79. JL to Frank Wise, 27 Nov. 1930.
80. Thorpe, *General Election of 1931*, *passim*, to which this account is indebted. Nearly half of Labour's 1929 seats were won on a minority vote in three-party contests, and a fifth of its seats were vulnerable to a tiny swing.
81. Later a Deputy Speaker and then Lord Kilmany.
82. JL to C. P. Trevelyan, n.d. (Feb.? 1931).
83. Ibid., 13 Oct. 1931; JL to Frank Wise, 12 Oct. 1930, 2 Oct. 1931.
84. Scurr's amendment was carried by 284 votes to 251, Jan. 1931. Sir Charles Trevelyan resigned as Minister for Education. John Scurr (MP for Stepney) had been a Poplar councillor and poor law guardian, imprisoned with Lansbury in 1921. Lee, *My Life*, 81; see also Gordon Brown, *Maxton* (1986), 238.
85. JL to Frank Wise, 22 Oct. 1931.
86. JL to Frank Wise, 29 Oct. 1931.
87. Jean Mann organized a public meeting of 600 of them to meet Jennie, but she failed to turn up. Mann, *Woman in Parliament*, 105.
88. C. P. Trevelyan to Lady Trevelyan, 23 Oct. 1931.
89. JL to Suse, 2 Nov. 1931.
90. *Wishaw Press*, 16 Oct., 23 Oct. 1931. For a sour summary of the policy disputes between PLP and ILP, see the ILP Annual Conference Report, Scarborough (April 1931), appdx 14.
91. Government: Tories 470, Libs 33, Nats 3, Lib Nats 35, Nat Labour 13; Opposition: Lab 46, Lloyd George Lib 4, ILP 3, Unendorsed Lab 3, Irish Nats 2, others 3. Thorpe, *General Election of 1931*, 279.
92. JL to C. P. Trevelyan, 29 Oct. 1931; JL to Frank Wise, 29 Oct. 1931.
93. JL to Suse, 2 Nov. 1931.
94. JL to C. P. Trevelyan, 30 Oct. 1931.
95. Brown, *Maxton*, 239.
96. *New Leader*, 25 March, 10 Apr. 1932.
97. Frank Wise, ILP Annual Conference Report, Blackpool (Easter 1932), 46–7.
98. M. Bondfield, *A Life's Work* (1949), 307.
99. For the background correspondence between Henderson and Maxton, see Labour Party Annual Report (1931), app. VIII.
100. Brockway, *Inside the Left*, 242–3. The ILP reversed that decision in 1934, but the damage had been done. The militants were organized in a Revolutionary Policy Committee that wished the ILP to become an explicitly Marxist party, but one which unlike the CP, was not chained to Moscow. The logic was a united front with the CP. See ILP Annual Conference Report, Derby (April 1933), 17. Dowse, *Left in the Centre, passim*; see also R. K. Middlemas, *The Clydesiders* (1965), 259–84.
101. Mann, *Woman in Parliament*, 106.

102. Lee, *My Life*, 80, 96; Brockway, *Inside the Left*, 237 ff.
103. Lee, *Tomorrow*, 175–7.
104. JL to Suse, 30 Aug. 1931; JL to C. P. Trevelyan, 3 Aug. 1932.
105. JL to Mr Lashley, North Lanark DLP, 5 Aug. 1932. She published a version of this letter in the *New Leader*, 2 Sept. 1932, thus burning her bridges very publicly.
106. F. Wise to C. P. Trevelyan, 3 Sept. 1932
107. ILP Annual Conference Report, Scarborough (April 1931), 95; *New Leader*, 25 March 1932; JL to Frank Wise, 12 Jan. 1931; JL to Suse, 25 July 1932.
108. Lee, *Tomorrow*, 151.
109. *Lochgelly Times*, 17 Aug. 1932.
110. Dowse, *Left in the Centre*, 193; ILP Annual Conference Report, Derby (Easter 1933), 17. The RPC, having pushed the ILP into abortive negotiations with the CP, resigned from the ILP in December 1935.
111. The Grand Old ILP (tune: The Church's One Foundation). I owe this reference to Denis Healey.
112. 1935 was a disappointing result: on a 9.4 per cent swing, Labour only gained 154 seats.
113. *The Jennie Lee Election Special*, Nov. 1935: Con: 22,301; ILP: 17,267; LP: 6,763.
114. JL to C. P. Trevelyan, 31 July 1935; Lee, *Tomorrow*, 198, 200–1; JL to C. P. Trevelyan, 4 Sept. 1935.

Chapter 3

1. C. P. Trevelyan, Memorial lecture on E. W. Wise, undated typescript, Trevelyan papers; *Manchester Guardian*, 6 Nov. 1933; *Morning Post*, 6 Nov. 1933; *Leicester Chronicle*, 11 Nov. 1933.
2. Interview Lady (Barbara) Castle.
3. Mary Murray to JL, 14 Dec. 1980; interview Mrs Mary Murray (née Wise).
4. Dorothy Wise to JL, 12 Nov. 1933.
5. A Soho club founded by Frank's friend J. A. Hobson, for 'advanced' men and women in literary and political life—such as Bertrand Russell, Olive Shreiner, and E. M. Forster. As its premises were dingy, its locale dubious, and members' fees often unpaid, the club closed in 1931. Hobson, *Confessions*, 115. It celebrated the Kerensky revolution of the spring, not the Lenin revolution of October.
6. Interview A. Roth. (The Tredegar books were a gift from the USA.) Archie Lush went to Oxford University.
7. Foot, *Aneurin Bevan*, *passim*; J. Campbell, *Nye Bevan and the Mirage of British Socialism* (1987).
8. Interview Mrs Arianwen Bevan-Norris.
9. Lee, *My Life*, 69, 72–3; *Observer* interview with Kenneth Harris, 3 Dec. 1972.
10. JL to Frank Wise, 22 Oct. 1931.
11. Foot, *Aneurin Bevan*, vol. 1, 61–2.
12. JL to Frank Wise, 27 Nov. 1930.
13. Ibid., 8 Dec. 1931.
14. Frank Wise to C. P. Trevelyan, 23 Nov. 1931.
15. Interview Mrs S. Saemann.

16. Interview Mrs S. Saemann.
17. F. Brockway, *Tribune*, 14 Nov. 1980.
18. *New Leader*, 19 Feb. 1932; *Lochgelly Times*, 13 Apr., 10 Aug., 30 Nov. 1932; *Sunday Mail*, 28 Jan., 4 Feb., 11 March 1934; Lee, *Tomorrow*, 153 ff.; *Wishaw Press*, 19 Feb. 1937.
19. JL papers, diary, 1936–8; Lee, *Tomorrow*, 162.
20. JL to Frank Wise, 6 Jan. 1932.
21. Lee, *My Life*, 100–1; JL to C. P. Trevelyan, 25 Aug. 1932.
22. JL to C. P. Trevelyan, n.d. (Apr.?) 1932.
23. JL to Frank Wise, 8 March 1933.
24. For the Socialist League, see R. Dare, 'The Socialist League', D.Phil. thesis, University of Oxford (1972); P. Seyd, 'Factionalism within the Labour Party: The Socialist League 1932–1937', in A. Briggs and J. Saville (eds), *Essays in Labour History 1918–1939* (1977); M. Cole, 'The Labour Movement between the Wars', in D. Martin and D. Rubinstein (eds), *Ideology and the Labour Movement* (1979); B. Pimlott, *Labour and the Left in the 1930s* (1977). The SSIP, Cole's new Fabian Research Bureau, started in March 1931, and Gaitskell and Dalton's XYZ Club, founded in 1932 to develop financial policy and diffuse Keynesian thinking, had learnt the lesson of 1929–31. The think-tanks sought to develop Labour's medium-term strategic thinking: see Pimlott, loc. cit., 36–40. Never again would Labour find itself with a policy vacuum. It came to office in 1945 well equipped.
25. R. Eatwell and A. Wright, 'Labour and the Lessons of 1931', *History*, 63 (1978).
26. Frank Wise to C. P. Trevelyan, 3 Sept. 1932. Trevelyan papers, MS 145.
27. Foot, *Bevan*, vol. 1, 156–7. Nye joined when Cripps, his friend, became leader.
28. Seyd, 'Factionalism', 219
29. C. P. Trevelyan to Lady Trevelyan, 6 Nov. 1933, Trevelyan papers, MS 127.
30. JL to Suse, 10 Nov. 1933.
31. Dorothy Wise to JL, 12 Nov. 1933. Frank left no money. The family had to move to a smaller house and Mrs Wise went to work full time. Eventually she remarried a gentle man whom she met on a train. Her daughter noted that she did not marry the same man twice. Interview Mrs Mary Murray.
32. JL to Suse, 27 Dec. 1933.
33. JL papers, MS 13 May 1987.
34. Lee, *My Life*, 104.
35. *Scarborough Evening News*, 12 Sept.; *Edinburgh Evening Dispatch*, 14 Sept.; *Daily Express*, 11 Sept. 1934.
36 *Daily Express*, 26 Oct. 1934.
37. Interview Lady Mallalieu.
38. JL to Mrs Pauline Dower, 5 Apr. 1977.
39. For the NUWM, see R. Hayburn, 'The National Unemployed Workers Movement, 1921–36', *International Review of Social History*, 23 (1983); Stevenson and Cook, *The Slump*. The NUWM, which was strongest in South Wales, Lancashire, and Scotland, had 50,000 members in 1932, the CP just 9,000.
40 *The Times*, 9 Nov. 1936, qtd in Campbell, *Nye Bevan*, 59.
41. JL papers, diary, 1936–8 undated MS.
42. He was soon to have an operation to remove his appendix.

43. Lee, *Tomorrow*, 222.
44. *New Leader*, 15 Jan. 1937.
45. Brockway, *Inside the Left*, 337–40. See also M. Ceadel, *Pacifism in Britain 1914–1945* (1980).
46. Jennie's version of their views in *My Life* is misleading. She suggests that official Labour, blind to the menace of Hitler, blocked the rearmament that the left was calling for; see 126–7.
47. The Club was launched in May 1936 and published books (largely by Communist writers) chosen by Laski, Strachey, and Victor Gollancz. Local discussion groups had some 50,000 members, drawn from all shades of the Left. It became increasingly a propaganda and political body, publishing some three million books.
48. The Constituency Party Association successfully campaigned to change Labour Party rules in 1937: the seven constituency delegates on the NEC would be elected by the constituency parties alone and not by the whole (trade-union-dominated) Conference. Cripps was its chairman. The constituency section became the home of the Bevanite Left in the 1950s.
49. Until it was dissolved by the NEC in 1936, a South Wales Council of Action united all sections: the Labour Party, the Miners' Federation, the ILP, the CP, and the NUWM. F. Jupp, *The Radical Left in Britain 1931–1941* (1982), 180.
50. The CP was founded in 1920. It spent the next twenty years denouncing the treachery of Labour leaders, while simultaneously seeking affiliation to the Labour Party, and entry into Labour's affiliated organizations. In 1924 the Labour Party Conference rejected affiliation; in 1925 it excluded communists from individual membership of DLPs; from 1928 Communists were forbidden to attend Conference even as trade-union delegates. They were distrusted by the ILP for their rigid obedience to instructions from Moscow; and detested by trade-union leaders for fomenting unofficial strikes which fragmented trade-union loyalty. Herbert Morrison regarded them as the termites of the Labour movement. See H. Dewar, *Communist Politics in Britain: the CPGB from its Origins to the Second World War* (1976); F. Beckett, *Enemy Within. The Rise and Fall of the British Communist Party* (1995); Stevenson and Cook, *The Slump*. Ben Pimlott's splendid *Labour and the Left in the 1930s* sets the CP in the context of socialist sectarian politics, as does Jupp, *The Radical Left*.
51. Qtd in Dewar, *Communist Politics in Britain*, 100, 151.
52. Foot, *Aneurin Bevan*, vol. 1, 247.
53. Ibid., 291.
54. Ibid.
55. Fenner Brockway to JL, 2 Sept. 1938; Dowse, *Left in the Centre*, 198–200.
56. JL to Fenner Brockway, 7 Oct. 1938.
57. Lee, *This Great Journey*, 185.
58. J. Carmichael to JL, 16 July, 29 Aug. 1936; *Wishaw Press*, 2 Oct. 1936.
59. Lee, *This Great Journey*, 181.
60. Lee, *Tomorrow*, 258–64.
61. V. Gollancz to JL, 5 June, 1 July 1939. The American edition was *This Great Journey*, to which Jennie attached an additional chapter taking the book forward into the war.

62. J. B. Priestley to JL, 22 Oct. 1939; H. G. Wells to JL, 23 Oct. 1939; JL to H. G. Wells, 24 Oct. 1939.
63. For a fuller discussion of this, see pp. 216–17.
64. JL papers, diary, 1936–8.
65. A. E. Housman, *A Shropshire Lad*, verse XLVIII.
66. Lee, *This Great Journey*, 187–8.

Chapter 4

1. A. J. P. Taylor, *Beaverbrook* (1972), 321.
2. JL to A. J. P. Taylor, 21 May 1971.
3. Lee, *This Great Journey*, 193–4.
4. J. Lee, 'Democracy begins in the Workshop', *Tribune*, 11 Apr. 1941.
5. Lee, *My Life*, 129 ff.; Taylor, *Beaverbrook*, 421.
6. J. Lee, '1200 Gallant Women', *Evening Standard*, 26 Aug. 1940.
7. JL to Beaverbrook, 22 Oct. 1940.
8. JL to Beaverbrook, Beaverbrook to JL, 24 Oct. 1940; JL wartime diary (3 March 1941).
9. JL papers, wartime diary (3 March, 17 March 1941).
10. JL papers, American diary jottings (24 Sept., 30 Oct. 1941).
11. A. J. P. Taylor, *English History 1914–1945* (1970), 532.
12. J. McNair to JL, 16 June 1942.
13. JL to J. McNair, 15 June 1942.
14. JL to C. P. Trevelyan, 16 Nov. 1942.
15. Qtd in P. Addison, *The Road to 1945* (1977 edn.), 61.
16. *Tribune*, 26 Jan. 1940.
17. P. Addison, 'By-elections of the Second World War', in C. Cook and J. Ramsden (eds), *By-Elections in British Politics* (1973), 165–90, on which this paragraph draws.
18. T. Driberg, *The Best of Both Worlds* (1953), 182; 27 Labour seats fell vacant, 8 were contested; 59 Tory seats fell vacant, 46 were contested: loc. cit., 164–7.
19. For the alternative view, which argues that Labour increasingly dominated domestic policy, see Addison, *The Road to 1945*; S. Brooke, *Labour's War. The Labour Party during the Second World War* (1992).
20. J. Lee, 'Labour: Guerilla or Mass Army', *Tribune*, 5 Feb. 1943.
21. T. Driberg, *Ruling Passions* (1977), 180–1; and, more generally, Addison, *The Road to 1945*.
22. R. Mackay, *Left*, Jan. 1944, qtd in A. Calder, 'The Common Wealth Party, 1942–1945', Ph.D. thesis, University of Sussex (1968), 158.
23. Many of the electioneering practices exploited by Labour in 1945 were pioneered by Common Wealth. Local parties disliked canvassing and preferred public meetings. Common Wealth ran election schools, and devised the 'Reading' system of canvass sheets which Ian Mikardo was to publicize at Reading. They had a squad of experienced election agents whom they could offer constituencies and a head office of 30 staff.
24. This paragraph draws on Calder, 'The Common Wealth Party', *passim*.
25 The 1941 Committee included Edward Hulton, publisher of *Picture Post*, Kingsley Martin, Thomas Balogh, and J. B. Priestley. It was a quasi-Fabian

Educational group, founded in 1941, lobbying for planning, nationalization of transport and mines, and rationing. Of its 50 local branches, 30 joined Common Wealth.

Common Wealth could not survive outside the abnormal situation of an electoral truce. When normal party politics began to unfreeze in late 1944, Common Wealth applied to affiliate to the Labour Party, which rejected it, fearing it would set a precedent for the CP. Reluctant to stand against Labour, Common Wealth ran 23 candidates in 1945; only one was elected. Calder, 'The Common Wealth Party'.

26. JL to C. Trevelyan, 4 Jan. 1943; JL to King Gordon, 27 Feb. 1943; 'Common Wealth. An Appeal to the British People', election leaflets, Apr. 1944.
27. Calder, 'The Common Wealth Party', 293; Minutes 30 July 1942, qtd Calder op. cit. 113.
28. *Bristol Evening Post*, 21 Dec. 1942; Sir R. Acland to author, 3 Dec. 1989.
29. *Bristol Evening Post*, 4 Jan. 1943.
30. J. Lee, 'Labour: Guerilla or Mass Army?', *Tribune*, 5 Feb. 1943.
31. *Western Daily Press*, 19 Feb. 1943; JL to Sir Charles Trevelyan, 4 Jan. 1943.
32. JL to King Gordon, 27 Feb. 1943.
33. Interview Mervyn Stockwood. He chaired Jennie's election campaign.
34. *Bristol Evening Post*, 11 Jan. 1943.
35. See Brooke, *Labour's War*, 145 ff.
36. W. Beveridge, *Social Insurance and Allied Services* (1942), para. 460.
37. Calder, 'The Common Wealth Party', 121 ff.
38. *Western Daily Press*, 18 Jan. 1943.
39. *Bristol Evening Post*, 15 Feb. 1943.
40. Chuter Ede Diaries, BM, Add. Mss. 59696, vol. 7 (19 Feb. 1943). I owe this reference to the kindness of Dr M. Sanderson.
41. Interview Mervyn Stockwood; see also M. Stockwood, *Chanctonbury Ring. The Autobiography of Mervyn Stockwood* (1982).
42. Lee, *My Life*, 144; see also M. De-La-Noy, *Mervyn Stockwood, A Lonely Life* (1996), 41–2.
43. C. M. MacInnes, *Bristol at War* (1972), 168.
44. Calder records that in 8 of the 12 contests with a Common Wealth-supported candidate, they acquired a better vote than the Labour Party had done in 1935, and in 3 seats a higher vote than Labour got in 1945. They did remarkably well. 'The Common Wealth Party', 180–1.
45. Ibid., 182; *Bristol Evening Post*, 19 Feb. 1943.
46. G. R. Shepherd to JL, 9 Dec. 1944.
47. Foot, *Aneurin Bevan*, vol. 1, 310–11. G. R. Strauss rejoined with Nye. Cripps was outraged by the undertaking he was asked to sign, insisted that the Party and not he had been guilty of past mistakes, and stated he would remain an Independent for the period of the war.
48. J. Lee, 'As I Please', *Tribune*, 13 Apr. 1945.
49. Lee, *My Life*, 132.
50. Undated galley proofs for an obituary, JL papers. Jennie contested any suggestion that Nye was a 'miniature Churchill. There were odd moments when they enjoyed each other's company as well as periods of bitter private and

public conflict. But I very much keep in mind that the two men not only had completely different backgrounds, but also utterly different values. During the Second World War Winston was fighting for all that he fundamentally believed in, which was in essence to restore the world of the past. Nye was fighting for what he fundamentally believed in, which was an entirely different future. Nye, most of his political life, was an outcast and a nobody'; JL to Kenneth Harris, 20 Apr. 1971.

51. *Tribune*, 18 Oct. 1940.
52. Foot, *Anenrin Bevan*, vol. 1, 439 ff. Perhaps the worst time of Nye's ministerial career was operating this regulation as Minister of Labour in 1951.
53. Ibid., 345, 330.
54. JL to C. P. Trevelyan, 16 Nov. 1942.
55. For the political context of Beveridge, see Nicholas Timmins's magnificent *The Five Giants. A Biography of the Welfare State* (1995).
56. Chuter Ede Diaries, BM, Add. Mss. 59696, vol. 7 (19 Feb., 21 Feb 1943).
57. J. Lee, 'Labour: Guerilla or Mass Army,' *Tribune*, 5 Feb. 1943.
58. Brooke, *Labour's War*, 168 ff.
59. JL to Jack Evans, 2 March 1945.
60. Founder and leader of the local Labour Party, an USDAW man with roots in the Co-operative movement, and an urban and county councillor.
61. Jack Evans to JL, 5 March 1945.
62. W. Adamson to A. Hampton, 22 Apr. 1945.
63. *Cannock Courier*, 21 Apr. 1945; interview Ernie Roberts, Jack Holston.
64. Interview Joan Loverock.
65. A. Mitchell, *Election '45* (1995), 41.
66. Lee, 'As I Please', *Tribune*, 1 June 1945; Mitchell, *Election' 45*, 69.
67. Letter Mr Smallshire; interview E. Roberts.
68. Mitchell, *Election '45*, 44, 67.

Chapter 5

1. Only 9 women in total were returned at the previous election in 1935: 1 Labour (Ellen Wilkinson), 1 Liberal (Megan Lloyd George), 1 Independent (Eleanor Rathbone) and 6 Conservatives. The 1945 Labour cohort also included Alice Bacon (Leeds NE), Bessie Braddock (Liverpool Exchange), Barbara Castle (Blackburn), Grace Colman (Tynemouth), Freda Corbet (Camberwell), Caroline Ganley (Battersea South), Barbara Ayrton Gould (Hendon North), Peggy Herbison (North Lanark), Jean Mann (Coatbridge & Airdrie), Leah Manning (Epping), Lucy Middleton (Plymouth Sutton), Muriel Nichol (Bradford North), Lady Noel-Buxton (Norwich), Florence Paton (Rushcliffe), Mabel Ridealgh (Ilford North), Clarice Shaw (Kilmarnock), Dr Edith Summerskill (Fulham West), Edith Wills (Birmingham Duddeston).
2. Castle, *Fighting All the Way*, 109. None the less, they were close enough for Barbara and Ted Castle to celebrate their wedding lunch at the Savoy in July 1944 with four guests, two of whom were Jennie and Nye; loc. cit., 120.
3. Brooks, *Women at Westminster*, 153. See also Harrison, 'Women in a Men's House', 623–54; E. Vallance, *Women in the House. A Study of Women Members of Parliament* (1979).

4. Mann, *Woman in Parliament*, 11.
5. Castle, *Fighting All the Way*, 126.
6. Qtd in M. Phillips, *The Divided House* (1980), 61.
7. Interview Viscount Davidson. Her father was Willougby Dickinson, MP for St Pancras.
8. Lee, 'As I Please', *Tribune*, 28 Dec. 1945, 19 Dec. 1952; see also Mann, *Woman in Parliament*, 143–5. MPs' salaries were raised to £1,000 p.a. in April 1946. Jennie still argued in the House that they were underpaid; see, e.g., *Hansard*, House of Commons, 7 June 1951, cols 1245–7.
9. Lieut. J. Callaghan, Major D. Renton, qtd in Mitchell, *Election '45*, 107.
10. *Hansard*, House of Commons, 16 Aug. 1945; qtd in Mitchell, *Election '45*, 111.
11. Mann, *Woman in Parliament*, 107.
12. Ibid., 106.
13. Ibid., 13. A pun, of course, on that wartime security slogan: 'Be like Dad and Keep Mum', about which women MPs had sharply complained.
14. 'The Work of the CHAC', *Municipal Journal*, HLG (1951) 36/9. Its 30 members met quarterly; its detailed work was done by its subcommittees, some of whose reports (on rural housing, on housing for special needs, or on housing management) had circulations of over 30,000 and were highly influential.
15. Silkin worked alongside Nye to produce his 1946 New Towns Act, which planned for 8 towns beyond London's green belt and a further 6 in regional development areas. By the 1990s they were home to 2 million people. See P. Hennessy, *Never Again, Britain 1945–1951* (1992), 173.
16. Jennie attacked tied cottages. She did not believe the government should subsidize their repair; the money should be used to build rural council houses instead. CHAC Minutes, 18 Oct. 1946, HLG 36/20.
17. Foot, *Aneurin Bevan*, vol. 2, 82.
18. Lee, 'As I Please', *Tribune*, 26 Oct. 1945; *Hansard*, House of Commons, 26 Nov. 1945, col. 954. On average, each house took between 1 and 1½ man-years to build.
19. CHAC Minutes, 21 Sept. 1945, HLG 36/19; 15 Nov. 1949, HLG 36/23.
20. Qtd in Timmins, *The Five Giants*, 147.
21. Lee, *Hansard*, House of Commons, 16 March 1949, col. 2149.
22. CHAC Minutes, 1 Oct. 1946, HLG 36/20. A 16-point standard, requiring hot water, heating, and storage, replaced the 8-point standard.
23. 'Subjects for Future Discussion', CHAC, HLG 36/7.
24. Qtd in K. Morgan, *Labour in Power 1945–51* (1984), 163.
25. Building labour fell from 206,000 to 145,000; by October 1947 Nye still needed an extra 70,000 building workers 'and the prospects of obtaining them are not good'. The Minister's Report, CHAC Minutes, 2 May, 24 Oct. 1947, HLG 36/21.
26. Michael Foot, e.g., is unnecessarily defensive of Nye's record; see also Morgan, *Labour in Power*, 168–9, who gives more credit to Dalton than departmental papers might suggest.
27. There were 730,621 new permanent houses, 125,000 temporary houses, 129,000 conversions, 144,000 renovations of unoccupied war-damaged houses; CHAC quarterly statistics, HLG 36/25.

28. CHAC Minutes, 16 May 1950, HLG 36/24. 'Controversial' presumably because rebates entailed a differential rent policy, with some tenants cross-subsidizing others. Subsidizing the tenant rather than the house has helped to create today's poverty trap.
29. CHAC Minutes, 30 May 1951, HLG 36/25.
30. Lee, *My Life*, 178.
31. Morrison argued prophetically in Cabinet on 12 October 1945: 'It is possible to argue that almost every local government function, taken by itself, could be administered more efficiently in the technical sense under a national system, but if we wish local government to thrive—as a school of political and democratic education as well as a method of administration—we must consider the general effect of each particular proposal. It would be disastrous if we allowed local government to languish by whittling away its most constructive and interesting functions.' Qtd in Hennessy's fascinating *Never Again*, 139.
32. A. Bevan, *In Place of Fear* (1952), 107–8.
33. Ibid., 106.
34. *Cannock Courier*, 17 Feb., 24 Feb. 1950.
35. JL papers, undated MS jottings.
36. The 1946 redistribution transferred 40,000 voters to Wolverhampton in the south, 20,000 to Brierley Hill (Seisdon RDC) in the south-west, while taking in 9,000 voters from Stafford (Cannock RDC) to the west. After the 1951 election, the boundaries changed again. Cannock lost Brownhills UDC to the new county seat (Aldridge-Brownhills), but took in Wednesfield UDC to the south, because there was 'nowhere else to put it'. *Cannock Advertiser*, 18 Sept. 1964. Only Cannock UDC remained with Jennie throughout.
37. M. J. Wise, 'The Cannock Chase Region', in *Birmingham and its Regional Setting* (1950); *Cannock and Hednesford Official Guide*, n.d., *c.*1953.
38. J. Hilton, *English Ribbon* (1950), 226–8; Lee, *My Life*, 154.
39. *Workers Voice*, no. 1, June 1945; *Labour Gazette*, Jan. 1947.
40. *Cannock Courier*, 10 Jan. 1947.
41. Ibid., 19 July 1946.
42. Ibid., 14 June 1958, 27 Aug. 1959; *Cannock Advertiser*, 13 Dec. 1958.
43. *Cannock Advertiser*, 2 Aug. 1958.
44. *Cannock Courier*, 18 Jan. 1946; *Labour Gazette*, Feb. 1946.
45. *Labour Gazette*, 3 March 1946.
46. Ibid., Apr. 1946, Apr. 1949, Apr. 1950, July 1951.
47. *Cannock Courier*, 18 June 1970.
48. JL to Alf Allan, 6 Oct. 1977; Alf Allan to JL, 5 March 1980.
49. *Labour Gazette*, Feb. 1949. This was not Jennie's hand: she loathed the word 'charming'.
50. JL to Alf Allan, 12 Dec. 1961.
51. *Labour Gazette*, Feb. 1946.
52. Lee, *My Life*, 154.
53. JL to Jack Evans, 20 Apr. 1945; interviews, Mrs Rowley, John O'Leary; Mrs Rowley to JL, 20 Dec. 1974.

54. In 1952 the figure was 43 per 1,000 and rising, while the England and Wales figures were dropping to 27 per 1,000.
55. *Labour Gazette*, May 1949.
56. *Cannock Advertiser and Courier*, 25 Sept. 1964.
57. Interview E. Roberts.
58. *Labour Gazette*, Apr. 1951; JL to Jack Holsten, 6 Sept. 1953; interview E. Roberts.
59. *Labour Gazette*, Sept. 1947; *Cannock Courier*, 27 Jan. 1950; 3, 17, 24 Feb. 1950.
60. Castle, *Fighting All the Way*, 141. Jennie herself noted: 'I said more openly in public what Ni was saying in Cabinet', JL papers, undated MS.
61. J. Schneer, *Labour's Conscience. The Labour Left, 1945–51* (1988), 56
62. *Hansard*, House of Commons, 18 Nov. 1946, cols 546–7; 16 March 1949, col. 2148.
63. Ibid., 16 March 1949, cols 2150–4; 30 May, 1949, col. 1860.
64. See, for example, her foreign affairs speech, ibid., 12 May 1953, col. 1090.
65. Interview Neil Kinnock.
66. The terms of the American loan required full convertibility between dollars and sterling on 15 July 1947.
67. For a remarkably vivid account, see Hennessy, *Never Again*, 300 ff.
68. *New Statesman*, 26 July 1947.
69. Vallance, *Women in the House*, 83.
70. E. Summerskill, *A Woman's World* (1967), 143 f. Local Catholic priests agreed that they would have put her on the rack if they had had their way.
71. Harrison, 'Women in a Men's House', *The Historical Journal*, 646; Vallance, *Women in the House*, 85.
72. Qtd in P. Thane, 'Women of the British Labour Party and Feminism', in H. L. Smith (ed.), *British Feminism in the Twentieth Century* (1990).
73. J. Lee, 'Post Office Wives', *Tribune*, 29 May 1953.
74. Barbara Castle saw the issue. She tried to amend the National Insurance Bill and require married women at work to pay the full rather than a reduced insurance stamp, and thereby receive benefits in their own right. Thirty years later she abolished the reduced stamp. *Fighting All the Way*, 135.
75. Vallance, *Women in the House*, 62–3.
76. Mann, *Woman in Parliament*, 14.
77. Summerskill, *A Woman's World*, 208–11.
78. Mann, *Woman in Parliament*, 111.
79. Braddock, *The Braddocks*, 90–1, 203–16.
80. Interview Eirene White.
81. J. Lee, 'As I Please', *Tribune*, 23 March 1945. Jennie's description of the WCG women has echoes of Virginia Woolf's extraordinary introduction to *Life as We have Known It*, ed. Margaret Llewelyn Davies (1931), where she describes a WCG conference in 1913.
82. J. Lee, 'I'd be a Suffragette', *Tribune*, 27 July 1951; *Hansard*, House of Commons, 8 May 1953, col. 830.
83. B. Castle, *Hansard*, House of Commons, 16 May 1952, col. 1836; interview B. Castle.
84. J. Lee, 'Are Women a Priority?', *Tribune*, 13 June 1947. See also J. Lee, 'A New

Life Opens Out for Women', *Picture Post*, 1 Aug. 1942. For the equal pay campaign, see Pugh, *Women and the Women's Movement*, 298 ff. By 1951 Jennie was publicly regretting that Labour had not done more to advance equal pay. Rab Butler agreed in 1954 gradually to introduce equal pay into the civil service. A year later equal pay was conceded to teachers, and in 1956 to NHS workers.

85. J. Lee, *Hansard*, House of Commons, 8 May 1953, col. 830.
86. JL papers, undated MS notes from the 1970s.
87. H. Dalton, *High Tide and After. Memoirs 1945–1960* (1962), 3. Castle, *Fighting All the Way*, 176.
88. I. Mikardo, *Back-bencher* (1988), 88: 'Every single one of us in that round-table group [in the Smoking Room] had come into the Commons bursting to help our leaders to carry out, against all the mountainous obstacles resulting from the war, the programme on which we had been elected.' His worries deepened as he noticed no boldness and urgency in the Government's economic planning; little attention paid to the interests of the workers; above all, a foreign policy that was taking them into the Cold War; loc. cit., 94–5.

    There is another critique of those years coming from the Right and the writings of Corelli Barnett: that Britain spent heavily on welfare and housing, and also on defence (under the illusion it was a great power). The country could afford either but not both. In consequence industry was denied investment and the country's late-twentieth-century decline assured. C. Barnett, *The Lost Victory. British Dreams, British Realities 1945–1950* (1995).
89. D. Howell, *British Social Democracy* (1976), 159.
90. J. Lee, 'Keeping to the Left', *Tribune*, 9 May 1947.

Chapter 6

1. Only 80 seats were not affected by redistribution. Jennie's Cannock, for example, was cut from 110,000 to 56,000. Redistribution meant that a swing of 3.3% to the Tories had given them a 40% increase in seats. Postal votes (pvs) probably broke two to one in favour of the Tories. H. Nicholas, *The British General Election of 1950* (1951), 4–8.
2. House of Commons, 27 Oct 1948, qtd in D. Rubinstein, 'Socialism and the Labour Party' in D. Martin and D. Rubinstein (eds), *Ideology and the Labour Movement* (1979), 243.
3. Interview D. Bruce.
4. D. Butler, *The British General Election of 1951* (1951), 271. The Tories' 48% of the vote gave them 52% of the seats; Labour's votes piled up in their safe seats.
5. Morgan, *Labour in Power, 1945–1951*, 414–15.
6. See B. Brivati's fine biography, *Hugh Gaitskell* (1996).
7. 'As I Please', *Tribune*, 24 Oct. 1952.
8. This account draws heavily on Dr C. Webster's meticulously researched official history, *The Health Services Since the War* (1988), vol. 1, ch. 5.

    1948/9 original net parliamentary estimates (9 months) for England, Wales, Scotland £149.7m., final £208.2m. (full year effect £198m./£275m.); 1949/50 original £259.7m., final £358.5m.; 1950/1 original £392.9m., final £392.9m.; 1951/2 original £398.1m., final £399.5m.; loc. cit., 136.

9. *The Times*, 26 Oct., 16 Nov. 1949.
10. Campbell, *Nye Bevan*, 219.
11. Brivati, *Hugh Gaitskell*, 112.
12. Morgan, *Labour in Power*, 433.
13. Of the planned defence estimates of £4,700 million for the three years 1951–4, only £3,878 million could be spent. Churchill conceded this in a defence debate: *Hansard*, House of Commons, 6 Dec. 1951, col. 2601.
14. Health and housing had been split: Dalton, in the Cabinet, combined housing with local government, Marquand, not in the Cabinet, ran health.
15. Foot, *Aneurin Bevan*, vol. 2, 292; note from H. Wilson to JL on the health charges controversy 1950–1, JL papers.
16. Nye did not forgive Gaitskell for getting Attlee to overturn a Cabinet decision that distanced Britain from America's hard line on Communist China, by quietly threatening his resignation. The Labour government had recognized Mao, the Americans would not. Gaitskell demanded that they support the USA in branding China 'the aggressor' in Korea; Nye and the constituency parties were in revolt. H. Dalton, *The Political Diary of Hugh Dalton*, ed. B. Pimlott (1986), (9 Feb. 1951), hereafter Dalton, *Diary*; A. Roth, *Sir Harold Wilson* (1977), *passim*.
17. G. Thomas, *Mr Speaker* (1985), 69. This was before his public meeting in the East End. He had written to Cripps to the same effect the previous summer.
18. Dalton, *Diary* (6 Apr. 1951); Thomas, *Mr Speaker*, 70.
19. Morrison was acting leader while Attlee was in hospital. He 'saw the situation as offering a brutal choice between Gaitskell and Bevan'. He unequivocally supported Gaitskell and pressed Attlee to do the same. B. Donoughue and G. W. Jones, *Herbert Morrison, Portrait of a Politician* (1973), 491.

    Barbara Castle, who later led the opposition to Gaitskell on the NEC, never forgave Gaitskell 'for precipitating a damaging split in the party which need never have taken place if he had been willing to show the slightest flexibility . . . Gaitskell considered Nye to be not only expendable but a positive liability . . . [Gaitskell showed] unyielding hostility to anyone who disagreed with him . . . For many years his mixture of pedantry and prejudice led him to errors of political judgement which kept the party at war with itself.' Castle, *Fighting All the Way*, 193.
20. Brivati, *Hugh Gaitskell*, 118.
21. By, e.g., Tomlinson, Minister of Education; Bevin; Morrison; Gordon-Walker; Chuter Ede, Home Secretary; and Attlee.
22. H. Gaitskell, *The Diary of Hugh Gaitskell*, ed. P. Williams (1983) (30 Apr. 1951), hereafter Gaitskell, *Diary*. Gaitskell did not keep his diary between 16 Feb. and 30 Apr. when he wrote a long retrospective note. Williams writes that Gaitskell resisted a cap 'as a dishonest [*why?* author] dodge to avoid charges—without which the Health Ministers knew [*really?* author] they could not keep within the ceiling, and which he knew would never be accepted except in the Budget speech'; quite. *Hugh Gaitskell, A Political Biography* (1979), 252.
23. Gaitskell, *Diary*; Dalton, *Diary* (10 Apr. 1951).

24. Dalton, *Diary*; Roth, *Sir Harold Wilson*, 133; Williams, *Hugh Gaitskell*, 266; Lee, *My Life*, 190.
25. Dalton, *Diary* (10 April 1951).
26. Qtd in Foot, *Aneurin Bevan*, vol. 2, 324.
27. Ibid., 326.
28. Dalton, *Diary* (12 April 1951); *Tribune*, 20 April 1951. The editorial board of Jennie and Michael Foot would not have published it without Nye's consent.
29. Gaitskell, *Diary* (4 May 1951).
30. Dalton, *Diary* (5 April 1951); Foot, *Aneurin Bevan*, 319.
31. Gaitskell, *Diary* (4 May 1951).
32. Minutes of meeting, 26 Apr., 3 May 1951 (Richardson papers).
33. Wyatt, *Confessions*, 211. Interview, W. Wyatt.
34. When Gaitskell won the leadership, Nye told Bowden, Chief Whip: 'There ought to be no *election* to the deputy leadership, Gaitskell should *appoint* me as deputy leader. I am the leader of the Party in the country.' Dalton, *Diary* (27 Oct. 1956).
35. *The Backbench Diaries of Richard Crossman*, ed. J. Morgan (1981) (22 June 1956), hereafter Crossman, *Diaries*.
36. Dalton, *Diary* (17 April 1951).
37. Dalton, *Diary* (17, 25 Nov. 1953). The elections had been on 5 November.
38. Interview D. Bruce.
39. I. Mikardo, *Labour Weekly*, 5 Oct. 1973.
40. Foot, *Aneurin Bevan*, vol. 2, 557.
41. Crossman, *Diaries* (12 Oct. 1954, 27 Sept. 1957); Dalton, *Diary* (13 Apr. 1954).
42. J. Lee, 'Keeping to the Left,' *Tribune*, 9 May 1947.
43. Ibid. She doubted, e.g., whether an Anglo-French alliance which excluded Eastern Europe could be the cornerstone of a third way.
44. Mikardo, *Back-bencher*, 118–19.
45. Keep Left minutes, 25 July 1949–17 Apr. 1951, Jo Richardson papers. Nye and Jennie did not feature by name in their minuted discussions until 27 Feb. 1951. See also Roth, *Sir Harold Wilson*, ch. 5, *passim*, for an absorbing account of the Bevanites and Wilson's role.
46. With Crossman and Silverman, Donald Bruce had helped to form the original Keep Left Group in 1947. When Nye learnt of this, Bruce was given 'a bollocking', and told that it was incompatible with his position as Nye's PPS. Continue, and 'you will be out'. So when it reformed, Bruce kept a low profile and Nye in ignorance. Interview D. Bruce.
47. Foot, *Aneurin Bevan*, 340.
48. Dalton, *Diary* (1 July 1951). He especially lamented that John Freeman had become 'a wonderful scalp for the uglies. I had heard Mikardo exulting over him in the entrance to a lavatory'. *Diary* (25 April 1951).
49. Keep Left minutes, 30 Oct., 6 Nov. 1951; 22 April 1952. See also Crossman, *Diaries* (30 Oct 1951). It was also a way of excluding fellow-travellers.
50. Keep Left minutes, 5 Feb. 1952. Of the group's 58 minuted meetings between April 1951 and October 1952, Nye attended 36 of them, Jennie 37.
51. Mikardo, *Back-bencher*, 120.
52. J. Lee, 'Keeping to the Left', *Tribune*, 9 May 1947.

53. Peggy Duff, *Left, Left, Left* (1971), 44–5; Mikardo, *Back-bencher*, 123–5.
54. Interview Elizabeth Thomas.
55. D. Hill (ed.), *Tribune 40. The First Forty Years of a Socialist Newspaper* (1977), on which this paragraph draws; together with JL papers, '*Tribune* file.'
56. Duff, *Left, Left, Left*, 26.
57. Ibid., 29; R. Edwards, *Goodbye Fleet Street* (1988), 35.
58. Duff, *Left, Left, Left*, 36.
59. Interviews Mervyn Jones, Elizabeth Thomas. Samuel divorced and then remarried his wife. She suffered breakdowns; he eventually committed suicide by walking into the sea.
60. J. Lee, draft, *My Life with Nye*, JL papers.
61. See pp. 192–3.
62. Interview Elizabeth Thomas. She was Michael Foot's secretary from 1951, before becoming *Tribune*'s gifted literary editor. She and Jennie warmly encouraged each other. When Jennie became Minister for the Arts in 1965, she relied on Elizabeth to tell her what was happening 'on the Left of the Arts', ensured she attended her press conferences, and put her on the literary panel of the Arts Council. Elizabeth Thomas helped Jennie edit *My Life with Nye*, lengthening her somewhat staccato sentences into narrative.
63. Edwards, *Goodbye Fleet Street*, 38.
64. Ibid., 39.
65. *Tribune*, 21 Dec. 1956.
66. Interview R. Clements; M. Foot to JL, 21 March 1958, n.d. (23 March?) 1958; JL papers.
67. Interview Mervyn Jones. In hindsight, Michael Foot believes that Jennie's instinct was right, and her distrust of Tito and her support for Djilas correct.
68. Interview Ian Aitken, Geoffrey Goodman.
69. Interview Ian Aitken, Mervyn Jones.
70. M. Jones, *Chances. An Autobiography* (1987), 131; interview R. Clements.
71. JL to Michael Foot, to Jill Craigie, n.d., JL papers.
72. M. Foot to H. Samuel, 27 March 1958; H. Samuel to M. Foot, 31 March 1958; H. Samuels to M. Foot, 2 April 1958; M. Foot to JL, 6 April 1958; JL papers, *Tribune* file. Interview Mervyn Jones, R. Clements; Foot, *Aneurin Bevan*, 578, 602.
73. Lee, *My Life*, 238. Dick Clements observed that Nye did not so much want 'a balanced discussion' on the H-bomb, 'as no discussion at all'. As it was, the pro-Nye letters had often to be fabricated by Michael, under fake names, to give a semblance of debate.
74. Interview Jill Craigie.
75. Memo M. Foot to JL, n.d. (late Oct.?) 1959; scribbled note by JL, n.d., JL papers.
76. Until 1955, members of the Parliamentary Committee did not hold individual portfolios. They were an Opposition, not a shadow government. Members roamed across the field of policy, allowing Right–Left splits to appear on any issue, without the discipline of being restricted to an official brief. It was an invitation to caucus. R. Crossman, 'Shadow Cabinet or Caucus?', *New Statesman*, 25 June 1955.
77. In 1955 the six great unions, TGWU, NUM, GMW, AEU, USDAW, NUR had

3.58m. of the 5.5m. trade-union and 6.8m. Conference votes. The TGWU, NUM, and GMW never deviated from the right, the other three sometimes did so, as did the smaller unions. L. Minkin, *The Labour Party Conference* (1978), 23–6.

78. Lee, *My Life*, 207, repeating a well-known jibe. Will Lawther of the NUM described Bevan as 'a man with his feet in Moscow and his eyes on 10 Downing Street'. *The Times*, 8 Oct. 1952, qtd in S. Haseler, *The Gaitskellites* (1969), 26.
79. Brivati, *Hugh Gaitskell*, 161.
80. Kingsley Martin, 'The Issue of *Tribune*', *New Statesman*, 28 Feb. 1953.
81. Crossman, *Diaries* (26 Nov. 1951). When, in 1954 and 1955, local Bevanite CLPs did attempt to deselect right-wing MPs, such as Bessie Braddock, Elaine Burton, and Arthur Skeffington, the NEC would not permit their deselection.
82. A. Bevan to R. Evans, 28 June 1954, JL papers.
83. 'The End of Bevanism', *New Statesman*, 12 Oct. 1957; Crossman, *Diaries* (6 May 1954).
84. *Tribune*, 12 Sept. 1947.
85. Donoughue and Jones, *Herbert Morrison*, 370, 384; P. Seyd, *The Rise and Fall of the Labour Left* (1987).
86. 'What happened at Morecambe', *New Statesman*, 4 Oct. 1952; Crossman, *Diaries* (28 Sept. 1952); B. Pimlott, *Harold Wilson* (1993), 179.
87. Dalton, *Diary* (29 Sept., 1 Oct. 1952).
88. Roth, *Sir Harold Wilson*, 167.
89. Speech at the Festival Hall, *The Times*, 13 Oct. 1952.
90. Interview Lord Cledwyn Hughes; Crossman, *Diaries* (23 Oct. 1952).
91 Ibid. (14 Oct. 1952); Keep Left minutes, 15 Oct. 1952, Richardson papers.
92. Campbell, *Nye Bevan*, 274.
93. Crossman, *Diaries* (4 Dec. 1951).
94. Castle, *Fighting All the Way*, 193.
95. Mikardo, *Back-bencher*, 108.
96. Castle, *Fighting All the Way*, 193. Crossman, *Diaries* (15 Oct. 1952).
97. *Tribune*, 17 Oct. 1952.
98. Crossman, *Diaries* (28 June 1955; 28 Apr. 1954); P. Ziegler, *Harold Wilson* (1963), 97; A. Howard, *Richard Crossman. The Pursuit of Power* (1990), *passim*.
99. Mikardo, *Back-bencher*, 108; E. Shinwell, *The Labour Story* (1963), 193.
100. Crossman, *Diaries* (23 July 1952).
101. Ted Castle, Ian Aitken, Peggy Duff, Bob Edwards, Jo Richardson (Mikardo's secretary).
102. *Tribune*, 22 Oct. 1954; Morgan Phillips to JL, 27 Oct., 12, 24 Nov. 1954.
103. *New Socialist*, March/April 1982.
104. Crossman, *Diaries* (24 March 1955). For a fuller account, see E. Shaw, *Discipline and Discord in the Labour Party, 1951–1987* (1988), *passim*.
105. J. Young, *Winston Churchill's Last Campaign. Britain and the Cold War, 1951–1955* (1996), 310.
106. That the House 'regrets that the Statement on Defence, 1955, while recognising that thermonuclear weapons have affected a revolution in the character

of warfare, and that until effective world disarmament has been achieved it is necessary as a deterrent to aggression to rely on the threat of using thermonuclear weapons, fails to make proposals for the reorganisation of H.M. Forces and of Civil Defence, to indicate what future defence expenditure may be called for; or to explain the grave and admitted deficiencies in the weapons with which H.M. Forces are at present furnished, in spite of the expenditure of some £4,000m. for defence purposes over the past three years.' *Hansard*, House of Commons, 1 March 1955, col. 1917.

107. Ibid., 2 March 1955, col. 2116 ff.
108. Crossman, *Diaries* (16 March 1955).
109. A senior party agent was reported as saying in the last week of the campaign, 'Issues? issues? There are no issues. This is just a national census to see who's Labour and who's Conservative.' D. Butler, *The British General Election of 1955* (1955), 164.
110. Crossman, *Diaries* (15 July 1955).
111. Jennie's papers contain the following undated note: 'transcending even his passionate, protective concern for the Health service, was his obsessional interest in international relations. Always a major concern but the devastating effect as the full impact of nuclear war risks invaded his sensitive radioactive intelligence made this top priority. If we allowed the world to become polarized between America and the Soviet Union, danger maximized. If a third force could gather strength, it might stop the proliferation of nuclear material. Nenni & Mendes France at Asheridge. Nehru, Tito and many others could be involved. Accepted the responsibility of preparing to become foreign secretary if Labour had won the 1959 election. Subordinated every other interest to this over-riding urgency. He might not have succeeded but certainly it would have altered the course of international affairs. British governments Labour as well as tory, too subservient to America. Friendly yes, sycophancy no. This one reason for his resignation in 1951.'
112. Ian Aitken, *Daily Express*, 1 Oct. 1956.
113. G. Goodman, *The Awkward Warrior: Frank Cousins* (1979), 158; Foot, *Aneurin Bevan*, vol. 2, 581, 570; Jones, *Chances*, 145; interview M. Jones. Jennie always insisted that CND was a middle-class cause.
114. By which, Jennie pointed out to Jack Hylton, Nye meant not 'naked' of bombs, but naked of alliances. He was referring 'to the network of international agreements that existed when one government gives place to another'. JL to Jack Hylton, 16 June 1964; JL papers.

    Nearly ten years later, Jennie offered yet another version in a letter to a friend: 'We were on the run-up to a General Election, and always Nye and those most closely associated with him closed the ranks at such times. He had either to speak as Shadow Foreign Secretary officially at the Annual Party Conference, or once more have the Party split wide open. He got most of his way in the compromise resolution, but this was misunderstood by many of the delegates. What he in fact said was that he had opposed Britain having the bomb; had opposed the testing of the bomb, and hoped that a Labour Government could lead a non-nuclear club that would prevent smaller countries from attempting to become nuclear powers.

'When he talked about "don't send me naked into the Conference Chamber" he was saying "give me something with which I can negotiate." In other words, Britain had no power to influence either Russia or America, but might well have given a lead to other countries . . . Nye was obsessed with the atomic menace of those years.' JL to Muriel (Box?), 3 Dec. 1973.

115. F. Brockway, *Towards Tomorrow* (1977), 227.
116. JL to M. Foot, 17 Oct. 1965.
117. Goodman, *The Awkward Warrior*, 237. Nye thought only fifty Labour MPs were socialists; Foot, *Aneurin Bevan*, 623.
118. P. Williams, *Hugh Gaitskell*, 559; 'Truce at Blackpool', *New Statesman*, 5 Dec. 1959.
119. Goodman, *The Awkward Warrior*, 237. 'After Gaitskell's speech, Bevan told me that G. would have to go and that either he or I would be leader, probably me', Wilson later told a confidant. Qtd in Roth, *Sir Harold Wilson*, 235.
120. Williams, *Hugh Gaitskell*, 558; Brivati, *Hugh Gaitskell*, 344 f.
121. B. Pimlott, *Harold Wilson*, 259.
122. Mann, *Woman in Parliament*, 106–7.
123. Interview G. Goodman.
124. Crossman, *Diaries* (28 April 1953).
125. Qtd in Foot, *Aneurin Bevan*, 43.
126. JL papers, undated diary notes 'written 1945–50 Govt'.
127. JL to C. P. Trevelyan, 4 Dec. 1950.
128. Lee, *My Life*, 168.

Chapter 7

1. Lee, *My Life*, 228.
2. Ibid., 117–18; interviews Mrs S. Saemann, Mrs Arianwen Bevan-Norris.
3. Lee, *Tomorrow*, 104–6.
4. Lee, *My Life*, 162.
5. Interview Constance Cummings; Benn Levy's Introduction to Lee, *This Great Journey*.
6. Foot, *Aneurin Bevan*, vol. 2, 439.
7. JL to Arianwen Bevan-Norris, 27 Nov. 1951; Tommy to JL, 15 June 1947; to Ma Lee, 15 Jan. 1958.
8. Interview Cannock Women's Council.
9. Interview Mrs Arianwen Bevan-Norris; undated jottings 1970s.
10. JL to Mrs Bevan-Norris, 16, 21 Aug. 1950.
11. Interview Mr Robert Norris.
12. Interview Lord Ardwick (John Beaven).
13. JL papers, jottings, dated 16 Jan. 1964.
14. Lee, *My Life*, 104.
15. JL papers, undated jottings, 1972.
16. Lee, *Tomorrow*, 170.
17. JL papers, jottings, dated 3 Dec. 1967.
18. Lee, *My Life*, 147.
19. F. Wheen, *Tom Driberg, His Life and His Indiscretions* (1990), 13. Driberg was a

fantasist. However, similar rumours circulated in the theatre world. There is also Nye's remarkable letter to John Strachey during the 1929 Parliament: 'As this friendship grows, and becomes more and more a part of me, I find myself becoming fearful . . . It is your generous nature that moves me to speak, even though I know that speech would bruise where it would caress.' Qtd in H. Thomas, *John Strachey* (1973), 89.

20. Interview Constance Cummings.
21. JL papers, undated jottings.
22. Private information to the author; interviews Jill Craigie, Barbara Castle; Castle, *Fighting All the Way*, 109.
23. *Daily Sketch*, 19 Apr. 1954; Lee, *My Life*, 205. Jennie was in no position to complain about Nye's driving. Driving their Humber one day in 1954 she careered across the road, knocked down the wall of a house, and hospitalized a Mr Shrubsall. She visited him in hospital bearing tulips; and was fined £10 for careless driving.
24. Interviews Jill Craigie, Mrs Ushe Adams; private information to the author.
25. Interviews Shirley Williams, Mrs S. Saemann, Mr Bevan-Norris.
26. Nye to JL, 12 Feb. 1953, n.d., 29 March 1957, n.d. 1959.
27. *Enfield Weekly Herald*, 15 July 1960.
28. Interview Mrs Bevan-Norris. Arianwen believed that Jennie was worried about her figure. Jennie told Suse it was a choice between children and a career. She chose the career over children (and Nye over the career).
29. JL papers, jottings, dated 26 May 1978.
30. *The People's Journal*, 18 Nov. 1961.
31. *Daily Mirror*, 14 Aug. 1945.
32. Interview Constance Cummings.
33. Interview Lord John Mackie; *News Chronicle*, 17 July 1954.
34. Lee, *My Life*, 210.
35. Their net loss for 1955–6 was £1,133, for 1956–7 it was £197, for 1957–8 £2,593 (when pig disease cost them dear). Asheridge was sold in 1968 for £40,000, excluding livestock and implements.
36. Tax and farm accounts, JL to Mr Rubens, 20 March 1956; see also draft accounts 1957–8, 1958–9.
37. JL to A. Goodman, 7 Dec. 1967.
38. Financial papers, JL to and from Chesham Builders, 2 Nov. 1957, 14 Jan., 14 Feb., 18, 24, 26 March, 23 Apr., 7, 17 May 1958.
39. John Buchan, 'Portrait of Aneurin Bevan', BBC, 21 Aug. 1961.
40. Interview John Mackie.
41. MP's salaries were £1,000 p.a. from 1946, £1,250 p.a. from 1954, £1,750 p.a. from 1957, and £3,250 p.a. from 1964.
42. JL to A. Goodman, 12 Sept. 1962.
43. Interview Woodrow Wyatt. He asked Nye who was his NHS doctor: 'I'll use the same one.' Nye replied, 'I don't use one. I go to Dan Davies, the Queen's physician.' Sir Dan was an old friend from Tredegar days who smoothed Nye's political relations with consultants in 1947–8. He lovingly cared for Nye during his last illness. In hospital, Nye and Jennie were always NHS patients.

Jennie used NHS GPs for her mother and later for herself, but would check into the London Clinic or Harley Street for any specialist medical problems.

44. Djilas was sentenced to house arrest in January 1954 for 'hostile propaganda', then tried and imprisoned in December 1956 and again in October 1957 for 'slandering Yugoslavia' in his books. For a critical view of Djilas and his 'wild denunciation', see B. Castle, 'Yugoslavia after Djilas', *New Statesman*, 10 Feb. 1957. For discussion of Yugoslavia in *Tribune*, see pp. 179–80.
45. J. Lee, 'Tito the Giant-Killer', *Tribune*, 13 Feb. 1953.
46. Memorial Meeeting for Jennie Lee, House of Commons, 17 Jan. 1989.
47. Lee, *My Life*, 197.
48. *Daily Express*, 7 Jan. 1954.
49. Transcript interview, J. Lee with B. R. Nanda, 1 Aug. 1967, JL papers.
50. Foot, *Aneurin Bevan*, vol. 2, 391.
51. Lee, *My Life*, 222; JL to Archie Lush, 20 Jan. 1963.
52. Lee, *My Life*, 240.
53. JL to Archie Lush, 20 Jan. 1963; Foot, *Aneurin Bevan*, vol. 2, 616.
54. JL papers, undated jottings (?1978).
55. Interview Michael Foot.
56. JL to M. Foot, 25 Jan. 1962.
57. *Daily Express*, 7 July 1960.
58. Interview Jill Craigie.
59. Lee, *My Life*, 248. In *My Life with Nye*, she tells the story straight but she cannot surely have been unaware of its heavy symbolic charge.
60. Archie Lush to JL, undated MS (1960).
61. Interview John Mackie, Ian Aitken (Mackie's brother-in-law).
62. Interview Jill Craigie, Arianwen Bevan-Norris.
63. John Buchan, who nursed Nye and also knew the truth, believed they had successfully kept it from him, and that they were right to do so. J. Buchan, 'The Member for Ebbw Vale. A Portrait of Aneurin Bevan', BBC, full transcript 21 Aug. 1961, transmitted extracts 3 Oct. 1961; Lee, *My Life*, 253.
64. Interviews Michael Foot, Eirene White, John Mackie, Ian Aitken. The exception was John Buchan.
65. JL to Archie Lush, 8 Nov. 1961.
66. JL to M. Foot, 25 Jan. 1962; Lee, *My Life*, 263.
67. *Sunday Telegraph*, 16 Nov. 1980.
68. JL to M. Foot, 6 July, T. Driberg to JL, 7 July 1960.
69. Foot, *Aneurin Bevan*, vol. 2, 655.
70. Interview Lord Parry.
71. JL papers, MS jottings, 22 Jan. 1962; diary notes, 23 Aug. 1972; MS jottings, 1960 onwards, n.d.
72. *Daily Express*, 27 July 1960.

Chapter 8

1. JL papers, MS jottings, 1960, 29 Jan. 1961; typed notes, 12 Sept. 1962.
2. JL to Archie Lush, 8 Nov. 1961.
3. Interview Vincent Stafford; draft letter to Arnold Goodman, JL papers, n.d.
4. Interview Mrs Bettina Stafford, Vincent Stafford.

5. Mervyn Stockwood to JL, 'Saturday'; JL to Mervyn Stockwood, 11 July 1962; see also, J. Lee, 'Labour and the Public Schools', *Tribune*, 20 Feb. Public schools 'stamped class labels . . . on the very souls of children'; *Tribune*, 19 June 1953.
6. JL to Mervyn Stockwood, 11 July 1962.
7. JL to Archie Lush, 8 Nov. 1961.
8. JL to Archie Lush, 20 Jan. 1963. It is a description which has strong echoes of her account of Ma and Nye in the farmhouse kitchen; Lee, *My Life*, 227, 232.
9. Interview Mrs Bettina Stafford.
10. Interview Dorothy Vernon.
11. JL to M. Foot, 17 Oct. 1965.
12. M. Foot to JL, 'Tuesd', 'Thursd' (n.d.); JL to M. Foot, 28 July 1960.
13. JL to M. Foot 17 Oct. 1965. Jennie was by then a minister.
14. JL to Archie Lush, 8 Nov. 1961; *The Listener*, 22 May 1982.
15. Minutes of the Aneurin Bevan Memorial Foundation, and associated correspondence, 1966–87, JL papers, *passim*. For Djilas, see J. Lee to Goodman Derrick, 8 Oct. 1975. By the mid-1970s, the fund had £100,000 in assets, which by 1987 had risen to £187,000. This generated trust fund income of some £7,000 rising to £15,000 p.a.
16. Compare Nye's own words to Michael Foot in hospital: 'Never underestimate the passion for unity, and don't forget it's the decent instinct of people who want to do something', words that Michael quoted when he was elected leader of the Labour Party. Jennie's plea did not stop the 1960 Conference being one of the rowdiest for years, with Gaitskell defeated on nuclear weapons.
17. *Tredegar Express and Star*, 27 Nov. 1964.
18. *Sunday Times*, 20 Aug. 1972.
19. *Daily Telegraph*, 27 Oct. 1960.
20. *Daily Express*, 9 Nov., *Manchester Guardian*, 9 Nov., *The Times*, 16 Dec. 1960.
21. *Hansard*, House of Commons, 8 Feb., 15 Feb. 1961.
22. Ibid., 26 Feb. 1962, col. 1018.
23. *Tribune*, 14 June 1962; *Hansard*, House of Commons, 8 Nov. 1962, col. 1212.
24. Ibid., 19 Dec. 1963, cols. 1556 ff.
25. Interview Mrs Vera Timberlake.

Chapter 9

1. *Listener*, 12 July 1945.
2. Qtd in A. Sinclair's splendid *Arts and Cultures* (1995), 33; CEMA Bulletin, July 1940, qtd by E. White, former staff member of CEMA, in *The Arts Council of Great Britain* (1975), 31, on which this account draws.
3. *Listener*, 12 July 1945.
4. Ibid. John Reith, first Director-General of the BBC (1928–38), laid down the public service ethic of the BBC.
5. Nineteenth Report of Select Committee on Estimates, 1948–9.
6. R. Hutchison, *The Politics of the Arts Council* (1982).
7. Ibid., 60–1 (my emphasis)
8. Ibid., 41.

9. Ibid.
10. *Hansard*, House of Lords, 22 March 1972.
11. Interview A. Goodman.
12. *Guardian*, 13 Jan. 1966.
13. A. Goodman, *Evening Standard*, 25 June 1970; D. Eccles, letter to author.
14. Party Political Broadcast, 19 March 1966.
15. A. Briggs, *The BBC: The First Fifty Years* (1985), 358.
16. For a fascinating account of the pop culture of the 1960s, see R. Hewison, *Too Much. Arts and Society in the 1960s* (1986); and *Culture and Consensus, England, art and Politics since 1940* (1995).
17. Interview A. Wesker; P. Coppieters, 'Arnold Wesker's Centre 42', Ph.D. thesis, Rijksuniversiteit (1971–2); this account draws heavily on both these sources.
18. Wesker lecture, 'Two Snarling Heads'.
19. *Encounter*, Feb. 1962.
20. Interview M. Stockwood.
21. JL, reported in *Sunday Times*, 14 June 1970; Crossman, *Diaries* (28 Oct 1964).
22. In 'The Open University re-examined', BBC broadcast, transmitted 1 Feb. 1983. Interview K. Jeffery; J. Lee, 'Power Politics', n.d. See also H. Wilson's review of Gaitskell's *Diary*, *Guardian*, 8 Sept. 1983.
23. JL papers, undated MS jottings.
24. H. Jenkins, contribution to Revised Policy Statement on the Arts RD 561/ Nov. 1963.
25. Interview K. Jeffery, A. Goodman; JL papers, desk diary jottings for Oct. 1964; misc. jottings, n.d.
26. A. Part, *The Making of a Mandarin* (1990), 112.
27. Ibid., 113.
28. Minutes of the Home Policy Committee, 11 March 1963; 11 May 1964; RD 429, March 1963; RD 561, Nov. 1963; RD 748, May 1964.
29. *Let's Go with Labour*, 18.
30. Part, *Making of a Mandarin*, 113.
31. As Raymond Williams said, reviewing the White Paper, this was not just an administrative change. Jennie's temporary home at the MPBW flagged arts as 'prestige and preservation', and Treasury control suggested that art was 'a minor object of patronage and subvention. Any real policy for the Arts is an educative one: part of a whole growth and activity.' The White Paper, he said, could be read in two ways. Part of it 'proposes bodies we do not want or approves of bodies we already have. But part of it was also about real places and real people—except where it refers to the younger generation as "more hopeful material." They are nobody's damn material' (JL papers, undated press clipping).
32. HM Treasury, *Government and the Arts, 1958–64*; quoted in White, *The Arts Council*, 71–2.
33. Interview A. Goodman; JL papers, misc. jottings, n.d.; A. Goodman, *Tell Them I'm On My Way*, 265.
34. See p. 227.
35. Goodman, *Tell Them I'm On My Way, passim.*
36. Ibid., 274.

37. Letter to author.
38. Interview A. Goodman.
39. Noel Annan, Gala tribute to Goodman, 21 Dec. 1986.
40. Interview K. Jeffery.
41. *Daily Telegraph*, 27 Feb. 1965.
42. The issue of the English language for opera performance, as well as the personal hostility between Drogheda and Harewood, meant there was little co-operation between the two companies (interview A. Goodman). Subtitles were not then in use.
43. As the Arts Council stated in its 21st Annual Report (1965–6): 'Money, rough-hew it as we may, is the subject of all our Annual Reports. Everything else apart from the Accounts might properly be called "extraneous matter".'
44. This account draws on interviews with K. Jeffery, N. Summers, A. Goodman, and H. Jenkins; JL's correspondence, JL to P. Gordon-Walker, 29 Feb. 1968, White, *The Arts Council*, *passim*; J. Cook, *The National Theatre* (1976), *passim*. The five sites were at Bloomsbury, then at Cromwell Road, and then three different sites on the South Bank.
45. Interview D. Plummer.
46. *Hansard*, House of Commons, 5 Feb. 1970, col. 716.
47. G. Drogheda, *Double Harness* (1978), 309.
48. Drogheda to JL, 8 Nov. 1969.
49. Peter Heyworth, *Observer*, 26 June 1965; Goodman, *Tell Them I'm On My Way*, ch. 12, *passim*.
50. Arts Council Annual Report 1958, qtd in Annual Reports 1964–5.
51. Letter to author.
52. Interview A. Goodman.
53. Interview A. Wesker.
54. Goodman, *Tell Them I'm On My Way*, 211–12.
55. Interviews A. Wesker, H. Willatt, A. Goodman; Coppieters, 'Arnold Wesker's Centre 42'.
56. Letter, Dr B. Simpson to author.
57. Letter, N. Reid to author.
58. *The Times*, 8 April 1968.
59. Letter to author.
60. Letter to author.
61. K. Tynan, 'The Royal Smut Hound', in *Tynan Left and Right* (1967), *passim*.
62. Interview G. R. Strauss.
63. Goodman, *Tell Them I'm On My Way*, 66.
64. Elizabeth Thomas to JL, 2 Nov. 1970; interview A. Goodman.
65. J. Lee, 'Theatre and the State', *Hutchinson's Theatre Annual*, 1970–1.
66. Interview N. Stuart; letter N. Reid to author.
67. N. Reid to JL, 30 Nov. 1970; Edward Heath to R. Sainsbury, 1 Dec. 1970.
68. *The Times*, 15 Feb. 1969.
69. White, *The Arts Council*, 287–8.
70. Interview A. Goodman; White, *The Arts Council*, ch. 11, *passim*; E. Thomas to JL, 4 May 1970.
71. *TES*, 19 June 1969; *Sunday Times*, 14 June 1970.

72. JL to H. Wilson, 22 July 1971.
73. J. Lee, entry in *Hutchinson's Theatre Annual* for 1970–1.
74. Letter to author.
75. Jan. 1967
76. *Scotsman*, 15 Apr. 1967.
77. DES, Reports on Education, Music and the Young. Sept. 1967, no. 39. HMIs found in 1964 that of 162 LEAs, 45 had drama advisers, 46 had art advisers, 70 had music advisers; by 1969, there were 70 drama, 50 art, and 80 music advisers.
78. J. Richards and A. Aldgate, *The Best of British Cinema and Society, 1930–70* (1983), 159–60.
79. National Film School (The Lloyd Report) 1967, para. 53.
80. To the original membership of the Lloyd Committee was now added Denis Forman of Granada, Huw Wheldon of the BBC, and Ted Willis; along with Richard Attenborough who offered his services, and Lord Goodman, chairman of British Lion, who was pressed into offering his.
81. *Today's Cinema*, 8 Dec. 1970. The BFI's budget rose from £107,000 in 1963–4 to £625,000 in 1970.
82. Letter H. T. Bourdillon to Mr Brierey, 16 Oct. 1969.
83. Carl Foreman in the brochure for the Cannes Film Festival.
84. JL to Colin Young, 8 July 1971.
85. H. Jenkins, *The Culture Gap* (1979), 134.
86. *Listener*, 12 July 1945.
87. Qtd in White, *The Arts Council*, 243.
88. Ibid., 241–2.
89. Arts Council, Annual Report 21, 1965–6; 24, 1968–9.
90. 'Government and the Theatre', *Hutchinson's Theatre Annual*, 1970–1.
91. Lord Redcliffe-Maud, *Support for the Arts*, Gulbenkian Report (1976), 74.
92. JL papers, undated MS.
93. Arts Council Annual Report 22, 1967–8.
94. Interview H. Jenkins.
95. Interview A. Goodman.
96. Interview H. Willatt.
97. JL to P. Gordon-Walker, Secretary of State for Education., 8 Dec. 1967. Diamond was referring to the Public Expenditure Survey Committee.
98. JL to Wilson, 12 Dec. 1967; and his undated memo of reply.
99. Roy Jenkins warned his Chief Secretary not to get 'dug in too far' as he would not be able to sustain it (interview R. Jenkins).
100. JL to Jack Diamond, 10 Feb. 1969; AG to JL, 7 May 1969.
101. DES, Report on the Arts, *A Growing Concern*, Sept. 1968.
102. Interview A. Goodman; interview H. Willat; Goodman, *Tell Them I'm On My Way*, 280–3.
103. The figures are extracted from the Arts Council's annual reports. The DES analysed the Arts Council budget for 1968–9 thus: 32% on the four national companies, 5% on Housing the Arts, 5% on central administration, 14% on London, 29% on English regions, 9% on Scotland, 6% on Wales; Report on the Arts, *A Growing Concern*, DES (Sept. 1968).

104. *Tribune*, 21 July 1967.
105. Arts Council Annual Report, 1967–8.
106. *Birmingham Post*, 25 Oct. 1969; *Northern Echo*, 26 Jan. 1970.
107. Redcliffe-Maud, *Support for the Arts*, 110–12.
108. White, *The Arts Council*, 86–7.
109. *Sunday Times*, 20 Feb. 1966.
110. JL papers, undated misc. jottings, 1985?
111. Goodman, *Tell Them I'm On My Way*, 289.
112. Ibid.
113. K. Tynan, 'The National Theatre', in *Tynan Left and Right*.
114. 'The Culture Confusion', *Focus* (March 1965).
115. *Sunday Times*, 20 Feb. 1966.
116. Interview C. Cummings.
117. Attenborough to JL, 5 July 1970; Olivier to JL, 22 June 1970; E. Boyle to JL, 23 June 1970.
118. *TES*, 19 Sept. 1969; *Evening Standard*, 25 June 1970.

Chapter 10

1. *The Times*, 9 Sept. 1963.
2. *The Economist*, 14 Sept. 1963. *The Economist*, under its former editor Geoffrey Crowther, did not like Oxbridge, nor the WEA, had grave reservations about the BBC, but had given generous support to the new universities. Letter Asa Briggs to author.
3. *TES*, 13 Sept. 1963.
4. *Listener*, 3 Oct. 1963.
5. *Learn and Live*, 3.
6. Preface to W. Perry, *The Open University* (1976), xi–xii.
7. The UK figure rises to 8.5% of the eligible age group in 1962 if teacher-training and other advanced colleges are included. H. Perkin, *Innovation in Higher Education. New Universities in the UK* (1969), 45.
8. J. W. B. Douglas, *The Home and the School* (1964); and *All Our Future* (1968).
9. *The Times*, 3 Oct. 1967.
10. Robbins showed that until 1959, about 75% of those with university qualifications went to university. By 1961, this had fallen to 60%. During the mid 1960s he calculated that there would be a deficiency of 78,000 university places. Between 1928 and 1947, 8.9% of middle-class boys had gone to university, and 1.4% of working-class boys; in 1960, the comparable percentages were 16.8% and 2.6%. *Robbins Report*, App. 1, 38, 47, 54.
11. *The Pilkington Report into the Future of Broadcasting*, June 1962, 46, 67, 273–7.
12. B. Sendall, *Independent Television in Britain*, vol. 2 (1983), 274 ff. Universities were also experimenting with closed-circuit TV; Strathclyde wanted a full broadcasting licence for its outreach work.
13. Even if ETV broadcast 18 hours a day, 7 days a week, that provided only 5,000 teaching hours p.a.; a medium-sized technical college like Ealing offered 35,000 teaching hours p.a. to its students. VCRs (not yet available) would soften, but not overcome the problem.
14. 'Educational Television. Future Developments and proposed pilot experi-

ment.' Memorandum prepared by the DES for the inter-departmental working party on educational broadcasting, n.d. summer 1964.

15. Wilson may have exaggerated the effectiveness of the Chicago scheme. Of its 53,000 participants, only 1,100 obtained a credit, and just 122 went on to take a degree.
16. Interviews E. Short, R. Jenkins, J. Callaghan; T. Benn, Open University interview, 19 Mar. 1982.
17. Pimlott, *Harold Wilson*, 513–14.
18. Anon. (Brian Jackson?), 'The Open University, MY's contribution', undated typescript; M. Young, 'The Origins of the Open university', supplementary note to the author, 2 Apr. 1992; 'Notes on the University of the Air', confidential Labour Party discussion paper, May 1964 RD/776; 'Towards an Open University', *Where?* (autumn, 1964). At the same time, he was coaxing Anglia TV into its Dawn University and drafting educational papers for Transport House.
19. M. Young, letter to author, 29 Dec. 1992.
20. *Sunday Times*, 30 Jan. 1977.
21. Interview A. Christodoulou.
22. Michael Young, 'The Story of the National Extension College', typescript; letter Asa Briggs to author.
23. Interview Ralph Toomey.
24. BBC Forum on the Open University, 10 Feb. 1975; JL papers, misc. jottings, 1985.
25. Interview Ralph Toomey.
26. J. Tunstall (ed.), *The Open University Opens* (1974), *passim*.
27. *Education*, 15 Mar. 1968.
28. *Spectator*, 28 Apr. 1967; *The Times*, 22 Sept. 1967.
29. *TES*, 5 Feb. 1965.
30. *TES*, 4 Mar. 1966.
31. Stuart Hood, *The Times*, 22 Oct. 1967.
32. Walton Hall lecture.
33. Interview Bill Hughes; TUC/OU Conference on Education for Adults, 2 May 1978; B. Jackson, *Guardian*, 22 June 1965.
34. See letter Tom Kelley, secretary of the Universities Council for Adult Education, to *The Times*, 7 March 1966; the WEA submission to the Planning Committee, reported *TES*, 26 Apr. 1968; Roy Shaw in his Jennie Lee Memorial Lecture 1989; interview Richard Hoggart; Neil Kinnock, Jennie Lee Memorial meeting, 17 Jan. 1989.
35. They pointed out that as many people were doing degree-level work in FE colleges and CATs as in universities, and five times as many were in subdegree courses. Their task should be to help students get satisfaction and advancement in their jobs. 'The technical colleges' effort is central to social and economic life and to the needs of working class people', unlike the WEA which was all about personal cultivation and therefore 'crammed with the bourgeoisie'. *Guardian*, 23 June 1968.
36. Note by the Secretariat, for meeting of CVCP with JL, 7 July 1967; minutes of

meeting of CVCP with JL, 19 July 1967; letter Peter Venables to Dr Christopherson, chairman, CVCP, 11 Sept. 1967.

37. *New Statesman*, 11 March 1966.
38. Interview R. Hoggart.
39. JL to A. Christodoulou, 12 Jan. 1971; JL to W. Perry, 28 Jan. 1974.
40. Perry, *The Open University*, 24.
41. Professor K. J. Alexander, Professor of Economics, University of Strathclyde; Lord Annan, Provost, King's College, Cambridge; Dr E. W. Briault, Deputy Education Officer, Inner London Education Authority; Dr Brynmor Jones, Vice-Chancellor of the University of Hull; Mr D. J. G. Holroyde, Director, University of Leeds Television Centre; Mr Peter Laslett, Fellow of Trinity College, Cambridge; Professor F. Llewellyn-Jones, Principal, University College of Swansea; Mr N. MacKenzie, Lecturer in Sociology, University of Sussex; Mr A. D. Peterson, Director, Department of Education, University of Oxford; Dr O. G. Pickard, Principal, Ealing Technical College; Mr J. Scupham, retired Controller of Educational Broadcasting, BBC; Professor H. Wiltshire, Professor of Adult Education, University of Nottingham.
42. JL papers, misc. jottings, June 1985.
43. Minutes of the Advisory Committee, 8 June 1965.
44. Ibid., 23 June 1965.
45. Minutes, 14 June 1965; i.e. a 'secondary modern university', rather than a 'grammar school university'.
46. JL to Marcia Williams, 4 Aug. 1965.
47. BBC1 transmitted from 9.20 a.m.; BBC2, apart from half an hour in the morning, from 7.20 p.m.; ITV was confined to 8 hours a day, from 2.30 p.m.
48. Benn, T., *Out of the Wilderness. Diaries 1963–7* (1987) (10 May 1966), hereafter Benn, *Diaries*.
49. Its membership in May 1965 included the Home Secretary (Sir Frank Soskice and then Roy Jenkins); the Secretaries for Scotland and Wales; the Minister for Housing and Local Government (Richard Crossman); the PMG (Tony Benn); the Attorney-General (Sir Elwyn Jones); the Chief Whip (Ted Short); the Financial Secretary to the Treasury (Niall MacDermot, and then Jack Diamond); Bill Rogers from the DEA, George Darling from the Board of Trade, Lord Snow from the Ministry of Technology, and Jennie Lee. Frank Longford was there from the Lords. It was chaired by the Lord President of the Council, Herbert Bowden.
50. Interview E. Short.
51. Interview R. Jenkins.
52. Interview JL's private secretary.
53. Interview R. Toomey.
54. J. Lee, lecture at Walton Hall, Feb. 1975.
55. Correspondence JL and Jack Diamond, 3, 7 Feb. 1966; JL to H. Wilson, 3 Feb. 1966.
56. Benn, *Diaries* (8 Feb. 1966).
57. Goodman, *Tell Them I'm On My Way*, 413.
58. Ibid., 412. Goodman was to meet Bundy again in May 1967, and Jennie, with

help from the Treasury, put in a very large bid to the Ford Foundation. It fell through.

59. Sir Hugh Greene to Lord Goodman, 29 March 1966; Planning Committee Minutes of the OU, 12, 6 Feb. 1969.
60. Memo R. Toomey to N. Summer, 11 Aug. 1966.
61. Interview R. Toomey.
62. *Teacher*, 11 Mar. 1966.
63. Mr Bryan, *Hansard*, House of Commons, 3 Mar. 1966.
64. Perry, *The Open University*, 22.
65. B. MacArthur, in Tunstall, *The Open University Opens*, 9. The Sussex connection was significant: Fulton was Wilson's mentor, and Vice-Chairman of the BBC; and it provided allies in Norman MacKenzie and Asa Briggs; Edward Boyle was Pro-Chancellor (information, Asa Briggs).
66. Memo R. Toomey to author.
67. Interview R. Toomey.
68. JL papers, misc. jottings, 1985.
69. Interview W. Perry, R. Toomey, A. Briggs.
70. Interview M. James; Jennie and her private office describe 38 Belgrave Square as empty; the Schools Council for Curriculum and Examinations subsequently claimed they were evicted on a week's notice. *Evening Standard*, 9 Nov. 1968.
71. JL papers, misc. jottings, 1985.
72. Minute, R. Toomey 17 Jan. 1967; Noel Annan to JL, 17 Jan. 1967.
73. *Hansard*, House of Commons, 27 Jan. 1969.
74. Interview Lord Hailsham.
75. Reported in *Daily Telegraph*, 17 Feb. 1969.

Chapter 11

1. Venables to JL, 15 Aug. 1969.
2. JL to Venables, 25 Nov. 1970.
3. M. Thatcher to R. Toomey, n.d. 'Thursday'.
4. Letter, M. Thatcher to author, 27 Sept. 1991.
5. According to Chris Price, if Thatcher had cut the OU, she would not have had to cut school milk or force up the price of school dinners.
6. Interview W. Perry.
7. Interview David Grugeon.
8. Interview A. Christodoulou.
9. Interview N. Stewart.
10. Ibid.
11. J. Byron, 'Provision for the University of the Air', conference paper, 1966. See also *Local Government Chronicle*, 11 May 1966.
12. Interview Chris Price, A. Christodoulou.
13. J. Ferguson, *The Open University from Within, passim,* on which these paras draw.
14. W. Ismay to W. Perry, 3, 17 Dec. 1968.
15. The deal consisted of the purchase of Walton Hall, plus a commercial lease on

15 acres of building land, and the rest of the site at a peppercorn rent; Perry to Ismay, 13 Feb. 1969.

16. Interview Lord Campbell.
17. Perry, *The Open University*, 39.
18. Interview Jane Drew.
19. Ibid.
20. *New Society*, 31 May 1973.
21. Perry, *The Open University*, 43–4.
22. Gardiner to JL, 20 Sept. 1972; OU misc. papers.
23. Interview Steven Rose.
24. See the thanks expressed to him by the Planning Committee, 25 Sept. 1968.
25. W. R. van Straubenzee, 'Whither the Open University', a lecture to Bristol OU students, 9 Apr. 1976 (I am grateful to Naomi McIntosh for this reference).
26. J. Lee, lecture at Walton Hall, January 1978.
27. *Learn and Live*, 14.
28. Interview Lord Campbell.
29. Perry to JL, 26 March 1974.
30. *Hansard*, House of Lords, 23 May 1974, 5 May 1975, 31 March 1976.
31. *Guardian*, 27 Jan. 1978.
32. *Hansard*, House of Lords, 18 June 1975, col. 969.
33. Information, N. McIntosh.
34. Perry, *The Open University*, 189.
35. J. Horlock, *The Open University After Fifteen Years* (1984).
36. *Hansard*, House of Lords, 31 March 1976, col. 1126.
37. *Hansard*, House of Lords, 23 May 1974, col. 1605.
38. He had produced for the Planning Committee (6 Feb. 1969) a draft quota system by occupation—of the first 10,000 places, 3,000 should go to teachers, 1,000 to civil servants, 2,000 to manual workers, 1,000 to 'housewives'.
39. Close to the overall proportion of women (28%) in conventional universities in 1970–1, and less than the new intake in 1971 of whom 34% were female (N. McIntosh, 'Women and the Open University' (1973). Around a quarter of mature students, and only 21% of part-time students were women. In 1969–70, 35% of Birkbeck's students were women.
40. *Hansard*, House of Lords, 23 May 1974, col. 1609; 18 June 1975, col. 970. When Naomi McIntosh, who chaired the OU Admissions Committee, tried to increase the proportion of women by fast-tracking their applications for science and maths, the EOC was obliged to take an interest.
41. *Sesame*, Sept. 1974.
42. M. Griffiths, 'Women in Higher Education—A Case Study of the Open University', *Schooling for Work*, Survey Research Dept. Paper 161 (1979).
43. Robbins estimated that by 1970–1, 386,000 teachers were needed to bring secondary classes down to 30, primary schools down to 40; 407,000 for ROSLA; 482,000 to reduce primary classes to 30; App. 1, para. 103 ff. Of 262,000 teachers (England and Wales) in 1961–2, 56,000 were graduates, 219,000 were non-graduates (7,000 were part time).
44. Brian Jackson, 'I feared the OU might basically become a super teachers'

training college, converting two-year diplomas into degrees that were career coinage.' (*Sesame. The First Ten Years*, 25.) By 1987, the percentage of applicants with teaching certificates had fallen to 7%.

45. JL letters, 28 Jan. 1974.
46. *Hansard*, House of Lords, 23 May 1974, col. 1607.
47. In 1989 the overall early drop-out rate was 28%, but for the unqualified and unemployed it was 42%. N. McIntosh, 'Open Admission—an Open or Revolving Door', *Universities Quarterly*, vol. 29 (spring 1975); N. Sargant, 'The Open University', in R. Fieldhouse, *A Modern History of Adult Education* (1997).
48. D. Harris, *Openness and Closure in Distance Education*, 1987.
49. Perry, *The Open University*, 189.
50. *Sesame*, Nov. 1977.
51. N. McIntosh, *A Degree of Difference* (1977). In 1971, 29% of conventional students and 52% of OU students had fathers in manual occupations.
52. Letters in *Sesame*, 1970–80.
53. JL papers, misc. jottings.
54. *Hansard*, House of Lords, 23 May 1974, col. 1607. Two years later she told the Lords that in 1975 there were 1,200, and in 1976 1,400 disabled students with the OU; loc. cit., 31 Mar. 1976, col. 1126.
55. *Sesame*, *The First Ten Years*, 21.
56. *Sesame*, Dec. 1978.
57. Ferguson, *The Open University from Within*, 108.
58. *Sesame*, May/June 1973.
59. *The Seafarer*, Winter 1963.
60. J. Tunstall (ed.), *The Open University Opens*, 78–99.
61. R. Thompson, 'OU at UEA', 1971 MS; JL papers.
62. *Hansard*, House of Lords, 23 May 1974, cols 1606–9.
63. Tunstall (ed.), *The Open University Opens*.
64. Ferguson, *The Open University from Within*.
65. *Sesame*, 'The First Ten Years', 1979, 15.
66. Interview J. Callaghan.

Chapter 12

1. Interview Shirley Williams.
2. JL papers, misc. jottings, 1985.
3. A. Crosland to JL, n.d., 'Monday'; Simon Jenkins, *Evening Standard*, 9 Nov. 1968.
4. Interview Dennis Howell.
5. JL papers, undated jottings, 1982–5.
6. A. Crosland, Woolwich speech, 27 Apr. 1965.
7. A. Crosland, to JL, 7 Sept. 1967.
8. Interview, K. Jeffery.
9. JL to P. Gordon-Walker, 18 Mar. 1968.
10. Ted Short wanted a modest expansion of nursery education. The Chancellor (Roy Jenkins) gave him a choice: nursery schools or the OU. Both knew that as the OU had Wilson's support, nursery education would have to be sacrificed.

11. Goodman, *Tell Them I'm On My Way*, 275, 280.
12. Interview R. Toomey. Toomey brilliantly fudged her position in the White Paper (Feb. 1966) by deploying both languages—the university of the air 'can' be established, and arrangements 'will be made'—a discrepancy Toomey was anxious not to resolve and hopeful that no one else would spot.
13. Letter to author from Sir William Reid.
14. Interview K. Stewart.
15. Roy Shaw, letter to author.
16. Nicholas Tomalin, *Sunday Times*, 20 Feb. 1966.
17. JL papers, MS jottings, 29 May 1978.
18. The farm was sold the following year for £40,000 gross (£20,000 net). The lease on Chester Row cost £200 a year.
19. Linda Christmas, *TES*, 19 Sept. 1969,
20. Unlike all the other divisions of the NEC, the women's section was elected by the entire conference, not by its separate sections, so the trade unions commanded 90% of the vote. Jennie would have added the women's reserved seats to the constituency section.
21. Jean Mann resigned over the choice of Scottish woman's organizer. She was not unfriendly to Jennie and timed her resignation to help Jennie come on to the NEC. She briefed Jennie. 'Heavens. I'm terribly busy this week. Why didn't you wait?' Mann, *Woman in Parliament*, 114.
22. Crossman, *Diaries* (9 March 1953).
23. Interview Lord Longford.
24. NEC minutes, 22 March 1961.
25. Ibid., 28 Feb. 1962. They lost by five votes to eighteen.
26. Jennie had also to deal with internal party matters, such as the breakaway Pembroke CLP and its MP Desmond Donnelly; changes in senior staff and in committee structure. See ibid., 1967–8.
27. *Observer*, 7 Jan. 1968; *Manchester Guardian*, 11 Jan. 1968; *The People*, 14 Jan. 1968; PLP minutes, 21 March, 8, 29 May; Liaison Committee minutes, 22, 31 Jan., 7 Feb., 6 Mar., 10 Apr., 1 May; NEC minutes, 21 Feb., 24 Apr. 1968.
28. *Sun*, 3 Sept. 1968.
29. G. Goodman, *Sun*, 3 Sept. 1968.
30. *Guardian*, 30 Sept. 1968; *Evening Standard*, 30 Sept. 1968.
31. Interview Lord Carter, A. Watkins, 'The Art of Conferencemanship', *New Statesman*, 4 Oct. 1968.
32. *Sun*, 5 Oct. 1968.
33. John Vereker, a Warwickshire councillor; *Cannock Advertiser and Courier*, 18, 25 Sept. 1964.
34. *Cannock Avertiser*, 31 Mar. 1966.
35. Information David Ennals, who was nursing an adjacent seat.
36. Interview Mrs Renée Short. P. Norton and D. Wood, *Back from Westminster, British Members of Parliament and their Constituents* (1993), *passim*.
37. Interview Mrs Timberlake.
38. Norton and Wood, *Back from Westminster, passim*.
39. Doreen Andrews to D. Davis, 20 Sept. 1969.
40. *Cannock Labour Party Minute Book*, 10 Nov. 1969.

41. *Cannock Advertiser*, 9 July 1970.
42. Ibid., 18 June 1970.
43. Information, David Ennals.
44. The 1969 Representation of the People Act lowered the voting age to eighteen; young voters formed 10% of the Cannock electorate, though they were less likely to be registered and less likely to vote than their parents.
45. Renée Short's majority fell from 8,102 to less than 2,000. The median swing in the 30 seats with Powellite candidates was 5%, only 0.2% above the national average swing of 4.8%. However, the National Front had done well in the May local elections in Wolverhampton; and of the 10 seats with the highest swing against Labour, 5 of them were in the Wolverhampton area: Cannock (11%), Brierley Hill (9.5%), Renée Short's Wolverhampton N-E (9.1%), George Brown's Belper (8.8%), and Wolverhampton S-W (8.7%). When after the election NOP asked voters whether Powell had made them more or less likely to vote Conservative, 37% said more, 23% said less. D. Butler and M. Pinto-Duschinsky, *The British General Election of 1970* (1971), 161, 328, and App. 1.

    More recent research suggests that *nationally* Powell's views brought a swing to the Tories of between 1.3% and 1.5% in 1970, without which Wilson would have held on. 'Powell's impact during the campaign is indisputable', says his latest biographer. 'Powell had not created the antipathy towards immigrants in Britain, but he had channelled this hostility into votes for the Conservatives.' R. Shepherd, *Enoch Powell* (1996), 399–403; R. W. Johnson, 'Stick to the Latin', *London Review of Books*, 23 Jan. 1997. Without Powell, and with the national swing to the Tories reduced by 1.5%, Jennie might just have held Cannock by 200 votes or so.
46. Interview D. and M. Davis, J. Sunley; draft election addresses among JL papers.
47. *Cannock Advertiser*, 4 June, 25 June 1970.
48. Ibid., 25 June 1970. See also endnote 45.
49. Ibid.
50. Interview Mr and Mrs Sunley.

Chapter 13

1. B. Castle to JL, 23 June 1970; B. Wootten to JL, 24 June 1970; H. Wilson to JL, 30 July 1970.
2. JL to L. Jeger, 17 Feb. 1978.
3. *Hansard*, House of Commons, 20 Sept. 1948, col. 579 ff; 14 Nov. 1949, col. 1764 ff. See also J. Lee, 'The House of Lords and All That', *Tribune*, 14, 28 May 1948.
4. 'The Future of the House of Lords', *Parliamentary Affairs* (winter 1953–4), 13.
5. Lord Salisbury had drawn up proposals for life peers at the behest of the National Government in 1932, but they had been abandoned.
6. *Hansard*, House of Commons, R. Butler, M. Lloyd George, 12 Feb. 1958, cols 402 ff; J. Lee, 13 Feb. 1958, cols 610 ff.; J. Lee, 2 Apr. 1958, col. 1254.
7. Interviews J. Waine, Sir Colin Cole. Mrs Stafford insists that Jennie borrowed her dark velvet trouser-suit for the occasion. The staff remember a pink suit. Technically, Jennie was a woman peer, not a peeress (i.e. the wife of a peer).

8. L. Shackleton to H. Wilson, 1 Dec, H. Wilson to L. Shackleton, 4 Dec 1970; interview Lord Strabolgi.
9. Summerskill, *A Woman's World*, 219.
10. J. Lee, *Hansard*, House of Lords, 22 Nov. 1971, cols 867–76.
11. J. Lee to M. Williams, 5 Sept. 1970.
12. ABSA was created (and chaired) by Goodman in 1976. As business sponsorship money flowed into the Arts Council in the early 1970s, the Treasury began to eye its grant. The Council, in some panic, hived off the business monies into an arms-length trust. Jeffery liaised between ABSA and the Arts Council to ensure consistency, e.g., that ABSA did not fund a company that was about to be chopped by the Council. Information K. Jeffery.
13. J. Lee, *Hansard*, House of Lords, 22 Nov. 1971, cols 873–4.
14. Interview Vincent Stafford.
15. JL to Mr and Mrs Tisdall, 21 Oct. 1970.
16. On her death, Jennie left around £220,000 gross in savings (none of it from property), which went to Bettina and Vincent. She had spent almost another £100,000 in recent years assisting Vincent.
17. Mrs Delia Lennie and her family, to whose information and copies of correspondence I am indebted.
18. A. Fox, *Completely Foxed* (1989), ch. 9, 'The Visitors'. Angela Fox accepts that when she later ran into them, 'I find they both look back on those days as having the Colour of the Rose', loc. cit., 126.
19. JL to *Amrita Bazar Patrika* (India's oldest English language paper) 10 Nov. 1964; J. Lee, *Tribune*, 30 Nov. 1962, 5 June 1964.
20. JL to M. Djilas, 8 Oct. 1975.
21. It was financed by Swraj Paul, an Indian industrialist, chairman of the Caparo Group, who had invested in Ebbw Vale, and became in 1996 a Labour life peer. Eldon Griffiths, Peter Shore, Michael Foot, and Jennie were prominent in it. Jones, *Michael Foot*, 403.
22. Benn Levy back in 1940 had quarrelled 'with your bland confession that to you liberty is merely a means to material betterment. This implies that if a more promising means seems to offer itself, liberty would be sacrificed . . . How I abominate that old deceptive defence of evil as a temporary expedient for ultimate good. Always we are left with the expedient and the Good remains ultimate' (Benn Levy to JL, 5 Apr. 1940).
23. *Guardian*, 20 Aug. 1975; *Observer*, 25 Apr.; 2 May 1976. See also David Holden, *Sunday Times*, 28 Dec. 1975; *Guardian* (editorial), 19 Feb. 1976. Dr David Selbourne of Ruskin College was awarded the Bevan memorial fellowship in 1975; on his return from India and to Jennie's dismay he wrote an article for the *Guardian* sharply critical of the state of emergency and its effect on universities.
24. Bevan, *In Place of Fear*, 61–2.
25. Mrs Gandhi to JL, 6 Dec. 1976; JL to Mrs Gandhi, 14 July 1978; JL to R. Aiyar, 7 Oct. 1977; JL to V. Reuther, 21 Jan. 1978.
26. Mrs Gandhi to JL, 6 Dec. 1976, 12 Mar. 1978.
27. *Indira Gandhi* (Vikas Publishing House PVT, 1985), 270–2.

28. JL papers, jottings, 20 Feb. 1972; Lee, *My Life*, 265–6. The publishers chose the title. Jennie had wanted *A Portrait of Nye*. Interview Elizabeth Thomas.
29. *Daily Express*, 19 Nov. 1981 (review of paperback edn.); *Guardian*, 20 Nov. 1980; *Sunday Times*, 16 Nov. 1980; *The Tablet*, 3 Jan. 1981.
30. Ken Morgan, *TLS*, 14 Nov. 1980; Janet Morgan, *FT*, 15 Nov. 1980; F. Brockway, *Tribune*, 14 Nov. 1980; *The Economist*, 15 Nov. 1980; Ben Pimlott, *New Society*, 13 Nov. 1980; P. Whitehead, *Now*, 21 Nov. 1980.
31. *Birmingham Post*, 7 Nov. 1981; *Sunday Standard*, 1 Nov. 1981.
32. Serialization in the *Observer* brought £25,000, and royalties in 1981–2 a further £16,000.
33. *Evening Standard*, 7 Dec. 1982.
34. JL papers, notes, 3 Feb. 1981.
35. Letter Dr S. Bryans to author.
36. JL papers, notes, 4 June 1985.
37. *Sunday Standard*, 1 Nov. 1981.
38. Letter Mrs Delia Lennie to author.
39. JL to M. Foot, 13 June 1985.
40. JL to Mrs Delia Lennie, 14 Aug., 14 Sept. 1984.
41. JL papers, notes, 13 Nov. 1986.
42. *Western Mail*, 28 Nov. 1988. Jennie died 16 Nov. 1988.

SELECTED BIBLIOGRAPHY

Papers

Tony Benn papers (private possession)

Cannock Constituency Labour Party papers (in possession of Mr and Mrs D. Davies)

Chuter Ede papers, British Museum

Common Wealth pamphlets, Bristol Public Library

Housing and Local Government (HLG) files, PRO 36 (2–32); 37 (52, 75–80)

Independent Labour Party, Annual Conference Reports, 1929–1933

Labour Party papers (NEC, PLP, Liaison Committee minutes, etc.), National Museum of Labour History

Jennie Lee papers (to be held by the OU)

Open University papers (minutes, proceedings, and papers of the Advisory and Planning Committees), Milton Keynes

Jo Richardson papers, National Museum of Labour History

C. P. Trevelyan papers (Newcastle Public Library)

Books, theses, articles, selected newspapers

ADDISON, P., 'By-elections of the Second World War', in C. Cook and J. Ramsden (eds), *By-elections in British Politics* (1973)

—— *The Road to 1945* (1975; 1977 edn.)

—— *Now the War is Over, 1945–51* (1985)

ALDERMAN, R. K., 'Discipline in the PLP 1945–51', *Parliamentary Affairs* 18 (1965), 'Parliamentary Party Discipline in Opposition: the P.L.P. 1951–64', *Parliamentary Affairs* 21 (1967–8)

A Policy for the Arts. The First Steps, Government White Paper, Cmnd 2601 (1965)

APPLEYARD, B., *The Culture Club. Crisis in the Arts* (1984)

ARNOT, R. PAGE, *A History of the Scottish Miners* (1955)

The Arts Council of Great Britain, Annual Reports, 1963/4–1971

—— *The Glory of the Garden. The Development of the Arts in England* (1984)

—— *Partnership. Making Arts Money Work Harder* (1986)

'The Arts'. A Discusssion Document for the Labour Party (1975)

Association of District Councils, *Arts and the Districts* (1989)

BALDRY, H., *The Case for the Arts* (1981)

BARNETT, C., *The Lost Victory. British Dreams, British Realities 1945–1950* (1995)

BBC Education, *Further Education. A Report on the use of Broadcasts in FE Colleges* (1976)

—— *Living Decisions in Family and Community. A Retrospective Impression of an Experimental 'Open Learning' Project for Adults* (1976)

—— *Trade Union Studies. A Partnership in Adult Education between the BBC, the TUC and the WEA* (1978)
BECKETT, F., *Enemy Within: The Rise and Fall of the British Communist Party* (1995)
BENN, T., *Out of the Wilderness. Diaries 1963–7* (1987)
BEVAN, A., *In Place of Fear* (1952)
BEVERIDGE, W., *Social Insurance and Allied Services* (1942)
BONDFIELD, M., *A Life's Work* (1949)
BOOTH, A., 'The Labour Party and Economics between the Wars', *Bulletin Society Study of Labour History* 47 (1983)
BRADDOCK, J. and E., *The Braddocks* (1963)
BRAILSFORD, H. N., HOBSON, J. A., JONES, A. C., WISE, E. F., *The Living Wage* (1926)
—— *The Life-work of J. A. Hobson* (1947)
Lord BRIDGES, 'The State and the Arts'. The Romanes Lecture (1958)
BRIGGS, A., 'The Role of the Open University', Ritchie Calder Memorial Lecture (1985)
—— *The BBC. The First Fifty Years* (1985)
—— *History of Broadcasting in the UK: Sound and Vision*, vol. 4 (1979); *Competition*, vol. 5 (1995)
BRIGGS, A., and SAVILLE, J. (eds), *Essays in Labour History*; vol. 3, *1918–39* (1977)
Bristol Evening Post, 1942–3
BRIVATI, B., *Hugh Gaitskell* (1996)
BROCKWAY, F., *Inside the Left* (1941)
—— *Outside the Right* (1963)
—— *Towards Tomorrow* (1977)
BROME, V., *Aneurin Bevan* (1953)
BROOKE, S., *Labour's War. The Labour Party during the Second World War* (1992)
BROOKES, P., *Women at Westminster* (1967)
BROWN, G., 'The Labour Party and Political Change in Scotland, 1918–1929. The Politics of Five Elections.' Ph.D. thesis, University of Edinburgh (1981)
—— *Maxton* (1986)
BROWN, P., 'History of Coalmining in Lochgelly', typescript, n.d.
BRULEY, S., 'Women against War and Fascism: Communism, Feminism and the People's Front', in Fyrth, J. (ed.), *Britain, Fascism and the Popular Front* (1985)
BRYON, J. F. W., 'Library Provision for a University of the Air', conference paper typescript (1966)
BUTLER, D., *The British General Election of 1951* (1951)
—— *The British General Election of 1955* (1955)
BUTLER, D., and PINTO-DUSCHINSKY, M., *The British General Election of 1970* (1971)
BUTLER, D., and ROSE, R., *The British General Election of 1959* (1960)
BUTLER, R. A. B., 'The Difficult Art of Autobiography', The Romanes Lecture (1967)
CAIRNCROSS, A., *Years of Recovery. British Economic Policy 1945–51* (1985)
CALDER, A., 'The Common Wealth Party 1942–1945', Ph.D. thesis, University of Sussex (1968)
CAMPBELL, J., *Nye Bevan and the Mirage of British Socialism* (1987)
Cannock and Hednesford Official Guide, n.d.
Cannock Advertiser, 1945–70

Cannock Constituency Labour Party Minute Book, Oct. 1969–Sept. 1970
Cannock Courier, 1945–70
Cannock Labour Gazette, 1945–70
Petition of Cannock UDC for Incorporation as a Municipal Borough (1953)
CASTLE, B., *Fighting All the Way* (1993 edn.)
CAZALET-KEIR, T., *From the Wings. An Autobiography* (1967)
CEADEL, M., *Pacifism in Britain 1914–1945. The Defining of a Faith* (1980)
—— 'Labour as a Governing Party: Balancing Left and Right', in Gourvish, T., and O'Day, A. (eds), *Britain Since 1945* (1991)
CLARKE, P., *Liberals and Social Democrats* (1978)
—— *The Keynesian Revolution in the Making, 1924–1936* (1988)
—— *A Question of Leadership. Gladstone to Thatcher* (1991)
COLE, M., 'The Labour Movement between the Wars', in Martin, D., and Rubinstein, D. (eds), *Ideology and the Labour Movement* (1979)
Common Wealth, *Again? Common Wealth Says No* (1944)
—— *Richard Acland of Common Wealth has a Personal Message for You* (1944)
—— *An Appeal to the British People* (1944)
Conference of Commonwealth Arts Councils, *The Arts Council Phenomenon: A Report* (1980)
—— *Patron or Paymaster: The Arts Council Dilemma* (1982)
COOK, J., *The National Theatre* (1976)
COPPIETERS, F., 'Arnold Wesker's Centre 42', Ph.D. thesis, Rijksuniversiteit Gent (1971/2)
CROSLAND, S., *Tony Crosland* (1982)
CROSSMAN, R., *The Backbench Diaries of Richard Crossman*, ed. Morgan, J. (1981)
DAICHES, D., *Sir Herbert Grierson, 1866–1960*, Proceedings of the British Academy (1960)
DALTON, H., *High Tide and After. Memoirs 1945–1960* (1962)
DARE, R., 'The Socialist League', D.Phil. thesis, University of Oxford (1972)
DE-LA-NOY, M., *Mervyn Stockwood. A Lonely Life* (1996)
DES, *A Policy for the Arts. The First Steps* (1965)
—— *Report of a Committee to Consider the Need for a National Film School* (1967)
—— *Report of the Robbins Committee into Higher Education* (1963)
—— *Report on the Arts, A Growing Concern* (1968)
—— *Report on the Arts. Partnership in Patronage* (1966)
DEWAR, H., *Communist Politics in Britain: The CPGB from its Origins to the Second World War* (1976)
Ditchley Park Conference, Proceedings (May 1964)
DOCHERTY, M., *A Miner's Lass* (1992)
DONNACHIE, I., HARVIE, C., WOOD, I. (eds), *'Forward!'. Labour Politics in Scotland, 1888–1988* (1989)
DONOUGHUE, B., and JONES, G. W., *Herbert Morrison, Portrait of a Politician* (1973)
DOUGLAS, J. W. B., *The Home and the School. A Study of Ability and Attainment in the Primary Schools* (1964)
—— *All our Future. A Longitudinal Study of Secondary Education* (1968)
DOWSE, R., *Left in the Centre. The Independent Labour Party 1893–1940* (1966)

DREWRY, G., and BROCK, J., *The Impact of Women on the House of Lords*. Studies in Public Policy, 112 (1983)

DRIBERG, T., *The Best of Both Worlds* (1953)

—— *Ruling Passions* (1977)

DROGHEDA, G., *Double Harness* (1978)

DUFF, J. (ed.), *The Education of an Englishman. An Autobiography of Sir Godfrey Thomson*, Moray House College of Education.

DUFF, P., *Left, Left, Left. A Personal Account of Six Protest Campaigns 1945–65* (1971)

DURBIN, E., *New Jerusalems. The Labour Party and the Economics of Democratic Socialism* (1985)

DURHAM, M., 'The Left in the Thirties', *Bulletin Society Study of Labour History* 46 (1983)

EATWELL, R., and WRIGHT, A., 'Labour and the Lessons of 1931', *History* 63 (1978)

—— *The 1945–51 Labour Government* (1979)

ECCLES, D., *Politics and the Quality of Life*, Conservative Political Centre (1970)

Edinburgh University Calendars, 1922–7

Edinburgh University Labour Party Minute Book, 1921–9

EDWARDS, R., *Goodbye Fleet Street* (1988)

FERGUSON, J., *The Open University from Within* (1975)

FOOT, M., *Aneurin Bevan*, 2 vols (1975 edn.)

—— *Loyalists and Loners* (1986)

FOX, A., *Completely Foxed* (1989)

GARSIDE, W. R., *British Unemployment 1919–1939, A Study in Public Policy* (1990)

GODFREY, R., 'The Bevan–Gaitskell Rivalry', Ph.D. thesis, University of Sussex (1986)

GOODMAN, A., 'The Public and the Arts', Address to the RSA (1968)

—— *Not for the Record. Selected Speeches and Writings* (1972)

—— *State Subsidies and Artistic Freedom* (1977)

—— *Tell Them I'm On My Way* (1993)

GOODMAN, G., *The Awkward Warrior: Frank Cousins* (1979)

GRAVES, P., *Labour Women. Women in British Working-Class Politics 1918–39* (1994)

GRIFFITHS, M., 'Women in Higher Education—A Case Study of the Open University', *Schooling for Work*, Survey Research Dept. Paper 161 (1979)

GUTTSMAN, W., 'Changes in British Labour Leadership', in *Political Decision-Makers*, vol. 3 (1960)

HAMILTON, M. A., *Remembering My Good Friends* (1944)

HARRIS, D., *Openness and Closure in Distance Education* (1987)

HARRISON, B. H., 'Women in a Men's House. The Women MPs 1919–1945', *The Historical Journal* (1986)

—— *Prudent Revolutionaries. Portraits of British Feminists between the Wars* (1987)

HARRISON, J. F. C., *Learning and Living, 1790–1960. A Study in the History of the English Adult Education Movement* (1961)

HASELER, S., *The Gaitskellites. Revisionism in the British Labour Party, 1951–64* (1969)

HAYBURN, R., 'The National Unemployed Workers Movement, 1921–1936', *International Review of Social History* 28 (1983)

HENNESSY, P., *Never Again, Britain 1945–1951* (1992)

HENNESSY, P., and SELDON, A. (eds), *Ruling performance. British Government from Attlee to Thatcher* (1987)
HEWISON, R., *Too Much. Arts and Society in the 1960s* (1986)
—— *Culture and Consensus. England, Art and Politics since 1940* (1995)
HILL, D. (ed.), *Tribune 40. The First Forty Years of a Socialist Newspaper* (1977)
HILTON, J., *English Ribbon* (1950)
H.M. Treasury, *Government and the Arts, 1958–64*, (1964)
HOBSON, J. A., *Confessions of an Economic Heretic* (1938)
HOGGART, S., and LEIGH, D., *Michael Foot: A Portrait* (1981)
HOLMAN, R., *The History of Cowdenbeath, 1890–1940* (n.d.)
HORLOCK, J. H., *The Open University after Fifteen Years*, Manchester Statistical Society (1984)
HOULT, D., 'The Open University: Its Origins and Establishment, Sept 1963–June 1969', M.Ed. thesis, University of Hull (1975)
HOWARD, A., *Richard Crossman. The Pursuit of Power* (1990)
HOWELL, D., *British Social Democracy* (1976)
HUTCHISON, R., *The Politics of the Arts Council* (1982)
JAMES, R. RHODES, *Robert Boothby* (1991)
JENKINS, H., *The Culture Gap* (1979)
JENKINS, M., *Bevanism. Labour's High Tide. The Cold War and the Democratic Mass Movement* (1979)
JOHNSON, R. W., 'Stick to the Latin', *London Review of Books* (23 Jan. 1997)
JONES, M., *Chances, An Autobiography* (1987)
—— *A Radical Life. A Biography of Megan Lloyd George* (1991)
—— *Michael Foot* (1994)
JUPP, F., *The Radical Left in Britain 1931–1941* (1982)
KING, M., 'The Labour Movement in Cannock Chase 1910–1930', typescript (1990)
KNOX, W., *James Maxton* (1987)
Labour Gazette
The Labour Party, *Leisure for Living* (1959)
LAYBOURN, K., *The Rise of Labour. The British Labour Party, 1890–1979* (1988)
LEE, J., *Tomorrow is a New Day* (published in the USA as *This Great Journey*) (1939)
—— *Russia our Ally* (1941)
—— *My Life with Nye* (1980)
Leicester Chronicle, 1926–33
Lochgelly Times, 1925–35
MACDOUGALL, I. (ed.), *Essays in Scottish Labour History* (1979)
MACDOUGALL, J. D., 'The Scottish Coalminer', *The Nineteenth Century* (Dec. 1927)
MACINNES, C. M., *Bristol at War* (1972)
MCCALLUM, R. B. and READMAN, A., *The British General Election of 1945* (1947)
MCINTOSH, N. E., with MORRISON, V., 'Student demand, progress and withdrawal: the Open University's first four years', *Higher Education Review* (Autumn 1974)
MCINTOSH, N. E., 'Open Admission—an Open or Revolving Door', *Universities Quarterly* (Spring 1975)
—— 'Women and the Open University', in *Women in Higher Education* Conference Papers, Staff Development in Universities Programme (1973)

McIntosh, N. E., with Calder, J. A., and Swift, B., *A Degree of Difference. The Open University of the U.K.* (1977)

Macintyre, S., *Little Moscows. Communism, and Working Class Militancy in Inter-war Britain* (1980)

McKibbin, R., 'The Economic Policy of the Second Labour Government 1929–1931', *Past and Present* (68) (1975)

McLean, I., 'The Labour Movement in Clydeside Politics 1914–1922', D.Phil. thesis, University of Oxford (1971)

Mann, J., *Woman in Parliament* (1962)

Manning, L., *A Life for Education* (1970)

Marquand, D., *Ramsay MacDonald* (1977)

Marwick, A., 'The Independent Labour Party in the 1920s', in *Bulletin of the Institute of Historical Research* 35 (1962)

—— *Clifford Allen. The Open Conspirator* (1964)

Mason, A. J., *Lochore, A Playground for Fife*, pamphlet (n.d.)

Middlemas, R. K., *The Clydesiders. A Left Wing Struggle for Parliamentary Power* (1965)

Middleton, L., *Women in the Labour Movement* (1977)

Middleton, R., *Towards the Managed Economy. Keynes, the Treasury, and the Fiscal Debate of the* 1930s (1985)

Mikardo, I., 'The fateful, hateful Fifties', *New Socialist* (Mar./Apr. 1982)

—— *Back-bencher* (1988)

Minkin, L., *The Labour Party Conference. A Study in the Politics of Intra-Party Democracy* (1978)

Mitchell, A., *Election '45* (1995)

Moffatt, A., 'Successes in the Scottish Miners' Struggles', *Labour Monthly* (Mar. 1934)

Morgan, K. O., *Labour in Power 1945–51* (1984)

—— *Labour People. Leaders and Lieutenants: Hardie to Kinnock* (1987)

—— *The People's Peace. British History 1945–1990* (1992)

Morris, A. J. A., *C. P. Trevelyan 1870–1958. Portrait of a Radical* (1977)

Motherwell Times, 1928–36

New Leader

New Statesman

Newman, M., 'Democracy versus Citizenship', Labour's Role in the struggle against British Fascism, 1933–6, *History Workshop* 5 (1978)

Newsom, J., *Half our Future* (1963)

Nicholas, H. G., *The British General Election of 1950* (1951)

North Lanark Labour News

Northern Echo

Norton, P., and Wood, D., *Back from Westminster. British Members of Parliament and their Constituents* (1993)

Oldfield, A., 'The ILP and Economic Planning', *International Review of Social History* (1976)

The Open University, *Report of the Planning Committee to the Secretary of State for Education and Science* (1969)

—— *Review of the Open University.* Conducted by DES and OU (1991)

PART, A., *The Making of a Mandarin* (1990)

PELLING, H., *America and the British Left* (1957)

—— 'The 1945 General Election Reconsidered', *The Historical Journal* 23, 2 (1980)

PERKIN, H. J., *New Universities in the UK. Innovation in Higher Education* (1969)

PERRY, W., 'The Open University', Friday Evening Discourse at the Royal Institute (6 Nov. 1970)

—— *The Open University. A Personal Account by the First Vice-Chancellor* (1976)

PHILLIPS, M., *The Divided House. Women at Westminster* (1980)

PICTON-TURBERVILLE, E., *Life is Good. An Autobiography* (1939)

The Pilkington Report into the Future of Broadcasting (1962)

PIMLOTT, B., *Labour and the Left in the 1930s* (1977)

—— *Hugh Dalton* (1985)

—— (ed.), *The Political Diary of Hugh Dalton 1918–40, 1945–60* (1986)

—— *Harold Wilson* (1993)

PUGH, M., 'Pacifists and Politics in Britain 1931–5', *Historical Journal* 23 (1980)

—— *The Making of Modern British Politics 1867–1939* (1982)

—— *Women and the Women's Movement in Britain, 1914–1959* (1992)

Rebel Student

REDCLIFFE-MAUD, Lord, *Support for the Arts in England and Wales*, Gulbenkian report (1976)

REISMAN, D., *Anthony Crosland. The Mixed Economy* (1997)

—— *Crosland's Future. Opportunity and Outcome* (1997)

RICHARDS, J., and ALDGATE, A., *The Best of British Cinema and Society 1930–70* (1983)

ROTH, A., *Sir Harold Wilson. Yorkshire Walter Mitty* (1977)

RUBINSTEIN, D., 'Socialism and the Labour Party: The Labour Left and Domestic Policy, 1945–50', in Martin, D., and Rubinstein, D. (eds), *Ideology and the Labour Movement* (1979)

SARGANT, N., 'The Open University', in Fieldhouse, R., *A Modern History of Adult Education* (1997)

SCHNEER, J., *Labour's Conscience. The Labour Left, 1945–51* (1988)

SELKIRK, R., 'Fife Miners and the Communist Party', *The Communist Review* (March 1929)

SENDALL, B., *Independent Television in Britain*; vol. 1, *Origins and Foundation 1946–62* (1982); vol. 2, *Expansion and Change 1958–62* (1983)

Sesame. The First Ten Years, 1969–79

Sesame. The Newspaper of the Open University, 1972–8

SEYD, P., *The Rise and Fall of the Labour Left* (1987)

—— 'Factionalism within the Labour Party: The Socialist League 1932–1937' in Briggs, A., and Saville, J. (eds), *Essays in Labour History*; vol. 3, *1918–1939* (1977)

SHAW, E., *Discipline and Discord in the Labour Party. The Politics of Managerial Control in the Labour Party, 1951–87* (1988)

SHEPHERD, R., *Enoch Powell* (1996)

SHINWELL, E., *Conflict without Malice* (1955)

—— *The Labour Story* (1963)

SIEFF, I., *Memoirs* (1970)

SINCLAIR, A., *Arts and Cultures. A History of the Fifty years of the Arts Council of Great Britain* (1995)

SKIDELSKY, R., *Politicians and the Slump. The Labour Government of 1929–1931* (1967; 1994 edn.)
SMITH, H. L. (ed.), 'Sex versus Class: British Feminists and the Labour Movement, 1919–1929', in *The Historian* 47 (Nov. 1984)
—— *British Feminism in the Twentieth Century* (1990)
SNELL, H., *Men, Movements and Myself* (1938)
SNOWDEN, P., *An Autobiography*, vol. 2, *1919–1934* (1934)
STEVENSON, J., and COOK, C., *The Slump. Society and Politics During the Depression* (1979 edn.)
STOCKS, M., *Eleanor Rathbone* (1949)
STOCKWOOD, M., *Chanctonbury Ring. The Autobiography of Mervyn Stockwood* (1982)
The Student, University of Edinburgh, 1921–9
SUMMERSKILL, E., *A Woman's World* (1967)
TAYLOR, A. J. P., *English History 1914–1945* (1970)
—— *Beaverbrook* (1972)
THOMAS, E. (ed.), *Tribune 21* (1958)
THOMAS, G., *Mr Speaker. The Memoirs of Viscount Tonypandy* (1985)
THOMAS, H., *John Strachey* (1973)
THOMPSON, G. (ed.), *Third Statistical Account of Scotland. The County of Lanark* (1960)
THORPE, A., *The British General Election of 1931* (1991)
—— *Britain in the 1930s* (1992)
TIMMINS, N., *The Five Giants. A Biography of the Welfare State* (1995)
H.M. Treasury, *Government and the Arts 1958–64* (1964)
The TUC, *The Arts, a Consultative Document* (1975)
TREVELYAN, K., *Fool in Love* (1962)
Tribune
TUNSTALL, J. (ed.), *The Open University Opens* (1974)
TURNER, A. LOGAN (ed.), *The History of the University of Edinburgh 1883–1938* (1938)
TYNAN, K., *Tynan Right and Left* (1967)
VALLANCE, E., *Women in the House. A Study of Women Members of Parliament* (1979)
VAN STRAUBENZEE, W. R., 'Whither the Open University', Lecture to OU Students' Association at Bristol, typescript (9 Apr. 1976)
VERNON, B., *Ellen Wilkinson* (1982)
WATKINS, K. W., *Britain Divided. The Effect of the Spanish Civil War on British Public Opinion* (1963)
WEBB, B., *The Diary of Beatrice Webb*, eds MacKenzie, N. and J., 7 vols (1982–5)
WEBSTER, C., *The Health Services since the War*; vol. 1, to 1957 (1988)
WESKER, A., *Fears of Fragmentation* (1970)
West Fife Echo, 1925–35
Western Daily Press, 1942–3
WHEEN, F., *Tom Driberg, His Life and His Indiscretions* (1990)
WHITE, E., *The Arts Council of Great Britain* (1975)
WILKINSON, E., *Peeps at Politicians* (1930)
WILLIAMS, P., 'Foot-faults in the Gaitksell–Bevan Match', *Political Studies* 27 (1979)
—— *Hugh Gaitskell. A Political Biography* (1979)

WILLIAMS, P., 'The Labour Party: The Rise of the Left', in Berrington, H. (ed.), *Change in British Politics* (1984)

WISE, M. J., 'The Cannock Chase Region', in *Birmingham and its Regional Setting* (1950)

Wishaw Press and Advertiser, 1928–35

WYATT, W., *Confessions of an Optimist* (1985)

WYMER, I., *The Open University and Adult Students* (n.d.)

YOUNG, J., *Winston Churchill's Last Campaign. Britain and the Cold War, 1951–1955* (1996)

YOUNG, M., 'The Leadership, the Rank and File, and Mr Bevan', *Political Quarterly* 24 (1953)

—— 'Is your Child in the Unlucky Generation?', *Where* (Autumn 1962)

—— 'The Story of the National Extension College', typescript (in author's possession)

ZIEGLER, P., *Harold Wilson* (1993)

INDEX